THE
Royal
R·A·J·P·U·T·S

THE
Royal
RAJPUTS

STRANGE TALES
AND
STRANGER TRUTHS

MANOSHI BHATTACHARYA

Rupa & Co

To

Ma

ACKNOWLEDGEMENTS

It has taken me close to three years to weave together from several historical sources a nearly uninterrupted tale. The inspiration behind the work lies in Lt Col Tod's *Annals and Antiquities of Rajasthan*.

It is time to thank the following people:

HH Brijraj Singh, Maharao Raja of Kotah, who from a very early stage involved himself with the book and went through it with a fine toothcomb. To him I am indebted for the numerous historical corrections and help in channelling my thoughts; Kaushik who first sowed the germ of the idea in my mind; Roopa whose exact words were, 'Never let your reader be forced to pick up a second book to make sense out of yours'; Randhir for flying to the rescue everytime; Andrew Cook for his help in locating Lieutenant Colonel Tod's service documents; Smita Singh for sharing my vision and Milee Ashwarya for seeing it through to the end; Aruna Chakravarty for the quick lessons in English grammar; Commodore Asoke Kumar Bhattacharya and Jayashri Bhattacharya – my parents, and my maternal grandfather, Shri GC Mukherji, for building up my repository of tales – both historical and mythological.

KOTAH

Preface

The Royal Rajputs – Strange Tales And Stranger Truths renders in simple language and in a concise form the story of Rajasthan. Dr Manoshi Bhattacharya has worked at untangling a web of myths, legends and folklore skilfully woven by the bards of Rajasthan – one that would test the skills of many a reputed scholar. She has also read many learned narratives on the subject and produced a fine book.

Napoleon once remarked: *what is history but a fable agreed upon*, where history fails one turns to legends. Epics are passed down from generation to generation with a certain element of truth, weaving a fabric that holds a people together. The celebrated bards of Rajasthan kept this tradition alive. It was this tribe of wandering minstrels who recited and sang the tales of glory with vigour and passion infusing the haughty Rajputs' blood with a surge of adrenaline and boundless pride driving them to acts of reckless gallantry. Fuelled with the traditional cup of fiery spirits and a generous dose of amal (opium), the Rajput warrior was a fearsome sight and a formidable adversary capable of prodigious feats of valour. They yearned only for victory or death. Glory was assured in any case.

This book will help the tourist – both Indian and foreign -- to understand the history and legends of Rajasthan, the proud traditions and customs of the Rajputs. Those with a greater interest in history will perhaps be enthused to read and appreciate the real stuff that discerns fact from fable.

MAHARAO BRIJ RAJ SINGH OF KOTAH

CONTENTS

INTRODUCTION

Kolkata 26 August 1799: A seventeen-year-old disembarked at the rain-lashed port and looked about with interest. The new land was far from alien. His thoughts strayed for a fleeting moment to the little island home he had left behind. Beyond the stormy oceans lay the United Kingdom of Great Britain still reeling from the effects of the Napoleonic wars, as mad King George[1] clung tenuously to his throne and mourned the loss of his American colonies. But turmoil was not limited to Europe and America alone. The great Mughal Empire of India, that had been a constant and lucrative trading partner for two centuries, writhed in the throes of a downfall. The blind emperor, Shah Alam, held onto the throne of Delhi, propped up by the Scindias, the foremost among the Maratha warrior clans that had issued like a scourge from their distant home in the hills of Maharashtra. Rapidly gaining control over the northern lands, they had dominated the political scenario wherever they managed a foothold. As Mughal India crumbled, politically important fragments declared independence defying the powers of Delhi. The time was ripe for the realisation of British

---

1. His Majesty King George III ruled the United Kingdom of Great Britain from 1760 – 1820. He suffered from porphyria the symptoms of which first became apparent in 1788. The excitement and delirium that is associated with the disease was mistaken for insanity and by 1811 he was no longer fit to rule. The prince of Wales acted as regent until the death of the king.

dreams. For many long years the British East India Company had had its army poised in the wings, biding time. In the biggest corporate takeover ever, they planned to grab the Grand Mughal's possessions, a jewel that the British crown would then begin to lust after. It was on the shores of this land that James Tod stood; he was going to love her as dearly as his own.

The Tods were a widely travelled lot. James Tod Sr. had left his native Scotland to marry Mary Heatly of New York. Hers was an important family, her brothers having held posts as members of the prestigious civil service of the East India Company. James Sr too sought his fortune in India working as an Indigo planter at Mirzapur (Uttar Pradesh) and then retired to a comfortable life in England. His son, however chose a different path. Not for him the life of buying and selling indigo. Armed with a letter from his uncle, Patrick Heatly, James Tod Jr reported to the Company's headquarters.

Young James was attached to the 2nd Bengal European Regiment: an infantry regiment, which comprised entirely of European soldiers. He was promoted to lieutenant a year later and after a brief stint with the 14th Native Infantry Regiment, rejoined the 2nd Bengal. It was at this stage that he became involved with the initial efforts of the British in the survey and mapping of India. The Survey of India that had been set up thirty-two years ago had a gigantic project simmering for a while and on 10 April 1802 it was launched from Chennai as 'The Great Indian Arc of the Meridian'. All surveyors, whether upon land or sea, contributed to the charting of the Indian subcontinent. Names like Lambton, Everest and Radhanath Sikdar, the man who would first calculate the height of Mount Everest, were to go down in history. Together the surveyors divided the land surface into a gigantic web of triangles that spanned mountains, torrents and raging seas. The surface of the earth was to be mapped in one long concerted effort. These peaceful progressive activities were to witness a dramatic shift in 1803. In a swift movement, Lord Lake occupied Delhi and the blind old emperor now ruled in name alone, a pensioner protected by the army of the East India Company.

That year the 2nd Bengal was transformed into a Marine Regiment and setting sail on board the Mornington, Lieutenant Tod left to serve in the Molucca Isles. He returned in 1805, and volunteered to join the 25th Bengal Native Infantry, which had been attached as escort to the British embassy, led by Resident Envoy Graeme Mercer[2] Esq., to the court of the Maratha leader, Daulat Rao Scindia. Scindia, who had recently lost his hold over Delhi, had encamped in the town of Rashmi, in Mewar – a state, which at the time, remained largely unmapped. Lieutenant Tod undertook the survey and charting of the routes used by the escort and the first to be completed was the 'Chittaurgarh to Udaipur' route map.

In a letter to the government, Lieutenant Colonel RH Colebrooke, the surveyor general, noting that the lieutenant did this more from zeal to promote useful knowledge than from any pecuniary motive, recommended a surveyor's allowance, of one-and-a-half-thousand rupees, for the period of employment. The remainder was to be calculated once the field book and journals were submitted. But the government seemed to think otherwise. The remuneration due to an assistant surveyor, that is, a sum of hundred rupees per month was deemed sufficient.

With a party of twenty men, Lieutenant Tod followed Scindia's camp, spending his time exploring the regions through which the Maratha army marched. In his usual fashion, Scindia spent the greater part of the year harrying and ravaging wherever he went. Agents were recruited to collect data from areas the lieutenant could not personally visit. Places as far as Hyderabad (now in Pakistan), Sind and Multan were covered. The map of the area between the Yamuna and the Narmada was compiled by 1809. Though it opened up a veritable treasure trove, life under the canvas open to the extremes of Indian weather affected his health drastically. He wrote to Surveyor General Colonel John Garstin, that year:

Nothing but the very bad state of my health could have for so long a period prevented me replying to your favour of the 7th June last, so delaying the protraction of Scindia's camp of my route, to the provinces. So little has my health benefited by a residence in them, that I have been under the necessity of applying for an extension of leave for two

---

2. Graeme Mercer had begun his career in the Bengal Service as assistant surgeon.

months, and as I generally feel better during the cold weather, I hope to resume my labours about its commencement. I have however much doubt whether I shall not be under the necessity of making a voyage to sea, at the commencement of the next hot season, my health having suffered so much, during near 4 years residence in camp, from the nature of my employment and the peculiar situation of being subject to the inclemencies of all weather under the canvas. It is my sincere wish however, that I may be enabled to delay any further temporary absence, till the commencement of 1811, by which period I hope to have my map finished.

The employment of agents, presenting official gifts to people in the petty states and purchasing instruments from England, proved too expensive for his hundred rupees per month allowance, but the recommendation that Lieutenant Tod be put on half a surveyor's allowance was once again turned down. To ease the burden on the lieutenant, the surveyor general opined that very different qualities were required to make a survey, take the levels of canals, estimate the cost of undertaking a project and execute the digging, as opposed to the contracting of local help and the supervision of the work. Lieutenant Tod was recommended for the former while Lieutenant J Macartney was placed in charge of the latter. Between 1810 and 1811, the land between the Yamuna and the Ganga was surveyed for the construction and repair of canals in the Doab. In 1808, the governor general appointed Lieutenant Tod to the office of postmaster, taking advantage of the peculiar manner in which he was qualified. It enabled the lieutenant to collect a host of geographical information, which aided his work as a surveyor.

By 1812, he was put in command of the escort he had served with during the last seven years, and was promoted to captain on 26 October 1813. That year saw the completion of the charting of the junction of the Chambal and Yamuna, but the effort took its toll upon his health. Submitting the map to Surveyor General Colonel Crawford, he wrote:

This map will since long have reached you; it has cost me any amount of pain and trouble…The consequence was an illness which nearly carried me off and the effects of which I still feel… My geographical pursuits occupy a wide range as far as the Indus to the west and the Narmada to the south. If my health permits, I may next year apply for permission to visit the western deserts; this is a part I have long had in contemplation; but I must consult my health, which is much broken since I have been in this camp. I have had the command of this escort nearly two years and look forward to the expiration of eight years more to join my father in England.

Backbreaking research had been required to fill in the bits that were missing from the map of the central and western Rajput states, and it was on the eve of a general war in 1815, that the first comprehensive map of Rajasthan was presented to the Governor General Marquess of Hastings[3]. It formed the basis of the war campaign.

From 1815 onwards, Captain Tod served as 2nd assistant to the resident at the court of Scindia at Gwalior and on 18 May 1816, was upgraded to 1st assistant, the governor general noting that he was known to the government by his indefatigable activity and conspicuous merit in collecting and arranging historical information concerning the regions of central India, of which so little accurate knowledge was previously possessed, and which was likely to become at no distant period the theatre of the most interesting operations.

In 1818, Captain Tod was selected to represent the Marquess of Hastings at the maharana's court. The very thought tickled the imagination of his overtly indophile colleague and friend, Ochterlony, the British resident at Delhi.

Tod was too much of a Rajput to deal with the Rajputs.

---

3. In 1812, while a replacement was being sought for Governor General Lord Minto, the prince of Wales, seeking a lucrative place for his elderly friend Lord Hastings, struck a deal with the directors. The fifty-nine year old general, who had had but a mediocre career in the army, proved himself to be a strategist of outstanding ability. The one-time gambler and man of fashion looked after the Company's assets with great care and revealed a genuine concern for the welfare of the people.

Ochterlony himself lived and dressed like a Mughal nobleman.

As resident and political agent to the Western Rajput States, Captain James Tod became responsible for the agreements that were to be signed between them and the British government of India. In 1819, the integrated princely Rajput states came to be known as Rajputana.

On integration with the Indian Union in 1948, the name Rajputana was changed to Rajasthan.

Rajputs of India

Rajasthan, the land of the kings, that lies in the hot dry part of north-western India, evokes visions of a golden desert bathed in brilliant sunshine. Tall men sport luxuriant moustaches, their aquiline features reminiscent of a regal past. In their large, brightly coloured turbans, white kurtas or tunics and short knee-length dhotis, they go about their business. The women of Rajasthan walk tall, ghagra-cholis -- colourful skirts and blouses, swinging about their knees, silver anklets tinkling and water pots piled one on top of the other balanced gracefully on their heads. The picture of Rajasthan is incomplete without a mention of the camels that wander in herds or as a part of disciplined caravans, bells ringing on their feet, their noses held high. There is an aroma about them that is warm and not unpleasant. Clouds of dust rise as men and beasts walk, making no attempt to look for a bit of shade for the short thorny kikar, that abounds amidst the dunes, has little to offer. These are the descendents of valiant warrior clans, who once thrilled to the clash of steel, the wind that whipped past and the steeds that strained at their bits.

They call themselves Rajputs -- the sons of kings. Their bards sing of valour, of love and of great battles fought since time immemorial. It was these songs that so captivated the heart of Captain Tod, that he added his name to the list of the bards of Rajasthan.

Some Rajputs had nomadic horsemen as their ancestors, who belonged to the inhospitable grasslands of central Asia. A very long time ago,

His years of study and love for the land and its people led to a deep respect and understanding of the history, customs and traditions of the Rajputs. Based on his knowledge and his deciphering of ancient family trees and lineages, quarrels over lands and titles were settled and the Rajputs learnt to trust the British government that was taking over power.

What nation on earth, could have maintained the semblance of civilization, the spirit or the customs of their forefathers, during so many centuries of overwhelming depression, but one of such singular character as the Rajpoot?

Huns and Gujjars were on the look out for a new home. Hoping for an entry, they waited at the gates of India for close to a century. It was at the close of the fifth century AD, that the stage was set.

Deep within Hindustan, in what is present-day Bihar, lay the once powerful kingdom of the Guptas. The mighty king Samudra Gupta, who had come to power in the fourth century AD, had chosen to extend his dominion all the way across the land, engulfing the smaller tribal states that lay on the border of Hindustan. These peripheral kingdoms played the very important role of buffer, keeping foreign invaders out, a fact that Samudra Gupta had completely failed to recognise. Alternating between the roles of a ruthless conqueror in quest of power and that of a magnanimous emperor, he allowed the humbled border chieftains to continue ruling their states. Weakened by attacks from within, these buffer states could no longer withstand those from outside. Within 150 years, both the Gupta Empire and the buffer kingdoms were in a state of decay. The opportunity the nomadic central Asian horsemen were looking for, presented itself.

Their frustrations had been unleashed in the meanwhile upon the empires of Europe. Though backed by waves of lesser invaders that followed in their wake, the long wait had fortunately tempered their ferocity and India, unlike the Roman Empire, survived the onslaught. The cattle herding Gujjars settled in Bhinmal (Rajasthan) and in Baruch (Gujarat). Toramana, leading his dreaded Huns, settled in Madhya Pradesh, while Mihiragula Hun chose as his capital Sialkot in Punjab. It is now commonly believed that the Gujjars and Huns are related tribes sharing similar warlike characteristics. That the borders of India had given way was now common news and the Maitrikas from Persia lost no time in occupying the rich kingdom of Vallabhi in Gujarat. From their new bases, the invaders spread through the land, some peacefully and others through sheer aggression. Some battles were lost some were won and in the end it was the Gujjar that could boast of the most extensive dominion. Rajasthan and Gujarat[4] became their base.

Many indigenous clans rose to prominence during the chaos that followed. With the demise of the old dynasties and with an invader declaring himself king every now and then, many landowners took to arms. In defending

---

4 Gujjar desh or Gujarat received its name from the Gujjars who made it their home.

their properties, they recognised their chance to become one of the new generation kings. Brahmins who had received their lands as grants from their ex sovereigns, tribal chiefs who defended their hill tracts and forest lands and merchants whose investments lay in property, all put forward their claims to royalty and sought admission into the warrior caste. Some left behind their names for posterity, while a thousand others perished with no record of their ever having ever existed. Some assumed new names when the parent clan fell out of power and often turned out to be unrelated to the others who laid claim to the same name. Those that rose to power and achieved some measure of permanence, illuminate the history of the period. Their sudden appearances in the pages of texts are a record of the moment when fortunes turned. The prologue of struggles and agonies remain silent dark passages. The names that illuminate the histories unfolding in various parts of the country, are a testimony to largescale migrations and conversions.

By the middle of the sixth century AD, Mihiragula Hun was chased north to Kashmir while the Chalukyas (Solankis), made an appearance in the highland territories of Maharashtra and Karnataka – the Deccan. The Chalukyas of the Deccan, it is maintained, are no relatives of their namesakes in Gujarat who rose to prominence some 400 years later at Anhilwara Patan. The Tomar Rajputs made their first mark in Delhi in AD 1024, with the building of the Kila Lal Kot. In it they planted the famous fifth century AD iron pillar imported from Vishnupada hill in Kurukshetra, signifying a deep desire to be linked to India's past and heritage.

The new generation of kings faced a peculiar problem in Hindustan. It was easy to rule 'Hindus' but it was impossible to become one of them, for the 'Hindus' considered themselves descendents of the first sages that inhabited the earth. These people, with their ancient lineage, divided themselves into workforces: teachers or Brahmins, warriors or kshatriyas, businessmen or vaishyas and those that supported and looked after the first three – the shudras. A king without an Indian lineage could rule by force, but without a legitimate position in the working order could garner no respect. Never being permitted to feel 'at home', the Rajputs decided to incorporate themselves into the 'Hindu' way of life.

The options were to claim descent from the mythical heroes of Hindustan, or lay claim to a divine origin. Mythical beginnings, befitting their royal stature, were fabricated and 'the sons of kings' began their lives afresh.

Modern history records Rajput presence in states other than those traditionally associated with them. The Chandel Rajputs rose to prominence in the tenth century AD at Bundelkhand (Madhya Pradesh) building their capital at Khajuraho, while the Kalachuris, who lived close to Jabalpur, overthrew their Pratihara (Gujjar) rulers to become independent in the eleventh. The Rajputs spread down to the south of India. The sixth century Rajput, who made it to the history books, was Pulakesin Chalukya (Solanki) I, who set up his capital at Vatapi in Mumbai. His descendents expanded their territories and occupied those of the Kadambas in neighbouring Karnataka. This powerful dynasty ruled through the seventh century, repelling two attacks by Harsh Vardhan of Thaneshwar (Haryana) who was then the most formidable ruler in northern and central India. Their fame drew to their court the Chinese philosopher, Hieun Tsang, who wrote extensively about them. The Chalukyas were powerful enough to take on the mighty kingdoms of the south. Pulakesin II was however killed in AD 612, during a battle with the king of Kanchipuram, Tamil Nadu, but his death was avenged in AD 674, when his son occupied Kanchipuram. But this first of the greatest Rajput kingdom of the south.was on its last legs and about eighty years later, in AD 757, Danti Durga Rashtrakuta, a distant ancestor of the Rathores – who were destined to rule Jodhpur some time in the future – took over the kingdom. The Rashtrakutas had ruled for over 200 years when they were defeated by Mularaja Chalukya. A second Chalukyan rule was set up which lasted for another two hundred years and with their demise the sway of the Rajput clans in the south came to an end. The kingdom of the Deccan was divided between the Yadavs and the Hoysalas, who lost it to the invading Muslims in AD 1328. After nearly 350 years of Islamic rule, a young Maratha declared himself an independent ruler within this region. At his coronation, his bards recounted his ancestry: Shivaji Raje Bhosle, king of the Marathas, was a descendent of the ranas of Mewar. His ancestor had left for the Deccan soon after Alla-ud-din Khalji's[6] sack

---

6 The Khalji or Khalj dynasty is known to popular historians as the Khilji dynasty.

The genealogical memory of Rajasthan lies in the custody of the Bhats and her traditional lore in the songs of the bards:

A long time ago, the kings of the earth fell into evil ways. Sage Parasuram was so enraged that he exterminated the race of the kings and warriors, the kshatriyas, twenty-one times. With no warriors left to protect the common man, the demons wreaked havoc, disturbing Brahmins at prayer, defiling their sacred areas by dragging in carcasses of dead animals and killing helpless priests and teachers.

The Brahmins soon realized that they would have to recreate the warrior class. A great fire was lit at Mount Abu and while the Brahmins chanted, the gods helped create new warriors. Out of the fire or Agni, were born the four Agnikul races.

Lord Indra, the king of the gods, created the Parmar king. He was given the lands of Abu, Dhar and Ujjain to rule and protect.

Lord Brahma, the creator, created the Chalukya or the Solanki and he was granted the land of Anhilwara Patan (Gujarat).

The Sun God, Rudra, created the Purihara or the Pratihara, and he became the guardian of the gates and the king of the Gujjars.

Lord Vishnu made the four-armed Chauhan in his own image and he ruled from Gurha Mundila spreading diagonally across Rajasthan along the tracts of the Luni into Ajmer[5]. The Chauhans went on to conquer the Deccan plateau ruling Golconda and Asirgarh, and further south to Sri Lanka; but the seat of Chauhan power remained in Ajmer.

---

5 Contemporary historians claim that the Chauhans began their rule at Shakambari (Sambhar district) initially subject to the ruling Pratihara dynasty. Independent branches established themselves at Nadol, Ranthambhor, Jalor, Sanchor and Ajmer. Essentially the Agnikul Rajputs established themselves upon Pratihara lands.

of Chittaurgarh. The Rajputs of the Deccan were to once again play a prominent role in the politics of Hindustan.

Drawn from bardic traditions, Captain Tod's version takes the reader back to the second century AD. Rajputs appear limited to north-western India. It is for the reader to identify those tales that belong to the realm of mythology and those that could be a historical possibility. The captain's tales confine themselves to the Rajputs of Rajasthan and Gujarat. The bardic stage opens with the Parmars ruling the largest territory – Abu in Rajasthan, large parts of Gujarat including Dwarka, and Dhar and Ujjain in Madhya Pradesh. The Chalukyas (Solankis) appear established in Anhilwara Patan in Gujarat and the Chauhans in Ajmer. In the second century AD, the descendents of Lord Ram's son Luv moved from their home in Lahore in west Punjab (now Pakistan) to Gujarat. Their cousins, descended from Luv's twin – Kush, settled in Narwar (Madhya Pradesh). The Tomars in the third century, ruled from Delhi, while Mandor[7], appeared to be occupied by the Purihara or Pratiharas (the royal branch of the Gujjars) from the fourth century onwards.

---

7 Mandor, near modern-day Jodhpur, is an ancient city. Tradition claims that Mandodari, the princess of Mandor, was the queen of Raavan, the king of Lanka (modern Sri Lanka) who fought the legendary battle with the Aryan prince, Lord Ram, in the Indian epic *Ramayan*. But the Aryans, finding themselves at the losing end, resorted to invoking the goddess of the Dravidians who offered a glimpse of herself on the sacred moment of crossover between the eighth and the ninth day after the new moon. And Raavan was struck on the tenth – the day of victory, the Vijay Dashami. Mandodari fell at Ram's feet. Unaware of her identity he bestowed upon her the traditional Indian blessing: 'may you never know widowhood'. But the situation could not be undone. The only way out was to ensure that Raavan's pyre was never allowed to cool, for until then a wife cannot assume widowhood. The Lord's vow cannot be broken and even today, on every Vijay Dashami fire is added to Raavan's pyre.

Captain Tod referred to thirty-six royal Rajput races. The list, however, varies from source to source. The races that play a prominent part in this book are:

1. Sisodias and their relatives:
   Gehlote
   Guhilot

2. Jadon (Yadu, Jadu) and their relatives:
   Bhati
   Jareja (Jadeja)
   Tomar (Tuar /Tanwar): Although acknowledged to be of Yadu descent, they are often designated as the thirty-sixth race claiming descent from the Pandav Bhim, of the *Mahabharat*.

3. Rathore

4. Kachwaha

5. Agnikul Rajputs: Each branch of the Agnikul Rajputs is counted as a royal race.
   – Parmar: (Pramar/Puar/Pawar/Panwar) Of the thirty-five Parmar branches the famous ones are the Moris, Sodas and the Dor or Dode
   – Chalukya or Solanki
   – Purihara or Pratihara
   – Chauhan: The main branch ruled from Shakambari and Ajmer. The line counts thirty-nine princes from the first prince who was created upon Mount Abu to the last – Prithviraj Chauhan. Of the twenty-four branches, the most famous are the Hadas of Bundi and Kota, Kinchis, Deoras and the Songaras.

RAJPUT TIMELINES

Delhi	Mewar	Marwar	Bikaner	Bundi	Kota
	1st capital: Chittaur 2nd capital: Udaipur	1st capital: Mandor 2nd capital: Jodhpur			
No documented history.	No documented history.	No documented history.	No documented history.	No documented history.	No documented history.

Dhundhar	Jaisalmer	Pune	Ujjain Gwalior	Indore
1st capital: Amber 2nd capital: Jaipur				
No documented history.	Raja Balbandh 229 – 279	No documented history.	No documented history.	No documented history.
	Raja Bhati 279 – 295 Capital Salbahanpur			
	Raja Bhupat Bhati 295 – 338 Capital – Bhatner			
	Raja Aterao 338 – 340			
	Raja Bhim 340 – 361			
	Raja Saterao 361 – 399			
	Raja Khemkaraṅ 399 – 438			
	Raja Narpat 438 – 467			
	Raja Baj 467 – 468			
	Raja Gaj 468 – 477 Second saka of Ghazni and the first saka of the Bhatis – 479			
	Loman Rao 474 – 479 saka of Bhatner – 479			
	Raja Ren Singh No kingdom 479 – 499			
	Raja Bhoj Singh No kingdom 499 – 519			
	Raja Mangal Rao 519 559 Built Fort Mammanvahan in 519 Lost it and had no kingdom			
	Raja Mandam Rao 559 – 610 Re-occupied Mammanvahan and built Fort Marot – 599			
	Rao Sursen 610 – 645			

Delhi	Mewar	Marwar	Bikaner	Bundi	Kota
	Rawal Kalbhoj Bappaditya (Bappa Rawal) 734 – 753				
Dhillika built by Tomar Rajputs AD 736					
	Shakti Kumar 977 – 993				
Anang Pal Tomar rules in the 11th Century AD. Kila Lal Kot is built in 1024.					

Dhundhar	Jaisalmer	Pune	Ujjain Gwalior	Indore
	Capital: Marot			
	Rao Raghu Rao 645 – 655			
	Rao Mulraj 655 – 682			
	Rao Udai Rao 682 – 729			
	Rao Manjham Rao 729 – 759			
	Rao Kehar 759 – 805			
	Rao Tanno 805 – 820			
	Yuvraj Vijay Rao – Churala 820 – 841			
	Rawal Sidh Deoraj 909 – 973			
	Rawal Mundha 973 – 998			
	986 Ghazni occupied by Subuktigen – a Turk Mahmud Ghazni 997 – 1030			
	Rawal Bachu 998 – 1044			
	Rawal Dusaj 1044 – 1122			
Duleh Rai of Dausa 1096 – 1136				
Kankal 1136 –...	Rawal Lanjha Beejy Rao 1122 – 1147			
Rao Maidal (dates unknown)	Rawal Bhoj Dev (Bhojdeo) 1147 – 1152			

Delhi	Mewar	Marwar	Bikaner	Bundi	Kota
	Kshem Singh 1168 – 1172				
Prithviraj Chauhan III 1170: builds Kila Lal Pithora in Delhi. 1175: abducts Sanyukta, daughter of Jaichand of Kannauj.	Rawal Samant Singh 1172 – 1179				
	Kumar Singh 1179 – 1191				
1192: Prithviraj is killed by Sultan Mohammad Ghuri of Ghazni (1173 – 1206). Delhi becomes part of the Ghaznavid and Ghur Empire.	Mathan Singh 1191 – 1211	Qutub-ud-din Aibak helps Mohammad Ghuri kill Jaichand of Kannauj. Jaichand's descendents migrate to Rajasthan and call themselves Rathores.			
Qutub-ud-din Aibak becomes independent. He establishes the Slave Dynasty in 1206.					
Iltutmish 1211 – 1236	Padam Singh 1211 – 1213				
	Jaitra Singh 1213 –· 1253				
		Rao Sihoji of Pali 1226 – 1273			
Rukn-ud-din Raziya Sultana 1236 – 1246					
Nasir-ud-din 1246 – 1266					

Dhundhar	Jaisalmer	Pune	Ujjain Gwalior	Indore
Rao Huna Deva (dates unknown)				
	Rawal Jaisal 1152 – 1167 builds Jaisalmer in 1156			
Rao Kantal I (dates unknown)				
	Rawal Salbahan II 1167 – 1189			
Rao Pujanadeva 1185 – 1191				
	Rawal Kalan 1189 – 1218			
Rao Malesi 1191 – ...				
Rao Byala (dates unknown)				
Rao Rajadeva (dates unknown)				
Rao Khilan (dates unkown)				
	Rawal Chachik Deo 1218 – 1242			

Delhi	Mewar	Marwar	Bikaner	Bundi	Kota

Tej Singh
1261 – 1267

Balban
1266 – 1286

Rawal Samar Singh Rao Asthan of
1273 – 1302   Kher
41st rawal to rule 1273 – 1292
Chittaurgarh

Kaikabad
1286 – 1290

Jalal-ud-din
Khalji   Rao Duhad
1290 – 1296   1292 – 1309
establishes the
Khalji Dynasty.

Alla-ud-din
Khalji
1296 – 1316

Rawal Ratan Singh
1302 – 1303
Alla-ud-din Khalji
sacks Chittaur in
1303..   Rao Rai Pal
                      1309 – 1313
Rana Ajay Singh, the
only survivor of the Rao Kanha Pal
royal family dies in 1313 – 1323
1314.

Unstable period
when the sons of
Alla-ud-din were
used as puppets
and placed on the
throne by those
with   vested
interests.

Ghias-ud-din
Tughlak
1321 – 1325
establishes the
Tughlak Dynasty.

Dhundhar	Jaisalmer	Pune	Ujjain Gwalior	Indore
	Rawal Karan 1242 – 1270			
	Rawal Lakhansen 1270 – 1274			
	Rawal Punpal 1274 – 1276			
Rao Kantal II 1276 – 1317	Rawal Jait Singh 1276 – 1293			
	Rawal Mulraj 1293 – 1295			
	Rawal Duda Jasod Bhati 1299 – 1315			
Rao Jansi 1317 – 1367				

Delhi	Mewar	Marwar	Bikaner	Bundi	Kota
Mohammad bin Tughlak 1325 – 1351	Maharana Hamir occupies Chittaur 1326 – 1366	Rao Jalhansi 1323 – 1328			
		Rao Chhadha 1328 – 1344			
				Rao Deva 1342 – ...	
Feroze Shah Tughlak 1351 – 1388		Rao Tida 1344 – 1357		Rao Samar Singh (dates unknown)	
		Rao Salkha 1357 – 1374		Rao Narpal (Napoo) (dates unknown)	
	Maharana Kshetra Singh (Khaitsi) 1366 – 1382				
		Rao Biramdeo 1374 – 1384			
	Maharana Lakha 1382 – 1421	Rao Chunda 1384 – 1423		Rao Hamoo 1384 – 1400	
Anarchy follows Feroz Shah's death Taimur-i-lang invades and remains in Delhi for a year in 1398.					
				Rao Bar Singh 1400 – 1415	
Daulat Khan Lodi		Rathore occupation of Mandor 1406			
Sayyid Dynasty 1414 – 1451				Rao Biroo 1415 – 1459	

Dhundhar	Jaisalmer	Pune	Ujjain Gwalior	Indore
	Rawal Garh Singh Bhati 1331 – 1361			
Rao Udaykaran 1367 – 1389	Rawal Kehar II 1361 – 1396			
Rao Nar Singh 1389 – 1413	Rawal Lakhansen 1396 – 1427			
Rao Banbir Singh 1413 - 1424				

Delhi	Mewar	Marwar	Bikaner	Bundi	Kota
	Maharana Mokal 1421 – 1433	Rao Kanha 1424 – 1427			
		Rao Ranmal 1427 – 1438			
	Maharana Kumbha 1433 – 1468	Rao Jodha 1438 – 1489			
Buhlol Lodi 1451 – 1489					
	Uday Hatiaro 1468 – 1473	Jodhpur founded in 1459	Rao Bando 1459 – 1503		
	Maharana Raimal 1473 – 1509		Rao Bika 1472 – 1504		
Sikander Lodi 1489 – 1517		Rao Satal 1489 – 1491	Foundation of Bikaner laid in 1488.		
		Rao Surajmal (Suja, Soojo) 1491 – 1515			
			Rao Nara 1504 – 1505	Rao Narayan Das 1503 – 1529	
			Rao Lunkaran 1505 – 1526		
	Maharana Sanga 1509 – 1529				
Ibrahim Lodi 1517 – 1526		Rao Ganga 1515 – 1532			

Dhundhar	Jaisalmer	Pune	Ujjain Gwalior	Indore

Rao Udha Rao
1424 – 1453

Rawal Ber Singh
1427 – 1448

Rawal Chachagdev
1448 – 1467

Rao Chandrasen
1453 – 1502

Rawal Devidas
1467 – 1524

Rao Prithviraj Singh
1502 – 1527

Delhi	Mewar	Marwar	Bikaner	Bundi	Kota
Babar 1526 – 1530					
	Maharana Ratan Singh 1529 – 1531			Rao Surajmal 1529 – 1531	
Humayun 1530 – 1542					
	Maharana Bikramjeet 1531 – 1537			Rao Surtan 1531 – 1531 Rao Arjun 1531 – 1535	
		Rao Maldeo 1532 – 1562			
				Rao Raja Surjan 1535 – 1585	
	Banbir 1537 – 1540				
	Maharana Uday Singh 1540 – 1572				
Sher Shah Sur 1542 – 1545			Rao Kalyanmal 1542 – 1574		
Islam Shah Sur 1545 – 1553					
Mohammad Adil Shah 1553 – 1555					
Humayun (restored) 1555 – 1556					
Akbar 1556 – 1605					
		Rao Chandersen 1562 – 1565			
	Maharana Pratap 1572 – 1598				
			Raja Rai Singh 1574 – 1612		

Dhundhar	Jaisalmer	Pune	Ujjain Gwalior	Indore
	Rawal Jait Singh II 1524 – 1528			
Rao Puran Mal 1527 – 1534	Rawal Loonkaran 1528 – 1550			
Rao Bhim Singh 1534 – 1537				
Rao Ratan Singh 1537 – 1548				
Raja Bharmal 1548 – 1574	Rawal Maldev 1550 – 1562			
Raja Bharmal gives his daughter in marriage to Akbar in 1562 and becomes an amir in the Mughal court.	Rawal Har Raj 1562 – 1578			
Bhagwan Das 1574 – 1589				

Delhi	Mewar	Marwar	Bikaner	Bundi	Kota
		Raja Uday Singh 1583 – 1595		Rao Raja Bhoj 1585 – 1608	
		Sawai Raja Sur Singh 1595 – 1620			
	Maharana Amar Singh I 1598 – 1619				
Jahangir 1605 – 1627				Rao Raja Ratan Singh 1608 – 1632	
			Maharaja Dalpat Singh 1612 – 1613		
			Maharaja Sur Singh 1613 – 1631		
	Maharana Karan 1619 – 1628	Raja Guj Singh 1620 – 1638			
					Rao Madhu Singh 1624 – 1656
Shah Jahan 1627 – 1666	Maharana Jagat Singh 1628 – 1654				
			Maharaja Karan Singh 1631 – 1667	Rao Raja Chhatra Sal 1632 – 1658	
		Raja Jaswant Singh 1638 – 1678			
	Maharana Raj Singh 1654 – 1682				

Dhundhar	Jaisalmer	Pune	Ujjain Gwalior	Indore
	Rawal Bhim Singh 1578 – 1624			
Mirza Raja Maan Singh 1589 – 1614				
		Maloji Bhosle made raja of Pune by the nizam of Ahmadnagar in 1595.		
Mirza Raja Bhao Singh 1614 – 1621				
Mirza Raja Jai Singh I 1621 – 1667				
	Rawal Kalyan Das 1624 – 1634			
		Shahaji Bhosle declares independence in 1629.		
	Rawal Manohar Das 1634 – 1648			
	Rawal Ramchandra 1648 – 1651			
	Rawal Sabal Singh 1651 – 1661			

Delhi	Mewar	Marwar	Bikaner	Bundi	Kota
					Rao Mokund Singh 1656 – 1658
Aurungzeb 1658 – 1707				Rao Raja Bhao Singh 1658 – 1682	Rao Jagat Singh 1658 – 1669
			Maharaja Anup Singh 1667 – 1698		
					Rao Kishore Singh 1669 – 1685
		Maharaja Ajit 1679 – 1724			
	Maharana Jai Singh 1682 – 1700			Rao Raja A n i r u d d h Singh 1682 – 1696	
					Rao Raja Ram Singh 1685 – 1707
			Maharaja Sarup Singh 1698 – 1700	Maharao Raja Budh Singh 1696 – 1724	
	Maharana Amar Singh II 1700 – 1710			M a h a r a j a Sujan Singh 1700 – 1735	
Azam Shah 1707 – 1707 Bahadur Shah 1707 – 1712					Maharao Raja Bheem Singh 1707 – 1720
	Maharana Sangram Singh II 1710 – 1734				
Jahander Shah 1712 – 1713					

Dhundhar	Jaisalmer	Pune	Ujjain Gwalior	Indore
	Maharawal Amar Singh 1661 – 1702			
Mirza Raja Ram Singh 1667 – 1688				
		Shivaji Bhosle enthroned at Raigadh. 1673 – 1680		
		Sambhaji Bhosle 1680 – 1689 R a j a r a m (S a m b h a j i ' s brother) 1689 – 1700 Shahu Shivaji II (son of Rajaram) was defeated by Raja Shahu (Sambhaji's son) and the Maratha empire was split into two with Shahu Shivaji II ruling from Kohlapur		
Mirza Raja Bhishen Singh 1688 – 1699				
Sawai Maharaja Jai Singh 1699 – 1743				
	Maharawal Jaswant Singh 1702 1708	Raja Shahu (Sambhaji's son) 1700 – 1749		
	Maharawal . Budh Singh 1708 – 1722			
		Appointed Balaji Vishvanath Bhat as peshwa (prime minister) 1712 – 1721		

Delhi	Mewar	Marwar	Bikaner	Bundi	Kota
Farukhsiyar 1713 – 1719					
Syyed brothers set up puppet emperors Muhammad Shah (Rangila) 1719 – 1748					Maharao Raja Arjun Singh 1720 – 1724
		Maharaja Abhay 1724 – 1750		Maharao Raja Dalil Singh 1724 – 1734	Maharao Raja Durjan Sal 1724 – 1757
	Maharana Jagat Singh II 1734 – 1751			Maharao Raja Budh Singh (restored) 1734 – 1735	
			Maharaja Zorawar Singh 1735 – 1746	Maharao Raja Dalil Singh (second tenure) 1735 – 1749	
			Maharaja Gaj Singh 1746 – 1787		
Ahmad Shah 1748 – 1754		Maharaja Ram Singh 1750 – 1751			Maharao Raja Umed Singh 1749 – 1770
	Maharana Pratap II 1751 – 1754	Maharaja Bakhta Singh 1751 – 1752			
		Maharaja Beejy Singh 1752 – 1753			
		Maharaja Ram Singh (restored) 1753 – 1772			

Dhundhar	Jaisalmer	Pune	Ujjain Gwalior	Indore
	Maharawal Akhai Singh 1722 – 1762	Baji Rao Peshwa I 1721 – 1740		
			Ramji (Ranoji) Scindia 1726 – 1745 founder of the clan established himself at Ujjain.	
		(Raghuji Bhosle set up an independent dynasty at Berar and moved to Nagpur.) 1730		
				Malhar Rao Holkar 1733 – 1766
Sawai Maharaja Ishwari Singh 1743 – 1750		Balaji Baji Rao (Nana Sahib Peshwa) 1740 – 1761 Raja Shahu Bhosle died in 1749 and the peshwa became supreme.	Jai Appa Scindia 1745 – 1755	
Sawai Maharaja Madho Singh 1750 – 1768				

Delhi	Mewar	Marwar	Bikaner	Bundi	Kota
Alamgir II 1754 – 1759	Maharana Raj Singh II 1754 – 1761				
					Maharao Raja Ajit 1757 – 1759
Shah Jahan III 1759 – 1760					Maharao Raja Chattra Sal 1759 – 1766
Shah Alam II 1760 – 1806 Shah Alam ruled as a puppet under the Rohilla Afghans until 1788.	Maharana Ari Singh 1761 – 1773				
					Maharao Raja Guman Singh 1766 – 1771
				Maharao Raja Ajit Singh 1770 – 1773	Maharao Raja Umed Singh 1771 – 1819
		Maharaja Beejy Singh (restored) 1772 – 1793			
	Maharana Hamir II 1773 – 1778			Maharao Raja Bhishen Singh 1773 – 1821	
	Maharana Bhim Singh 1778 – 1828				
1788 – 1803 the emperor ruled as a puppet under Mahadji Scindia.			Maharaja Raj Singh 1787 – 1787 Maharaja Pratap Singh with Surat Singh acting as regent. 1787 – 1787 Maharaja Surat Singh. 1787 –		
		Maharaja Bheem 1794 – 1803			

Dhundhar	Jaisalmer	Pune	Ujjain Gwalior	Indore
			Scindias establish themselves at Indore in 1754	
			Jankoji Scindia 1755 – 1761	
	Maharawal Mulraj Singh II 1762 – 1820	Madhu Rao Peshwa 1761 – 1772	Kadarji Rao 1763 – 1764	
			Manaji Rao 1764 – 1768	
				Malerao Holkar 1766 – 1767
Sawai Maharaja Prithvi Singh II 1768 – 1778			Mahadji Scindia 1768 – 1794	Ahilya Bai Holkar 1767 – 1795 Tukoji Holkar (Ahilya Bai's second husband and co-regent) 1767 – 1797
		Narayan Rao Peshwa 1772 – 1773 Raghunath Rao or Raghoba (Balaji Baji Rao's brother) 1773 – 1774		
Sawai Maharaja Pratap Singh II 1778 – 1803		Sawai Madhu Rao Peshwa (son of Narayan Rao) 1774 – 1795		
			Daulat Rao Scindia 1794 – 1827	

Delhi	Mewar	Marwar	Bikaner	Bundi	Kota

In 1803, the emperor was brought under the protection of the British East India Company, evicting Daulat Rao Scindia from Delhi.

Maharaja Maan Singh
1803 – 1843

Akbar Shah II
1806 – 1837

Maharao Raja Kishore Singh
1819 – ....

Maharao Raja Ram Singh
1821 – ...

Maharana Jawan Singh
1828 – 1838

Bahadur Shah
1837 – 1857

Dhundhar	Jaisalmer	Pune	Ujjain Gwalior	Indore
		Baji Rao Peshwa II (son of Raghunath Rao) 1795 – 1802		
				Kashi Rao 1797 – 1799
				Khande Rao Holkar (Jaswant Rao Holkar acting as regent) 1799 – 1806
Sawai Maharaja Jagat Singh 1803 – 1818				
				Jaswant Rao Holkar 1806 – 1811
				Malhar Rao Holkar II 1811 – 1834
Sawai Maharaja Jai Singh III 1819 – 1835			Gwalior became the Scindia capital in 1814.	
	Maharawal Guj Singh 1820 –			
			Jankoji Scindia appointed raja (with Daulat Rao Scindia's wife, Baiza Bai, acting as regent until 1832) 1827 – 1843	

Rajput & Islamic Timelines

The empire of Islam	Tomar	Guhilot	Chauhan	Bhati
Hazrat Mohammad b. 570 600 – 632				
Khalifa Abu Bakr 632 – 634				
Khalifa Omar 634 – 644 conquest of Persia & Egypt				
Khalifa Othman 644 – 656				
Khalifa Ali 656 – 661				
Khalifa Muawiya – Ommayad Dynasty 661 – 680 His followers called themselves the Sunnis – the orthodox Muslims. The followers of Ali became known as the Shias (from the Arabic word meaning sect).				
The capital is moved to Damascus. Persia and Egypt are conquered.				
Khalifa Walid I 705 – 715 The empire stretches from the western border of Tibet to the Atlantic Ocean. Sind becomes a part of the empire. Defeated by the armies of Leo III of Constantinople.				
				Rao Manjham Rao of Marot 729 – 759
732: General Abdur Rahman met the Franks at Tours and was defeated by Charles Martel.	Dhillika built by Tomar Rajputs AD 736.	Rawal Kalbhoj (Bappa Rawal) 734 – 753	Manik Rai Chauhan of Ajmer & the Chauhans of Asi and Golconda.	

The empire of Islam	Tomar	Guhilot	Chauhan	Bhati
Khalifa Ab-l-Abbas – Abbassid Dynasty 750 – 754				
Khalifa Al Mansur 754 – 775 shifts capital to Baghdad in 762.		Rawal Khuman I 753 – 773		Rao Kehar 759 – 805
Khalifa Haroun-al-Rashid (fifth Abbasid khalifa) 786 – 809		Rawal Mattat 773 – 793		
		Rawal Bhert Pat I 793 – 813		Rao Tanno 805 – 820
Mamun the Great (sixth Abbassid khalifa) 813 – 833		Rawal Sinha 813 – 828		Yugraj Vijay Rao – Churala 820 – 841
The first signs of disintegration appears.		Rawal Khuman II 828 – 853		
Khalifa Al Mutasim 833 – 842 Employs Turks as personal bodyguards.				
By AD 850, the empire of the khalifas begins to break up.		Rawal Mahayak 853 – 878 Rawal Khuman III 878 – 942		
				Rawal Sidh Deoraj 909 – 973
		Rawal Bhert Patt II 942 – 943		
		Rawal Allat 951 – 953		
				Rawal Mundha 973 – 998
				986 Amir Subuktigen – a Turk from Ghazni raids Bathinda
				Mahmud Ghazni 997 – 1030

TIMELINES OF THE SULTANATES OF GUJARAT & MALWA

Mewar	Malwa	Gujarat
	1398: Malwa independent after Taimur's invasion. Dilavar Khan Ghur left as governor.	1391 – 1403: Muzaffar Shah I (Zafar Khan – last governor to be appointed from Delhi)
	1405 – 1435: Dilavar's son declares himself Sultan Hoshang Shah.	1403 – 1407: Tatar Mohammad Shah
		1407 – 1411: Sultan Muzaffar Shah I (restored and becomes the first sultan of Gujarat)
Maharana Kumbha 1433 – 1468	1435 – 1436: Sultan Muhammad Shah I (leaves the government in hands of his second cousin Mughith).	1411 – 1442: Sultan Ahmad I (Muzaffar's grandson)
	1436 – 1469: Sultan Mahmud Khalji I (Mughith's son).	
	1442: marches to punish Maharana Kumbha of Chittaurgarh for having assisted Umar Khan – the son of Muhammad Shah I.	1442 – 1451: Sultan Mohammad Karim Shah
	1446: Mahmud again invades Mewar. On the way, he obtains submission from the commanders of the fortresses of Ranthambhor and Mandalgarh and Bayana.	
	1455: Invasion of Mewar, conquering the district of Mandsaur, Ajmer, and the fortress of Mandalgarh.	1451 – 1458: Sultan Qutub-ud-din Ahmad Shah II
		1458 – 1458: Sultan Daud Shah 1458 – 1511: Sultan Mahmud I Begara (The Prince of Cambay)
Maharana Uday Singh I (Ooda the Hatiaro) 1468 – 1473	1465: An envoy arrives at Mandu from the shadowy 'Abbasid caliph of Egypt with a robe of honour and patent of sovereignty. Despite the hollowness of such a gesture, the patent is gratefully received.	
Maharana Raimal 1473 – 1509	1469 – 1500: Sultan Ghiyas-ud-din Shah (Mahmud's son). Maharana Kumba had been murdered by his son, Ooda, and this had led to a civil war in Mewar with one of the parties seeking the aid of the Malwa sultan. Ghiyas-ud-din provided military assistance but without success.	
	1500 – 1510: Sultan Nasir Shah	
Maharana Sanga 1509 – 1529	1510 – 1531: Sultan Mahmud II Medini Rai, a Purbiya Rajput who is appointed as minister dominates the sultan.	1511 – 1526: Sultan Muzaffar II

Mewar	Malwa	Gujarat
	1514: Mahmud tries unsuccessfully to assassinate Medini Rai	
	1517 : The sultan made his way to Gujarat to seek the aid of Muzaffar II against Medini Rai and his ally Maharana Sanga. Medini Rai flees. Mahmud re-enters his capital and thinks it best to attack Medini Rai at his headquarters at Gagraun, before the Rajput can really consolidate his position. But a strategic blunder allows Maharana Sangram Singh to capture him and keep him in captivity in Chittaurgarh. Mahmud pays a hefty ransom before he can secure his release and is forced into recalling his troops from Gagraun. Malwa, as a result, breaks up.	
	1519: The Mandsaur area passes into the hands of Maharana Sangram Singh and Chanderi is occupied by Medini Rai.	
		1526 – 1526: Sultan Nasir Shah
		1526 – 1526: Sultan Sikandar Shah (elder son of Muzaffar II)
Maharana Ratan Singh 1529 – 1531		1526 – 1535: Sultan Bahadur Shah (younger son of Muzaffar II)
Maharana Bikramjeet 1531 – 1537	1531: Sultan Bahadur Shah of Gujarat declares himself sultan of Malwa.	On 28 March 1531 Bahadur declares himself sultan of Malwa.
		1534: Sultan Bahadur sacks Chittaur
		1535: Gujarat occupied by Emperor Humayun
	1536 – 1537: Mallu Khan governs Malwa	1536 – 1537: Sultan Bahadur Shah restored. He is murdered at the hands of the Portuguese.
	1537 – 1542: Mahmud Shah II of Gujarat appoints Mallu Khan as Qadir Shah of Malwa.	1537: Miran Mohammad 1537 – 1554: Mahmud Shah II
	1542 – 1554: Sher Shah occupies Malwa and places Shujaat Khan in overall command.	
	1554 – 1561: Baz Bahadur	
	1561: Malwa is annexed by the Mughal Empire.	1554 – 1561: Ahmad Shah III
		1561 – 1573: Muzaffar Shah III
		1573: Gujarat is annexed by the Mughal Emperor Akbar.

What nation on earth,
could have maintained the semblance of civilization,
the spirit or the customs of their forefathers,
during so many centuries of overwhelming depression,
but one of such singular character as the Rajpoot?

James Tod

Remnants of the kingdoms of Rajputana within modern Rajasthan.
Districts of Rajasthan that were once included in the kingdom of Mewar.

CHAPTER 1

MEWAR

The princely state of Mewar occupies the southern corner of Rajasthan, sharing borders with both Gujarat and Madhya Pradesh. Ruled by one of the oldest dynasties in the world, it is steeped in antiquity, tradition, valour and romance. Through the pages of history, Mewar had held its own as the premier 'Hindu' nation and its maharana as the Hindupati – the defender of the ancient Indian way of life[1]. He was the senior-most of all Rajput kings and granted honours and titles, a right that belonged to the most powerful ruler in all Hindustan.

---

1. The ancient way of life was comprised of Hinduism, Jainism, Buddhism and the tribal faiths that had survived the test of time. By their side, were the Parsees, the followers of Zarathustra who arrived soon after the Islamic conquest of Persia and the Jews who, as legend put it, had made many settlements since the time of King Solomon (962 – 922 BC). Technically, they all formed the ancient way of life practised in India. Perhaps all of them, barring the Jews who were recognised as followers of The Book, were viewed as a single entity, by the Arabs Muslims. Unable to pronounce the alphabet S, the Arabs referred to the land that lay along and beyond the banks of the river Sindh as the land of Hind. Its people quite naturally came to be known as 'Hindu'. Islam arrived on the shores of India with the Arab invasion of Sind in AD 712, but was not actively propounded until the late twelfth century AD. Christianity arrived with the Portuguese in the early sixteenth century AD.

The Hindupati, Maharana Bhim Singh Sisodia had inherited the fortunes of a falling house. Over the ages, India had been besieged by numerous warring factions and his dynasty had laboured to maintain their independence. But no sooner had one predator out-lived its allotted time when another reared its head. The 'barbarians'[2] strove to erase from living memory the very identity of the Indians[3]. They set up many empires within Hindustan, ruling from the coveted city of Delhi. While destinies throughout India were rewritten with every change that took place in Delhi, the Rajputs struggled with their karma and clung to their possessions with a tenacity that defied the predatory powers. But a great change had taken place since those early years. Rajput kingdoms, that would have once bled for the preservation of Mewar, now leagued with the powers of Delhi. New-found wealth and offices at the imperial courts led them to challenge the age-old authority of the Sisodias.

To the court of Maharana Bhim Singh came the thirty-six-year-old British Political Agent Captain James Tod. The year was 1818 and Bhim Singh had completed forty years on the gaddi of Mewar. It had been destiny, once again that placed him – as an eight-year-old boy – upon the throne. Murder and conspiracy, that had been no stranger to the house of the Sisodias, had dealt yet another hand. A dominating stepmother, reluctant to hand over the reins of power, Afghan and Maratha marauders and petty infighting between neighbouring Rajput kingdoms cast long shadows upon his life. The days were past when the chivalry of Mewar would have rallied to his side preferring to join the leading family in death, rather than compromise the honour of Mewar. Eight years had passed since the day the maharana had been forced into reminding his sixteen-year-

---

2. The term 'barbarian' is a subjective one. Invaders and vandals, regardless of the heights to which their civilisations may have reached, were viewed as 'barbarians' by the people whose culture and identity they tried to destroy. No doubt, the Rajputs, upon their arrival, were also viewed as 'barbarians' by the Indians of the time. In due course the Rajputs became part of accepted Indian society.

3. The word Indian has been used to denote the residents of India. Invaders, who chose to make this land their own, were not considered to be Indians until they merged with the Indian way of life or ceased ostracising and being ostracised by the older established population. Generally a sense of kinship developed over time or made itself felt when a common enemy came into the picture. The word has expanded today to incorporate the many faiths and races that have made India their home.

old daughter, Krishna Kumari, of her royal duty. For Maharaja Maan Singh of Marwar and Maharaja Jagat Singh of Jaipur, in their quest for her hand, had threatened Mewar with destruction.

James Tod's first visit to Mewar had been as a young lieutenant in the year 1806, when he accompanied the British embassy, led by Graeme Mercer Esq, to the court of Daulat Rao Scindia. Since that fateful day in 1803, when the army of the British East India Company occupied Delhi and relieved Scindia of his duty as protector, the Maratha had sulked in his camp at Rashmi. For nine years he had enjoyed the honour, one that his predecessor, Mahadji, had assumed in 1788, imposing upon Shah Alam – the blind puppet emperor of the ailing Mughal dynasty. Lieutenant Tod's official duties had included the survey and charting of Mewar. In the course of his duties, he studied the characteristics of the land as only a surveyor can but his passions extended to more than mere survey. His work evolved into a detailed and sensitive study of the people, their history, customs and traditions.

The extensive travelling that were a part of his days of survey gave way to the stillness of life in the political agent's camp supervising negotiations between the princes and the government of British India. It was a year before the treaties had all been signed and the captain was free to tour the states that came under his political supervision. His work had been a labour of love and Rajputana yielded to the captain the most intimate of her secrets.

Here was a race of people completely unknown to the western world. 'India had no history of her own,' proclaimed their scholars. Surrounded by these ancient peoples, whose lives were no less driven by the very emotions that enslaved the Europeans, the captain felt a sense of kinship, one that he resolved to share with the world. The peoples of Rajasthan could not have found themselves a better spokesman. Determined to record every aspect of their lives, the captain began a study of ancient Indian texts. His passion for his new home gave release to talents that had until now lain dormant and he became at once antiquarian, historian, anthropologist and archaeologist to Rajputana.

Since his appointment as political agent to the Western Rajput States in 1818, he had spent two years in Udaipur at the court of Maharana Bhim Singh. One wing of a lavish two-storeyed palace had been allotted

Rampiyari's lavish villa, stands close to the Shiv Niwas Palace. A part is occupied by the government of Rajasthan and the other by Rawat Surendra Singh Saktawat of Bohera who runs the adjoining Mahendra Prakash Hotel.

to him. It had once been the residence of the late queen mother's chief confidant, Rampiyari, who with her nose for intrigue, had played a crucial role in the politics of Mewar. The captain began a tour of the kingdoms that came under his personal supervision. The geographical observations of his early days as surveyor had resulted in the first detailed map of Rajasthan. His time was now devoted to a study of the people and their heritage. It provided a rich insight into the glorious tales that had been compiled over twenty-two years of service in India.

Mewar stretched lengthwise, slanted in a north-easterly direction with Gujarat at its base and Ajmer to the north. The Aravalli range that formed the western border widened towards its southern end spanning the width of almost the entire kingdom. The northern end tapered, the high mountains with their deep narrow passes, forming the border with the desert kingdom of Marwar. The Sisodia castles of Udaipur and Kumbhalgarh lay along its crest. Between Kumbhalgarh and Ajmer intervened Merwara, the land of the savage mountain tribes – the Mers. The plains of Bhilwara, the land of the Bhil tribe, lay to the east of the mountain range, where a rich mercantile township bustled with activity. Beyond Ajmer, the Aravalli broke into fingers that traversed the region of Shekhawati and Alwar, gradually losing height until it terminated in Delhi.

Upon the eastern border of the kingdom rose the plateau of central India, a grand natural boundary rising 400 feet above the plains. Beyond, lay the Hada kingdoms of Bundi and Kota. As recently as sixty years ago, Mewar had stretched from Godwar on the western side of the Aravalli, to beyond the plateau, its eastern boundary terminating upon the banks of the Chambal.

Captain James Tod stood at the summit of the plateau surveying the view. Mewar in its entirety lay at his feet. Ancient Chittaur stood to his right while straight ahead, across the plains, nestling at the base of the gigantic Aravalli, lay Udaipur. The rest of the land right up to the foot of the plateau and beyond, lay under Maratha and Pathan occupation;

though Kanera, which lay close to where the captain now stood, had been extricated with great difficulty and returned to the maharana. Beyond the Aravalli lying upon the edge of the desert was Godwar, which had been lost to Marwar half a century ago.

The great ancestor of the kings of Mewar, or so claim the bards, was Luv[4], the son of Lord Ram, the hero of the epic *Ramayan*. Having abandoned his father's kingdom in Ayodhya (Uttar Pradesh), Luv had travelled to western Punjab (now Pakistan) where he lived out his days. Around his cottage, Lah-koot (Lahore), developed a township, where his descendents, the Ikshavaku Suryavanshis – the dynasty of the sun, ruled.

It wasn't until the second century AD that Kanak Sen, the reigning Suryavanshi king, set out in the search of a new home. He marched south wards into the lands of the Parmars. Within viewing distance of the sea he stopped. In the land that would later earn itself the name Gujarat he resolved to establish himself. Brute force wrested for him a small piece of land and here the city of Birnagar came up. Four generations later, Kanak Sen's dynasty was flourishing. Three great cities had been established – Vijaypur, Vidarbha and Vallabhi (modern Vala). Vallabhi became famous as a great centre of Jain learning. The peaceful Jains thrived under the patronage of the Suryavanshi kings.

King Siladitya who ruled Vallabhi in the middle of the sixth century AD was invincible. Mystical powers lay at his disposal. At his command, the chariot of the sun god drawn by seven horses, the Sapta aswa, would arise from the sacred fountain of the sun, the Surya Kund. But Siladitya was not without enemies. Many eyed the prosperity and peace enjoyed by Vallabhi; and among the varied aspirants were the Maitrikas, said to be of Iranian descent. A wicked minister in Siladitya's court revealed to the foe the secret of the fountain. The crafty enemy polluted the Surya Kund with blood and the sun god could no longer send his chariot for the defence of Vallabhi. In vain did Siladitya call upon Sapta aswa, but

---

4.   The Sisodias claim descent from the Suryavanshi dynasty, though it is now thought that they started life as the Brahmins of the village of Sesoda, who assumed kshatriya status.

the charm had been broken. The city was ravaged and with it sank the Suryavanshi dynasty of Vallabhi[5].

Of all the royals, Queen Pushpavati alone survived. She had been away on a pilgrimage when news of the massacre arrived. Her husband was dead and all his queens had sacrificed themselves on his funeral pyre. The baby she was expecting had now no crown to claim. Pushpavati, the daughter of the Parmar prince of Chandravati, took refuge in a cave. There she delivered a son who was named Guha (one who is born in a cave). The infant was handed over to a brahmani of Birnagar and immolating herself, Queen Pushpavati left to join her dead lord.

Kamlavati, the brahmani, cared for Pushpavati and Siladitya's child, bringing him up as a young Brahmin: but the Rajput blood was difficult to hide. The growing child shunned his mild mannered companions and chose to hunt the small birds and beasts in the woods. His adventures led him deeper into the forests of Idar where none but the savage Bhil dared to venture. His daring won him friends amongst these children of the forest but it was a game that changed the course of his destiny. A young Bhil cut his finger one day, and streaked Guha's forehead with his blood. The teeka acclaimed the prince's right to kingship. What in all probability began as sport, soon acquired a gruesome dimension. Guha took up his role in all earnestness but his reputation was to be stained with ingratitude forever. He slew his benefactor and ruled over the forest tribe with an iron hand. His sons succeeded him upon the forest throne, adopting the name Guhilot. In time it softened to Gehlote[6].

Guha's descendents ruled these mountainous regions of Gujarat on the

---

5. Vallabhi had been a centre of Jain culture. With the sack of Vallabhi, her Jain population escaped to Rajasthan where they continued to practise their way of life. The largest numbers settled in the desert land of Marwar forming a successful mercantile community. The first sack of Vala, during the reign of Siladitya, was by non-Muslims. The birth of Islam took place around AD 600, and the successors of Hazrat Mohammad – the khalifa's – then took to establishing the empire of Islam. Arab Muslims arrived upon the shores of the Indus and in AD 712, Sind became the first Indian kingdom to fall. Gujarat was the next target and the Islamic conquest of Vala is dated to AD 770, ending the rule of the Maitrikas. What is interesting is that the Maitrikas were also sun worshippers related to the Zoroastrians.

6. Rawal Guhil is known to have ruled from AD 569 – 603. He was succeeded by Rawal Bhoj (AD 603 – 615), who ruled from the Bhomat district in Idar.

The tales of young Bappa's life are many.

It was Jhul Jhulni, the festival of swings, and Bappa chanced upon the daughter of the local Solanki chieftain. With her friends, she was trying to set up swings in the forest. The Guhilot offered to help, provided they played a game with him first. The Solankini's scarf was tied to Bappa's garment and all the village girls joined hands forming a long chain. Together they danced around a tree and in all the merry-making the girls failed to keep count of the number of revolutions that were performed. The game over, Bappa and his friends set up the promised swings.

This light-hearted frolic led to a chain of events quite out of Bappa's control. The chieftain's daughter soon received an offer of marriage and a priest from the prospective bridegroom's family came to check the fortunes in store for the young bride. He looked at the girl's palm and declared that she had already been married. Alarm swept through the Solanki village and though Bappa had sworn his friends to secrecy, it was difficult to keep such a large number of girls quiet.

Bappa fled. With him went two childhood companions, Baleo, the Bhil and Dewa, the Solanki. Together they remained in hiding and became life long companions.

Bappa's little game caused his flight from Nagda and resulted in his greatness. At the same time though, it burdened him with 600 damsels whose descendants ascribe their origin to a prank played around the old mango tree of Nagda.

southern border of the land that would come to be known as Mewar. The descendants of Kamlavati continued their role as family priests. When Guha's grandson came to the throne, the Bhils, tired of foreign rule, killed him. Kamlavati's descendants came to the rescue once again and escaped with the three-year-old prince, Nagaditya. They settled in a valley ten miles north of present-day Udaipur and named it Nagda after their prince. The Guhilots lived quietly in their little hamlet until their name was raised out of oblivion by the eighth prince of the line – Kalbhoj or Bappaditya. Born in AD 734, the child was barely a toddler when his father died. He romped the valley and the forests of Nagda with friends and like all young lads his thoughts were devoted only to the making of mischief.

Chittaurgarh was ruled at the time by a Mori prince of the Parmar race. It was in AD 725, that Chitrang Mori of Morwan, a subordinate of the imperial Parmars of Dhar (Malwa), had unearthed the philosopher's stone in his fields. The blade of his plough re-emerged from the dirt, having turned to gold. Morwan prospered. The newfound wealth was used to repair the ruins of a fort atop a hill close to the plateau. Chitrang's abode came to be known as Chitra-koot and later Chittaurgarh.

Aware that he was a nephew of the Chandravati Parmars of Gujarat, Bappa sought employment at the court of Chittaur. The Mori prince allowed him to lead the army against the foreign foe that had appeared on their borders. They were none other than Khalifa Walid I's Arabs[7], who had

---

7. The presence of the Arabs caused ripples through the Rajput world. But it was unlikely that they were aware of the colossal might of the invader. By AD 700, the empire of Islam stretched from the western border of Tibet, through Afghanistan, Persia, Egypt and Carthage in northern Africa to the Atlantic Ocean. Leaving Persia the Parsees fled to the shores of India, as Islam began replacing the local religions. In 711, Walid's general, Tariq-ibn-Ziyad, crossed the strait of Gibralter (bequeathing his name to the Mount of Gibralter or Jebel-al-Tariq) and took Spain from its Visigoth king, Roderick. If Dahir Despati of Sind received aid from his 'Hindu' counterparts, we have no record but he lost his life a year after Roderick. His daughters were amongst the booty that made its way to the khalifa. But the spirited girls were determined to have their revenge. Mohammad bin Kasim had had his pleasure they declared and the enraged khalifa had his general arrested even as he prepared to embark upon an expedition to Kannauj. The hapless Kasim was sown up in rawhide and transported to Damascus. But the march of Islam did not cease. The Bhati rao of Marot, Manjham Rao, became an accomplice; Manik Rai Chauhan died defending Ajmer and his kinsmen, the Hadas of Golconda, held their jauhar. The Chawura prince, evicted from his island on the coast of Saurashtra, established for himself a new kingdom – Anhilwara Patan.

An illustrious race must always be crowned with its proper mythology. The strange source of Bappa's good fortune is a story, which, in Mewar, is sacrilege to doubt.

Bappa found employment as a cowherd. While grazing his master's cattle in the valleys of Nagda, the royal cowherd was accused of stealing the milk of a favourite cow.

The indignant Bappa followed the brown cow and found her standing at a site by herself, her udder spontaneously pouring its milk into the thicket and shrubs. He looked further and found a hermit lost in a divine trance.

Aroused by the impetuous Bappa, Harita, the hermit, revealed the symbol of the great God Shiva at the sacred site[8]. Bappa related to the hermit all that he knew of himself and received his blessings.

From that day he paid Harita a daily visit with offerings of milk, washed his feet and collected for him the poisonous wild flowers used in the worship of Shiva. In return, he was initiated into the mysterious rites of the deity and received the title of regent or diwan of Eklinga. Bhavani, the consort of Shiva, bestowed upon Bappa a set of celestial arms, marking him as the favourite of the heavens, while Gorakhnath, the hermit of the forest of the Tiger Mount or Nahara Magra, presented to him a double-edged sword which, with the proper incantation, could sever rocks.

---

8. On this spot the temple of Eklinga was erected and the descendents of Harita continued with their priestly duties. At the time of Lt Col Tod's visit, the sixty-sixth descendant was found holding office.

occupied Sind in AD 712. Though Walid I and his famous general, Mohammad bin Kasim died within the next two years, their myrmidons continued with the process of annexing Indian territories in the name of the khalifa. In trying to secure the ports of Gujarat, they targeted Rajput forts in the vicinity that could prove to be a nuisance to Indo-Arab trade.

The Arabs were vanquished and the victorious Guhilot chased them all the way to Gujarat. But on his return, instead of professing gratitude to his king for the opportunity to prove his prowess, he snatched the crown of Chittaur. In AD 734, Bappa became the first rawal of Chittaur, a title borne by his descendents until the accession of the Sisodia branch of the Guhilot family when the title was changed to maharana. Baleo the Bhil – the companion of his youth, claimed the privilege of drawing the teeka of sovereignty with his own blood on Bappa's forehead. The Bhils of Ondari have since continued to exert this right[9].

Bappa had returned from Gujarat bringing back with him the princess of Bunderdhiva (Diu). Of the numerous children born of this marriage some returned to Gujarat while five others settled in the desert of Marwar.

Bappa's career had a strange ending. The legends claim he abandoned his children and his country and left for Khorasan[10]. There he established himself and married new wives from among the 'barbarians'. His 130 children came to be known as the Naushera Pathans and each founded a tribe in the name of the mother. His ninety-eight 'Hindu' children came to be known as the sun born fire worshippers or the Agni-oopasi Suryavanshi. In all twenty-four tribes claimed descent from Bappa.

His death gave rise to a dispute. His 'Hindu' subjects wished for a cremation whereas his 'barbarian' followers clamoured for burial. The two quarrelling groups arrived to claim the body but when they raised the shroud, they found in its place a thousand lotus blossoms. Bappa's children divided the flowers equally between themselves[11].

---

9. The Solanki chieftain of Oghna continues to take the prince by the arm and seat him on the throne while the Ondari Bhil holds the silver salver of spices and rice and applies the teeka with his own blood.
10. The lands to the west of the river Indus were called Khorasan.
11. The Persian Noshirwan is said to have had a similar ending. The king of Jaipur, writing at a later date, felt Bappa and his descendents were all of Persian descent

The semicircular plateau alternated between flat table-like surfaces and clustering ridges. Beginning at Mandalgarh, which stood on an isolated hill, it encompassed the area up to Chittaur. Chittaurgarh exploited its strategic position atop a solitary hill close to and yet distinct from the plateau. The edge could be followed to Jawad, Rampura and Bhanpura in Madhya Pradesh (ancient Malwa), traced past the Mukandara Pass down to Gagraun and across to the point where the Parbati broke into Kota on its way to the Chambal, through Shahbad terminating upon the banks of the Chambal. From the point of its outset at Mandalgarh, the plateau lost much of its table-like features extending in a north-easterly direction through the capital of Bundi, Dablana, Ranthambhor and Karauli terminating in Dholpur Bari.

> Here the geologist may read the book of nature in distinct character. The tract from Rampura to Kota being the most interesting for the antiquarian, the geologist and the lover of nature.

Standing close to the summit of the plateau, the captain's gaze passed westwards over the plains of Mewar across to where the Aravalli rose. In the distance, two great lakes were visible. The Pichola lay, surrounded by the hills, eighty feet above and six miles to the west of the Uday Sagar. A minor lake high up in the village of Suhaila-ka-bari fed the Pichola, which in turn fed the Uday Sagar. The outlet of the Uday Sagar formed the Berach, which crossed the plains to wind past Chittaurgarh. Gathering the waters of the Gambhiri, which was the ancient capital's own rivulet, it made its way due north emptying itself into the Banas. Perennial streams from the Aravalli ensured a constant supply of water to both lakes. The captain gazed upon the ancient kingdom, contemplating his favourite subject – the linking of Chittaur and Udaipur by canal. In his mind's eye, the trains of oxen, treading slowly with their merchandise, were replaced by boats gliding swiftly along the canal and the fields on either side irrigated by lateral cuts instead of creaking water wheels.

It had taken him fifteen days to reach this far. The march had begun on 29 January 1820. Leaving Udaipur, the captain, accompanied by Captain Patrick Waugh, Lieutenant Cary and Dr Duncan, had ridden through the highlands of Toos and was making his way eastwards towards the kingdom of Bundi. An extensive retinue was in attendance. Elephants, camels and horses bore the camp ware while the cooks, stewards and helpers marched on foot. A cavalry division provided the armed escort.

The course of the first day had taken them fifteen miles to the banks of the lake of Kheroda, near Bhindar. A little temple of Mandeswar (Shiva) had been discovered on the banks of the Berach, exploration of which had revealed it to be a miniature of the celebrated temple of Chandravati near Mount Abu. Kheroda itself, situated on the high road between the ancient and modern capitals, had always been the bone of contention during civil wars. Its fortress boasted an interesting set of protective double ditches that could be filled, at will, from the river.

Nine miles of fertile black loam lay between Kheroda and Hinta. The dark soil – the mal (dirt) – extended to the neighbouring kingdom (modern Madhya Pradesh) bequeathing to it the name Malwa. Hinta, which once belonged to one of the infants of Mewar, had been taken by a chief noble of Mewar – the Saktawat. But the deed had taken place post 1766 and by the agreement of 4 May 1818, the land was due for restitution. The chief, however, claimed the right to retain it pleading that his clan had held it for more than half a century. Warm and emotional discussions had been held as a consequence.

Travelling through the fiefdom of Hinta, the captain arrived at Morwan. Nikumbh, Marla and Nimbahera lay ahead. Another nine miles would take them to Kanera. The only traversable route thereafter lay through three steppes, that lent to it the appearance of a miniature Russian Tartary, winding its way through Ratangarh and Singoli towards Hadavati.

Morwan with its stronger claim to antiquity stood upon the border of Mewar, near the modern-day town of Mangalwar. Here stood the ruins of a fort that, tradition maintained, was once Chitrang Mori's castle – the one that he occupied before the move to Chittaur. The ancient township laboured, at the time, under Maratha occupation.

An accident occurred on 2nd February which compelled a longer halt. The morning had been frosty and clear with not a cloud in the sky. The officers had risen with the sun and Captain Waugh had set out to hunt nilgai (blue buck). At the very point of spearing the prey, neither horse nor rider paid attention to the fact that they had entered the thickest part of the jungle. The horse dashed into a tree and the captain was thrown with some violence onto the ground. There he lay unconscious until villagers brought him home on a charpai. Fortunately, no bones were broken and in the absence of leeches for application, rest and ointments were all that could be advised.

Captain Tod had himself returned, that day, with no game except for two black partridges and a batten quail for the large brilliantly plumaged rock pigeons had proven too wild for even his gun.

The annual supply of good things arrived later that day and the officers had settled down after dinner to enjoy a bottle of some delicious Burgundy and La Rose when violent screams from the direction of the village roused them. Help was despatched immediately. The anxious wait ended with the arrival of two men, a young boy carrying a pitcher of milk and a strange tale.

It seemed that the three had gone several miles as usual for their daily supply of milk. On the way back the boy had lagged a couple of steps behind. A sudden scream of 'oh, uncle, let go – let go – I am your child, uncle let me go,' startled the men who turned around to discover a large tiger hanging on to the boy's clothing. Raising their walking sticks, the men attacked the beast lending their voices to the child's pleas. Soon the whole village -- men, women and children, armed with every missile conceivable -- had joined in. Pelted by shoes, vegetables, sticks and stones and confused by the sheer noise, the tiger let go and bounded away. Never had a lethal weapon been raised against the lord of the black rock of Morwan. In return, it was said, that he never preyed upon man and if he ever seized one erroneously, the endearing term of mamoo, would induce him to let go.

The leeches arrived the next day from Nimbahera and the patient felt greatly relieved by their application. That night, clouds gathered and the wind changed direction. The thermometer dropped at daybreak to four degrees below freezing point. Huddled inside his tent, the captain used the time to update his journal.

Reader do you envy me my bon vin de Bourgogne et murailles de coton, with not even a wood fire, labouring under a severe pulmonary affection, with work enough for five men? Only three days ago, the thermometer was 86°F at noon, and today it is less at noon than yesterday at daybreak. Even old England with all her vicissitudes of weather, can scarcely show so rapid a change as this.

It was two days before the patient felt well enough to travel. The weather had worsened considerably and ice blocked the mouths of the leather water bottles. Shards of ice floated on the surface of shallow streams. All along the way, men and cattle huddled morosely around fires. The cotton crop had already been blighted at the onset of the winter and all hopes had been strung on the young gram that would have been ready for harvest within a month. The sudden frost had now dashed all prospects for the coming year.

Guhilot rawals

Khuman, who succeeded Bappa, ruled from AD 753 – 773. He strongly resisted the invading Arabs as his father had done before him and Chittaur had been both lost and regained in his time. The thirteenth Guhilot rawal, Khuman II, who ruled in the latter half of the ninth century, was a name famous in the history of Mewar, for it was in his time that Chittaur had faced a nearly overwhelming invasion by the army of Islam. The princes of Chittaur had, thereafter, assumed the name Khuman as an additional title. But *Khuman Rasa*, that was to be compiled in AD 1715, in celebration of the defence of Chittaur, introduced the name of Mahmud two centuries before the actual invasion by Mahmud of Ghazni.

By 951, Chittaur was lost to the Parmar king of Malwa, Munja Raja. Rawal Allat moved to his new capital at Ahar, close to the modern capital, Udaipur, and Chittaur remained in the hands of the Parmars for close to 200 years. The Solanki Rajputs of Gujarat appear to have held the fort for short periods in between, and the illustrious Raja Bhoj Parmar[12] (AD 1010 – 1055), a favourite character in Hindi literature, also laid claim to having ruled the greatest Rajput fort of all time.

Twenty-two generations of princes ruled from the time of Khuman to that of Samant Singh. An important event had taken place in the intervening period. In 1168, when Kshem Singh succeeded Rawal Karan Singh to the throne of Ahar, his brothers Rahup and Mahup chose to go their own way. Mahup conquered Dungarpur, while Rahup attacked the Purihara prince of Mandor, near modern-day Jodhpur, snatching from him the rich district of Godwar and with it his title of rana. Changing his name from Guhilot to Sisodia[13], Rana Rahup continued as an independent junior branch of the Guhilots of Ahar. Dungarpur was brought under the direct rule of the rawal by Samant Singh (Samantsi) who came to the throne in AD 1172. In this period, the Chauhans of Ajmer and the Guhilots alternated between being friends and foes.

Prithviraj Chauhan had not long ago inherited the coveted Tomar throne of Delhi, driving the other aspirants wild with passion. The Guhilots, however, chose to cement their relationship with the most powerful prince in India through the bonds of matrimony. Rawal Samant Singh sought the

---

12. Bhoj lent his name to the city of Bhopal in Madhya Pradesh and is credited with the excavation of its famous lake – the Bada Talab or Badi Jheel – the waters of which have healing properties and the university of Dhar – the Bhojshala. Around him spawned a generation of legends, among which the *Singhasan Battisi* – the throne with thirty-two tales – has remained a favourite with the puppeteers of Rajasthan. 'Word was brought to the king of the fame of a village lad who delivered the most rational and spectacular of judgements while seated upon a mound of earth. The king ordered the site be excavated and it unearthed a throne that bore thirty-two female statuettes. It was identified as that of his legendary ancestor, Vikramaditya (56 BC – AD 78). But as Bhoj was about to take his place upon the great throne the statuettes spoke up. Every day the king was regaled with a story of the great Vikramaditya. In the end, Bhoj was forced to admit that he was not a worthy occupant of the throne.'

13. Bardic sources recount a delightful tale about the origin of the name Sisodia. An ancient member of the royal Guhilot family once sat down to a feast that followed a hunt in the wilds of Bhainsrorgarh. The ravenous prince swallowed a piece of meat without noticing the gadfly that was feeding on it. The fly tormented the prince's stomach and the royal physician came to his rescue. The tip of a cow's ear was cut off and attached to a string. The prince was made to swallow it and the gadfly attached itself to the bait. The string was withdrawn and the gadfly removed. The grateful prince was nevertheless horrified that a piece of forbidden flesh had passed his lips and he swallowed a mouthful of boiling lead (sisa) to cleanse himself. The lead passed through him like water leaving him unaffected. The prince's descendents then changed their name to Sisodia.

hand of the Chauhan's sister, Pritha. The two brothers-in-law were close friends and Prithviraj invited Samantsi's help when treasure was discovered at Nagaur. This deposit of ancient treasure worried the princes of Anhilwara Patan and Kannauj. The Chauhan would become exceedingly powerful. They invited Mohammad Ghuri, the new sultan of Ghazni, to help humiliate the Chauhan. To cope with the emergency, Prithviraj sent Chand Pundir, the vassal chief of Lahore, to Samantsi. Chand kept detailed records of the gifts that he carried and the speech that he made.

Samantsi appeared dressed as the regent of Shiva. He wore a necklace of lotus seeds, his hair was braided and he referred to himself as Jogindra, the chief of the ascetics. As he was also related to the prince of Patan through marriage, it was decided that he would engage the sultan, while Prithviraj marched against Patan. The invader was repelled and though Samantsi declined any share in the treasure, he permitted his chiefs to accept the gifts of the Chauhan.

Many years elapsed before Samantsi was called once again to defend Delhi and its prince. Prithviraj Chauhan's arrogance, ambition and success followed by periods of disgraceful slothfulness had invited invasions. Jealousy and revenge had rendered the princes of Patan, Kannauj, Dhar and the minor kingdoms, indifferent. They stayed away from the contest that was designed to overthrow them all.

In 1191, the sultan occupied a fort on the border of Prithviraj's kingdom – it was either Sirhind or Bathinda. Prithviraj's army, led by his a vassal chief, Govind Raja of Delhi, rushed to its defence. The first Battle of Tarain was a tremendous success, but instead of following the sultan to his lair the Rajputs sat back contented. With the next year came the second Battle of Tarain. Prithviraj was backed by a large Rajput army. By his side was Rawal Mathan Singh, who ruled from Nagda. It was the decisive battle. The sultan of Ghazni forwarded his terms – convert or fight. The latter was accepted, and the staff of Islam was planted in the heartland of Hindustan – Delhi.

Some say that Prithviraj had been blinded and taken to the sultan's capital where he was later beheaded; some that his faithful bard had come to the rescue, entering the sultan's court while an archery contest was in progress and, through his songs, guided the blind Chauhan's arrow to where the sultan sat upon his throne; some that he died at the site of

The songs of Chand describe Samantsi's departure from Mewar. Mewar was entrusted to the favourite son. The frustrated elder son left for the Deccan where he was welcomed by the Habshi Padshaa, the Abyssinian chief who had set up an independent kingdom.

The last book of Chand *The Great Flight*, describes Samantsi in detail. His arrival at Delhi was hailed with songs of joy. Prithviraj and his court came seven miles to greet him and while the king of Delhi was reunited with his sister, chiefs on either side greeted each other rekindling old friendships. Samantsi chided his brother-in-law on his unprincely inactivity. Chand's narrative devotes equal attention to Samantsi as it does to Prithviraj:

Samantsi was brave and calm, skilful in fight, prudent, wise and eloquent in council, pious and decorous, beloved by his own chiefs and revered by the Chauhans. He could explain the omens better than any augur, dress the squadrons for battle and guide his steed and his lance better than any hero of his time. At the end of the day's battle, all leaders would flock to his tent delighting in his eloquence and drawing upon his wisdom. From the lips of Khuman they would learn the art of good governance.

Three days before the battle ended, Samantsi was slain. With him were lost his renowned chieftains and 13,000 troops of Mewar.

His beloved Pritha on hearing the news – her husband dead and her brother captive, the heroes of Delhi and Mewar 'asleep on the banks of the Ghaggar, in the wave of steel' – joined her lord. She did not wait to witness the invader as he swept through Delhi nor the death of her nephew, Prince Rainsi[14] – the last of the Chauhans, who defended the walls of the city till the end.

14. Historians maintain that Prithviraj's brother – Hariraj Chauhan – continued to wage war against the sultan and against Govindraj – a younger son of Prithviraj – who had defected and had been granted Ajmer. Despite Aibak's support Govindraj was forced to leave Ajmer. He established himself at Ranthambhor and a few generations later his successor managed to shake off the Islamic yoke. Hariraj, who had succeeded in temporarily occupying Delhi, was driven out and eventually took his own life when Ajmer was besieged by Aibak's forces.

battle, upon the banks of the Ghaggar. The victorious Mohammad and his Turkish slave, Qutub-ud-din Aibak, turned upon Kannauj and Jaichand, the traitor, met his fate in the waters of the Ganga. No one was left to contend with the sultan of Ghazni. The invader's men poured into the land. The noble Rajputs fought with enduring courage and though the land was moistened by the blood of both invader and defender, it was to no avail. Those were desperate days. Entire tribes were swept away leaving nothing but a memory of their existence and formal glory.

The great Chola empire of the south and the Rajput Chalukya kingdom of the Deccan, exhausted as they were warring with their 'Hindu' neighbours, had considered themselves too far removed. Bengal, ruled by the last of the Sen dynasty, was to pay the price almost immediately.

As for Sultan Mohammad Ghuri, his end lay not in the glory of the battlefield but lurked instead in the blade of a fellow Muslim – an Ismaili fanatic. Having inherited his brother's dominion of Ghur, Mohammad, now sultan of Ghur, Ghazni and Hindustan, was recalled to deal with the powerful Khokar tribe of Punjab. In March 1206, having dealt with the revolt in the manner of the day, he was in full march, towards Ghazni, when fate overtook him.

It was Rawal Jaitra who succeeded in recovering Chittaur from the Parmars during the early half of the thirteenth century. Chittaur was reinstated as the capital of Mewar. The forty-first rawal, Samar Singh, ruled from AD 1273 – 1302. He witnessed the throne of Delhi pass from the hands of the slaves of the sultan of Ghur into those of the Khalji generals. His son Kumbh Karan left for Nepal where he spread the Guhilot line, and it forms the present-day Rana family of Nepal[15].

The still of the plateau rang with the clash of steel from bygone eras. Silent arrows had once flown through the depths of the jungle and unseen

---

15. The modern-day Nepalese royal family are of Parmar descent. The Ranas were among the leading nobles and rose to prominence in 1846, with Jung Bahadur Rana establishing a line of hereditary prime ministers.

eyes had followed every move. It was home to the Meena and the Bhil. The ancient claimants of the land were still as possessive and though the passage of time had reduced their ferocity, a traveller would be wise to call for an armed escort. The plateau had changed hands many times. The Sisodias, the Hada-Chauhans had once all put forward their claims. As business boomed, forts sprang up along the way to protect caravans that plied the route between Mewar and Hadavati. Though Mewar lost the tableland to the Pathan and the Maratha, the indomitable native continued to hold his ground. Despite the years of domination by Rajputs, hounded and driven to extinction in many parts, the strong-willed tribes had survived. From Jahazpur, in the northern-most part of the plateau, to Mandalgarh, Bijolia and Begun they had left their indelible stamp.

Bijolia or Vijyavalli lay ten miles to the north of Menal. The frontier town was held, by a rao of the Parmar tribe, as a fief of Mewar. In ancient times it had been known as Ahaichpur and had once been ruled alternately by the Guhilots of Mewar and the Chauhans of Ajmer. Half a mile to its east stood Morakara, where amongst the ruins of a fort, survived a palace together with five temples to Parasvanath, the twenty-third Jain teacher. The rivulet here was the Mundagni – the fire extinguishing stream. The Rewati Kund remained well preserved, and notable amongst the inscriptions that survived was the one engraved by Rahil, the Gohil chief.

Whosoever shall bathe in the fountain of Rewati shall surely be the beloved of her lord and bear many children.

The modern castle of Bijolia had been built entirely out of the ruins of the shrines of Morakara.

Menal (Mahanal) occupied the great cleft on the western face of the plateau. The ancient Meena capital had been overrun by Raja Hun who had declared himself lord of the plateau at a time when Bappa struggled for recognition. Both had served the lord of Chittaur, Chitrang Mori, saving the great fort from the Arabs that coveted it. Temples stood to either side of the 400-foot drop, one bearing the name of Prithviraj Chauhan and the other that of Samantsi. Menal had served as summer capital for the two brothers-in-law. To one who had immersed himself in its legends, the ruins of Menal appeared enveloped in melancholic charm.

Rawal Ratan Singh

Ratan Singh came to the throne in AD 1302, at a time when Alla-ud-din Khalji, the visionary sultan of Delhi, was busy securing the trade route that led to the ports of Gujarat. The riches of India tempted many and they had to be kept at bay. Since AD 1298, hordes of Mongols had begun crossing over into India. The sultan's energies were devoted completely to keeping them out. Some were granted refuge and they settled in Delhi as the New Mussalmans. But in 1299, Kutlugh Kwhaja arrived with a large force. He passed through leaving the countryside undamaged. The Mongol had come determined to win himself an empire. The sultan bore the brunt by himself arriving at the realisation that the Rajputs could not be counted amongst his friends. In 1301, Hamir Deva Chauhan of Ranthambhor paid with his life for having sheltered a few Mongols and Ranthambhor passed out of Rajput hands for many long years. For Alla-ud-din's trade route to be truly secure, the powerful Rajput forts would have to go. Jaisalmer had already been taken care of by Alla-ud-din's uncle, Jalal-ud-din Khalji, in 1294. Alla-ud-din had himself razed the Chauhan stronghold of Asirgarh the very next year. Chittaurgarh's turn had come.

Among the friends and relatives that assembled for the defence of Chittaur, was the rawal's cousin Rana Lakshman Singh (Lakumsi). He brought with him his twelve valiant sons. For six months, the fort withstood a siege. Then provisions ran low. A terrible battle followed. Despite all the aid that poured in, it soon became evident that the fort could no longer be saved. The saka of Chittaurgarh was announced and a jauhar commanded. Husbands bade farewell to wives and children, promising faithfully to meet them the next day in heaven. A great fire crackled and blazed in a cavern. To the chanting of verses from the *Bhagwad Gita* the wives of Rawal Ratan Singh led the women and children of Chittaurgarh to their deaths. By the dawn of 25 August 1303, the men had been set free. Earthly bonds no longer stood in their way.

Lakumsi spent a troubled night. The women were all gone and the only men that survived would fight to the last. The coming of the morning would spell doom for Chittaur. As he rested at his post upon the ramparts, the night loomed darker than ever before. Lakumsi's heart was filled with pain. There seemed to be no way in which he could preserve at least

Rawal Ratan Singh ruled Chittaur for but one year. By his side was the dark-skinned Padmini, the daughter of Hamir Sank Chauhan (or perhaps Gandharv Sen and Champavati – as claimed in the Padmavat, written by poet Malik Mohammad Jayasi) of Lanka (Sri Lanka). She was as radiant as the lotus she had been named after and her beauty was renowned through the land. But the queen of Chittaur was to be the cause of unnumbered woes for Mewar[16].

Alla-ud-din Khalji the sultan of Delhi was determined to have her for his harem. A direct attack on Chittaur would have been of no avail, for the greatest fort in Rajasthan stood its ground firmly. Alla-ud-din came instead, on a friendly visit. He sent word to the Rajputs that he would be satisfied with a mere sight of the lady, his motives were chaste and he would henceforth consider himself a brother to Padmini.

Relying on the famed Rajput word of honour, Alla-ud-din entered the fort lightly guarded. The queen of Chittaur was reluctant to meet him and her husband decided that the sultan would have to make do with a glimpse of her reflection upon the waters of a pond, keeping the queen out of direct line of vision. But the reflection itself was bewitching. The eighteen-year-old queen of Chittaur was indeed a treasure among women. A glimmer of desire lit the sultan's eye. In a flash, Ratansi cast his goblet into the water. The ripples broke the spell and the sultan was stunned into recovery. Regaining his composure, he prepared to leave.

Ratansi escorted Alla-ud-din down the winding path, while his guest made many polite noises at the trouble he was taking. Just as Alla-ud-din had

---

16. No evidence has been found to validate this tale. Padmini may well have been the creation of bards trying to justify Alla-ud-din's savage attack on Chittaur. But the bards of Jaisalmer claim she was a Bhati girl, the daughter of the exiled Rawal Punpal whose descendents occupied Pugal. She had been born while her father was in exile, a misfortune that spared her from the first jauhar and saka of Jaisalmer.

Some versions claim that it was a glass mirror in which Alla-ud-din received his first glimpse of Padmini and that the mirror was shattered by her husband who threw his goblet at it. Mirrors with a metallic backing had come into use nearly a century ago and would have been in use during this period.

risked his life by entering the fortress alone, the rawal took with him no personal guards. As they bade each other farewell, imperial soldiers, who had been lying in wait just outside the walls of the fort, fell upon the rawal. The horrified Rajputs received word from the sultan's camp: the rawal would be released once Padmini had been surrendered.

Chittaur was in despair. Padmini conferred with her Chauhan relatives – her uncle Gorah and her nephew Badal – who had accompanied her from Sri Lanka. The Chauhans devised a scheme that would save their prince, without having to sacrifice Padmini. A message was sent to the sultan that the queen would be handed over but in a manner befitting her high station.

She would be accompanied by maids and highborn Rajput ladies who would wish to pay her their last respects. The sanctity and privacy of these women would have to be observed by the Islamic army.

Shielded from Islamic eyes, 700 covered palkis proceeded to the imperial camp. Ratan Singh was to be permitted one last interview with his wife. He would then have to return to Chittaur. Alla-ud-din, who had no real intention of releasing the rawal, waited impatiently. Ratan Singh was spending more than his allotted time with the woman who now belonged to the sultan of Delhi. Alla-ud-din approached the tent. As he drew near, a troop of Rajput soldiers sprang out and in the confusion that followed, the rawal escaped.

The loyal Rajputs covered their sovereign's retreat, perishing in the attempt, but Ratan Singh ascended the fort in safety.

While the sultan ranted and raved, threatening Chittaur with destruction, a call was sent out and Rajputs from far and near rushed to its defence. A siege of Chittaur began, the likes of which had never been witnessed before. The city remained secure as long as its defendants lived but there was no end to the tragic news that kept pouring in. One by one the best warriors of Chittaur were lost. Paying no heed to the wounds that he had sustained, Badal, then a stripling of twelve, escaped to announce to the women that Chittaur could no longer be saved. The women prepared for jauhar.

A great fire was lit in a subterranean retreat. The last defenders of Chittaur watched their women – mothers, wives and daughters – led by the queens, proceed to the cavern to save themselves from dishonour.

'Tell me Badal, how did my piya behave?'

Badal stood beside Padmini and recounted to her the manner in which her lord conducted himself during the battle.

'He was the reaper of the harvest of battle. I followed his steps as a humble gleaner of his sword. On the gory bed of honour, he spread a carpet of the slain, a 'barbarian' prince his pillow, he has laid himself down and sleeps surrounded by the foe. Oh, mother! How further can I describe his deeds, when he left no foe to dread or admire him.'

Padmini smiled farewell to the boy saying, 'my lord will chide me for my delay,' and sprang into the flames.

one of his sons. A voice broke in on his solitude.

'Mai bhooki hoo.' 'I am hungry.'

Raising his eyes, he beheld the Kangra Rani. The terrifying form glowed from among the shadows.

'Not satiated,' exclaimed the rana. 'Though 8,000 of my kin were offered to you?'

'I must have regal victims,' said the guardian goddess of Chittaur. 'And if twelve kings bleed not for Chittaur the land will pass from the line.'

She appeared once again the next night to make her demand. This time the council of ministers waited at the appointed site.

'On each day enthrone a prince. Let the parasol, the red umbrella and the yak tail whisk proclaim his sovereignty and for three days let his decrees be supreme. On the fourth day let him meet the foe and his fate.'

Ari Singh (Ursi), the rana's firstborn, claimed his right and eleven sons followed in the same manner. Eventually the contest arose between Ajay and Lakumsi. The favourite son was prevailed upon to make good his escape, while the rana, satisfied that his line was not extinct, followed his brave sons.

Of the fantastic tales woven by the bards, little is true but fact remains that Alla-ud-din took possession of the celebrated fort, committing every act of barbarity, destroying temples and works of art. A palace, attributed co Padmini, is said to have alone escaped his wrath. The Sisodia ranas of Mewar stepped into the shoes of the rawals and swore to regain Bappa Rawal's throne. Alla-ud-din's son, Khizr Khan, was made governor of the fort and it was re-named Khizrabad[17]. In 1311, Khizr Khan handed the fort over to Rao Maldeo, the Songara-Chauhan chief of Jalor.

---

7. A bridge of ten arches that dates from this period, still stands across the Gambhiri. It is said to be the work of either Khizr Khan or Rana Ari Singh, the father of Maharana Hamir.

Days were spent in idleness at Morwan, waiting for Captain Waugh to recover. A man was sent, in the meanwhile, to copy the inscriptions within the temple of Mama Devi at Palode. The following legend was brought back:

A wealthy Jain had built the shrine for one of the tirthankaras (Jain pontiffs) but as soon as it had been completed, the mother goddess appeared in a dream and expressed her desire to occupy the temple. The Jain was unable to deny the goddess but he refused to violate the rules of his order. He would not carry out animal sacrifices. The goddess then instructed him to go to the Songara chieftain of Chittaur who would attend to the installation rites.

The inscriptions upon the temple wall corroborated a fact that had been unearthed amidst the ruins of Chittaur. It proved that that the Solankis had once made a conquest of Chittaur. In the winter of AD 1151, the Solanki ruler of Chittaur had come to worship at the temple of Mama Devi and had recorded, for posterity, his visit upon its walls. It also proved that there had been an ancient temple at the site, which the Jain had wished to embellish and rededicate to his own guru but had been prevented from doing so by Rao Maldeo the Songara-Chauhan governor at Chittaur.

Rana Ajay Singh

Rana Ajaysi was the only survivor of Chittaurgarh. Setting up his capital at Kelwara, a town situated in the heart of the Aravalli mountains, he sent for Hamir, the son of his eldest brother, Ursi. It had been Rana Lakumsi's desire that Hamir succeed Ajaysi when the latter had attained a hundred years.

Of Ajaysi's own sons, one had already died at Kelwara. The other Sujansi, (Sujan Singh) was capable of inciting civil war and therefore needed to be banished. Sujansi left for the Deccan with bitterness in his

Hamir was the son of Ursi and a Chundano Rajputni.[18]

With a few friends, Ursi had been out hunting in the forests of Ondwa when the boar they were chasing escaped into a field of maize. It disappeared from sight, lost amongst the dense growth. Each stalk grew close to ten or twelve feet from the ground. Hunting the boar down would have led to ruining the crop.

A young woman came up and offered to drive out the game. Seizing the tallest stalk of corn, she climbed onto a raised platform. Casting her gaze upon the field she waited until she detected a slight trembling amongst the leaves and then, raising her arm took aim. As sure as a spear, the stalk found its mark and within minutes the impaled beast was dragged squealing and writhing before the hunters.

The Rajputs were used to feats of heroism from their nervous and delicate women, but this was unusual. As they sat by a stream to prepare the day's feast, the conversation hovered around the fair arm that transfixed the boar.

Quite suddenly a ball of clay came singing through the air. The stray sling shot fractured a leg of the prince's steed. Looking in the direction

---

18. The Chundanos were by this time an impoverished branch of the Chauhans.

from where it came, they saw the same woman on her elevated stand, chasing crows from her ripening field.

Seeing the mischief she had caused, she descended to express her apologies and returned to her duties.

They spotted her yet again in the evening, a vessel of milk balanced on her head, leading two buffaloes by the hand. Wickedly, they decided that it was the moment of payback. Hoping to upset the milk she carried, one of the prince's companions dashed past, too close for comfort. Displaying no alarm, the Chauhani stepped aside at the very last moment pushing one of her buffaloes directly into the path of the jester. Both horse and rider were brought to the ground.

Ursi returned the next day to ask for her hand and was surprised when the proud father refused the match. The old Chundano was, however, scolded soundly by the more prudent mother and made to recall the refusal.

Born in 1291, Hamir remained in his maternal home, leading a rustic village life until the catastrophe of Chittaur changed his destiny.

heart. His descendants[19] would one day right the wrong done to him by Mewar.

Mewar was lost. Despite the ills that afflicted the dynasty of the Khaljis and their successors, the Tughlaks, the garrisons of Delhi remained in occupation of Chittaur. The plains were abandoned and farmlands neglected as the peasants took to the hills.

Ajaysi was kept busy battling the tribal chiefs of the mountains, the most formidable amongst whom was Munja Balaitcha. Fatally wounded, he summoned Hamir, who promised to return successful or not at all.

In a few days, Munja's head was laid at the rana's feet and Ajaysi anointed Hamir's forehead with a teeka drawn with Munja's blood.

Mewar lost more than just Chittaur. Territories that had been under her control were reclaimed by the original tribal occupants of Rajasthan. The Meenas settled once again in the plateau.

The survivors of Ajmer, the Hada-Chauhans, who had taken sanctuary in Mewar since 1192, now saw an opportunity to create a kingdom of their own. They targeted the plateau. The Meenas were driven out and independent Bhil lands taken over.

As Mewar recovered, lost lands were regained. Although the Hadas were forced to vacate the plateau and move into the Meena lands of Bundi and the Bhil valley of Kota, they retained their position as one of the great vassals of Mewar.

The plateau and the surrounding lands changed hands again 400 years later. Until 1760, the entire area right up to the Chambal had belonged to Mewar but had since fallen into the grip of the Marathas. Kanera alone had been extricated with great difficulty and returned to the maharana.

The frost had spared the crops upon the plateau that winter but it was

---

19. Shivaji Raje Bhosle, the Maratha, was of Sujan Singh's line. This young man set up the independent kingdom of Satara in Maharashtra, amidst Mughal domination, in the seventeenth century. The Marathas eventually proved to be the ruin of Rajasthan.

From the histories, it is known that the first Mughal emperor, Babar, had introduced melons and grapes to India and Akbar, following his example, had brought in gardeners from Persia who had succeeded in growing peaches, almonds and pistachio. Jahangir had introduced tobacco but no mention was to be found regarding the cultivation of poppy for the express purpose of producing opium for trade.

with some sadness that Captain Tod recorded the increase in the cultivation of poppy. As to who had introduced the plant to Indian cultivators, there was no clue. Though its use in medicine had long been known its abuse seemed to be a recent phenomenon. The culture, that had been first confined to the tract between the rivers Shipra and Chambal, the original poppy nursery, had spread throughout Malwa and into parts of Rajasthan, especially Mewar and Hadavati. The cultivation of opium appeared to increase in direct proportion to poverty and oppression. The poppy, as opposed to barley or corn, allowed easy payment of taxes, sparing villages from destruction. The opium produced was exported to China for sale and the Marathas encouraged its farming.

The uncultivated regions of the plateau continued to be well wooded with abundant streams, every glen and fountain being associated with the worship of Shiva. The temple of Sukhdev (the god who grants happiness) lay in a deep recess upon an ascent, guarded by a waterfall. Several caves existed, but the most conspicuous object was a projecting ledge known as Dyte-ka-har or the giant's bone. Those in search of happiness would jump onto the ledge from above giving it the name Viraj hamp or warriors leap. There were records of a few that had not perished in the attempt.

Maharana Hamir

Hamir succeeded in 1326, and was destined to become the saviour of Chittaurgarh. On the day of his teeka[20] ceremony, he plundered and captured the territory of his enemy Munja.

Hamir made forays into Chittaur, laying bare the countryside and occupied all but the fortified towns. He appealed to those loyal to him to move to the hills and abandon Chittaur. Together they carried out a guerrilla-style warfare retreating each time to the safety of the Aravalli.

As long as the fort of Chittaurgarh lay in enemy hands, farmers stayed away. Mewar was on the verge of ruin when a coconut – a proposal

---

20. This teeka-dowr was an ancient custom practised by the princes of Chittaur. Should there be no enemy or indifferent acquaintance, a mock raid would be carried out on a neighbouring kingdom. For many years, after the princes of Jaipur united their fortunes with those of Delhi's, the border town of Malpura became the object of such raids by the newly crowned maharanas of Mewar.

Bardic lore has a colourful and a fairly improbable tale about Hamir's Songara-Chauhan queen who turned out to be the brains behind the recovery of Chittaur.

As stipulated by the governor, Hamir brought with him only 500 horsemen. As they approached Chittaur, five sons of the Chauhan advanced to meet them. The city was without decoration, no torna strung above the gates and not one woman to shower him with flower petals or greet him with songs. An unsatisfactory answer was all that was forthcoming, and Hamir's mind grappled with possibility of treachery as he mounted for the first time the steps of Chittaur.

In the hall of his ancestors, Hamir was received by Rao Maldeo, his son Banbir and their chiefs. The bride was brought in without ceremony and the corner of their garments knotted together. Their hands were united in the traditional manner but there were none of the usual solemnities practised on such occasions.

The couple was left to retire. Hamir discovered to his horror that he had married a widow. The very idea was inconceivable at the time and the young Sisodia could never have imagined that a fellow Rajput could have descended to such a level. His bride had long ago been married to a chief of a Bhati tribe who had been slain soon thereafter. She had been too young to even recall his face. But she understood her new husband's plight and with her kindness and vows of fidelity, overcame Hamir's sorrow.

Exercising a bridegroom's privilege to request a favour, and as instructed by his wife, Hamir asked for the services of Jal Mehta, a civilian officer and scribe. Together they returned to Kelwara.

A romantic tale confirmed Hamir's legitimacy.

Once on the throne of Chittaur, Hamir began a search for Bappa Rawal's sword. In a dream, the mother goddess of Chittaur appeared. Hamir was led into a subterranean cavern.
The floor writhed with snakes, the air was putrid and in the heat of their lair, demonesses moaned the chant of the Kangra Rani. Hamir's antecedents were verified and the sword that they had guarded since the fall of Chittaur was handed over to the true descendent of Bappa.

In the ancient Parmar temple, that Bappa had dedicated to Surya, Hamir installed the mother goddess – Kalika Mata.

of marriage – arrived from Rao Maldeo the governor of Chittaur. Was it a trap or a means of humiliation? Every possibility of danger was looked into. The prince's advisors were firmly against it.

'My feet shall at least tread on the rocky steps on which my ancestors have moved,' said Hamir and he accepted the coconut.

The wedding took place and in due course a son[21] was born. Rao Maldeo celebrated by making over the entire hill tracts to Hamir. The young mother wrote to her parents. She begged permission to lay her child before the shrine of the mother goddess.

Mother and baby arrived at a time when Maldeo was away with his chiefs. Hamir's wife and Jal Mehta managed to win the hearts of the remaining troops and Hamir was allowed entry. Though a sudden resistance from Maldeo's soldiers nearly ruined the plan, Hamir was able to force his way through and the oath of allegiance (aan) to the rightful rana of Mewar was proclaimed from the palace of his forefathers.

Maldeo returned to find the fort occupied and he personally carried the account to Delhi. Mohammad bin Tughlak, the sultan who now occupied the throne of Delhi, hurried to recover his lost possession and found the standard of the sun flying once more from the walls of Chittaur. The old citizens had re-emerged from the hills and the hiding places. Streams of men poured out into the valleys as every heart rejoiced. It is said, that the sultan was made captive and confined within Chittaur, that he obtained his release only after the surrender of Ajmer, Ranthambhor, Nagaur and Sooe Sopoor. In addition, fifty lakhs of rupees and 100 elephants were gifted to Mewar.

Hamir assumed the title of maharana and was the sole 'Hindu' prince of power left in India. The princes of Marwar and Jaipur paid him homage, as did the chiefs of Bundi, Gwalior, Chanderi, Raisen, Sikri, Kalpi and Abu. The Sisodias became the ruling family of Mewar.

Hamir died full of years, having ruled wisely and well, a gallant prince of Mewar; his name was to be remembered and honoured forever.

---

21. It is not known whether Hamir's successor, Kshetra Singh (Khaitsi), was this child.

The towers of Chittaur rose in the distance. Led by their elders, the villagers had all turned out to greet the visitors. Marla was home to the charuns (bards), of the tribe of the Kachhelas who were Banjaras (carriers or couriers) by profession, but poets by birth. Like genealogists and priests, poets have been revered by all in India. The sanctity of their persons gave to them an immunity, which extended not only to their personal belongings but also to the goods they carried. In time, the charuns became the free traders of Rajputana.

Graceful charunis waved their scarves high over the heads of their esteemed guests. The husbands dressed in white with high loose folded turbans inclined to the side, looked on as the colourful scarves of the muses of Marla held the captain and his men captive. Mischievous and bright-eyed, the women had dressed themselves in dark skirts and colourful bodices. Gold ornaments had been worked into their dark tresses and ivory bangles covered their arms from wrist to shoulder. Heavy gold necklaces distinguished the elders. The natural dignity and bearing of the charuns bespoke of a proud race that, despite the homage they paid, expected a full measure in return. Never was there a nobler subject for the painter in any age.

The village elders arrived at the camp in the afternoon and it was then that the captain learnt of his escape from the silken bonds of the charunis. For 500 years, this community had enjoyed the privilege of making prisoner any king of Mewar who should pass through Marla. He was kept in bondage until he had provided the women with a feast. As the maharana's representative the captain had been in jeopardy. But unsure of an Englishman's reaction to this light-hearted bullying, they had allowed him to pass. Delighted with the custom, Captain Tod sent money to the ladies with his respects and a request that they should hold their feast.

The charuns claim to have accompanied Maharana Hamir as he returned from the coast of Makran, having completed his devotions at the shrine of Hinglaz Mata (now in Baluchistan, Pakistan). It was on his way to the shrine, as he made his way through Gujarat, that a young charuni had taken charge of feeding all the maharana's men insisting that she had been commanded to do so by the mother goddess. In return for her kindness, Hamir had induced her family to move to Mewar and bestowed upon them the village of Marla.

Maharana Kshetra Singh (Khaitsi)

Maharana Hamir's son succeeded in AD 1366, to a well-established kingdom. Khaitsi extended the borders, capturing Ajmer and Jahazpur and re-annexing Mandalgarh, Dasar and all of Chappan from the Bhils. A spirited warrior, he was said to have defeated a sultan of Delhi at Bakrole, but lost his life in a brawl with a vassal chief, Lallaji – a Hada rao of the plateau, whose daughter he had promised to wed. A misunderstanding led to the abandonment of the bride at the altar and the groom had returned in a few years at the head of the army of Mewar. The Hada refused to give battle but was sought out in the depths of the forest during the joyous occasion of the spring hunt. It proved disastrous for both father and son-in-law. But the greatest tragedy was that of the anguished bride who had never known her husband. Her dying shrieks carried through the land: Were a Sisodia and a Hada ever to forget the agony of the virgin sati and meet for the spring hunt, they would do so at their peril.

The annals of Hadavati recount the names of four maharanas who ignored the prophetic warning only to suffer its consequences.

Maharana Lakha

Lakha mounted the throne in AD 1382 and proceeded immediately to subjugate the entire mountainous region of Merwara, destroying its stronghold in Beratgarh. Beratgarh grew into the city of Badnor and it was here that he encountered and defeated the sultan of Delhi. The southern wild lands of Chappan were rich in tin and silver and Maharana Lakha was the first of his race to enter this exclusively Bhil region and begin the work of mining. Chavand in the Chappan area was named after the heir apparent Choonda. Mewar prospered and Lakha's numerous children formed great clans, notable amongst which were the Choondawats, Dulawats and the Lunawats.

A strange event transferred the crown of Mewar from his firstborn, Choonda, to his youngest son Mokal. Maharana Lakha was by then getting on in years, his many sons and grandsons were settled upon their own lands having fathered powerful clans, when a coconut arrived from the court of Mandor in Marwar. Chunda, the Rathore rao, was offering his daughter's hand in marriage. Choonda was absent at the time and Lakha received the emissary. His son would soon return and accept the coconut for surely, the invitation was for the heir of Chittaur and not for an old greybeard like himself. But Choonda turned down the proposal. His sense of delicacy had been offended. Lakha could marry the princess for all he cared. Incensed with his son's obstinacy and unable to return the coconut at the risk of greatly insulting the Rathores, the old man agreed. But Choonda would be made to pay. Were a son to be born of this last marriage it would be to him that the throne of Mewar would belong. Choonda swore by Eklinga to honour his father's wishes.

Mokal was born of this union and when he was in his teens, Maharana Lakha decided to undertake the final pilgrimage of his life – to free the holy city of Gaya (now in Bihar) from its 'barbarian' conquerors. In a last attempt to salvage the situation, he conferred with Choonda.

'Which territories were to be granted to Mokal?'

'The throne of Chittaur,' was the reply.

And, to set all suspicions to rest, Choonda insisted that Mokal be installed upon the throne before their father departed.

In 1398, Taimur-i-lang (Tamar the lame – the Mongol prince from central Asia) invaded Delhi. That this event is not recorded in the annals of Mewar reflects how far removed they were from the ongoing politics in the rest of the country. The annals however, record an attempted invasion by the king of Delhi, erroneously referred to as Feroz Shah the grandson of Taimur. Maharana Mokal is said to have met him beyond the passes in the field of Raipur and compelled him to abandon his mission.

Maharana Mokal

With the young Mokal on the throne, Choonda carried out the affairs of the state wisely and well. But he reserved the right to be the first among council members. No grant was valid unless the lance, the symbol of Choonda, accompanied the king's signature. Choonda's descendants came to be known as the Choondawats and the leader of the clan was commonly referred to as Salumbar after the estate that served as his abode.

The queen mother, Raj Mata Hansa Bai, was jealous of Choonda's powers at court oblivious to the fact that had it not been for his sacrifice, her son would have never become maharana. Upbraiding the queen for her suspicions, Choonda left, leaving her as the guardian of the Sisodia throne. The queen mother's Rathore relatives from Mandor were now free to enter. They were glad to leave behind the arid desert land of Marwar and live in the fertile luxurious plains of Mewar.

Mokal, a prince worthy of the name Sisodia, was not destined to rule for long. He had ascended the throne in 1421, and secured the territory of Sambhar and its salt lakes. The borders of his kingdom were extended which, in the wake of Taimur's invasion, was easily accomplished. Lakha's palace, now a mass of ruins, was repaired and a shrine erected to Chaturbhuj, the four-armed deity.

Mokal had three sons and a daughter – one so lovely that she was called Lal Bai[22] or the ruby of Mewar. As he gave her away to the Kinchi chieftain of Gagraun, he promised to stand by them in the event of an attack. The time to redeem himself arrived quickly, for Hoshang Shah of Malwa attacked the little Rajput kingdom. The maharana was in Madaria, putting down a revolt of the mountain dwellers, when the news arrived. The flames of jauhar threatened his precious child and Mokal

---

22. Some accounts claim that Lal Bai was Maharana Lakha's daughter and that a marriage had been contracted with the crown prince of Jaisalmer, Jait Singh, who had been adopted by Rawal Kehar. Mehraj Sankhla Parmar, who held a jagir near Abu, joined the wedding band and proceeded to defame the princess. Falling prey to the words of the augers, Jait Singh abandoned the alliance with Mewar. The rawal of Jaisalmer was furious and disinherited the crown prince, while Lakha, suffering the blow to his dignity quietly, married his child to the Kinchi chieftain of Gagraun. Hoshang Shah of Malwa attacked and occupied Gagraun twice – once in AD 1408, and a second time in AD 1422, a year after Mokal had come to the throne.

hurried to reach her side. Accompanying him were his uncles, Chacha and Maira, who led a cavalry of 700. They were Maharana Lakha's half-brothers, born of Khaitsi's Khatan rani – a carpenter's daughter.

As was tradition, the brothers of the maharana, held positions below the third class of nobles. Appanages were bestowed upon them, which were to be resumed if a natural heir failed to be born. Sons and brothers born of commoners, though treated with respect and entrusted with confidential duties possessed no rank. They were termed the fifth sons or babas (infants).

A jealous Chauhan chieftain in Mokal's army was on the look out for trouble and when the maharana asked for the name of a particular tree, he found the perfect opportunity. Feigning ignorance, the Chauhan whispered that the maharana ask his uncles. Artlessly, he did so. The uncles took offence certain that aspersions were being cast. Later that day, while Mokal was at prayer, a blow severed his arm from his body while another stretched him lifeless.

Nimbahera lay seven miles from the hamlet of Marla. The passage lay through Ranikhera, the largest township in the district. Built by the mother of Maharana Bhim Singh, it boasted of a fine temple, a reservoir and paved streets. The top-soil in the area had worn away revealing the blue schist rock of the plateau which extended into the beds of the rivulets and showed up through the clear rippling water. Schools of small fish abounded, but it was the speckled trout flashing about in the background of blue that caught the eye.

Although within the jurisdiction of Amir Khan, the Pathan commander, the village elders thronged the gates. The captain lent a patient ear to the woes of the subjects of Mewar, who though unhappily under the Turk, still considered themselves children of the maharana. The carcass of a pig had been cast into the reservoir of Baiji Raj, the queen mother (a term also used for the mother of the head of the Saktawat clan). Two communities of Bhangis, the class entrusted with the cleaning of refuse, had quarrelled over a business deal and a member of the affected party

The uncles fled and went into hiding. The dissolute lives that they led, however, gave them away for they abducted a young Chauhan girl. The girl's father traced the villains to their lair and informed the new maharana.

Kumbha's men accompanied by their Rathore allies followed the Chauhan to the hideout. In the dead of the night, they scaled the walls. As he hoisted himself on to a ledge the Chauhan found himself face to face with a tigress. The Rathore prince, who had come up beside him, buried his sword in its heart. It could not have been a better omen.

A loud crash woke Chacha's young daughter. The drummer who had accompanied the assaulting party had slipped. The drums, that were to sound the victory, had rolled all the way down.

'It is only the thunder and rains of Bhadon,' said Chacha as he comforted his child. 'Fear no one but God.'

As he uttered these words, the Rathore rao entered the room. While the Chauhan cleft Chacha into two, the rao laid Maira at his feet had given vent to his frustration by contaminating the tank and fleeing to the safety of Bhindar. But what could possibly be done to a wretch who had already lost an arm, a leg and his nose for previous misdeeds? The only solution lay in blackening his face, parading him through the town mounted on an ass with a garland of shoes about his neck. He could then be drummed out from within the limits of Ranikhera, all this provided the villagers could first lay their hands on him. The reservoir, in the meanwhile, was in the process of being drained and once empty it would have to be washed with the pure waters of the holy Ganga. A 100 Brahmins would have to be fed before the purification ritual could be considered complete.

The captain could not resist a little peep into the rani's temple. An inscription caught his eye. Kistna, the sculptor had, at his own expense, repaired the altars and, for this pious act, had been promised, a grant for all time to come. Six thalis of spices, saffron, oil and butter and several pieces of money were to be handed over, to Kistna and his descendents, every year during the village fair.

The hakim of Nimbahera had arrived with his cavalcade and had been waiting patiently for the citizens of Ranikhera to release the captain. He was the son-in-law of Amir Khan, the nawab of Tonk. The governor general, Lord Hastings, in a bid to control the predatory forces that ravaged north India had targeted the Pathan forces of Amir Khan, the Pindaris and the Marathas. The result was a gigantic operation that had begun soon after the monsoons of 1817. By the end, several treaties had been signed. Amir Khan had been offered the lands he occupied as a price of disarmament and he had styled himself the nawab of Tonk.

The Pathan cavaliers mounted on their impatient chargers filled the interlude contesting with matchlock and spear. The middle-aged khan was a gentlemanly Pathan, courteous and affable unlike his predecessor, the one-eyed Jamshid, who as the first lieutenant of Amir Khan, had become a byname for torture and cruelty. There was a friendly dustabazee – the shaking of hands, without having to dismount – and the khan welcomed the captain in true oriental style. 'Nimbahera,' he said, 'belonged to the captain. Nawab Sahib Amir Khan had sent word that the captain be treated with every honour due to Amir Khan himself.' The khan visited the captain's tent that afternoon and a long discussion followed, concerning the welfare of his charge and the peace of the borderline.

Maharana Kumbha

In 1433, six-year-old Kumbha was crowned maharana. The Rathores of Mandor were jubilant. Taking his sister's grandson upon his knee, Rao Ranmal sat upon the throne of Bappa Rawal. And when the child scampered off to play, the wily Rathore was left all by himself, upon the ancient Sisodia throne, the royal flag of Mewar fluttering over his head.

The royal nurse, a proud and patriotic woman, could stand it no longer. She accosted Hansa Bai, accusing her of allowing her own grandson to be cheated of his throne. Hansa Bai was alarmed. The creed of the Rajput was to acquire kingdoms. The means mattered little. She could not deny the fact that her own brother and nephew were now potential enemies. Her fears were enhanced when her stepson, Raghudev, was murdered.

Raghudev owned the lands of Kelwara and Kowaria and lived away from the court. A dress of honour arrived one day. It was sent by Rao Ranmal. Etiquette demanded that he put it on immediately. Raghudev died within a matter of hours and it was assumed that the new clothes had been coated with poison. The death of the beloved prince became an act of martyrdom and he received a place amongst the deities of Mewar. Since then, his altar has received homage twice a year from the poorest farmer to the richest nobleman.

The grandmother's thoughts turned to Choonda. Panic stricken, she realised that her kinsmen were now in occupation of every important post in Chittaur. The principal post was held by a Bhati Rajput of Jaisalmer, who was loyal to her brother. Word was sent to Choonda and he advised that the young king be brought out everyday for a public audience. Feasts were to be held in the villages and the maharana was to attend each one without fail. Gradually the distance from the palace was to be increased.

'The festival of lamps,' said Choonda, 'would be celebrated far away from the palace.'

Every instruction was followed carefully. Diwali arrived and the feast was attended but Choonda failed to appear. With heavy hearts, the royal entourage began their homeward journey, when a group of forty horsemen overtook them. A secret sign was used to pay homage to the young sovereign. Choonda and his men reached the Ram Pol unchecked. Claiming to be neighbouring chieftains, who had been granted the honour of escorting the young maharana home after the feast, they gained entrance, but as the main body of the Choondawat army rode up, the alarm was sounded. Salumbar unsheathed his sword. Though the Bhati's dagger succeeded in drawing blood, he had been taken by surprise. Chittaur's gates were thrown open and the Rathores slaughtered mercilessly. Rao Ranmal was slain, but Jodha, who was in the lower town at the time, managed to escape. Not satisfied with having chased him out of Mewar, Choonda followed him to the gates of Mandor.

Abandoning his capital, Jodha fled into the desert as Choonda's sons Konto and Munja occupied the throne of Mandor. With the maharana safe in the palace, Choonda returned to Mandu. Mandor remained occupied by Mewar for the next twelve years.

Jodha wandered the great desert garnering support. Eventually he succeeded in assembling a sizeable army. The sons of Choonda were surprised to find themselves surrounded. Even the citizens of Mandor had risen against them. While the elder was slain, the younger fled. Munja was pursued and killed on the border of Godwar. Two sons of Chittaur had fallen for one rao of Mandor and Jodha sought no further revenge. Mewar was by far the superior power and Jodha sued for peace. The place where Munja was struck down was accepted as boundary. Godwar became Mewar's and the two kingdoms separated forever.

The sultanate of Delhi had weakened steadily since the days of the Tughlaks and it was during the last years of Maharana Hamir's life, that the kingdoms of the Deccan had broken away to form the 'Hindu' Vijaynagar and the Islamic Bahmani[23] kingdoms. They survived until the

---

23. The Bahmani kingdom was founded on 3 August 1347, by a Turkish governor, Ala-ud-din Bahman Shah, who had revolted against Sultan Muhammad bin Tughlak of Delhi. It included all the southern states of the Delhi sultanate and its southern border was marked by the banks of the Krishna. The capital was at Gulbarga (now in Karnataka). It reached its peak around the late 1400s and was reponsible for large scale massacres and destruction of temples overshadowing the atrocities committed by the ruling Muslims of the north. After 1518, it broke up into five Deccan sultanates – Ahmadnagar (now in Maharashtra), Berar (or Vidarbha now in Maharashtra), Bijapur (now in Karnataka), Bidar (now in Karnataka) and Golconda (now in Andhra Pradesh).

The contemporary 'Hindu' Vijaynagar kingdom that was set up in AD 1336, occupied all of peninsular India south of the river Krishna. It was destroyed by the confederation of the Deccan sultanates in 1565. 'Hindu' rule was thereafter confined to the south of the river Tungabhadra.

Having enjoyed his opium, Rao Ranmal had fallen into a deep sleep. A maid, who had been in attendance that evening, quietly and gently bound him to the bed with his own Marwari turban.

When Choonda's men burst into the room, the old rao tried to rise. His head still befuddled with sleep, he made many attempts to stand pulling the bed up with him, but his feet would not touch the ground. Reaching out he grabbed a brass pot. Several assailants were brought down before he was killed.

In memory of that fateful day, Rathores have always slept on short beds with their feet sticking out.

coming of the Mughals. Taimur's invasion in AD 1398, rung the death knell for Delhi and Malwa, Gujarat and Jaunpur asserted themselves. With a youth on the throne of Mewar, the vultures looked for easy pickings.

In 1422, the powerful kingdoms of Malwa and Gujarat joined forces and Kumbha met them at the border with his vast army of foot soldiers, horses and elephants. Sultan Mahmud Khalji I of Malwa[24] fell into the hands of the victorious Rajputs, who held him prisoner for six months at Chittaurgarh. Eleven years later, Kumbha decided to celebrate the event and the building of a victory tower began. It took ten years to complete. The tower was said to be the ringlet on the brow of Chittaur, which made her look down upon Meru with derision. So impressed was Sultan Mahmud that he raised an identical one at Mandu. The outcome of the battle, he said, had been indecisive, as he put forward his claim to victory, but his tower, it is said, could not be made to stand. Malwa, nevertheless, proved a worthy adversary and Ranthambhor, Mandalgarh, Mandsaur, Ajmer and Bayana interchanged hands probably more times than is on record. It is also suggested that the two joined hands to defeat the sultan of Delhi at Jhunjhunu, which added Hisar (Haryana) to Mewar's crown.

Kumbha mixed gallantry with warlike pursuits. He is reputed to having abducted the daughter of a Jhala chieftain, who had been promised to the prince of Mandor. This renewed the old feud and the Rathore made many attempts to regain his lost bride. When the rains of the month of Bhadon cleared the air of dust, they made the towers of Kumbhalgarh visible. In the gloom of the night, the light from the lamp of the pining Jhali would radiate far. The young Rathore managed to cut his way through the forests in the night.

'Though, he cut his way through the jaal,' sang the bards 'he could not reach the Jhali.'

Perhaps the greatest king and statesman in the history of Mewar, Kumbha, a poet and lover of the arts, ruled for nearly half a century, triumphed over his enemies and fortified his kingdom. To his credit are

24. Sultan Mahmud Khalji I paid a hefty ransom amongst which was included his jewelled crown. It was this crown that Babar mentions having received from Sanga's queen, to supplant the rightful heir of Chittaurgarh.

Ranakpur or Rana-ka-pur was named after Kumbha, who had granted the land to Seth Dharan Shah, a wealthy merchant of the area. The temples were dedicated to Adinath, the first of the twenty-four Jain tirthankaras.

two encyclopaedias of music – *Sangeetraja* and *Sangeet Ratnakar, Eklingji Mahatmya* and a commentary on the *Geet Govind*.

His was, however, a tragic end, for in his fiftieth year (1469), as he worshipped in the temple at Kumbhalgarh, he was assassinated by his son, Ooda (Uday Singh), who was forever to be known as hatiaro or murderer.

The heir apparent, Raimal, had been away, banished for his impertinence. It is said that since his victory over the king of Delhi at Jhunjhunu, Kumbha indulged in a mysterious ritual. Before taking his seat upon the throne he would wave his sword in circles, three times around his head and utter an incantation. Raimal had been unable to contain his curiosity. Others suggest that perhaps it was his patronage of the bards, who had lost favour with Kumbha, that led to the falling out.

Maharana Uday Singh I (Ooda the Hatiaro)

Shunned by everyone, Ooda, bribed dependent princes with gifts of land. The Deora prince became independent in Abu. Rao Jodha claimed Sambhar and Ajmer as well as the hand of Maharana Mokal's daughter. Raimal returned and Ooda ran to Buhlol Lodi, the sultan of Delhi, offering him a daughter in marriage. Fate was on Mewar's side that day, for as Ooda stepped out of the Lodi's palace, he was struck by a bolt of lightening[25]. Five years of his rule had resulted in considerable loss to Mewar.

25. According to historian GH Ojha, Raimal mounted a defence and routed the armies of Ooda and the sultan of Delhi. Ooda escaped to Sojat and then making his way through Bikaner approached Ghiyas-ud-din Khalji of Malwa. The Malwa army was defeated and the sultan sent a second force under the command of Jafar Khan. Raimal, who by now had been declared maharana, faced and routed the Malwa army, assisted by his five sons, which included Crown Prince Prithviraj, Jaimal and Sangram Singh. The sons of Ooda – Soorajmal and Sheshmal – earned their pardon and made peace with the maharana.

Of the eighty fortresses of Mewar, Kumbha built thirty-two. He fortified
a strategically located hill (Kumbhalmer, traditionally called Komulmer) in
the hamlet of Kelwara upon the Aravalli, that looked down upon Marwar.
Kumbhalgarh was said to have been raised at the site of an ancient fortress
built by a Jain mountain king, Sumpriti Raja, who claimed descent from
Chandragupta Maurya. Within the ancient Parmar fortress of Mount Abu,
Kumbha erected a citadel. An alarm tower was raised in his name and
within a little temple, receiving the devotions of the people, were bronze
statues of Kumbha and his father, Mokal. Besides the repair and
construction of forts, he also built the Kumbha Shyam temple at Abu and
contributed towards more than half the cost of the temple to Rishub Deva.
The foundation of this grand temple had been laid in AD 1438, by a Jain
minister of Mewar. Granite columns, forty feet high, supported its three
storeys while the interiors were inlaid with mosaics of cornelian and agate.
It was estimated to be worth more than a million pounds sterling but
because of its location, in the Sadri pass leading from the highlands of
Mewar, Rishub Deva had escaped the notice of bigots. That he was unable
to visit it remained one of the captain's greatest regrets.

The swampy tracts enroute to Kumbhalgarh turned out to be disastrous
for the elephants. That particular morning it had been the turn of the
elephant that carried breakfast supplies. The retinue and the advance party,
that had left in the small hours of the morning, were still in the midst
of extricating the animal when the officers caught up with them. A couple
of hours later, they were once again able to pick their way through the
prickly shrubs. Mid morning found them at the village of Gurha, upon the
banks of a serpentine river that meandered through the alpine valley. The
hillsides were thick with mango groves and the riverbank abounded with
peach, custard apple and fig, while tall tamarinds and sacred peepul offered
their generous shade. The village of Samecha lay at the base of a mountain
called Rana Paj. It was by this path that the maharanas made good their
escape when harried by the Mughals.

Settled in the region were the Kumbhawats. These descendents of

Maharana Kumbha came to pay their respects and brought with them kakri (the famous desert cucumber), curds and a young goat. Dressed in ordinary farming clothes, the tall robust figures with their aquiline features and flowing beards drew exclamations of admiration. Their quiet dignity compelled respect. Together they sat and relived the days of yore. Recounting the deeds of their ancestors never failed to win the hearts of Rajputs. The memory of their glorious past was something they could never resist nor outlive.

Maharana Raimal

Raimal succeeded to the throne of Chittaur in AD 1473, having defeated the joint armies of his brother Ooda and the sultan of Delhi. The chiefs of Girnar and Abu supported their legitimate prince and together they defeated the king of Malwa who had chosen this opportune moment to declare war.

Of Raimal's thirteen sons, the three eldest were – Prithviraj, Jaimal and Sangram[26]. Sangram was cautious and brave; Prithviraj impulsive and thirsting for action while Jaimal was a hothead. An argument arose between them one day. Which one of the brothers would make the most suitable ruler? They decided to consult the oracle at the temple of the Tiger's Mount, Nahara Magra.

The three brothers, accompanied by Maharana Raimal's uncle, Sarangdeo[27], arrived at the temple where their ancestor Bappa Rawal had received the sword of investiture from Gorakhnath. Prithviraj and Jaimal were the first to enter the dimly lit temple and they seated themselves upon a pallet. The nervous Sangram, whose eyes had not adjusted to the dark, sat down in a hurry. He failed to notice that it was the leopard skin rug of the priestess that he had occupied. Sarangdeo, who had knelt behind his youngest grandnephew, planted a knee on a corner of the leopard's hide. As soon as Prithviraj uttered the nature of their mission, the priestess pointed to the leopard skin indicating thereby that Sanga was the future

---

26. Many versions of the story claim that Sanga was the eldest but they fail to explain why Prithviraj and Jaimal felt so cheated when Sanga was declared heir.

27. In the legend it is said to be Surajmal of Bari Sadri – Maharana Raimal's brother.

ruler and that their granduncle would also have a portion of Mewar. Prithviraj would have had the oracle declared as false had Sarangdeo not stepped in between and prevented him from attacking Sanga. The priestess fled as Prithviraj grappled with his uncle. Sanga managed to escape with five sword cuts and an arrow in one eye and he fled towards the sanctuary of Chaturbhuj. At Sevantri, he came across Bida Udaywat. The Rathore had scarcely helped the wounded heir of Mewar upon his steed when Jaimal galloped up in hot pursuit. Bida gave up his life keeping Jaimal at bay while Sanga fled.

Compelled to live in disguise amongst goatherds, Sanga was found too stupid to tend goats. Fortunately, few faithful Rajputs discovered him and together they took up service with the Parmar chieftain, Karamchand. One day, as his companions prepared the mid-day meal, Sanga rested beneath a banyan tree. A passing goatherd noted the prince's face lit up by a ray of sunlight that had found its way through the dense foliage. A cobra had uncoiled itself against the warmth of his body and had spread its hood over the royal head. A bird of omen, chattering loudly, had perched upon the serpent's hood. Though the goatherd's homage was declined, the Parmar chief learnt of the identity of his royal servant and offered him his daughter's hand in marriage. Sanga's secret was maintained until he was able to claim his rightful place. Not one to forget his friends, Sanga, upon his accession, granted his friend and father-in-law the jagir of Bambori and the title of rao.

When the maharana heard of the quarrel that nearly deprived him of a son, he banished Prithviraj from Chittaur. With five horses, Prithviraj made for Baleoh in Godwar, confident that he could prove to his father that he had access to resources independent of his birthright. Godwar's native population consisted of the aboriginal Meenas over whom Rajput interlopers ruled. However, in the recent past, a rawat of the Meena tribe had regained a part of his ancestral lands and was holding court at Nadol. Prithviraj enlisted himself and his band of Rajputs in the service of the Meena. The festival of the hunters, the Ahairea, arrived and the vassals received permission to rejoin their families. Prithviraj, who had also obtained leave, hid by the gate of the town. When everybody had left, the Rajputs attacked. As the Meena fled past the gate, Prithviraj gave chase. His lance transfixed the rawat to a tree. The Meena towns and villages were torched

With Sanga in hiding and Prithviraj banished to Godwar, Jaimal was looked to as the heir of Mewar. He was desperate to marry the beautiful Solankini, Tara Bai, but her father had laid down a condition. Rao Surtan had been expelled from his lands of Tonk[28] and Toda by Pathans and recovery of his dominion alone could earn the hand of his daughter. Having agreed to fulfil the conditions, Jaimal assumed that it had earned him the right to Tara Bai's favours. His arrogance cost him his life.

'He who has thus dared to insult the honour of a father, and that too a father in distress, richly merits his fate,' declared the magnanimous maharana. Badnor was granted to Rao Surtan.

Jaimal's death resulted in Prithviraj's recall and he gallantly went to Rao Surtan's aid, winning thereby for himself the hand of the beautiful and brave Tara Bai. The Amazonian Solankini, dressed in a soldier's uniform, accompanied Prithviraj's band of 500. They arrived at Toda.

---

28. This Solanki tribe, descendants of the Balhara Kings of Anhilwara, was chased from their land by Alla-ud-din Khalji. In the thirteenth century they took possession of Tonk and Toda upon the Banas, from the tribe of Tak or Takshak, one of the thirty-six tribes of royal Rajputs. The town of Takshshila Nagar evolved into Taktipur and Toda. From the ruins of their architecture it has been postulated that perhaps Chittaur was also once under them. It is also supposed that King Porus, who had faced the army of Alexander in 326 BC, was of the race of the Taks. The Babar Nama, the life of Emperor Babar, refers to another Takshshila Nagar west of the river Indus at the modern-day site of the city of Taxila.

The ceremonial tazzia (bier), in the memory of Hasan and Hussain, the martyrs, had been laid in the city square. They joined the procession and as it passed below the palace balcony, Lilla, the Pathan chief noticed the strange horsemen. He had but pointed them out when the lance of Prithviraj and an arrow from the bow of the fair Tara brought him to the floor. By the time the panic had ceased, the cavaliers were well beyond the gates. The Afghan army had lost its leader and with it, its morale. They could no longer stand up to the Rajputs and Rao Surtan was reinstated.

The nawab of Ajmer declared his intention to chastise the Sisodia, determined to vindicate the honour of a fellow Muslim.

Prithviraj did not wait for the nawab to come after him and instead advanced to meet him in the great citadel of Gurh Beetli. A great slaughter followed and Rajputs, whose hearts were set afire by the love of glory and devotion, flocked to the banner of Prithviraj Sisodia.

and Godwar fell into Prithviraj's hands – all except Madraicha Chauhan's stronghold of Desuri. Raimal Solanki, whose ancestor had escaped the destruction of Patan and had sought refuge in Mewar, was encouraged to grab Desuri from his Chauhan father-in-law. Murder solved the issue and Desuri was granted in perpetuity to the Solankis. Forbidding the future generations of Sisiodias from ever attempting a reclamation, Prithviraj included a curse within the grant itself. Order was restored in Godwar and Prithviraj earned his recall.

With Sanga in hiding, Surajmal of Bari Sadri, who was the maharana's first cousin, assumed that he was now the next in line. This brought him into conflict with Prithviraj. Prithviraj was also unable to comprehend his father's policies. Arguments arose over the grant of Bhainsrorgarh to Sarangdeo. Fuming, the prince marched off to reclaim the jagir and Sarangdeo saw wisdom in quitting the castle peacefully. But he joined hands with Surajmal and together they applied to Ghiyas-ud-din, sultan of Malwa, for aid. A rapid occupation of the lands close to the southern border began. As they approached Chittaur, the maharana descended to meet them at the Gambhiri. Leading his army from the front, Raimal fought alongside the common soldier. He had already received twenty-two wounds and was on the verge of collapse when Prithviraj arrived with a 1,000 fresh horses.

Prithviraj gave the rebels no rest until his uncle called a truce saying, 'if you are killed what will become of Chittaur? My face will be forever blackened.'

The swords were sheathed and Prithviraj asked his uncle to accompany him to the temple of Kali in the morning. But Surajmal sent Sarangdeo in his stead. Having sacrificed a buffalo, Prithviraj was preparing to slay a goat when without warning he turned upon Sarangdeo. The head of the traitor was laid before the goddess.

Surajmal fled south. Abandoning Mewar, he rode through the wild lands of Khanthul. Here an omen made him stop and subduing the aboriginal tribes, he set up a town that came to be known as Pratapgarh Deolia. Here his descendents remained, enjoying British protection, even at the time of the captain's visit.

Maharana Raimal soon followed his gallant firstborn in death.

Fighting by his father's side, Prithviraj targeted his uncle. By the time the day's battle ended, Surajmal had been covered in wounds. Prithviraj went across to meet him.

The barber had just finished stitching up the wounds but Surajmal rose and came forward, as if nothing had happened, though the effort caused some of the stitches to give way.

'Well,' said Prithviraj, 'uncle, how are your wounds?'

'Quite healed, my child, since I have had the pleasure of seeing you.'

'Kaka,' said Prithviraj, 'I have not seen the diwanji (the maharana) yet. I ran over first to see you, and I am very hungry, have you anything to eat?'

Uncle and nephew sat down to dinner and ate off the same plate with Prithviraj accepting the paan that was individually presented.

'You and I will end our battle in the morning, uncle.'

'Very well, child, come early.'[29]

They met in the morning and the rebels were defeated. Many battles were fought between uncle and nephew, with the latter threatening to drive Surajmal from the land and the uncle retorting that he would allow Prithviraj only as much land as could be occupied by his lifeless body.

---

29. Exchanges like these were common in those days, for the Indians believed that all hostilities ended with sundown and enemies were entitled to honourable treatment.

Prithviraj discovered the ambassador of Malwa, one day, addressing his father with unusual familiarity. The prince marched off with his band, kidnapped the sultan from his capital at Mandu, and dragged him to Chittaurgarh. The sultan fell at Raimal's feet, begging forgiveness while his ambassador looked on helplessly. He was released after a month with every demonstration of honour but his ransom was extracted in the finest horses bred in Malwa.

Prithivraj made Kumbhalgarh his residence and lived out his life in daring exploits.

A letter arrived from his sister, begging to be restored to her father's house. Her husband, she complained, indulged freely in opium and when overcome by the flower, forced her to sleep on the floor. Prithviraj gave up his persecution of Sanga and left for Sirohi.

Scaling the walls of the palace at midnight, he roused his brother-in-law, with a dagger at his throat. Despite her letter, his sister pleaded for her husband's life and Prithviraj relented. The Sirohi, however, could not be left unpunished. He was made to touch his wife's feet, beg forgiveness and place her slippers upon his head. Death would have surely been a better option.

As Prithviraj prepared to leave, his brother-in-law packed some confectionary for the way. Nearing the border of Kumbhalgarh, the gallant Sisodia stopped to refresh himself. He had barely reached the temple of Mama Devi when the poison began to take effect.

A message was sent to the palace, but before help could arrive, the brave prince was no more. At the head of Prithviraj's sixteen wives, came Tara Bai. Taking their husband's body into their arms, they followed him to the mansion of the sun.

Maharana Sangram Singh (Sanga)

Sangram Singh took Mewar to the pinnacle of prosperity. To place this celebrated prince upon the throne, Mewar forsake, for the first time, the tradition that prevented a cripple from ascending the throne.

The sultanate of Delhi was weak. Malwa and Gujarat together could not stand up to Sanga. Into his hands fell the sultan of Mandu, who, backed by the forces of Sultan Muzaffar II of Gujarat, had attempted to chastise his ally, Medini Rai of Gagraun. Sultan Mahmud Khalji II spent a few months luxuriating in the splendour of captivity at Chittaur and then having presented Sanga a magnificent ransom, was permitted to return to Mandu. But Malwa's power had been broken. Mandsaur passed into Sanga's hands by 1519 and Chanderi (now in Madhya Pradesh) into Medini Rao's.

The storm of Ranthambhor, pried the ancient Chauhan fortress out of imperial hands, bringing Sanga to the forefront. Khanua became Mewar's northern border and here was raised Sanga's new palace.

Eighty thousand horses, seven rajas, nine raos and 104 chieftains followed Sanga into battle accompanied by 500 war elephants. The princes of Marwar and Amber acknowledged him as the principal authority in north India, while the raos of Gwalior, Ajmer, Sikri, Raisen (now in Madhya Pradesh near Bhopal), Kalpi (now in Uttar Pradesh on the banks of the Yamuna), Chanderi, Bundi, Gagraun, Rampura, and Abu all followed him into battle.

Of the eighteen battles that he had won against the sultan of Delhi, two were fought with Sultan Ibrahim Lodi leading his army in person. Mewar's northern limit had been extended to the banks of the Peela Khal or the yellow river near Bayana. But at its peak, Mewar was to encounter her worst enemy.

Thrown out of his home country in Ferghana, Babar, carrying the blood of both Taimur-i-lang and Genghis (Chingis) Khan, was on the lookout for an empire. For the last twenty-three years, he had made a home out of the cold desolate mountains of Kabul. The loss of Ferghana and Samarkand gnawed at his soul and the rich lands of Hindustan titillated constantly. Not averse to treason, the Rajput creed of 'get land, no matter at what cost' suited him well.

He welcomed Sanga's emissaries[30]. If Babar would take on Delhi, Sanga promised to march upon Agra. Sultan Ibrahim Lodi was left to deal with Mughal all by himself. But Sanga failed to uphold his end of the bargain and the Mughal marched onto Agra dispatching, that very day, his heir, Humayun, to Gwalior. Raja Vikramaditya Tomar[31], who had earlier been forced to submit to Sultan Ibrahim Lodi, had died at Panipat and the grieving family surrendered. Humayun returned flushed with success and presented to his father the most prized diamond[32] in all the world. It had been expected that Babar, like Taimur, would leave having once helped himself to the empire's treasures and leaving the Lodi's hold over Delhi broken. Sadly, it was not to be: for Babar, unlike Taimur, did not have an established empire and a home to go back to. Sanga's inertia still remains a matter to be lamented.

The battle began at Khanua, a year after Babar had occupied Delhi. An ambassador had been sent offering undisputed ownership over Delhi and its dependencies, provided the Peela Khal was respected as the future boundary of their respective dominions. But the Mughal had had a taste of success and Silhadi, the Tomar chieftain of Raisen, Sanga's most trusted general, returned empty handed. What Sanga did not know was that his ambassador had been promised the independent kingdom of Malwa.

Sanga stood at the head of the combined Rajput forces. Despite a few initial setbacks, Babar was not discouraged. But his men had been away from home too long. They were tired and outnumbered. Muhammad Sharif, the astrologer, addressed them.

'It would be best for the emperor not to fight, for the constellation

---

30. Sanga's invitation, as recorded in Babar's memoirs, had not been the only one to arrive. The governor of Punjab, Daulat Khan Lodi, and Alam Khan, Sultan Ibrahim Lodi's uncle, had also sent similar proposals. Two reconnaissance missions had been carried out in 1517 and 1519. In November 1525, the invasion of Punjab began and in the First Battle of Panipat – 21 April 1526 – the forces of the sultan were overcome.

31. He was the son of the famous Raja Man Singh Tomar of Gwalior who, with his Gujjar queen Mrignayani, had established the famous school of music that trained the likes of Tansen and Baiju Bavara – men who graced the court of Akbar. Man Singh Tomar became known as the father of Dhrupad – the oldest existing form of classical music in northern India.

32. The name Kohinoor (mountain of light) was given in 1739, by the Persian invader Nadir Shah. It lies today in the Tower of London.

Sakkiz Yildoz (Eight Stars) is in opposition.'

An air of despondency fell upon the army. Seeing this, Babar called out to his men.

'Do you not know that there lies a journey of some months between us and the land of our birth? If our side is defeated – God preserve us from that day! God forbid it! – where are we? Where is our birthplace? Where our city? We have to do with strangers and foreigners. It is in every way best for each man to set resolutely before himself the two alternatives: if we win, we are the avengers of the cause of God; if we lose, we die martyrs. In either fate lies our salvation.'

Relinquishing wine and the pleasures of life, Babar swore his men on the *Koran* to conquer or perish. The next morning, which was the 16th of March 1527, they took to the field once again. Sanga, a month short of his forty-fifth birthday, and Babar, who had two days ago celebrated his forty-fourth, faced each other. This time it was Sanga who faced a reversal of fortunes, for Babar put to use – for the first time in Indian history – field guns. His artillery created havoc. With his best chieftains dead, Sanga, himself severely wounded, was forced to flee.

Among the dead were Uday Singh of Dungarpur, Ratna of Salumbar, Raimal Rathore – the son of Rao Ganga of Marwar, the Merta leaders – Khaitsi and Ratna, Ramdass – the Songara-Chauhan, Ajja – the Jhala[33] who had been granted the jagir of Bari Sadri, his brother Sajja who had received Delwara, Gokuldas Parmar, Chanderbahan and Manikchand - the Chauhan chiefs of the first rank in Mewar, Hasan Khan of Mewat (Haryana) – a vassal of the last Lodi King of Delhi, and a host of others. When Sanga retired from the field, the chiefs turned to Ratan Singh

---

33. Known originally as the Makwanas of Kirtigarh, Sind, the ancestor of the Jhalas, Harpal Makwana, established the kingdom of Halvad in Kathiawar, Gujarat, in 1506. Two sons of Raja Raj Singh of Halvad came to Mewar during the reign of Maharana Raimal. Ajja was granted Bari Sadri and Sajja Delwara. Both brothers were permitted to use the title raj rana. The brothers lived to furnish the annals with tales of gallantry and abiding loyalty. 'What is the history of India if not the history of Rajasthan, and what is the history of Rajasthan if not the history of Mewar, and what is the history of Mewar if not the history of the Jhalas.'

Choondawat-Salumbar. Salumbar refused. His ancestor Choonda had given up the crown and Ratan Singh would not go back on the word of his forefather. Ajja then raised the royal insignia above his own head and led the last charge. The responsibility, of these precious articles, has since remained with the Jhalas of Bari Sadri.

A pyramid, made with the heads of the slain, was erected on the battlefield and the conqueror assumed the title ghazi. Sanga retreated, swearing that he would enter Chittaur only in victory.

Babar moved on to occupy Chanderi, held for Sanga by Medini Rai. The jauhar over, the sacking of the fort began and he went on to take Bihar and Bengal. He outlived the gallant maharana by a year, handing over to his son, Humayun, an empire that included Badakshan, Afghanistan, Punjab, Delhi, Bihar and the forts of Bayana, Ranthambhor, Gwalior and Chanderi.

Had he lived, Sanga would surely have redeemed his vow; but he died at Baswa on the frontier of Mewar. Rumours of poison never quite faded. Sanga had nurtured a not so secret ambition to rule from Delhi and perhaps his exhausted nobles had just had enough.

A cenotaph marks the spot where the celebrated prince of Mewar was cremated. Sanga was succeeded by his son, Ratan Singh (Ratna).

Maharana Ratan Singh

Ratna (Ratan Singh) came to the throne in 1527, determined to make the battlefield his capital. Like his father, he possessed all the martial skills of his race. He ordered that the gates of Chittaur be forever left open, boasting that its portals were Delhi and Mandu.

Arrogant and lacking in wisdom, this impetuous prince was always on the lookout for trouble. Even before the death of his elder brother, he had secretly sent his double-edged sword, as a symbol of marriage, applying for the hand of the daughter of Rao Prithviraj of Amber. Bhojraj's death left him to succeed Sanga. So overcome was he by this stroke of good luck that he delayed in redeeming his proxy and bringing home his bride. Surajmal, the Hada rao of Bundi, had in the meanwhile, unaware of Maharana Ratna's intentions, also applied for her hand. The princess herself

Though he referred to him as a pagan, Babar wrote of Sanga with utmost respect in his memoirs.

Rana Sanga attained his high status by his own valour and his sword.

A man of medium height, he had a powerful build, a fair skin with unusually large eyes – a feature inherited by all his descendents. At his death, he was but a fragment of his former self. Blinded in one eye by his brother, an arm lost in the action against Sultan Ibrahim Lodi, a leg shattered by a cannon ball, Sanga had a total of eighty wounds to be counted on various parts of his body.

During the reign of Maharana Bhim Singh, the palace possessed a collection of full-length portraits from Samantsi to the ruling maharana, which truthfully reflected the appearance of each prince and made an interesting study of costumes worn down the ages.

Maharana Sanga had seven sons, Bhojraj, Karan Singh, Krishna Singh, Parvat Singh, Ratan Singh (Ratna), Vikramaditya (Bikramjeet) and Uday Singh.

Bhojraj, the heir of Chittaur, sought the hand of the daughter of the Rathore of Merta. It was a favourable alliance and a great honour for the house of Rao Duda, son of Rao Jodha – the founder of Jodhpur.

Duda's granddaughter, the only child of his second son had grown up in the seclusion of the palace at Merta. As talk of marriage and ceremonies dominated the women's chamber, little Mira had tugged at her mother's sleeve.

'But whom will I marry?'

The mother had led the child to the image of Krishna. 'Worship Girdhar Gopal,' she had said. 'He will be your husband.'

Mira's mother unfortunately did not live to see the day when her daughter's hand was sought by the heir of Mewar. Maharana Sanga's sister who had married Rao Biramdeo – Duda's eldest son – arranged the match between her nephew and her niece.

Heart wrenching tales have been spun by her devotees and though little distinction remains between truth and fiction it is a known fact that the bride of Krishna was handed over to the Sisodia prince in AD 1516.

The saintly Mira remained immersed in the worship of Krishna and was unable to involve herself in domestic life. She was his first daughter-in-law and Sanga gave in to her every whim. A large temple was designated for her exclusive use. Mira's temple was open to all. Devotees, who hoped to seek Krishna through Mira's intervention, flocked to her side and Mira sang and danced before her Gopal in divine ecstasy.

The indulgent Bhojraj died in 1521, and Mira horrified the Rajputs by refusing to commit sati. The bride of Krishna declined the garb of a widow and continued with her devotions.

Legend speaks of a donation, of a surprisingly large value, that was made to her temple and the Sisodias suspected the hand of a Mughal prince[34]. He must have been present in disguise. That the widowed daughter-in-law of the Sisodias had sung and danced before a Muslim was unthinkable.

The persecution of Mira Bai began in the reign of Maharana Ratan Singh and was continued by his brother Vikramaditya (Bikramjeet). Matters came to a head when Mira attached herself to Ravidas – a low caste cobbler turned saint. Dressed in the garb of a lowly maidservant, she would attend his religious discourses in the village. The maharana deputed a female cousin to bring her back to her senses but instead, Uda Bai turned into a devotee. The royal family despaired.

---

34. Legend claims that the mysterious visitor was Emperor Akbar – a highly improbable conjecture considering the fact that Akbar's birth did not take place until 23 November 1542.

Cups of poison and beds of needles made their way to her but the beloved of Krishna survived them all. Vikramaditya's relentless torture forced her to flee. Little did Bikramjeet realise that he was infact helping Mira escape the horrors that were about to visit Chittaurgarh – Sultan Bahadur Shah's invasion. Unwelcome even at Merta, she took to wandering by herself and made her way to the holy city of Dwarka, the kingdom of her Lord.

It is said that when Uday Singh succeeded as maharana he sent a delegation of Brahmins to Dwarka with instructions to bring her back home with every honour due to the wife of his eldest brother. Reluctant, Mira requested permission to spend one last night in the temple of her Lord. But when morning came, she was nowhere to be found[35]. Her few material possessions lay upon the floor. Amongst them was the golden image that she had worshipped all her life.

The image of Girdhar Gopal was brought back and it remained with the royal family until it found a place in the temple of Pitamber Rai, within the queens' palace (zenana mahal) at Udaipur.

Mira died in 1546, but even in death, her following grew and her hymns lived on recognised for the beauty of their lyrics.

---

35. It would have been the Brahmins and the pandits of Mewar who, antagonised and threatened by Mira Bai's saintly status, had pronounced the death sentence. It resulted in driving her away. Mira's departure was followed by a saka. The jauhar that accompanied it deprived Mewar of all its royal women. It then fell to these very Brahmins to bring her back for perhaps the people had begun to believe that this terrible fate had be-fallen them because a royal saint had been tortured and driven from their land. It seems hardly surprising that the Brahmins returned without her. Mira, in all probability, had been murdered. Nor did Chittaurgarh go unpunished. Twenty-two years later, this grandest of all Rajput forts was served the deathblow.

was, in all probability, tired of waiting for Ratna to claim her and saw no reason to declare her secret or refuse the Hada prince's offer. Although, the Hadas were close allies, this unintentional offence rankled. And despite having married the Hada's sister and given him his own sister in return, Ratna sought Surajmal out at the Ahairea spring hunt. Revenge resulted in the death of both rivals.

Ratna was king for only five years but he lived to see the death of Babar, the founder of the Mughal Empire, and was succeeded by his brother, Bikramjeet.

Maharana Vikramaditya (Bikramjeet)

Bikramjeet, who ruled from 1531 – 1537, had the turbulent and arrogant nature of his brother but none of his endearing qualities. The fourteen-year-old was insolent, passionate, vindictive and paid no heed to the respect due to his nobles. Guiding him was his mother, Raj Mata Karmavati – a manipulative woman, who had engineered his accession. Bikramjeet preferred to spend his time among wrestlers, prizefighters and foot soldiers. Like the Muslims, he had begun to realise the growing importance of the infantry. With the advent of artillery, the lance of the warrior astride his steed had become of little use. His nobles were unable to accept the change and unwilling to equate themselves with cheap foot soldiers. They preferred the glory of being mounted cavalry warriors.

The result was a falling out with the nobles. The police were despised and the hill tribes carried off, with impunity, cattle from the very slopes of Chittaur. The cavaliers refused to give chase, taunting the maharana to send his foot soldiers instead. Popa Bai-ka-raj, was a proverb commonly used during these times recalling the mismanaged rule of an ancient princess.

Bahadur Shah, sultan of Gujarat, thought it a good time to avenge past insults. In March 1531, he had deposed Sultan Mahmud Khalji II of Malwa and occupied the fort of Mandu. Many exiles, from the former Lodi court of Delhi, held high positions in his court. 'Defy Humayun,' they urged.

In 1534, reinforced by the troops of Mandu, twenty-eight-year-old Sultan Bahadur Shah marched against Mewar and set up camp in the Bundi

Legend speaks of Queen Mother Karmavati's ambitions. On Sanga's death, she had taken the liberty of writing to Babar – the enemy of all Hindustan. She offered to recognise him as sovereign if only he would place her son, Bikramjeet, upon the Sisodia throne. With it Karmavati offered to surrender the fortress of Ranthambhor and the jewelled crown and belt won in 1518, from Sultan Mahmud Khalji II of Malwa.

But it was destiny, and not Babar, that seated her son upon the throne for Maharana Ratan Singh died unexpectedly. Karmavati continued to make regular use of bribes to keep Mewar's enemies at bay.

For a while Mewar was left alone. But it served only to whet Sultan Bahadur's appetite. When a saka looked imminent, a Rakhi[36] was sent by messenger to the Mughal emperor.

Humayun responded but in a leisurely manner. By the time he arrived, the women of Chittaur waited no longer for him. Nor did their eyes strain at the horizon for a glimpse of dust raised by approaching horses.

His unhurried entrance caused Sultan Bahadur's flight and having expelled the foe from Chittaur, Humayun took Malwa by force. Then sending for Bikramjeet, Humayun invested him, in the manner of the Mughals, as king in the citadel of Mandu.

---

36. This famous story too is said to have been a fabrication of the bards. Humayun had come to punish the errant Sultan Bahadur Shah of Gujarat who had annexed Malwa and declared independence during his absence. When he learnt that Sultan Bahadur had embarked on a jehaad, he waited patiently until the holy war was done with. In AD 1535, Humayun deposed the sultan and occupied Gujarat for about a year driving Bahadur into the arms of the Portuguese. Bassein was surrendered and a treaty signed. Bahadur regained his kingdom but found himself in bed with the devil. In February 1537, Governor Nuno de Cunha invited him on board a Portuguese vessel to deliberate over the important trading port of Diu. Both sides were keenly aware that the other was bent on the use of treachery. As Bahadur jumped overboard a sailor struck him on the head.

During the festival of Rakhi or Raksha Bandhan, Rajput women bind threads of delicate silk around the wrists of men they choose to honour as brothers.

This pretty ceremony has crossed all barriers of race, religion and time with sisters claiming the right to summon the gallant brothers to their defence. Many stories of gallantry are woven around this age-old custom and the chivalrous ritual of the Rajputs had been embraced enthusiastically by the Grand Mughals themselves. Two letters written by Emperor Aurungzeb to the queen mother of Udaipur were remarkable for their elegance and delicacy.

Although never permitted to see them face to face, Captain Tod had himself received several Rakhis from the queens of Udaipur, Bundi and Kota besides Chand Bai, the maiden sister of Maharana Bhim Singh. Conversations were limited and held across the purdah, the Rakhi itself being delivered by the hands of a family member or priest.

As political resident he was in the enviable position of doing good and had restored many an ancient family from degradation.

His greatest reward and the only one that he would accept remained the honour of being considered a Rakhi bandh bhai – a Rakhi bound brother.

territory. Though faced with an overwhelming army, Bikramjeet did not hesitate to give battle but his mercenary foot soldiers turned out to be weak defenders and his chiefs decided to remain aloof. They marched off enmass to defend Chittaur and thirteen-year-old Uday, the youngest son of Sanga.

The name of Chittaur conjures magic in the breast of the Rajput. When threatened, her defenders come from the most inexplicable quarters. Rawat Bagh Singh (Baghji), the heir of Surajmal, gave up the security of his capital at Pratapgarh Deolia and arrived to save the home of his forefathers. Rao Maldeo of Marwar sent a select division of Rathores, Rao Arjun[37] of Bundi came with a band of 500 Hadas as did the Songara-Chauhans and the Deora raos of Jalor and Abu. Sajja Jhala of Delwara swore never to stir from his post at the Hanuman Pol; Bhairav Das, the son of Raimal Solanki of Desuri, stood guard at the second gate from the bottom of the ascent – a gate that would bear his name forever. Allies poured in from all Rajwara.

This was the most powerful and concerted effort made by any invader. The sultan brought with him Portuguese artillery and engineers. Labri Khan of Frengan, the engineer, was instrumental in the success of the storming of Chittaur. A mine placed at the Beeka Rock blew up forty-five cubits of the rampart where the Hadas had been posted. Rao Durga, and the Choondawat chieftains Sutto and Doodo moved in swiftly to defend the breach while, to set an example, senior queen mother – Rathorni Rani Jawahar Bai – donned her armour and led a sally. When she was slain, Queen Karmavati, the mother of Maharana Bikramjeet and Uday Singh took charge.

As the invaders gained ground, an emergency meeting was held to find a way to save the youngest son of Sanga. Uday Singh was placed in the care of Rao Surjan Hada of Bundi and guarded personally by the faithful Chakka Sen Dhundera. Maharana Bikramjeet left with a handful of soldiers to carry out guerrilla styled attacks. The main body of the army donned saffron robes while the women prepared for jauhar. A royal sacrifice was required or Chittaur would be lost. Baghji of Deolia was crowned maharana and the changi, of black feathers with its central disc

---

37. Some historians claim that Rao Arjun never really ascended the throne of Bundi.

of gold, raised above his head. Time was running short and Karmavati, sister to gallant Arjun Hada, led 13,000 women to the rapidly prepared reservoirs of explosives and gunpowder. As soon as the lives of the women were extinguished, the gates were thrown open and the Deolia chief rushed out to meet his fate.

Bahadur entered Chittaur to find her burning and strewn with the dead and dying. Every clan had lost its chief and 32,000 warriors lay dead. He remained but a fortnight when news of Emperor Humayun's arrival sent Bahadur running, to save his recently liberated kingdom from falling once again into the hands of the Mughals. Mewar's allies redeemed the great fort.

Never one to learn from experience, Bikramjeet renewed his insolent ways and alienated his chiefs. Of still greater consequence was his lack of reverence for the elderly, causing him to strike in open court Karamchand – the protector of his father, during the days of misfortune. The chiefs rose as one and left. Unwilling to let another teenager bring disaster to Mewar, they approached the illegitimate child of Sanga's eldest brother, Prithviraj. Banbir, in a show of virtue refused to be solicited and agreed only on repeated entreaties to act as regent until Sanga's youngest came of age.

Banbir

The cries of the women in the palace announced the assassination of Maharana Bikramjeet. In the nursery, Panna Dhai[38] was instantly aware that a second murder would follow. Quickly, she placed the sleeping Uday in a fruit basket and covered him with leaves. A faithful palace barber smuggled the basket out of Chittaurgarh. Panna had barely lain her own son in his playmate's bed when Banbir burst into the nursery. Unable to speak, she could only point and watch as the cold steel plunged into the heart of her son. Panna, the emerald lady, allowed her tears to cool her child's ashes before she hurried to the riverside where the sovereign of

---

38. Tradition grants the role of the royal wet-nurse to Gujjar women. That Panna belonged to the clan of the Kinchi-Chauhans, as stated in *Annals and Antiquities of Rajasthan*, appears to be a mistake.

Mewar awaited her. She then took the fifteen-year-old on a long and arduous walk. They travelled south to Deolia but dreading the consequences of detection, went on further to Dungarpur. Despite a desire to help, the chief felt insecure. Panna then made her way up to Kumbhalgarh. Laying the boy on the lap of the governor, she pleaded with him to protect the life of his sovereign. Assa Sah, a Jain of the Depra tribe, was alarmed, but, urged by his mother, accepted the responsibility. Panna left and the king of Chittaur was declared the governor's nephew.

Three years elapsed before the secret was revealed. Young Uday's bearing and dignity left no doubt that he was no nephew to the governor and rumours abounded about the heir of Sanga. The nobles gathered at Kumbhalgarh and, having heard the testimony of both Panna and the barber, placed the young prince in the charge of Akhai Raj, the Songara-Chauhan chief of Jalor, a senior noble of Mewar. The Jalor rao did not hesitate to affiance his daughter, Jayawanti, to the prince, breaking the law laid down by Hamir four hundred years ago. Tricked into marrying a widow of this family, Hamir had forbidden marriages with the Songara-Chauhan family of Jalor. Uday received the teeka in the Badal Mahal of Kumbha and the homage of all the nobles.

Unaware of Uday's existance, Banbir failed to hold his office with the humility it deserved. Instead, he tried to behave as a legitimate maharana would. He sent a portion of food – the doonah – from his own plate to Salumbar. It should have been a great honour, all eyes should have been riveted on the favoured person and his good fortune should have dominated the talk of the table. But the chief of the Choondawats refused. This open refusal to accept Banbir as maharana, united the chiefs in a common cause. They set out for Kumbhalgarh to hail the legitimate son of Sanga. Banbir held on to the capital for as long as he could but was eventually compelled into relinquishing the throne peacefully[39].

---

39. Banbir's army was defeated at Mavli. Some claim that he died on the battlefield while others maintain that he left for the Deccan and that the Bhosle's of Nagpur claim descent from him.

Kumbhalgarh served as refuge everytime the Sisodias were driven from their capitals. The path led past the elephant's pool in the valley and the Sati-ka-makan. Tents were pitched for the night upon the slopes. Arait Pol, the first of the gates leading to the fort lay 500 feet above. The governor, Maharaja Daulat Singh, a baba of Mewar and a close relative of the maharana, came to welcome the captain.

Tiers of battlements rose beyond the great wall that enclosed the fort. On the summit stood the Badal Mahal or the cloud palace. The way in was through a succession of gates – the Arait Pol, Halla Pol, Hanuman Pol, the gate of victory, the gate of blood, Ram's gate and lastly the Chougan Pol. The Hanuman Pol bore an image of the deity that had been brought all the way from Nagaur. Kumbha's cloud palace stood 600 feet high. This was the birthplace of Uday's firstborn, Pratap, the grandson of Sanga and here the nakarras had sounded the accession of Sanga's heir, Uday. As the new sovereign's eye passed over sandy desert tracts and cacti covered mountains, Rajput women would have showered his path with flowers, bathing his feet continuously with water from their pots as the joyful strains of the 'farewell to Kumbhalgarh' announced the beginning of a new reign.

The peak of Kumbhalmer stood 3,353 feet above sea level. The day was spent the day completing sketches of the fort and a Jain temple with a vaulted dome and colonnaded portico. The extreme want of decoration stressed upon its antiquity. Chiselled from the very rock on which it stood, the temple bade defiance to time. A second Jain temple stood out in stark contrast. It was three stories high, each tier decorated with numerous low columns.

Looking down from the temple towards the pass, the eye followed the narrowing gorge until it disappeared into the distance. It was filled with a mass of ruins. But two stood out prominently – the temple of Mama Devi and the shrine where the ashes of Prithviraj Sisodia and the beautiful Tara Bai reposed. Prithviraj, the troubadour of Rajasthan, had filled the pages dedicated to valour and romance in Mewar.

Recorded upon the black marble walls of Mama Devi's temple was the history of the princes who contributed to the temple.

Maharana Uday Singh

Eighteen-year-old Uday Singh was seated upon the Sisodia throne in 1540. The maharana had brought with him, from Kumbhalgarh, his newborn son and heir, Pratap.

To preserve the line of the illustrious Sanga, many lives had been laid down. Great rejoicing accompanied the restoration of this prince and the song of joy composed on this occasion remained a favourite at Udaipur. For centuries to come, on the festival of Ishani, women would chant the 'farewell to Kumbhalgarh.'

The evil days of Mewar had begun with Sanga's death. The fiery valour of Ratna and the irresponsible conduct of Bikramjeet and the officiating Banbir had only accelerated the decline. Mewar now hoped for a respite; but the sadly, their precious prince turned out to be the biggest coward they were to know. Uday's lack of kingly qualities led to internal discord.

Having dealt with Rao Maldeo of Marwar, Sher Shah turned his attention towards Mewar. Uday Singh had been on the throne for four years but his court was still ridden with problems. He opted for peace. No sooner had the Afghan set up camp at Jahazpur that keys of Chittaurgarh were presented to him. Sher Shah accepted and left a deputy behind at the Sisodia court. But the days of Sher Shah's dynasty were numbered and the throne of Delhi was returned to Akbar in 1556.

Haji Khan, a former slave of Sher Shah, who had made himself the ruler of Ajmer and Nagaur had successfully, with Mewar's help, warded off Rao Maldeo's attack. But Uday and Haji Khan soon had a falling out over a pretty dancer and Haji teamed up with Maldeo. In 1557, at the Battle of Harmoda, they met and defeated Uday's forces.

Chittaurgarh's vulnerability was obvious and the maharana looked for a new capital. By 1559, it was established in the circular valley of the Aravalli.

Soon Akbar, then twenty-five years of age, was drawn to the fame

Two years after Uday's coronation, Akbar was born in the desert kingdom of Umarkot.

His father, Humayun, had lost the empire that had been created by Babar and had been on the run ever since, living the life of a fugitive. The first ten years of his life as emperor, had been spent in perpetual strife with his brothers who as custom demanded had been placed as subordinate governors.

Sher Shah, the Afghan noble made most of the chaos. Chasing the weakened Mughal out, he declared himself emperor of India. His descendents styled themselves as the Sur dynasty which was later corrupted to Suri.

Let down by his own people, Humayun pleaded in vain with even his foes. That he received no help from Jaisalmer is of little wonder but even Rao Maldeo of Marwar, to whom he had applied for succour, attempted to have him imprisoned. Humayun fled into the desert where he was sheltered by the Rajput Soda-Parmar prince of Umarkot.

Akbar was trained in the army from his early years. When Humayun regained the crown of Hindustan, Akbar was permitted to command the army. He was thirteen when his father died and had just been declared emperor, when Delhi and Agra were wrested away from him. With the help of his energetic teacher and general, Bairam Khan, the lost territories were recovered.

He soon turned his attention towards the Rajputs and it was against the Rathores that he first advanced. Merta was stormed and occupied, as was a second city in Marwar.

Raja Bharmal of Amber and his son Bhagwan Das pre-empted an attack on Amber by enrolling themselves as vassals of the Mughals and offering a daughter in marriage.

of Chittaur. He longed to be known as her conqueror and his first attempt remained immortalised in bardic lore. That Uday Singh was no friend was made amply clear from the sanctuary he granted Baz Bahadur[40]. Dressed as a man, the maharana's favourite wife, who hailed from a common background, led the soldiers into the very heart of the Mughal camp and on another occasion right up to the emperor's tent. Mewar owed its independence to this courageous woman, declared Uday Singh. The chiefs were infuriated. A slur had been cast on their abilities and they conspired to kill her.

After a year-long siege, Akbar was ready to lead the second attack. The site of his camp or ordo[41] occupied a ten-mile wide area. A pyramidal column, that served as a beacon, was set up and a large mound of earth was piled up close to the southern end from where the cannons could fire directly onto the walls of the fort. Mohur Magri is so named because the emperor paid a gold coin for every basket of earth that was brought in to raise the mound. Despite tremendous odds, covered ramps, that extended right up to the wall of the fort, had been successfully built. Covered by Mughal artillery, at the same time safe from Rajput gunfire, they were to conduct Mughal soldiers through the wall as soon as it had been breached. Directly above was the emperor's observation post.

Akbar had barely settled into his camp when Uday Singh felt compelled to leave. It certainly was not due to a lack of defenders, for Sai Das, leading the Choondawats, was at his post at the gate of the sun. There he fell fighting to the last and there his altar still stands where the rock was drenched with his blood. Rawat Dooda of Madaria led the Sangawats — a branch descended from Choonda Sisodia — while the Baidla and Kotario

---

40. Sultan Baz Bahadur of Malwa was known for his romantic liaison with Rupmati – a Rajputni who did not give up her 'Hindu' faith. The couple were famous for their musical skills. When Akbar's army led by his foster brother, Adam Khan, invaded Malwa, the sultan fled leaving instructions that his wives be killed before the Mughals entered his palace. Rupmati, who was left to her own devices, committed suicide to avoid degradation at the hands of Adam Khan. Eventually Baz Bahadur found himself a place in Akbar's court.

41. The word 'horde' is a corruption of the Turkish word 'ordo.' In the days of the sultanate, the officers in the camps spoke Persian while soldiers spoke Hindi. A language using a combination of both soon developed and was in use by the army It borrowed the Arabic script and included several Turkish words. This camp language used by the hordes was named Urdu. It gained popularity during the reign of the later Mughals.

Chauhans descended from Prithviraj Chauhan of Delhi, the Parmar of Bijolia, the Jhala of Sadri, a son of the Deolia, the Songara-Chauhan of Jalor, Ishwaridas Rathore, Karamchand Kachwaha, Dooda Sadani of the Shekhawat subdivision and the Tomar prince of Gwalior were amongst those who rushed to Chittaur's aid. This time, however, there was no regal sacrifice for the Kangra Rani. Uday Singh left Chittaurgarh in the hands of his commanders – Sai Das (Salumbar), Jaimal Rathore, Putta the Jaggawat chief of Amet and Kalla Rathore.

When Salumbar was slain at his post – the eastern gate (Suraj Pol) – the responsibility fell on the sixteen-year-old Putta, a descendent of Choonda. His father, Jagga, had died in the struggle to replace Banbir and his mother had kept herself alive to rear their only son. She now commanded him to put on his saffron robe and die for Chittaur. No question of surrender had entered the Rajput mind until a shot struck Mira Bai's cousin, the sixty-one-year-old Jaimal Rathore – erstwhile chieftain of Merta[42], who when ousted by Rao Maldeo of Jodhpur, had been granted sanctuary and the jagir of Badnor by Maharana Uday Singh. The day's battle had ended at sunset and Jaimal had climbed the rampart of Lakhoti Bari, to inspect the ongoing repairs, when a lone marksman picked him out. His thigh was shattered and his soul revolted, for a death that did not take place upon a battlefield denied a soldier salvation. As the life force ebbed, he called for Putta and handed over charge of the fort. The siege continued until 25 February 1568. All diplomatic negotiations had failed. The only promise that Akbar was prepared to make was to cremate the dead Rajputs in the manner of the 'Hindus'. Realising that all hope was lost, Putta and Jaimal signalled the end of the war by commanding that the jauhar be lit. To the chanting of verses from the *Bhagwad Gita*, women, dressed in bridal finery, led the children, the elderly and the servants to the mahasati. While the flames consumed them, 8000 Rajputs ate their last beera together. The seven western gates were thrown open. Jaimal, though wavering upon the brink of death, insisted upon a honourable end. Kalla, the descendant of Mallinath of Jasol – the spiritual leader of the Rathores, who had left his home in Jasol (Barmer) and had been

---

42. Rao Biramdeo of Merta had married Maharana Sangram Singh's sister. It is this lady who had arranged the marriage of her nephew Bhojraj with Biramdeo's brother's daughter, Mira, and it was most probably she who was mother to Jaimal, which would explain his close bond with the house of Mewar.

granted Bhainsrorgarh by Uday Singh, hoisted him up. Down the steep slope, at the head of the army, rode Kalla bearing before him the wounded Jaimal. Emperor Akbar, who was greatly influenced by 'Hindu' thought, beheld the vision. Like Vishnu, wielding weapons with all four arms, the pair descended. Behind them poured out a flood – the clans dressed in saffron, a sprig of sacred basil held between clenched teeth. With them, lance in hand, was Putta's mother and wife. The defenders of Chittaur saw the young bride fall, fighting by her mother-in-law's side. When wives and daughters performed such feats, Rajputs were spurred on to greater deeds of valour.

Jaimal fought on even after Kalla was beheaded and fell eventually at the Bhairav Pol. Putta, who stood guard at the Ram Pol, was caught in the trunk of an enraged war elephant. Akbar entered Chittaur. All clans had lost their chiefs except for the Tomars of Gwalior. Curling tendrils of smoke were all that remained of the women and children of Chittaur. Nine queens and five princesses were to be counted amongst those that had perished. In a childish fit, Akbar defaced all temples and palaces and ravaged the works of art that both Alla-ud-din and Bahadur had spared. Then he did something totally out of character – one that was to leave an indelible stain on his reputation. Thirty-thousand peasants who had gathered to protect the fort were condemned to death. The credit of slaying an experienced warrior like Jaimal was claimed by the emperor himself and the matchlock, that helped him fire that fatal shot, was honoured with the title Sangram. An ardent admirer of valour, Akbar had statues built to honour Jaimal and Putta. The images seated on elephant back found a place at the gate of the Red Fort of Agra[43].

Among the royals who survived the saka were Crown Prince Pratap[44], just two months short of his twenty-eighth birthday and his nine-year-old son Amar. Having first found sanctuary with the Gohils of Rajpipla, the

---

43. The elephants remain where they were positioned but the statues are now preserved in the Delhi Museum.

44. The annals of Mewar fail to document Pratap's contribution in this last siege of Chittaur where both elderly and teenage warriors including women distinguished themselves. The suggestion that the royal family forbade him to participate and save himself for the future fails to ring true especially in the light of the fact that Jagmal was the heir Uday Singh had in mind. Pratap's inertia must have invited unfavourable comments from his peers – notably Kanwar Maan Singh of Amber.

royals made their way to the girwo where Bappa had lived before the conquest of Chittaur. Soon after the birth of Amar, the maharana had built himself a summer palace, the Moti Mahal on the banks of the Pichola, a dam on the Berach and the Uday Sagar (lake) excavated. Upon its banks came up the first of the Udaipur palaces – the Nauchauki Rajya Angan. Here he lived for four years and his descendents came to be known as the Ranawats. But on his deathbed, the forty-nine-year-old maharana named his youngest – the son of his Bhatiani rani – successor. Pratap, it appears, gave in to his father's wishes. As was custom, Jagmal took possession of the throne even before the cremation. The Jalor rao, whose sister was Uday's first wife and the mother of Pratap, demanded of Salumbar an explanation. Together, Rawat Kishan Das – the leader of the Choondawats – and the ex-prince of Gwalior held Jagmal[45] by the arms and, gently but firmly removing him from the throne, placed him on a cushion on the floor.

'You have made a mistake maharaj,' said Salumbar. 'The throne belongs to your brother.'

And girding Pratap with the sword, he touched the ground three times and hailed the thirty-two-year-old king of Mewar.

Every chief followed Salumbar's example. The ceremony over, the newly crowned king and his chiefs joined the Ahairea to slay a boar Gauri's name, for the ancient custom could never be forgotten. Mewar rejoiced and looked forward to happier days.

---

45. To avoid quarrels between royal brothers, Mewar followed the tradition of never investing the brothers or younger sons of the maharana with political authority. They are infact ranked after the sixteen chief nobles of Mewar and are referred to as the infants or babas of Mewar. Jagmal was the grandson of Rawal Loonkaran of Jaisalmer. The Bhati royal family, which included Uday's own sister, had all perished eighteen years ago in the half saka of 1550. Jagmal subsequently defected to the Mughal side, received the jagir of Jahazpur and was appointed ruler of Sirohi by Emperor Akbar. His sister, Kika, built the Bhatiani Bazaar in Udaipur to honour their mother – Dheer Bai.

CHEETORE – My heart beat high as I approached the ancient capital of the Seesodias, teeming with reminiscences of glory, which every stone in her giant like kangras attested.

Outside the town stood the relic of the last day of Chittaur where Emperor Akbar, the greatest monarch that India has ever known, pitched his tent and flew his green flag. The Chirag dan or Akbar ka Dewa (Akbar's lamp), still in place at the time of the captain's visit, was built of limestone. This pyramidal column was thirty-five feet high with each face measuring twelve feet at the base. At its summit, a huge lamp was placed to serve as a beacon. A stairway led to the very top.

The lower town of Chittaur, the Tulaiti, was situated to the west of the fort. The ascent being steep, the captain was forced into abandoning the comfort of his palki and making his way up by elephant. Passing through five gates, each time stooping involuntarily though there was more than enough space above his head, he made his way to the Surya Kund (the fountain of the sun) where tents had been pitched for the night. The captain spent the rest of his day gazing upon the wrecks of the ages until the last beam of sunlight fell upon the ringlet of Cheetore illuminating its grey and grief-worn aspect, like a lambent gleam lighting up the face of sorrow. The lonely and majestic columns called out to him in a language that needed no interpretation. Together they recalled deeds which should not pass away unrecorded, of names that ought not to wither and the ghost of Chittaur withheld a sigh for its departed glories. How, wondered the captain, did a city so full of people become so lonely and desolate?

How was it that she, who was a princess among nations and provinces, had now become a widow?

Lying in bed that night, he read from *Khuman Rasa*. Set in the ninth

In the days of the *Mahabharat*, the Pandav, Bhim, went looking for the paras patthar – the philosopher's stone. It lay in the custody of two sages – Yogi Nirbhaynath and Yati Kukareshwar who lived upon an isolated hill close to the central plateau of India.

Nirbhaynath put forward a condition. If the hill could be fortified before the coming of the morning, the stone would belong to the Pandav brothers.

The brothers set to work and laboured through the night. A magnificent fort rose with astonishing speed. It was nearing completion. All that was left was a bit at the southern end. But dawn was yet to come. The brothers redoubled their efforts.

Yogi Nirbhaynath watched in horror when Yati Kukareshwar, who shared his name with the rooster, came to the rescue. The loud jeering cry of a cockerel rang through the still dark night. The sun was shamed into releasing the first of his rays.

The Pandavs stopped. Bhim stamped his foot in frustration, leaving behind what is now the Bhim Lat reservoir (also credited to Bhim, a Mori-Parmar). The Bhim Godi marked the spot where his knee rested. Where Yati Kukareshwar sat was to forever bear his name. But the work of fortification had to stop. The fort atop the hill, that was to one day bear Chitrang Mori's name, remained incomplete – its southern end forever remaining its sole weakness.

century, the story of Rawal Khuman describes Chittaur as the supreme royal abode in India. She was second to none.

> *Chitra-koot is the chief amongst eighty-four castles, renowned for their strength; the hill on which it stands rising out of the level plain beneath, the tilak on the forehead of the earth. It is within the grasp of no foe, nor can the vassals of its chief know the sentiments of fear. Ganga flows from its summit and so intricate are its paths of ascent, that though you may find the entrance, there would be no hope of return.*

According to the Khuman Rasa, eighty-four bazaars, many schools and colleges, many scribes and eighteen varieties of artisans existed within Chittaur.

Between the isolated hill of Chittaur and the rise of the plateau was a densely wooded belt of about three miles in which lay the estates of Gwalior, Bijipur and a part of Begun. Deep woods extended all the way from the base of the hill to the summit. Here in the early 1800's, tigers, lions, deer and hog were in abundance. The Tulaiti was crowded with splendid monuments – the triumphal column, the palaces of Chitrang Mori and Maharana Raimal, Maharana Mokal's temple and the mansions of Jaimal and Putta.

Emotion overcame the captain as he wandered through the hallowed grounds. Every inch had a powerful tale to recall. He paused at the spot where Jaimal received the fatal shot and offered flowers at the cenotaph of Sai Das (Salumbar) near the Suraj Pol, and at the palace of Putta from where emerged that brave Sisodia mother and her young daughter-in-law.

The crest of Chittaur stood at 400 feet and the eastern face near the Suraj pol, or the gate of the sun, at 300 feet. The narrow southern face was lower and this was the chink in Chittaur's armour. It was the very spot exploited by Akbar. Tradition has it that he had had the level raised beginning with a copper for every basket of earth deposited and a gold coin per basket when nearing the top.

The gates of Chittaurgar.

Eastern Gate:

Suraj Pol: The oldest gate.

Seven western gates said to have been either built or re-built by Maharana Kumbha:

Ram Pol: Here stands the cenotaph of Putta.

Lakshman Pol

Jorla Pol

Ganesh Pol

Hanuman Pol: Here died Sajja of Delwara and Sinha of Bari Sadri during the second sack of Chittaurgarh.

Bhairav Pol: This was named after Bhairav Das Solanki of Desuri who gave his life during the second sack. Here, stand the cenotaphs of Jaimal and Kalla.

Padan Pol: Here, at the first gateway at the bottom of the road stands a memorial to Bagh Singh of Deolia who gave his life during the second sack of Chittaurgarh.

Lakhoti Bari: A small gate in the north-eastern rampart where Jaimal was shot by Akbar.

It was at the fourth gate of Chittaur, the Hanuman Pol, that Jaimal and Putta lost their lives[46]. At the sacred spot stood a cenotaph for Jaimal and a sculpture of a warrior on horseback, lance in hand, in the memory of Putta the young Jagawat (Choondawat) chief of Amet. A second cenotaph with a simple dome supported by light elegant columns was dedicated to Raghudev. Three gates lay before the Ram Pol, which led to the Durri Khana – the hall of carpets – where the princes of Chittaur met on grand occasions. In a recent inscription on the Ram Pol, Bheem Singh Choondawat of Salumbar had, in his sovereign's name, abolished forced labour. The orders in the inscription concluded with a grant of land to a carpenter who at his own expense had furnished the Ram Pol with a new gate. The very same Bheem had later attempted to usurp the throne of Mewar.

Walking along the western face, the captain came upon the small antique temple of Tulsi Bhavani, the goddess of the scribes, that stood next to the Tope Khana Chaori, the square park that housed the relics of the cannons from the last time that Chittaur had been plundered. The buildings around had been used to accommodate priests, the master of the horse and other officers.

The first imposing building to catch the eye was the Naulakha Bhandar or the treasure store. It was a citadel by itself, with massive walls and towers and said to have once been the residence of the traitor Banbir. The Sringar Chaori, a richly sculptured little temple, lay at the north-eastern corner. The north-western face was a castle by itself and judging by its looks, was thought to be a very old palace of the Moris and the early rawals. Though attributed to Maharana Raimal, it appeared architecturally far older. Plain with crenellated battlements as its only ornamentation, it was a good example of Rajput architecture prior to the influx of Islamic influence. The vaulted chamber, the projecting balconies and the gentle exterior slope of the walls were characteristic of the architecture of Chittaur.

A courtyard surrounded the palace in which stood a small temple to Deoji. Maharana Sanga had attributed all his victories to this deity. Deoji,

46. This is from Lt Col Tod's personal narrative. However, the cenotaphs for Jaimal and Kalla stand at the Bhairav Pol and that of Putta inside the Ram Pol.

chief of the Bagrawats, was a warrior named Bhoj, born of a Chauhan father and a Gujjar mother. Deoji was on his way to avenge an ancient feud with the Puriharas of Ram Binai. He stopped at Chittaur and Maharana Sanga, who was aware of his divinity, welcomed him with great respect and honour. In return Sanga was given a pouch and was instructed to wear it always around his neck. Using a peacock feather Deoji raised to life Sanga's dead soldiers. Fortified with the blessings Sanga pursued his conquests. The one-time that the pouch slipped off his neck was while he was bathing, in the Peela Khal at Bayana. A voice had immediately warned him of a mortal foe at hand. The foe turned out to be none other than Babar the founder of the Mughal Empire. Deoji obtained for himself a niche in the Sisodia pantheon and never, despite the waxing and waning fortunes of the Sisodias, have the lamps in his temple been extinguished.

Two immense temples to Krishna had been built by Maharana Kumbha and the celebrated princess, the chief poetess of the age – Mira Bai. Both had been constructed from materials collected from the ruined shrines. In front lay twin reservoirs, each a hundred and twenty-five-feet long and fifty feet in width and depth. These had been constructed to celebrate the wedding of the Kinchi chieftain of Gagraun and the ruby princess of Mewar. On the day of the wedding they had been filled with the ghee that was to be served during the feast.

The Vijay Stambh or the tower of victory had been erected by Maharana Kumbha, at the cost of nine lakhs of rupees, to celebrate the defeat of the joint armies of Malwa and Gujarat. Though taller, the Qutab Minar in Delhi would have to be called inferior. Kumbha's tower stood at a hundred-and-twenty-two feet, each face measuring thirty-five feet at the base and seventeen-and-a-half feet at the apex immediately under the cupola. Its nine stories bore openings on every face and every door opened into a colonnaded portico. The richly carved tower exhibited every deity and character from Indian mythology. The ninth storey was devoted exclusively to Krishna and his gopis and decorated with a richly carved scroll fringed with birds – the Indian sarus (phenicopteros). Black marble tablets had been placed all around recounting the genealogy of the kings of Chittaur.

Adjoining the Brahma temple was the Charbagh where the ashes of

One tablet at the Vijay Stambh alone survives the desecration of 'barbarians'. The 172nd and 183rd sloka carved on it recorded the following:

Shaking the earth, the lords of Gujjar Khand and Malwa, both the sultans with armies overwhelming as the ocean, invaded Medpat. Koombhkarna reflected lustre on the land: to what point can we exalt his reknown? In the midst of the armies of his foe, Kumbha was as a tiger, or as a flame in a dry forest.

While the sun continues to warm the earth, so long may the fame of Rana Kumbha endure. While the icy mountains of the north rest upon their base, or so long as Himachal is stationery, while ocean continues to form a garland round the neck of Awini (the earth), so long may Kumbha's glory be perpetuated! May the varied history of his sway and the splendour of his dominion last forever! Seven years had elapsed beyond 1500 when Rana Kumbha placed this ringlet on the forehead of Chittaur. Sparkling like the rays of the rising sun, is the torna, rising like the bridegroom of the land.

The imposing temple of Brahma, also said to have been erected by Kumbha, bore an inscription pertaining to the temple that lay within the victory tower.

In Samvat 1515, the temple of Brahma was founded and in this year on a Thursday on the 10th tithi and Pookhia Nakshatra, in the month of Magh the Kirat Stambh was finished. What does it resemble, which makes Chittaur look down on Meru with derision? Again what does Chitra-koot resemble, from whose summit fountains are ever flowing, the circular diadem on whose crest is beauteous to the eye: abounding in temples to the almighty, planted with fragrant trees, to which myriads of bees resort and where soft zephyrs love to play. This immovable fortress (Achil Durg) was formed by Maha Indra's own hands.

heroes from Bappa's day to that of Uday Singh's were entombed. A rugged path led to a sequestered spot in the deep cleft of a rock that lay in the shade of a banyan tree. From the cleft issued a spring called the Gomukh or the cow's mouth. A tunnel to the side was said to lead to the cave where Padmini committed jauhar.

Climbing further, the captain came upon edifices named after Jaimal and Putta and the shrine of Kalika Devi. This shrine was said to have been in existence since the days of the Mori, the dynasty that preceded the Guhilots. The vaulted cenotaph of Choonda, the chief of the Choondawats who gave up his throne to humour his aged father, lay ahead. Further down, were the palaces of Bhim[47] and Padmini and beyond lay a stone enclosure where the victorious Kumbha had imprisoned the king of Malwa. Adjoining it was the palace of the raos of Rampura. To the south was the tank and the palace of Chitrang Mori, the ancient Parmar prince – the founder of Chittaur. The tank had been divided into compartments. The sculptures here, though in very good taste, did not compare with those of Baroli. Next lay the palaces of the vassal princes of Sirohi, Bundi, Sont and Lunawarra. The chaogan or the field of Mars continued to host the Dushera festival celebrated by the army posted at Chittaur. Close at hand lay a reservoir a hundred-and-thirty-feet long, sixty-five-feet wide and forty-seven-feet deep with richly carved sides.

The Kirti Stambh (also called the Khawasan Stambh or Jain Pillar), a seventy-five-feet tall square pillar carved with Jain figurines was dedicated to Adinath the first of the twenty-four Jain leaders and dated to AD 896. A temple and fountain that dated back to AD 755, were said to have been built by Raja Kukareshwar. Jain inscriptions abounded in the ruins but in them Captain Tod failed to discover any further leads.

---

47. Popular lore as well as the Annals and Antiquities of Rajasthan claim that Bhim Singh was husband to Padmini, while modern historians claim that it was Rawal Ratan Singh who was besieged by Alla-ud-din Khalji.

Maharana Pratap

Pratap succeeded in 1572, to the titles and glory of an illustrious house. He had no capital city, no money and his followers were broken-hearted. But the spirit of the proud race endured. Chittaur had to be recovered. She had been lost and regained many times before. The wheel of fortune had to turn just a bit and Pratap was certain he would win back the lost honour of Mewar.

Akbar, however, was a crafty opponent. Not only was he going to fight the maharana on the battlefield, he was going to fight him at an emotional level. And he succeeded in filling Pratap's heart with anguish. He preyed upon the maharana's allies and relatives. Amber, Bikaner, Marwar and even Bundi defected to the Mughal faction. Not even were Pratap's own brothers left alone. Sagar[48] and Sakta soon joined the wily Mughal.

But Pratap was not one to give in. For twenty-five years, single-handedly, he withstood the combined efforts of the Mughal Empire. Hiding with his family in the hills and forests, surviving on wild grain and fruit, entrusting the care of his children to the tribes of the forests, Pratap harried the Mughal forces in the hills, in the valleys and on the plains. His surprise attacks caused great destruction and before a counter attack could be launched, he would have retreated into the safety of his native hills. The memories of his brilliant acts are enshrined in every rock of these hills and in the heart of every true Rajput. They are too many to recount. Where the eloquence of oral tradition is still alive, the recollections of the deeds of this forefather still bring tears to many an eye.

---

48. Sagarji's descendants formed the clan of Sagarwats. He held the lands and fortress of Kandhar, which remained with the Sagarwats till Maharaja Sawai Jai Singh, who occupied an influential position in the Mughal court, took it away, for the Sagarwats had refused to intermarry with the house of Amber. That Sagar Singh's son gave up the faith of his forefathers taking on the Islamic faith and went on to become the famous and daring General Mahabat Khan in the service of the Emperor Jahangir appears to be bardic fantasy quoted in the *Annals and Antiquities of Rajasthan*. A history written by Mahabat Khan's son claims that they were Sayyeds of the Razwiya stock that had descended from Moses. That his grandfather Ghuyur Beg Kabuli had moved from Shiraz to Kabul and had taken service with Emperor Akbar distinguishing himself in the sack of Chittaur. That his father Zaman Beg had entered the service of Prince Salim and for the murder of Raja Uchaina had received the title Mahabat Khan. But it was a troop of trusted Rajputs that Mahabat Khan led and it was with their help that he imprisoned Jahangir and Noor Jahan at the tail end of their lives.

Pratap was nobly supported. Though constantly tempted with wealth and fortune, his chiefs did not abandon him. The sons of Jaimal Rathore and the house of Salumbar shed their blood for their prince. The Jhala chief of Delwara earned his place as Pratap's right hand man.

Pratap and his followers decided to forsake every article of luxury until the day that Chittaur was redeemed. Pots of gold and silver gave way to simple vessels put together from leaves. They chose beds of straw, left their beards untouched and the martial nakarras were made to follow in the rear. So ingrained were these signs of depression that they would never cease to exist. Beards would continue to grow freely and though the future generations would eat off plates of gold and silver and sleep on comfortable beds, they would tuck leaves under one and straw beneath the other. Alliances with Rajput royal families that chose to associate with the Mughals[49] were renounced. As for a daughter of the royal house of Mewar stepping into a Mughal's harem, well, that was just never to be.

The rajas of Amber had long joined the Mughal camp. Raja Bharmal, who had submitted to Humayun had reaffirmed his ties with Akbar, a move made well in time for Ajmer attacked the little Kachwaha kingdom and would have completely destroyed them had it not been for the Mughal's timely intervention. A grateful Bharmal gave his daughter, Heera (Harka) Bai[50], in marriage to Akbar. The princess of Amber became mother to the heir apparent, Salim. Raja Bhagwan Das followed in the footsteps of his father, as did his nephew and adopted son, Maan Singh. Mughal ties with Amber grew stronger than ever, as Maan Singh became

---

49. This was revoked after a gap of 150 years when Maharaja Ajit of Marwar and Maharaja Sawai Jai Singh of Amber wrote personally, humbly requesting that they may be readmitted to the honourable Rajput society despite the fact that they had submitted to the Mughals. Matrimonial alliances, they pleaded, should be permitted once more.

50. Harka or Heera, the diamond princess of Amber, erroneously referred to by popular historians as Jodha Bai, was mother to the Mughal heir – Salim. Salim in turn married two princesses of Amber, Maan Singh's sister Maan Bai, who became mother to his eldest son Khusro, and Maan Singh's grand daughter whom he married after he succeeding to the throne as Emperor Jahangir. Three Rathore princesses were married to Salim, the first of them being Jagat Gosain – daughter of Raja Uday Singh of Jodhpur and mother to Khurram (later Emperor Shah Jahan) – followed by the daughter and granddaughter of Raja Rai Singh of Bikaner who were also members of the house of Jodha. Akbar had himself wed two Rathornis in his later years – a daughter and a great granddaughter of the late Raja Maldeo of Jodhpur. All Rajput princesses who married into the Mughal family, regardless of their origins, have until now been carelessly labelled Jodha / Jodh Bai.

the most powerful general in the Mughal court. His courage and talent were legendary and to him Akbar was indebted for more than half his triumphs.

Kanwar Maan Singh, for he was still the crown prince of Amber, invited himself to an interview with Pratap. Though he wished to establish peace, Pratap was unwilling to become an officer of the Mughal court and Mewar's independence was not negotiable. Akbar's first emissary had returned unsuccessful. Maan Singh had also tried his hand twice. This was to be his third attempt. The two men were of exactly the same age, both having been born on 9 May 1540, yet one was a king with no kingdom and the other, though a great general in his Mughal master's army, still a prince-in-waiting. Maharana Pratap descended from Kumbhalgarh for the occasion and a great feast was prepared on the banks of the Uday Sagar, but at the appointed hour it was Crown Prince Amar, nineteen years his junior, who waited upon the crown prince of Amber. His father suffered with a headache he pleaded, begging Maan Singh to wave aside ceremony and start his meal. The Kachwaha was outraged. He would not eat unless the maharana shared the meal with him. Polite excuses were useless and Pratap was forced into expressing regret. He would not eat with one who had given his sister in marriage to the Mughals and had broken bread with them. Tucking into his turban the few grains of rice, a portion of his meal that he had offered to the Gods, the humiliated Kachwaha turned to Pratap, who had put in an appearance at the last moment.

'If I do not humble your pride, my name is not Maan.'

That he would always be happy to meet him, was the curt reply, while someone in a less than dignified tone invited Maan Singh to bring along his phoopha[51].

The ground on which Maan Singh sat needed to be purified. The soil was broken up using spades and shovels and sprinkled with holy water

---

51. Phoopha or uncle refers more specifically the husband of one's father's sister. The heckler was referring to Akbar who had married Maan Singh's aunt — Heera (Harka) Bai, daughter of Raja Bharmal. Akbar was, however, two and a half years younger in age than both Maan Singh and Pratap.

from the Ganga. The chiefs, who had been present at the feast, bathed and changed their clothes as if polluted by the presence of an apostate. Every act was reported to the exasperated Akbar. The emperor determined to step up his efforts at subjugating Mewar. Both Raja Bhagwan Das of Amber and Raja Todarmal[52] took turns at convincing Pratap but to no avail. The result was the battle of Haldighati, which succeeded in immortalising the name of Pratap.

The Mughal army, led by General Asaf Khan[53] and Kanwar Maan Singh, made their way easily from the plains in the east, encountering little resistance, until they reached the chief pass in the mountains. Here Rajputs were posted on every rock and pinnacle that overlooked the turmeric yellow plains of Haldighati. The faithful Bhils[54] waited armed with boulders ready to be rolled down upon the intruders. For the first time in history an Afghan led the Rajput army. Hakim Khan Sur had committed himself to the preservation of Mewar. The Rajputs fought gloriously, with every man trying to emulate his maharana. Pratap tried in vain to engage Maan Singh but was denied the luxury of a hand-to-hand combat. The bards were present that day to witness the events as they unfolded. A large number of lives were lost as Mughals and Rajputs rushed to the defence of their princes. Pratap was singled out easily because of the royal umbrella above his head, which he stubbornly refused to relinquish. Thrice he was rescued from the midst of the enemy and at one point, when he had nearly been overwhelmed, Raj Rana Mana (Bida), the Jhala chief of Bari Sadri, in an act reminiscent of the events at Khanua, had snatched the royal umbrella and made off

---

52. Raja Todarmal became famous for successfully organizing the revenue systems.
53. Asaf Khan was the son of the Persian noble Ghiyas Beg whose father – an imperial officer – died soon after Shah Tahmasp was poisoned. The family fled and sought refuge in Hindustan. Tahmasp's kindness in helping Humayun regain his empire had not been forgotten and Mirza Ghiyas was appointed first as Akbar's treasurer then promoted to wazir on Jahangir's accession, receiving the title of Itimad-ud-daula. Asaf succeeded to his father's office of prime minister. His widowed sister, Mehrunissa (Noor Jahan), became twenty-seventh wife to Emperor Jahangir and his daughter, Arjumand (Mumtaz Mahal) wed Khurram.
54. Rana Punja, the Rajput chief of Panarwa, who led the Bhil army, was considered a Bhil by his men. Having proved themselves at Haldighati, Punja's Bhils were declared equal in status to the citizens of Mewar. This recognition was said to be the first of its kind in the history of the tribal population of India.

Severely wounded, Chetak flew bearing his injured master from the plains of Haldighati. Leaping across mountain streams, he left the pursuing Mughals far behind. As the horse weakened, sparks from the hooves of a steed shadowing them caught Pratap's eye. It continued to follow closely across the hard flint rock of the Aravalli.

The pursuer called out in his native tongue, 'Ho! Neela ghora re sawar.' 'Ho! Rider of the blue horse.'

Pratap glanced over his shoulder. It was a lone horseman – his brother Sakta.

Personal enmity had driven Sakta into the Mughal's camp. But as he watched his wounded brother fly from the battlefield, remorse and affection filled his heart. He joined the pursuers only to slay them during the chase and now for the first time in their lives the brothers embraced in friendship. Chetak collapsed exhausted and as Pratap removed the saddle and reins, the loyal steed breathed his last. At this site, Chetak's memorial was raised and his memory kept alive forever.

Sakta returned to the Mughal's camp having gifted his own horse, Unkarro, to Pratap. An explanation was demanded of him with a promise of pardon if he would speak the truth.

'The burden of a kingdom is upon his shoulder and nor I could witness his danger without defending him.'

Dismissed from the imperial army, Sakta redeemed himself, by freeing his old estate of Bhainsrorgarh from the Mughals, before joining Pratap at Udaipur. Bhainsror was granted once more to Sakta and it long remained the abode of the head of the Saktawats.

Baiji Raj, the queen mother, left to manage Sakta's household. The mother of the head of the Saktawat clan has since been referred to as Baiji Raj.

Sakta was the second of Maharana Uday Singh's twenty-four sons. As a five-year-old he had displayed a fearless temperament testing the sharpness of a new dagger on his own little hand. No surprise or pain was betrayed when blood gushed out on to the carpet.

Predicted to be the bane of Mewar, Uday had commanded the child be put to death. Salumbar, who was childless, begged for his life and adopted Sakta as his own.

Later in life, having borne children in his old age, Salumbar wavered and Crown Prince Pratap sent for his brother. A relationship that began on an amicable note ended on the field with the brothers contesting for the position of best lancer.

As they charged at each other, the court pundit rushed in imploring them not to endanger the illustrious house. His appeal was in vain and he realised that the only way he could put an end to the contest was to plunge his dagger into his own breast. As the priest fell down lifeless, the brothers stopped in horror. The blood of a Brahmin was on their hands.

Appalled, Pratap retired waving to Sakta to quit his lands and leave. Sakta carried his grievances to Akbar. A repentant Pratap, carried out the ceremonies for the Brahmin, granting Salaira to his son.

with it. The enemy wheeled around and gave chase. With the changi raised over his own head, the faithful Mana and his soldiers bore the brunt of the battle.

On the 7th of Savan (July 1576), a day ever memorable in her annals, the best blood of Mewar irrigated the pass of Haldighati. Five hundred of the maharana's relatives died that day. The Tomar prince of Gwalior, who had been granted sanctuary in Mewar since his expulsion by Babar, accompanied by his son and 350 clan members, paid their debt of gratitude.

The rains bought temporary peace for Pratap. The imperial army left the hills elated with joy. Pratap had but a few months to recuperate before the foe returned with the spring. Another defeat was suffered and Pratap took up his post at Kumbhalgarh. A gallant and protracted defence was conducted with the Rajputs holding out until the drinking water became infested with worms. The contamination of the Noguna well was attributed to the treachery of the Deora chief of Abu, who had defected to the Mughal's camp at the behest of Raja Rai Singh of Bikaner. Rai Singh, a Rathore descended from the house of Jodha, had as a crown prince led expeditions under the imperial banner against the then independent Rathores of Marwar.

Pratap withdrew to Chavand, in the heart of the mountainous territory of Chappan. The Songara-Chauhan chief remained behind and held on to Kumbhalgarh till his last breath but with its fall, the castles of Dhurmeti and Gogunda gave way to Maan Singh and Udaipur to Mahabat Khan. The Mughals invaded Chappan, approaching Chavand from the south.

Hounded from all sides, Pratap managed with secret signs to reassemble at the most surprising spots, assailing the Mughal army when they least expected it. Khan Farid, the general whose only dream was to capture Pratap alive, found himself suddenly trapped, cut off from his army amidst gorges and ravines. Unaccustomed to such warfare, the mercenary Mughal army was frustrated. The periodical rains, which caused the mountain streams to swell, gave the Rajputs much needed respite.

Years rolled by. Pratap's resources depleted steadily while his misfortunes continued to rise. His family was a chief source of worry. He dreaded their falling into enemy hands. On more than one occasion they had been saved by the faithful Bhils. Deep within the tin mines of

Zawar, large wicker baskets were suspended from trees by rings the bolts driven firmly into the upper branches. These were the royal cradles that preserved the children from the tiger and the wolf.

Yet, in the midst of adversity, Akbar's spies reported to him a picture of the maharana and his chiefs seated at a scanty meal. The doonah, though comprising wild fruit, was offered and accepted by the most deserving of the chiefs, an act reminiscent of Mewar in her days of glory. Akbar's soul was touched. Neither he nor his council could withhold their admiration.

'All is unstable in the world, land and wealth will disappear, but the virtue of a great name lives forever. Putto[55] abandoned wealth and land, but never bowed his head,' exclaimed the khan-e-khana[56].

There were, however, moments when Pratap despaired for his family. Food was scarce and his queen insecure. His children, who were heirs to luxury, wept with hunger. The Mughals chased them so relentlessly that there were days when five hot and ready meals had to be abandoned in a row. His queen and his daughter-in-law spent their time collecting seeds of the wild grass and grinding them into a flour-like powder that was baked into bread. A loaf was given to each member: a part was to be eaten and a part saved for a future meal. A piercing shriek roused the maharana. A wild cat had stolen a portion of the food, driving his starving child hysterical. Until now, Pratap had witnessed sons and relatives fall in the battlefield without emotion, but the sight of the little ones lamenting over food was too much for him to bear. He wrote to Akbar.

---

55. Referring to Pratap.
56. Khan-e-khana (the senior-most of the Mughal generals) was Abdur Rahim, the son of Akbar's regent and mentor Bairam Khan. When Bairam Khan, who had been dismissed in 1560, died, Akbar married his widow, which made Abdur Rahim his stepson. Four years after Haldighati, twenty-one-year-old Amar surprised the Mughal by occupying Mewari township of Phulia, which later came to be known as Shahpura. Chief among his booty were the begums of Abdur Rahim. But Pratap was not impressed and the dutiful son escorted the ladies back.

But in his last years Abdur Rahim's fidelity to the emperor wavered. He leagued with Malik Ambar of Ahmadnagar against Jahangir and finally allied himself with the rebellious Khurram.

Akbar's name is linked with that of Pratap's in many verses that honour them both.

Rajasthani bards while singing Pratap's praises will often say that Akbar alone could compare with him.

Mughal historians who, understandably, refrain from ever criticizing Akbar write:

If he sometimes did things beneath the dignity of a great king, he never did anything unworthy of a good man.

The hopes of the 'Hindu' rest on the 'Hindu' yet the rana forsakes them. But for Pratap, we would have all been reduced to the same level by Akbar.

Our chiefs have lost their valour and our women their honour. Akbar has purchased us all from the flesh market but the son of Uday proved far too expensive. Despair drove many of us to permit ourselves to be sold but from such infamy the descendant of Hamir alone has been saved. Akbar, the merchant who is buying up the Rajputs, cannot live forever.

Our race will then look to Pratap and his children to provide a pure breed of Rajputs with which we will rebuild Rajasthan.

The Mughal court was overcome with joy. Akbar announced public celebrations. The Rajput chiefs at court congratulated the emperor but their hearts were downcast. Prithviraj, brother to Raja Rai Singh of Bikaner, a state carved out of Marwar, was a secret admirer of Pratap. The desert kingdom of Bikaner, small and with no natural advantage had been amongst the first to join the Mughals.

'It is forgery,' he insisted and obtained permission to verify the truth. Prithviraj – poet and warrior, counted as one of the nine gems of the imperial court – wrote to Pratap.

This one letter was equal to encouragement by 10,000. Prithviraj's letter roused Pratap into action. All Rajput eyes, he realised, were fixed on him. He worked out a new strategy. He would abandon Mewar and leave for Sogdoi on the banks of the Indus. Mewar he would reduce to a desert. There would then be nothing left for the Mughals to covet.

As Pratap came down from the hills, a minister came forward. Bhama Sah's family had held office as minister for many generations. He placed before Pratap all the accumulated wealth of his family. It is said, that the money could have maintained 25,000 men for twelve years. Mewar preserved forever the name of Bhama Sah as her saviour.

The Mughal army garrisoned in Mewar assumed Pratap was leaving and would make his way out through the desert. Taking them by surprise, Pratap recovered nearly all of Mewar except for Chittaur, Ajmer and Mandalgarh. Determined to teach Maan Singh a lesson, he invaded Amber and sacked its business centre, the town of Malpura.

The rest of Pratap's life was spent in comparative ease. Huts constructed on the banks of the Pichola marked the spot for the future palace of Udaipur. The Mughals busied themselves with campaigns elsewhere. Some degree of sympathy and admiration for Pratap prevailed in Akbar's heart and in the minds of the Rajput chiefs at the Mughal court. The inactivity however preyed upon the mind of Pratap. It was compassion and not glorious victory that had earned him this repose. A wound sustained at Chavand continued to fester and the poison spread. The maharana worried about Mewar's future. Crown Prince Amar was getting used to the easy living. It was a source of great worry. For the

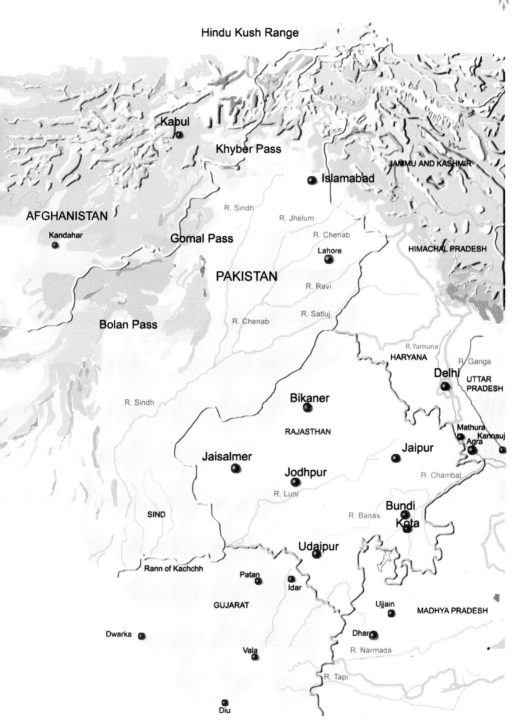

The descendents of Luv abandoned Lahore to set up the Suryavanshi dynasty of Vallabhi (Vala). Mohammand Ghauri of Ghazni overcame the forces of Prithviraj Chauhan and occupied Delhi.

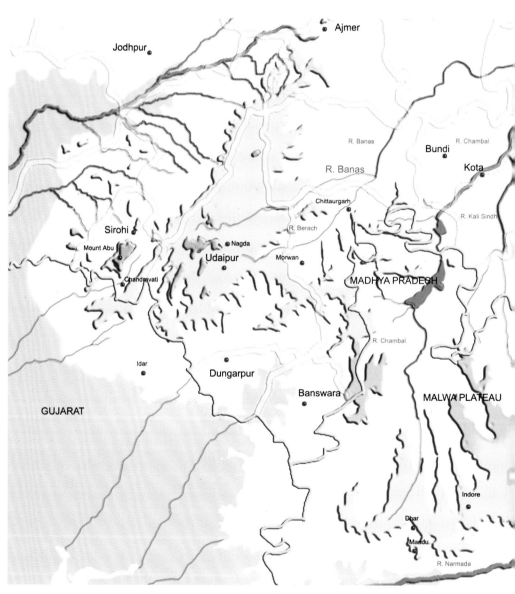

Siladitya and Pushpavati's son ruled in the forests of Idar. His descendents settled in Nagada. Morwan, in Bappa Rawal's time, was ruled by the imperial Parmars of Dhar.

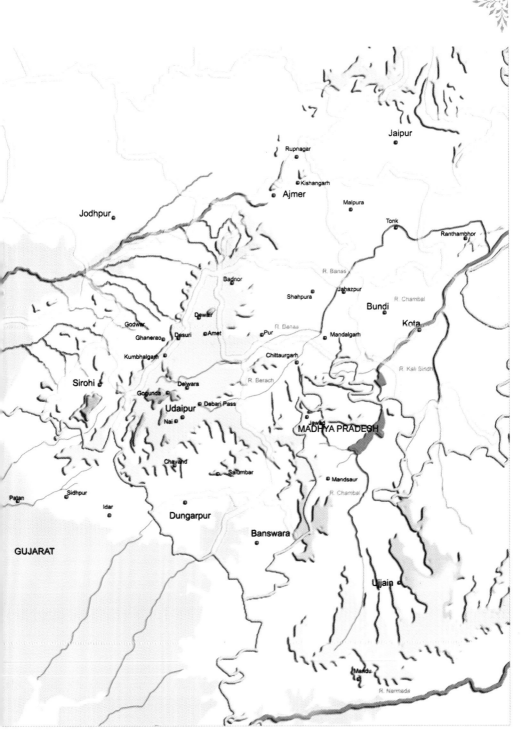

Battles fought in the passes of the Aravalli

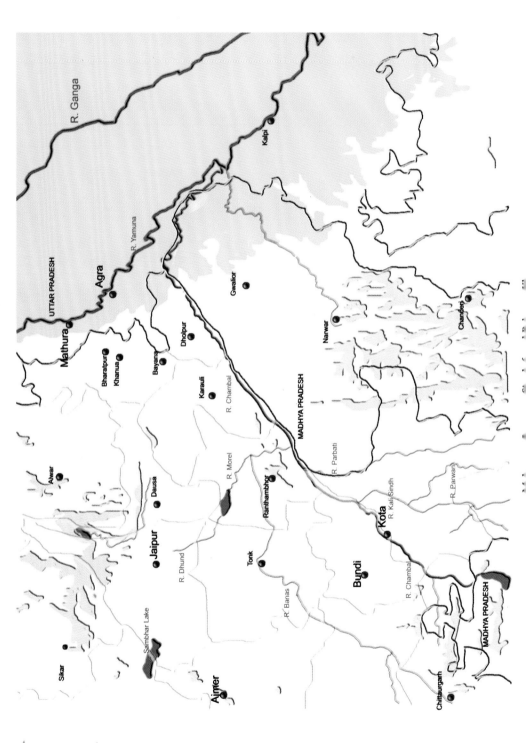

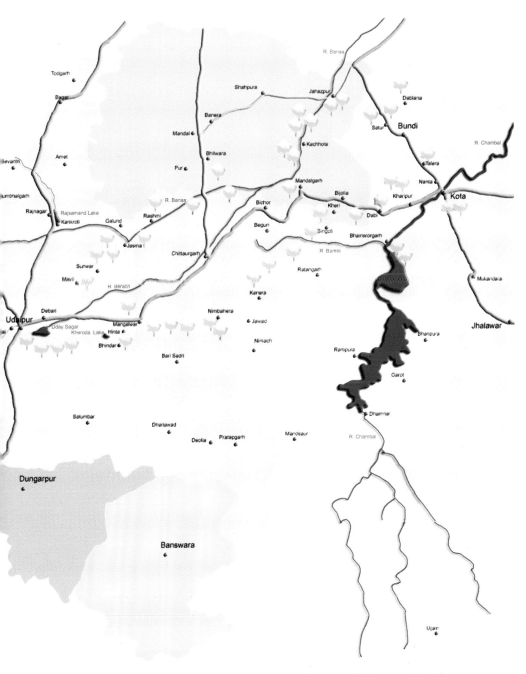

Trail followed by Captain Tod across the plateau between Udaipur and Bundi

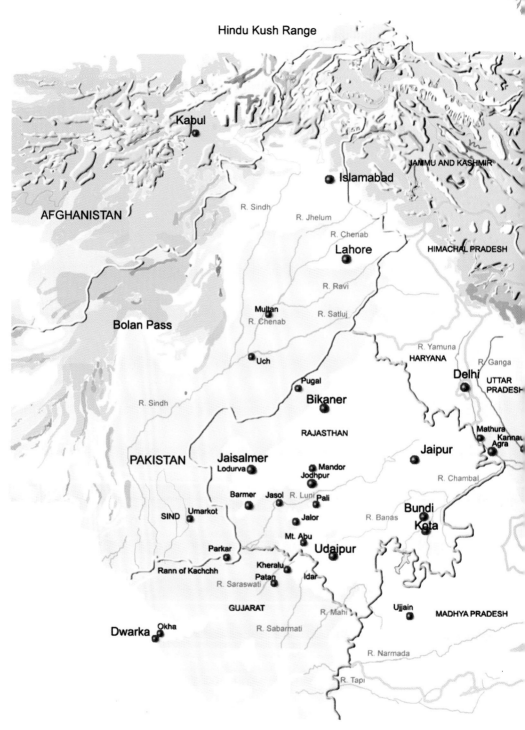

Sihoji's descendents settled in the desert. The nine Parmar castle –
the nau kothi Maroo – gave way to the nine Rathore castles.

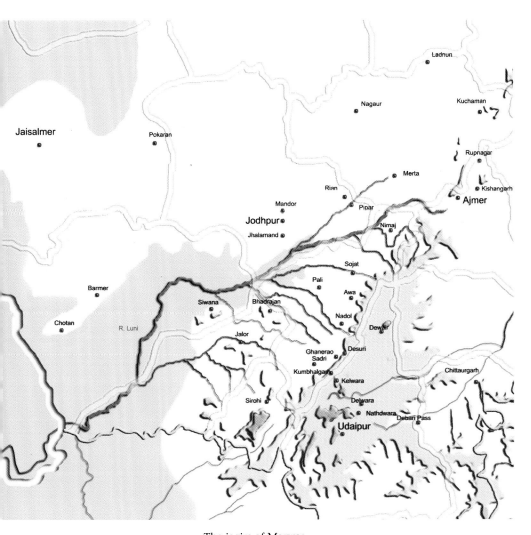

The jagirs of Marwar

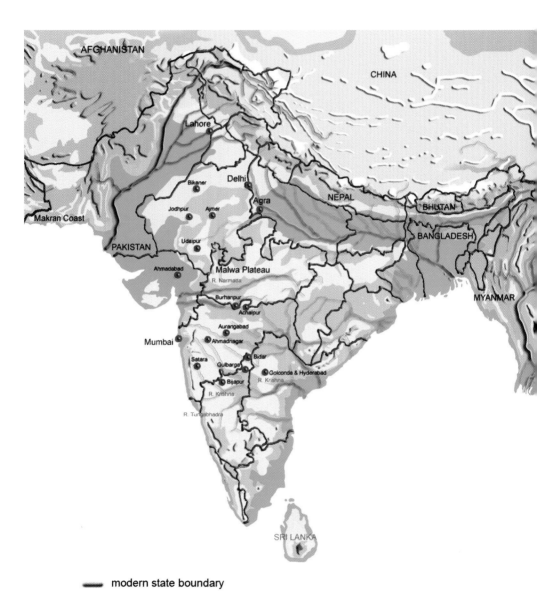

modern state boundary

Mughal campaigns in the Deccan

prince, unwilling to give up his regal posture, would frequently catch his turban on the bamboo that projected from the makeshift roof. Would such a prince keep up the struggle for Mewar's independence? Would he not trade the trials of a battlefield for a more comfortable existance?

'These sheds,' said the dying Pratap, 'will give way to sumptuous palaces. The independence of Mewar, for which we have all bled, will be sacrificed to the love for ease and luxury.'

The chiefs pledged by the throne of Bappa Rawal that they would not let Amar, or for that matter any maharana rest, or indulge in building palaces until Mewar was independent.

Maharana Pratap died and his soul was at peace.

The castle of Bhainsrorgarh that had long been the jagir of the Saktawats had a turbulent tale to recount. It lay on the plateau just beyond the territory of the Meghawats close to the border with Bundi. To visit the famous fort the course of the Bamni would have to be followed. Cutting their way through the dense forests, hatchets in hand, the party descended guided by the roar of the mighty waters. The Bamni came into view cascading fifty feet down the rocky hillside. Weeds that had been deposited during the last monsoon swell of the river remained entangled amongst the uppermost branches of the trees. A heap of stones, a memorial to a Rajput who had fallen defending his post against the Meenas of the area, caught the captain's eye and he dutifully added his contribution to the growing pile.

Situated on the extreme point of the ridge was the castle, bound by the Chambal on the eastern side and Bamni on the west. Mewar's territory extended to the east of the Chambal, up to a small stream known as Kurb-ka-khal that divided the lands of the Hadas from those of the Sisodias.

Standing guard upon a trade route, the castle had been built by two business partners, a merchant, Bhainsa Sah and a Banjara charun, Rora, to protect their caravans from lawless mountaineers. Its early history had long been lost. The list of gallants that held the castle, before Mewar first made itself the master, is not known, for the famous destroyer Alla-ud-din Khalji had also paid a visit. When the plateau was lost to the Meenas in the early fourteenth century, the Hada-Chauhans redeemed it in the name of Mewar. For a while Bhainsrorgarh remained with them.

Two inscriptions were discovered by the captain. They had been reversed and applied as common building material but could be dated to AD 1123. Of those that had held it subsequently there was ample evidence. The name of Dodeah was preserved among the ruins. He was succeeded by Mohandas, a Rathore of Mehwa, whose father – Bagh Singh – had lost his life at Haldighati and his brother in the service of Maharana Amar I. They were the descendents of Kalla, who had laid down his life during the last sack of Chittaur. Mohandas received command of the castle and the hand of the maharana's niece. The new rani of Bhainsrorgarh, however, was unhappy and leapt to her death from the battlements into the Chambal lending to the site its new name – Ranigutta. Mohandas was to soon lose his life in battle. The castle was then occupied by Parmar Rajputs and was lost subsequently as a result of a feud with the neighbouring Meghawats. Bhainsror came into the hands of Lal Singh Choondawat, the younger son of Salumber, in the late 1700's.

Lal Singh was a beacon in the annals of crime and was held out as an example to those who would barter a good name, and the hope of life to come, for the evanescent gifts of fortune.

Lal Singh conspired with Maharana Ari Singh II (Ursi), who had gained the throne having murdered his infant nephew and sovereign. Ursi lived in constant fear. Thoughts that his own uncle, Nathji of Bagar, could possibly entertain similar notions, served to torment him. Receiving wind of the maharana's suspicions, Nathji instantly renounced material life and retired to his abode within the Aravalli. He entertained himself by writing poetry and growing melons in the bed of the river that washed his castle walls.

Lal Singh and Nathji had once long ago exchanged turbans and pledged friendship at the altar. It was midnight and Nathji was at his prayers when a voice broke in on his devotions. None other could have claimed such a privilege. Making his final prostration, Nathji called out to his friend to enter and scarcely had the words passed his lips that the dagger of the traitor struck his neck. For this Lal Singh received Bhainsror and a place among the sixteen chief nobles of Mewar, the rights of the Saktawat chief – who laid claim to Bhainsror since the days of Maharana Pratap – being cancelled to accommodate him. But Lal Singh did not enjoy the honours long and died of disease, vilified in living memory while Nathji lived on in death sanctified by all.

It was with some surprise that the captain discovered that the grandsons of the victim and murderer had resolved their differences and joined in celebrations together. Maharaja Sheonath Singh, the grandson of Nathji continued the cultivation of melons, many of which were enjoyed by the captain.

Maharana Amar

The eldest of Pratap's seventeen sons, came to the throne. From the age of eight, Amar had accompanied his father on every campaign and learnt the art of mountain warfare. Pratap's greatest enemy, Akbar, had outlived him by eight years. Akbar did not trouble Mewar again and Amar wisely realised that it would be foolish to challenge the Mughal's colossal might. He enjoyed the peaceful years building his palace, the Amar Mahal, making new laws and redistributing lands and responsibilities.

Salim, now Emperor Jahangir, had spent four years on the throne. The internal problems of the royal household had been sorted out and Jahangir looked to a great victory that would serve as a signal start for his reign. The subjugation of the only prince who held out against the might of the Mughals was just what he required.

The Mughal army marched towards Mewar. Amar hesitated, torn

between his love for comfort and his reputation. There were many, standing in court that day, who advised him to give in to the emperor and accept the royal firmaan, when Salumbar, remembering the oath given to Pratap, threw a brass ornament shattering a beautiful European mirror. He pulled Amar up by the arms and commanded everyone to mount their horses. Roused by Salumbar's words, the chiefs, forced the young maharana on to his horse. Anger gave way to tears but Amar soon recovered. He took charge of himself and thanked his chiefs for acting in time. At Dewair, they encountered the imperial army as it entered the pass. After a long and bloody battle, the enemy was completely routed. Kana[57], Amar's uncle, was the hero of the day. The Mughals returned in the spring of 1666 and were again successfully engaged in the sacred pass of Rampura. All Mewar was flushed with glory and the crimson banner floated proudly once more.

Jahangir was alarmed. He determined to divide the people loyal to the maharana. A new maharana would have to be appointed and Sagar, a brother of Pratap, was chosen. Sagar who had defected to the Mughal camp was girt with the sword of investiture and sent, in the company of an armed escort, to reign among the ruins of Chittaur.

For seven years, Sagar sat upon the gaddi of Chittaurgarh listening to the silent reproach of his ancestors. The victory tower of Kumbha reminded him of his own unworthiness. He could not plant a foot on an inch of ground or a rock that did not call out to him recalling a heroic deed performed in the defence of Chittaur. He sent for his nephew, the legitimate maharana, and handing over possession of the fort, retired to Kandhar. Jahangir had Sagar sent to Bihar, though legend maintains that he stabbed himself before the emperor.

The acquisition of Chittaur increased the enthusiasm in Mewar. Another eighty chief towns and fortresses were taken by assault. Clans quarrelled among themselves for the honour of leading the vanguard.

Jahangir now put together an overwhelming force. His son, Parvez, was in command, and the imperial army gathered in Ajmer. The Mughal flag flew high. Expecting surrender, Jahangir had instructed his son in advance

---

57. His descendents were known as the Kanawats.

that the maharana be treated with utmost respect and that Mewar be spared from all damage. However, no thought of submission had crossed Amar's mind. The imperial army was met at the pass of Khamnor and was dealt a terrible blow. All historians, whether Rajput or Mughal, agree that it was a glorious day for Mewar. Parvez was recalled. But his son was asked to remain behind to keep an eye on the maharana. Parvez's son, a student of the great Mahabat Khan, was hunted down and slain.

Amar had fought seventeen pitched battles since the death of his father. However, the steady loss of his skilled officers and the lack of time to rear new ones led to a steady decline of his powers while the Mughals kept up a steady inflow of reinforcements. The army was reorganised under Prince Khurram. His cousin, Guj Singh, the crown prince of Marwar, joined him with his Rathores. Both Khurram's mother and grandmother had been Rajput princesses. His Rajput blood gave rise to a deep-seated admiration for his kinsmen. Though Maharana Amar and his son, Karan, collected the might of the hills, all they could muster were a handful of warriors. This time, the crimson banner, that had waved for more than 800 years in proud independence, was taken down by Jahangir's son.

The surrender of Mewar came as a great blow to the house of the Sisodias. Amar died a bitter man. Jahangir's considerate behaviour served only to torment him. But it was Khurram that Amar heaped curses on; a Mughal prince of Rajput blood and an ardent admirer of Rajput valour, Khurram had demanded friendship as the price of peace, offering to withdraw every Muslim from Mewar, if only the maharana would accept the firmaan from the emperor's own hand. Proud Amar could not bring himself to do so, even in defeat. Abdicating his throne and anointing Karan with the teeka in the presence of his chiefs, he shut himself away at Nauchauki crossing its threshold only in death. His ashes were set to rest at Ahar[58].

Maharana Amar Singh was the last independent maharana of Mewar.

---

58. Maharana Amar Singh was cremated at Ahar, where his son Maharana Karan Singh built for him a magnificent cenotaph. Ahar became the royal cremation site for the future generations. A mahasati was constructed for the queens to immolate themselves. Amar became the first to die at Udaipur, his father having died at Chavand and his grandfather at Gogunda.

From Jahangir's Diary

In the eighth year of my reign (AD 1613), I decided to go to Ajmer and sent my son Khurram ahead to meet the maharana. I gifted my son a magnificent khelat, an elephant, horse, sword, shield and dagger and sent Azam Khan along with him accompanied by an army of 12,000 horses.

In the beginning of my ninth year, Khurram captured the maharana's favourite elephant Alum Guman along with seventeen other elephants. They were all sent to me. I went out seated on Alum Guman and distributed large sums of gold to celebrate the occasion.

I had also received the welcome news that the maharana had expressed his wish to surrender to Khurram. He sent word requesting that he be pardoned and that he would send his son, Karan, to attend the imperial court. However, there was one condition. The maharana of Mewar and his successors would be exempted from having to enter the Mughal court for all time to come[59]. I was very happy to have accomplished this during my reign. I commanded that Mewar should not be taken away from its proud and ancient possessors. After all Maharana Amar and his ancestors, had never neither seen nor submitted to any king of Hindustan. I did not want the opportunity to slip away and I instantly forgave the maharana and sent him a friendly firmaan assuring him of my protection and care. As a symbol of my sincerity, I marked the letter with a print of my whole hand. I also wrote to my son to treat the 'illustrious one' according to his own heart's wish.

On Sunday the 26th, the maharana paid his respects to my son and presented him with a celebrated ruby, many kinds of weapons inlaid with gold, seven elephants and nine horses. He touched Khurram's knee and begged forgiveness. My son, with princely generosity and courtesy, raised his head and assured him of his protection, presented him with khelats, an elephant, horses and a sword.

Karan and Khurram arrived at Ajmer the next day. Khurram requested that Karan be seated on my right hand side. I presented him with suitable khelats. Karan was shy and

---

59. Henceforth the heirs-apparent of Mewar would attend the Mughal court but would eease to do so on becoming maharana.

*unused to the ways of the court. He had spent his years
in the hills always with the army. I took him under my wing
and to reassure him of my regard and protection I would
present him something every day. On his second day, I gave
him a jewelled dagger and a richly caparisoned steed from
Iraq on the third. Empress Noor Jahan gifted him many
khelats, a horse, elephant and sword. I gave him a pearl
necklace and another elephant. I wanted to give him the
choicest gifts. Three royal hawks and three gentle falcon's
trained to the hand, a coat of mail, chain and plate armour,
two rings of great value and on the last day of the month
carpets, state cushions, perfumes, vessels of gold and a pair
of bullocks from Gujarat. In the tenth year of my reign, I
allowed Karan leave to return to his jagir[60]. I gave him
an elephant, a horse and a pearl necklace worth 50,000
rupees (5,000 pounds). In the time that he had spent with
me, I had given him gifts worth ten lakhs of rupees apart
from the 110 horses and five elephants. Khurram made
additional gifts. Later in the year, Karan was made a
munsubdar of 5,000. His twelve-year-old son Jagat arrived
at court, that same year, with his teacher Haridas Jhala.
In my eleventh year, the statues of the maharana and his
son Karan were sculpted in white marble and placed in the
gardens at Agra. Later that year, Itimad Khan gave me the
news that Khurram had visited the maharana. From the
tribute of seven elephants, twenty-seven horses, trays of jewels
and gold ornaments Khurram accepted only three horses
returning the rest. He made only one demand: that Prince
Karan and 1,500 Rajput horses remain with him in the wars.*

*In the fourteenth year of my reign, I received news that
Maharana Amar had passed away. His grandson Jagat Singh
and younger son Bheem Singh were at court at the time.
To them I gave khelats and sent Raja Kishoridas with the
firmaan conferring the title of maharana and a letter of
condolence and choice horses to Karan.*

---

60. Ancient, independent and sovereign Mewar had been reduced to the status of a jagir or
a fief. Mewar now belonged to the Mughal emperor. The maharana was granted the right
to govern Mewar on behalf of the emperor in the capacity of a mere jagirdar. This
possibly explained Karan's quiet demeanour, which was referred to as shyness.

Maharana Karan Singh

Fighting by his father's side, Karan had proved himself to be a skilful general. During the troubled years when they desperately needed money, he had taken it upon himself to find a solution. With a small band of men, Karan had broken through the enemy lines and plundered Surat, carrying off a rich booty. The whole operation had been carried out with such unparalleled rapidity that it defied comprehension. But now as a maharana under the Mughal yoke, he had little scope to utilise his military skills. The thirty-five-year-old's talents and energies were used instead to fortify the capital, enlarge the dam and build the rawala. Of Karan's additions to the City Palace were the Moti (pearl) Mahal, Manik (ruby) Mahal and the Dilkhush (heart-warming) Mahal.

Karan's younger brother Bheem Singh had become friend and advisor to Khurram, who had earned himself the title of Shah Jahan for bringing down the fort of Ahmadnagar in 1616. At Khurram's behest he was made raja of Toda (Tonk). The new raja built his palace on the banks of the Banas but Jahangir was to soon have a taste of his spirit. Keen to separate him from the rebellious Khurram, who aspired to the crown, he posted Bheem to Gujarat. Bheem refused to go.

Evil days were at large and Khusro, Jahangir's eldest, his proclaimed heir, the blind prince beloved of the people, died in January 1622. The circumstances were indeed suspicious for he had been in the care of his half-brother – Khurram. The rebellion was out in the open. Refusing to obey his father's commands Khurram let Kandahar slip into the hands of Shah Abbas the Great, emperor of Persia. It was to be the first great loss of Jahangir's reign. Keen to separate Bheem from his rebellious son, Jahangir had him posted to Gujarat but the order was ignored. Greatly worried the emperor considered shifting the treasury from Agra to the safety of Lahore. But Khurram threatened to intercept the convoy were any such move to be attempted.

Jahangir summoned his second son Parvez to his side and named him heir apparent. Together they advanced to put down the rebellion. Unsure of the Rathores, who were after all Khurram's cousins, the emperor allowed Jaipur to lead the van. Offended at the aspersions cast on his fidelity, Guj Singh of Marwar took down his banners, and decided to become a spectator.

Under Karan's roof, Khurram remained until he was ready to leave for the Deccan. With him were his Persian wife Arjumand (later Mumtaz Mahal) and their two sons Dara and Aurungzeb.

Rooms in the city palace had been assigned to him but his followers, disregarding Rajput sentiment, took over an entire island in the Pichola lake. Here Karan had begun the construction of a magnificent palace the previous year. The unfinished complex was handed over to Khurram who set about making it his own.

A dome was raised and adorned with a crescent. Its interiors were decorated with mosaic, onyx, cornelian, jasper and agate. Rich carpets from Turkey were strewn on the floors and a throne carved from a single block of serpentine, supported by quadriform female Caryatidae, adorned the centre.

A little chapel was erected to the Muslim saint Madar. Here Khurram lived and his every wish was attended to. Such was Rajput gratitude for Khurram, who, when he was triumphant over them, had worked ceaselessly to mitigate their misery over the loss of independence.

Karan and Khurram exchanged turbans as a symbol of brotherhood.

The rest of the palace complex was finally completed by Maharana Jagat Singh and Khurram's palace became a part of the opulent Jag Mandir.

When Captain Tod visited the palace, he was surprised to see the lamp still burning in Madar's chapel. Khurram's turban and shield were brought down from their niche. The folds of the orange coloured turban had been preserved in their original state. The British political agent bowed his head before the turban of Shah Jahan, once emperor of Hindustan. Despite the unrelenting and barbaric persecution that followed under the reign of Khurram's son, oil never went wanting in the Muslim chapel.

As the armies approached, the impetuous Bheem called out to Guj Singh. The Rathores had been standing by the edge of the field seething with rage but as the lalkar, calling out to their manhood, rang through the air, the cohorts wheeled slaying Bheem and his army. Khurram fled to the security of Udaipur. His rebellion, however, did not come to an end and in 1623, he was chased by General Mahabat Khan to the Deccan. By October 1626, Parvez had died a mysterious death (attributed later by Aurungzeb to his father) and Khurram married, rather hastily, Parvez's Rathorni widow – his own first cousin Manbhavati – sparing her the sorrows of widowhood.

Karan reigned in perfect tranquillity for nine years. The sanctuary he offered Khurram did not disturb Jahangir, for he believed that the maharana could never have sanctioned Bheem's behaviour.

Maharana Jagat Singh

Jagat Singh, the lion of the world, succeeded to the throne in 1628. Jahangir had died the previous October, and it had been Jagat who had sent the news to the Deccan. His brother and a band of Rajputs had gone to Surat to receive the new emperor, who came directly to Udaipur. It was in the Badal Mahal that Khurram had first been saluted as emperor. In return five districts had been restored, Maharana Karan presented with a ruby of great value and Jagat permitted to fortify and repair Chittaur. His first cousin, Maharaj Sujan Singh, who devoted himself to Shah Jahan, was granted the jagir of Phulia in 1631. Phulia was renamed Shahpura.

Jagat ruled peacefully for twenty-six years. The Jag Mandir that had been begun by his father was completed and Shah Jahan's Gul Mahal retained. The most striking feature was the courtyard of black and white marble, the lush gardens, cooling fountains and marble walkways. The Jagdish temple was built and dedicated to Lord Jagannath. Recorded on the walls of its sanctum was the genealogy of Mewar traced from the days of Bappa Rawal.

Jagat, remembered for his dignity and benevolence, had the satisfaction of saving the ancient capital from ruin. He restored the Mala burj, a chaplet bastion blown up by Akbar and replaced the pinnacles on the temple of Chitra-koot.

Maharana Raj Singh

The royal lion mounted the throne in 1654. In Raj Singh, the martial blood of the Sisodias would not lie dormant. He signalled his accession by the age-old ritual of teeka-dowr, plundering the town of Malpura. Shah Jahan, when he received the news, responded with an indulgent smile. 'It is only a folly of my nephew,' he said. But when the maharana began to fortify Chittaur, Shah Jahan moved his army. A gift of elephants and horses and a detachment that was to join in the Mughal campaigns in the south helped soothe the frayed nerves.

But Mewar was yet to experience the turbulence that was shaking the entire country. The sons of Shah Jahan[61] had begun fighting for the throne even before their father had passed away. Their unmixed foreign blood bought them no Rajput sympathies. Mewar inclined towards Dara Shikoh, Shah Jahan's firstborn and the legitimate heir, as did nearly the entire Rajput race. Maharaj Sujan Singh of Shahpura laid down his life along with those of seven of his eight sons. But the battle of Fatehabad gave Aurungzeb the lead. He was prepared to sacrifice his brothers, his father and even his sons to further his own ambitions. In 1658, Aurungzeb declared himself emperor even as his father languished in the Agra Fort. Shah Jahan would spend the next seven years imprisoned by his son.

---

61. Shah Jahan and his Persian wife Mumtaz had four sons – Dara Shikoh, Muhammad Shuja, Aurungzeb and Murad Baksh. Of all the the Mughal, Aurungzeb appears to have been victimized by the bards for historians maintain that Akbar's religious tolerance and Jahangir's indifference had given way to religious intolerence during the time of Shah Jahan. But Shah Jahan's extravagant tastes turned out to be his redeeming feature for he gave to India the Taj Mahal – the grand mausoleum built for Mumtaz – after whose death he lapsed into scandalous licentiousness. Aurungzeb who, ordered the mass destruction of temples and converted a handful of timid 'Hindus' to Islam, earned himself a terrible reputation but was by comparison the mildest and the least cruel of the Mughals. Capital punishment was done away with in his time and slaughter abated. He remained a humble emperor, one who had considered renouncing his throne to become a religious recluse.

Seven years after Raj Singh's accession, famine and pestilence raged through Mewar. As the months of Asar, Sawan and Bhadon passed without a drop of rain, the maharana went to implore the favour of the four-armed goddess. Driven to madness by hunger, the people resorted to stripping trees of their bark while children were hawked to acquire but a handful of grain. Bright stars shone relentlessly every night and even insects perished for want of food. To alleviate the miseries of his starving population, the maharana and his chiefs contributed a sum of 11,50,000 pounds sterling towards a national project. Twenty-five miles north of Udaipur, a small stream, the Gomti, was arrested and confined by a huge embankment to form the Rajsamand (royal sea) lake. The relief operations began in 1662, and continued until 1676. White marble steps led down to the water's edge. Along the embankment were built pavilions with ornate arches, commissioned by Rani Charumati. The temple of Kankroli, one of Krishna's seven forms, came up below the dam. Inscribed within was a genealogical sketch of the Sisodias. To its south lay the upcoming town and the fortress of Rajnagar.

They had barely been released from the grip of the famine when Aurungzeb chose to unleash his religious warfare. He targeted old and famous temples. The 'Hindus' rushed to salvage as much as possible. The statue of the boy Krishna (Nath) that is said to date from the eleventh to twelfth century BC was rescued from Mathura. In 1671, Raj Singh offered to take responsibility. On its way to Udaipur, the carriage wheels sank into the swampy grounds. It was a sign. A temple was built to house the deity and the area named Nathdwara.

Riddled with religious intolerance, Aurungzeb, introduced the hated jaziya. So long as Mirza Raja Jai Singh of Amber lived, Aurungzeb dared not offend him by taking such a measure but with his death and Jaswant Singh of Marwar posted beyond the Attock, there was no one at the Mughal court looking out for the welfare of the 'Hindus'. The maharana, as the head of the Rajput states, wrote a letter of remonstrance in a style of such uncompromising dignity, gently rebuking and yet benevolent and tolerant at the same time, that Aurungzeb was driven to a fit of passion.

With the death of Jaswant Singh of Marwar, the mother of the infant Ajit, a princess of Mewar, had appealed to Mewar. Sanctuary was offered,

Born of a Persian mother, Aurungzeb was acutely concious of the lack of Rajput good will. He was determined to rectify it. His own heir was born of a 'Hindu' Kashmiri princess. Then at the height of his power, Aurungzeb demanded the hand of the princess of Rupnagar.

The Rathore kingdom of Kishangarh, that lay to the north of Ajmer, had broken away from the parent kingdom of Marwar in 1611. Kishan who established Kishangarh was the son of Raja Uday Singh of Jodhpur. The fifth king of Kishangarh, Rup Singh, conquered lands to the north of Kishangarh and built the magnificent capital city of Rupnagar. The rajas of Kishangarh allied themselves with the Mughals and in June 1658, Rup Singh lost his life at Samugarh, fighting against Aurungzeb. To the daughter of Rup Singh came the summons.

Two thousand horses and a royal litter were sent to escort the princess back. For the emperor of Hindustan, this was the greatest honour that he could bestow upon the 'Hindu' race and there was no question that the Rathores would feel anything but honoured. But the haughty princess indignant at such a demand appealed to the chief of the Rajput race. The family priest carried her message,

'Is a swan to be the mate of the stork, a Rajputni pure in blood, wife to the monkey faced 'barbarian'!'

Charumati threatened to kill herself if not saved from this dishonour. In this appeal to his gallantry, all the valour and recklessness of the Sisodias burst forth. Laying caution to the winds and risking the lives of the people of Mewar, the maharana rode swiftly to Rupnagar and, from before the very eyes of the imperial guard, carried the Rathorni away. All Rajasthan rejoiced and gathered once more about the crimson flag.

Charumati wed Raj Singh in 1660. But her brother Man Singh, who had succeeded to the throne, was intent on keeping the peace. The following year, their sister Amrita married Aurungzeb's heir Muazzam.

Amrita's grandson was to later mount the imperial throne as Emperor Farukhsiyar.

and the infant king of Marwar was assigned Kelwa as his residence while his mother took care of his kingdom[62].

The Mughal assembled all his resources. His sons were re-called, Azam from Kabul and Akbar from Bengal. So vast were his preparations against Mewar, that in it he paid the Rajputs the highest tribute possible. On 3 September 1679, the formidable army entered Mewar from the east. Cities and forts of the low-lying areas were occupied with ease. Experience had taught the Mughals that these were difficult to defend. Chittaur, Mandalgarh, Mandsaur, Jiran and several others fell after the usual amount of resistance.

Maharana Raj Singh sent a call to all who supported the cause of the 'Hindu'. The tribes gathered with thousands of bows and arrows. Raj Singh divided his forces into three. Of his two sons, Jai Singh was posted on the crest of the Aravalli; Bheem in the west kept up communications with the outlets to Gujarat, while the maharana himself led the main body. Raj Singh waited in the Nai defile, ready to trap the enemy as they entered the mountains.

'Let the emperor have free entrance through the passes, shut him in, and make famine his foe,' advised Garib Das, chief of the Saktawats.

Aurungzeb was counselled against entering the Debari Pass. He camped on the banks of the Uday Sagar with his son Azam while Prince Akbar was deputed to occupy Udaipur. General Delhire Khan entered the mountains, at the same time, through the Desuri Pass in the north. The maharana moved his forces to Rajsamand to counter the Mughals approaching from the north. As Akbar entered Udaipur, not a soul interrupted his progress. The palaces, islands, gardens and lakes had all been abandoned. Accustomed to the Mewari custom of desertion, Akbar was lulled into a false sense of security. His soldiers rested, some were at their prayers and the others occupied with games of chess when the heir of Mewar surprised them. Jai Singh had deftly positioned himself between Udaipur and Debari. An unrelenting slaughter followed and Akbar

---

62. The annals of Marwar relate the incident differently. It is said that the queen immolated herself at Delhi, while a faithful Muslim acting under Durgadas's instructions carried the infant prince to a monastery in Abu.

Aurungzeb had engaged both the armies of Mewar and Marwar. As the imperial army approached from the low lying eastern front,

Chittaurgarh and Mandalgarh fell with relative ease as the Rajputs withdrew into the Aravalli.

As the Mughal army wound its way slowly through the maze of the hills, Aurungzeb found himself quite suddenly at a dead end. The pinnacles rose high around him forming an impenetrable wall and the Rajputs closed in from behind. Large trees were felled blocking the way out and from their vantage points upon the heights they prevented the Mughals from clearing the blockades.

Udaipuri Begum[63], who had accompanied Aurungzeb, found herself trapped in yet another mountain gorge. Her retinue, fearing for her safety, surrendered. The maharana received her with every courtesy due to the wife of an emperor.

The emperor, in the meanwhile, had starved for two days and it was decided that it was time to set him free. As soon as Aurungzeb was out of danger, the maharana had his wife escorted back. There was but one accompanying request: the emperor refrain from destroying the sacred cattle that may have been left out in the fields.

There had been several occasions when the Rajputs could have redeemed Hindustan but a misplaced sense of honour and gallantry only added to the sorrows of the land.

---

63. Udaipuri Begum was a slave from Georgia and had been confiscated from the harem of Dara Shikoh. Some believe her to be the daughter of a Sisodia thakur from Jodhpur. She lived to become one of Aurungzeb's favourites and mother to his son, who was quite literally the gift of love for he was named Kam Baksh after Kam Dev the 'Hindu' god of love.

The skill of a Bhil as an archer is legendary. In the days of the *Mahabharat*, when Bharatvarsh was ruled by the dynasty of the Kurus, Pitamaha Bheeshma – the patriarch who presided over the royal family – obtained the services of Guru Dronacharya, a grand-master in the art of weaponry. The grandsons of the family were placed in his care. Among them were the 100 sons of the blind king Dhritarashtra, and his wife Gandhari – a princess of the 'Hindu' kingdom of Kandahar (now a part of Afghanistan) – and the five sons of his younger brother Pandu, the Pandavs.

Arjun, Pandu's third son, had been promised that Dronacharya would ensure that no one in the land would ever surpass his skills as an archer. A youth arrived one day attracted by the great guru's fame and pleaded to be allowed to join the classes. But he was not from the right caste and Dronacharya declined to accept him as a disciple. Downcast the boy made his back to the forests from where he had come.

In time, Arjun became a true master of his skill. The guru took his students into the forest one day, and came upon a young man at his prayers. A dog, accompanying the princes, ran barking towards the stranger. The young man turned around shooting several arrows into its open mouth and then seeing the great guru fell at his feet. With Arjun bristling with envy by his side, Dronacharya asked the young man to name his guru.

'It is you,' replied Eklavya the Bhil. 'Since the day you denied me admission at your school I have been practising before your image.'

'Then it is time for my fees,' said Dronacharya. 'As Guru dakshina I demand the thumb of your right hand.'

Eklavya lost his thumb that day and took to drawing his bowstring with his middle finger a practise followed, ever since, by Bhil archers.

tried to escape to Marwar by the way of Gogunda. It turned out to be the worst decision he could have taken, for the Bhils were waiting for him. At a point when death beckoned Akbar from every direction, ill judged humanity on the part of Prince Jai Singh, saved Akbar. He allowed him to escape to the safety of Chittaur.

Delhire Khan, who was making his way through the Desuri Pass, was allowed to proceed unmolested until he was well inside a long gorge. Waiting for him were Bikram Solanki of Roopnagar[64] and Gopinath Rathore, the chief of Godwar. A bloody conflict followed and a rich booty fell into the hands of the Rajputs. The mountain warfare turned out so successful that the maharana turned his attention towards Aurungzeb and Azam who had moved to Debari to watch the outcome of the operations. Durgadas, with the best Rathore swordsmen (Tulwaren Rathoran), spurred by the memory of the injustice meted out to Marwar, fell upon the tyrant. Despite the European guns manned by French mercenaries, Aurungzeb was forced to flee. The imperial standard, elephants and horses fell into the hands of the Saktawats. From 1679 to 1681, Aurungzeb remained in Ajmer directing the operations from within its safety. His sons were left to lead the army. Commanding his forces to gather below the walls of Chittaur, Aurungzeb sent to the Deccan for his heir. Muazzam was ordered to abandon the war with Shivaji. The Rajput wars were deemed more important.

Sawaldas of Badnor, the descendent of the illustrious Jaimal Rathore of Merta, had in the meanwhile cut off the communication lines between Chittaur and Ajmer. Azam and Akbar were left with instructions to wait until reinforcements arrived. Rohilla Khan arrived with 12,000 men to tackle Sawaldas but was chased, by the spirited Rathores, all the way from Pur Mandal to Ajmer.

While the maharana and his heir had been notching their successes,

---

64. The Solankis of Roopnagar, near Godwar, claimed descent from Raimal Solanki, whose ancestors had fled the destruction of Anhilwara Patan. Raimal Solanki, who traced his descent from Sidh Raja Jai Singh Solanki and had in his possession the sacred war conch that belonged to the celebrated monarch, had been granted Desuri by Maharana Raimal. His sons had acquitted themselves honourably: Shankar, the eldest, founded the Jilwara Solanki clan; Samant Singh the Roopnagar clan; while Bhairav Das, who sacrificed his life during the second sack of Chittaur, had the Bhairav Pol of Chittaurgarh named after him.

Prince Bheem had not remained idle. Realising that their rapidly depleting treasury needed replenishment, he invaded Gujarat. It served as a powerful diversion. Capturing Idar and expelling its resident Mughal garrison, he passed through Birnagar and appeared without warning at the home of the Mughal governor of Patan. Patan and Sidhpur were plundered and he was in full march towards Surat when the benevolent maharana recalled him. Raj Singh was all sympathy for the fugitives who begged for mercy.

Aurungzeb's utter faithlessness compelled the Rajputs to retaliate and behave in much the same manner as him. Dayal Singh, a civil minister, carried out an expedition that ravaged Malwa. Sarangpur, Dewas, Sironj, Mandu, Ujjain and Chanderi were plundered and numerous imperial garrisons were put to the sword. Chaos reigned in the cities as husbands, wives and children abandoned each other. What could be carried off was looted and the rest torched. For once, the Rajputs avenged themselves in imitation of the tyrant. Kazis were bound and shaved and *Korans* thrown into wells. The minister rendered Malwa a desert and the booty replenished Mewar's treasury.

Flushed with success, Dayal Singh joined Prince Jai Singh in giving battle to Azam outside Chittaur. With their Rathore and Kinchi allies by their side, theirs was a glorious victory. Azam managed to escape and locked himself up in the fortress of Ranthambhor. The outcome was just, for it had been Azam who had taken Chittaur from them the previous year. The remnants of the imperial army were expelled from Mewar and a fresh campaign began in Ghanerao, the chief town of Godwar. Prince Bheem and the Rathore army engaged Akbar and General Tyber Khan. A Rajput chief, who had earlier captured 500 Mughal camels, conceived the idea of fixing flaming torches to their sides and setting them loose in the Mughal camp. The chaos that followed was unimaginable.

The maharana and his allies decided it was time to dethrone Aurungzeb and place Akbar on the throne of Hindustan. The way Aurungzeb had treated his own father, had not been lost upon Akbar and he received the proposal favourably. Backed by the Rajput army and supported by Tyber Khan, he was but a day's march away when the very astrologer, who had foretold the day that was to exalt Akbar, disclosed the plan to Aurungzeb. The emperor had no time to lose. Attended by only his personal guards, his sons Muazzam and Azam yet far off, he penned a letter to Akbar. The letter fell into the hands of Durgadas quite by design. To the Rajputs it seemed that a secret plan had been hatched. This was the very scheme that had once helped Sher Shah escape from the clutches of Rao Maldeo of Jodhpur. The Rajputs abandoned the prince who appeared to have betrayed them. With everyone stalling, Tyber Khan despaired. He determined to carry out the plot by himself. But it had all fallen apart by then and Tyber Khan merely sacrificed himself. Before anything further could be achieved, Muazzam and Azam arrived. The Rajputs offered Akbar sanctuary but, insecure with his father in the vicinity, he chose to leave for the Deccan accompanied by Durgadas and an escort of 500. They were well on their way when 40,000 gold coins arrived. There was no accompanying message, but the intent was obvious. Durgadas spurned Azam's offer and under the protection of the Maratha leader, Sambhaji, Akbar boarded a British ship and made his way to Persia.

Maharana Raj Singh died of his wounds in 1682, having made overtures for peace at the behest of Shyam Singh of Bikaner, a retired Mughal officer. Inordinate delays, however, took place during the negotiations, by which time Aurungzeb had regrouped his broken forces.

October 1819: Having spent two years in what he called 'the most romantic place in India,' the captain set out for Jodhpur. It was an excellent opportunity to tour the Aravalli that had once trapped the mighty Aurungzeb and threatened the imperial army with destruction.

The valley of Udaipur lay surrounded by an irregular elliptical segment of hills, fourteen miles in length and eleven in breadth, with only the Pichola intervening between the city and the base of the mountain. The pinnacles of the girwo (the circular range) rose in diverse primitive shapes ranging from 800 to 12,00 feet. The western hills stood 2000 feet above the plains. Three passes led to the plains, the northern-most being Delwara, Debari the central and Nai the southern, that led into Chappan.

Captain Waugh, Lieutenant Cary and Dr Duncan, prepared for the march. Two companies of foot soldiers and sixty Skinner's Horse[65] made up the escort besides the usual retinue of cooks, stewards and helpers trudging alongside the baggage elephants and camels. Passing Eklingji, Delwara and Haldighati they made their way towards Nathdwara. It lay across a swampy stretch of land. Brown granite hills striped with veins of quartz encircled the valley of Krishna. Camp was struck on the banks of the Banas. For the express purpose of dinner, the river was crossed, the chickens slaughtered and the feathers given a quiet burial. The sacred valley could not be defiled with blood.

Treacherous swamps made travel difficult and the trek to Usarwas

---

65. James Skinner, born of a Scottish father and a Rajputni mother, led an irregular cavalry division. Rejected by the British for his Indian blood, the eighteen-year-old found employment with the Marathas. In 1803, as the Marathas prepared to take on the British, they were forced to discharge all those with foreign blood, despite their proven loyalty. Whereas the Holkars beheaded theirs, the Scindia general – Perron – preferred to discharge his lot. Skinner leaves behind a graphic account of his vain attempt to get himself reinstated. Perron's words were, 'Go away Monsieur Skinner. I no trust.' The same fears prevented him from receiving a commission in the Company's service but eventually Lord Lake, the British commander in north India, permitted Skinner's Horse to fight as an irregular cavalry troop. As the Company's mounted guerrillas, their job was to ride ahead of the main force and worry the enemy cutting off their supply lines. In time, Skinner's Horse was absorbed into the Company's army and James received the rank of captain.

proved disastrous. As the men laboured their way through, Fateh Bahadur – the victorious warrior – found himself knee deep in a bog. The old elephant, who religiously tested the ground, thumping it with his trunk, had signalled several times indicating the danger that lay ahead. His warnings had gone unheeded and the animal found himself floundering. In a fit of rage, for it was clearly the mahout's fault, Fateh tried to pick his way out. With the approaching sunset, the thought of the thirty kilograms of cakes and butter that made up his dinner aroused great passion within his breast but exercising admirable patience he awaited the arrival of wooden planks and logs. Grabbing hold of them with his trunk, he pulled the planks towards himself. Placing them directly in front, he positioned his feet firmly upon them and then with a colossal heave hauled himself up and out of his miry prison. Aware that the fault was not his, he shook off his load leaving the men to cope as best as they could.

As the reloading began, the captain set off on a short walk, accompanied by his greyhound. Mysterious shapes darting about in the dusk proved too much for Belle to bear and she bounded off to investigate. The path was too difficult to follow but the dog was soon found scampering down a height, delighted at having spotted her master. At her heels were two great wolves. It was clear that their initial flight had been an attempt to draw Belle further into the jungle and away from her human companion. Wolves like these had long dogged the camps. Scores of gray blurry shapes lurked teasingly in the shadows, always just beyond reach. Scattering and regrouping time and again they would never relinquish the watch and though they had never attempted to make a meal of the humans, there would be news, now and then, of a child being carried off.

Tents were pitched on the banks of the Banas. The chill of the night had set in. The cook had managed to get a great roaring fire going. Above it sizzled a leg of mutton. The men gathered around. It was a heart-warming sight that added to the romance of the land. In the ancient days when the river and the ground were hallowed, an unknown arm had been known to rise from the depths of the river to accept a coconut. But since the day, a 'barbarian' cast a stone into the outstretched hand, the arm had been withdrawn and the river declined from accepting any further offering. The blazing logs were shielded by tents that kept out the mountain air. The men drew about themselves warm blankets shielding themselves from the heavy dew of the night.

Winding through Samecha and Kelwara, the path led to ancient Kumbhalgarh. Then passing below the castle, the descent into Marwar began.

Lying to the west of the Aravalli, in the shadow of Kumbhalgarh, Godwar had been a part of Mewar's territory since the days of Choonda Sisodia and Rao Jodha of Mandor. Greed and treachery had lost the Rathores the only fertile lands they could call their own. For three centuries Godwar remained alienated until the hand of destiny played its card. And Maharana Ari Singh, beset with treachery, trusted the desert lord with its safekeeping. But fifty years had passed since that fateful day and despite all appeals Godwar had not been restored. The matter continued to rankle in the hearts of those loyal to the Sisodias. Quite recently the capital city, Ghanerao, had been deprived of its walls by the army of Maroo, for the defiant Rathore chieftain had preferred to have his sword of investiture bound on him by the maharana's hand. The thakur remained unabashed and came to meet the British envoy, fully aware that it would excite the passions of his jealous sovereign.

An invitation to visit Ghanerao was diplomatically turned down but Kishendas, the thakur's envoy, who arrived almost immediately, wasted no time in pleading his case.

'Restore Godwar', was his abrupt salutation.

It irked the captain for the case was beyond his powers and it sparked off a lively debate. The natural features shared by Mewar and Godwar were pointed out. But the boundary of Mewar, asserted Kishandas, extended to wherever the aonla put forth its yellow blossoms, for the desert kingdom was permitted to boast of nothing but the thorny stunted babul.

Maharana Jai Singh

Twenty-seven-year-old Jai Singh, the victorious lion, concluded the treaty with the Mughals. Prince Azam and Delhire Khan were present on the emperor's behalf. The maharana was attended by 10,000 horses and 40,000 foot soldiers. Over a 100,000 gathered to view the proceedings. The treaty was concluded on the spot and a shout of joy went up at the prospect of being able to live in the plains once again. However, a nominal fine for aiding Akbar's rebellion was levied and three districts were confiscated. The Sisodias were left with the hint that they would be better off were the use of the crimson flag and umbrella be discontinued. Delhire's sons were left in the Jai Singh's care as a symbol of good faith and his gratitude to Maharana Raj Singh whose generosity had spared him from certain death. Though a kind of treaty did take place, Aurungzeb would not permit peace in Mewar. It served to empty the treasury.

Jai Singh immersed himself in civil works. A mountain stream was dammed forming the largest lake in India – the Jaisamand or the sea of victory. Here he built the summer palace for his favourite queen, Komala Devi (possibly Karmeti Bai). Komala the roothi rani, or the petulant queen, was a Parmar princess. She was, unfortunately, the reason for the estrangement between Jai Singh and his heir. For Amar, who was the son of the Bundi princess, Rang Kanwar (sometimes called Ganga Kanwar) and the grandson of Rao Raja Chhatra Sal, resented having to watch his mother's fall from grace.

When some measure of peace was achieved at last, a tired Jai Singh chose to seclude himself. All he desired was a life with Komala. Crown Prince Amar was left in the care of the Pancholi minister at the capital. The impetuous prince was one day rebuked for setting a 'must' elephant loose in the town and in turn let fly insults at his esteemed guardian. The maharana came down to Udaipur. Unwilling to face his father, Amar fled to Bundi.

He returned at the head of 10,000 men. Jai Singh, wisely, retired to Godwar and the Ghanerao chieftain was sent to reason with the prince, who was already on his way to secure the treasury at Kumbhalgarh. Unsuccessful, for the Depra governor was loyal to his sovereign, and aware that the Rathores would use any opportunity to regain Godwar, Amar agreed to meet his father at the temple of Eklinga. By the terms agreed upon, Maharana Jai Singh returned to the capital and Amar was exiled to a new palace. There he would remain for as long as his father lived.

Jai Singh died at the age of forty-five, a tired and mentally unstable man.

Jai Singh and his brother Bheem had been born a few hours apart[66].

According to custom, the father acknowledged his son by tying a band of the amardhoop grass around the arm of the newborn. Perhaps out of greater affection for Jai's mother or by sheer oversight, Maharana Raj Singh tied the band of grass on the arm of the younger son first.

As the boys grew to manhood, the father worried about possible dissension between the brothers. Placing his sword in Bheem's hand, he suggested that perhaps it would be better to use it on his brother at once rather than jeopardise the throne at a later date. This appealed to Bheem's generous nature and he swore by his father's throne to uphold his brother's rights as sovereign and, to set all fears to rest, left Udaipur at once.

Bheem disappeared from the pages of history to live on through the songs of the bards.

---

66. In the light of what is known today, it appears that Bheem was the fourth son of Maharana Raj Singh. He left Mewar and went over to the Mughal side. Muazzam, the Mughal heir, granted him the jagir of Banera. Aurungzeb concurred and soon Bheem's title was raised to that of raja and Banera made independent of Mewar. Shahpura followed suit in 1706 with the maharana granting his cousins special seats at his court.

Maharana Amar Singh II

Twenty-eight-year-old Amar succeeded in 1700, a brilliant man, but one who carried the burden of his youth. In the early days itself, Amar had helped himself to imperial favours by making a private treaty with the Mughal heir apparent and the Mewar contingent had been pledged to accompany Muazzam to the lands west of the Indus.

Rao Gopal, a kinsman of the maharana who held the jagir of Rampura, was serving at the time in the Deccan. His son, who remained at home, withheld revenue due to his father. The unhappy father complained to Aurungzeb and the crafty son realised, that to keep the emperor happy and retain Rampura for himself, all he had to do was to convert to Islam. Rao Gopal fled the imperial camp and made an unsuccessful attempt to redeem his estate. He applied to Maharana Amar for refuge. This grant of asylum was interpreted as a sign of revolt and Prince Azam was ordered to keep an eye on Mewar.

Muazzam succeeded to the throne of Hindustan, as Shah Alam Bahadur Shah, to discover the irreparable damage that had been done by his father. His 'Hindu' subjects had been estranged forever. Despite being born of a 'Hindu' Kashmiri princess – Nawab Begum Anuradha Bai, the daughter of the Raja Chatar Sen of Rajauri – and possessing many virtues that could have endeared him to his subjects, Bahadur Shah was not permitted the luxury of time. He had barely subdued his brothers, Azam and Kam Baksh, when the Sikhs of Lahore revolted. On its heels, came the news of a mutiny brewing in Rajasthan. Sawai Jai Singh of Amber and Ajit of Marwar, who had both had their kingdoms confiscated and had been ordered to the Deccan, took the opportunity to desert and it was to Udaipur that they headed. The three most powerful princes of Rajasthan united to form a federation against the Mughals.

This treaty against the common foe was solemnised by intermarriages between the three royal houses and Princess Chandra Kanwar, the daughter of Amar's heir Sangram, married Jai Singh. Since the days of Pratap, Rajput houses that had chosen to associate with the Mughals had been denied marital alliances with the Sisodias. Re-admission to this honour meant the acceptance of a new clause. Children born of Sisodia princesses would, henceforth, have special privileges: their sons would be heirs, overriding the rights of other brothers, and their daughters never dishonoured by being married to a Mughal. This sacrifice of the right of primogeniture would prove to be catastrophic. The domestic strife it was to produce would call up an umpire – a foe that would turn out to be worse than the Mughal.

The emperor had meanwhile unwisely supported the apostate chief of Rampura, Ratan Singh, now known by his new name, Raj Muslim Khan. Ratan Singh had successfully warded off the maharana's attempt to liberate Rampura and had been rewarded generously by the emperor. The Rajput federation flew into action and Sawaldas Rathore, the descendent of Jaimal of Merta, attacked Pur Mandal and, though he lost his life in the attack he succeeded in driving the governor, Feroze Khan, to Ajmer. Rampura was won back, but only temporarily.

Sadly, the Rajput federation did not last long. The first to defect was Ajit, now maharaja of Marwar, who not only gave a daughter in marriage to Emperor Farukhsiyar, but also agreed to pay tribute, all for a share of power at the tottering Mughal court. Sawai Jai Singh, who had also assumed the title of maharaja, maintained his position as the emperor's officer. Nor was Maharana Amar going to remain an idle spectator. He redoubled his efforts for personal independence and with it that of the Rajput states. Concluding a treaty with the emperor, he asked for the abolishment of jaziya, accepted a munsub of 7,000 and offered the emperor protection from insubordinate Rajput chiefs. He offered sanctuary and a pension to Durgadas Rathore, Ajit's loyal protector, who found himself abandoned in his old age. Maharana Amar Singh II outlived Emperor Aurungzeb by three years, dying at the age of thirty-eight.

A great change had come since the days of the first Amar. All Rajput states had risen in status and now considered themselves to be Mewar's equals.

Maharana Sangram Singh II

The lion of battle succeeded, in 1710, at the age of twenty. Under the brilliant minister, Bihari Das Pancholi, Mewar regained a large part of her lost territory, and with it her respect. But their combined skills were unable to stem the tide of the Maratha invasion, which commenced with the death of Sangram.

The birth of the Maratha had taken place 300 years ago, with Alla-ud-din Khalji's sack of Chittaur. Three Sisodia princes had survived: Ajay Singh, his son Sujan Singh and Ajay's nephew Hamir. While Hamir succeeded as maharana, the disappointed Sujan had been banished. Uttering curses upon his faithless clan, Sujan had left for the Deccan. The founder of the Maratha empire was Sujan's own descendent, Shivaji Raje Bhosle. But while Shivaji concentrated on the foreign foe – the Mughals – his successors intoxicated with their own genius for conquest chose a life style of devastation instead of consolidated government. Their initial severe and frugal lifestyle linked with dynamic patriotism had been transformed into low cunning. Though connected by a common creed, of 'get land no matter how,' to the Rajput the Marathas turned out to be far more degrading for Rajasthan than even the despots of Delhi.

Maharana Sangram Singh's reign was an honourable one and beneficial to Mewar. During his years, he commissioned the writing of *Khuman Rasa* – an account of Mewar since the day of Rawal Khuman to that of Maharana Raj Singh I. But it was to classify more as historical fiction. He was the last prince to have upheld the dignity of the throne of Bappa Rawal and with his death began the rise of the Maratha.

Maharana Jagat Singh II

The eldest of the four sons of Sangram succeeded in 1734. The beginning of his reign signalled the revival of the Rajput federation. This time it included all the minor states and was signed at Hurda, a town on the border of Mewar and Ajmer. The twenty-five-year-old maharana was invested with paramount control. Of the other members, Maharaja Abhay of Jodhpur was thirty-two and had been on the throne for ten years, while Sawai Maharaja Jai Singh at forty-six was both brother-in-law and father-in-law to Abhay, brother-in-law to Jagat as well as father to Sisodia princess Chandra Kanwar's six-year-old, Madho Singh. The federation was the most powerful 'Hindu' authority in India but despite the family ties that

Troubles that were to become the bane of Mewar had grown apparent in Sangram's time. Ambitious queen mothers, reluctant to let go, held on to the reins of power, emotionally blackmailing their sons for as long as possible. Even strong characters like Sangram had their own crosses to bear. Having inherited the throne as a minor, he had been accustomed to letting his mother take decisions on his behalf. Long after he had attained manhood, he still found it difficult keeping her from interfering in court affairs.

The chieftain of Dhariawad who had had his estate confiscated knew there was no point in appealing to the maharana, for Sangram never punished nor pardoned from sheer emotion. He carried his petition, instead, to the queen mother. At her request, the maharana returned the lands instantly. He did not wait, not even for the customary period of eight days between the acceptance of a request and the actual promulgation of the order. Within a matter of hours the eight supreme nobles of Mewar, without whose consent the document would not be valid, had attached their seals. Placing the document respectfully in his mother's hands, Sangram left the rawala. He never returned. Not even for his meals. At first, the queen mother was surprised. A few days later, she sent him a personal message to which she received a ceremonious reply. The lady fumed and fretted but her son would not visit her. She vented her fury on her ladies in vain and then announced that she wished to go on a pilgrimage to Mathura. Though a befitting escort was commanded to accompany her, the son declined to see her off. The queen mother stopped at Amber and Sawai Maharaja Jai Singh of Amber, who had married Sangram's daughter, came to pay his respects. He put his shoulder to her palki and promised to escort her personally during the return to Udaipur. He would plead with his father-in-law on her behalf. The laws of hospitality were strict and the mahrana would never have denied a fellow king his request.

When they arrived at Udaipur, Sangram advanced to greet them. He met his mother first, escorted her back and then returned to greet the sawai maharaja. Family matters were to be kept strictly within the family.

Remembered for being wise and just, Maharana Sangram Singh II was as steady as he was inflexible.

The Chauhan of Kotario, one of the highest ranking chieftains, suggested one day that an additional fold be added to the royal robe. His wish was accepted, according to the traditions of the court. The Chauhan left, satisfied that the ancient customs of Mewar continued to survive and that his office still held all its power. He reached home to discover that the mahrana had confiscated two of his villages. 'But what is my fault?' he pleaded. 'None, raoji,' said the maharana, 'but on minute calculation I find that the revenue from these villages will just about cover the cost of the additional fold to my ancient robe. As all my costs are borne by the state you must bear the cost of your suggestion.'

Once, perhaps by oversight, the maharana himself broke one of his own laws. A village attached to his household had been reassigned elsewhere. Each branch of the household had been allotted appropriate funds and expenses for the kitchen, wardrobe and the queens were drawn from the revenues generated from specified villages. Seated at a banquet with his chiefs, the maharana found the curds served without sugar.

'Unnadaata,' said the cook, 'the minister has said that you have given away the village set apart for sugar.'

'Just,' said Maharana Sangram as he ate the unsweetened curds.

The first signs of disloyalty among the great chiefs of Mewar began to make an appearance in Sangram's time. Troublemakers attempted to break the fabric of Mewari society that had been its strength until now. It needed the moral strength of a man like Sangram to recognize the importance of his chiefs and hold it together.

A mischief-maker in the court of Udaipur had been looking for an opportunity to create trouble between the maharana and Salumbar. The Choondawat leader, having just returned victorious from Malwa, had taken leave to visit his family. Although he was certain that the insinuations were false, Sangram Singh dispatched a messenger recalling Salumbar. The battle worn chief had just given leave to his officers and men and was on the point of entering the rawala when the messenger handed him the maharana's letter. The chief asked for his horse, a dozen men and returned immediately to the capital.

It was midnight when he arrived. Hot food from the royal kitchen awaited him at his official residence. The next morning Salumbar arrived at court. The maharana was unusually gracious and lavished upon him gifts of land, horses and jewels. The descendent of Choonda refused to accept any of it, remarking that had he even lost his life for his king it would not merit such a reward. But to preserve the memory of that day, when he had been assured of his sovereign's trust and goodwill, Salumber requested a favour. In times to come Choondawat leaders responding to summons would find waiting for them the exact same number of dishes cooked in the royal kitchen. It was granted.

It was night when news arrived. The Malwa Pathans had invaded Mandsaur. The maharana pushed aside his dinner plate and called for his armour and his chiefs. The gallant band assembled quickly and insisted that petty matters, such as this, were best left in their hands. As they turned to leave Sangram noticed the chief of Kanor.

He had left a sick bed in response to his sovereign's command and would not be persuaded to remain behind. The foe was overcome that day but the chief of Kanor did not return. His son returned wearing his battlescars like medallions. From the hands of the maharana, he received a beera.

It was deemed ample reward for the wounds he had received and was testimonial to his father's worth.

bound it, the Rajputs found it difficult to remain united–especially now.

The once mighty Mughal Empire was on the verge of disintegration. In 1724, nizam-ul-mulk voluntarily gave up his office and retired to his province. He became known as the first nizam of Hyderabad and founded his own dynasty, which in time came to be known as the Asaf Jahi dynasty of the nizams. In an attempt to destabilise the grip of the kingmakers upon the throne of Delhi, he conspired with the Rajputs and instigated Balaji Vishvanath Bhat – Baji Rao Peshwa, the militant priest of the Marathas – to snatch Malwa and Gujarat. By 1732, the calculating Sawai Jai Singh, who had been entrusted with the defence of Malwa, let it fall to the Marathas, as did Abhay who, following Amber's example, allowed Gujarat to share the same fate. Both helped themselves, at the same time, to the border villages. Like swarms of locusts, the Marathas crossed the Narmada. Holkars, Scindias, Puars and other lesser names thronged under Baji Rao's banner.

Having conquered Malwa and levied a chouth (one-fourth) upon its revenues, Baji Rao arrived at Mewar. His arrival caused great alarm. Hoping to avoid a personal meeting, Jagat sent Salumbar and Prime Minister Bihari Das Pancholi as ambassadors. A long meeting ensued, the chief issue being the mode of reception at court. It was decided that Baji Rao would be seated in front of the throne in the place assigned for the raja of Banera, the descendent of Bheem who had abandoned his rightful place upon the throne in deference to the wishes of his father, Maharana Raj Singh. A treaty followed and Mewar agreed to pay tribute. Then a letter arrived. An imbecile was on the Satara throne and the peshwas were in the process of usurping power. Acknowledging the ties of blood that linked his sovereign with the Sisodias, Baji Rao requested that the Maratha throne be filled by a Sisodia. Court intrigues, however, stopped the accession of Jagat Singh's younger brother, for the maharana dreaded creating a superior from within his own family.

In 1735, Baji Rao crossed the Chambal and appeared in Delhi. He would not leave before securing for himself a chouth of the empire's revenue. It was apparent that the Maratha no longer required the nizam's support. Their sudden rush of success alarmed the nizam and he engaged Baji Rao's army, occupying Malwa. It was under these conditions that Saadat Khan, the nawab of Avadh and his Persian son-in-law –

Safdarjung, invited Nadir Shah of Persia to invade India. It was Emperor Muhammad Shah Rangila himself who had raised these parasites to the status they enjoyed and in an instance of the basest disloyalty – for though it marked an increase in the personal fortunes of the Persian ministers of Delhi – served the Mughal Empire a final stab. The Rajputs, as a body stayed away and Delhi witnessed the bloodiest sacking in its history. Shah Jahan's Peacock Throne and his prized diamond – the one Nadir Shah christened Kohinoor – were among the loot that made its way to Persia. The Mughal emperor did not lose his life but was reduced to being no more than a minion of the shah of Persia.

Sawai Maharaja Jai Singh died two years after Nadir Shah's invasion and his son, Ishwari Singh, was proclaimed maharaja of Jaipur. For the time Madho Singh held his peace. Acknowledging that the treaty had faltered, Jagat Singh granted his nephew the jagir of Rampura. But Madho Singh continued to be addressed as cheema or heir apparent of Jaipur. Seven years after Ishwari Singh came to the throne, Madho Singh and Maharana Jagat Singh put forward their claims. The first round went in Ishwari Singh's favour, who had enlisted Scindia's help. But Ishwari's persecution of Bundi and his own arrogance earned him many enemies. Imitating Jaipur's example, Mewar and Bundi together invited Malhar Rao Holkar. Mewar offered Holkar sixty-four lakhs of rupees for the deposal of Ishwari Singh who, to avoid degradation, took recourse to suicide. The cup of poison gave to Madho Singh the throne of Jaipur, Bundi its independence, Holkar his bribe and the Marathas a firm grip on Rajasthan. The maharana's nephew mounted the throne as the new sawai maharaja of Jaipur and during his private negotiations with Holkar, callously gave away the jagir of Rampura. This was the first major loss of territory for Mewar.

Jagat Singh died in 1751. He had been given to a life of luxury, completely unsuited for the governance of Mewar in these difficult times. His elephant fights took up more of his time than the control of the Maratha menace. He indulged in the arts and embellished the islets of the Pichola. A small fortune had been spent on additions to the Jag Mandir and the City Palace but the triumph of Jagat's reign had been the building of the opulent Jag Niwas (now the Lake Palace Hotel). It had taken three years to build and was inaugurated in 1746. Marble had been used in abundance. Stately columns, luxurious baths and reservoirs made it the grandest of palaces. Fountains abounded, lit by the sunlight that passed through panels of coloured glass. Paintings depicting the history of Mewar adorned the walls. Scented groves of orange and lemon were planted and tall tamarinds spread out wide branches offering their luxurious shade. Mewar, that had known strife for so long, basked in grandeur and peace. By the water's edge, lulled by soft ripples, the chiefs slept off their noonday opium to the strain of bards who sang of glories of days long past. Cool breezes wafted over them, scented with the fragrance of the lotus blossoms that left not an inch of the Pichola uncovered. The days could not have been pleasanter. In the far distance where the wooded margin of the great lake terminated, stood the temple of Brahmpuri looking down upon the pass in the Aravalli, which had been their forefathers' field of exploits.

The villas and festivals devoted to idleness remained Jagat's contribution to Mewar.

Maharana Pratap Singh II

The three years that this maharana ruled were devoted to war with the Marathas. As a youngster he had, against his father's wishes, granted the jagir of Lakhola to Deep Singh – the younger brother of Maharao Raja Umed Singh of Bundi. For that he had been thrown into prison by his father's younger brother, Nath Singh of Bagar. The uncle was then seized with paranoia. The crown prince was bound to earn a pardon sooner or later. Nath Singh attempted, unsuccessfully, to have him poisoned but found to his surprise, that his mild mannered nephew harboured no ill will.

Pratap's son, by a princess of Jaipur, succeeded him.

Maharana Raj Singh II

Raj Singh succeeded at the age of eleven. The child was credited with a cruel unattractive nature and the seven years of his tenure were marked by seven Maratha invasions, exhausting the kingdom. So destitute was

Mewar that Raj Singh was forced to borrow for his own wedding.

Emperor Nadir Shah of Persia had been murdered in 1747, and his Afghan underling Abdalli (alias Durrani) had doubled back to lay claim to his master's possessions in India. He obtained a formal cessation of Punjab as soon as Muhammad Shah Rangila died; returned to enforce discipline by sacking Delhi and Mathura in January 1757; then declaring his intended retirement took back with him to his mountains two lovely young Mughal princesses – the daughter of Muhammad Shah Rangila for himself and the daughter of Alamgir II for his son and heir. The summer of 1757 saw the Afghan leave but in distant Bengal, far from the notice of the Mughals and the Rajputs, history was taking a new turn. Encouraged by the Afghan's victories, Robert Clive used treachery to win the Battle of Plassey. By 1764, Bengal was to be handed over to the Company on a platter.

In 1759, the Maratha government, in response to the invitation sent out by imad-ul-mulk of Delhi, put out a call for the invasion of northern India. Maratha clans flocked to the standard of the peshwa's son – Vishvas Rao – and his advisor Sadashiv Bhao. Lahore was occupied but standing at Panipat, waiting for them, was Ahmad Shah Abdalli. A decisive battle took place on 13 January 1761, and the notion of a Maratha empire of Hindustan was permanently erased. No longer united, the Marathas roamed the country in predatory bands. Prowling for prey, they set up puppet princes vying for power in the great Rajput royal houses.

Maharana Raj Singh died suddenly and quite unexplicably. The hearts of the nobles were filled with dread, for Ari Singh, the man next in line, spelt trouble for Mewar. Terror so gripped the inmates of the palace that even the zenana denied the Jhali queen's pregnancy.

On 3 April 1761, a murderer sat upon Bappa Rawal's throne.

Maharana Ari Singh (Ursi)

The ungovernable temper of this maharana was to prove fatal to Mewar.

Malhar Rao Holkar had attempted to depose Pratap II and set up his brother Nathji. In the confusion that had followed, Holkar had succeeded in grabbing large territories and laid claim to the tribute that had been due to Baji Rao Peshwa. But the Marathas had themselves broken the clause that prevented them from occupying land in Mewar and Ari Singh justifiably withheld payment. Malhar sent several threatening letters and then proceeded to march into Mewar. He was stopped from occupying Udaipur by an agreement that promised to pay him fifty-one lakhs of rupees. The treasury was exhausted but the evil days of Mewar were not over. Famine struck the land. After four years of deprivation, civil war broke out.

Some nobles hoped to throw the Marathas out. Others were against Maharana Ursi who, they claimed, had unfairly occupied the throne. His insolent behaviour annoyed and estranged many who had long been loyal to the Sisodias. Five of the sixteen chief nobles formed a party and in 1768, set up a youth named Ratan Singh declaring him to be the posthumous son of Maharana Raj Singh by the daughter of the chief of Gogunda. Salumbar, who had initially joined the cause of the pretender or the fitoorie, abandoned the rebels probably because he was denied the supremacy he desired. The pretender was installed as maharana in Kumbhalgarh. Without a thought for the well-being of Mewar, the chiefs invited Scindia to dethrone Ursi. A bribe of a crore and twenty-five lakhs of rupees was offered.

Maharana Ursi, at the time, laboured under the domination of the Jhala raj rana of Delwara who had helped him get to the throne. The raj rana would have to go and a commoner from the Jhala clan came to the rescue. Zalim Singh was the son of the military governor of Kota. Having fallen from his prince's favour, he had been exiled but was intent on climbing the rungs of success. The raj rana was relieved of his life and a grateful Ursi conferred upon Zalim the title of raj rinna and the lands of Chitarkhaira. The new raj rana, for Zalim had quietly changed his title from rinna to rana, called for the Maratha leaders, Raghu Paigawalla and Daula Mia, and had the ancient Pancholi ministry handed over to Aggarji Mehta.

A large army was put together in 1769. Salumbar was in charge of the maharana's forces. The rajas of Banera and Shahpura led their own armies and Zalim joined them with his Maratha allies. Together they engaged the pretender who was encamped on the banks of the Shipra backed by Mahadji Scindia's forces. Scindia was driven from the field but as the victorious Rajputs indulged in plundering Ujjain they were taken by surprise by a body of fresh troops that had been rushed in by Peshwa

Amar Chand Burwa, of the mercantile class, had held office as minister during the previous reigns. Pratap had treated him like a father. Banishment of corruption and disorder marked his years of administration. Out of office for the last ten years, Amar Chand now came forward.

Maharana Ursi was in the process of fortifying the hill of Eklingarh. His men struggled with a gigantic cannon that was to be placed upon its summit. The scraggy ascent baffled the engineers. As Ursi watched helplessly, Amar offered to complete the task for ' a few rations of grain and some days.' Assembling the working population, he had a road laid and in a few days the guns of Eklingarh saluted the maharana.

While Amar Chand had been out of office, the country had become dependent on Muslim Sindi mercenaries led by Adil Beg. The Sindis had established themselves on lands forfeited from ancient clans. Discontentment ran high at the cost of patriotism. Even those who did not join the pretender remained sullenly at their castles. The pretender's army surrounded Udaipur and all was dependent upon the fidelity of the mercenaries from Sind.

But at this very moment, the Sindis were clamouring for pay and were audacious enough to grab at Ursi tearing his robe. His chiefs had no worthwhile advice to offer and the maharana realised that the only one man that could save him was Amar Chand.

Madhu Rao to reinforce Scindia. Salumbar and the rajas of Banera and Shahpura lost their lives while Daula Mia, Raja Maan of Narwar and Raja Kullian – the heir of Sadri – were severely wounded. Zalim Singh's horse was killed under him and he became a prisoner of Trambak Rao Ingle, the father of the celebrated Ambaji.

The pretender's party incited Scindia to occupy Udaipur and with a large force, they appeared outside the capital. Udaipur was an unfortified city. There was neither a ditch nor a wall that could protect her. Ursi's cause appeared to be lost.

Summoned to court to take charge of the desperate affairs, the ex minister, Amar Chand Burwa said, 'You know my temper admits no control. Wherever I am I must be absolute, there will be no secret advisors and no counteraction of measures. If you wish that I take charge of your empty coffers and your disobedient army then swear that all my orders will be supreme.'

The maharana swore by Eklinga.

'Should you even demand the queen's necklace or nose ring, the very symbol of her marriage, it will be granted.'

Amar Chand had all the gold and silver in the treasury converted to money and the arrears of the mercenaries were cleared. For every one who signed up as a soldier, six months provision of grain was provided. The Sindis reaffirmed their loyalties to Maharana Ari Singh with such enthusiasm that it drew tears from the eyes of all who stood as witness.

In the meanwhile, Scindia offered to abandon the pretender for a sum of seventy lakhs of rupees. Amar Chand agreed and the greedy Maratha instantly upped the price by an additional twenty lakhs. Furious Amar tore up the agreement and called for his army. The enthusiasm of the Sindis alarmed the Maratha and he agreed to settle for sixty-three and a half lakhs. Thirty-three lakhs were handed over as ready cash and the districts of Jawad, Jiran, Nimach and Morwan were mortgaged to be jointly superintended by officers of both governments. The understanding was that once the balance owed was recovered from the revenues of these districts, they would be returned to Mewar. But Scindia was not one to keep his word. In a few years he dismissed the Mewari officers and refused to return the lands. The Maratha clans had shaken off the peshwa yoke and established states for themselves. Morwan was occupied by the Holkars, who bullied the maharana in much the same way that Scindia had.

The pretender returned to Kumbhalgarh, while most chiefs returned to the maharana's service. Territories lost to the pretender were recovered but Kumbhalgarh had a direct access to Godwar. To keep the pretender from it, Maharana Ari Singh handed it over for safe-keeping to Maharaja Beejy Singh of Jodhpur. Until the time it was withdrawn, Jodhpur promised to provide Mewar with 3,000 men. Godwar, that had been won from the Purihara prince of Mandor along with his title of rana, and whose northern boundary had been confirmed by the blood of a Choondawat, was finally back in Marwar's custody.

Maharana Ursi was slain by Maharao Raja Ajit of Bundi, during the spring hunt. Nearly 500 years ago the sati of Bambaoda, the virgin bride of Maharana Kshetra Singh, had laid a curse on the spring hunt. Hada raos and Sisodia maharanas who dared hunt together were certain to lose their lives. Ursi had earned himself another curse: yet another sati, the wife of his own premier noble, Salumbar. A victim of suspicion, Salumbar had accepted the poisoned beera from his sovereign's own hand. Ajit slew Ursi driving his lance through his heart. Some say it was an accident while others feel it was a part of conspiracy involving the disgruntled chiefs of Mewar. Ajit died of injury and remorse while his father and the entire Hada nation denounced him.

As soon as the death was announced, the mercenaries of Sind threw away their garb of loyalty and occupied Udaipur. The young chief of Salumbar was imprisoned. The Sindis were about to seat him upon large heated plates used for baking bread when Amar Chand arrived from Bundi. Salumbar was saved.

Emperor Shah Alam II, who had clung for thirteen years to the security of Avadh, had returned to Delhi a year before Ursi's murder. At the auspicious hour in January 1772, he had entered escorted by his Scindia bodyguards. The Rohilla Afghan appointed by Abdalli had died in 1770, but in the time that the emperor had taken to build up courage, a Persian adventurer, Mirza Najaf, had seized control.

Several trips had been made across the tableland as Captain Tod toured between the kingdoms of Mewar, Bundi and Kota. The route was varied every time, scouring the plateau accommodating ancient settlements and the diverse geographical features. The illnesses that bred in the summer of 1820 had been unfortunate. But labouring under the mistaken notion that this was to be his last journey across the plateau, the captain, despite the cholera and chronic malaria that assailed him, routed his return to Udaipur through areas that had been missed earlier.

The fortress of Jahazpur came into view as they negotiated the pass that led from Bundi to Mewar. It stood guard at this most important point of entry. The local population comprised Meena tribals who could turn out an army of 4,000 bowmen. Here the Meena remained the sole proprietor of the land: the rights belonging to him who first cleared and tilled it. Not even the maharana dared lay claim to anything besides tribute. Were he to attempt more, he would have been brought to his senses by one of their various methods of defence, which could range from setting the lands or themselves alight, to mass abandonment of the area. Wherever original Indian customs and traditions existed, as opposed to the laws of the Islamic conquerors, the rights of the cultivators were the same as those of freeholders in England.

Dr Duncan and Lt Cary, who had been very sick that summer, continued to be bedridden. That night only two officers sat down to dinner – the captain and his cousin Captain Patrick Waugh. All appetite lacking, the captain decided to try a corn cake and he had eaten but scarcely two mouthfuls when a strange sensation developed. His head, throat and tongue appeared to swell up and he was left gasping for breath. Captain Waugh ran for the surgeon, who thrust some ether and other compounds down his throat. They worked magically and induced a massive vomit. The patient then sank into a deep sleep and awoke completely recovered. Since the question of poison could not be ruled out, the baker had to be discharged.

Early next day, the captain set out towards Mandalgarh leaving his sick friends to nurse each other. Too weak to walk or ride, he was forced to travel in a palki, accompanied by a few men and a small escort drawn from the Skinner's Horse. The kirar, or the tract of land on either side of the Banas, belonged to the Meenas. It was a peaceful land to travel through as opposed to what it had been three short years ago.

The route lay through a narrow valley, the slopes thickly covered with trees amongst which the wild cock loudly announced its presence. Half expecting to stumble upon a bear at any given moment, the party crossed the Brahmin township of Kajuri. The castle of Amirgarh lay a few miles ahead. The chief, a baba of Mewar, was away at the time and had left Amirgarh in the care of his uncle, Pahar Singh – the mountain lion – who was there ready with a welcome. Too unwell to make the climb, the captain declined the visit. Of the castle, he writes:

> It is quite unassailable being built on an isolated rock, and, except by a circuitous path on one side, there is no passage through the dense jungle that surrounds it: a mode of fortifying recommended by Manu.

In the centre of the valley stood the cenotaph of Maharana Ari Singh and in the distance rose the blue ridge of Mandalgarh.

Pahar Singh astride his Panch Kalian, a name given to horses with four white legs and a white nose, escorted the captain to the border.

By the time they reached Kachhola, the captain was in the grip of a violent fever, accompanied by an enlargement of the spleen. A week's halt was forced upon him. Entire populations had turned out along the way, their damsels bearing gleaming bronze pots of water upon their heads, but the song of the Suhailea failed to charm. Too weak to respond or even return their kindness, the captain could only determine to try to get through the work that brought him this far.

Two days were spent at Mandalgarh and it was with much regret that an invitation to the fort was declined. The festival of Dushera was upon them and there was feasting and merrymaking but the joy of the occasion was lost upon the captain, who had been unable to keep any food down for the past nine days. Captain Waugh arrived a few days later, looking very sick himself, and found the captain lying on his charpai with sixty

Mandalgarh had been named after Mandoo the Bhil who, while guarding his sugarcane fields from the wild boar, had come upon one that lay fast asleep. To make certain that his arrow would pierce the hide, Mandoo began to sharpen his arrowhead upon a stone that lay nearby. The arrowhead turned to gold and the bewildered Bhil ran to his chief, a Solanki (Chalukya) of the Balnote tribe. The pair returned and the moment they snatched the paras patthar (philosopher's stone) the boar disappeared.

Mandalgarh was raised with the blessings of Vishnu who had appeared in the Varaha avatar – the boar form. It eventually fell in to the hands of Mewar and though the descendents of Balnote were reduced to the status of petty landlords, they continued to carry the distinctive title of rao.

leeches applied to the abdomen. His enlarged spleen had become rock hard, causing him tremendous discomfort. The Indian physicians had offered two alternatives – the application of leeches or cautery. Having chosen the lesser of the two evils, the captain lay, surrounded by Bhumias and Patels – landowners who were in the process of getting their land records documented. Several groups of men stood, outside the tent, waiting their turn. The result of the exercise was a detailed understanding of the agricultural aspects of the area.

Rejoining his friends who waited for him by the banks of the Banas, they marched through the most fertile plains in Mewar, crossing the towns of Birslabas, Amba and Hamirgarh, which had once been known as the ancient city of Bakrole. These were Ranawat lands belonging to the descendents of Maharana Amar. The lakes were thick with wild duck that moved about unmolested amongst the lotus and water chestnut. Brightly coloured chintz, used for turbans and fine veils, were strung out to dry along the way, marking the colonies of the weavers and dyers.

Skirting the banks of the Banas, they followed the gentle waters till Jasma when the river parted company, taking a right for Galund. Camp was set up and the exhausted men settled for the day. Dr Duncan looked a shade better but Lt Cary remained precariously ill. The waters abounded with trout, each seventeen-inches in length and nine in girth, but the wily fish outwitted the fly and in the end were netted in revenge. The panchayat and elders of each village turned out in large numbers to pay their compliments. Each one was met with personally and satisfied with the day's proceedings, the captain marked his last entry for the day.

Now for coffee and the charpai.

Maharana Hamir Singh II

Maharana Ursi left behind two sons. Hamir and Bhim, and Amar Chand was determined to secure the rights of the young princes. Wisdom and experience told him that his actions would be construed as an attempt to usurp power. Putting all his money, property and possessions right down to his clothes together, he had them sent to the queen mother. He would not accept any of it back. For the time, suspicions were laid to rest.

The imperious queen mother, Sardar Kanwar Jhali, was determined to assume control during her son's minority and as a result clashed with both Salumbar and the head of the Saktawats – two men who wished to play the same role. Amar Chand died a sudden and inexplicable death. The role of poison was never ruled out. Mewar instituted an award in his memory designating acts of valour and integrity as an Amarchanda.

In 1775, two years after Hamir came to the throne, the Begun chief, head of a grand division of the Choondawats – the Meghawats – rebelled. Crown lands were usurped and the queen mother turned to the Scindias. Mahadji recovered the lost lands and imposed a fine of twelve lakhs of rupees on the errant noble. However, instead of returning the lands to the maharana, he retained them for himself handing a few over to Ahilya[67] Bai. The maharana lost annual revenue worth six lakhs of rupees. The Marathas also claimed large sums for participating in the wars. What could not be paid in cash was exacted in the form of land.

Hamir died before he attained the age of eighteen leaving the throne to his half-brother – Bhim.

---

67. Malhar Rao the founder of the Holkar clan had chosen eight year-old Ahilya – the daughter of Mankoji Scindia – as his daughter-in-law and groomed her as a future leader and general. Ahilya's husband died at war and the twenty-nine-year-old – who had borne a son, Malerao, and a daughter, Mukta – did not join her husband and his nine junior wives on the pyre. Instead, she re-married as soon as the period of mourning was over. Thirty-two year old Tukoji, was a first-cousin to Malhar Rao's father. Ahilya's son, who had begun showing signs of insanity, succeeded on his grandfather's death but died within a year. In 1767, Ahilya Bai and her second husband assumed leadership of the clan ruling as co-regents and soon emancipated themselves from the central authority at Pune. Remembered as a saint who built temples and forts and saved existing ones from desecration, Ahilya encouraged education, helped widows retain their right to their husband's property and adopt children. Sadly she was unable to save the women of her own family. Mukta's only son – Nathoba Rao Phanse – who had been adopted by Ahilya as the Holkar heir died of consumption in 1790, and was joined by his wives on the pyre. Mukta, herself, committed sati. Ahilya's death in 1795 left Tukoji as the sole ruler for the next two years after which he abdicated in favour of his son – Kashi Rao (said also to be Ahilya's son). But it was to be Jaswant Rao – who was recognized as Tukoji's natural son – who would make the Holkars a force to contend with.

From the pass of Bichor that led to the plains of Mewar, to the highest peak on the plateau, Kala Megh (Black Cloud) of Begun had once held sway. He was a Sangawat, one of the early subdivisions of the Choondawats. Kala Megh's descendents styled themselves as the Meghawats and formed numerous clans. Unfortunately for them nearly all their lands had been lost to the Marathas.

The passage to Bundi took the captain through ancient Meghawat lands. The path descended from Kanera to Dhareshwar. A clear stream ran ahead leading the way through forests of fine timber past several little hamlets. One of these belonged to a colony of charuns. They were distant cousins to the muses of Marla and had not forgotten their privilege. Choosing to drop five rupees in one of their bronze vessels the captain rode on for the group was composed only of elderly matrons There would have been no amusement in the captivity, he mused.

The stream led towards Ratangarh Kheri. Scindia's officer, the komasdar of Kheri, arrived to conduct the British to their tents. The township had been allotted to Mahadji Scindia, to pay off a war contribution incurred during the time the maharana had enlisted his services against the chief of Begun who had turned traitor. The land was to be returned once the promised sum had been recovered but the revenue the land yielded was never accounted for, and the Marathas held on indefinitely. With Begun mortgaged, Mewar had lost some of its prime property.

The fort of Chota Attoa (Little Attoa) lay eight miles uphill. A keen wind cut straight from the north as the party climbed in the company of Attoa's chief, Doongar Singh. Short, dark and rugged the young chief was perfectly good humoured and frank. He regaled the captain with tales of his land. Doongar, who traced his ancestry from Kala Megh, had long been the terror of the countryside. 'Doongar Singh aya – the mountain lion comes,' the cry was sufficient to drive peaceful occupants from their properties or take up arms against him for Doongar Singh made his living by raiding lands held by the Marathas. Farmlands that rightfully belonged to him had been confiscated during his grandfather's time. Doongar and his father sought revenge and with a band of like-minded braves led raids not only into Begun and neighbouring Maratha territories but deep into the heart of Malwa, which had been declared Maratha country for close to a hundred years.

A British envoy had once admonished the chief, for there had been several complaints. 'I must have bread,' was the simple answer.

Writes the captain:

> Had every chieftain of Mewar acted like Doongar, the Maratha would have had fewer fields.

Doongar, whose cause had been warmly espoused by the captain, was restored to a part of his ancestral property. In return, he exchanged his lance for the plough.

Maharana Bhim Singh

Bhim Singh succeeded his brother in 1778, and was the reigning maharana during Captain Tod's time. He was but eight-years-old at the time of his accession and remained under his stepmother's control long after attaining the age of majority. The queen mother, who had dominated while Hamir was king, continued with her imperious ways. Her confidant and assistant was her female companion, Rampiyari, who dearly loved palace intrigues and gossip.

Mewar continued to be the hot bed of trouble. Kumbhalgarh lay in the grip of the pretender. The Choondawats and Saktawats remained involved in a bitter feud. Bheem Singh of Salumbar, the arrogant head of the Choondawats, openly defied authority and land was parcelled out amongst his Sindi mercenaries without the sovereign's consent. The Marathas made the most of the disorder and played havoc at will. Large tracts of the best revenue yielding lands were grabbed by Scindia's lieutenant – Shivaji Nana.

In 1784, Salumbar attacked Bhindar – the castle of Mokhim Singh, the chief of the Saktawats. With him were Oorjun Singh of Korabar and Pratap Singh of Amet. Sangram Singh, a junior Saktawat, had just returned from a feud, having successfully captured the Poorawat castle of Lawa. Brimming with confidence, he created a diversion by attacking Korabar and in the ensuing action Salim Singh, the heir of Korabar, lost his life. Oorjun Singh withdrew from Bhindar. Casting his turban from his head, he swore never again to wear it until he had had his revenge. He made his way to Seogarh, the home of Sangram's father, Lalji. Deep within the forests of Chappan, hidden away in the mountains, the seventy-year-old Saktawat had built his retreat. The castle was considered to be in a safe and inaccessible place. Sangram's own family was at their grandfather's home. The old man fought bravely and fell defending his family. Sangram's children were dragged out and butchered as Lalji's wife climbed onto her husband's pyre.

Mirza Najaf, the Persian, who ruled Delhi, had died·in 1782 and Emperor Shah Alam II, considering himself liberated, appointed in 1785, Mahadji Scindia as vakil-i-mutlaq or regent. Mahadji used the opportunity to invade Rajasthan on the pretence of collecting taxes.

Where the maharana for want of funds was obliged to borrow money for his own wedding, Salumbar spent more than a 100,000 pounds on his daughter's wedding. The queen mother turned to the Saktawats for aid and they in turn appealed to Zalim Singh, the military commander and prime minister of Kota. Zalim, who longed to control Mewar as he did Kota, became once again a part of Mewar's forces. With him came Lallaji Bellal, the Maratha. Salumbar took up his post in Chittaur, surrounded by his Sindi garrison.

Such were the state of things when news arrived from Lalsot. Mahadji Scindia had been defeated at the hands of the combined forces of Jaipur and Jodhpur. All of Rajasthan was jolted awake and the chiefs of Mewar galvanised into action. Ancient lands that had been lost to the Marathas were reoccupied. Mewar was elated, but her newfound joy drew the attention of the saintly Ahilya Bai, queen regent of the Holkars. She united with Scindia and 5,000 horses were sent to support the Maratha lieutenant, Shivaji Nana. Gallant and unwise as always, the Rajputs had spared the lives of Nana's men. The troops of Mewar were taken by surprise and slaughtered. Territories that had been recovered were lost once again.

But Mahadji's defeat at Lalsot turned out to be the gust of wind that blew out the flickering Mughal lamp. Taking advantage of the Maratha's temporary weakness, a Rohilla Afghan, the grandson of the protector appointed by Ahmad Shah Abdalli (Durrani), seized Delhi. The youth, in a fit of madness, blinded the hapless emperor. Mahadji rushed to the rescue and had the Afghan executed but the fall out was that Delhi now fell completely into Scindia hands. The year 1788, marked the end of the Mughal Empire and the beginning of the Kingdom of Delhi, which was ruled by Mahadji Scindia and the puppet emperor Shah Alam.

The chiefs of Mewar had all united in this patriotic struggle with the singular exception of Salumbar. The Choondawats continued to defy the queen mother and the newly appointed minister, Somji. At length, Rampiyari came to pacify the stubborn Salumbar and he condescended to pay his respects to the young maharana. Pretending to cooperate with Somji, they reorganised the jagirs of Mewar. Somji was in his office one day, when Oorjun Singh of Korabar and Sardar Singh of Bhadesar burst in. Sardar Singh plunged his dagger into the minister's breast, claiming revenge for lands lost during the reorganisation. The brothers of the slain minister rushed to the maharana pleading for protection. Behind them came Oorjun, his hands still stained with Somji's blood. Unable to punish the insolent chief, Maharana Bhim Singh ordered him out branding him a traitor. Salumbar returned to Chittaur with his fellow conspirators while Somji's brothers took up their new ministerial appointments and joined the Saktawats against the rebels. Every battle led the country further into ruin. Farmers abandoned their fields and merchants left in search of peace. Those that remained sought private protection. Every Rajput, who could afford a horse and a lance, had his clients. No camel load of merchandise could pass the abode of such a cavalier without paying a fee. The results were disastrous.

Zalim Singh Jhala, who had readied himself to play the role of a lifetime, prompted Maharana Bhim Singh to employ Scindia and expel the Choondawats from Chittaur. Scindia's army had been recently reorganised by the French mercenary, De Boigne, and tested against the Rathores at Merta and the Kachwahas at Patan. Zalim Singh, who had become regent of Kota, nurtured the secret hope of commanding the joint forces of Hadavati and Mewar. He enjoyed a good rapport with the chiefs of

Marwar and could have well been the one to lead Rajasthan and change the destiny of India. Disguising his ambitions, Zalim pretended to have Mewar's best interest at heart. The cost of sending an army to Chittaur, it was decided, would be extracted from Salumbar.

In 1791, Scindia's lieutenant, Ambaji Ingle, arrived with a strong army. Zalim and Ambaji moved towards Chittaur, targeting on the way those estates against which Zalim bore a grudge. They positioned themselves at Chittaur where the main body of Scindia's army was to join them. But Mahadji Scindia's vanity needed pandering and Zalim was forced into persuading the twenty-one-year-old maharana to personally meet with the sixty-four-year-old Maratha. Scindia and Zalim went to Udaipur to escort Maharana Bhim Singh to Chittaur. Neither was aware that behind their backs Ambaji and Salumbar had leagued together. Having divined Zalim's real intentions, Ambaji was keenly aware that he would always play second fiddle unless the regent of Kota was removed from the scene. Bheem Singh Salumbar's personal enmity with Zalim encouraged the private negotiation. No sooner had the maharana arrived at Chittaur that Salumbar descended from the fort to meet him. A picture of humility, Salumbar begged pardon, offering to surrender the fort provided Zalim Singh Jhala was ordered to retire. This suited all parties, especially Scindia who, was keen to return to Pune for the control of Delhi and its emperor no longer whetted his appetite. It was the control of Pune that he desired[68]. Zalim was taken completely by surprise. He had been outwitted by a man whose father he had held in great esteem, for Zalim Singh would not have lived to see the day had it not been for Trambak Rao, who had saved him on that fateful day at the battle of Ujjain. Salumbar touched the maharana's feet. Scindia departed, leaving Ambaji behind as the sole

---

68. The Pune court had become a hotbed of troubles. Young Madhu Rao Peshwa, who had succeeded in establishing central control with the help of Nana Fadnavis, had died prematurely in 1772. His brother Narayan Rao, who had succeeded, had been murdered by his uncle Raghunath Rao. Caught in the interpersonal rivalry between the Bengal and Bombay factions of the East India Company, Raghunath Rao, though ousted by the Company's intervention, received refuge in Mumbai (Bombay). Both Mahadji Scindia and the Holkar co-regents – Tukoji and Ahilya Bai – seized the opportunity to free themselves of Pune. But both parties wished to control the peshwa – the son of Narayan Rao – who ruled under the regency of Nana Fadnavis. In 1792, Scindia defeated the Holkars and his heart's desire would have surely materialised had he not died within a span of two years.

arbitrator of Mewar. Though he extracted two million pounds sterling (two crores of rupees) he gave to Mewar a measure of peace and tranquillity to which she had long been a stranger.

Scindia's instructions to Ambaji were:

Restoration of the maharana's authority and the crown lands occupied by the rebel chiefs and the Sindis.

Expulsion of the pretender from Kumbhalgarh.

Recovery of Godwar from the maharaja of Marwar.

Settlement of the feud with Bundi over the murder of Maharana Ari Singh.

The crown lands and Kumbhalgarh were redeemed but not those held by the Marathas. Though the dispute over Godwar and the Bundi incidence remained unresolved, Ambaji assumed the title of subedar of Mewar.

The ministers at court lived in fear of a Choondawat revival. In Ambaji's hands, they felt secure. They made a second agreement with him. The cost was a piece of land that yielded revenue worth eight lakhs of rupees a year. Mewar's finances were in such a state that the maharana was obliged to borrow from the Maratha to pay for his sister's wedding. Five years later, Ambaji was appointed as subedar of Hindustan – the viceroy in north India. Ganesh Pant was left behind as his deputy. But the maharana's own officers who were to help the maratha collect revenue did so with such ferocity that Ambaji was forced remove Pant and appoint the celebrated Rai Chand in his place. The clans did not yield to Rai Chand and a focus of mistrust and discontent was created. The country lay open to terrorism by the Marathas, the Rohilla Afghans and the French. The Choondawats with their Sindi allies roamed the country like ordinary dacoits. For a price of ten lakhs of rupees, Ambaji agreed to recall his lieutenant and support the Choondawats. Salumbar once again took the lead at court. The Saktawats were attacked and the stipulated ten lakhs raised from their estates.

The death of Mahadji Scindia was followed by the accession of his brother's grandson, the fifteen-year-old Daulat Rao. Scindia infighting began and it spilt over to Mewar. Daulat Rao's youth and inexperience strengthened Ambaji's position as the subedar of Hindustan and the Shenvi Brahmins and the wives of Mahadji hotly contested the issue[69]. Lakhva Dada, a Shenvi Brahmin, wrote to the maharana to overthrow Ambaji's yoke and expel his lieutenant while Ambaji ordered his lieutenants, Ganesh Pant and Shivaji Nana, to evict all Shenvis from Mewar. Ganesh Pant set up a meeting with the chiefs.

The chiefs of Mewar decided to play the game. They appeared to agree with Pant but sent word to the Shenvis to advance promising support. The two groups battled among themselves, Mewar becoming their arena[70]. In 1800, word arrived that Ambaji had been replaced by Lakhva Dada. The Shenvi Brahmin was now the viceroy and he marched into Mewar. The Choondawats returned to power. Having exacted twenty-four lakhs of rupees from Mewar, Lakhva Dada left for Jaipur, appointing Jaswant Rao Bhao as his lieutenant. The Choondawats used the opportunity to appropriate the most valuable of the crown lands.

Holkar[71] occupied Ujjain in 1801 and advanced into the Deccan. The next year in Indore, he suffered a defeat at Scindia's hands, and was pursued to Mewar. Ratlam he plundered on his way but was stopped from ravaging Bhindar and Udaipur. Taking refuge in Nathdwara, Jaswant Rao

---

69. Daulat Rao allowed himself to be influenced by Sarza Rao Ghatge, the father of his third wife – Baiza Bai. Ghatge terrorized Pune to raise money, which led to protests by Lakhva Dada and the widows of Mahadji. Nana Fadnavis died in 1800, and Daulat Rao became the peshwa's chief minister. The civil war in the Scindia household ended in May 1801, with Lakhva and the widows being driven out.

70. The chiefs of Mewar covertly supported Lakhva Dada and the unsuspecting Shivaji Nana – who had been joined by the raja of Shahpura and the British adventurer George Thomas – faced many reversals. Bala Rao, Ambaji's own brother, accepted money from Lakhva and opted out. The raja of Shahpura abandoned Ambaji's camp and received the district and fortress of Jahazpur, for which he paid the maharana two lakhs of rupees in an underhand deal. Jahazpur was sold later to Lakhva Dada for a sum of six lakhs and it made its way eventually into the possession of Zalim Singh of Kota.

71. In 1799, Kashi Rao Holkar was deposed by his half-brother – a natural son of his father – the brilliant but erratic Jaswant Rao. Jaswant placed Khande Rao – the one-year-old posthumous son of Kashi Rao's own brother – as head of the clan and named himself regent. By September 1806, Khande Rao had died of cholera and thirty-year-old Jaswant Rao had taken his place as the new head. But by 1808, the signs of insanity could no longer be ignored and Tulsi Bai, Jaswant's mistress, assumed control.

threw himself before the image of Krishna, berating the deity for his failures and levied a fine of three lakhs upon his priests. Damodar, the high priest, turned to Kotario-Chauhan, who smuggled the image to Udaipur for safekeeping. As they returned, they were accosted by Holkar's men, who demanded the surrender of their horses; but the descendents of Prithviraj preferred death to dishonour. Hamstringing their horses, they dismounted to fight the unequal battle. The image of Krishna, finding insufficient security, took another flight to the mountains of Gassyar, where the high priest threw up fortifications and called upon the services of 400 cavaliers.

Holkar made his way to Ajmer distributing a part of Krishna's largess among the followers of Khwaja Pir and then carried on to Jaipur. His pursuers gave up the chase at Udaipur and stayed to extract three lakhs of rupees. The unfortunate maharana had no option but to raise the money by selling his household goods and jewels.

Disgraced by his prince, Lakhva Dada died in 1803, while in sanctuary at Salumbar, and his place was taken by Ambaji's brother, Bala Rao. Both the Saktawats and Zalim Singh allied themselves with Bala Rao expelling the Choondawats for control over the maharana. Bala Rao, who exacted money with ferocity, arrived at the palace with his demands. An ingenious minister managed to imprison the Maratha leaders. And they should have all been put to death, but that would have meant enraging the entire Maratha nation. Zalim Singh was determined to save his friend and with the Saktawats in tow advanced to the Chajja pass. The maharana led a band of Sindis, Arabs and Goseins and, supported by the brave Jai Singh and his Kinchis, held the pass for five days. But in the end he was forced to liberate Bala Rao. Zalim manoeuvred for himself the entire district of Jahazpur before returning to Kota, while Bala Rao bled Mewar for war contributions.

Having put together his shattered forces, Holkar advanced towards Udaipur, plundering and looting all that came his way. He had just done with ravaging Bhindar when the maharana's ambassador arrived. Holkar put forth a demand for forty lakhs of rupees of which one-third was to be paid up immediately. The palace was denuded, its women deprived of their personal articles of luxury and taxes levied upon the citizens. Against the rest Holkar accepted royal hostages as security. After a stay of eight months, having milked the towns of Lawa, Badnor and Deogarh to his heart's content Jaswant Rao had just moved on to Shahpura when Scindia entered Mewar. Rajasthan was to be made to pay for the successes that the East India Company was in the process of enjoying.

A common foe in the form of the British united the Marathas. To them, the Marathas had lost their power in Hindustan and territories north and south of the Narmada. On 30 December 1803, Daulat Rao Scindia had been forced to hand over Delhi, Gwalior and a large number of forts. Sardar Singh arrived to represent the Choondawats at Scindia's camp. Ambaji, who headed Scindia's council, ranted and raved against the support given to Lakhva Dada. He demanded Mewar be divided among the Marathas but fortunately, Baiza Bai was sympathetic and she wielded tremendous influence.

Sardar then went to the Holkar camp where Sangram Singh Saktawat was present and put forward the dilemma. Was Mewar to be sold? Touched by his distress, Jaswant Rao assured him it would not come to that. He advised the clans to declare peace and enjoy opium together. He would himself befriend Scindia, and recalling the blood shared by Shivaji and Mewar's royal family, offered to renounce the mortgaged crown lands.

Incessant rains hampered communications between the two camps for a while and then Holkar received news: Maharana Bhim Singh had entered into negotiations with the British; Lord Lake was already present with his troops in Tonk. Throwing the newspaper in the ambassador's face, he asked if this was the way that Mewaris kept faith.

'I cared not to break with Scindia in support of your master while combating the firangis when all 'Hindus' should be as brothers. Your rana, who boasts of never having acknowledged the supremacy of Delhi, is the first to enter into arms with them.'

Alikar Tantia, the minister upbraided Jaswant. He advised reconciliation with Scindia.

'Let Ambaji be the subedar of Mewar and let us have nothing more to do with the Rajputs.'

Jaswant Rao left, leaving Daulat Rao with a warning: The rights of the maharana were inviolable and that Scindia would be held answerable. As he proceeded northwards, he was chased into Punjab by Lord Lake. News of his misfortune resulted in an instant levy of sixteen lakhs on Mewar.

The British embassy led by Graeme Mercer, which included James Tod, entered Mewar in the spring of 1806, following Daulat Rao Scindia and his Marathas. Mile after mile, nothing but desolation met the eye. Wherever the Maratha camped annihilation within twenty-four hours – a sheer force of habit – was guaranteed. The march of destruction continued leaving a trail of burnt villages and fields. The British flag fluttered weakly in its wake. Ambaji was forced to disgorge his spoils. This officer who had overthrown Daulat Rao's mantle of authority was subject to every indignity possible. Manacled inside his tent, small torches were applied to the tips of his fingers but Ambaji remained resolute. He even tried to commit suicide with the aid of an English penknife. But a British surgeon stitched up the wounds and fifty-five lakhs were eased from his coffers. Mewar was entrusted once again to his hands but Ambaji did not have long to live. It was said that the rest of his wealth made its way into the hands of his old ally – his father's friend – Zalim Singh of Kota.

It would be reasonable to think that the maharana's lot could not get any worse. In June 1806, joyous news came Mewar's way. An offer of marriage had come from Jaipur for their twelve-year-old princess. But scarcely had Maharaja Sawai Jagat Singh's proposal been accepted when Maharaja Maan Singh of Marwar sent word that the hand of the princess had been promised to his predecessor. She was, theoretically speaking, betrothed to the occupant of the throne of Jodhpur. He threatened vengeance should Krishna Kumari choose otherwise. Scindia, who had been denied a pecuniary demand made on Jodhpur, joined the Kachwaha camp. Maharana Bhim Singh had little choice but to cancel the wedding and the Jaipur prince prepared to avenge the insult.

Rival Rathore clans fighting for the throne set up a pretender and joined the armies of Jaipur. Most Marwari chiefs went over to the pretender's side and a dejected Maan Singh tried to plunge the dagger into his own breast. He was prevented from taking his own life by a few faithful chiefs and together they fled, pursued by the joint forces of Jaipur and the pretender of Marwar. The fort of Mehrangarh was besieged for six months but Jodha's castle did not fall. The mighty army of Jaipur wasted away in the desert and Jagat Singh eventually decided to go home empty handed.

Amir Khan, the Afghan marauder, until now a notorious enemy of Maharaja Maan Singh, accepted a generous bribe to switch sides. He arrived at Udaipur. The princess would have to marry the desert lord failing which her death alone would ensure peace in Rajasthan. The khan took vicious pleasure in tormenting the father, a man no older than himself. Krishna, it appeared was doomed. At the age of nine, she had narrowly escaped having to climb the pyre with Maharaja Bheem of Jodhpur. Every alliance that her father sought for her seemed to end in disaster. This time her fate was to embroil her country. Maharana Bhim Singh was faced with no other choice. On 21 July 1810, Mewar opted for death. Maharaj Jawan Singh, a natural brother, was convinced by the court that no ordinary hand could perform the deed. He prepared himself, but when the sixteen-year-old appeared before him, the dagger fell from his hand. The deed was left to the rawala. A cup of poison was prepared and presented to the princess in her father's name. Krishna drained her cup. The inconsolable mother soon followed her child. Even the ferocious khan was shocked. Was this the famous Rajput valour?

Krishna's grieving father turned her room into a shrine and the Krishna Mahal, with its delicate fresco work, remained a memorial to the girl who had sacrificed herself for her people.

The next year Bapu Scindia arrived with the title subedar of Hindustan and rendered what was left a desert. Mewar was liberated, from the Maratha menace and the ceaseless infighting, by a treaty with the British in 1817. To be rid of predators, all Rajput states, with the exception of Jaipur, eagerly embraced the invitation.

Tragedy, that had dogged the Mewaris for years was finally put to rest and Rajasthan came together to celebrate a multiple wedding. On 3 July 1820, Maharana Bhim Singh gave in marriage his daughters Ajab Kanwar and Deep Kanwar to the heir of Bikaner, Yuvraj Ratan Singh, and his brother Maharajkumar Moti Singh respectively while Maharawal Guj Singh of Jaisalmer claimed Roop Kanwar's hand. The fourth princess was the maharana's granddaughter, Kika Bai, who wed Yuvraj Mokkam Singh of Kishangarh.

October 1820: As they made their way back from Bundi, a decision was taken to pay a visit to the celebrated field of battle: the Khet Kuraira, where Rawal Samarsi had faced Bhola Bhim Solanki of Anhilwara Patan. The defeated Solanki was said to have retreated southwards beyond the Berach. The site lay seven miles from Rashmi and nine from Sunwar. Among its ruins was a temple, a specimen of twelfth century architecture built at a time when the arts had gone into a decline. But it could still be described as imposing. Its two domes were supported by numerous massive columns, the stone used being a species of porphyry, which though exceedingly difficult to carve is capable of taking on a fine polish. The priests of the twenty-third Jain apostle, Parasvanath, though poor and ignorant were in the process of transcribing its history. Some distance away the Berach joined the Banas and a third stream to form a triveni. At the confluence stood an altar to Shiva. Even until thirty years ago, these plains had been covered with crops of jowar so tall and thick that an elephant would have been lost from sight. The fields had now given way to tall grass and the annoying thorny babul.

From Sunwar, which belonged to a baba of Mewar, they passed into Mavli, which was the appanage of the maharana's sister. An inscription favouring the Jains, reads thus:

The oil mills of Mavli will not work during the four rainy months.

The ostensible purpose was to lessen the destruction of animal life. The tired horses picked their way through the desolate landscape, but as they approached the heights of Toos and Mairta their ears pricked up. Holding their heads low and defiant, instinctively aware that they were nearing the journey's end, they were unwilling to accommodate even the smallest of deviations.

Coaxing the reluctant Bajraj, the captain turned to the ruins of Nahara Magra: the tiger mount and ancient hunting seat of the Sisodias, the site where their ancestor, Bappa, had received the enchanted sword. The ancient palace had crumbled, choking the Berach, which murmured sorrowfully to the stones. The nakarras of Toos sounded and as the villagers poured out, women came forward with gleaming pots of water chanting the usual strain of welcome. The captain had been away since the 29th of January and had missed the royal weddings that had taken place in Udaipur. For many years, happiness had eluded Mewar and the shadow of Krishna's death had loomed over its people. However, a great change had taken place since then.

But it wasn't a joyous homecoming. Lieutenant Cary had been left behind, entombed upon the heights of Mairta, while Dr Duncan, half dead from the Kota Fever and tormented by a guinea worm infection, looked to catching a ship to the Cape of Good Hope. For his part, Captain Tod resolved never to stir from Udaipur until it was time for him to return home to Britain. His health, always poor, had suffered greatly that year. The winter of 1820 passed uneventfully, but the cholera epidemic returned with the spring. It raged through the early months of the year, making no distinction between its victims. The captain wavered upon the brink of death and Maharana Bhim Singh, who lay upon the sickbed himself, had his nakarras hushed with many a rupee's worth of saffron pledged to the deities pleading for the life of the one that had become so dear. While the captain recovered, the maharana continued to suffer. In a court that had assembled for the distribution of swords and coconuts, Captain Tod was forced to ask for a personal favour. Smiling, the maharana replied that it had already been granted, when he was entreated to give up the sapta dhatu — a mixture of seven metals — that was being administered to him by his physician cum astrologer, a Brahmin who managed the princess royal's estates. That the year would spell evil for the maharana, had already been foretold by the same man. The poisons were abandoned and under Dr Duncan's care the maharana made a quick and visible recovery.

Times were bad, for though Captain Tod made a slow and painful recovery, his good friend the maharao raja of Bundi lost his personal battle and left his son and heir in the care of the British envoy. Bundi had to be reached post haste despite the poor health that tormented him.

The commercial centre at Bhilwara had been the captain's own brainchild, 'the work of his own hands' as he put it. 'Tod sahib ki basti' was how the maharana good-humouredly put it. Despite its rapid strides to prosperity, feuds between the merchants had earned the captain's displeasure and he had threatened never to enter Bhilwara until the differences had been sorted out, firmly denying permission to change its name to Todgunj. His sudden requirement once again at Bundi brought with it the opportunity to visit his repentant protégés. The reception was quite Asiatic. The entire population, headed by the chief merchants, waited a mile outside the city limits. Women preceded them bearing pots of water upon their heads. Where there had been not one dwelling a few years ago, there existed now streets lined with shops all displaying the most expensive silks and brocades. The captain was escorted to his tent and once breakfast was over streams of visitors poured in. The walls of the tent had to be removed for it would not accommodate even a tenth of those who wished to meet him. Plans for the future were discussed and promises made in the maharana's name. Bidding his last farewell to Bhilwara, the captain left, a silent prayer playing upon his lips.

The remainder of the year had been spent among the Hadas and it was time, at last, to return once again to Mewar. The 26th of February 1822, had been marked for the restoration of Begun to its rightful chief. Begun had been granted to Govind Das: a son of Khengar Choondawat, who had served as the sixth Salumbar, in the time of Maharana Pratap I. It had been held by the Scindias illegally, for over thirty years. Scindia, who should have returned the lands once he had recovered his dues, held onto them despite having exacted twice the amount. Appeals had only produced endless discussions and the frustrated chief had eventually taken the law into his own hands. With his band of Meghawats he had attacked and driven out the Marathas. The British government had found it necessary, for the sake of formality, to punish him. Begun had been put under the maharana's flag and the chief submitted in good grace. An excellent case had, however, been made out on behalf of the Meghawats and Captain Tod arrived with pomp and ceremony, on behalf of Maharana Bhim Singh, to hand over the keys.

Every son of Kala Megh had turned out for the occasion. The castle of Begun boasted of a remarkably wide moat with a wooden bridge. As the first elephant of the cavalcade made its way through to the archway at the end, the captain's mahout expressed doubts. The height of the howdah would present a problem. Heedlessly, Captain Tod chose to press on. They could always stop if a collision looked imminent. But the vibrations of the bridge and the water below spooked the animal and she broke into a run. Efforts at stopping her were futile. The gateway loomed upon them. With superhuman strength, the captain reached out and clung to the frame of the archway as the elephant charged through. The back of the howdah gave way and he dropped senseless upon the bridge narrowly missing the spikes that lined it. He recovered his senses to find himself lying on a pallet, badly bruised and the ancient gateway – built by Kala Megh himself – torn down. There had been no listening to the voice of reason. The Meghawats were resolute in their decision. It had attempted to take the life of the one who had restored life to them.

Body sore and limbs weary and though confined to a palki, he desired one last look at Chittaur.

8 March 1822: The party returned for the last time to the capital of the chief of the 'Hindu' race. A few days had been spent at Mairta where the captain had been building himself a home overlooking the sparkling waters of the Berach. The building was close to completion, the gardens flourishing, the lime and orange in full bloom. Exotic fruit trees gathered from various parts of India, a result of numerous postings spanning fifteen years of service in this land, had taken root. Nostalgic memories had come flooding back of peaches relished in Gwalior, custard apples, and pomegranate and bananas that had held his attention during the years in Agra, Lakhnau (Lucknow) and Kanpur. The influence of the surya of Mewar was evident in the robust vitality of all that grew in the land.

Accompanied by his son and courtiers, Maharana Bhim Singh had advanced to receive him. 'Aap ghur aye – You have come home,' was his simple greeting. His eyes scanned each face. A great deal had changed. Captain Waugh and Dr Duncan were both missing, as was Bajraj, the royal steed – a gift from the maharana himself. 'Hai Hai Bajraj,' he exclaimed. Bajraj lay entombed in Kota, neath a cenotaph so magnificent that his master· could never have dreamt of such a one for himself. The regent of Kota had valued horses above everything else.

The captain looked forward to days of ease, sailing his cutter among the islets of the Uday Sagar but the company's doctor would not agree. A certificate of sickness was filled out and preparations were made for the captain to return home to England[72]. Filled with grief, Maharana Bhim Singh insisted that he would grant the captain no more than three years of leave, while his sister Rajkumari Chandji Bai insisted that this time around the captain should bring back a wife, one whom she would equally love and pamper.

Sickness could not dampen the spirit, for instead of catching the next ship to England Captain Tod chose to visit the sacred mountain of Abu. During the course of his explorations he stumbled upon the ruins of an ancient city that lay on the border of Marwar. The ancient capital of the Balhara kings of Gujarat was visited and having respectfully marked his presence at the temples and shrines of the land, he embarked at last at Mumbai in March 1823.

Captain James Tod returned home, picking up the rank of major on 1 May 1824. He went on to serve in the 49th Native Infantry moving as lieutenant colonel to the 51st Native Infantry. His retirement had come into effect since 28 June 1825 and he applied for an extension of two years taking up his post as lieutenant colonel librarian to the Royal Asiatic Society. On 16 November 1826, at St George's Hanover Square London, he married Julia, the daughter of the London physician, Dr Clutterbuck, and retired permanently in 1827.

It was with mixed feelings that his last words were penned ten years since the day he had concluded his wanderings. On 8 March 1822, he

---

72. Captain Tod had openly blamed the woes of Rajputana upon the non-interference policies of Lord Cornwallis – who had served in the dual capacity of governor general and commander in chief from 1786 to 1793, and was known for his anti Indian stance, a viewpoint supported by later historians. His attitude drew criticism. His sympathy for the princes of Rajputana resulted in suggestions of corruption, a charge that was later proven completely baseless. Disgusted with the British government of India, Captain Tod cited reasons of ill health and opted for a premature retirement.

had ended his journey by entering Udaipur and it was on 8 March 1832, that he added the finishing touches to his manuscript. The book was ready to appear before the public. March had been a significant month in his life, for he had been born in the month of March, embarked for India in March and had the last glimpse of its coastline in March.

Captain Waugh returned to England some six months later. The cousins once again had the opportunity to serve together, but even amidst the splendours of London, Belgium and France, Rajputana was a theme they reverted to constantly. Patrick Waugh returned to India as a major commanding the 10th Light Cavalry Division. On a march between Mathura and Mau (Madhya Pradesh) he sustained an injury, which necessitated a surgery. Two days later, feeling considerably improved, the major continued with his journey but at the end of the march was found dead behind the curtains of his palki. Major Patrick Waugh's ashes found a home in Mewar.

A chronic chest condition obliged Lieutenant Colonel Tod to take up residence in Italy where he spent the last year of his life. He returned to his mother's house at Hampshire, hoping to settle down once and for all. A delightful property had been identified on Regent Street and process of buying had begun, but two months later, on the day of his sixteenth wedding anniversary while transacting business at his banker's, a sudden apoplectic stroke rendered him comatose for over twenty-four hours. He expired in the afternoon of 17 November 1835.

Seated amidst the ruins of ancient cities, I have listened to the traditions respecting their fall; or have heard the exploits of their illustrious defenders related by their descendants near the altars erected to their memory....Could I impart to the reader but a small portion of the enthusiastic delight with which I have listened to the tales of times that are past, amid scenes where their events occurred.

— JAMES TOD

Remnants of the kingdoms of Rajputana within modern Rajasthan.
Districts of Rajasthan that were once included in the kingdom of Marwar.

CHAPTER 2

MARWAR

The great desert of Rajasthan could sustain no life. It was called Maroowar (Marwar) or death's own land. Barring the ancient tribes none would venture onto the scorching sands. Only the desperate sought refuge here. When Vala (Vallabhi)[1] in Gujarat was overrun by the Maitrikas in the sixth century AD, the Brahmins and Jains fled to the desert in the north. Here, in the depths of the wasteland, they built new towns. Foundations of new temples were laid and the old way of life was resumed once more. From the meticulous records, maintained by the Jain priests, Captain James Tod was able to draw the history of Maroo.

The largest part of the desert came to be ruled by the Rathores and though there were other contenders in the vicinity, it was the Rathore who declared himself lord of the land of death. Their origin was indigenous, the Rathores having descended from the Rashtrakutas who had ruled the Deccan for close to 200 years. The ancients had proved to be a match for the great empires of the north for on more than one occasion, they had snatched Kannauj from its Pratihara rulers. Two

---

1. Vallabhi had become a centre of Jain culture. With the sack of Vallabhi, her Jain population escaped to Rajasthan where they continued to practise their way of life. The largest numbers settled in the desert land of Marwar forming a successful mercantile community.

   The first sack of Vala, during the reign of Siladitya, was by non-Muslims. The birth of Islam took place around AD 600, and the successors of Hazrat Mohammad -- the khalifas -- then took to establishing the empire of Islam. Arab Muslims arrived upon the shores of the Indus and in AD 712, Sind was the first Indian kingdom to fall. Gujarat was the next target and the Islamic conquest of Vala is dated to AD 770.

Prithviraj was in love with Jaichand's daughter, Sanyukta. The vindictive Jaichand not only did not invite Prithviraj to his daughter's swayamvar, where the princess was to choose her own groom from among the many princes in attendance, he had his likeness placed at the doorway.

Unknown to everyone, Prithviraj had had the image removed. In its place stood the king of Ajmer and Delhi himself. The unhappy princess garlanded what she thought was the wax image of her beloved and was snatched up from before the very eyes of her father and every suitor present and carried away to Delhi.

The event has been dated to AD 1175.

The bards of Maroo created the Rathore dynasty of Kannauj.

Nayan Pal Rathore, having slain the last ruler, became the first Kannauji Rathore or Kamdhuj. His sons and grandsons spread far and wide, throughout India, and though they assumed various names they acknowledged their descent from Kamdhuj.

The last Rathore king of Kannauj was Jaichand who ruled in the latter half of the twelfth century AD.

hundred and fifty years after their demise, a kinsman rode into the desert. He did not acknowledge the great ancestors of the south but, quite strangely, fabricated a beginning from the ashes of Kannauj. Its last Gahadwal king was proclaimed his grandfather.

On the banks of the Ganga, as it winds it way through the modern state of Uttar Pradesh, stands Kannauj, ancient Kanyakubja, the capital of the empire of the north since the early seventh century AD. The city of the 100 hunchback maidens had been claimed by the Pratiharas, in the ninth century, who after 200 years of rule were routed by the sultan of Ghazni. The Turk, who had established himself in the desolate mountains of Afghanistan, made a living by raiding kingdoms in India. Kannauj and the Pratihara empire were occupied by Gahadwals, relatives of the Chandels of Bundelkhand (in Madhya Pradesh).

Distantly related to the Tomar kings of Delhi, Jaichand of Kannauj hoped to inherit their throne. Unluckily for him, Prithviraj Chauhan, the king of Ajmer, who was yet another cousin[2], turned out to be the chosen one. Jaichand became Prithviraj's sworn enemy.

But a far more powerful enemy was gathering strength in the distant mountains of Afghanistan. The power of the old empire built by Mahmud of Ghazni had been broken by the growing empire of the Seljuk Turks. Several Turkish tribes had been displaced and compelled to leave in search of lands to occupy and one such tribe had forced the last of Mahmud's descendents to retire to Lahore in 1160. Thirteen years later Mohammad – a Turkish prince of Ghur – who had served as governor to the last Ghazni sultan succeeded in pushing out the interlopers.

The new sultan of Ghazni established himself and began his Indian operations with a successful raid on Multan in 1175 followed by the occupation of the Bhati fort of Uch. However, not every mission was a success. Having suffered a terrible defeat at the hands of Bhimdev II the Solanki king of Gujarat in 1178, he sent a diplomatic mission

2.   It was said that the mothers of Prithviraj and Jaichand were sisters – the daughters of the Tomar of Delhi. However, historians have found no evidence to support this. Prithviraj's mother may have been a Kalachuri-Chedi princess named Karpur Devi.

to Delhi. Scorned and rejected at the Chauhan court, the sultan targeted Prithviraj himself.

The kings of Hindustan did not comprehend the implications of this contest. Complacence and malice coloured their attitudes. In 1192, Mohammad Ghuri, the sultan of Ghazni, occupied the throne of Delhi and then turned his attention upon Kannauj. Jaichand had failed to unite with the Chauhans at the crucial moment that could have kept the 'barbarians' out of Hindustan. In a desperate attempt to escape, he drowned in the sacred river and the Gahadwal dynasty of Kannauj came to an end[3].

Udaipur, 12 October 1819: the time of departure had arrived. Since his appointment as political agent, Captain Tod had remained stationed in Udaipur, overseeing the signing of the agreements between the princely Rajput states and the East India Company. Nearly two years had been spent in the most romantic spot in India. The valley had been explored until every rock, tree and tower had become familiar. It was time to pay an official visit to the court of the desert king, Maharaja Maan Singh, who ruled from Mehrangarh, the great fort of Jodhpur.

The mission included the captain's cousin, Captain Patrick Waugh, Lieutenant Cary and Dr Duncan. Accompanying them was a large retinue of cooks, stewards and helpers, baggage camels and elephants, while two companies of foot soldiers and sixty Skinner's Horse formed the escort. Trumpets sounded at the crack of dawn and the men were ready to move. Skinner's yellow boys and their Indian commandant looked cheerful. Smartly turned out in bright yellow tunics and scarlet turbans with silver edged girdles and black shields, they were the most orderly and efficient of soldiers in the Company's service. The palace drums sounded. Maharana Bhim Singh had sent a guard of honour to see off his British friends.

---

3.   Kannauj passed into the hands of the Chandels of Bundelkhand (Madhya Pradesh).

Dismissing the guard at the pass, the officers rode on. The destination for the day lay thirteen miles away – the villages of Mairta and Toos.

By the light of the rising moon, the St George's flag was raised and tents pitched upon the heights that gazed upon ancient Chittaur. The Berach gleamed with a silver sheen, its surface rippling with leaping trout. Could there be a spot more pleasant, a place more perfect to build a home? The camels fitted with pack-saddles for the first time groaned – voicing their complaints for the day – lamenting the hardship thrust upon them. Blissfully unaware, that on leaving the fertile plains of Mewar they would have only the thorny mimosa to nibble on, the desert fleet settled for the night.

The peace of the dawn was broken by the discordant yells of a hundred camels and as elephants squeaked their delight, the camp prepared for departure. Men yelled at the top of their lungs in an attempt to be heard and young elephants free of all restraints and unburdened with load enjoyed getting up to mischief. One little fellow, no more than eight years of age, made sport of sneaking into the sepoys' baggage and making off with bags of flour. The owners gave chase, while shouts of laughter added to the morning's commotion. This little elephant, no higher than twelve hands, would choose to wander among the cooking fires with not a thought to the discomfort he caused his trusted human companions. For those watching, he was an infinite source of amusement and a lovable pet.

Nathdwara lay across a swampy stretch of land. Brown granite hills striped with veins of quartz encircled the sacred valley of Krishna. Through the bogs of Usarwas, across the river Banas and past Samecha, the party wound its way to Kelwara. It had been the abode of the ranas during the times that they had been driven from Chittaur. Passing below the castle of Kumbhalgarh, the British mission prepared to enter the kingdom of Maharaja Maan Singh.

Sihoji

Eighteen years after the sack of Kannauj (AD 1212), a young man rode into the desert looking for a kingdom to call his own. Two hundred faithful soldiers accompanied Sihoji (Shivaji) Rathore. Though he was a distant relative of the ancient Rashtrakutas, who boasted of a glorious two hundred year reign in the Deccan, Sihoji's bard linked him to Raja Jaichand Gahadwal of Kannauj. The grandson of Jaichand was to begin his new life with a pilgrimage to Dwarka (Gujarat).

Upon the banks of the Luni, Sihoji chanced upon the Dabeys of Mehwa (Barmer), one of the thirty-six royal races. They were in the middle of a feast when the Rathores fell upon them, slaying the unprepared men. Flushed with success and obedient to the Rajput creed of 'get land no matter what the cost,' Sihoji then turned his attention to the Gohils who lived across the river. Mahesh Das, the Gohil chief, fell by the sword of Jaichand's grandson. In the sands of the Luni, Sihoji planted his flag.

As a Rajput prince who led a powerful band of men, Sihoji was looked to for protection by the peaceful citizens of the area. Among them were the Paliwal Brahmins, refugees from Garh Nan-na, who on being driven from their homelands by the 'barbarians' of Multan and Uch had settled in this inhospitable land 700 years ago. The Paliwal Brahmins, of the desert city of Pali, appealed to the Rathore warriors. The Mers and the Meenas, the original natives of the desert, constantly worried the little community. As the troublesome and resilient tribes returned time and again, the Brahmins offered the Rathores a permanent home within their city. It was here, that Sihoji's Solanki wife bore their son, Ashwathama (Asthan). The Solankini, now a proud mother, demanded that Sihoji make himself lord of Pali. The Rathore waited until the full moon rose heralding the festival of Rakhi. The little community, quite oblivious to the traitor that had bred upon their hospitality, immersed itself in the rites that reaffirmed the ties between brothers and sisters. As they celebrated, the unsuspecting elders were summoned and beheaded. Sihoji claimed Pali for himself.

While Asthan succeeded to the throne of the desert, his brothers, Soning and Ajmal, occupied Idar from a branch of the Dabeys and

Setram and his son Sihoji rode into Gujarat. Bhim Dev II, the Solanki king of Anhilwara Patan, received his royal guests with kindness and Setram offered him their services.

The little township had been subject to raids by Lakha Phulana, the chieftain of the Jareja[4] tribe of Phulra. From the banks of the Sutlej to the ocean, the Jarejas roamed terrifying the people. Father and son made their way to castle of Phulra that stood deep within the sand dunes of Maroo. Though Setram lost his life that day, the Rathores returned victorious. The grateful Solanki gave his sister in marriage to Sihoji.

It was during his return from Dwarka, that Sihoji chanced upon the dreaded Lakha. The Jareja was in the thick of a foray in Anhilwara Patan. It was not just the love of glory or the ambition of maintaining the reputation of the Rathores but sheer vengeance that drove Sihoji to a confrontation. His father's blood was avenged and the chieftain of Phulra killed in a single-handed combat.

---

4. The Jareja or Jadeja is the most important tribe of the Yadu (Jadu) race next to the Bhati. Several beliefs regarding their origin exist. Some claim direct descent from Krishna (Shyam), some from his son Shambo and the rest from Raja Bhati's son Samba. The descendents of Raja Bhati refer to themselves as the clan of the Bhatis, which includes the Jareja branch. The modern Jareja has so mixed with the Sindis, that in confusion they often claim origin in Shyam or Syria and their descent from Jamsheed, the Persian. Shyam has been converted to Jam, which remains the name of a Jareja estate – Jamnagar in Gujarat.
Jam Lakha Phulana Jareja Bhati came to the throne of Kerakot in AD 844, and was never a contemporary of Sihoji Rathore. Several Lakhas succeeded him, but none attained the supernatural attributes of this great ancestor. Down the ages it became every Rajput's quest to be victorious over the mythical Lakha.

Okha from the Chawura Parmars respectively. Ajmal's line forever earned the title of badhail or slayer from his act of beheading the Parmar chief.

The Rathores set up base in the land of Mehwa (Barmer). Abandoning the old city of Kher, they built a new capital at Jasol.

Asthan left behind eight sons. Each became the head of a reputed clan. The growing family eyed lands as yet unconquered.

Doohar, who followed Asthan, made several unsuccessful attempts to recover Kannauj.

Mandor, the central and the most important of the nine forts that protected Maroo, was ruled at the time by an Indu-Purihara prince. To become lord of Mandor was a tempting proposition and the successive generations of Rathores that attempted to possess it could only boast of having watered the sands with their blood.

Rao Chunda

The seventh generation that descended from Doohar was the first to shed Rathore blood. Overcome by the guilt of fratricide, Mallinath renounced the throne of Mehwa in favour of his younger brother, Biramdeo, and turned to religion. But Mallinath's son, unable to come to terms with his father's choice, drove his uncle from the land. Biramdeo died in exile, leaving his title to his six-year-old son, Chunda.

Mallinath's spiritual awakening turned the fortunes of the Rathores. He came to guide his nephew and collecting all tribes that bore the name Rathore, Rao Chunda assaulted Mandor.

The Purihara dynasty, ruling Mandor since the earliest days, had lost their title of rana and the rich province of Godwar, to Rahup Sisodia of Mewar in AD 1201. But the dynasty had held on until it was evicted by the sultan of Delhi. Rup Singh Purihara – whose daughter had wed Chunda's grandfather, Rao Salkha of Kher – had fled seeking sanctuary with Rawal Jait Singh of Jaisalmer. Chunda, who had himself taken a wife from the Purihara clan, redeemed Mandor.

In 1406, the banners of Kannauj (Kamdhuj or Kamdhwaj – literally the banners of Cupid) flew atop the new capital of Maroo. Firmly set upon the path to success, Chunda took Nagaur[5] or Nag Durg, the castle of the serpent, from the garrisons of Delhi and ventured into Godwar, planting his flag in the capital city of Nadol. His daughter, Hansa Bai, he gave in marriage to the ageing Maharana Lakha of Mewar who gifted him forty villages. Chunda lived to see his grandson, Mokal, seated upon the throne of Chittaurgarh.

Although he was the firstborn, Ranmal, was disinherited by his father and he chose to move to Chittaurgarh while his brother, Kanha, was named heir. With Chunda's death, Nagaur was lost to the sultan of Delhi, as was the ancient Chauhan capital – Ajmer. Ranmal masterminded the recovery of Ajmer. A match was arranged between his own daughter and the sultan's governor at Ajmer and under the pretence of conveying the girl to her matrimonial home, the army of Mewar was introduced into Taragarh. The sultan's garrison was put to the sword and Ajmer attached to Mewar.

Born of a Gohil mother whose clan was related to the Sisodia ranas of Mewar, Ranmal was a giant of a man, powerfully built and quite easily the best athlete of Marwar. He was named first chief of Mewar[6]. Fortune favoured Ranmal and in AD 1427, when Kanha died without an heir, the throne was returned to him. The event coincided with the birth of the heir of Chittaurgarh.

The last act of Rao Ranmal's life was, however, a controversial one. While the annals of Mewar scream treachery, those of Marwar swear that any treachery that did take place was indeed by the Mewaris themselves. Maharana Lakha had abdicated and Mokal, the son of Lakha's Rathorni rani – Ranmal's sister Hansa Bai – was assassinated in 1433. Six-year-old Kumbha succeeded. Around him gathered the Rathore princes of Mandor. Ranmal and his son, Jodha, took over the reins of administration. Officers loyal to the Marwaris occupied key positions. With his grandnephew upon his knee, the old rao took to

---

5. Nagaur the castle of the serpent finds a mention in the *Mahabharat*. The castle moved from Chauhan hands to those of Mohammad Ghuri, the sultan of Ghazni. Around 1242, Nagaur, Mandor and Ajmer were governed by Muzaffer Balban Kishlu Khan who, for want of support, was unable to claim the throne of Delhi. Kishlu Khan met his death at the hands of Rawal Karan Singh of Jaisalmer. Nagaur was then placed under the more famous Balban who led his troops against Ranthambhor, Bundi and Chittaur, and eventually became sultan of Delhi.

6. Marwar was at the time a vassal state of Mewar acknowledging the supremacy of the maharana.

sitting on the throne of Bappa Rawal and when the child scampered off to play, the flag of the Sisodias would wave over the head of the Rathore. The palace watched with bated breath. It was but a matter of time before the primeval instinct of the Rajputs would overcome every modicum of civilised behaviour. Blood had never stood in the way of the Rajput creed – 'get land no matter what'. Nervous palace nurses and maids accosted Hansa Bai. Her grandson was in danger and her thoughts turned to her stepson, Choonda Sisodia. Time was of importance for Choonda's brother, Raghudev Sisodia, who led a secluded life far from the intrigues of life at court had already been murdered. Whispers of a poisoned robe gifted by Rao Ranmal were making their rounds[7].

Choonda was summoned and he sent word that the young maharana be made to hold a public audience every day. Official tours of villages were to begin increasing the distance between Kumbha and the palace. Every festival was to be celebrated amidst the people. The Diwali celebrations had come to an end when a group of horsemen appeared at the gates of Chittaur. They were local chieftains who had been granted the honour of escorting their young sovereign home. Once inside, Choonda's men threw off their disguises and war was declared. Rao Ranmal, who had enjoyed his opium that evening, lay fast asleep when a palace maid crept into his room. Taking the Marwari turban from his head she bound the sleeping Rathore to his bed. Aroused by Choonda's men, Ranmal did his utmost to hoist himself up. But the foot of the bed extended way beyond. Try as he might, his feet would not touch the ground. His powerful arms succeeded in bringing down several of his assailants but in the end he was slain. Jodha escaped. Though he crossed the border into his own lands, the sons of Choonda Sisodia followed at his heels. The Rathore capital of Mandor and the rich lands of Godwar fell to the Choondawats. Since that fateful day, Rathores have taken to sleeping on short beds ensuring that their feet always stick out from the end of their beds.

---

7. Several versions of this story exist. It is said that Choonda Sisodia entrusted his brother, Raghudev, with the care of young Mokal. This led to a clash with Rao Ranmal. When Mokal was murdered, Ranmal pursued and slew the assassins and ordered that the women of the offending clan be given in marriage to the Rathores. Raghudev protested for the women were after all Mewaris and Ranmal slew Raghudev in open court. Choonda Sisodia arrived to avenge his brother's murder and drove the Rathores out of Mewar.

Noon, 20 October 1819: the descent into the region of death began. The retinue, carrying the camping gear, moved three hours in advance. The entrance to Marwar was a mountain pass just wide enough to allow the passage of a single loaded elephant. Here sounds echoed until they magnified into thunderous proportions, the path steep, angled at 55 degrees.

Leading the horses by the mouth, the men picked their way with the aid of hatchets. Streams roared by on either side, drowning all conversation. The officers caught up with the slowly moving advance party. The gallant Manika, a gift of the Bundi prince, had missed his footing and had rolled all the way to the bottom. He was fortunately, none the worse for his experience except that he had broken the cantle of his saddle. Further down the slope sat the cook, lamenting over his implements that lay scattered, as his camel bemoaned the replacement of the kitchen baggage that he had so recently managed to dislodge. The officers rode on ahead.

The mile that passed below the tower of Kumbhalgarh was gentle. The cool air, the magnificent view of the noble forests and the serpentine torrent that repeatedly crossed their path invigorated the spirit and the horses needed but little urging as they leapt over boulders of granite. At one point the waters formed a pool. Lt Cary decided to trust his horse to carry him across but to everyone's horror, both horse and rider disappeared beneath the surface. Fortunately, the shock was momentary and a good ducking the only result. Leaving the drenched Cary in the care of the retinue, the officers rode onto Hathidwar. But the proposed site for the night's halt afforded little space to set up tents and orders were passed to the rear to stop and await the morning.

The shades of night descended fast and the party proceeded in utter darkness guided by the sounds of the gushing stream. Near the end of the descent, the path widened and the waters assumed a hoarse tone as they glided into the plains of Marwar. Stars, unusually brilliant, shone through the few visible patches of night sky that arched over towering cliffs. The party descended in silence, their thoughts drawn to the dangers that could befall the straggling retinue. Men and animals were constantly at the mercy of the ferocious tigers and plundering mountaineers that abounded in these hills.

A gleam of light flashed through the dense foliage, revealing a band of dismounted horsemen seated around campfires. A thrill ran down the spines of the onlookers. Thirty tall and well-armed men sat in groups, passing the pipe from hand to hand. Their long black hair and typically styled turbans confirmed that they were from Maroodesh. The chief reclined against an altar, built to a fallen hero of bygone days. A band of gold ran through his turban, distinguishing him from the others. The chill of the night aided by hunger pangs sharpened the imagination. A council of war was called and after much deliberation a decision was taken against moving any further that night. The Englishmen revealed themselves, greeting the chief and his band of men with the usual Ram Ram. In keeping with local courtesy, the health of the chieftain of Ghanerao was inquired after. Ghanerao, the capital city of Godwar, lay on the border of Marwar and Mewar. The latter had lost Godwar over fifty years ago. The site had been the scene of many battles where brave cavaliers had fallen while defending the pass. Altars, raised to their memory, marked the spots where the heroes last stood.

Dr Duncan and Captain Waugh rolled themselves up in the broadcloth used for housing the elephants and joined the chief for the night, resting on the ashes of the brave, while Captain Tod sat with the men. They passed the night smoking and recounting tales and experiences. Writes the captain:

> It would have required the pencil of a master to paint the scene. It was a subject for Salvator Rosa; though I should have been perfectly satisfied with one of Captain Waugh's delineations, had he been disposed at the moment to exert the pictorial art.

The morning was greeted with reverence and the doctor and the captain uncoiled themselves from their wrappings. Thirst and hunger had dulled the senses, rendering the picturesque surroundings unappreciated. Accompanied by their Marwari friends, the officers rode on for about five miles where they found waiting for them the chieftain of Ghanerao, Thakur Ajit Singh. He had travelled at the head of his retinue to welcome the British officers. At the risk of incurring the displeasure of his king; he had come nevertheless, for a feeling of reverence for his ancient sovereign, the maharana of Mewar, still ran strong in his veins. Quite recently, for having preferred to have his sword of investiture bound on him by the maharana, Ghanerao had had its walls blasted. Yet, should Mewar's envoy ever cry, 'Remember Kumbhalgarh!' the chieftain of Ghanerao would not turn a deaf ear.

The thirty-year-old thakur, a tall man with a noble bearing, sat astride his horse like a true Rathore cavalier. Related by blood to the maharana, this nephew of Mewar politely invited the British to visit him at Ghanerao. It was diplomatically refused, to save the young thakur from the wrath of the desert lord. Excuses, of fatigue and the necessity of an early march the next morning, were made.

The next day brought a visit from the Solanki chief of Roopnagar. His ancestor Samant Singh who had founded Roopnagar was the son of Raimal Solanki who had arrived at the court of Maharana Raimal seeking refuge. With the sacred war conch that had once belonged to the celebrated Sidh Raja Jai Singh Solanki of Anhilwara Patan he had established his credentials. His ancestors had been on the run since that fateful day in 1197 when Mohammad Ghuri had occupied their lands. Maharana Raimal permitted him to occupy the ancient Chauhan property of Desuri. These were kinsmen to the brave and beautiful Solankini – Tara Bai, the star of Badnor, the bride of Maharana Raimal's first born son Prithviraj. On Prithviraj's insistence a curse, directed at the future generations of Sisodias, had been included within the grant. It was to strike at those that attempted an annexation. Like Ghanerao, Roopnagar too owed a divided allegiance to the courts of both Mewar and Marwar.

Kishendas arrived as the party prepared to march. The confidential officer of the thakur of Ghanerao, had come to escort the British through the territory of Godwar. The old man, known for his integrity and wisdom, was a mine of ancient lore.

'Restore Godwar', was his abrupt salutation.

It sparked off a heated debate, for the government had forbidden interference in this particular matter.

Testily the captain replied, 'why did you let them take it? – where has the Sisodia sword slept this half century? God Almighty never intended that the region this side of the mountains should belong to Mewar; nature's own hand has placed the limit between you.'

The old man's blood boiled at the very thought.

'Even on this principle, Godwar is ours, for nature has marked our limit by features far stronger than mountains. Take note of the shrubs and flowers that are common to Mewar, cross the border of Godwar into the land of Marwar and you will find that they are all lost. *Aonla Aonla Mewar, Babul Babul Marwar.* The yellow blossoms of the aonla mark the territory rightfully belonging to Mewar while the stunted babul is all that grows in the land of death.'

The small town of Indara lay on the border of Godwar and Marwar. The character of the land changed completely from this point onwards. The yellow blossoms were nowhere to be found and the giant fig gave way to the dwarfish shrubs of the desert. Streams were shallower; their beds white with salt and fine sand replaced the hitherto fertile soil. Even the villages looked different. Huts were surrounded by fences made of thorns fortified at intervals by stacks of chaff some twenty or thirty-feet high. Coated with dung to protect them against the weather, the stacks would come in use as cattlefeed during the months when the earth would yield no grass. The stark landscape brought to mind a satiric stanza of a bard who came from a more favourable land:

Ak ra jhopra	Huts of sugarcane stalks
Phok ra bur	Barriers of thorn
Bajra ra rooti	Bread of millet
Moth ra dal	and mung bean soup
Dekho ho raja, teri Marwar	Look raja, this is your Marwar

A smile of quiet satisfaction lit the face of old Kishendas.

Mandor was open to attack, for it had no natural defence. Jodha looked for a site to build a new city. During his wanderings he came across an ascetic in the desert. The yogi pointed out Bakar Cheeria, the hill that was home to nesting birds. On 12 May 1459, upon this auspicious spot, Jodha laid the foundation. It was re-named Jodhagir – the hill of strife. Four miles south of Mandor, Jodhagir commanded a clear view right up to the southern border of Marwar. The summit of the Aravalli was visible on a clear day while in every other direction the desert stretched for miles. The impregnable fortress of Mehrangarh was raised upon these steep slopes. The ongoing construction disturbed the hermitage and the pleas of the yogi went unheard. Incensed, he pronounced that the great fort would always suffer the lack of drinking water.

Many successive generations attempted to find a source of fresh water but in vain. The memory of the yogi remained preserved in the water wheel that drew water from a lake at the base of the hill. The apparatus was controlled from within the fort and was inaccessible to the enemy.

The city of Jodhpur grew around the great fort. Hurba Sankhla and the warriors of the desert who helped in redeeming Mandor earned Jodha's everlasting gratitude. Their images, carved in stone, stood for posterity at Mandor.

Rao Jodha

With no kingdom to call his own, Jodha was forced to wander the great desert with a handful of followers. For twelve years, Mandor was denied to the Rathores. The generosity of the dwellers of Maroo kept the small band of warriors alive while they dreamt of their lost glory and made futile plans for the future.

Hurba Sankhla, a pious soldier who lived in the desert, held the feast of Shudh Vratt, the pure fast, every year. During this feast, food was offered to all who came but alas, by the time Jodha arrived, the food had all been distributed. With no provisions available at such short notice, Hurba quickly had a porridge of flour, sugar and spices, cooked. A piece of red wood was added, to lend it colour. The young rao and his 120 followers ate a hearty meal and drowned their sorrows in the comfort of sleep. Morning arrived and Jodha's men stared at each other. Their moustaches had all taken on a deep red hue. It appeared to be as good an omen as any and they shared their hopes with Hurba. The aid of Cousin Pabooji of Mehwa, a descendent of Mallinath, was enlisted. With him came his famous charger Kesar Kali and a fleet of hundred steeds. Jodha found himself strong enough to recover his capital.

The sons of Choonda were taken by surprise. The citizens of Mandor, who had until then submitted quietly to their rule rose to drive them out of Marwar. While the elder brother was struck down almost immediately, the younger, Munja, made it to the border of Godwar. But he went no further, for the Rathores caught up with him. Munja's blood sealed forever the border of Mewar and Marwar. Two sons of Chittaur had fallen and Jodha sought no further revenge. He wisely reflected on their own initial aggression and the superior power of Mewar, as well as his dependence on outside help. Jodha sued for peace and as the price of blood, accepted the place where Munja fell as the future boundary of the two states. Godwar became a part of Mewar legally and without contention. Mewar and Marwar were separated as a result of this incidence and remained apart ever since.

With twenty-four brothers and twenty-four sons, Jodha divided the land of Marwar into jagirs and issued rules of succession. Each became the head of a clan. Nine of the most powerful clans formed the Nau Kothi Maroo claiming for themselves the semicircular chain of the nine ancient Parmar castles that guarded the northern, western and southern frontiers of the desert. The central castle of Mandor had changed hands several times. It had been ruled successively by the Parmars, Puriharas and Rathores.

Of Jodha's sons, Satal built the fort of Satalmer. With the death of his elder brother, Satal soon found himself the heir of Jodhpur. Duda, the fourth, established himself on the plains of Merta and his clan earned its reputation as the 'first swords of Maroo'. He was the grandfather of the celebrated devotee of Lord Krishna, Mira Bai: mystic poetess and wife to the eldest son of Maharana Sanga of Mewar. He was also grandfather to Jaimal of Badnor, who fell in the defence of Chittaur in 1568. Bika[8] relinquished his claim to the throne and joined by his uncle, Rawat Kandhal, left to seek his fortune. Conquering lands belonging to six Jat tribes, he established himself in the wild lands – Jangaldesh. Rao Jodha lived to see his son raise the fort of Bikaner.

Of Jodha's brothers, Akhai Raj (Kumpa), the eldest, who had renounced his claim to the Rathore throne in favour of Jodha, became the thakur of Bagri and the head of the Kumpawat clan. Kandhal went on to establish the clan of the Kandhalotes, who voluntarily joined with Bikaner, and Champa the clans of Champawats of Awa and Pokaran. The Champawats rose to become the 'first nobles of Maroo'. So powerful were they that they could make princes on the throne of Marwar tremble. Kurmsi led the Kurmsotes and Jodha's grandson Uday the Udaywats.

Together they formed the asht thakoorait or the eight lordships of Marwar. Lesser properties were conferred upon the remaining brothers, sons and grandsons. These were all hereditary and could never be withdrawn. Their entitlement to their lands was as sacred as that of the rao to his throne. Within three centuries, Sihoji's descendents had regained their lost glory. Jodha ruled for another thirty years and beheld with satisfaction his sons and grandsons flourish in the land of Maroo.

---

8. The annals of Marwar claim that Bika was the eleventh son of Jodha. Some maintain, however, that he was second in line to the throne, which made him the senior-most Rathore alive when Satal died without an heir. In accordance to the promise extracted from his father, while relinquishing his right to the throne of Jodhpur, the emblems of Kannauj became rightfully his. The sandalwood throne and the white stallion of Kannauj remain in the possession of Bikaner.

He died at the age of sixty-one and his ashes were buried beside those of his fathers' in the ancestral abode of Mandor.

Rao Satal

Satal succeeded Jodha but ruled for no more than three years. Though he died with no heir to succeed him, Satal lived on in song. He is remembered, traditionally, during the annual teej fair, for the gallant rao had lost his life at Pipar, rescuing 140 maidens from the hands of marauding Pathans.

Rao Surajmal (Sujo)

Sujo, the third son, succeeded to the gaddi of Jodhpur. His brother Bika, who had relinquished his rights to the throne, returned to claim the royal emblems of Kannauj. Though Bikaner would remain the junior Rathore kingdom, its king laid claim to the privileges of the senior-most Rathore. The sandalwood throne and the white stallion were amongst the heirlooms that made their way to Bikaner.

In his twenty-seven years, Sujo preserved the land of Marwar from the depredations of the Lodi kings. Sadly his heir, his second son, Bagh Sahib, died in 1514, leaving behind seven sons and seven daughters. Three of the girls were given in marriage to Maharana Sanga of Mewar and a fourth, Ketu, to Rao Narayan Das of Bundi. Of the sons, the third, Biramdeo, was named successor, much to the displeasure of the eldest – Ganga. ͵

Rao Biramdeo

Within days of his accession Biramdeo was deposed, for his mother, a hot-headed Deora princess of Sirohi, dared insult the thakur of Bagri. A war of succession broke out.

Pipar, a prosperous little town, was said to be the ancient settlement of the Takshaks (an aboriginal tribe of India known as the race of snakes) and Parmar Rajputs. The soil was rich and dark and good water was available at the Sampoo or the snake's lake.

Legend speaks of a Paliwal Brahmin, Pipa, who worshipped the sacred serpent that lived on the banks of the lake. Pipa made daily offerings of milk and in return was rewarded each day with two pieces of gold. One day Pipa was obliged to leave town and he sent his son, with the milk. The greedy youth thought it a good opportunity to grab the snake's treasure and struck the serpent violently as it emerged. Injured, the snake retreated into its lair. The boy's mother worried that the snake would have its revenge and arranged to have him sent away. Forbidding him to leave his room, she went to arrange for a bullock cart. At first light, she got up to wake her son and set him on his way but to her horror, found instead a huge serpent coiled up in his bed.

The devastated Brahmin rushed home as soon as he heard the news but his son was gone forever. Throwing himself before the serpent, he begged forgiveness. The serpent relented. Pipa's devotion was rewarded and he was made master of the serpent's wealth. A memorial to the incident was raised at the serpent's command and the town of Pipar grew around it.

The lake was named Sampoo after its benefactor.

Rao Ganga

It was a trail that reeked of poison and death that led Ganga to his throne. The chief of Bagri swore fealty, running his right thumb over the edge of his sword and anointing the new sovereign with his blood. A custom was thus born and adopted for posterity.

His uncle Saga (Shekha), would not however concede his right to the gaddi and called upon Daulat Khan Lodi – the sultan who had not long ago wrested Nagaur away from the Rathores. Not more than fifty-five years had passed since Jodhpur had first become the symbol of Rathore independence and already the sons of Jodha had been marshalled against one another. Relying on the best swords of Maroo, Ganga gave battle. Saga was slain and the sultan defeated.

Twelve years went by, the sons of Jodha were called upon by Maharana Sanga. This time against a foreign foe – Babar, the Mongol. Ganga, whose sister Dhan Kanwar was mother to Sanga's successor, Ratan Singh, rallied to the call. Sadly the Rajput confederation was defeated on the fields of Bayana and an Islamic Mongol empire, which was to become famous as the Mughal Empire, took root in India.

Ganga died four years later. The body was found beneath the palace balcony. Perhaps he had had too much opium or, as it was whispered, had been pushed. He was joined in death by five wives, but his second wife, Maharana Sanga's daughter, Padmavati, chose to return home to Chittaur. She was to end her life in the flames of jauhar that were lit as Sultan Bahadur Shah of Gujarat took possession of the grandest of all Rajput forts.

Rao Maldeo

Delhi had changed hands and with the new masters, the Mughals, looking to claim fertile lands, the desert lay unnoticed. In Maroo, Babar found no temptation. Maharana Sanga was dead and the misfortunes of Mewar multiplied. The Mughals, the sultans of Gujarat and Sher Shah – who longed for an empire of his own – beset Mewar with worries, which her incompetent kings were incapable of handling.

Maldeo was left as the strongest prince of Hindustan. Twice, he sent aid to Mewar – the first time to ward off Sultan Bahadur Shah of Gujarat and the second to help young Uday take his place upon the Sisodia throne.

Rao Maldeo expanded his own territories. Nagaur was taken in 1534 followed by Ajmer, Jalor, Siwana and Bhadrajan. Two years later, he grabbed Bikaner from the sons of Bika and compelled the rebellious Mehwa Rathores and the settlers along the Luni to accept him as their chief. The Bhatis he engaged in war and conquered Bikampur. Branches of his family were settled in Mewar and Dhundhar. Chatsu, twenty miles south of Amber, was fortified and Sirohi grabbed from his maternal grandfather. Maldeo built a number of forts and enclosed the city of Jodhpur within high walls. A palace was built within Mehrangarh and towers and bastions added to the fort itself. The fort of Merta he re-named Malkote and dismantled Satalmer to fortify Pokaran.

Until this time, every child born to a noble house had an appanage assigned to him at birth. Maldeo realised that the continuous subdivision of Maroo would have to stop. A number of fiefdoms were resumed. It was even applied to Merta[9] and Jaimal, the heir of Merta, allied himself with Maharana Uday Singh of Mewar who granted him Badnor.

---

9. Duda's eldest, Biramdeo – who was married to Maharana Sanga's sister and had given his niece Mira in marriage to Sanga's eldest son – had captured Ajmer in 1535, from the sultan of Gujarat. Maldeo put forward an immediate demand but Biramdeo would not yield. The result was the confiscation of Merta. Biramdeo fled to Ajmer and sent his henchmen to murder Maldeo's appointee at Rian, which lay within the territory of Merta. Maldeo lashed out by occupying both Ajmer and Rian. Biramdeo lay low for a while and resorted to scheming. He is said to have treacherously fostered Maldeo's belief that the Rathore chiefs had turned traitor and defected to Sher Shah's side. The result was the disaster of Samel in 1544. Sher Shah was victorious and Merta was restored. When Biramdeo died in 1553, Maldeo seized Merta once again but Jaimal, the heir of Merta, supported by Rao Kalyanmal of Bikaner succeeded in winning it back. In January 1557, it was lost again as a result of the Battle of Harmoda, in which Jaimal supported his cousin Uday Singh of Mewar against the combined forces of Maldeo and Haji Khan (Sher Shah's former slave who had made himself master of Nagaur & Ajmer after his master's death). But the boy emperor Akbar's meteoric rise had already begun. That year Nagaur and Ajmer fell to the Mughals. In 1562, Jaimal approached Akbar. Merta was targeted and occupied by the Mughal.

Ten years of undisturbed peace followed. Babar was dead and his son Humayun had lost his empire to the Afghan governor Sher Shah. The fugitive emperor appealed for asylum in the name of his pregnant wife but Maldeo bade him begone. Little did Maldeo realise that his fortunes were linked to that unborn prince for whom Humayun had sought protection. The infant Akbar was to see the light of day in Umarkot at the far edge of Maldeo's desert kingdom. He was soon to avenge the inhospitable treatment meted out to his distressed father.

Close on the heels of Humayun, came the usurper with 80,000 men. Sher Shah, revelling in his newly acquired status as emperor of India, decided to stay on even after he realised that his quarry had given him the slip. Humayun was gone but Maroo, he decided, was to become the latest addition to his crown. The Rathores withdrew and refused to give battle. The imperial army would not give up the chase. Lured into the depths of the desert, Sher Shah repented his rashness. For a month, the armies lay within sight of each other. The desert was merciless and, as the Rathores expected, the imperial army's condition grew worse by the day. The moment Maldeo had been waiting for had arrived, but the crafty Afghan was yet to be beaten. Sher Shah wrote a letter pretending to correspond with the chiefs of Marwar. It was allowed to fall into the hands of Maldeo's spies.

. Perhaps the recent confiscation of estates weighed heavily on Maldeo's mind and he had been expecting a betrayal. When the call came, the rao failed to respond. In a display of devotion with which the annals abound, the chiefs attacked the imperial camp at the head of 12,000 men. Maldeo was convinced of their loyalty a little too late. Though the Battle of Samel was counted as a victory for the Afghan, the risk he had taken had been driven home in no uncertain measure. For but a handful of millet he had nearly lost the crown of Hindustan. The confession was an ever-lasting tribute to the descendents of Sihoji.

Sher Shah moved swiftly leaving garrisons behind in Jodhpur, Pali, Phalodi, Sojat, Jalor, Nagaur, Abu, and Ajmer. Ranthambhor had already been taken the previous year. Chittaurgarh and Amber quickly surrendered and agreed to pay tribute. Within ten months nearly all of Rajasthan had submitted to the Afghan. On 22 May 1545, Sher Shah suffered a fatal injury during the siege of Kalanjar and Rajasthan slipped out of imperial control.

Maldeo outlived Sher Shah and witnessed the imperial crown of India once more encircle the brow of Humayun. Unfortunately, for the Rathores this mild mannered man did not live long. Maldeo had by then re-established himself recovering some of his lost estates including Merta. But Jalor remained in the hands of Sher Shah's governor, Malik Khan, and his Bihari Pathans. The nineteen-year-old Akbar, perhaps nursing a grievance against Maldeo, invaded Marwar. Nagaur, Ajmer and Merta were occupied. Keeping Ajmer for himself, he bestowed the rest, by and by, upon Rai Singh of Bikaner. Bikaner was established as a state independent of the parent state of Jodhpur.

The year 1568 saw the greatest attack ever in the history of Chittaurgarh. Rajputs from all over the land put aside their woes to rush to her defence. Leading from the front was sixty-year-old Jaimal Rathore of Badnor, Rao Jodha's great-grandson – the deposed chief of Merta. But the Mughal had brought in every resource at his disposal and despite the tremendous defence mounted by the Rajput nation, Chittaur was doomed. The question of surrender had not entered the Rajput minds until a shot struck Jaimal. Akbar personally claimed the honour of bringing down the Rathore. Horrified at the thought of an inglorious death caused by a distant blow and realising that there was no hope of salvation, Jaimal signalled the end of the war. Jauhar was commanded. While the flames consumed the women, 8,000 Rajputs ate their last beera together. An ardent admirer of valour, the emperor immortalised the Rathore, raising a statue to him and honouring the very matchlock that took Jaimal's life. It received the title Sangram – a tribute to both Jaimal and the universally admired Maharana Sangram Singh (Sanga).

In 1569, Maldeo succumbed. His younger son, Chandersen, was sent with gifts to Akbar. Perhaps Chandersen had been chosen especially for the mission, keeping in mind that he was related to the emperor by marriage for both Akbar and Chandersen had taken a wife each from amongst the daughters of Rawal Har Raj of Jaisalmer. But Chandersen failed to charm and peeved because Maldeo did not come personally, the emperor not only guaranteed free possession of Bikaner to Rai Singh, the heir apparent of Bikaner, but also presented him with a firmaan for Jodhpur. Rai Singh was not just a rival, being a Rathore who could lay claim to the throne of Jodha, he was, to add insult to injury, married to yet another of Rawal Har Raj's daughters. The three brothers-in-law were set against each other. Uday Singh, the heir of Marwar, rushed to court and managed to ingratiate himself with the emperor.

Uday Singh was invested with the titles of mota raja or fat raja and raj rajeshwar or king of kings. Jodhpur was saved but Marwar was lost. The name Uday Singh had consistently spelt disaster in the annals of Rajasthan. Maldeo was at least spared the indignity of seeing a daughter bestowed upon his enemy. He died that very year.

Rao Chandersen

Twenty-one-year-old Chandersen seized the throne in his brother's absence. Jodhpur was as a result subject to a siege of seventeen months. It is said that Chandersen had been his father's chosen heir and that the aggrieved older brothers had defected to the Mughal side, organising the resistance.

The imperial army led by Rai Singh succeeded in driving out the usurper but Chandersen and his men preferred to cling to independence and took up post in Siwana. Negotiations with Akbar failed and pursued by Yuvraj Rai Singh of Bikaner, the deposed king of Maroo was driven into hiding for the last seven years of his life. Chandersen, who was to be emulated by Pratap of Mewar, maintained his right to the gaddi till the end.

That Chandersen's right was upheld by the princes of Rajasthan, was evident from the marriages he had contracted. He was the son-in-law of Maharana Uday Singh of Mewar, Maharawal Har Raj of Jaisalmer and Rao Surjan of Bundi. Even as an exile, he was not a social outcaste. Rajput society looked out for the welfare of his daughters. Two were given in marriage to Uday Singh of Mewar, while Maan Singh of Amber and his son Sabal came forward to accept a wife each. For all those years, Rathore loyalty remained divided between the two brothers.

But Maldeo's eldest, Ram Sahib, was bypassed and it was Uday who found himself upon the throne confirmed at last by Akbar. Jodhpur, that had been governed until then by Rai Singh of Bikaner, was handed back.

Raja Uday Singh

The powerful clans of Marwar would not accept Uday Singh's accession. The Mughal flag now floated above the Panchranga, the flag with five colours that had led the Rathores to victory in the years gone by. The raja had become an officer of the emperor and led his army to wherever it was that the emperor commanded but their deeds of bravery did earn them generous favours in the imperial court. Emperor Akbar used the Rathore army to subjugate the independent Muslim states of the Deccan. Though a part of the spoils of Golconda and Bijapur made its way to Jodhpur, embellishing its palaces, the Rathores were keenly aware of their degraded status. Resentment gave vent to emotion at times before the emperor himself.

The clans accepted Uday only on Chandersen's death. Marwar prospered while Maharana Pratap in Mewar struggled to maintain his independence. Uday gave his daughter Jagat Gosain[10] (Manvati Bai who was renamed Taj Bibi) in marriage to the Mughal heir apparent, Salim, and the emperor restored all lands that had been wrested from them. Ajmer was the only exception. The Grand Mughal insisted on keeping for himself the key to Marwar. Instead, he gave them several rich districts in Malwa. In 1581, Akbar took two royal Rathornis as brides. One was the granddaughter of Uday's older brother, Ram Sahib, and the other Rukmavati, the daughter of Maldeo and his Muslim wife Tipu Paswan.

---

10. Rathore princesses, since the time of Jodha, had married into ruling Muslim families. Rao Maldeo had given a daughter in marriage to Sher Shah as a precaution against the Afghan's return. The fact that he had himself married a Muslim lady, Tipu Paswan, is also on record. Tipu bore him two sons and a daughter. Maldeo's grandson, Raja Guj Singh, also had two Muslim wives: Anguri Rai and Anara Begum. Anara Begum, the widow of a nawab of Delhi, is credited with the building of many beautiful structures in Jodhpur. Her influence was not to be underestimated, for it is said that it was she who had pushed her husband into disowning his eldest, Umra, and naming Jaswant Singh heir.

Uday used his new power to clip the wings of the powerful Marwari clans. Jagirs were confiscated and Uday's own sons established new clans. Some settled in Malwa beyond the Marwar border and some in the wild lands within Rajasthan. Of the independent kingdoms thus established, Kishangarh and Ratlam shot to prominence. Matrimonial alliances were made with kingdoms allied with the Mughals. Uday's daughters married into Bundi and Jaipur. Among his sons-in-law was Chhatra Sal, the heir of Bundi.

Uday was far too overweight to participate in battles personally. His Rathores served him well and his son and heir was a brilliant general. Sur Singh had been dignified by the hereditary title of sawai raja during the lifetime of his father. Considered to be a quarter more as valuable than the others in the imperial court, the emperor awarded him the status of sawai.

In 1573, Sur Singh was commanded to take charge of Rao Surtan, the arrogant Deora prince of Sirohi. Secure in his inaccessible mountain kingdom, Surtan had steadfastly refused to acknowledge any superior. This suited Sur Singh perfectly as he had a private feud to settle with him. The opportunity was used to plunder Sirohi and Surtan was left with not even a bed of straw to sleep on. So humiliated was the Deora, that he shot an arrow at the sun for daring to shine on him in his hour of misery. Then meekly accepting the imperial firmaan agreed to follow Sur Singh to Gujarat. A terrible battle followed and though many brave Rathores lost their lives, Muzzaffer Shah III was defeated and chased to his stronghold of Jalor[11]. The pitch of the battle intensified, for the castle of Jalor had been captured from the Rathores in the recent past and wounds were as yet raw. Though the Rathores of both

---

11. The Parmar fort of Jalor (ancient Jabalipura) stood upon the mountain of gold – Sonagir. It came into the hands of Kirtipal, the youngest son of the Chauhan of Nadol, in 1181. Kirtipal Chauhan's descendents took the name Songara after Sonagir. Jalor defied Iltutmish but fell to Alla-ud-din Khalji in 1311. With the sons of Sihoji establishing themselves in the desert, Jalor became a part of Marwar. Rao Maldeo, who annexed it in 1534, lost it to Sher Shah. In the sixteenth century it fell into the hands of the sultan of Gujarat but with the Mughal conquest of Gujarat, Jalor was added to Akbar's list of forts. It was returned to Ajit of Marwar in 1704, when Emperor Aurungzeb's granddaughter, who had been in the care of the Rathores, returned home.

Marwar and Bikaner were involved in the campaign it was the brilliance of Sur Singh's young son, Guj, that brought about the surrender of the ancient Chauhan castle. Gujarat became a permanent part of the Mughal Empire. The spoils of 17,000 towns were sent to the emperor but Sur Singh kept a large portion for himself. The money was used in embellishing Jodhpur. The Sur Sagar, or the warrior's lake was excavated in the middle of the desert.

The sawai raja was in command of the imperial forces at Lahore when the news of his father's death reached him.

Sawai Raja Sur Singh

Sur Singh succeeded in July 1595 and to celebrate, a wedding was arranged. The daughter of Raja Uday Singh's brother Raimal was given in marriage to Akbar's son Danial. On 30 October 1595, Shobha Devi, the adopted daughter of Emperor Akbar, gave birth to the heir of Maroo, Guj Singh.

Akbar increased the number of troops at Sur Singh's command. The sawai raja received a sword, a khelat and a grant of fresh lands. Sur was then sent to the Deccan. With 13,000 horses, ten large guns and twenty elephants he fought three grand battles. On the banks of the Rewa (Narmada), he defeated Umra Balecha, the Chauhan and for this service, received the kettledrum and jagir of Dhar.

On Jahangir's accession to the throne, Sur Singh's son and heir, Guj Singh was recognised for bravery. In the escalade of Jalor, the heir of Maroo had outshone the rest. Guj Singh was girded with a sword by the emperor's own hand while the bards immortalised the event. 'What took Alla-ud-din years, Guj accomplished in three months. He scaled the walls of Jalindra, sword in hand and though many a Rathore of fame lost their lives, Guj put to sword 7,000 Pathans.'

Guj, who was quite a hero by then, was ordered against Mewar. His cousin, Prince Khurram, who was in charge of the operation negotiated a surrender with Maharana Amar Singh – the last of the independent Rajputs.

Sur Singh died in the Deccan. Since his youth, his life had been spent in the service of the emperor. His native land had barely seen him and the heart of the king of Maroo craved for the simple desert fare – green pulses and maize porridge. The imperial banquets left him cold. In exasperation, he commanded a pillar be erected. Engraved upon it was a curse applicable to his descendents were they ever to cross the Narmada. In his lifetime he had greatly added to the beauty of his capital.

Making their way through the mercantile town of Pali, the British mission arrived at Jhalamand. Here, ten miles short of Jodhpur, they were obliged to make a halt. The tricky business of the manner of reception of the governor general's envoy was yet to be decided. The desert court was aware of protocol required for an ambassador sent directly by his majesty, the king, but was greatly puzzled by the mode of reception required in this case. The commanders of the Scindia and Holkar armies demanded great privileges for themselves as did Amir Khan, who expected the same treatment that was reserved for princes. It was decided eventually that the maharaja, seated in his palki, would receive the mission at the central barrier of the descent. Salim Singh, the Champawat chief of Pokaran and Surtan Singh of Nimaj, chief of the Udaywats, the two most important chiefs of the court of Marwar arrived to personally escort the party of British officers.

The sands across the Luni lay thick and heavy, and while men and horses laboured their way across, the Marwaris with their light-footed camels moved with ease. In the distance, Mehrangarh – the great fort of Jodha – shimmered into view, an isolated projection from a low range of hills towering above every surrounding object. Strong walls with numerous round and square towers encircled the crest of the hill. Seven gates marked the circuitous ascent, the first bearing cannon ball scars: a reminder of the days spent quarrelling with Jaipur over Krishna Kumari, the teenage princess of Mewar. Below the walls lay the Rani Talab or the queen's lake and the Gulab Sagar or the rose water sea.

A mechanism of buckets drew water constantly into the fort from the sea of roses, which despite its pretty name, yielded brackish water. Many splendid buildings and palaces lay within the fort each standing testimony to the architectural tastes of the rajas who had ruled since the day of Rao Jodha.

The maharaja received the mission at the alarum or the nakarra darwaza, the second gate from the top, and having exchanged pleasantries, left to prepare for the next meeting. The mission advanced slowly through the lines of Rathore clansmen to the main reception area. The amazing display of grandeur could be matched by the imperial court at Delhi alone. The Rathores had long held important posts at the court of the Grand Mughal and had imbibed many of their customs. Lines of gold and silver mace bearers roared:

'Raj raj Iswara,' 'The king of kings'.

The thundering announcement echoed around the great fort as the British officers were ushered into the royal presence.

A mysterious silence, typical of Indian courts, filled the thousand-pillared hall. The king of Maroo rose from his throne and advanced a few paces. Here he received the envoy and formal introductions were made.

In deference to Indian customs, all shoes were left outside and heads remained covered. White linen covered the delicate carpets that were to be used for seating the officers. Above the royal cushion, was raised a richly embroidered canopy supported by silver columns. To the maharaja's right, in the positions of maximum honour, were seated the chiefs of Nimaj and Pokaran. Palms were put together to receive attar, the essence of roses, from the august hand and the paan was acknowledged by a salute, the officers bringing their right hands sharply to their cocked hats. The maharaja presented the captain with an elephant, a horse, necklaces, brocade and draped ornate shawls about his shoulders. Officers, who had accompanied the mission, received gifts proportionate to their ranks.

Three days were spent in the maharaja's company. Less than a year apart in age, the younger man, realised the captain, was far more intelligent than he allowed his court to discover. Remarkably well read, he engaged his guest in many varied discussions. A copy of the family's history was received as a gift and was forwarded to the library of the Royal Asiatic Society.

Raja Sawai Guj Singh

Guj Singh came to the throne of Marwar in 1620. He had been born in Lahore, where his father had been serving at the time and when the news of his father's death was announced, he had once again been far from home. The sword of investiture arrived at the imperial camp of Burhanpur (now in Madhya Pradesh). The son of the khan-e-khana arrived with the news and as the emperor's proxy.

Besides the nine castles of Marwar, Guj Singh inherited seven districts in Gujarat, Jhalai in Dhundhar and Masuda in Ajmer. This last acquisition was of great consequence, being counted amongst the lost heirlooms of the Rathore dynasty. He was appointed viceroy of the Deccan and as special testimony of imperial favour, his horses were spared the imperial dagh. By his side in every battle was his older son, Umra. This gallant prince contributed to the splendid display of Rathore valour.

The sons of Jahangir were soon battling among themselves. They sought to manipulate themselves into powerful positions even during their father's lifetime. The Rajputs were drawn against their will into the power struggle. Gaddi ki aan, or the principle of allegiance to the rightful possessor of the throne, kept the Rajputs on side of Jahangir.

Khurram, who had earned the title Shah Jahan in 1616, attempted repeatedly to bring Guj to his side. But this first cousin, three and a half years his younger, stuck stubbornly to his Rajput principles. In frustration, Khurram murdered Govindas, the Bhati chief who was Guj Singh's principal advisor. Disgusted, the king of Maroo left the Deccan and marched back home.

In 1622, Bheem, a prince of Mewar, instigated Khurram into open rebellion. Earlier that year in January, Jahangir's eldest son and heir,

Khusro, had died an unexplained death while with his half-brother Khurram in the Deccan. Khurram's open defiance and lack of cooperation resulted in the loss of Kandahar to Shah Abbas the Great of Persia in June. His son's attitude preyed upon the emperor's mind. Paying minimal attention to the recovery of Kandahar, Jahangir decided to move the treasury from Agra to the safety of Lahore. Khurram sent word threatening to intercept the convoy were such a move to be attempted. The idea was dropped. Proclaiming his second son, Parvez, his heir, Jahangir mustered his faithful Rajputs. The enthusiastic response of the Rathore so touched the emperor that he took the raja's hand and kissed it. But despite Guj Singh's show of fidelity, the emperor was still a little unsure, for after all Guj and Khurram did share ties of blood. Amber's eleven-year-old Mirza Raja Jai Singh was asked to take the lead and offended, Guj Singh pulled out of the battle. The Rathore moved to a side and took down his banners. Bheem tried one last time to spur the Rathore into joining their side. His arrogant taunt rang through the battlefield and the lord of the desert, his passions inflamed, whirled around, massacring Bheem and his men. Khurram was not destined to be emperor that day. His forces were routed and he fled to Mewar. From the security of Udaipur, Khurram continued to fuel rebellion ransacking Bihar and Bengal but in a few short months was chased to the Deccan. In 1624, at the battle of Hazipur, Guj Singh, Jai Singh and Ratan Singh Hada of Bundi led by Mahabat Khan and Parvez inflicted a crushing defeat driving the prince into the arms of his one-time enemy – Malik Ambar. A grateful Jahangir granted Guj Singh the jagirs of Phalodi and Merta. But Khurram was far from disheartened and by October 1626, Sultan Parvez had died a mysterious death. Manbhavati, Guj Singh's own sister, had been widowed in less than a year of marriage. Silent fingers pointed at first cousin Khurram. In quick succession Khurram married both Manbhavati and another of her sisters, Lilavati.

On 28 October 1627, Emperor Jahangir passed away and the grandson of Raja Uday Singh, the first raja of Maroo, ascended the Mughal thone of Hindustan as Emperor Shah Jahan.

Guj Singh died in 1638, slain in an expedition against Gujarat. He was survived by two valiant sons, Umra and Jaswant.

Umra (Amar), the elder, was troubled by a turbulent nature. His energetic spirit served him well during battle and he drew about him like-minded warriors. Together they furnished the annals with many accounts of gallantry. Times of peace, however, drew many complaints and the father was forced to banish his firstborn. In a ceremony of mourning, the feudal lords of Maroo assembled, Umra's birthright was taken away and assigned to his younger brother. His citizenship of Marwar was lost forever.

Mounting him upon a black horse, Maroo bid its prince farewell. Umra left, but not alone. With him went members of several clans, men who were alike in spirit and who regarded Umra as their future lord.

Though the emperor approved of the banishment, he offered Umra employment. His gallantry soon won him the title of rao, a munsub of 3,000 and the grant of Nagaur as an independent domain. But the arrogant and uncontrollable spirit of Umra continued to trouble him. He absented himself from court at will and when reprimanded was impudent enough to declare that he had been off chasing wild game for over a fortnight. The emperor threatened him with a fine but placing his hand on the hilt of his sword, Umra proclaimed that that was all he had. Salabat Khan, the bakshi (paymaster general), went to Umra's quarters to collect the fine but was unceremoniously thrown out. Shah Jahan was enraged. He summoned the Rathore to court. On that fateful day in 1644, it was to be held at the house of the Mughal heir apparent, Dara Shikoh.

With blood shot eyes, the Rathore strode past the umaras of five and seven thousand and with a dagger, hidden in his sleeve, stabbed the bakshi who was at that moment engaged in addressing the court. Then drawing his sword, Umra lunged at his horror-stricken cousin. It splintered on impact but missed its intended victim. Prince Dara fled and Umra, oblivious to consequences, continued with his work of death, indifferent to upon whom the blows fell. He had taken the lives of five eminent Mughal chiefs when his brother-in-law, Arjun Gaur, approached uttering words of comfort. Umra paused and Arjun stabbed him. He continued to ply his dagger until all signs of life were extinguished.

Bulloo Champawat and Bhao Kumpawat, two loyal retainers of Umra, donned garments of saffron and a fresh bout of carnage ensued within the Lal Kila (Red Fort) of Agra. The faithful band continued with the slaughter until the last man fell. Umra's wife, a princess of Bundi, arrived. She claimed her husband's body and cradling his head upon her lap sat with him until the flames of the pyre consumed them both. The Bukhara Gate, by which they had entered, was henceforth known as the Umra Singh Gate.

Shah Jahan, an ardent admirer of valour shared Umra's Rathore blood. He chose not to be vindictive. Umra's son, Rai Singh, he installed in Nagaur and it remained in the family until Inder Singh of the second generation, lost it to Jodhpur. Umra's daughter – by the sister of Mirza Raja Jai Singh of Amber – Rajkumari Anup Kanwar Baiji Lall Sahiba was married to Dara's son Suleiman Shikoh[12].

For a very short while in 1759, Rai Singh had been appointed by Aurungzeb as raja of Jodhpur but was quickly removed on popular demand. His descendents made several attempts at regaining Jodhpur without success.

---

12. Iffat Jahan Banu Begum and Kandhari Begum traced their descent from Ismail Shah I, the founder of the ruling Safawi dynasty of Persia, and were married to princes Parvez and Khurram respectively. Their fathers had defected to India in 1594, during the reign of their second cousin – Shah Abbas the Great – surrendering their governments, which included Kandahar, to Akbar. Parvez's daughter by this marriage was Nadira who married Dara Shikoh in 1633 and became mother to Suleiman and Siphir Shikoh. Kandhari Begum became mother to Khurram's daughter Pariz Banu. Arjumand Banu Begum (Mumtaz Mahal), a Persian woman of common origin, married Khurram in 1612 and bore fourteen of his sixteen children. Of Mumtaz's children four sons and three daughters survived. Safawi girls continued to be regarded as first choice as brides for the Mughals. Iffat Banu's father – Rustam Iffat Khan – did particularly well for himself and seven girls from his family were chosen as brides for Mughal royals. Amongst them was his granddaughter Dilras Banu Begum who became Aurungzeb's chief queen, and mother to his sons, Akbar and Azam, and two great-granddaughters who wed Jahandar Shah. The Bibi ka Maqbara (the lady's tomb also known as the poor man's Taj) was built at Aurangabad as a tomb by Azam for his mother.

Maharaja Jaswant Singh

'Jaswant,' sang the bards, 'was unequalled among the princes of his time. Stupidity and ignorance were banished and the sciences flourished. Many were the books composed under his benevolent eyes.'

The first imperial service performed by Jaswant was in the war of Gondwana. He led twenty-two different contingents of the army under Aurungzeb. Jaswant continued to play a subordinate role for a while until Prince Dara, Shah Jahan's firstborn, was named regent. He was then nominated as viceroy in Malwa and his munsub was increased to that of 5,000. On 6 January 1654, Shah Jahan granted Jaswant the personal title of maharaja.

The sons of the ailing Shah Jahan began their struggle for the throne and the loyalties of the Rajputs were once more put to the test. While Mirza Raja Jai Singh of Amber was commanded to oppose Shuja, the viceroy of Bengal, Jaswant was entrusted with putting down the ambitions of Aurungzeb.

Jaswant marched from Agra at the head of the united troops of Rajasthan and the imperial guards. Like a great glittering snake, the army wound its way southwards and camped fifteen miles south of Ujjain. He soon received news of Aurungzeb's approach. Jaswant could have crushed Aurungzeb with ease but he took a decision that was to cost him dearly. He allowed Murad time to join Aurungzeb from a vainglorious desire to crush two Mughal princes at one go. On 15 April 1658, the armies met at Dharmat. The two brothers had managed to sow distrust in the imperial camp and as soon as the battle began the Mughal guard deserted the field. Jaswant found himself suddenly abandoned, left alone with his 30,000 Rajputs.

Astride Mahboob, Jaswant, charged spear in hand. Though 1700 Rathores fell, 10,000 Muslim lives were claimed. Every clan of Rajasthan had dead to mourn. By a stroke of sheer luck, Aurungzeb and Murad managed to get away. Covered in blood, Mahboob and his rider let them escape. Aurungzeb cared not to renew the combat nor interfere with the retreat of Jaswant's troops. Although every noble house was covered in grief that day, it was counted as an event glorious in the history of Rajasthan. The Rajputs had displayed their fidelity to the ageing Shah Jahan, whose salt they had eaten. Of all the acts of heroism, Ratna of Ratlam's deeds were considered to be the greatest. He was a great-grandson of Raja Uday Singh. The Rathore blood had certainly not degenerated. But Jaswant returned to find the gates of his capital closed. His queen[13], the daughter of Rao Raja Chhatra Sal of Bundi, had barred his entry into Jodhpur, for he had abandoned the field and lost his chance to redeem Hindustan. Aurungzeb was to later commemorate the events of Dharmat by renaming it Fatehabad – the city of victory.

On 29 May 1658, Aurungzeb and Murad met and overcame Dara's army at Samugarh near Agra. Dara fled, leaving matters in hands of the faithful Rajputs. Rao Raja Chhatra Sal laid down his life that day. Aurungzeb wasted no more time. Shah Jahan was imprisoned and the treasury secured. All that remained was the elimination of his brothers, his nephews and his eldest son. Shahzadaa Muhammad Sultan Mirza – born of the Kashmiri princess, Anuradha Bai of Rajauri – had foolishly defected to his uncle Shuja's side.

Having seated himself upon the throne, Aurungzeb sent a letter, by the hand of the raja of Amber, to Jaswant. He assured him of his forgiveness and invited him to help defeat Shuja. Jaswant saw a chance to avenge himself. He agreed to join Aurungzeb and at the same time communicated the plans to Shuja. The hostile armies met at Khajuwa, thirty miles north of Allahabad. On 7 January 1659, the battle began. Leaving the two brothers to a contest he heartily hoped would destroy them both, Jaswant concentrated on plundering the imperial camp, loading his camels with valuable trophies, before he left for Agra. His appearance in Agra caused such panic that had he but made a demand,

---

13. Interestingly Jaswant's first wife – Jasrup, the daughter of Rawal Manohar Das of Jaisalmer – was eleven years his junior, while Kalyan Bai – the daughter of Rao Raja Chhatra Sal of Bundi – whom Jaswant renamed as Jaswant Devi, was but a year younger. The wedding had been a turning point in his life for the very next day Raja Sawai Guj Singh, at the age of forty-two, was slain in the Gujarat campaign. Suddenly Jaswant was king. There was obviously a special bond between Jaswant and Jaswant Devi for this spirited Hada queen could publicly chastise her husband and get away with it. From among his twelve queens, it was she who was named maharani on 22 April 1670. There appears to be no record of the children she bore, nor is her name listed amongst the queens who committed sati. Possibly she had predeceased her husband.

Shah Jahan would have been liberated. But he did no such thing and instead awaited Dara's instructions. At this crucial moment, Dara faltered, loitering on the southern border of Marwar unable to make up his mind. Thus did Dara Shikoh lose forever the crown of India.

Jaswant returned to Jodhpur and displayed his trophies, which included Aurungzeb's tent, at Mehrangarh.

Aurungzeb crushed Shuja's army and returned to overwhelm every last opponent that could possibly lay claim to his throne. His eldest son and heir was marked for death. In June 1659, Aurungzeb declared himself emperor. It was the first coronation to be held in the Shalimar Gardens of Delhi. This time prayers were read in his name and new coins struck, erasing the name of Shah Jahan, who languished within the Agra Fort. The crafty prince preferred stratagem to overt war. Though for a few short months he had deprived Jaswant of his throne, conferring it upon Umra's son, Raja Rai Singh of Nagaur, he wrote nevertheless to Jaswant. All was forgiven. Offering Jaswant the viceroyalty of Gujarat, Aurungzeb humbly requested him to forsake Dara and take on a neutral stance. Jaswant accepted and agreed to lead the Rajput contingents under Prince Muazzam – Nawab Begum Anuradha Bai's second son, who had now been declared heir – against the Maratha Raja Shivaji Bhosle who was bent upon reviving the independence of the western and southern parts of the country.

As soon as Jaswant reached the Deccan, he sent word to Shivaji. Together they planned to eliminate the Mughal general, Shaista Khan. Aurungzeb received the details of the plot from his spies. He well understood the role Jaswant hoped to play. He wrote warm congratulatory letters without betraying emotion and quite suddenly Jaswant found himself superseded by Mirza Raja Jai Singh of Amber.

Shivaji was persuaded to surrender in 1666. Jai Singh agreed to send Shivaji to the Mughal court provided his safety was guaranteed. The war in the Deccan was brought to a quick conclusion but when Jai Singh realised that Aurungzeb had no intention of keeping his promise and that the life of young Maratha was at risk, he personally helped Shivaji escape. Aurungzeb was forced to remove Jai Singh from his post and re-establish Jaswant.

The Rathore began plotting once again and inspired Muazzam with

There had been many great chiefs in Jaswant's service.

To be recognised for bravery was the greatest honour that could be bestowed upon them. Together the Rathores made a formidable team. To Nahar (tiger) Khan, chief of the Kumpawats[14] – the descendent of Rao Jodha's brother, Kumpa – Jaswant was deeply indebted.

Mokundas, for such was Nahar Khan's name, had earned the displeasure of the emperor with a reply that had been considered disrespectful. Aurungzeb had awarded a punishment and Mokundas was ordered to enter a tiger's den unarmed. The angry Rathore fortified himself with opium and strode right in. The savage beast that had been pacing its lair came face to face with its intended victim. Unaccustomed to such a visitor, it stole its gaze from the blazing eyes and slunk away.

'You see,' cried the Rathore, 'he will not even look me in the eye. It is against the creed of a true Rajput to attack an enemy who does nor dare to confront him.'

Aurungzeb was amazed. 'Do you have children like you,' he asked. 'How can we have children when you keep us away beyond the Attock far from our families?'

The same freedom of speech earned the 'tiger lord' the shahzadaa's displeasure. The heir of Hindustan once commanded the Rathore to ride at full gallop and, while passing under the branch of a tree, to grab and cling on. The 'tiger lord' flatly refused. He was not a monkey, he said. 'If it was Nahar Khan's prowess that the shahzadaa wished to test, he would have to allow him the use of his sword.' Nahar Khan was ordered against Surtan, the Deora prince of Sirohi.

---

14. The annals of Jaisalmer claim that the Bhati fort of Pokaran was granted to Nahar Khan Kumpawat by Shah Jahan. Nahar Khan had been sent as royal emissary to install Sabal Singh as rawal upon the throne of Jaisalmer. Pokaran later became the property of the junior branch of the Champawat clan – descendants of Rao Jodha's brother Champa. The annals of Marwar, on the other hand, count Pokaran amongst the crown properties since the days of Raja Sur Singh.

This fiercely independent branch of Chauhans acknowledged no man as superior. The Deoras, secure in their native hills were taken by surprise. Oblivious to the challenge that had been accepted, they had failed to tighten their levels of security. Stabbing the guard at the door, Mokundas entered. Tying up the sleeping prince with his own turban, he sounded the alarm. Their prince was safe, he informed the Deoras, but were they to attempt a rescue they would most certainly lose him.

'My sole objective in giving the alarm,' said Nahar Khan, 'was so that you may witness me carrying off my prize.'

Surtan was taken to Jaswant who insisted he appear at court. The Deora was adamant. He was never going to bow his head before any man. The Rathores worked out a strategy. To appear before the emperor, Surtan would have to pass through a gate that was knee-high. It would be impossible to negotiate it without resorting to a crawl. In a flash, the Deora lay down and wriggled through the gateway feet first, his head being the last to emerge before the emperor.

His stubborn pride coupled with Jaswant's interventions to ensure his well-being earned him the emperor's favour. Boldly Surtan asked for the restoration of Achilgarh, the fortress of the Deora princes of Abu and Sirohi. Never ever did the Deoras rank themselves among the vassals of the empire.

Leaving Marwar in the hands of his eldest son, Pirthi Singh, Jaswant left for the Khyber Pass accompanied by his wives and children. With the father out of the way, Aurungzeb commanded Pirthi Singh to court.

He was greeted with all the customary dignities due to his position. Then one day, with unusual familiarity, the emperor called him to his side. Pirthi Singh advanced, his hands folded in the traditional 'Hindu' salutation, the namaste.

Grasping both his hands firmly, Aurungzeb said, 'Well Rathore, I am told you are as great a warrior as your father. What can you do now?'[15]

'God preserve your majesty,' said the Rathore, 'when the sovereign of mankind lays the hand of protection on the meanest of his subjects, all his hopes are realised, but when he condescends to take both of mine, I feel as if I should conquer the world.'

'Ah! Another Khootan,' said Aurungzeb, using a term he reserved for Jaswant.

Affecting to be pleased with the reply, he ordered a splendid garment for Pirthi Singh. As was custom Pirthi Singh appeared before the emperor in his new robe and left with the certainty that his would be an exalted career.

That day was his last. He was ill even before he reached his residence. The poison from the robe burned its way into his flesh and he died in great agony.

The heir of Maroo was dead but the emperor had not finished with Jaswant.

---

15. This appears to be Aurungzeb's favourite question. It was put to many Rajputs and the answer was always the same — a tutored one but its outcome varied with the emperor's moods. The same reply won Raja (later maharaja) Jai Singh II of Amber the hereditary title of sawai, a title that the kings of Marwar had earned during the reign of Akbar.

grand designs. Aurungzeb was compelled yet again to have him superseded and this time Delhire Khan was sent as general to the Deccan. Delhire arrived at Aurangabad and that night would have surely been his last for Jaswant and Muazzam had been lying in wait. Delhire Khan fled, chased beyond the Narmada and Aurungzeb realised that keeping Jaswant in the Deccan was only adding to his troubles. He sent Jaswant to take over as viceroy of Gujarat.

Jaswant arrived at Ahmedabad to realise that the Mughal had outwitted him. There were orders waiting for him to continue marching north. He had been posted to beyond the Attock and it was understood that he would have to remain there permanently. The nearly savage race of Afghans would keep him busy leaving him no time nor opportunity to indulge in intrigues.

In 1671, leaving his eldest in charge of Marwar, Jaswant, accompanied by his two younger sons, embarked on his assignment. The Mughal's master plan worked perfectly. While Pirthi, the elder, fell victim to poison, seven years of the emperor's wars claimed the lives of the two younger princes. Grief claimed Jaswant.

He died in 1678 amidst the snow clad mountains of Jamrud (Peshawar) without an heir to avenge the house of Marwar.

Maharaja Ajit (Dhunni)

Two queens and nine wives of common rank mounted the pyre in Jamrud. Uday Kumpawat forcibly withheld the two youngest. They were soon to become mothers. Jai Sukh Devi, the Chandravati queen, who had remained behind in the capital, took a turban of her dead husband and committed sati at Mandor. The 'Hindus' were in despair. Jaswant's presence had kept Aurungzeb's excesses in check. The bells in the temples lay silent, as did the sacred conch.

On 19 February 1679, Jas Kanwar, the granddaughter of the maharaja of Karauli, gave birth to a son and he was named Ajit, the invincible. The Rathore contingent prepared to return to Jodhpur. Accompanied by his family, the infant Ajit began his first journey. At Lahore, a second son was born to Jaswant's youngest Kachwaha queen.

Sadly, the newborn did not survive the hardships of the journey to Delhi.

They had barely entered Delhi when summons arrived for the Rathore chiefs. The emperor offered to divide Marwar between them. All they needed to do was to hand the infant over. The emperor's guards had had them surrounded. The Rathores prepared to defend their honour. Ritual offerings were made to the gods and a double dose of opium issued to all. All women and children, including those of Jaswant's family, were led into a room filled with gunpowder. The torch was applied and the men were ready to give battle. Every clan did its duty and the day's events were likened to a pilgrimage.

The heir of Maroo had been smuggled out hidden in a basket of sweets and entrusted to the care of a faithful Muslim. At an appointed place in the depths of the desert, they waited until the gallant Durgadas and a few survivors, who had managed to cut their way out of Delhi, arrived to take charge of the infant. Ajit was taken to a monastery in Abu. The child grew up ignorant of his own identity but rumours persisted that a son of Jaswant still lived. The mere mention of the name Dhunni (lord) became a rallying point for his defence.

The Indu-Puriharas, the ancient sovereigns of Maroo, took the opportunity to fly their flag on the walls of Mandor. Inder Singh of Nagaur, the descendent of Umra Singh, made an attempt to regain the throne but the clans faithful to the memory of Jaswant would not have either of them.

Times were troubled for the 'Hindu' kingdoms. Aurungzeb led his army personally into Marwar. Jodhpur was occupied and plundered, as were the jagirs of Merta, Didwana and Rohit. Temples were torn down and every symbol of Hinduism trampled. Mosques were erected where temples once stood and nothing short of forcible conversions satisfied the tyrant. Seventy thousand men under Tyber Khan were commanded to destroy the Rajputs. Aurungzeb settled into Ajmer to watch and wait. The Merta clan arrived at Pushkar and engaged the imperial army. Before the temple of Varaha, the first swords of Maroo laid down their lives. Tyber continued to advance. The common people fled into the hills. Marwar decided to join forces with Maharana Raj Singh of Mewar. Feelers were sent to Aurungzeb's son, Akbar: the throne of

Delhi needed a new occupant. Akbar's interest was aroused, but the wily emperor soon received wind of the plot. The imperial army was within the control of Akbar and Tyber Khan and they both had agreed that assassination was the need of the hour. With the rest of his sons still far away, Aurungzeb took recourse to his wits. A letter was drafted; it appeared to be a secret communication between father and son. It was allowed to fall into the hands of the Rajput spies. As expected the reaction was that of hysteria and though Tyber went ahead at the appointed hour, he was alone and unsupported. The Rajputs had lost their opportunity.

Akbar chose to flee, making his way through the Deccan to Persia. He left his youngest daughter[16], Safiat-un-nisa, in the care of Durgadas who had escorted him all the way until he was safely in the care of Sambhaji Raje Bhosle, the Maratha king.

The clans clamoured for a glimpse of their prince. Mokund Kinchi could resist their pleas no longer. In an auspicious hour on the last day of the month of Chait, the prince was made known to the world. Durjan Sal Hada, an ex-chieftain of Bundi, was the first to lift his hand in salutation. Like the lotus bud that blossoms with first rays of sunlight, the heart of every Rathore brimmed over.

Inayat Khan, the emperor's minister, carried the tidings to Aurungzeb.

'If they could fight for so long without a head what is to be expected now?'

Inayat demanded reinforcements.

The young raja was brought to Awa, the seat of the premier noble of Maroo. The Champawat chief of Awa held a vessel of pearls, circling it over his head slowly. The badhoo over, the raja was presented with horses and preparations made for the teeka-dowr. Raipur, Bilara and Bharunda were taken and having visited the abodes of the

---

16. Prince Akbar had married his cousin Salima, the daughter of Suleiman Shikoh and his Rathorni wife – Anup Kanwar (daughter of Umra Singh by the sister of Mirza Raja Jai Singh of Amber). Their son – Nekusiyar – was to have his turn upon the imperial throne albeit for a very short while.

senior chiefs of Maroo, Ajit arrived at Pokaran. Here he met Durgadas, who had just returned from the Deccan.

Inayat Khan was alarmed. Aurungzeb set up a pretender[17]. The pretender did not survive the journey to Jodhpur and Sujait Khan was appointed hakim or governor of Marwar. Bands of Rathores resorted to guerrilla tactics and when the son of Inayat Khan left Jodhpur for Delhi, he was attacked by Jodha Harnat. Deprived of his wives and his wealth, he fled to the Kachwahas for aid. Sujah Beg, who set out from Ajmer to help him, was murdered by the Champawats.

Durgadas targeted Sefi Khan, hakim of Ajmer. Sefi took up position within a pass but was so badly cornered that he had to flee to the safety of Ajmer. The news reached Aurungzeb. He wrote to the khan.

'If you can control Durga I will raise you above all the khans. If not, be gracious enough to accept a gift of choories (bangles).'

Sefi tried to redeem himself. He wrote to Ajit that Aurungzeb had agreed to restore to him the lands of his father, that Sefi was in possession of the imperial orders and all Ajit needed to do was to come and collect them personally. Ajit marched at the head of 20,000 Rathores. Mokund Champawat rode ahead. The snare was detected.

'Let us at least have a sight of Ajaydurg now that we are so near,' said Ajit and they rode into the city.

At the sight of the Rathores the hakim lost his nerve. Trembling with fear Sefi Khan submitted to the raja of Marwar.

The hakims of Jodhpur, Jalor and Siwana combined their forces. Ajit retreated into the hills and prepared for a prolonged battle. With each year of Ajit's life, Rathore hopes grew and Aurungzeb turned increasingly anxious. Prince Akbar's daughter had been left in Durgadas's care. With every passing year, the grandfather pressed upon Sujait, the hakim of Jodhpur, to secure the princess's honour. Negotiations continued and

---

17. Listed amongst the sons of Maharaja Jaswant Singh, is Muhammadi-Raj who was born in 1675, and educated at the imperial court. He died of plague, at Bijapur, in November 1688 and is buried there. This was probably the pretender that Aurungzeb had in mind.

though Durgadas took nothing for himself, he demanded the return of Jalor, Sewanchi, Sanchor and Tharad. In 1696, the fifteen-year-old princess was returned and even Aurungzeb was all praises for the honourable treatment meted out to his granddaughter. Though Akbar had betrayed the family, his daughters were far from neglected. The six of them found husbands among their cousins, the sons of their uncle Muazzam.

In 1701, Ajit won Jodhpur back. He sacrificed a buffalo at each of its five gates but lost it two years later to Prince Azam. Ajit relocated to Jalor. The tyrant devoted himself to terrorising the ancient people of the land. The sacred cow was slaughtered in the holy cities of Mathura, Prayag and Okha. Ascetics chanted and invoked the heavens and the common man prayed to have his land cleansed of the 'barbarian'. In the month of Magh when the sun was in Gemini, Ajit's Chauhani queen gave birth to a son. He was called Abhay Singh.

From 1705, the star of the foe began to decline. The Rajputs were able to hold their ground and the imperial troops suffered increasing losses. Murshid Kuli Khan was appointed hakim of Jodhpur. On his arrival he presented Ajit with the firmaan of Merta, an honour which Mohkam, son of Inder Singh of Nagaur, had expected to receive. Infuriated, Mohkam wrote to the emperor to nominate him to the command of Marwar. The traitor's letter was intercepted by Ajit's men.

The good news came in March 1707. Aurungzeb was dead. Ajit rode to Jodhpur and sacrificed at the gates. The imperial garrison fled and those left behind faced the wrath of the Rathores, who were entering their homes after twenty-six years. Abandoning the wealth they had amassed over the years and invoking the names of Sita Ram and Har Govind, the Muslims took flight. Mosques were re-converted to temples and Ajit announced a shaving allowance to better distinguish his men from the Muslims. The faces of Rathores have sported no beards ever since.

Muazzam succeeded to the throne of Delhi as Emperor Shah Alam Bahadur Shah. On receiving news that Ajit had occupied Jodhpur, he hurried to Ajmer. Advised to resolve the situation peacefully, he sent Ajit the imperial firmaan for Jodhpur. Ajit arrived at Pipar to meet with the emperor who honoured him with the title Teg Bahadur or the warrior's sword. But there was villainy underfoot. Even as the meeting was in progress, Mairab Khan was sent on the sly to take possession of Jodhpur. The traitor Mohkam led the way. Ajit burned with rage. Compelled to hide his anger, he agreed to serve in the Deccan under Kam Baksh.

On his way, also proceeding to the Deccan was Jai Singh, the sawai raja of Amber, another man in the clutches of discontentment for the emperor had had a garrison and governor placed in his capital. The two rajas waited till the imperial army had crossed the Narmada and then without a word to anyone turned around and made their way to Udaipur. Maharana Amar Singh II advanced to meet them and there was a joyous reunion. With the chaori waving over their heads, a Rajput federation was created. Jodhpur and Amber regained the right to marry into the Sisodia royal family.

From Udaipur, the two rajas made their way to Jodhpur. Mehrangarh was surrounded by 30,000 Rathores. Mairab Khan was allowed an honourable retreat and Ajit entered his capital once again.

Jai Singh camped on the banks of the Sur Sagar until the monsoon months were past. The two rajas then made their way to Amber. When they reached Merta, Agra and Delhi trembled. As they approached Ajmer, the Mughal governor sought sanctuary and willingly paid the contributions demanded. Like a falcon, Ajit snatched up Sambhar and the chiefs and vassals of Amber gathered around Jai Singh's flag. As the imperial army approached, the Kumpawats led the charge. A desperate battle followed and the Muslims fled. The Indu-Purihara chief of Mandor fell into Ajit's hands and the Rathores were once again in possession of the ancient city. Jai Singh was restored to the throne of Amber.

Ajit targeted Bikaner and Nagaur. Inder Singh of Nagaur (Umra's grandson and the father of Mohkam) came and embraced Ajit's feet offering him the city of Ladnun. Ajit insisted upon Nagaur and Inder went to complain to the emperor. Jai Singh and Ajit united once again. The emperor arrived at Ajmer and sent a message of goodwill. The two rajas met him at Ajmer. Ajit was formally granted the nine castles of Maroo and Jai Singh, Amber. Paying their respects at the holy lake of Pushkar, the two rajas made their way home. That year Ajit married the Gaur princess and ended the feud that had begun with Arjun's slaying of Umra Singh in the Red Fort of Agra.

In 1713, Emperor Shah Alam Bahadur Shah passed away. The long patient wait under the shadow of his highly dominant father had earned him the nickname Shahi Bekhabar (royal ignoramus). But, to be fair to him, in the six years that were at his disposal, he had sought to undo the mischief created during his father's tenure. Alas, it was not to be and the house of Chagatai spiralled downhill into a mess of blood and turmoil. The unfortunate Jahandar Shah was declared emperor but was soon murdered by the kingmakers, the Syyed brothers Abdulla and Hussain Ali. Ajit was made the viceroy of Gujarat and Farukhsiyar emperor.

The Syyeds were now all powerful. Headstrong and arrogant, they summoned Ajit's seventeen-year-old son, Abhay, to court. Aware that the traitor Mohkam was at Delhi, Ajit sent, instead, a band of trusted men who slew the traitor in open court. This brought the Syyeds with their army to Jodhpur. All merchants fled, carrying their gold in quickly tied bundles of cloth. Ajit and his family took refuge in the desert. Jodhpur was occupied and the Syyeds demanded Abhay as hostage and Ajit's presence at Delhi. Reluctantly, Ajit agreed. Abhay became an officer of the court and was given a munsub of 5000.

Ajit followed and was forced into signing a treaty. His office of viceroy was renewed and he permitted to return to Jodhpur. The sight of the altars raised over the ashes of those brave Rathores who died trying to save his life filled him with pain and anger.

In an attempt to be rid of the controlling Syyed brothers, the emperor brought back Inayat Khan. With him came the ills of times of Aurungzeb, including the hated jaziya. The 'Hindus' despaired. In bargaining with the Syyed brothers for a share of power at court, Ajit abandoned the Rajput federation. He agreed to pay tribute and gave a daughter in marriage to Emperor Farukhsiyar. Durgadas, Ajit's loyal protector, found himself abandoned in his old age. With nowhere to go, the old man sought sanctuary in Mewar. A pension of 500 rupees a day was granted to him by Maharana Amar Singh II.

Soon there was war between the Syyeds and their opponents. Hussain Ali busied himself in the Deccan and Abdulla wrote letter after letter to Ajit. They plotted against Jai Singh and the Mughals. When Farukhsiyar heard that his father-in-law was in Delhi, he gave him a grand reception. Ajit was granted a munsub of Haft Hazari (7,000

Before his wedding with Maharajkumari Shri Indira Kanwar Baiji Lall Sahiba, HM Abu-l Fath Nasir-ud-din Muhammad Shah Shahid-i-Marhum Farukhsiyar Padhshah-i-Bahr-u-Bar, emperor of India desired to be rid of a tumour on his back. The presence of the tumour delayed the wedding, for the court physicians had been unable to come up with a cure.

Mr Hamilton, the British surgeon from Surat, was brought in and the operation successfully performed. As his reward, Mr Hamilton humbly requested that British traders be allowed to trade once again in India.

To the doctor, the East India Company was forever indebted but he lies in an unmarked grave in Kolkata, forgotten by those who amassed their fortunes directly as a result of his intervention.

The wedding was held at Delhi on 27 September 1715, and was quite the event of the season celebrated with true Asiatic pomp. To this wedding is ascribed the rise of the British.

With the death of the emperor, Ajit's daughter returned home to Jodhpur and converted back to the 'Hindu' faith.

horses), the Mahi Maratib – the order of the fish – elephants and horses, a sword and a dagger, a diamond jewel to be worn in his turban, a plume and a pearl necklace. At the hands of his son-in-law, Ajit received the hereditary titles of maharaja and raj rajeshwar – king of kings. From the emperor's court, he went directly to Abdulla. They swore to stand together. Ajit presented Farukhsiyar with extravagant presents the next day but at the same time, a letter recalling Hussain Ali had been despatched.

There was a change in the atmosphere of Delhi. The sky was unusually red and donkeys brayed ceaselessly. The dogs on the streets howled and thunder rolled though there was not a cloud in the sky. The citizens of Delhi, who had until now no reason to be unhappy, felt a sense of foreboding. Hussain Ali arrived and the sight of him struck terror in every heart. His nakarra beat outside the palace like a death knell and Delhi was enveloped in the dust raised by the hooves of his horses. The trembling emperor sent him congratulatory messages and gifts. The Mughal chiefs kept to the safety of their homes. Jai Singh was like a lamp without oil.

On the second day, Ajit marched at the head of the Rathores to the palace. His soldiers took control over every post. Ajit looked like death himself. The crash, which announced the death of Farukhsiyar, reverberated through the land. Not a soul stirred. Not one chief came to the aid of his emperor. Maharaja Sawai Jai Singh of Amber fled. The jaziya was repealed and all 'Hindus' were grateful to the maharaja of Marwar.

Between Ajit and the Syyed brothers, they set up one puppet emperor after another. Not one ruled for more than a couple of months. Grisly deaths lay in store for each one. Then in 1720, came Muhammad Shah, the one who would be known as Rangila or the colourful one. Gratitude poured from his lips but vengeance clouded his heart. Too many royals of the Chagatai household had fallen victim to the greed of the Syyeds. But the Syyeds were not done yet. On their list was the sawai maharaja. Terrified, he came to Ajit pleading for sanctuary. Ajit took Jai Singh under his wing.

The emperor bestowed Ahmedabad on Ajit and gave him permission to go home. With Jai Singh of Amber and Rao Raja Budh Singh Hada of Bundi, he left for Jodhpur.

Winter passed, spring was in the air and the intoxicated peacock danced among the sands of Maroo. Songs of joy filled the hearts of men and the lord of Amber, dressed in saffron, married Surya Kumari, the princess of Marwar[18].

The rains had just set in and word came to Marwar that the Syyed brothers had been murdered. The Mughals were on the look out for Ajit. Ajit drew his sword and swore to take Ajmer. Within twelve days, he had slain the governor and claimed Taragarh. In the year 1721, Ajmer resounded with the chanting of Vedic hymns and call of the muezzin was silenced. Sambhar and Didwana were taken and Ajit ascended the throne. The umbrella of supremacy waved over his head. Coins were struck in his name and he established his own system of weights and measures. New laws were formulated and new ranks created for his chiefs. Standards and banners, every emblem of an independent sovereign was created. Ajit in Ajmer was equal to the emperor in Delhi.

A year passed and Muhammad Shah determined once again to regain Ajmer. General Muzzaffer advanced towards Marwar. Ajit left the warfare to Abhay, 'the shield of Maroo'. The fearless Abhay, with eight great vassals and 30,000 horses took to the field. To his right stood the Champawats and to his left the Kumpawats. The imperial army was met at Amber. At the sight of the Rathores, Muzzaffer locked himself within the walls of Amber. Exasperated at having no battle to fight, Abhay attacked Shahjahanpur, sacked Narnaul and levied contributions on Patan and Rewari. Villages were plundered and set afire. The Muslims fled from 'Dhonkul', the terminator.

Abhay remained behind at Sambhar and Ajit came to meet him. The father's heart was filled with pride, for his son had broken the spirit

18. Ajit's daughter, Surya Kumari, had been engaged to Maharaja Sawai Jai Singh II in 1708. The actual date of marriage has been recorded as 19 May 1720. Ajit had married two princesses from Mewar, Shri Rani Udot Kanwarji Maji Sahiba — daughter of Maharaj Shri Gaj Singh Sahib, the brother of Maharana Jai Singh of Mewar in 1694 — and in 1709, as his fourth wife, Shri Bada Sisodini Rani Kalyan Kanwarji Maji Sahiba — eldest daughter of Maharajadhiraj Maharawat Shri Prithvi Singh Bahadur of Pratapgarh. Both Mewari queens gave birth to daughters. It was Rani Udot Kanwarji's daughter, Indira, who was given in marriage to Emperor Farukhsiyar in flagrant violation of the stipulation imposed by the maharana of Mewar.

of the Mughals and made every 'Hindu' heart happy. The emperor sent his emissary, Nahar Khan, to deal with Ajit. His language was coarse and it offended the Rathores. The fields of Sambhar devoured the tiger lord and his 4,000 soldiers.

The son of Choraman the Jat claimed sanctuary with Ajit. Choraman was on his way to becoming the founder of the Bharatpur state.

The unhappy Muhammad Shah was tired of battles but his heart still ached for revenge. Collecting his army, he put them under Jai Singh and attacked Ajmer. Abhay marched out leaving the defence to his garrison. Ajmer held out for four months. In the end, Ajit was forced to listen to the emperor's stipulations through Jai Singh. Terms were sworn on the *Koran* and Ajit agreed to the surrender of Ajmer. The khans took Rao Inder Singh, the great-grandson of Umra Singh, by the arm and seated him in Nagaur.

Abhay Singh was presented at court. The heir of Marwar was received with the utmost honour. Assuming, that he would occupy his father's allotted seat, the arrogant youth strode past the assembled dignitaries. Not a thought had he for the etiquette of the proudest court in the world. One foot had already been planted on the steps that led to the throne when a nobleman stopped him. Abhay's hand was instantly on his dagger. The court waited with bated breath. The performance that the Agra court had witnessed seemed about to be repeated for Umra Singh and Abhay were related by blood. With unusual presence of mind, the emperor cast about Abhay's neck, his own jewelled necklace restraining him.

The annals of Marwar have a sad tale to recount at the end of Ajit's saga. He was murdered by his sons, both born of his senior Chauhan queen. Abhay sent instructions from Delhi and Bakhta carried out the dreadful deed.

Bakhta Bakhta bawara	Oh crazed Bakhta
Kyon mara Ajmal?	Why did you kill Ajit?
Hindwani ka sahara	The pillar of the 'Hindu'
Toorkani ka sal	The lance of the Turk

The bards of Maroo prefer not to dwell on the topic and say instead that Ajit took the road to paradise in 1724. Six queens and fifty-eight wives of common origin chose to burn with him. Dressed as new brides and chanting the name of Hari they climbed the pyre.

The gods above cried 'Dhanya Dhanya Ajit who maintained the faith and overwhelmed the Asuras.'

Forty-six years had been the span of Ajit's life.

The political situation of Maroo was to affect the fates of the sons of Ajit. Some were adopted by noble houses who, for the lack of an heir, looked to the house of their sovereign. The curious fact about these adoptions was that the issue of younger brothers adopted into a foreign or independent states maintained their claim to the throne while all such claims were nullified by adoption into a home clan.

Devi Singh was adopted by the head of the junior Champawat clan of Pokaran. Though he surrendered all claim to the gaddi of Marwar, he wielded tremendous power over the occupant of the throne.

Anand Singh had been adopted into the independent state of Idar and his descendents remained heirs-presumptive to the throne of Marwar.

While at the court of the desert king, a day was set aside entirely to be spent rambling through the ruins of Mandor. Five miles from Jodhpur lay the ancient capital. Escorted by the maharaja's men the captain set out on the road to Nagaur. Through the Sojat gate, past the Maha Mandir – that Maan Singh had built to celebrate his escape from Jalor – skirting the range of hills for nearly three miles they entered a gorge in the mountains. Almost perpendicular cliffs surrounded the narrow pass that led to the ancient capital of the Puriharas. Soon it widened a little and a glimpse of that which lay ahead arrested all attention. In a line stood lofty temples, each a cenotaph for a crowned head of Maroo, standing upon the site where the Rathore was cremated. A small stream of sweet water that arose at the mouth of the pass flowed past the monuments. In the simple shrines of Chunda and Jodha, the temple-like monument for Maldeo and the magnificent mausoleum for Ajit lay a mute testimony to the once simple desert kingdom, now ruled by the sons of Ajit in show of pomp and glamour.

Beyond the fortress, stood memorials to Rao Ranmal, Rao Ganga and Rao Chunda. At a distance of hundred yards, was the area that had been set aside for queens who had died natural deaths. From the cemetery of the Rathores a paved path led to the city of the Puriharas.

Halfway up the ascent stood a reservoir excavated from solid rock. It served as the memorial to Nahar Rao, the last of the Puriharas. The Purihara palace stood commanding the vantage point in the centre of the fortress, recalling the days of yore when long distance artillery warfare was completely unknown. Remnants of massive bastions and towers remained, the square shape a reminder of its antiquity. Much of the material had been re-used in the construction of Jodhpur and the cenotaphs. Symbolic figures used in Buddhist and Jain architecture as well as the hexagram of the worshippers of Shiva and Shakti adorned the walls. But no amount of hunting nor enquiry could reveal the site where the ashes of the Puriharas reposed.

A little distance to the north, lay the grave of a Muslim saint, Thana Pir – a disciple of Khwaja Qutub of Ajmer – a place revered by the mercenaries of Sind and Afghanistan.

Down by the glen of the Pushkunda, welled up the serpentine rivulet, the Nagda. Here in a cave lay the altar to Nahar Rao, who had defied the Chauhans of Ajmer. Strangely, it was a barber who performed the office of priest here. Here lay a piece of sculpture with nine figures that was said to represent Raavan, the king of that distant isle, Tambrapane (Sri Lanka), who came during the epic age to marry Mandodari, the princess of Mandor. Two gates stood nearby, one that led to Maharaja Ajit's palace and the other to the memorials to the heroes of the desert.

The archway leading to the memorials opened into a courtyard, which led to a chamber built into the side of the mountain. The roof

Nahar Rao, the Purihara lord, sent word to the Mers. The passes of the Aravalli needed defending, for Prithviraj Chauhan of Ajmer had announced his intention: the invasion of Mandor. The mountain tribes gathered and four thousand bowmen heard and obeyed. Men who never moved without an omen, whose arrows never flew in vain, concealed themselves in the dark recesses.

Tidings reached the Chauhan that the manly Mer stood in the mountain gorge. He called for Kana and bade him clear the pass.

Bowing Kana departed and advanced against the mountaineer who remained immovable. But the arrows carried death and warriors fell from their steeds. Dismounting, he resorted to a hand to hand combat. The lance flew through the breast appearing at the back, like a fish escaping through the meshes of a net. Evil spirits danced in the mire of blood. The hero of the mountain dealt Kana a blow. But like lightening it was returned.

The Chauhan band struck the Sindhu Raaga, the hymn of victory, and Nahar Rao arrived seeking vengeance for the blood of his brother. In person he sought out Prithviraj.

was supported by three rows of columns in the Jain architectural style. An enormous statue of Ganesh stood at the entrance accompanied by two statues of Bhiroo, the god of war; Chamunda, the goddess of destruction; and Kanakali, her eight arms bearing weapons of war. Nathji, the spiritual guide of the Rathores, stood next with rosary and churri in hand. Displayed within were statues of legendary warriors astride steeds with names as deathless as their riders. Carved out of the rock upon which they stood, robed in the costumes of their day and wearing expressions of grim defiance were Mallinath – astride his white charger, returning from a raid, lance over his shoulder, quiver resting against his horse's flank, being greeted by his queen, Padmavati; Pabooji astride Kesar Kali, his black steed and Ramdeo Rathore, who is honoured in every Rajput village. Hurba Sankhla, who had supported the exiled Rao Jodha and helped redeem Mandor, stood beside Goga Chauhan who, with his forty-seven sons, had stood against the armies of Islam defending the passage across the Sutlej. Mehwoh Mangulia Gehlote, a famous chieftain, brought up the rear.

Another chamber, larger than the last, displayed the gypsum and stone statues of the taintees cul devta rajasthan or the tutelary divinities of thirty-three races.

The second gate led to Maharaja Ajit's palace and gardens, of which the captain had but one word to say: 'superb.' The colonnaded halls were covered with sculptures of easy and even graceful execution, some with screens of lattice work to secure the ladies from public gaze. The gardens, delightfully cool even in the summer, with fountains, reservoirs and water-courses, boasted several varieties of exotic plants.

Let the reader imagine the picture of a solitary Englishman scribbling amidst the ruins of Mandor: in front of a group of venerable mango trees; a little further an enormous isolated tamarind, planted by the hand of a juggler in the time of Nahar Rao...and as the legend goes, from whose branches the juggler met his death: amidst its boughs the long armed

Goga ruled from the banks of the Sutlej to the plains of Haryana.

The powerful Chauhan despaired, for he had no children. His patron goddess offered two cobs of barley (jav) to be given to his queen. Goga gave one to his queen and the other to his favourite mare.

The mare gave birth to Javadia who was to become as famous as his master.

Captain Tod himself owned a steed named Javadia gifted to him by the maharana of Mewar.

*tribe, the allies of Rama, were skipping and chattering
unmolested; while beneath two Rathore Rajputs were stretched
in sleep, their horses dozing beside them, standing as sedately
as the statue of Kesar Kali: a grenadier sepoy of my escort
parading by a camp basket, containing the provender of the
morning, completes the calm and quiet scene.*

The captain concluded his evening with one last visit to the heroes
of the desert, inscribing his name at Kesar Kali's feet.

Maharaja Abhay Singh (Dhonkul)

In 1724, Emperor Muhammad Shah Rangila with his own hand applied
the teeka of investiture on Abhay's forehead. He girt him with the
sword, bound the torah upon his head and placed a dagger set with
gems in his belt. With chaoris, nobuts and nakarras he invested Abhay
as maharaja of Marwar. Nagaur was taken away from the line of Umra
Singh and bestowed upon Jodhpur.

Abhay's coronation did not bode well for the empire. Though not
directly responsible, it was carried out in an atmosphere of vibrant
animosity. Nizam-ul-Mulk Chin Qilich Khan who had also been
appointed to the post of wazir, unhappy at the disorder that had become
the way of life, retired voluntarily and left for his province. Though
he did not formally declare independence, he ruled from Hyderabad
and tolerated no interference. But his example ignited a chain reaction
and Avadh and Bengal followed suit.

On his way home, Abhay visited every village. Every chief and
village elder waited to greet the new maharaja. Women came forward,
one from every family. Shining brass pots of water were offered in
homage and the Suhaila – the song of joy – wafted on the air
throughout the land of Marwar. Karna, the bard, whose ancestor had
served the royal house of Jaichand of Kannauj, sat at the gate of
Jodhpur and added yet another chronicle to his work. The kavisvar,

lord of rhymes, was at once a politician, a warrior and a poet.

Young and ambitious, Abhay was the prime catch in Rajasthan. He had already proved his prowess as an army commander and was admired by all in the Mughal court and in Rajasthan. Barely had he become king of Maroo when Maharaja Sawai Jai Singh of Jaipur offered him his daughter's hand in marriage. Chatur Kanwar and Abhay were married within three months of his accession and it was not too long before Maharana Sangram Singh II of Mewar sought Abhay as a son-in-law.

The festivities over, Abhay prepared to take Nagaur back from his cousin, Rao Inder Singh. Soon after Holi the cannons were brought out and readied. Goats were sacrificed to Jwala Mukhi[19] and blood, oil and vermilion were sprinkled upon the cannons. The news reached Nagaur and Inder Singh brought out the imperial sanction with which went the personal guarantee of Jai Singh of Amber. Abhay paid no heed. Nagaur he bestowed on his brother Bakhta Singh.

In 1727, Abhay was summoned to court. The emperor welcomed him warmly. He was still at court when news arrived: a rebellion had broken out in the Deccan. An army of 60,000 Marathas had attacked and slain the imperial governors. Sirbulland Khan was appointed to quash to the rebellion. The khan marched at the head of 50,000 men and was defeated in the very first encounter. He then quickly entered into an agreement with the rebels and arranged to divide the country between themselves. Abhay was appointed viceroy of Gujarat and charged with the responsibility of putting down the rebellion. The new viceroy of Gujarat and Ajmer, drew arms from the imperial armoury and, with imperial legions under his command, left Delhi. But the first priority was to put his own affairs in order. He arrived at Ajmer, where Jai Singh of Amber was waiting for him. The two plotted the fall of the empire. At Merta, he was joined by his brother, Bakhta, and together they arrived at Jodhpur. The vassals of Jodhpur and Amber had already assembled beneath the walls of Mehrangarh.

Instead of making his way to the Deccan Abhay turned his attention

---

19. The mouth of flame is a volcano, which is regarded as a form of the mother goddess.

Seated upon his throne, Muhammad Shah Rangila was surrounded by seventy-two grand nobles when news arrived. Sirbulland Khan had turned against the empire. To every one at court it was obvious that were the situation not set right immediately, more revolts would follow and the empire would disintegrate.

But when the beera, on its golden plate, was passed around, not one of the mighty nobles accepted it. No one wished to contend with Sirbulland Khan. The almighty badshah, who could reduce an umara (noble) of 12,000 to a beggar and raise a beggar to an umara, was left without resource.

The beera was making its way back when the badshah's distress touched Abhay's heart and he, who was on the point of returning to Jodhpur, reached out for it. The visibly relieved emperor thrust the grant of Gujarat into Abhay's hands.

'It was your ancestors that upheld the throne of Jahangir when Khurram and Bheem rebelled. It will be you that will protect the honour of the throne of Muhammad Shah.'

The hearts of the nobles were as ready to burst with envy as a ripe pomegranate, overflowing with its rich red juice, that can withstand the hot summer sun no longer.

upon his neighbour, the gallant Deora-Chauhans of Sirohi. Cornered by the superior army, Rao Narayan Das offered a daughter in marriage and tribute that would fill the coffers of Jodhpur. The Deora contingents accompanied the royal army and the march began.

They halted on the banks of the Saraswati and an envoy was sent to Sirbulland Khan. The self-declared king of Gujarat ignored the warning. Each of his gates was manned by 2,000 men and five cannons of European design. His personal bodyguards were Europeans. Bakhta led the charge. A great battle followed, with huge losses on both sides but in the morning that followed, it was Sirbulland Khan who surrendered.

Leaving a garrison behind in Gujarat, Abhay returned to Jodhpur. He brought back with him the spoils of Gujarat, 4,000 crores of rupees and 400 guns of every description[20].

By 1732, Abhay and Maharaja Sawai Jai Singh had realised that the Marathas were more determined than they had been given credit for. Their kingdoms, they decided, came first. Baji Rao Peshwa was appointed subedar of Malwa and Gujarat was handed over, with Abhay keeping the border villages for himself.

With Malwa, Gujarat and Bundelkhand under their belt, the Marathas appeared suddenly in 1737, at the gates of Delhi. They were bought off for the moment. But the weakness at the helm did not fail to attract a Turk who had just murdered his way to the Persian throne. Nadir Shah arrived in 1739.

When Maharana Jagat Singh II ascended the Sisodia throne in 1734,

---

20. The trophies of the Gujarat campaign, including Sirbulland Khan's carriage, remain on display at Mehrangarh.

Abhay could now indulge himself and a magnificent palace was ordered in 1730. It was on a Tuesday in the month of Bhadon when the maharaja's men, in the search of timber to be used in the lime-kilns, arrived at the village of Khejarli. Amrita Devi, a Bishnoi woman, was quick to protest for living green trees were sacred to the Bishnoi faith. She clung to the tree that was being cut down and was beheaded in the process. Following their mother's lead, her three young daughters sacrificed their lives. The news spread like wild fire and the peaceful Bishnois gathered. Word reached the maharaja and he hurried to the troubled area. But by then, 363 members of the community had lost their lives. The maharaja put an end to the massacre and ordered that the laws of the Bishnoi sect be respected.

an abortive attempt had been made at re-establishing the Rajput Federation. Mewar had fallen far behind, both militarily and financially. Though outwardly Abhay maintained a pretence of submitting to the twenty-five-year-old's traditional authority, the federation proved to be an unqualified disaster

As the years sped by, Abhay's love for ease and opium increased. With it was a growing apprehension that his brother's true genius for warfare was being stifled. The high-spirited Bakhta was ambitious and Nagaur too small a field for his talents. A window of opportunity soon opened. Maharaja Zorawar Singh of Bikaner had given offence. Bikaner, though independent, accepted the maharaja of Marwar as superior and Abhay decided, in 1740, to teach his kinsman a lesson, while Bakhta found it to be just what he had been waiting for. Bakhta wrote to Jai Singh of Amber.

The sawai raja in his last years had grown fond of wine and had given orders that no official work was to be brought to him when he was under the influence of alcohol. Bakhta's envoy was clever man. He had a good friend in Vidyadhar Bhattacharya, a Bengali Brahmin who was the civil minister of state and the architect of the new city of Jaipur. Through him, he managed an audience while the raja was enjoying a glass of wine.

'Bikaner is in danger and without you it will fall.'

'My master,' he added, 'considers Jaipur his suzerain and not Marwar.'

Wine and vanity did the rest. Jai Singh put pen to paper. He wrote to his son-in-law to forgive Bikaner and to remove his army. As he picked up another cup of wine and twirled his moustache the envoy pleaded:

'Two more words maharaj, add just two more words.'

Jai Singh added: 'Or my name is not Jai Singh.'

Abhay's courage had been legendary as his contempt for the Kachwahas. The scholarly Jai Singh was often showered with sarcasm even in the presence of the emperor. Jai Singh decided that his son-in-law needed to be taught a lesson.

Taking his cue from the sawai maharaja, Kriparam, the emperor's favourite chess partner, praised the Rathore's dexterity in slicing off a buffalo's neck with a single stroke. So effervescent were his praises that it led to a request for a demonstration.

People thronged to the arena. A specially bred bull from the luxuriant fields of Haryana was led in. Taking one look at its enormous bulk, Abhay begged the emperor for leave. He returned, having taken a double dose of opium. As he grasped his sword with both hands and raised it above the buffalo's head, his eyes met those of Jai Singh's.

Abhay's eyes were red with rage and opium. He brought his sword down and as the massive head dropped onto his knees the Rathore was thrown backwards. Jai Singh leaned and whispered to the emperor – maintaining a safe distance from Abhay for a while would be advisable.

Never again did the emperor ask for a demonstration of Abhay's skills.

The overjoyed envoy sent off the letter by the swiftest camel in the desert. The letter was to reach Abhay before Jai Singh came to his senses.

Scarcely had the envoy left that the chiefs of Amber entered. Messenger after messenger was sent to intercept the letter but Bakhta's envoy had done his work well. Soon a reply came back.

'By what right do you dictate to me? If your name is the Lion of Victory mine is the Fearless Lion.'

The chiefs of Amber and Jaipur knew that there was no going back. A call was sent out to all vassals and friends. A hundred thousand men collected below the Amber Fort. They marched to Gangwani at the border of Marwar. Abandoning the war with Bikaner, Abhay rounded up his troops and left to defend Jodhpur. Bakhta was terrified. Never in his wildest dreams had he thought that his scheme would be blown so out of proportion. He had no desire to embroil his country in a war. He pleaded with his brother. With the vassals of Nagaur, he would bear the brunt of the battle. Abhay was not averse to seeing his brother punished.

Bakhta chose 8,000 Rajputs who had sworn to die for him. He handed out an infusion of opium and dipping his hand into a bowl of saffron water, placed the imprint of his right hand on each man's heart. Then he led them through a field thick with corn. 'Let no man come who is not prepared for victory or death. If any of you wish to return do so now.' Five thousand emerged from the field.

In a tightly packed group, the army of Bakhta charged and cut through the legions of Amber. Sixty emerged. The vassals with great difficulty led the reluctant Bakhta off the field.

One Rathore equalled ten Kachwahas and even the bards of Jai Singh could not refrain from singing the glory of Bakhta. Karna, the bard, prevented Bakhta from making another charge. It was when Jai Singh left the field that Bakhta realised the enormity of his loss. He wept, for he believed Marwar was lost and it was not until Abhay came to assure him that he regained his composure. The maharana of Mewar intervened to prevent the quarrel from going any further. The image of Bakhta's god had fallen into the hands of Jai Singh. It was married with great ceremony to the image of Kali of Amber and returned to Bakhta with Jai Singh's compliments.

Abhay Singh died in 1750, at Jodhpur.

It was in Abhay's time that Nadir Shah invaded India. Delhi had been sacked mercilessly but not a single Rajput prince stirred from his palace or sent aid to Muhammad Shah Rangila. In 1748, a month before the emperor died, Nadir Shah's Afghan minion, Ahmad Shah Abdalli (Durrani) had returned. Maharaja Sawai Ishwari Singh of Jaipur had been present that day at Sirhind when Wazir Qamr-ud-din Khan lost his life and Safdarjang saved the day by offering tribute. It was but a matter of months before Abdalli returned. Punjab was physically occupied. The Marathas decided that their turn at empire building had arrived. Their dreams of glory brought great pain to Mewar, Jaipur and Hadavati. Marwar remained hitherto unaffected.

The long shadows cast by the towering Aravalli inched along the gently undulating plains of Merta bent upon touching its western-most edge.

This land had been drenched on more than several occasions by the best Rathore blood, but it was the spires of Aurungzeb's mosque, rising high over the ruins of a 'Hindu' temple, that arrested the eye. Merta was home to the first swords of Maroo, whose celebrated daughter – Princess Mira Bai, mystic poetess and devotee of Krishna – had married the heir of the exalted Maharana Sanga of Mewar. Rao Duda who had established himself here had been Rao Jodha's fourth son and yet Rao Maldeo had not hesitated in annexing the land and renaming its great fort Malkote.

Merta's rightful heir, Jaimal, turned his back on Maroo forever. Mewar welcomed him with open arms and Maharana Uday Singh honoured the prince with the charge of his fort and the fief of Badnor. Badnor that had once been a Solanki property granted by Maharana Raimal to Tara Bai's father was handed to the Rathore for all time to come. When Emperor Akbar came for Chittaur, sixty-year-old Jaimal Rathore made the supreme sacrifice going down in Mewar's history as one of its greatest heroes.

Merta, that had given birth to legends and upon whose plains unfolded the drama of Marwar's destiny, lay uncared for, gradually becoming a part of the ever expanding desert.

Maharaja Ram Singh

Nineteen-year-old Ram Singh succeeded to the splendid kingdom that his father had put together from the tottering empire of the Mughals. He was at that dangerous age when the strong hand of a father is needed the most. Brash and immature, he almost immediately alienated his uncle, Bakhta, who held the fief of Nagaur and Jalor. Nor were the Champawats or Kumpawats spared the ire of their new sovereign.

Bakhta Singh absented himself from the coronation ceremony. Instead of personally anointing his sovereign's forehead with the teeka and swearing fealty, he sent his old nurse to do the needful. Ram Singh demanded an immediate surrender of his jagirs. The army was ordered to move. The old chief of the Champawats rushed to calm the newly crowned king. Scarcely had he taken his seat, when his sovereign turned upon him, expressing a desire to see as little of his frightful face in court as possible. The old man dashed his shield upon the carpet.

'Young man,' he cried, 'you have mortally offended a Rathore. I can turn Marwar upside down as easily as this shield.'

He rose and left.

It was past midnight when Bakhta heard of the arrival of the chief noble of Maroo at his border. He left immediately to welcome him. Stopping the attendants from waking the old man, Bakhta waited quietly by the foot of his bed. The Champawat awoke and as he called for his pipe, his eyes fell upon Bakhta. He scrambled to his feet. Sleep had cooled his rage and the realisation of the day's events hit him with full force.

'My head is now yours,' he said.

Ram Singh did not permit his uncle time to gather a force. The plains of Merta were fixed as the battle site. The first swords of Maroo rallied around their sovereign, as did the rest of the clans of Jodha. Most believed in loyalty to the throne, barring a few that chose to remain neutral. The Rathores of Bikaner, indebted as they were, took part in Marwar's civil war. Both Maharaja Abhay Singh and Maharaja Ram Singh had conspired against Bikaner time and again and Maharaja Gaj Singh was determined to cut out the canker once and for all.

The battle began with Bakhta's cannons saluting his sovereign and nephew but as friend encountered friend and brother crossed swords with brother all ties of kinship were forgotten. The first swords of Maroo sealed their fealty in blood, fighting till the clan was near extinction.

Unable to withstand Bakhta's artillery power, Ram Singh retreated to his barricaded city and fled in the dead of the night to enlist the help of the Marathas. Raja Shahu Bhosle had been dead these many years and his peshwa, Nana Sahib, controlled the Maratha nation. Jai Appa Scindia was deputed to fight Ram Singh's battles. Six battles followed but Ram Singh was defeated. He took sanctuary in Jaipur.

Maharaja Bakhta Singh

Bakhta was enthroned in Jodhpur and his aan was proclaimed through the land. The chief of Bagri applied the teeka and girded Bakhta with the sword.

The Maratha advanced from Ujjain and Bakhta proceeded to the mountain passes beyond Ajmer to meet him. When Scindia arrived to set Ram Singh upon the throne, he found to his surprise the choicest swords of Maroo arrayed against him. His primary intention of plundering Marwar

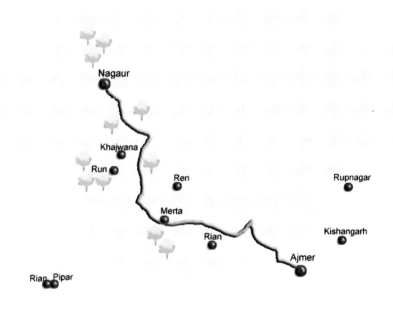

Nagaur

Khajwana

Run

Ren

Rupnagar

Merta

Rian

Kishangarh

Rian Pipar

Ajmer

odhpur

Modern district of Nagaur

Modern road from Ajmer to Nagaur

Beejy Singh fled from Merta to Nagaur

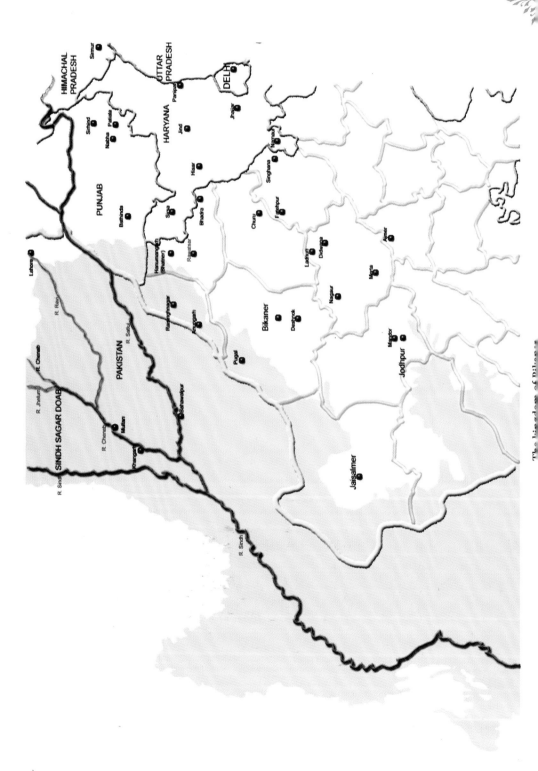

The kingdom of Bikaner

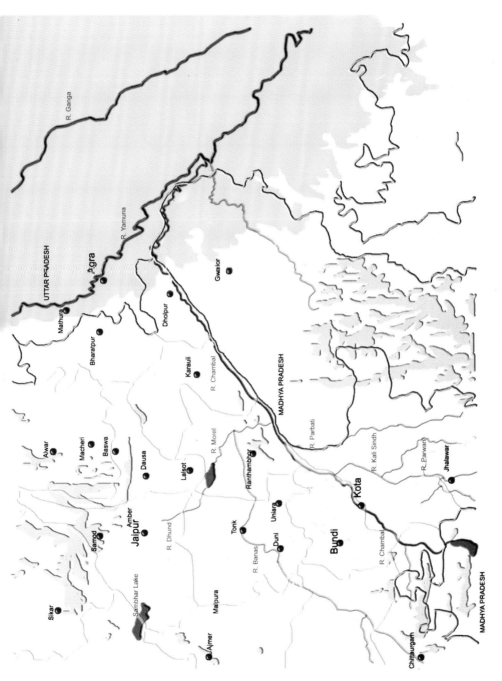

The jagirs of Hadavati

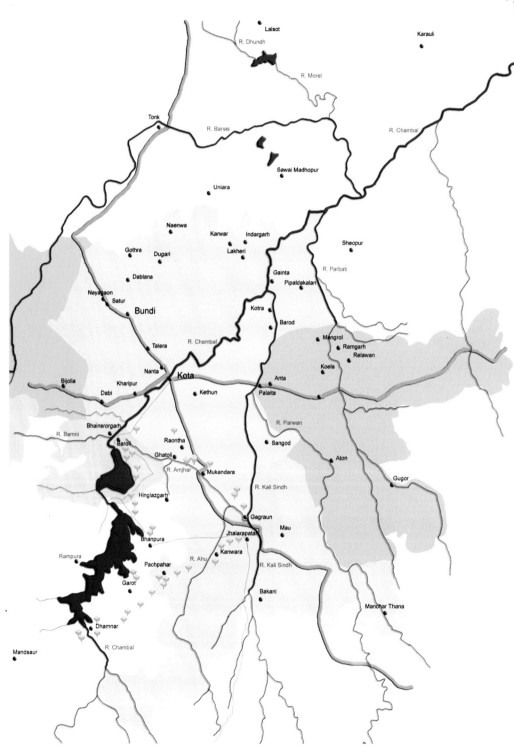

Trail followed by Captain Tod around Kota

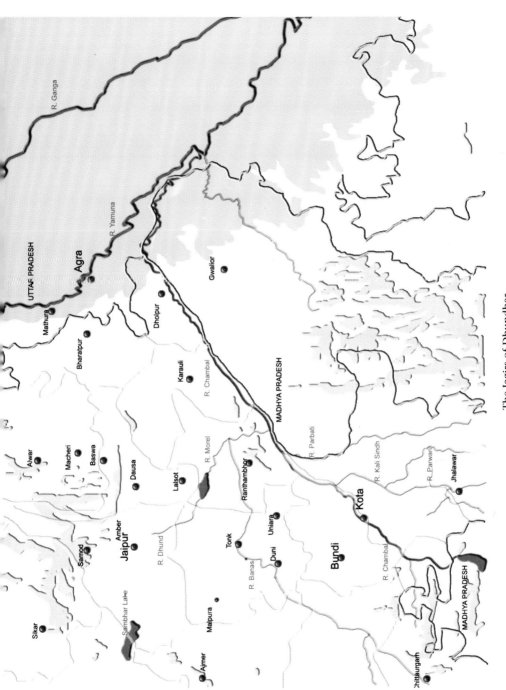

The Jagirs of Dhundhar

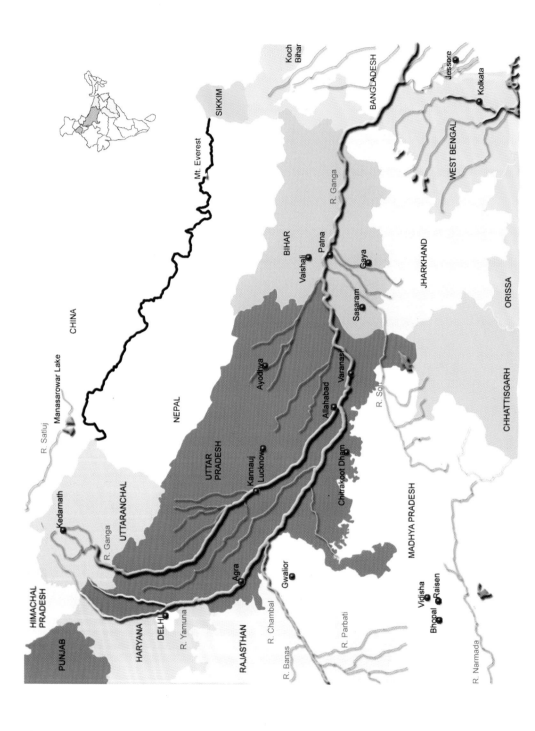

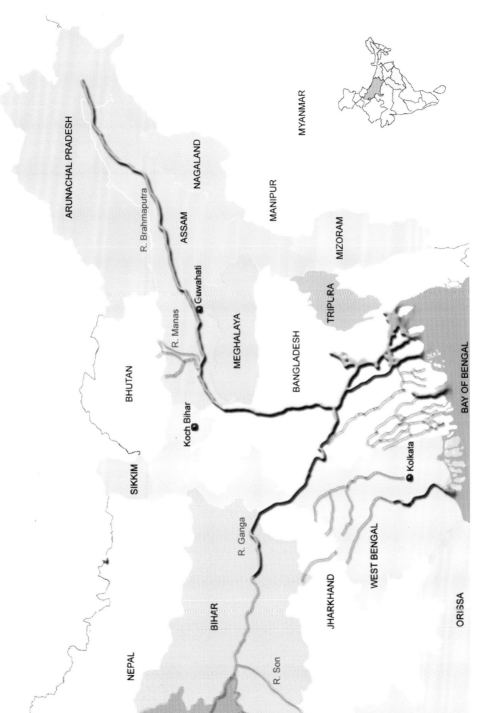

Mughal campaigns in Assam

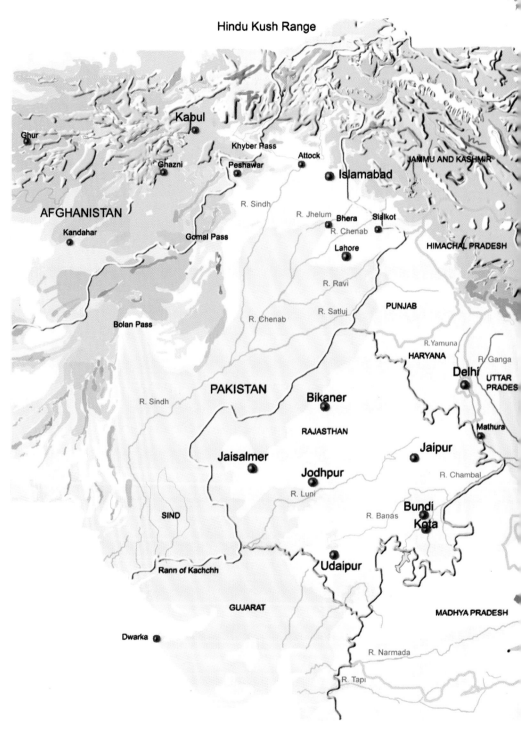

The descendents of Lord Krishna fled, abandoning Dwarka and Mathura, to set up kingdoms in the mountains of the north west – Bhera (Hill of Jud), Peshawar and Ghazni.

Of the gallantry of the sub vassals of Merta, the death of the heir of Mehtri lives on in verse.

Kan a moti bulbula	With pearls in his ears
Gula soni a mala	Gold necklaces about his
Assi kos kurro ho aya	Across eighty kos came
Kanwar Mehtri wala	The heir of Mehtri

The youth, who had long been engaged to the daughter of the chief of the Nirukas, was in the midst of his wedding when news arrived: the armies of Maharaja Ram Singh and Bakhta Singh had engaged. Though the knot had just been tied and their hands barely joined, his Merta blood was aroused and tearing himself away from the fair Niruki he left to court the apsara on the battlefield.

With pearls in his ears and gold beads about his neck, the heir of Mehtri arrived having ridden a span of eighty kos to join his father and brothers.

The bride's doli arrived to be greeted not by music and gaiety but by lamentations and tears. Commanding the pyre to be lit, she accompanied her new husband to the mansion of the sun.

To the aid of Ram Singh came five thousand Jarejas whose queen was skilled in the art of the augur. On the eve of battle, an inauspicious raven perched upon her tent but before it could crow thrice the queen had drawn her matchlock and shot it dead. The impetuous king was enraged at this show of disrespect and ordered her begone. The Rajputni pleaded to be allowed to stay and help but in the end was forced to leave. Sorrowfully, she predicted that her exile would cost the maharaja his crown.

was out of the question for every son of Sihoji had gathered to keep the Maratha from meddling in their internal affairs. Scindia refused to give battle.

Bakhta remained encamped in the passes, the vulnerable point, which gave the enemy access to Marwar. He sent word to Maharaja Sawai Madho Singh of Jaipur. The sawai maharaja was required to confirm allegiance or declare himself a foe for Ram Singh was the late Sawai Ishwari Singh's son-in-law. Madho Singh pretended to support Bakhta and sent his queen who was the daughter of Bakhta's own brother, Rai Singh. Rai Singh and his elder brother Anand Singh, both sons of Ajit's second Chauhani rani, had evicted their relatives who formed the royal house of Idar and jointly ruled the kingdom which comprised of Idar, Ahmadnagar, Morasa, Baad and Soor.

The Rathorni came bearing gifts, sweets and flowers. Among them was a poisoned robe to avenge the murder of her grandfather, Ajit.

The maharaja was soon in the throes of a fever, which the doctor claimed was beyond cure. Assembling his chiefs, he declared his son, the twenty-eight-year-old Beejy Singh, his successor. But before he closed his eyes he repeated the words that his mother had said to him as she led the satis to Ajit's funeral pyre.

'May your corpse be consumed in a foreign land.'

A cenotaph was raised over his cremation site and it came to be known as the Booro Dewul, the 'Shrine of Evil'.

But for that one foul stain Maharaja Bakhta was perhaps one of the finest princes of his race. He had been instrumental in the recovery of Gujarat from the hands of Sirbulland Khan. His elevation to the throne had never been considered usurpation for Ram Singh had been deemed incapable. All Maroo swore to uphold the rights of Bakhta's son, Beejy Singh.

During his two years as king, Bakhta found time to fortify the capital. His spoils from the Ahmedabad campaign were added to the collection at Mehrangarh and his throne became the seat for future investiture ceremonies.

During his rule, the Muslim's call to prayer was forbidden through out Marwar.

There was a joyousness about Bakhta's soul that attracted friends. A large man with a majestic bearing, Bakhta was well versed in literature and poetry. The clans loved him and he would have gone down in history, as one of the noblest princes of Rajasthan were it not for the fact that he bore the blood of his father upon his hands.

The nobles were happier with Bakhta but the royal priest, Jugga, was torn by his loyalty to Ram Singh. He went to the Deccan to enlist the aid of the Marathas. Bakhta wrote to Jugga.

'O bee, the flower that long gave you pleasure has now been shed. Not a leaf is left on the rose bush. Why do you cling to its thorns?'

He received an equally poetic rejection.

'The bee clings to the denuded rose bush in the hope that spring may return and the bush may flower once again.'

Bakhta was gracious enough to respect Jugga's feelings.

Despite the adulation they claimed, neither Abhay nor Bakhta were ever forgiven the heinous crime that set them upon Jodha's throne. At Pushkar, where both Abhay and Jai Singh were offering prayers, a bard unwilling to let people forget recited the following verse:

Jodhpur aur Amber	Jodhpur and Amber
Doono thap oot hap	Can dethrone the enthroned
Koorma mara deekro	But Koorma killed his son[21]
Kamdhwaj mara baap	And Kamdhwaj his father

---

21. Koorma or Jai Singh had supposedly killed his elder brother, Chamanji, to get to the throne. It appears that Chamanji was not Beejy Singh, the brother that Jai Singh had imprisoned. Chamanji's sister, Jai Singh's half-sister, was given in marriage to Maharao Raja Budh Singh of Bundi who then became a victim of Jai Singh's persecution. Though 'deekro' translates strictly into 'son,' there appears to be no evidence of Jai Singh ever having to kill a son. Shiv Singh, his son and heir, died while Jai Singh celebrated the wedding of Maharaja Abhay and his daughter, but that death is attributed to cholera.

Maharaja Vijay Singh (Beejy Singh)

Beejy was anointed at the Sringar Chowk of Mehrangarh on 31 January 1753.

The death of his Uncle Bakhta gave the ousted Maharaja Ram Singh a chance to reclaim his throne. Backed by Jaipur, he made a treaty with the Marathas. Sixteen great Maratha leaders took part in the negotiations and from Pushkar, where, the combined armies had halted, the Scindia general Jai Appa sent summons to Beejy:

'Surrender the gaddi of Maroo.'

Beejy Singh marched to meet the Marathas and surprised them with the dexterity of the Rathore army. Jai Appa, leading the combined Maratha army, was on the verge of giving up when two accidents took place. A chosen cohort of Rathores returning from a successful charge was mistaken as foe. They were mowed down by their own brothers-in-arms. But it was a second incident that turned the wheel of fortune in Scindia's favour.

Bahadur Singh had grabbed his elder brother's throne of Kishangarh in 1748. Both Abhay and Bakhta had remained indifferent to the troubles faced by their cousins. The magnificent city of Rupnagar, that had been built by Sawant and Bahadur's great-grandfather Rup Singh, as the personal jagir of the heir to the Kishangarh throne, continued to remain with Sawant Singh but he did not care to fight for his rights. Sawant Singh[22] turned to religion, abandoning worldly life. His young and spirited son, Sardar Singh, failed to understand his father's point of view.

'Having tasted the sweetness of life it is easy for you to give it up. I am still a stranger to the good things in life,' he said.

Determined to regain his estate, Sardar Singh joined Ram Singh's troops. Jai Appa called the young man aside.

---

22. Sawant Singh of Rupnagar, had married Bani Thani – a slave girl from Delhi. By his orders, it was her face alone that was to be used in paintings that depicted scenes from the life of Lord Krishna. This gave rise to the Bani Thani school of paintings.

'Your star is linked to Ram Singh's, which fortune does not favour.'

He would have to trick his countrymen into surrendering or else the Marathas would leave him stranded without an estate.

Sardar sent a horseman flying to the division of Rathores that were pressing them the most.

'Why do you fight,' asked the horseman, 'when Beejy Singh lies dead killed by a cannon ball?'

Easily disturbed and superstitious, Rajputs had fallen prey to such gimmicks many times in their history. Yet, they failed to learn. Grief and confusion overwhelmed them. Not one man thought of confirming the news. Instead, they withdrew enmass from the field and Beejy, in the thick of battle, found himself abandoned. The disaster broke the morale of the Rathore army.

Young and impressionable, Beejy was agreeable to allow age and experience to guide him. Advising a tactical retreat, Maharaja Gaj Singh of Bikaner, who had helped Bakhta gain the throne, marched off. A bewildered Beejy found the Marathas helping themselves to the Rathore guns. Bahadur, the Rathore raja of Kishangarh, seized the opportunity to desert. Beejy Singh was left with no option but to flee to Nagaur.

Within a few months Maharaja Ram Singh ascended the throne for a second time.

Maharaja Ram Singh

For six months, Beejy Singh defended himself gallantly in Nagaur. The Marathas who had had no experience of laying siege, suffered great losses. Encouraged, the courageous young man, who had inherited all the boldness of his father, decided to appeal for succour directly.

With a 1,000 men, astride a fleet of 500 camels, he broke unobserved through the enemy lines and within twenty-four hours was at the court of Bikaner. Realising that he would receive no help from this Rathore cousin, he made his way to Jaipur. But Sawai Maharaja

In the dark, Beejy probably took the wrong road, or perhaps he was misled, for he found himself near Run. The chieftain of Run, who had accompanied him thus far, begged leave to go home. He had to help his family escape. Too dignified to reply, the raja remained silent as the last of his companions abandoned him. With five soldiers, he continued on his way and had barely crossed Khajwana when his horse dropped dead. Nagaur was yet another sixteen miles. Leaving his worn out escort and disguising himself as a common man he convinced a simple Jat to convey him to Nagaur before daybreak.

The Jat drove a hard bargain. He would settle for no less than a princely sum of five rupees all to be paid in new coins issued in the name of Maharaja Beejy Singh. The king of Maroo was seated in an oxen cart beside the peasant.

Impatient to be within the safety of Nagaur, Beejy urged the beasts with the customary cry, 'Hank Hank!'

The honest Jat, aware that his oxen were doing their best, finally lost his temper.

'Who are you to cry hank hank? One would expect a sturdy man like you to be by Beejy Singh's side at a time like this instead of rushing off to Nagaur as if the Marathas were after you. So sit still for I will not go any faster.'

As dawn appeared, Nagaur was yet another two miles away. The Jat turned around, to get a better view of the impatient traveller, and jumped off the cart in horror. It was his sovereign who had been his companion through the night. The unpardonable crime of sitting at the same level as his king had been committed.

'I pardon you,' said Beejy mildly. The Jat took up the reins and did not stop his cry of hank hank until he was within the walls of Nagaur.

Letter from Kanwar Beejy Singh to Maharana Jagat Singh II dated to a full moon on a Thursday of Samvat era 1791 (AD 1735 – 1736).

Let my moojra (obediance) be known. You honoured me by sending Rawat Kesari Singh and Bihari Das, and commanding a marriage connection. Your orders are on your child's head. You have made me a servant. To everything I am agreed, and now I am your child; while I live I am yours. If I am a true Rajput, my head is at your disposal. You have made 20,000 Rathores your servants. If I fail in this, the Almighty is between us. Whoever is of my blood will obey your commands, and the fruits of this marriage shall be sovereign, and if a daughter, should I bestow her on the Turk, I am no true Rajput. She shall be married to a proper connection, and not without your advice; and even should Sri Bahoji (referring to his father), or others of our elders, recommend such proceeding, I swear by God I shall not agree. I am the Diwans, let others approve or disapprove.

Letters confirming the terms of this marriage, penned by Maharaja Abhay Singh and Bakhta Singh of Nagaur, remain in the possession of the palace at Udaipur.

Madho Singh I had planned to get rid of the son as he had done the father.

Jawan Singh, who had received the estate of Rian that had been confiscated from the leader of the first swords of Maroo by Maharaja Bakhta, accompanied Beejy Singh. He was from a younger branch of the Merta clan and his wife was the daughter of a great vassal chief of Jaipur. Fearing the impending bloodshed, the Jaipur chief cautioned his son-in-law. Under an oath of secrecy, the plot was revealed at the very last moment.

Madho Singh embraced the young Beejy Singh and sat him by his side upon his own gaddi. Jawan Singh seated himself behind the rajas and as if by accident upon the flowing skirt of Madho Singh's robe. Puzzled, for seat of the chieftain of Rian, who led the first swords of Maroo, was on the right hand side of his sovereign, Beejy looked up in askance.

'The day demands it,' was the reply. 'But you need to rise,' he added. 'Leave immediately for your life is in danger.'

As Beejy Singh rose, Madho Singh reached out for him but found himself restrained by a dagger at his throat. The astonished court watched with bated breath until word was brought back that Beejy was back in the saddle and awaited the presence of his chief. The dagger was sheathed and saluting the king of Jaipur, the chieftain of Rian left.

'What loyalty!' exclaimed Maharaja Madho Singh. 'Can one ever hope to succeed against men such as these?'

With none to support him, Beejy made his way back into Nagaur in much the same manner as he left it.

Most of the kingdom had fallen into the hands of Ram Singh and his Marathas except for Jalor, Siwana and Phalodi. It was now that an unusual offer presented itself. It seemed to be the only way out. Two foot soldiers, an Afghan and a Rajput who drew a measly pay in the army, offered to get rid of the Maratha leader, provided their sovereign promised to look after their families. The plot though it succeeded cost Marwar the brightest gem in its crown – the fortress and district of Ajmer.

The Marathas became side tracked for a while. The year following Ram Singh's restoration saw the imperial capital engulfed in crisis. A new nizam-ul-mulk, the grandson of the first nizam of Hyderabad, had been appointed which resulted in the ousting of Wazir Safdarjung; the blinding and deposal of Emperor Ahmad Shah; the murder of the blind Emperor Alamgir II, who had spent his five years on the throne in prayer during which time Delhi was subject to a sacking by Nadir Shah's Afghan minion – Ahmad Shah Abdalli (Durrani). Horror was heaped upon horror. So caught up were those watching the events unfold that they failed to comprehend the repercussions that were taking place in faraway Bengal. In June 1757, not even six months after Delhi had been sacked for the second time in history, the Battle of Plassey delivered Bengal from the hands of its nawab to those of the traders of Great Britain. Within seven years they were to become the unquestioned masters of that eastern corner of India.

The nizam-ul-mulk and wazir – who was more popularly known as imad-ul-mulk – attempted with Maratha help to recover the empire's possessions. Deluded by visions of his Indian empire, which was to reach beyond the Attock, Nana Sahib – Balaji Baji Rao Peshwa – ordered his Marathas to seize Punjab. It precipitated the Third Battle of Panipat in January 1761. The Afghan rushed back and the Rajputs took a back seat allowing the Marathas and the imad-ul-mulk to bear the brunt. Abdalli was victorious and the Maratha dreams evaporated. But destiny was not ready to end the Mughal Empire. Faced with a mutiny on his hands, Abdalli could not indulge himself and sit upon the throne of India. Grudgingly he crowned the absent Shah Alam II, who had escaped to Avadh the year before his father had been murdered. But a Rohilla Afghan was left behind in charge.

Broken in spirit, the Marathas, nevertheless, managed to keep the struggle in Marwar going for another ten years. The treaty of Sambhar decided the issue of tribute.

The deserted Ram Singh, whose second tenure had lasted nineteen years, was left out in the cold. He finally gave up his claims in 1772 and in return was granted the district of Sambhar, where he lived out

It is said that during the siege of Nagaur Jai Appa[23] fell seriously ill and Beejy Singh sent Surajmal the vaid – his own physician. The vaid refused at first saying that under no circumstances would he administer poison.

'On the contrary,' said his prince, 'let your skill cure in two days what would take you four, and I shall favour you.'

What was even stranger was that Jai Appa took the vaid's drugs without hesitation and recovered.

It was 25 July 1755 and Jai Appa was performing his ablutions in his tent oustside the walls of Nagaur when two camp settlers approached. Quarrelling loudly, they threw a bundle of account statements at his feet imploring him to intervene. As he listened to their story they drew nearer. Suddenly plunging their daggers into his breast, they cried out, 'This is for Nagaur, and this for Jodhpur.' The alarm went up. The Afghan was slain on the spot but the Rajput managed to escape.

Although the siege of Nagaur continued it proved expensive for the Marathas and soon the cause of Ram Singh was abandoned. As their general lay dying, the Maratha clans clamoured for vengeance. But the dying man's last words exonerated young Sardar Singh of Rupnagar.

For having spilt the blood of Jai Appa, Beejy Singh paid with the surrender of Ajmer and a tribute that was levied on all the lands of Maroo.

---

23. Jai Appa, or Jayaji Rao, was the eldest of the five sons of Ranoji Scindia (Shinde) who had conquered the Mughal province of Malwa. He was succeeded by his minor son, Jankoji while his brother, Dattaji, served his nephew as regent. Dattaji, who was a great general, was instrumental in the Maratha occupation of Punjab. He was slain near Delhi in January 1760. The Punjab war also claimed the life of Ranoji's third son. The Third Battle of Panipat that followed claimed the life of Ranoji's youngest, Tukoji, but his fourth son, Mahadji managed to escape, astride his loyal Bijli (lightening), despite being grievously wounded. These two youngest were born of Ranoji's Rajputni mistress – later referred to as Maharani Chima Bai. Tukoji's son – Kadarji – refused to accept leadership of the clan despite recognition by the peshwa and held the position only until the appointment of a relative – Manaji. Ranoji's only surviving son – Mahadji – who was childless, was eventually recognised by the peshwa in 1768. Mahadji proved to be the most successful of the Scindias and freed himself of the peshwa's control. After his death, the leadership passed to Tukoji's grandson – Daulat Rao.

In 1756, Sawant Singh was forced into formally signing Kishangarh and Khakarti over to his brothers – Bahadur and Veer. Then appointing his twenty-six-year-old son, Sardar Singh, as regent of Rupnagar, he retired to Vrindavan. Sawant Singh died in 1765. His son ruled as the raja of Rupnagar for three years and died having named his cousin – Amar Singh of Khakarti – heir.

But Rupnagar was occupied forcibly by his uncle Bahadur.

the rest of his days. He died within a year and is remembered as a tall, distinguished man with a princely bearing, scholarly and benevolent who had paid a great price for the intemperance of his youth.

Pushkar, the sacred lake where all creation had taken place, lay close to the British held city of Ajmer.

The return from Jodhpur had been routed through the towns of Nandla, Pipar, Madreo, Bharunda, Merta, Jharau and Alniawas. Two miles outside Jodhpur, the glimpse of the occasional red sandstone protruding from the deep sands was greeted with relief. The sightings became frequent. At last there was firm ground.

The Sabarmati[24], with its glistening mica bed, had been crossed half a mile west of Govindgarh. It issued from the Pushkar along with the Saraswati, which had been encountered at Nandla and for a second time at the entrance to the valley of Pushkar. Bulrushes, ten feet high, grew along its banks. Great cartloads of it were being carried away to be used as thatching and elephant fodder. The Boora (old) Pushkar, the actual source of the Saraswati, lay four miles to the east of the present lake: the one that had been excavated by the Puriharas of Mandor.

The sands that blew across the plains formed a bar across the mouth of the valley and the occasional sand dune. Mountains of deep rose coloured quartz sparkled to the left while on the right towered grey granite topped with white quartz. Pushkar, the most sacred lake in India, next only to the Manasarowar of Tibet, lay at the centre of the valley. Numerous shrines and cenotaphs studded its banks. Among them stood the memorial to Jai Appa Scindia, the commander of the combined Maratha forces, who had been assassinated at Nagaur sixty-five years ago. Here, every 'Hindu' family of rank had claimed a niche for itself. In these exclusive surroundings, undisturbed by the masses, they would practise their devotions.

---

24. Known locally as the Luni.

Upon this hallowed site, Brahma had assembled all celestials to perform a yagna to ensure the success of his project.

Mountains sprang up to protect the site while the work of creation was in progress. To the south rose Ratnagir, the hill of gems; Nilagir, or the blue mountain to the north; Kutchactargir to the east; and Sonachura, the golden mountain to the west. Nandi, Shiva's bull mount, guarded the mouth of the valley while Krishna (Kanhaiya) guarded the north.

The sacred fire was lit but, at the crucial moment, Sawantari, Brahma's wife, was found missing. The rites would not be complete without the female presence and a Gujjar girl took her place. That in a matter of moments she had been replaced, so upset Sawantari that she merged with the rocks on Ratnagir. A stream bearing her name gushes from the spot close to where her shrine now stands.

Lost in his own thoughts, Shiva neglected to put out the sacred fire, which spread, threatening to engulf the universe; but Brahma managed to extinguish it using sand. The sand was left behind to form the dunes of Pushkar.

Among the most conspicuous were temples built by Raja Maan Singh of Amber, Ahilya Bai Holkar, Jawaharmal of Bharatpur and Maharaja Beejy Singh of Marwar. Four years ago, Gokul Pak, Scindia's minister, had built a temple to the creator, Brahma, at a cost of 1,30,000 rupees (£15,000).

To the south of the lake stood the Nag Pahar – the Serpent Mountain, where the remains of the fortress of Ajay Pal Chauhan could still be found. Ajay Pal had abandoned this site to build himself a home on the other side of the range, on the hill that came to be known as Ajay-mer or Ajmer.

Making their way through mountains of granite, that lined the northern edge of the valley of Pushkar, the party headed towards Ajmer. Here the milky cactus and the yellow aonla of the border were abundant and the sand dunes loftier than those in the south. The steep path changed direction from north to east and a gap in the mountains suddenly opened up. As they negotiated the famous Dhar-l-Khair, the view that burst upon them was of startling magnificence. Shoulders of red granite rose on either side of the pass resting on a base of blue slate that glittered with mica. At their feet lay the vast lake of Vishal Dev Chauhan, set amidst a densely forested plain, beyond which rising 800 feet into the sky towered the fortress of Ajmer, in all its majesty, crowned atop the crest of an isolated hill.

Eight miles in circumference, the Vishal Talab was the source of the Luni, which flowed all the way westward across Rajasthan until it emptied into the delta of the Indus. Here upon its banks, in the comfort of the Daulat Bagh, the gardens that fringed the lake, Emperor Jahangir would have awaited the news of the surrender of the maharana of Mewar. Sadly the palace[25] in which he received the maharana and Sir Thomas Roe, the first ambassador sent by King James I, had long since decayed. To the east of the Vishal Talab lay the Ana Sagar named after the grandson of Vishal Dev Chauhan.

> *Ajmer had been too long the haunt of Mughals and Pathans, the Goths and Vandals of Rajasthan, to allow any preservation of its ancient heritage. Whatever time had spared, bigotry had destroyed or used it to build altars to itself.*

---

25. Jahangir's palace houses the Government Museum today.

It was only in the very first building of the Islamic conquerors, the Urai-din-ka-jhopra[26], that bits of ancient 'Hindu' architecture continued to survive.

The spiritual might of Roshan Ali, that had driven the army of Islam across the Indus, had been faced by the reigning king, Manik Rai Chauhan and the citadel of Ajmer had been lost for the first time in its history.

Though the ancient walls and towers raised by Ajay Pal continued to encircle the crest of the hill, the march of time had left its mark – a whitewashed mosque lifted its dazzling minarets into the sky. But fluttering above them all was the cross of St George, for Ajmer had been handed to General Ochterlony in 1818, ostensibly to protect it from disorder.

Maharaja Vijay Singh (Beejy Singh)

In 1772, at the age of forty-eight, Beejy Singh ascended the throne acknowledged by all the clans and the emperor of Hindustan. But he found himself dominated wholly by his uncle, Devi Singh, the Champawat chief of Pokaran.

Devi Singh, one of Ajit's fourteen sons, had been adopted into the house of Pokaran, a junior but powerful branch of the Champawat clan. Despite having to give up his claim to the throne, Devi Singh was determined to maintain his influence over his nephew and, together with the new chief of the Champawats of Awa, formed the royal bodyguard. In effect, the maharaja was completely isolated. Beejy discovered that he had no access to information and no say in the matters of state. Every time he raised an issue Devi Singh would have but one condescending reply.

'Why trouble yourself about Marwar? It is safe within the sheath of my dagger.'

---

26. The Urai-din-ka-jhopra literally translates into 'the hut that was built in two and a half days'. The conquering Islamic army constructed these temporary mosques to offer thanks. Little time would be invested and local material, collected from the vandalized 'Hindu' temples, was quickly put to use. As a result, blocks of stone bearing 'Hindu' carvings, symbols and even deities can be identified within the walls.

Beejy Singh's foster brother (Dhaibhai), Jaggo, was the only one he could confide in. Advising Beejy to put forward a happy face, Jaggo left in search of aid and returned with a band of Sindi mercenaries who had some knowledge of European tactics. The Sindi guards were shuffled between many posts until they came to their final positions at the gates of the castle. Jaggo and Beejy discussed means of bringing prosperity back to Marwar. Putting together an army from his limited resources, borrowing money from his own mother, Jaggo announced that he was off to curb the hill tribes of Nagaur. But as there was not enough money to buy horses and the arrogant cavaliers were too proud to walk, Jaggo was pushed into procuring carts to transport his army. Drawing guns from the armoury of Nagaur, they put up a show of attacking the mountain folk but on the return, in an unexpected move, occupied the castle of Seel Bukri. Alarmed, the clans of Maroo united. Civil war looked imminent.

Govardhan Kinchi, a Rajput of foreign origin, who had been recommended by the dying Bakhta to his son, came to the rescue. He convinced the maharaja that he needed to address the clans personally. Govardhan went ahead to prepare the chiefs. When Beejy Singh arrived, not one man came forward to meet him. He was taken straight to the tent of the Champawat of Awa, where the chiefs had congregated.

'Why have you deserted me?'

Beejy broke the silence. A long and tedious discussion followed. The clans demanded that the force of the Dhaibhai be broken up, the records of the jagirs be submitted to the clan elders and the court be moved from the citadel to the town.

The Champawats returned with the maharaja having regained their former position as the royal bodyguards. The situation remained unchanged until the death of the royal guru. The grieving Beejy ordered that the last rites be carried out within Mehrangarh itself. In a formal ceremony, the queens arrived to pay their last respects. As the chiefs mounted the rocky steps to Jodha's castle, the Champawat chief felt a sudden flutter in his breast. He wondered aloud if it seemed to be an unlucky day.

The last hours of Devi Singh Champawat were strange. He had after all been born a prince of Maroo and none would dare spill his blood. His death warrant arrived in an earthen jar with a command from his sovereign to make his own departure from life.

'What,' cried the proud chief, 'shall Devi Singh take his opium from a common clay pot? Let my golden cup be brought and it shall be welcome.'

This last request was denied and the son of Ajit dashed his brains out against the walls of his prison.

A voice taunted him. 'Where now, is the sheath of the dagger that holds the fortunes of Marwar?'

'In Subbula's girdle,' came the chilling reply.

The sheath of the dagger that lay with Devi Singh's son Subbula was to haunt Beejy's days.

Subbula went on a rampage. He attempted to pillage and burn the business town of Pali. Unsuccessful, he attacked the wealthy city of Bhilwara. It was a pointless exercise and the deranged grandson of Maharaja Ajit eventually received a fatal shot. His ashes were washed away by the waters of the Luni.

'You are the chief noble of Maroo. Who would dare harm you?' asked the others as they made their way up.

But when they reached the alarum or the nakarra gate they found it shut. Within minutes, the Dhaibhai's forces were upon them and the work of death began. Several chiefs were slain and the rest made captive. Their end came soon.

The tremendous sacrifice of chiefs who had bled so often for Marwar freed the sovereign from the shackles that had long bound him. The aristocracy in the Rajput states had played a powerful role. The first among the nobles who was usually a direct descendent of the royal family, asserted his right to be consulted in every decision and to tutor the rajas, especially if they were minors. No grant of land was valid unless the chief noble had signed the deed. In trying to break this bond Ram Singh had lost his crown and Beejy forced to take this drastic step.

The feudal system was reorganized and Beejy Singh ensured the fidelity of his chiefs by keeping them occupied. The hordes of the desert were conquered and Umarkot was taken, which gave him the key to the valley of the Indus. Lands were grabbed from Jaisalmer and most importantly, the rich province of Godwar, that had been left in custody, was never returned. The money generated from Godwar equalled that which was raised from all Maroo. In an attempt to safeguard it from the pretender that threatened the Sisodia throne, Maharana Ari Singh of Mewar had entrusted it to Marwar. But, despite all pleas, here Godwar stayed after five centuries of alienation. In 1775, Emperor Shah Alam II, restored the confiscated Jodhpur property of Raisina (where Rashtrapati Bhavan now stands) in Delhi.

Several years of peace followed, but the rapid strides of the Marathas caused the princes of Rajasthan to unite once again. The gaddi of Jaipur was occupied by the energetic Pratap Singh. Mahadji Scindia, a natural son of the founder of the clan, had succeeded once all the legitimate successors had had their turn. He reorganized the Scindia army, employing the services of the French mercenary De Boigne. Emperor Shah Alam who had sought refuge in Avadh, sometime before the murder of his father, picked up courage and returned to Delhi in 1772, accompanied by the Marathas. But Shah

Alam was to remain a puppet for the next ten years under a Persian adventurer who had occupied the Rohilla's post. In 1785, he offered Mahadji Scindia the post of vakil-i-mutlaq or regent of the empire. Mahadji took the opportunity to invade Jaipur in 1787 on the pretext of collecting taxes. With him came the Mughal army. Putting past grievances aside, the Rathores led by Jawan Singh of Rian, joined Maharaja Sawai Pratap Singh of Jaipur on the battlefield of Lalsot (Tonga). Pratap was quick to realise that the Mughal commanders were upset at being superseded by a Maratha and a generous amount of money won them over in no time at all. Together they charged De Boigne's forces, sobering the Maratha artillery commanders at their guns. Mahadji Scindia was compelled to abandon the field and Beejy redeemed the castle of Ajmer, freeing Marwar from having to pay tribute to the Marathas.

Mahadji's temporary lapse at Lalsot left him weak for the moment and the control of Delhi fell into the hands of Rohilla Ghulam Kader Khan, the grandson of the Rohilla appointed by Ahmad Shah Abdalli (Durrani). Here was the man who in a frenzied moment would plant both feet upon the emperor's breast and with his dagger gouge out his eyes. The day that the terrible deed was done – the 10th of August 1788 – spelt the official demise of the Mughal Empire. Mahadji rushed to the rescue and seized control. The offender was executed and the Kingdom of Delhi – in reality the Maratha Kingdom of Delhi – looked to its new future with Emperor Shah Alam acting as a figurehead.

Three years after Lalsot, Mahadji and De Boigne[27] were back in Rajasthan. The lethal combination of genius and talent was not to be underestimated. Their army now used modern European skills that

---

27. Count Benoit de Boigne (1751 – 1830), born at Chambry in Savoy, was the son of a fur merchant. He served in the Irish Brigade in France, then joined the Russian army, was captured by the Turks and finally lured by the wealth of India. De Boigne, who was never troubled by issues of loyalty, joined the British East India Company. He soon resigned to join Mahadji Scindia and was instrumental in the Maratha's rise to success. He was appointed governor of the Doab, which included the city of Agra and the restoration of the Taj Mahal, became an obsession even though it elicited a cool response from his 'Hindu' master. The Nabob of Savoy returned home in 1795, and had honours heaped upon him by Louis XVIII. He became a frequent visitor to Napoleon's court, where, it is believed, plots were hatched to bring the Mughal emperor under French control.

were new and strange. The legendary Rajput courage was no match for what was about to be witnessed. The Rathores marched out to meet the invasion, but differences with Jaipur led to the withdrawal of the Kachwahas. The battle of Patan in 1790 was a terrible disgrace.

The treacherous Maharaja Pratap Singh of Kishangarh (the grandson of Maharaja Bahadur Singh) who had lost Rupnagar in 1787 – due to the intervention of Beejy Singh – to Amar Singh of Khakarti, seized the opportunity to conduct the Marathas into Marwar. De Boigne's guns reduced Rupnagar and invested Ajmer.

Jodhpur suffered a levy of sixty lakhs of rupees and the loss of Ajmer. Beejy Singh sent word to Dumraj, the governor of Ajmer, to hand the fort over to De Boigne. Denied permission to defend Taragarh, the faithful governor enjoyed a last cup of wine laced with a pinch of diamond powder closing his eyes before the disgraceful surrender could take effect.

Mahadji remained in Ajmer while his army marched to engage the Rathores on the plains of Merta. But the heavy guns that had until now worked wonders sank into the deep sands of the Luni. Here was a golden opportunity for the Rathores, but interpersonal rivalry between the civil ministers, who represented the sovereign on the field, misled chiefs who had sworn to die for their land. The delay allowed the recovery of De Boigne's artillery and the frustrated chiefs on the battlefield found themselves under attack before the night was out. The civil commanders fled but 4,000 Rathores led by the Champawat chief of Awa decided to stand their ground. The gallant band charged, scattering the Marathas, but without an infantry to secure them, they were decimated by the skilful use of De Boigne's guns.

The best warriors of Maroo were lost. In the still of the night, a servant crept onto the battlefield. From amongst the dead, he drew out the still breathing chief of Awa. The dying man requested to lay his eyes upon his sovereign one last time. Maharaja Beejy Singh hurried to his side and there he remained until the chief noble of Maroo ceased to draw breath.

The last years of Beejy Singh's life were spent in the foolish pursuit of Gulab Rai, a young beauty from the Oswal tribe. Upon her, he lavished honours due to a legitimate queen, granting her the jagir of

Jalor and excavating the lovely Gulab Sagar in her name. But the girl took full advantage of her powers, often driving the maharaja from her presence with her slippers. Beejy was besotted. He placed in her lap his own legitimate grandchild, Maan Singh, adopting him as the heir of Marwar[28]. The real heir, his eldest son, Zalim Singh was left out in the cold. The chiefs of Marwar were invited to grace the occasion and acknowledge the new heir. The haughty nobles refused. The son of a slave would never be their lord. The clans assembled to plot against Beejy. Recalling his past success, Beejy Singh came forward to address his chiefs. The negotiations were proceeding successfully, or so he thought, unaware of what was taking place while he was thus occupied. The confederates had sent word to the chieftain of Raus to bring Prince Bheem (another of Beejy's grandsons) down from the castle. The chiefs also sent word to the young Oswali that the maharaja awaited her at the camp and that a guard of honour stood ready to escort her. As she entered her palki an unseen hand slew her.

The chieftain of Raus hurried with the young Bheem to where the confederates had assembled. Their motive was to at once dethrone Beejy Singh and enthrone Bheem. Beejy, however, received intelligence of the incident almost at the same time and rushed back. Bheem, he appeased, by giving him the lands of Sojat and Siwana and to his eldest son, Zalim Singh, the rich districts of Godwar with private orders to attack Bheem. Bheem received the news in time to confront and defeat his uncle. He then fled to Jaisalmer.

His sons and grandsons engaged in conflict, his chiefs in open rebellion and his favourite companion torn violently from him, Beejy lived out his years unhappily, dying in 1794.

---

28. Gulab Rai had two sons of whom one died early. The one that lived clearly would not have been acceptable to the clans. To make sure that she would be entitled to the rights of a queen mother, she influenced Beejy into naming his third son, Sher Singh, heir overriding the claims of the two older sons – Zalim and Bhom. Zalim appears to have had no children, which brought Bhom Singh's only son, Bheem, in line to the throne. Sher Singh, who had no sons of his own, adopted his youngest brother's only son, Maan. The throne when it passed into the hands of the third generation would have to go to either Bheem or Maan. Bheem took on the unpleasant task of getting rid of the uncles who would needlessly occupy the throne before he or Maan could get to it. Though Bheem got to the throne first, he was unable to bear a son in time.

Maharaja Bheem Singh

The news of Maharaja Beejy Singh's death was conveyed by express to his grandson, Bheem, at Jaisalmer. Within twenty-two hours he' had seated himself upon the gaddi at Jodhpur, while the rightful heir Zalim Singh awaited the auspicious hour to enter the capital. That hour never arrived. The people of Marwar received news of Bheem's enthronement by the sound of the nakarras that chased Zalim out of Marwar.

Maharana Bhim Singh of Mewar[29] offered Zalim Singh sanctuary and there he spent his days in literary pursuits; but in the end took his own life while still in the prime of youth.

To secure his throne Bheem, put to death all surviving male relatives. Of all the royal blood of Maroo only a single claimant remained, but young Maan Singh, the adopted son of the Oswali, was secure within the walls of Jalor.

The siege of the stronghold of Jalor was a difficult one. To maintain one over a long period at such a site was tedious. For those locked behind the walls it proved stifling and the restless and energetic Maan often broke through the imperfect blockade, plundering the surrounding lands for support. One such foray into Pali had nearly proved fatal. They were attacked while attempting to re-enter Jalor and Maan Singh had been unhorsed. He would have been captured, had it not been for the chief of Awa who pulled him up onto his own horse and bore him to safety.

To the turbulence of the chiefs of Marwar, Maan Singh owed his life. Bheem was as impudent as the dethroned Ram Singh and he raved and ranted against the chiefs who were in charge.

'Give them oxen to ride instead of horses,' he fumed.

The chiefs abandoned the siege and marched off enmass. Bheem retaliated by turning upon them confiscating several jagirs but in the

---

29. Zalim Singh's mother was Sisodini Rani Ratan Kanwar, the daughter of Maharana Jagat Singh II and Maharaja Beejy Singh's third wife. A translation of the letter signed by Beejy Singh, confirming the terms of the marriage, has been included on page 235.

end mercenary armies had to be procured to continue the siege of Jalor.

In 1800, Daulat Rao Scindia and Jaswant Rao – the Holkar regent – took to fighting each other. The opportunity was too good to lose. Bheem joined Sawai Maharaja Pratap Singh of Jaipur in initiating fresh hostilities, with a view to relieve themselves of their debts. But the battle of Malpura turned out otherwise. Rajput valour was outwitted by the smaller and more nimble Maratha army. In a show of bravado, a division of the Jodhpur cavalry charged, setting their Maratha counterparts to flight. The sudden and unexpected success went to their heads and the the enthusiastic chase was carried on till well beyond the battlefield leaving the allies exposed. Major Pohlman and James Skinner were quick to regroup the tattered Marathas and fell upon the Kachwahas. Sawai Pratap Singh's elephant was struck down and Jaipur withdrew.

Nevertheless, Jaipur upheld Bheem's right to the throne and in a show of support, Sawai Maharaja Pratap Singh gave him his daughter Anand Kanwar in marriage. Sadly, Anand Kanwar was to lose both her father and her husband within two years.

Jalor had withstood for eleven years but the end was approaching. All means of defence had been exhausted. A small supply of millet flour was all that was left for the garrison. Death was to arrive either by sword or starvation. Then as if by miracle, the news of Bheem's death was announced. Nobody believed it at first. It was not until Guru Devnath returned from a survey of the enemy lines with the happy news that not a single moustache was to be seen in the camp, that Maan Singh was hailed as the new head of the Rathores.

Maharaja Bheem Singh died on 19 October 1803. It would be a matter of days before the throne of Delhi was to come under a new master. Daulat Rao Scindia had succeeded to Mahadji's privileges at the same time that Bheem had gained the Rathore throne. The role of protector to the emperor in Delhi made the Maratha defacto ruler – a temptation that became too much for the East India Company to bear. In December that year, Lord Lake occupied Delhi and evicted Daulat Rao. The East India Company assumed the dignities for itself.

An invitation to dinner arrived from the palace. With it came a request, which would have appeared strange had it not been common practise at Scindia's camp. The cuisine of the British was to be sent to the palace incase the desert fare proved unpalatable. Accordingly, joints of mutton, fowl and some claret wine made their way. All the while the officers looked forward eagerly to the Jodhpuri delicacies that lay in store.

On the 13th of November the table was laid in the newly constructed Maan Mahal. It commanded an extensive view, the pinnacle of Kumbhalgarh being visible eighty miles to the east on a clear day. The table was covered with silver platters filled with curries and pulaus of both 'Hindu' and Muslim styles. There were exotic vegetables: miniature melons no larger than eggs and the famed kakri (cucumber) of the desert; but occupying the pride of place was the hurea-moong-Mandor-ra or the green mung bean soup of Mandor, beside the pot .of maize rabri, the porridge of the simple Rathore.

Great care was taken to ensure that the dinner was a success and it was singularly special as the food was served in vessels from which the 'Hindus' themselves ate. The tolerant Rajputs believed that a little fire would purify the silver plates from contamination. The same, however, did not apply to earthenware and unfortunately, a well-meaning but ignorant servant had used a handsome China bowl to serve the officers. As this bowl, no doubt a collector's item, could no longer be used by the palace it was brought to the captain's butler with the same message, 'keep this for it is no longer of any use to us'. Kali Khan was not a man to be trifled with. Knocking it right out of the servant's hands and over the battlements he observed that that was the only way to treat things that were useless. Perhaps, observed the captain, the maharaja did get to hear about the incident for barely a couple of months later the dominating Prime Minister Akhi Chand was flung to his death over the same battlements.

A few days later the king of Maroo returned the firangi vakil's visit, calling on the British camp. With expressions of good wishes the mission bade adieu to Maharaja Maan Singh and the capital of Marwar.

Maharaja Maan Singh

Sawai Singh, who had succeeded as chief of Pokaran, soon found an excuse to take offence over some trivial matter and turn hostile. He had assumed the position of the most powerful noble at court and in his possession lay the dagger that Devi Singh had bequeathed to Subbula. This great-grandson of Ajit could still control the fortunes of Maroo.

He announced to the chiefs that the queen of Maharaja Bheem was expecting. A council was called, in which Maan Singh was present. It was decided that were a male child to be born, his right as heir apparent to the throne would be upheld and he would be granted the forts of Nagaur and Siwana.

Posthumous births never fail to create discord and in due course, a male infant was born but the mother, alarmed for its safety, concealed the baby in a basket and had it sent it to Pokaran. The baby received the inauspicious name of Dhonkul, one who is born to strife: a name that had been borne by Maharaja Abhay Singh. For two years the birth was kept secret and had Maan Singh ruled wisely, the cause of the pretender may have well been forgotten.

But Maan Singh favoured friends who had been by his side since his days at Jalor. The rest were alienated. Two years later, Sawai Singh brought up the cause of Dhonkul once again. Maan Singh called for an examination of the child. Bheem's queen, who had remained behind in Jodhpur, was terrified. Concerns for her own personal safety overcame maternal affections and she disclaimed the child. The chiefs remained subdued for a while but within, a deeper plot was brewing.

Maharaja Bheem had applied to the maharana of Mewar for the

hand of his daughter Krishna Kumari but had died before the preliminaries could be concluded. The situation presented Sawai Singh with a perfect game plan. He induced Sawai Maharaja Jagat Singh of Jaipur to ask for the hand of the fair Krishna. No sooner had Mewar accepted the proposal that Sawai confronted Maan Singh. The throne of Maroo would be eternally disgraced were the wedding allowed to take place. The bride had been promised to the throne of Maroo and not to its occupant. The bait was swallowed and the Rathores intercepted the wedding gifts that were making their way to Jaipur. Jagat Singh was furious and war was declared.

Having initiated the drama, Sawai took Dhonkul to the court of Jaipur. The pretender was declared the true heir with a claim stronger than that of Maan Singh's. In recognition of his legitimacy, Maharaja Jagat Singh invited Dhonkul to eat from his own plate while his sister Anand Kanwar, the late Maharaja Bheem's Kachwaha rani, sat the pretender upon her knee declaring him to be her stepson.

Jaipur and the pretender brought more than a 100,000 men to the field. The ostensible issue of love and romance drew participants from far and near. The Marathas chose sides depending upon who carried the heavier purse. Daulat Rao Scindia, who had set up base in Mewar, joined Jaipur. But Jaswant Rao, the Holkar regent, was morally bound to Maan Singh who had sheltered his family when Lord Lake had chased him all the way to the Attock. Holkar, barely eighteen miles away, was due to join Maan Singh the next day, when he made a sudden detour to the south. It was a bribe of a 100,000 pounds, made from Sawai Singh's personal account, that effected the desertion.

As the armies approached, the Rathore chiefs rode up to salute their sovereign. It appeared to be a preliminary salute before they took up their positions. Instead, it was one of farewell. Maan was left abandoned on the battlefield but for four friends who stood resolutely by his side. The chieftains of Kuchaman, Ahor, Jalor and Nimaj and the auxiliary army of Bundi alone abided with him in this evil hour. Desperation caused him to pick up his dagger and he would have plunged it into his own heart had Surtan Singh Udaywat, the chief of Nimaj, and Seonath of Kuchaman not stopped him. Dragging him down from his elephant, they forced him onto one of their swiftest horses and helped him escape while they covered his rear. It was a moment Maan Singh would never forget. He had become the first of his race to have ever turned his back upon a Kachwaha.

Sawai Singh had calculated, and correctly, that Maan Singh would choose to ensconce himself at Jalor, abandoning Mehrangarh to its fate. In full flight towards Jalor, the maharaja arrived at Birsilpur where a civil officer in his train stopped him.

'There lies Jodhpur only nine kos to the right, while Jalor is sixteen further. If you cannot hold out in the capital what chance do you have elsewhere? While you defend your throne your cause is not lost.'

Maan Singh took the advice while Sawai Singh, confident in his prediction, halted at Merta for three days to prevent the maharaja's allies from entering Marwar.

There were 5,000 men waiting for their sovereign at Mehrangarh. From among these, Maan Singh sent garrisons to secure Jalor and Umarkot. A strange calm descended upon him. He now waited fearlessly. The four chieftains who were by his side when all the rest had deserted him pleaded for the honour of defending the ramparts of Mehrangarh but Maan Singh would not let them in. He had lost trust in all his kinsmen. Their fidelity in doubt, the spurned chiefs abandoned him. Joining the enemy, they occupied the city of Jodhpur.

The siege lasted for five months. The treasuries of Amber and Pokaran were drained. Amir Khan paid his men by plundering the estates nearby, estates that belonged to Rathore chiefs fighting alongside. The pretender's soldiers clamoured for pay and though he had been declared raja in the city of Jodhpur, the fort of Mehrangarh was still out of reach. The four chiefs who had earlier been faithful to Maan were asked to provide the money as a test of their loyalty. Silently, they withdrew and sent word to Amir Khan. It did not take much for the khan to defect. This was the right time, advised the chiefs, to plunder Jaipur as it lay unguarded.

Maharaja Sawai Jagat Singh chose this inopportune moment to take up the cause of the complaining Rathores and to punish Amir Khan. The commander-in-chief of Jaipur, Seolal, attacked putting a sudden stop to the deliberations going on in Amir Khan's tent. The Afghans were chased beyond the Luni. He surprised them once again at night, pursuing the khan to the very border of Jaipur. Seolal was amazed by his own success, little aware that the chase was in Amir Khan's chosen direction. Happy with a job well done, he left the camp and went to Jaipur to celebrate. The khan who was at Piplod near Tonk, called to his aid the heavy brigades of his Afghan counterparts. Jaipur lay unsuspecting and unprotected. Seolal's army was taken by surprise. The camp, guns and horses were looted and prompted by the four Rathores, led his Pathans to the gates of Jaipur. It was to Amir Khan that Maan Singh owed his salvation.

Trouble had been brewing for some time among the clans. The rajas of Bikaner and Shahpura had been feeling disgruntled for a while and withdrew from the confederacy. The lovelorn Kachwaha, who had set out to win a princess and a harvest of love and glory, withdrew on hearing that his army had been annihilated and his capital plundered by the khan and a handful of Rathores. The news had been kept from him by his prime minister and Sawai Singh but a special messenger sent by the queen mother of Jaipur had managed to get through. Enraged, perplexed and alarmed for his personal safety, he arranged to have the spoils, which included forty cannons, sent to Jaipur in advance. To the Maratha leaders he offered a 120,000 pounds to provide an escort and to Amir Khan a bribe of 90,000 pounds to stay him from intercepting the royal entourage. The humiliation Jagat Singh was to suffer was not yet over. The four Rathore chiefs, determined that no symbol of Rathore, disgrace was to enter Jaipur. The encounter that took place on the border was short and furious. All the spoils of war including the cannons were recovered and lodged in Kuchaman.

The cannon ball scarred walls of Mehrangarh remained as a reminder of the days when the rajas of Jodhpur and Jaipur battled over love. The Jai Pol or the gate of victory was raised in 1808, commemorating Maan Singh's triumph. But little Krishna's ordeal was far from over. For the next two years, her family was blackmailed. Mewar was threatened with destruction. Amir Khan arrived at Udaipur

Maharaja Maan Singh received Amir Khan with distinguished honours. He was granted a palace within Mehrangarh. Greater rewards were promised if he could extinguish the rebellion led by Sawai Singh. The khan and the maharaja exchanged turbans pledging brotherhood and with an advance payment of three lakhs of rupees tucked away in his pocket Amir Khan was on his way.

Sawai had brought the pretender, Dhonkul, to Nagaur, which was the jagir of the heir apparent of Marwar. Here future plans were in the process of being discussed when a message came from Amir Khan. He was some ten miles away and begged permission to visit the shrine of Pir Tarkeen, the only Muslim shrine that Bakhta had spared.

With a few men, the khan was permitted to perform his devotions and on his return, he came to pay his respects to Sawai Singh. Amir Khan looked unhappy. The king, he said, had not shown enough gratitude for the services he had rendered. Sawai swallowed the bait. 'Name your terms,' he said and offered twenty lakhs of rupees for the day that Dhonkul would be seated upon the gaddi of Jodhpur. With his hand on the *Koran*, the khan pledged himself. Sawai and Amir exchanged turbans. Amir Khan was presented to Dhonkul and he pledged himself to the pretender's cause. An invitation to the Pathan camp was accepted.

A large spacious tent had been pitched. Festivity hung in the air. Wine flowed freely while dancing girls and musicians prepared for the evening. Afghan hospitality was at its best. The guests arrived and turbans were exchanged and the evening wore on. The dancing was in full swing when the khan excused himself for a moment. The dancers swirled as the rhythm of the musicians reached a frenzied peak and as the lead singer uttered the word dugga, the tent came crashing down. Forty-two chieftains were slaughtered and those that tried to get away were brought down by cannon fire.

The heads of the chiefs were presented to Maharaja Maan Singh. Among them was that of Sawai's. The year 1808 was for Maan Singh the year of victory. The pretender alone managed to escape leaving his jagir, Nagaur, to be plundered by the Pathans.

Amir Khan was paid ten lakhs of rupees. He received the towns of Mundhiawar and Kuchilawas, which provided him with an annual rent of 30,000 rupees and a hundred rupees daily for table allowance.

The khan turned his attention upon Bikaner. The raja with his small army put up a feeble resistance and in the end, surrendered the town of Phalodi, which had been received as a reward for joining the confederacy. The khan was now the arbitrator of Marwar. He placed his garrison in Nagaur and partitioned the land of Merta among his followers. Another garrison he placed at the castle of Nava and this gave him the command of the salt lakes of Nava and Sambhar.

and took inordinate pleasure in asking the princess to choose between Maharaja Maan Singh or death for Mewar. Eventually Mewar opted for death. The sixteen-year-old girl took a cup of poison to spare her father further humiliation. The perverse pleasure that was being derived from the situation turned to one of absolute horror. Rajputs, throughout the land, cowered in shame.

The war between Jodhpur and Jaipur was now officially over and peace was signalled by intermarriages. On 3 September 1813, Maan Singh married Jagat Singh's sister Suraj Kanwar and the very next day gave his daughter to the sawai maharaja. The battle that began over the race for the hand of the fair Krishna, ended with both kings bringing home a bride.

Raja Kalyan Singh of Kishangarh, who had remained aloof despite being a Rathore, was asked by the victors to provide funds for the maintenance of Amir Khan's services. Two lakhs of rupees (20,000 pounds) were provided and Amir Khan pledged himself to Maharaja Maan Singh.

The maharaja kept to himself. He opened up to no one, trusted no one but Induraj, his minister and Devnath, his guru. They were the maharaja's only counsellors. The chiefs of Marwar resented their power and jealousy drove them to Amir Khan. For seven lakhs of rupees Amir Khan agreed to get rid of their enemies.

Devnath's death affected Maan Singh's reason. The king went completely mad. He stopped talking, would not attend to his duties and appeared not to comprehend anything. He refused to wash or shave and his face remained covered with hair. Eventually, he was persuaded to name his son Chattur Singh successor. With his own hand, he applied the teeka to his forehead but Chattur Singh, young and impetuous, died an early death. Maan Singh sank further into depression. He suspected everyone. His own queen, he believed, was trying to murder him. He would accept no food except that brought to him by one faithful servant. He had either become insane or pretended to be. The government was run by Salim Singh Champawat of Pokaran, the son of Sawai Singh.

In 1817, the British government invited the Rajputs to throw off the yoke of the predatory bands of the Marathas and the Pathans.

Chattur Singh and his ministers had sent an envoy to Delhi but prince died before the treaty could be concluded. In desperation, the ministers attempted to explain the terms of the treaty to Maan Singh and when at last he appeared to understand, he objected to the article, which specified that the armies of the vassals of Marwar would be at the disposal of the British. He was sane enough to recognise that this would cause further discord.

In December that year, a Brahmin named Beas Bishen Ram negotiated the treaty on behalf of Marwar. A year later, a British officer arrived. Jodhpur was in a terrible state. The mercenary bands of Sindis and Pathans had not been paid for three years. They had been reduced to begging in the streets. Law and order was lacking.

In 1819, another envoy was appointed. He sat with Maharaja Maan Singh and convinced him that the British government was aware of Marwar's history and understood the difficulties that Maan Singh had faced. With the British supporting him, Marwar could return to its former glory. Maan Singh suddenly threw off his cloak of insanity. He became possessed by a demoniacal spirit of revenge. Beginning with Akhi Chand – the diwan, who taking advantage of the king's madness had enriched himself by confiscating ancient jagirs – the maharaja did away with the heads of all the clans. A mad spell of killings were ordered and even those who had been loyal to Maan Singh were victimised. The feudal lords abandoned Marwar and the ancient system crumbled. But Maroo was to continue in the maharaja's grip for the next twenty-three years.

Eventually a dagger found its way to the heart of Maharaja Maan Singh. His queens left behind fifteen prints of vermilion stained hands as they trooped out of the innermost gate, the Lohapol, on their last journey to the funeral pyre of their lord.

Dhonkul, the pretender, was declared maharaja of Marwar.

Word had arrived at Ajmer: Maharao Raja Umed Singh of Kota had passed away. Despite his immediate instinct to rush to Kota via Shahpura and Bundi, urgent communication from the maharana desiring the captain's presence at Udaipur held him back.

Making his way past the newly raised castle of Bhimgarh, spending a little time at Bhilwara presiding over the quarrels of the merchants, a quick look at the picturesque castle of Bhunai, a long march through Banera and Mandalgarh and the captain was at Mairta where a deputation awaited him. Maharana Bhim Singh was to meet him at Ahar and escort him home.

But the oracle deemed otherwise. It would be inauspicious for the captain to enter Udaipur until three days later. Consequently two days were spent examining the cenotaphs at Ahar but on the third, the captain grew restless. The maharana arrived with his son, chiefs and ministers. It was a meeting of old friends. The words Ram Ram Tod sahib were on nearly a thousand lips.

Willing to compromise with the oracle, the captain allowed himself to be escorted a part of the way and then, while the maharana entered Udaipur by the gate of the sun, he made his way home by the southern entrance to the garden of Rampiyari.

Remnants of the kingdoms of Rajputana within modern Rajasthan.
Districts of Rajasthan that were once included in the kingdom of Bikaner.

CHAPTER 3

BIKANER

The modern districts Bikaner, Churu, Hanumangarh and Ganganagar make up what was once the Rathore kingdom of Bikaner. Though he compiled the annals of Bikaner, it was an area that Captain Tod did not visit personally and as a result it fails to find a mention in his personal narrative. The journals of Mr Elphinstone were used to provide a sense of the desert as it was in those days.

Napoleon had embarked recently on his Egyptian expedition unnerving the British who transferred, instantly, the perceived French threat from the south of India to the north-west. It was the formidable French army and not the navy that was feared. And they would now have access to a land route that could bring them to India. Governor General Lord Minto adopted a three-pronged game plan. Persia, Kabul and Punjab were to strengthened and used as British allies. Accordingly John Malcolm[1] was

---

1. John Malcolm, who had been sent to sign the treaty with Persia, had risen subsequently to the rank of major general succeeding Elphinstone to the post of governor to the Bombay Presidency.

dispatched to Persia, Montstuart Elphinstone[2] to Kabul and Charles Metcalfe[3] to Amritsar. Persia, which stood solidly in the way, agreed to deny any European power a passage to India provided Britain promised to help out with the Russian menace that loomed upon her border. Elphinstone secured a treaty with Shah Shuja of Kabul against the Franco-Russian menace but it all proved futile in the end for the Afghan was deposed soon after the treaty was concluded. Metcalfe took a while to convince Maharaja Ranjit Singh into withdrawing to the far bank of the Sutlej. The vacated portion was to become British held Punjab. But Ranjit Singh resisted giving up control over the lands between the Sutlej and the Yamuna and was won over only when the use of force was politely suggested.

Traditionally the route to Kabul lay through the plains of Punjab and the Khyber Pass – the only passage in the Himalayan range. The alternative was to go via Jaipur, Ajmer, Jodhpur and Jaisalmer. Diplomatically, Elphinstone chose his route bypassing all areas that could potentially spell trouble. The march that had begun from Delhi on 13 October 1808, led them through the 100 miles of British held territories

---

2. Monstuart Elphinstone, a civil servant who had served with the East India Company since 1795, had been present at Varanasi the day Nawab Wazir Ali was deposed. He lived to escape the massacre, become ambassador to the court of Peshwa Baji Rao II, conclude the treaty with Shah Shuja of Kabul and take the credit for the defeat of the peshwa at the Battle of Kirkee in 1817. In 1818, he became commissioner to the Deccan and served as governor to the Bombay Presidency from 1819 –1827. Steeped in the classics, Elphinstone believed that Britain's Indian Empire would not be long-lived and tried to aggressively push higher education for Indians at a time when Britain advised against it. He returned to England having refused the post of governor general twice. To his credit are *Account of the Kingdom of Kabul* and two volumes of *History of India*. Elphinstone College in Mumbai was named after him.

3. Charles Metcalfe was the second son of a major in the Bengal Army who became a director in the East India Company. Having graduated from Eton, Charles arrived, as a writer in Kolkata and studied Oriental languages at Fort William. His success with Maharaja Ranjit Singh earned him the reputation of a skilled diplomat by the age of twenty-four. In 1827, he was appointed member of the Supreme Council, and after the departure of Lord Bentinck, acted as provisional governor general until Lord Auckland was ready to take over. The highlight of his administration was the removal of restrictions imposed upon the Indian press – something that the directors of the East India Company did not take to kindly. It resulted in his resignation. Charles Metcalfe went on to become governor of Jamaica and later governor general of Canada.

It was Charles' brother, Thomas Metcalfe, who converted a tomb in the Qutub Minar complex at Delhi into his residence. It came to be known as Metcalfe's Folly.

to Kanor, which lay a few miles north of Narnaul (Haryana). From this point the Indian desert was said to begin. The desert's edge was approached with some apprehension, this being their first experience. The initial impression of the sands was likened to fresh snow. What were gentle piles to begin with, grew into hills that soon threw off the encroaching thorny bushes to revel in naked splendour under the noonday sun. The embassy followed the rather circuitous route through the northern sandy tracts of Shekhawati, Singhana, Jhunjhunu and Churu until it arrived at Bikaner.

The expanse of the Thar that would lead them to the Indus and the mountains beyond lay ahead. In comparison Shekhawati seemed to lose its entitlement to be included within the limits of the desert. This area could boast of not even one perennial stream, the local population being dependent upon two seasonal rivers, the Katli and Ghaggar. Water was a scarce commodity being raised from wells and harvested from the limited rainfall. Among the original inhabitants were the camel herders – the Raibaris, Bhatis, Mohil-Chauhans, Johiyas, Sankhlas, Parmars and Jats. Dominated by Rathores, they reared camels, horses and sheep, which made profitable trade during times of plenty. Famine and drought were features that were just taken in their stride.

Rao Bika

Jodha, the patriarch, viewed with satisfaction his growing tribe seated around the throne in the fabulous castle at Jodhpur. His brothers had stood steadfastly by his side during the days when the Sisodias of Mewar bayed for Rathore blood, accusing them of coveting the throne Chittaurgarh. Their father had been murdered at the hands of Choonda Sisodia and Mewar and Marwar had separated as a result. But they had all come a long way since then. Years of hardship and struggle had given them their own independent kingdom. Mandor had been recovered and the new capital raised at Jodhpur was into its sixth year.

Twenty-four sons, royal princes born of Jodha's queens, sat amidst their uncles and Bika[4] found himself next to Rawat Kandhal, the bravest of all his father's brothers. The whispered conversation between uncle and nephew did not escape the desert lord's notice. Perhaps it was a jest on his part or wilful negligence of his secondborn's rights but the heart of the father grew heavy with fear. How long would the martial blood lie quiet in the veins of his sons? Would the throne of Maroo fall victim to sibling rivalry?

Bika rose to announce that it was time he left Jodhpur and went in search of his fortune. Relinquishing his claim to the throne, he laid down but one condition; should Jodha's successor die without an heir, Bika would continue to stay away from the throne but, as the senior-most Rathore alive, would expect that the royal insignia, heirlooms cherished by the family since their days in Kannauj, be handed over to him.

On 30 September 1465, twenty-seven-year-old Bika left accompanied by Rawat Kandhal, who had sworn to help his nephew establish himself just as he did Jodha. Two brothers, several uncles, 100 cavaliers and 500 foot soldiers accompanied the prince. They arrived at Mandor to pay homage to the gods and ancestors. With an amulet of Shiva added to his treasured possessions, Bika turned north to where the sands grew deeper. The wild lands were known to the Rathores as Jangaldesh.

The men journeyed to Deshnok seeking the blessings of the charuni, Karni Mata, the clairvoyant who remained spiritually in touch with the mother goddess. Prostrating before her, Bika sought guidance.

'In these lands your fame will exceed that of your father's! But do not be hasty. Await my instructions,' said the lady as she placed her hand upon his head.

Bika rode on to Chundasar where the next three years were to be spent quietly training the army. His queen returned to Deshnok to give birth to Bika's heir. When the three years had passed Bika appealed once

---

4. Bika, according to the annals of Marwar, was the eleventh son of Rao Jodha. Some historians hold the view that perhaps he was second in line to the throne, which justified his claim as the senior-most Rathore to the emblems of Kannauj.

When Bika left, Karni Mata received yet another devotee. Rao Shekha, chief of a Bhati clan, came to complain about the Rathore's presence. War looked imminent. The Bhati clans and the Bhagodas had assembled under the eighty-year-old Kalikaran, ready to give battle. Rao Shekha asked for the lady's blessings but her words were to fill his heart with dread.

'The ultimate victory shall be Bika's. Give your daughter Rang Kanwari to Bika for his future is bright.'

Despondent, Rao Shekha abandoned the cause of the Bhatis. Undaunted by the betrayal, Kalikaran, leading his army of 300, went ahead with his plans and met with a hero's death. The Bhatis would not give up and instead took to guerilla tactics. Shekha tried to dismiss Karni Mata's words from his head. Bika had given up his rights to Jodhpur throne. He was nothing more than a struggling prince in search of a kingdom. Shekha would never give his daughter to such a man.

Rao Shekha was returning from a raid one day when the aggrieved party caught up with him. The rich booty was snatched back and Shekha found himself languishing in the dungeons of Multan. Shekha's queen appealed to Karni Mata who instructed her to go ahead with the wedding that had been destined and she, on her part, would make sure that Rang Kanwari's father would be there to give the bride away.

The moment the bridegroom struck the torna and was about to enter Pugal, a blaze of light lit up Shekha's cell. The goddess stood trident in hand. Meekly, Shekha submitted to her will and followed her home. The alliance between the Bhatis and the Rathores was sealed.

more to Karni Mata. Pleased by his devotion and self-restraint, she charted out the course of action:

'Proceed to Kodamdesar; build a temple to Bhairav (Shiva). Consider the act to be the laying of the foundation of your kingdom and begin the process of conquest.'

Bika did as he was bid but assuming that Kodamdesar was to be his capital, began the construction of a fort. This set up an immediate alarm amongst the neighbouring Bhatis and Bhagodas who prepared to give battle. Bika approached Karni Mata again.

He was not advised against giving up the fight but it was suggested that the castle be raised elsewhere. Since the Rajput code of honour allowed no retreat, the army geared up but at the same time Rati Ghati – the Red Pass, a site twenty-four kilometres east of Kodamdesar where the roads from Multan, Nagaur and Ajmer converged – was chosen as the new site.

The neighbouring Jat villages were occupied and soon Bika's kingdom extended up to the Punjab border. Discontent was however inevitable amongst the family members and Rawat Kandhal's grandnephews appealed to the sultan of Delhi. Their lands had been annexed by Bika's brother Bida. Sultan Buhlol Lodi ordered a restoration and Bika sought the intervention of his father. But help was not forthcoming for the desert lord was peeved. His son had not offered him a part of his first spoils, especially the newly conquered villages of Ladnun. Undaunted, Bika appealed to Bagha, the son of Rawat Kandhal. Reminding him of his father who had helped Bika establish a kingdom appealed to Bagha's generous nature. The matter was resolved peacefully.

Rawat Kandhal was in the meanwhile busy extending the boundaries of the new Rathore kingdom. With his sons, he advanced through the province of Hisar. Villages fell before him but at Sahwa, the armies of Sarang Khan put up a tough resistance. As the battle raged, Kandhal's saddle unexpectedly came apart and the seventy-year-old Rajput was dashed to the ground. His death brought the grieving Jodha and Bika together. Father and son joined forces to avenge their blood. The deeds of Rawat Kandhal lived on in the hearts of men and ballads were composed around the events of his last battle. The legacy of the great Kandhal lived on in his descendents, the Kandhalots.

In AD 1488, Karni Mata arrived to inaugurate the fort and named the new kingdom Bikaner. The chief of the Godara Jats anointed Bika's forehead: the beginning of a tradition that was to live on.

Rao Jodha survived for but another year and desiring peace amongst his sons reminded Bika of his promise. Sadly, Jodha's eldest did not enjoy the throne for long and died without an heir. Maroo passed into the hands of Suja. But Rao Suja was reluctant to part with emblems of Kannauj and an enraged Bika marched against his brother. Suja's mother intervened in time and the cherished heirlooms were brought to Bikaner. Amongst them were the sandalwood throne and the white stallion of Kannauj.

The lands of Rewari, which lay within the territory of the Lodi sultans of Delhi, beckoned to the restless Rathore and it was here that he received a fatal wound. Rao Bika died in 1504, leaving behind ten sons and a kingdom that bordered Jaisalmer to the west and Delhi to the east.

Rao Narayan Singh – Nara

Rao Bika's death was followed by the much expected turmoil as subdued neighbouring chiefs tried to reassert their independence. Nara had but a few short months at his disposal and those were spent suppressing the uprisings. The period of mourning for his father had not yet ended when Nara passed away, leaving the throne to his brother.

Rao Lunkaran

Thirty-five-year-old Lunkaran followed the aggressive policies of his father, annexing both Rajput and Muslim held lands adjoining his borders. Bikaner was now a power to contend with and Lunkaran found himself in a position to mediate between the ambitious Rao Ganga of Jodhpur and Mohammad Khan of Nagaur, while helping himself at the same time to the lands of Didwana, Narbad, Bagad, Kanthalia and Singhana.

Narnaul he desired at any cost and, refusing all offers of truce made by its nawab, Lunkaran went ahead with his battle plans. Realising that their king's ambitions knew no end, the chiefs withdrew. Lunkaran faced the forces of Narnaul alone, supported by his sons and a handful of men.

Though he died that day, Lunkaran's court was already being counted amongst the finest in the land. The Rathore was held in high regard by the princes of Rajasthan and his zenana was graced by a princess of Mewar, the sister of the legendary Maharana Sanga. The hand of his daughter, Apurva (Bala Bai), had been given to Rao Prithviraj of Amber and it was her son who had succeeded to the Kachwaha throne. Pomp and glamour were the boast of Bikaner.

Legend remembers him as the gallant who marched his armies to Jaisalmer demanding retribution, for his charun had brought back tales of the Bhati's flippant attitude towards the nascent Rathore kingdom. Both rao and rawal had declared peace by taking home a princess each.

Lunkaran's daughter became wife to Loonkaran Bhati, who was due to succeed to the throne of Jaisalmer. His granddaughter, the daughter of his heir, Yuvraj Jait Singh, married Maldev Bhati – Loonkaran's younger son. Destiny had it so worked out that the throne of Jaisalmer remained earmarked for the line of Maldev that resulted from this marriage.

Rao Jait Singh

Rao Jaitsi came to the throne in 1526, a few short months before the first battle of Panipat, which was to irrevocably change the destiny of Hindustan. Babar overcame the forces of Sultan Ibrahim Lodi and then prepared to take on the greatest 'Hindu' prince of the time – Maharana Sanga of Mewar.

But Jaitsi did not pause to think about such matters. He had one little detail to set right first. His father's death needed to be avenged and he marched to Dronpur. But by the time he arrived, the errant chieftain had fled. Appointing the culprit's grandson as the new chieftain, Jaitsi rushed back home, for more pressing matters were coming to a head. Babar had placed his sons as governors of his dominion and they, with the zeal of new conquerors, targeted the border kingdoms. When Humayun succeeded to Babar's throne, his brother Kamran[5], governor of Kabul and Kandahar, treacherously helped himself to Punjab declaring himself independent.

Greedily Kamran eyed Bikaner. Rawat Kandhal's grandsons had extended the north-western limits of the kingdom eating away resolutely into Bhati territory. In 1538, Kamran's forces overcame those of the Kandhalots. The Bhati fort of Bhatner[6] that had been won in 1527, from Rawal Jait Singh, fell to the Mughal. Jaitsi received a demand for tribute and acknowledgement of overlordship. The Mughal was spurned and Bikaner found itself surrounded. Jaitsi rushed to Deshnok. Karni Mata was invoked and Bikaner made ready for the long night that was to follow.

The ringing of anklet bells roused the Mughal's camp. The only light available on that pitch-dark night came from a few flaming torches. Then, in what appeared to be an invasion by women, a great slaughter followed. Believing that they had been attacked by charunis with magical powers the Mughal army took to its heels. So great was their terror that Kamran's royal umbrella was abandoned near the village of Chotriya where it remained preserved for posterity. Bikaner was saved. Perhaps it was the doing of Karni Mata, or perhaps the miracle had been brought about by strings of bells wound about the bodies of Rajput soldiers. Whatever be the case, Jaitsi bequeathed Chotriya upon the charuns of Bikaner.

Things were not going well for the Rathore kingdom of Jodhpur. Maldeo, the heir apparent, grew exasperated with his father's easy-going policies that let slip prized territories from their grasp. Rao Ganga was found dead one day beneath a palace balcony and the new rao marched his powerful army towards Bikaner. Realising that Maldeo was infact a more dangerous foe, Jaitsi made his peace with Sher Shah Sur, the Afghan

---

5. Humayun a cultivated gentleman, though not lacking in ability, had been deprived of his father's energetic versatility. He was unable to keep his nobles in order who were swayed by the other centres of power namely the emperor's three brothers. On his accession, Humayun had reconfirmed Kamran as governor of Kabul and Kandahar. To Askari he had promised Multan and to Hindal, the youngest, Mewar. But the treachery of his brothers cost him his crown and kept him from regaining it. For ten years, Humayun was unable to take any decisive action but in the end was forced into doing so. Hindal had already died in a skirmish with Kamran's men; Askari was sent in chains to Mecca and Kamran who was blinded made to follow.

6. Bhatner was subsequently occupied by the Chayal Rajputs and was back in Bikaner's possession by 1560.

The Karni Mata temple in Deshnok is famous for the numerous rats that have overrun it. They are a revered lot: said to be the souls of deceased charun clan members awaiting re-birth into the same clan.

The rats that live in the little temple are free to share food off the plates of devotees and receive their daily tilak and rations of milk from the priests.

who had just relieved Emperor Humayun of his throne. But by the time Sher Shah arrived, Jaitsi had been slain and Bikaner occupied.

About the time that Rao Jaitsi died, Karni Mata decided to take leave of the world. At Hardian Talai, she sat down to meditate and as she went into a trance her aged body burst into flames and was reduced to ashes.

Rao Kalyanmal

While Jaitsi faced the Rathores of Jodhpur, his family took refuge at Sirsa. Kalyanmal, the twenty-three-year-old heir, accompanied by the faithful minister Nagaraj, had been sent on ahead to meet with Sher Shah. The fallen Mughal emperor, Humayun, chose this very moment to plead with Jodhpur for sanctuary. His wife was expecting a child. Unknown to all, Humayun had been pleading for the life of the unborn Akbar. Though Maldeo was cold and unrelenting, he let slip from his grasp the opportunity to incarcerate the Mughal. Sher Shah's arrival caused Humayun's flight but the sultan's army set up camp among the sands. Having come this far, and having missed their quarry, they were intent upon adding Jodhpur to their list of trophies.

Rao Kalyanmal's army joined Sher Shah at Merta, while one of his thakurs left to redeem Bikaner. In the desert of Marwar, where they had congregated, Sher Shah drew with his own hands the raj tilak of coronation upon Kalyanmal's forehead anointing him rao of Bikaner. The tie with the throne of Delhi was sealed.

Kalyanmal lived to witness the rise and fall of the fortunes of Delhi. Sher Shah died in May 1545, but Humayun re-entered Delhi only after ten long years. It had taken this long to put down his brothers and depose the descendents of Sher Shah. Humayun was at last re-seated upon his throne. But within months this mild mannered emperor met his death in an unfortunate accident. He was succeeded by his son, the thirteen-year-old Akbar. Kalyanmal sought diplomatic relations with the Mughal. His nephew, Bagha, won the emperor's favour and with it the lost fort of Bhatner.

In 1571, Akbar arrived at Nagaur, a castle that he had won ten years ago. Having paid his respects at shrine of Khwaja Moin-ud-din Chisti at Ajmer, he was making his way to Punjab. Kalyanmal and his heir, Yuvraj Rai Singh, attended him at Nagaur and returned to Bikaner having accepted the office of munsubdar. Lying in the desert with no natural protection, Kalyanmal wisely chose preservation over independence and bowed before the superior strength of the twenty-nine-year-old Grand Mughal. His brothers' daughters – Bhanumati and Raj Kanwar – were bestowed upon the emperor.

While Maldeo of Jodhpur resisted the might of the Mughal, Rai Singh was charged with safeguarding the road that led to the ports of Gujarat. It passed through Jodhpur. Rai Singh led the imperial army onto Jodhpur and evicted Chandersen who had declared himself rao while the rightful heir of Marwar, Uday Singh, was busy at the imperial court. Rathores were pitted against Rathores.

Raja Rai Singh

Rai Singh abandoned the title of rao and assumed the titles of maharajadhiraj and maharaja even though the emperor had not sanctioned their use. Already a distinguished warrior, the thirty-three-year-old raja commanded a large personal force estimated at 12,000 horse and 50,000 foot. He was related to the emperor by marriage, as was Chandersen of Jodhpur for that matter, for they had all married the daughters of Rawal Har Raj of Jaisalmer.

Rai Singh was honoured with a munsub of 5,000 and held the highest rank among the 'Hindus' at the imperial court. His brother Prithviraj, popularly known as Peethal, was chosen by the emperor to remain constantly by his side and was counted amongst the nine gems of Akbar's court. The princes had made their mark as quick-witted military commanders with exemplary skill in the craft of war and Akbar had grown to depend upon them. Their loyalty, never in question, won them the emperor's confidence. Gujarat had been annexed after a traditional long-drawn-out battle, but no sooner had the imperial army pulled out that Akbar's rebellious cousins reasserted themselves. The emperor sought to waste no more time. A clever and short second campaign was formulated by Akbar himself. Its success depended entirely on the speed with which it was carried out. Led personally by Akbar the second Gujarat campaign of 1573[7], was a brilliant success. Bikaner's Rathores were present alongside those of Marwar during the siege of Jalor, a feat that catapulted young Guj Singh – the son of Crown Prince Sur Singh of Marwar – to the forefront. For the part they played, the princes of Bikaner were amply rewarded. While Rai Singh became master of Junagarh, Saurashtra and Kathiawar, which brought nearly all of Gujarat under his control, Peethal received as jagir, the fort of Gagraun, for the military skills displayed during the imperial campaign at Kabul.

In Akbar's Rajput wars, Rai Singh continued to play a major role. Abu was occupied reducing the support available to Maharana Pratap. The battle of Haldighati followed in 1576, led by Kanwar Maan Singh of Amber, reducing the unfortunate maharana to dire straits. Akbar had been away at the time busy with the conquest of Bengal but the Mughal generals took it upon themselves to harry the beleaguered Sisodia and dreamt great dreams of taking him alive. At last, the tired maharana wrote a letter of surrender. The imperial court rejoiced. But Peethal declared the letter a fake. Taking permission to verify its authenticity, Peethal wrote to the maharana:

The hopes of the 'Hindu' rest upon the 'Hindu'...

The immortal lines exhorted the only independent Rajput to continue the fight. Pratap awoke a new man.

---

7. Gujarat had, historically, been a part of the sultanate of Delhi and this, Akbar had felt was reason enough to stake claim. In any case, it was too wealthy to be left alone. The local government had fallen into disorder and by sheer stroke of luck Akbar received an invitation to intervene. The campaign began in July 1572. Surat was taken and an elated Akbar returned home the following April. Hardly had he reached Fatehpur Sikri when word arrived of a formidable insurrection headed by his disorderly cousins known as the Mirzas. Akbar, then thirty-one, was at the height of his faculties. He rose to the challenge. A new force was made ready with such extraordinary rapidity, that he could rightly boast of having outdone all his contemporaries. No one could have gotten ready sooner than him. The Rajputs that went with the advance guard included crown princes Rai Singh of Bikaner and Bhagwan Das of Amber. Riding out on 23 August the emperor travelled the 600 miles, at hurricane speed, with a small army of 20,000, engaged the enemy at Ahmedabad on 2nd September and was back in his capital on 4 October 1573. Gujarat had become unquestionably a part of the Mughal Empire.

The hopes of the 'Hindu' rest on the 'Hindu', yet the Rana forsakes them. But for Pratap, we would have all been reduced to the same level by Akbar. Our chiefs have lost their valour and our women their honour. Akbar has purchased us all from the flesh market but the son of Uday proved far too expensive. Despair drove many of us to permit ourselves to be sold but from such infamy the descendant of Hamir alone has been saved. Akbar, the merchant who is buying up the Rajputs, cannot live forever. Our race will then look to Pratap and his children to provide a pure breed of Rajputs with which we will rebuild Rajasthan.

Late in life Akbar was to compose the following lines remembering friends that had passed away leaving him alone:

Peethal so majlis gayee	With Peethal went the pleasure of gatherings
Tansen so raga	With Tansen music
Hansibo-ramibo-bolibo	Laughter, good company and conversation
Gayo Birbal saath	Left to keep Birbal company

When Akbar's half-brother, Hakim Mirza, not content with his share of territory in Kabul snatched at lands that fell within Akbar's realm, Rai Singh was sent to put the greedy prince in place. He remained in Punjab for five years keeping an eye on the border. The Lakki area of Punjab was exchanged for Bhatner in 1585. Utilising the imperial favour that he enjoyed, Rai Singh began adding to Bikaner's territories. In 1586, he began building the fort of Junagarh on which he lavished five long years. That year saw yet another celebration. Rai Singh's daughter[8] was given in marriage to the Mughal heir, Salim.

Rai Singh remained at the battlefront all his life and so strong was his bond with Akbar that not even the rebellion of his brother, Amar Singh, could undermine it. The rest of the family conducted themselves admirably. His uncle Kaka Saran won for the emperor, at the cost of his own life, peace in Kashmir. Akbar was truly indebted to the royal house of Bikaner and when one of Rai Singh's many daughters was widowed the emperor went personally and counselled the young woman to concentrate upon the needs of her children and forgo the rituals of sati. A second visit was made to Rai Singh's residence to condole the death. It is thought that Rai Singh's position in court was second only to that of Maan Singh of Amber.

Yet emperors make difficult companions. One of Akbar's fathers-in-law, who visited Bikaner in 1597, complained of having received improper treatment. The price was the confiscation of the fort of Bhatner. It was bestowed upon Dalpat Singh, Rai Singh's trouble creating firstborn. Rai Singh rushed to reason with the emperor as Dalpat's men struggled with the take-over. The result was a spilling out secrets. It was discovered that Karam Chand Bachhawat, Rai Singh's minister, had secretly been aiding Dalpat's rebellion while the raja served at the war front. Karam Chand fled and his properties were confiscated and declared state land.

Karam Chand made his way to the imperial court. A shrewd and talented man, he used his skills at chess to win the emperor's ear. Weaving his web of intrigue and deceit, he poisoned the atmosphere and Rai Singh distanced himself. At last Akbar could stand it no more. His loyal friend had been away too long. He restored to him the jagir of Gujarat. But with it was

---

8. According to the *Imperial Gazetteer*, Rai Singh's daughter became mother to Emperor Jahangir's second son Parvez.

an order to move to the Deccan. Sentimental and prone to emotions, Rai Singh did not respond. He went home instead. The heart of the emperor relented and he called for his friend's presence in court receiving him with every honour that was his due. In his last years Akbar gave to his friend the coveted castle of the serpent, Nagaur, that had been taken from Sher Shah's crumbling empire.

Akbar died in 1605, and Rai Singh supported the accession of Prince Salim. His office was raised but Khusro's rebellion raised doubts about the longevity of Jahangir's reign. A Jain soothsayer added his proclamations to the confusion and Rai Singh, who had been given the honourable task of escorting the begums from Agra to the safety of Delhi, deserted his post. Khusro was overcome, blinded and thrown into the dungeons. His fellow conspirators all met with horrible deaths. Rai Singh made his way back to the imperial court and through many an intercession and reassurance won back the trust and favour of his son-in-law.

Like his brother, Prithviraj, Rai Singh was himself a scholar and to him is attributed the *Rai Singh Mahotsav* and *Bal Bodhini*.

Raja Rai Singh died in 1612, at Burhanpur.

Raja Dalpat Singh

Raja Rai Singh's death left Bikaner in a state of confusion. Dalpat, the firstborn, won the emperor's pardon and declared himself king while Sur Singh, the younger son, was left insisting that he was infact his father's chosen heir. It was his forehead that had been anointed; but Jahangir decreed otherwise – a decision that he would almost instantly be made to regret.

Dalpat's turbulent nature plagued the emperor. Ignoring imperial orders that posted him to Thatta, he began the construction of a fort near the northern border of Bikaner's territories driving local Bhati tribes to panic. A force of 3,000 Bhatis appeared and tore up the newly laid foundation. After a couple of attempts the Rathores were forced into abandoning the site but years later Maharaja Anup Singh would choose the same location to build the fort of Anupgarh.

Then acting on the advice of his minister, Purohit Man Mahesh, Dalpat confiscated his brother's jagirs. Sur Singh appealed to the emperor. Jahangir reconsidered the wisdom of his decision and ordered Sur Singh to occupy the throne.

The imperial army moved into Bikaner but the first offensive proved to be a disaster. It was, however, only a matter of time before the chiefs of Bikaner defected. The thakur of Churu, Bhim Singh Balbhadrot, who enjoyed a position of trust at Dalpat's court, looked for an opportune moment to imprison his prince. Bhim Singh, whose seat was immediately behind that of the king, waited until news arrived that the armies had engaged. Dalpat was transported to Ajmer and thrown into the dungeons. In a desperate bid to escape he lost his life but Emperor Jahangir's historian has it on record that Dalpat Singh was brought to Delhi and executed.

But Dalpat was not unloved, for at Bhatner six queens climbed the pyre. Nor were his children uncared for. Rup Manjari's wedding was arranged the following year and the emperor graciously accepted her hand.

Raja Sur Singh

Nineteen-year-old Sur Singh came to the throne in 1613. He had pledged by his father's deathbed to rid Bikaner of its enemies. Immediately after the coronation he left to pay his respects to the emperor. While at the imperial court he called upon Lakshmi Chand and his brother, the sons of Karam Chand Bachhawat. The head of Bachhawat family was invited to occupy once more the position of prime minister of Bikaner.

The Bachhawats could not resist the temptation and despite the stern warning their father had left them with, returned to Bikaner. Within the space of two months, they found themselves surrounded by the king's men. Though outwitted, they swore that none would benefit from their death. They barricaded themselves in and by the time they were dragged out, their women had committed suicide and all their gold and precious stones ground to dust. The men emerged from their homes dressed in saffron. Not one Bachhawat survived except for a boy who was away at his maternal grandfather's home. He never returned choosing to settle instead in Udaipur.

In 1624, Rawal Bhim Singh of Jaisalmer passed away. His wife, Rani Kamavati – who was Sur Singh's sister, worried about her son's fate, for it lay in the hands of the chiefs of Jaisalmer. Sur Singh left immediately but before he could arrive the youth had lost his life. In sheer disgust, he passed a royal decree banning marriages with the house of Jaisalmer for all time to come.

Sur Singh grew to become a kind and just ruler and the Mughal Empire benefited from his presence. He was called upon by the emperor on several occasions and received jagirs and other honours in recognition for his work. He was asked to help control the disturbances caused by Khurram's revolt and when Khurram ascended the throne as Emperor Shah Jahan, Sur Singh found himself included amongst the honoured and trusted 'Hindu' princes of the imperial court.

Sur Singh died at Burhanpur aged thirty-seven, a favoured and trusted officer of the Mughal Empire to whom Jahangir had taken to writing informally. 'To raoji our Ram Ram.'

Raja Karan Singh

Karan Singh came to the throne at the age of fifteen. When the young raja came to present himself at court, Emperor Shah Jahan upgraded his munsub to 2,000 foot and 1,500 horse while his brother was granted a munsub of 500 foot and 200 horse.

Karan Singh was among the campaigners who besieged the Deccan, annexed the fort of Parande and kept the rebellious Bundela Rajputs of Madhya Pradesh in check. Umra (Amar) Singh, the rebellious and disinherited son of Maharaja Jaswant Singh of Marwar who had been granted the jagir of Nagaur, clashed with Bikaner over the border territories. Emperor Shah Jahan wisely kept both princes at Delhi, keeping the situation under control.

Unfortunately for the emperor, the war of succession between his sons started in his own lifetime. Unwilling to be drawn into controversy, Karan Singh, who had been posted in the Deccan under Prince Aurungzeb, returned to Bikaner without permission. Though his sons, Kesari and Padam, supported the cause of Aurungzeb, Karan's lack of cooperation was held against him. Aurungzeb owed his life to the princes of Bikaner and bardic sources maintain that when the young men returned from the battle with Dara Shikoh, Aurungzeb welcomed them personally, wiping the dust off their armour with his silken kerchief. Aurungzeb bestowed his own sword with its gold scabbard upon Kesari and it remained a proud possession of the house of Bikaner.

But Aurungzeb nurtured his grievance against Bikaner and he wasn't going to let it pass. An imperial army marched towards the desert kingdom. Karan Singh, on the other hand, had no intentions of indulging in petty squabbles. He met the Mughal general and in his company proceeded to Delhi. The misunderstandings were ironed out and Karan Singh resumed his office of imperial munsubdar and his post in the Deccan.

Bikaner's bardic lore recounts the days of oppression under Aurungzeb's rule. A fanatical Muslim, he brought back the days of forced conversions – the payment of jaziya or death. Then came the day when all 'Hindu' princes were ordered to Iran. As they neared Attock, on the banks of the Indus, news arrived of the demise of the queen mother of Jaipur. A ten-day mourning was declared and the 'Hindu' princes halted while the imperial army continued on its way. At the 'Hindu' camp a strange visitor materialised. It was a fakir, one so famous that he was allowed to collect one paisa annually from every home in Bikaner[9]. He revealed to the august gathering the dark plot that lay within the emperor's heart: the conversion of all 'Hindu' princes, once they were beyond the reaches of Hindustan. Horrified, the princes turned to Karan Singh. But Karan demanded acknowledgement. Quickly a makeshift throne was put together and to the cries of 'Jai Jai Jangaldhar Badshah', victory to the emperor of the wild lands, Karan Singh was acknowledged as the supreme ruler in all Hindustan. The boats that waited to ferry the princes across were burnt and Bikaner readied itself to pay the price.

As the imperial army approached the border of Bikaner, Karan Singh rushed to Deshnok. Karni Mata was invoked. As if by miracle the emperor's army stopped and retreated. The expected destruction of Bikaner did not take place. Karni Mata had saved the day. But it was just a matter of time before summons arrived. The Rathores had good

9. A privilege his descendents would be permitted to enjoy until 1947.

cause to be alarmed for it was known that Karan Singh's son by a junior queen, Banmali Das, was in Delhi. He had presented himself before the emperor and offered to convert to Islam in exchange for the gaddi. Unsure of what the outcome would be, but fully expecting some form of treachery, Karan Singh arrived at Delhi with his sons, Padam and Kesari. The two young men, who enjoyed great favour with the emperor, sat on either side of their father. It was just another day at court. Were there any murderous plans afoot one would never really know but the father received thanks for having raised a son like Kesari, who had saved the emperor's life. Brushing all praise aside, Karan Singh observed that in all probability the miracle lay in the strength of the emperor's prayers and his continuous reading of the *Koran* especially during the critical moments. Karan Singh had appeased the emperor but was far from forgiven. He was ordered to the Deccan and there he remained until his last day.

Within Aurangabad Karan Singh was granted a betel leaf garden where the jangaldhar badshah built his abode and named it Karanpur. A temple was built to Karni Mata, which has since been maintained by the treasury of Bikaner. No one was permitted to stay with him but Thakur Sangram Singh wilfully gave up his own liberty to remain by his side. It was he who performed the last rites when Raja Karan Singh passed away in 1669. The words 'Jai Jangaldhar Badshah' were to remain a proud memory and would be emblazoned upon the Bikaner coat of arms and presented to Bikaner in 1877, by Victoria, empress of India

The princes of Bikaner were famed for their valour. Padam and Kesari were favourites. The successful hunting of a lion had earned Kesari his name and a grant of twenty-five villages. Of Mohan Singh, the fourth son, Lieutenant Colonel Tod writes:

The young desert chieftain, like all his tribe, would find matter for quarrel in the wind blowing in his face.

He picked a fight with a relative of the emperor and lost his life in a duel. Enraged by his brother's death, Padam slew the offender and lifting the body of his brother onto his shoulder sent out a call to Rajputs everywhere. The insult had to be avenged. The Mughal heir apparent sent a noble to negotiate with the Rajputs who had decided to abandon imperial service. The shahzadaa approved of Padam's actions he pleaded, but there was no soothing of Rajput tempers until Shahzadaa Muazzam arrived personally.

It wasn't long before Padam lost his life in the emperor's wars leaving behind a son and three daughters: one of whom he bestowed upon Bheem, the disinherited son of Maharana Raj Singh of Mewar. Kesari died two years later leaving the eldest, Anup Singh, to rule Bikaner. Among the gallant princes of Bikaner it was Kesari, who retained his place firmly in the hearts of his people. His sword remains an object of adoration and continues to be worshipped in his memory.

Maharaja Anup Singh

Anup Singh had become ruler of Bikaner during his father's lifetime. He had served the emperor in all the expeditions to the Deccan and had played an instrumental role in the storm of Golconda, which earned him the Mahi Maratib – the order of the fish, an honour granted only to independent princes of the first class. For services rendered at Bijapur he won for himself in 1675, the hereditary title of maharaja.

At home, however, Anup Singh continued to be plagued by problems. The Bhatis constantly worried the border territories and the maharaja's half-brother, Banmali Das proved to be thorn in his side. On behalf of the absent maharaja, three officers of Bikaner – Mukund Rai, Amar Singh Sringot and the loyal Bhati chief, Bhag Chand – besieged the fort of Churia where the Bhatis were holed in. The fort was won and work began on the construction of a new fort, Anupgarh, which was to become the northern bastion. Both Anup Singh and Banmali Das enjoyed Aurungzeb's favour: Anup Singh through his exemplary work in the Deccan which won him the posts of kiledar (officer-in-charge of the fort) and faujdar (officer-in-charge of the army) of Sagar in Bijapur and Banmali Das through the influence of Saiyad Hasan a close confidante of the emperor who managed to obtain for his protégé an imperial grant, which made him master of half of Bikaner. Maharaja Anup Singh who had hitherto tolerated his half-brother's ambitions realised that the time had come for decisive action.

Banmali Das arrived with an army of 3,000 and demanded to inspect the revenue records before making his choice. The accountants were reluctant to divulge information without the king's permission and it was at this moment that Uday Ram came forward with his services. He corresponded with the maharaja and had an order issued for the grant of Banmali's share. Together they set off to Chingoi where Banmali Das hoped to lay the foundation of his fort.

Three outlaws – an old thakur, his daughter and his assistant – sought out the new king and fell at his feet. They had been on the run for years and pleaded for protection. Banmali was happy to grant any enemy of Bikaner refuge and accepted the lovely girl as his bride. That wedding night proved to be his last for unknown to him he had entertained none other than one of the maharaja's fathers-in-law, an impoverished thakur who had sworn to come to his Anup Singh's aid when the time came. Having secretly liased with Uday Ram, Thakur Lakshmi Das Songara had brought along a slave girl and a loyal assistant. The demure bride slipped poison into her groom's drink while Aurungzeb's men, who had accompanied the would-be king, were silenced with lavish gifts of money.

The maharaja remained all the while at Adoni in the Deccan where, having contained the revolts, he acted as governor until his death in 1698.

Bikaner prospered in his time and scholars and poets fleeing Aurungzeb's fanatical discrimination sought refuge in the desert kingdom. Valuable 'Hindu' writings that had been saved from destruction at the hands of the emperor were preserved in Bikaner's museums and libraries. Maharaja Anup Singh's library of rare Sanskrit works remain housed at the Lallgarh Palace. The Karan Mahal that had been conceived by his father to celebrate his victory over Aurungzeb was completed during his time. Here within its regal splendour future generations, that were to take their place upon the sandalwood throne, would be anointed.

Maharaja Sarup Singh

Sarup Singh was by his father's side on that last day at Adoni. Though first-in-line to the throne, he was born of Anup Singh's second wife, a Sisodia princess. The regency passed into the hands of his mother while

Sarup moved from Adoni to the imperial court at Delhi.

Meanwhile mischief was afoot at Bikaner. The queen mother's trusted aide Lalit, led her to believe that a senior minister was plotting against her. Frantically, she sent word to her son asking, at the same time, her husband's trusted minister, Mukund Rai, to take care of the situation. Mukund Rai arranged to have the offender murdered. But the advisors in Delhi were alarmed. They warned young Sarup about the meddlesome Lalit.

Anticipating his fall from grace Lalit switched to the Rajawat rani's camp. Her sons being half-brothers to Sarup were next in line. Hysteria gripped the zenana of Bikaner. The boys were packed off to Delhi in Lalit's company for it was assumed no mischief could take place in the imperial presence. The anxiety, however, proved baseless for while they were on their way, word arrived – the maharaja had succumbed to an attack of small pox.

Eleven-year-old Maharaja Sarup Singh gave way to his ten-year-old half-brother Sujan Singh in 1700.

Maharaja Sujan Singh

Sujan Singh came to present himself at Delhi and there he remained until his coming of age ceremony while the regency passed into the hands of his mother. At the Mughal court he received lessons in statesmanship and military sciences.

Seven years after the maharaja's coronation, Emperor Aurungzeb died and the power of the Mughal was broken. Maharaja Ajit Singh of Jodhpur regained his kingdom at last and with the zeal of a new conqueror marched upon Bikaner that had enjoyed more than a 150 years of relative peace thanks to the alliance with the Mughals. The kings of Bikaner had earned the rank of maharaja long before the senior Rathore clan could lay claim to the title. Fortunately it was only a temporary loss and the thakurs of Bhukarka and Malsisar were able to win back Bikaner's independence.

Delhi's throne witnessed a quick succession of emperors. The Rajputs took pleasure in meddling in the politics of Delhi, fanning fires whenever possible. Bikaner beset with its own worries kept to itself and though Sujan

Singh remained completely occupied containing rebellions within his own dominion, he faithfully sent his soldiers to the aid of the emperor every time a demand was put forward. Sadly a rift appeared between him and his heir, for Zorawar, who had been trusted with the reins of administration, cared little for his father's policies.

The powerful thakurs of Bhukarka and Bhadra continued with their interpersonal feud and Maharaja Abhay Singh of Jodhpur, made a second unsuccessful attempt upon Bikaner. The maharaja's energies were spent in ensuring peace in his land and his health eventually gave way. He died at camp in Raisinghnagar in 1735.

Maharaja Zorawar Singh

Zorawar Singh came to inherit a kingdom weakened by border disputes. The internal system of administration had broken down and everyday more chiefs raised their heads in defiance. An attempt at disciplining Sangram Singh of Churu drove him into Maharaja Abhay Singh's arms. Restoring him to his lands only served to increase his impudence. Sangram did not care to present himself before his king. Enraged, Zorawar Singh stripped him of all honours and lands and Sangram, this time in the company of Lal Singh of Bhadra, made his way back to Jodhpur.

Maharaja Abhay Singh had long lusted after the crown of Bikaner. No explanations were due for Delhi was embroiled in its own personal struggle. Emperor Muhammad Shah Rangila, crippled by the circumstances that surrounded him, was in no position to intervene. In 1739, Nadir Shah, a Turk, who had murdered his way to the throne of Persia invaded India. The Rajputs sat back and watched. Delhi was subjected to the cruellest sacking in its history and, as was expected, it was the common people that fell to the Turk's sword by the droves. The Red Fort was turned inside out. The treasures of the empire were plundered and India lost its glorious Peacock Throne and its greatest diamond – the one that Nadir Shah named Kohinoor. The humiliated emperor received permission to rule his bleeding empire in the name of Nadir Shah of Persia.

Abhay seized the opportunity. But as he marched into Bikaner he found waiting for him his own brother. Bakhta Singh of Nagaur had rushed to the aid of his fellow Rathores. That day, Abhay desisted from picking a fight but he returned again in 1740, led by the thakur of Mahajan who had joined the dissidents – Sangram Singh and Lal Singh. They made their way to Deshnok to invoke Karni Mata but were turned out by the charuns. The merciless army inflicted their vengeance upon the people looting and killing indiscriminately and laid siege to the fort of Bikaner.

The desperate citizens scanned the skies for a sign. Karni Mata could not have forsaken them. And she hadn't; for high above a white kite was espied circling the troubled city. The miracle duly took place and word arrived that a three lakh strong army led by Maharaja Sawai Jai Singh of Jaipur, Abhay's father-in-law, stood waiting to give battle outside Jodhpur. Bakhta Singh had come once again to the rescue though more out a quirky desire to add to the troubles of his older brother. But Bakhta had not wished to embroil Jodhpur in war. What had been intended as a prank had gone horribly wrong. In an attempt to make amends, he took on the forces of Jaipur while brother Abhay looked on determined to let Bakhta learn his lesson. Though it was the army of Nagaur that was annihilated that day the sting had gone out of Abhay's operation. He withdrew from Bikaner.

The Bikaneri forces took the opportunity to storm their benefactor's stronghold of Nagaur. Bhatner was regained and Zorawar planned an offensive against Hisar. He walked barefoot to the shrine of Karni Mata and gifted her with a gold umbrella. Money, blankets and food were distributed;

Hisar was occupied; the miscreants upon the border chastised and a promise extracted from the chief of Bhatner never to rise against the parent kingdom. Pleased with himself Zorawar made his way home. He halted at Anupurra where he took mysteriously ill. Within a matter of two days he was dead. Rumours of poison were never put to rest.

Maharaja Gaj Singh

Zorawar's death led to a crisis for he died without an heir. The fort of Bikaner was quickly taken over by Thakur Kushal Singh and Mehta Bhaktawar Singh. The task of choosing the successor began. In line to the throne were Amar Singh and Gaj Singh, sons of Zorawar's uncle Anand Singh. Though Amar was the elder, Gaj was deemed the more capable and was anointed to the gaddi of Bikaner. But there was more. A secret pact was signed between the new maharaja and the kingmakers. Never were they to be questioned over the expenditure incurred during the siege laid by Maharaja Abhay Singh of Jodhpur.

Maharaja Gaj had some celebrity from the number of his offspring, having had sixty-one children, though all but six were 'sons of love'. Through the forty-one years of his reign he expanded the borders of his kingdom grabbing lands and villages from the Bhatis. From the khan of Bahawalpur he recovered the castle of Anupgarh and laid waste the frontier lands, filling the wells with sand, rendering them unapproachable.

Gaj Singh's older brother defected to Jodhpur and led its army against Bikaner. It was yet another unfruitful attempt, for morale in Bikaner ran high. Gaj Singh then took to scheming against the parent stronghold and encouraged Bakhta Singh into grabbing the throne of Jodhpur from his brother's son. Maharaja Abhay's son, Ram Singh, in trying to free himself from his dominating chiefs had succeeded in alienating them. Backed by his cousin, Gaj Singh of Bikaner, and the chiefs of Maroo, Bakhta ascended the throne of Maroo.

Though there was one threat less for Bikaner, trouble continued to brew at home. Gaj Singh remained occupied putting down rebellions among the Shekhawats of the Nohar region and sending aid to Emperor Ahmad Shah who struggled to maintain control even within the limits of Delhi. The grateful Mughal granted him Hisar and it was placed under the control of Bhaktawar Singh, a minister at the court of Bikaner. When Mansur Ali Khan Safdarjung, the prime minister at Delhi rebelled, Gaj Singh rushed the Hisar division of his army to Delhi. The Mughal throne was saved and the maharaja was granted new titles, an increased munsub and a royal robe of honour. He would henceforth be known as Sri Raj Rajeshwar Maharajadhiraj Maharaja Siromani Gaj Singh. His eldest son won for himself an independent munsub and Bhaktawar Singh was honoured with the title of rao.

Maharaja Bakhta Singh of Jodhpur died in 1752, and his son, Maharaja Vijay (Beejy) Singh, came to depend heavily upon Bikaner's aid. Despite its own problems with insurgency, Bikaner supported him both materially and financially. Beejy was deposed within a year and held out at Nagaur while Ram Singh occupied the throne for the next nineteen years backed by his Maratha allies. Beejy struggled to build alliances but when he chose to liase with the Jat leader, Jawaharmal of Bharatpur, relations with Bikaner grew strained. By 1761, the Marathas, who had taken a drastic beating on the battlefields of Panipat, grew weary of Ram Singh's cause. The Treaty of Sambhar decided the issue of tribute and Maharaja Ram Singh found himself out in the cold. In 1772, Beejy Singh ascended the throne of Jodhpur for a second time. It was now that Maharana Ari Singh of Udaipur pleaded with Gaj Singh to persuade Beejy into returning the rich lands of Godwar. These had been handed over to Jodhpur for safekeeping during the years that a pretender had threatened the Sisodia throne. Beejy turned a deaf ear. The maharana died within a year and Godwar continued in Rathore hands becoming the brunt of many a thorny debate.

In 1759, the Bhatis and the Johiyas took up arms again and Rao Bhaktawar Singh rushed to Bhatner to regain control. The maharaja personally led his forces against Bhadra and Rawatsar. Rebellions within Bikaner were subdued.

Five-year-old Maharaja Sawai Pirthi Singh II of Jaipur came in 1768, to take as his first wife the maharaja's granddaughter – the daughter of his heir, Yuvraj Raj Singh. Sadly the little princess died within a few months of becoming Rathorni maharani of Jaipur. In his last years, Gaj Singh found himself alienated from his heir. Raj Singh, who had permitted himself to become embroiled in a conspiracy, was caught and thrown into jail. His fellow conspirators turned out to be Bidawats and Bhatis acting together with Nawal Singh Shekhawat and Thakur Hari Singh of Churu – men who stood to benefit the most from the death of the maharaja.

Maharaja Gaj Singh passed away in 1787, having forgiven his son.

In his lifetime he had witnessed the dramatic changes in the fortunes of Delhi. Emperor Ahmad Shah, who had ascended the throne two years after Gaj Singh, had lost Punjab almost immediately to Ahmad Shah Abdalli (Durrani) – the minion of Nadir Shah of Persia, who had upon his master's death made himself independent in his native Afghanistan. The emperor had then been blinded and deposed by his own wazir, the imad-ul-mulk, whose imperialistic notions unleashed upon the citizens of Delhi, in 1757, another bloody sack. The echo that sounded in the distant corners of the land went unheard and upon the fields of Plassey Bengal, unnoticed by all, slipped from the hands of its nawabs into those of a trader turned army man – Robert Clive of the East India Company. But the militant merchants could be ignored for the moment. It was the Afghan that had to be mollified. Whatever it took was to be lavished upon him. Mughal princesses; jewels; money; promises were all bestowed but the wazir failed to learn. Upon his invitation, came the deluded Marathas whose occupation of Lahore brought Abdalli raving and ranting out of retirement. The frustrations of the would-be empire builders were vented upon the hapless Alamgir II but there was no avoiding the Third Battle of Panipat that brought to its end the Maratha union. Abdalli placed Delhi under a Rohilla Afghan protector while the successor to the imperial throne – Shah Alam II – preferred to stick to the safety of Avadh. Only thirteen years later, once the protector was dead, did Shah Alam return. But he did not come alone. By his side were his new bodyguards, the Scindias. Maharaja Gaj Singh lived to witness Mahadji's rise to the dignity of vakil-i-mutlaq – regent of Hindustan, but not the outcome of the Battle of Lalsot. Gaj Singh died in March 1787, four months before this turning point in history.

Maharaja Raj Singh

Twelve days after the death of his father, Raj Singh sat upon the sandalwood throne.

That Raj Singh would earn a pardon and live to see this day came as a shock to many. Those that had played a part in seeing him incarcerated fled Bikaner. Among them were three of his brothers. But Raj Singh's good fortune did not last for, unknown to even himself, the king had contracted a deadly illness. The maharaja took to his bed almost immediately. Not for one day was he able to administer his kingdom. Twenty-one days later he was dead leaving behind two minor sons – Pratap and Jai.

His death remained shrouded in mystery with historians implicating the hand of the mother of Surat Singh, Maharaja Gaj Singh's fifth queen.

Maharaja Pratap Singh

Pratap Singh succeeded upon birth, with uncle Surat Singh acting as regent. Surat's older brothers chose that day to flee to Jaipur. The regent, who during the next six months managed to successfully disguise his ambitions, eventually revealed his plans to two chiefs. Rao Bhaktawar Singh, whose family had held the post of prime minister, grew suspicious. He was thrown into the jail and all opposition was silenced.

Mercenary troops were brought in from Bathinda and the nobles of Bikaner ordered to attend the regent's succession. The two traitors were the only ones by his side that day. Instead of uniting to oppose Surat Singh, the nobles chose to foolishly remain at their estates. Surat Singh set out with his mercenaries and attacked them one by one. Some were imprisoned; some put to death; the rest coerced into accepting him and subjected to hefty fines. There remained now but one obstacle. But young Pratap, was watched over closely by his father's sister. This elderly aunt would not allow the regent physical access to the four-month-old infant.

Surat sent for the needy Kachwaha prince of Narwar. He was promised a dowry of three lakhs of rupees. In vain did the poor lady object – she was well past the marriageable age. Her protests made no difference. She then accused him publicly, but Surat stood his ground. He gave her his solemn word: he would personally look after his nephew's welfare. The wedding took place on 9 October 1787. The departure of the bride signalled the death of Maharaja Pratap Singh.

Bikaner wrapped up in its own intrigues and politics remained untouched by the events that were causing an upheaval in the rest of Rajasthan. Mahadji Scindia, the regent of the empire, had invaded Rajasthan in July on the pretext of collecting taxes. But the armies of Jaipur and Jodhpur surprised the Maratha at Lalsot. Even the trouble creating chiefs of Mewar laid aside their differences and hurried to redeem their lands. Taking advantage of Mahadji's temporary weakness, a Rohilla Afghan – a grandson of the first who had been appointed protector after Panipat – grabbed control of Delhi and the emperor of Hindustan.

Maharaja Surat Singh

Within a year of Maharaja Raj Singh's death, the gaddi of Bika was pressed by its seventeenth occupant – an assassin. His older brothers united against him. Their troops assembled at Bhatner but Surat put up a fierce defence and won a resounding victory. Three thousand Bhatis lost their lives and their hold over Dabli. Upon the battle site, Surat Singh built his castle of victory – Fatehgarh.

The next year was one of great change. On 10 August 1788, the Rohilla blinded Emperor Shah Alam II. That inauspicious day spelt the official end of the Mughal Empire. Mahadji Scindia rushed to the emperor's rescue and in the process assumed the role of protector himself. Daulat Rao Scindia, who succeeded Mahadji, enjoyed the honour until 1803, when the Marathas were unceremoniously evicted by Lord Lake. Shah Alam II was officially declared a pensioner on the rolls of the East India Company.

Maharaja Surat Singh entered into alliances with Jodhpur and Jaipur ensuring that border disputes were put to rest. Internal problems continued, but ignoring the restless chiefs of Bikaner, Surat Singh rushed to the aid of Maharaja Sawai Pratap Singh of Jaipur. George (Jhajh) Thomas[10], who

---

10. George Thomas, the sailor raja (jahazi sahib – ship sahib) from Tipperary, Ireland, had arrived at Madras (Chennai) as the quartermaster of a ship in September 1782. Weary of a subordinate career, he deserted and made his way to a post of honour in the lovely widow Begum Samru's (Sombre – for her first husband, Walter Reinhardt, a mercenary from Luxembourg, was said to have worn a sombre look) army at Sardhana (now in Uttar Pradesh). She had risen from a nautch girl to become the successful general of her late husband's army. In the face of his obvious attraction, she married another and dejected, Thomas raised his own forces, establishing himself in, what is today, Haryana. Despite being harried by the lady's army, which was often, the gallant rushed to her rescue whenever occasion demanded. He could be drunk for over a month but during action was known to remain stone cold sober. Although he was adopted by Appa Khande Rao – a Maratha adventurer who had been dismissed from Scindia's army – Thomas, because of his foreign blood, was denied the rights of a legal successor. Turning to king and country he offered to place Punjab into the kitty. But, because of his Maratha connections, the East India Company would not have him. Would a salaried post under Daulat Rao Scindia's French general, Perron, and a chance to lead his mercenaries against Holkar do? All that was required was the surrender of Jajhar. But had his adopted father not been slighted by the same set of people and was Perron not a man that served two masters? Among the men that Perron sent against Thomas, was James Skinner who left behind copious writings documenting the times. In the end, leaving his family in the care of Begum Samru and meekly accepting British protection, he made his way towards Kolkata. George Thomas died during the journey on 22 August 1802 aged forty-six.

had led the Marathas against Jaipur, backed off. But Bikaner was chosen as his next target. Perhaps he was invited by the Bhatis who chafed at the very sight of Fatehgarh. A full-scale offensive was launched. Faced with the firangi's determination, Surat Singh decided to buy him off. Two lakhs of rupees were promised. But the payments were not honoured and Jhajh sahib returned, unfortunately at a time when Surat Singh was away at war. Fatehgarh was razed to the ground. Bikaner teetered on the brink of destruction when a Sikh cavalry unit rushed to the rescue. Surat's diplomatic alliances had paid off. Jhajh sahib withdrew to Jhajhar (George-garh or Jahaz-garh in Haryana) and Fatehgarh was restored.

Surat Singh had established Bikaner's reputation as an independent and formidable force. Military aid was offered to all neighbours including Khuda Baksh of Bahawalpur. In 1802, an expedition was mounted against Khangarh and though the castle was ransacked its fabled wealth was never found.

Slowly and systematically insurgency was tackled. The rebellion in Churu was put down and tribute levied upon its chief. The Bhatis were next. Bhatner, the ancient Bhati fort, was renamed Hanumangarh. But it was the support that Surat extended to Dhonkul, the pretender to the throne of Jodhpur, that drove Bikaner to ruin. It taxed the chiefs heavily. Observed Tod dryly:

> In consequence of this, the usurper fell sick, and was at the last extremity; nay the ceremonies for the dead was actually commenced, but he recovered, to the grief and misery of his subjects.

The rise of the British could no longer be denied and the advantages of an alliance were becoming more and more obvious. In 1808, Monstuart Elphinstone was appointed ambassador to Kabul and as he made he made his way through Bikaner, Maharaja Surat Singh came to meet him. The keys to the fort of Bikaner were offered. Though these were politely declined it was evident that a treaty would soon take place. Agitation continued amongst the Bhatis and the thakurs of Churu. There could be no more waiting and the maharaja dispatched Kashinath Ojha to draw up a treaty with the East India Company. On 21 March 1818, a declaration of 'perpetual friendship, alliance and unity of interests' came into being.

Under the terms of the treaty, Bikaner was made to return lands grabbed from those who had bound themselves with the British. In return financial help was to be provided to suppress lawless acts within Bikaner's boundaries and though the Rathores would continue to maintain their own army they could also, against payment, borrow troops from the East India Company. The treaty had been signed in good time for soon there was another uprising: a powerful, concerted effort by the chiefs of Bikaner. The affair was left in the capable hands of General Alner. Twelve forts were occupied and returned to the maharaja while Bhadra was retained by the Company to pay for war expenses.

On 3 May 1820, at a multiple wedding ceremony in Udaipur, Surat Singh's sons took part. Yuvraj Ratan Singh took as wife Maharana Bhim Singh's daughter Ajab Kanwar and his brother Maharajkumar Moti Singh, Deep Kanwar. Maharawal Guj Singh of Jaisalmer married Roop Kanwar and Yuvraj Mokkam Singh of Kishangarh took as bride the maharana's granddaughter, Kika Bai. The three kingdoms reaffirmed their ties with Mewar and with each other.

At the durbar of 1827, a nuzrana of precious articles was presented by Bikaner to Governor General Lord Amherst. In turn, Maharaja Surat Singh received a robe of honour.

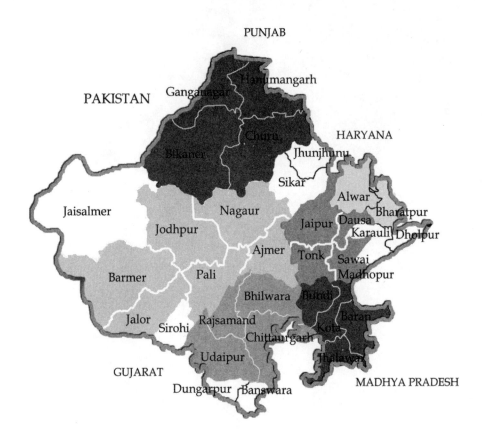

Remnants of the kingdoms of Rajputana within modern Rajasthan.
Districts of Rajasthan that were once included in the kingdom of Hadavati.

CHAPTER 4

HADAVATI BUNDI & KOTA

The south-eastern corner of Rajasthan belongs to the Hada-Chauhans. Upon the banks of the river Chambal, in the shadow of the central plateau extending all the way to the border of the modern Indian state of Madhya Pradesh, lies the region of Hadavati. For a while the Hadas had laid claim to the plateau but that was before Mewar reasserted her age-old authority.

The plateau had slipped out of Mewar's grasp in AD 1303, when Sultan Alla-ud-din Khalji of Delhi took possession of Rajput forts that could threaten the security of the trade route that led to the ports of Gujarat. A deathblow had been struck at Chittaur. As the kingdom of Mewar disintegrated, the tribes lost no time in reoccupying their ancestral lands. The plateau returned to its original inhabitants – the Meenas.

Alla-ud-din, like Mohammad Ghuri, the sultan of Ghazni, had also been responsible for displacing several Rajput clans. They had been forced to scatter seeking new homes and kingdoms to rule. Many had settled in Mewar, but the desire for independence continued to smoulder. Alla-ud-din's military campaigns threw up new opportunities and they did not go unrecognised. Wresting the plateau from the Meenas, the Hada-Chauhans set about constructing their castles. In no time at all, twelve castles dotted the landscape with the stronghold of Bambaoda at the centre. The valley of Bunda, the Meena chieftain, was conquered in 1341, and the spires of the palace of Bundi proclaimed the growing might of the Hadas. In 1364, Kota, the valley of the Bhils, was occupied and it became a jagir (fief) of Bundi.

However, as Mewar recovered, the Sisodia maharanas not only reclaimed lost lands but also eyed the new territories acquired by their one-time vassals. The Hadas were evicted from the plateau and though they openly accepted the supremacy of Mewar, they held on tenaciously to their possessions in the Bundi and Kota areas. Kota remained a fief of Bundi until 1624, when it was made independent and granted to a younger son of the royal family. The princely states of Bundi and Kota became a part of British India in 1817, and came under the political superintendence of Captain James Tod.

Captain James Tod had been stationed in Mewar since 1817. In October 1819, when the last of the princely Rajput states had signed the agreements with the East India Company, he began an official tour of the kingdoms. His geographical descriptions, the result of a surveyor's critical eye, remain the only record of the land as it had been in the early nineteenth century. His store of tales had been collected not only from the oral records of bards, priests and ascetics, but also from the written records that he was permitted to examine. Tinged with mythology and colourful imagination, oral tradition, as always, is the cause for many a historical debate. It remains nevertheless the most charming of accounts of the genealogy of the people of Rajasthan.

29 January 1820: Circumstances in Kota necessitated the captain's presence among the Hadas. This was an opportunity he could not lose, for it gave him the chance to write about the 'men and manners' of a region little known to Europeans. Maharao Raja Umed Singh had passed away the previous November, and the new king had been crowned in the captain's absence amidst great political upheaval and uncertainties.

The march began from the heights of Toos, which looked down upon the Berach as it flowed out of the Uday Sagar. An elaborate retinue replete with elephants, camels and horses carried the wares required to ensure a comfortable journey. Captain Patrick Waugh – cousin to the captain, Dr Duncan with his medical expertise and young Lieutenant Cary made up the company. Skinner's horse provided the escort.

Making most of the lovely weather, they marched fifteen English miles to reach the lake of Kheroda. The freezing temperatures of daybreak rose to 90 degrees Fahrenheit by noon and the cloudless sky flaunted its dazzling splendour at night. The route had been laid through Hinta, Morwan, Nikumbh and Marla to the Pathan occupied township of Nimbahera. Nine miles ahead upon the plateau lay Kanera.

Well wooded with abundant streams, every nook and glen of the plateau was devoted to the worship of Shiva.

The Chauhans of Ajmer and Delhi had been supreme in their time. Their glorious origin remains immortalised in the songs of the bards.

'Drawn out, by Lord Vishnu, from the sacred fire of Mount Abu, the first Chauhan was the image of his four-armed creator – Chaturbhuj. A celestial weapon was granted for each hand and he was pronounced king of Macavati Nagari (Gurha).'

Many generations later, a young prince, Ajay Pal Chauhan, left Gurha to settle on a hill, which came to be known as Ajay-meru or Ajmer. Here the Chauhans built their famous fort Taragarh. Ajay Pal's descendent, Manik Rai Chauhan, came to be known as the lord of Ajmer and Sambhar and it was he who made the name of the Chauhans famous.

Manik Rai's patron goddess, Shakambari, had promised him as much land as could be encompassed within the span of a single day warning him at the same time not to look back until the deed was done. Riding hard, he forgot the injunction and, as the western sky darkened to a deep shade of red, Manik Rai turned to gaze upon what was to be his future kingdom. The rich, fertile tract with its great lakes turned, before his very eyes, to a sparkling white. He had no one but himself to blame and the Chauhan acknowledged his patron by naming the salt lakes Shakambari or Sambhar. The Hadas, the most important branch of the Chauhans, claim descent from Manik Rai[1], the first Rajput who was said to have faced the might of Islam – the myrmidons let loose by Khalifa Walid I.

Of the famous Hadas of Asi, Hamir ruled peacefully but to his successor Rao Chand Hada, came Alla-ud-din Khalji as a messenger of doom. The walls of Asi, once said to be impregnable, could not withstand the invader and the fort was razed to the ground in AD 1295. The only survivor of the Hada race was two-year-old Prince Rainsi who had been away with his mother visiting her maternal home at Mewar.

Mewar had not escaped Alla-ud-din's notice either. Chittaurgarh had been lost, its ruling dynasty, the Guhilot rawals, wiped out, but the spirit had not dampened. The Sisodia ranas, who were cousins to the Guhilots, salvaged from amongst the wreckage a semblance of a kingdom – the recovery of Chittaur remaining never far from their hearts. With the leading family thus occupied, its dependent tribute paying jagir holders declared independence. The ancient castle of Bhainsrorgarh was captured by the Bhil chieftain, Doonga, who set it up as his mountain retreat.

Rainsi, as he grew to manhood, discovered himself to be a prince without a kingdom and offered to redeem Bhainsror. The rana granted the castle to his Hada nephew.

The plateau of central India had been home to the aboriginal Meenas. In ancient times, Raja Hun had driven them out making himself lord of the plateau. He held court at Menal and his memorials and temples lay scattered over the land, the exquisite workmanship of Baroli testimonial to his architectural skills. Here Angad Singh, lord of the Huns, had celebrated his wedding and it was he who had gone with Bappa Rawal to the aid of the Mori[2] prince of Chittaur. Chittaur had been saved from falling into the hands of the Arabs

---

1. Manik Rai Chauhan is supposed to have been a contemporary of Rawal Bappaditya of Mewar. Roshan Ali, who made his way to Ajmer, had his finger cut off for having dipped it into a pot of curds meant for the king. The finger flew to Mecca. It was recognized as that of the saint's and an army was despatched. Manik Rai's infant son was playing upon the battlements when an arrow struck him. A silver anklet had marked him out as target. Ajmer fell to the forces of Islam. While the child earned his place in the pantheon of the Chauhans, the wearing of a silver anklet remains forbidden amongst the children of the race.
2   The Moris were a principal branch of the Parmars.

Legend claims that the ancestor of the Hadas set up the kingdoms of Asi[3] and Golconda (Hyderabad, Andhra Pradesh). The two Rajput kingdoms were attacked by 'barbarians' from the wilds of Gujilbund (though it appears to be Gujni – Ghazni, it is supposedly the ancient name for Khambhat – Cambay, which had been occupied by the Arabs in the eighth century AD). The Chauhan clan of Golconda perished and as the women flung themselves into the flames of jauhar, Princess Surabhi stole away. She made her way to Asi only to find that it too had not been spared. Among the dead, lay Prince Ishtpal, the son of King Anuraj who had descended from the line of Vishal Dev Chauhan and Manik Rai. The grieving Surabhi took shelter beneath a peepul tree and awaited her own death.

'Be of good cheer,' said a voice.

Ashapurna Devi, the guardian goddess of the Chauhans, appeared before her.

'One of your own race has slain the demon.'

Surabhi was led to where Ishtpal lay and instructed to gather his bones (had[4]). The goddess sprinkled them with water and Ishtpal returned to life.

Together, Surabhi and Ishtpal recovered the fortress of Asi and their children came to be known by the name Hada.

---

3. The whereabouts of Asi are debatable. Some claim it is Hansi in Haryana.
4. 'Had' or bone, is pronounced as 'häd' with the ä being pronounced as in far, harm, hart etc. The 'd' at the end is pronounced as cross between a 'd' and a 'r' with the tongue being taken back as far as possible on the palette and then flicked forward back into position. The legend, though a pretty one, does not ring true for consanguinous marriages were never permitted. The Hada bards have yet another version on offer. The Hadas, they claim, descended from the Chauhans of Nadol and migrated after Qutub-ud-din Aibak occupied their kingdom. A scion of the family – Manik Rai II – settled in Mewar with Bambaoda as his base. Hado, a sixth generation prince, lent his name to his race.

Of Rainsi's two sons, Kolun and Kankul, Kolun was struck by an incurable disease and was advised to make a pilgrimage to Kedarnath, the abode of Lord Shiva.

The penance was a difficult one. The 1,000 odd kilometres would have to be measured by the length of his body. He would begin by laying himself down on the path with his feet at the starting point and marking the position where his head lay. Rising, he would place his feet at the spot marked out by his head and lie down once more. This tedious method would be repeatedly employed until he reached Kedarnath.

After six months of this painful journey, Kolun had barely reached Bunda-ka-nal – the valley of Bunda. Here he bathed in the Banganga rivulet and found himself greatly recovered. Amazed, he sank to the ground in prayer. Pleased with his devotions Lord Shiva appeared before him. Kolun was crowned king of the plateau: the Hadas had been granted a divine right.

but Bappa had used the victory to usurp the Mori throne. The Huns accepted the new lord of Chittaur and the plateau was included within the realm of Mewar. But with Alla-ud-din's coming, the aboriginal Meenas and Bhils regained the plateau once again.

Rao Bango

The grandson of Kolun, Rao Bango, overcame the Meenas and took possession of the ancient city of Menal. On the western face of the plateau, he built the fortress of Bambaoda. With Bhainsrorgarh on the east and Bambaoda on the west, the Hadas were in control of the entire plateau. Fresh conquests added Mandalgarh, Bijoli, Begun, Ratangarh, and Churetgarh to the wealth of the Hadas.

The twelve sons of Bango spread out over the region and the eldest, Deva, succeeded as the next rao.

Rao Deva

The wealth of the Hadas did not escape the notice of the sultan of Delhi who summoned Rao Deva to his court. Bequeathing Bambaoda to his son, Har Raj, Deva left for Delhi accompanied by his youngest, Samarsi.

The sultan was an ardent admirer of horses and the rao's steed was famous. He could leap across rivers without so much as wetting a hoof. The nuzzer of the sultan was upon the steed that had never failed to share the fortunes and the exploits of his master. Realising that he would not be in a position to refuse the emperor, Rao Deva decided to return. Taking the precaution of sending his family home in advance, he appeared below the sultan's balcony, lance in hand, seated astride his charger.

'Farewell king,' he said, 'there are three things your majesty must never ask of a Rajput – his horse, his mistress or his sword.'

In a flash, he was away and did not stop until he had reached the safety of the plateau.

Aloo Hada who had succeeded his father, Har Raj, was returning one day from a chase when he was accosted by a charun (bard). In return for his blessings, the bard would accept nothing but the turban worn by the chief. Wearing Aloo's turban, the charun made his way to Mandor, the capital of Marwar. Standing before the Rathore rao[5] he removed the turban before bowing his head. The Rathore was surprised and demanded an explanation.

'The turban of Aloo Hada bows to no one,' was the reply.

The king of the desert was enraged. Walking up to the bard he kicked the turban right out of his hands.

The charun returned woefully to Bambaoda with the turban tucked under his arm and Aloo, who until now had been peacefully occupied, berated the bard for having unnecessarily provoked this indignity. It would now need to be avenged. Gathering 500 of his clansmen, the mountain prince prepared to take on the king of the desert. It was going to be a desperate encounter and the Hada women, in anticipation, lit the flames of jauhar. The safety of Aloo's nephew, the heir of Bambaoda, was paramount for he alone would preserve the bloodline of Aloo Hada. The youth was locked in the castle behind the security of seven gates.

Well aware that he had called it upon himself, the rao of Mandor prepared both himself and Marwar. Confident that the Hadas would be detected and slain the moment they set foot in the desert, he made a haughty declaration. Lands that Aloo and his men should succeed in marching over would be given away as daan (donation) in perpetuity to the Brahmin community.

Aloo and his men, however, were not averse to strategy and disguising themselves as horse merchants, arrived undetected at the gates of Mandor. Before dawn, the nakarras of the mountain prince woke the

---

5. In all probability this would have been Rao Chunda of Mandor or his one of his sons – Rao Kanha or Rao Ranmal.

Rathore rao. The queen mother accosted her son.

'How did he now propose to keep his word?'

Impressed with their daring, the Rathore decided to give the Hadas a fair chance. He offered to meet them with only 500 men. A hand to hand combat was proposed.

As the warriors sized each other up, a youth, his horse panting for breath, galloped into the arena demanding to engage a gigantic Rathore. It was Aloo's nephew who, having found the locks of the seven gates mysteriously opened, had arrived to be by his uncle's side. The arrival of the headstrong heir drew exclamations of dismay but the youth's sword cleaved his opponent in two. Another took his place and shared the same fate. Aloo's nephew slew twenty-five Rathore braves before he was himself stretched on the ground. The Hadas were distraught.

The queen mother of Mandor watched in horror and her heart grew cold at the thought of the vengeance that was yet to come. Commanding an immediate end to the contest she offered a daughter in marriage to the lord of the plateau. Aloo's honour redeemed, he returned to Bambaoda with his bride. Vijayseni – the guardian goddess of armies, whose statue stood at the gate of the castle of Bambaoda, had saved the day by releasing the youth from behind the locked gates.

Destiny had however, decreed that the race of Aloo Hada was to perish and on the day of his daughter's wedding, a decrepit old woman came to join the feast. She insisted that she had been invited personally by the father of the bride. But the guards laughed her away.

Uttering a curse, Vijayseni left and the bloodline of Aloo Hada was soon extinguished.

Deva made his way to Bunda-ka-nal, where Kolun had found redemption. Here ruled the aborigine, Jaita Meena, of the Usara tribe. Secure in their little valley, the Meenas built their huts wherever fancy led them to. But this community, that had rushed to defend Chittaurgarh when Alla-ud-din Khalji had threatened, was now at the mercy of the Kinchi[6] Rao Gango. From his castle at Ramgarh (Relawan), Gango imposed himself upon the local tribes. To save themselves from his tyranny, the Meenas had agreed to suspend a bag filled with tribute over the gate to their village, on the full moon of every second month.

That day, Rao Gango appeared at the appointed time but found no bag.

'Who has been here before me?' he roared.

Deva appeared mounted on the steed so coveted by the sultan of Delhi. Gango of Relawan was astride a charger of equal fame. A fierce battle followed and the Hada was victorious. Gango turned and fled while Deva gave chase. The Hada followed him all the way to the banks of the Chambal and just when he thought he had his opponent cornered, Gango sprang from the cliff. Horse and rider disappeared beneath the waters of the flooding river and emerged moments later on the far bank. The spectacular sight amazed the Hada.

'Bravo Rajput! Let me know your name,' called out Deva.

'Gango Kinchi,' was the answer.

'And mine is Deva Hada. We are brothers and must no longer be enemies. Let the river be our boundary.'

In 1342, Jaita Meena and his tribe acknowledged Rao Deva as their lord. Bundi was built in the centre of Bunda-ka-nal or the valley of Bunda. The territory so described came to be known as Hadavati or Hadoti.

---

6.   The Kinchis are a branch of the Chauhans as are the Hadas.

As Aloo Hada's kinsmen settled the land around Bambaoda, twenty-four Hada castles came up on the plateau. One belonged to Lallaji, who sent a coconut offering his daughter's hand to Maharana Hamir of Mewar. The bearer of the coconut was the family priest and Hamir's refusal saddened the holy man. On the way back, he came across Kshetra Singh (Khaitsi), the heir apparent of Mewar, who was out hunting. The prince listened to the tale of grief and, taking the coconut from the priest's hands, promised to marry the Hada maiden.

With an escort befitting the heir of Chittaurgarh, he arrived at Bambaoda. With him came Bheemsen Bardai, the favourite bard of the court of Mewar. There was joy in the air and sounds of mirth rang through the castle walls. Gifts were lavished upon the priests and bards who had congregated for the wedding.

Richly caparisoned horses and elephants were on offer – gifts that the community is banned from accepting. Bheemsen, having made many an excuse, gave way to temptation. As shame overcame him, he buried his dagger in his own heart. Cries rent the air, 'The sacred bard of Mewar is slain.'

The news arrived just as the bride's hand was placed in that of the groom's. He dropped her hand and demanded compensation. The father of the bride was offended. This was the second insult compounding the one already proffered by the prince's father. The heir of Chittaurgarh was asked to leave.

When Khaitsi succeeded to Hamir's throne, the army of Mewar came to seek revenge. The Hadas refused to give battle but Khaitsi lay in wait. The month of Falgun arrived and with it came the festival of spring. Lallaji left his castle to hunt a boar in the name of Gauri and the maharana sought him out in the depths of the forest. Hada and Sisodia fought to the death.

Mother and daughter ascended their respective pyres: the mother her dead Hada lord's and the daughter that of Khaitsi, maharana of Mewar.

As she mounted the steps of the pyre, Khaitsi's bride gave vent to her anguish. The virgin sati pronounced death upon all Sisodia maharanas and Hada raos who dared forget her agony and meet for the spring hunt.

The bards of Rajasthan look back upon their history and recount the sad instances when the curse had been ignored.

Hamoo Mukul marya	Hamoo killed Mokal
Lalla Khaita Ran	Lallaji slew Kshetra Singh Rana
Soojo Ratna sengaria	Surajmal killed Ratan
Ajmal, Ursi Ran.	Ajit slew Ari Singh Rana

His Meena subjects far outnumbered the Hadas and Deva took recourse to a barbaric act. Summoning the Hadas of Bambaoda and the Solankis of Toda (Tonk), he declared war upon the native tribes determined to wipe them out.

Bundi was now granted to Samarsi just as Bambaoda had been granted to Har Raj. This was the Hada rao's second abdication. As tradition demanded, an effigy of Deva was consigned to the flames. He was no longer king nor subject of Hadavati and never again did he enter either of the two cities. He lived out the rest of his days in a village on the outskirts of the kingdom.

But while Bundi was destined for glory, fortune did not favour Bambaoda.

Sixty years ago, wrote the captain, the entire plateau right up to the Chambal belonged to Mewar. But that was then. It had since fallen into the hands of the Marathas. Kanera, the sole exception, had been successfully recovered and returned to the maharana. Making their way through Scindia land, that had once been the property of the Meghawats of Mewar, they entered the valley of the Bamni (brahmani). At the entrance to the thirty-mile-long valley stood the castle of Kala Megh. The Bamni coursed towards the Chambal watering its lush banks. Here lay Singoli: a town of 1,500 built around a castle that once had belonged to Aloo Hada. Though none of his line lived to tell the tale, the centuries had failed to erase his name. Of all his castles, Ratangarh alone had been left intact. Diwalgarh and Paroli had long been reduced to ruins. But it was Bambaoda that stood on the western crest of the plateau that remained the most famous.

Desolation reigned in the court of Aloo Hada. Bambaoda was shrouded in silence. The andheri kotri or the dark chamber, which had once been charged with preserving the life of Aloo's nephew, held on guiltily to its secrets. Amongst the ruins lay Jain and 'Hindu' temples and three tanks that had survived the passage of time. The peak of Bambaoda towered over the plains of Mewar, looking through the Arnio Ghati pass into the valley of Begun. Standing guard at the edge was a gigantic statue of Jogini Mata (Vijayseni). The queen of the pass looked down upon the sylvan landscape where 20,000 men would once have assembled. But no longer was there a foe to oppose nor a prince to guard, for Bambaoda, once a fiercely independent castle, had long been included within the fief of Begun

The path descended gently from Kanera to Dhareshwar. Two miles away lay the township of Ratangarh Kheri. A clear stream led the way through forests of fine timber. At Dhangermow three choices presented themselves. To the left was the celebrated Menal, to the right – but out of direct line – Bhainsrorgarh. Straight ahead lay Kota. A detour was taken and the course of the Bamni followed to visit the famous fort of Bhainsror. Using hatchets to cut their way through dense jungles the party descended. The roar of mighty waters echoed as the Bamni came into view cascading fifty feet into the valley below. The incredible volume of water that flowed during the monsoon was evident from the weeds that remained entangled upon treetops deposited during the last flood. A pyramid of stones caught the eye. It was a memorial to a Rajput who had fallen defending his post against the Meenas of the area. Every passerby added to the growing pile and the captain dutifully placed his contribution.

The castle of Bhainsrorgarh was situated on the extreme point of a ridge. On its eastern side, 200 feet below the face of the cliff flowed the Chambal. The monsoon swell had left its mark some thirty feet below the castle. To the west it was bound by the Bamni, the fury of its dark waters eroding the rock until the castle became positioned within the angle of confluence. Bhainsrorgarh could only be approached from the north. The waters of the Chambal, never gentle, rushed on, creating rapids and whirlpools along its way. Pebbles were ground and polished into oblong shapes and these with the help of a little red paint were consecrated as Bhiroo (Kartik), the elder son of Shiva. Mewar's territory extended to east of the Chambal with a small stream known as Karab-ka-khal dividing the lands of the Hadas from that of the Sisodias.

Bhainsa Sah – a merchant and Rora – a Banjara charun had built the castle of Bhainsrorgarh to protect their caravans from lawless mountaineers. The list of gallants that had held the castle before the Hadas made themselves its master is not known, for the famous destroyer Alla-ud-din Khalji had paid it a visit. Two inscriptions were discovered dating to AD 1123. These had been reversed and applied as common building material. The castle of Bhainsa and Rora then became the property of Mewar.

A visit to the fascinating whirlpools of the Chambal being a must, a special visit had been organized at a later date from Kota. Approaching the river from Baroli, a path had to be hewn through the forests for the horses and camels to pass, using the ascending pitch of the rushing waters as guide. Camp was pitched on an elevated site commanding a view of the river. Behind, lay deep woods while the cliffs of the plateau rose up ahead. To the left, the river expanded into a calm, unruffled lake fringed with trees while nearly a mile to the right the Chirmitti – the cleaver of soil, a classical name for the Chambal – shrank into a bed so deep and narrow that a man could plant his feet on either side. At this point the falls began, one rapid succeeding the other, their roars increasing in ferocity until the spot where the river split into four murmuring channels. There in the centre lay a large rock, flat as a table, rising above the turbulent waters, played upon by a fine spray and brilliant sunlight. A little beyond, the waters united once more cascading down sixty feet into a large basin, the white foam bubbling up against the masses of black rock. The table rock was used, by the thakur of Bhainsror, for holding feasts during the summer months, a tree trunk being laid across the chasm for the purpose. The captain reclined upon the rock, drawing in his mind's eye a picture of Rajputs, enveloped in the rising mist, sipping from their goblets amrit drawn from the churning waters.

The whirlpools comprised of caverns thirty to forty feet in depth, some connecting with others through subterranean channels. The waters that issued from within were gentle and shallow to begin with but picked up velocity by the time they reached the softer rock below Bhainsrorgarh. Here the strength of the river was sufficient to set a ship afloat. It then wound its way towards Kota, piercing its rocky bed with little whirling vortices that whittled away at the pebbles.

Rao Samar Singh (Samarsi)

Of Samarsi's three sons, the eldest, Napooji, succeeded to the throne of Bundi. Harpal, the second, obtained Jajawar and his descendents called themselves the Harpalpotas. The youngest, Jait Singh (Jaitsi), spread the name of the Hadas to beyond the Chambal.

Jaitsi had been to visit the Tomar chief of Kaithun[7]. On his way back, he chanced upon a long and deep ravine on the banks of the Chambal. Here lived an ancient community of the pure blooded Ujala Bhils. Jaitsi took them by surprise and occupied their valley.

At the entrance to the ravine, where Koteah – the chieftain of the Bhils – fell, Jaitsi erected a memorial. It was shaped like an elephant and dedicated to Bhiroo (Kartik), the god of battle. Koteah and his Bhils would never be forgotten. Dedicating the new conquest to their memory, Jaitsi's son Surjan named it Kota. Twelve lakes were excavated by Surjan's son Dheerdeo, the most beautiful of which was the Kishore Sagar that stood in the eastern part of the city. Dheerdeo was succeeded by Kandul, who was followed by his son Bhunak Singh. Bhunak Singh was to later lose Kota to his cousin, Rao Surajmal of Bundi.

Rao Napooji had three sons and his eldest succeeded him.

Rao Hamir (Hamoo)

Hamoo succeeded to the throne of Bundi in 1384.

Mewar was in the process of re-establishing control over the great vassals who had grown noticeably powerful. Since the time they had vacated the plateau, the Hadas considered themselves independent even though they acknowledged the supremacy of the gaddi of Mewar. Bundi had never been granted to them as jagir. It had been conquered independently.

The maharana would not admit that the temporary lapse in power released erstwhile vassals from age-old promises. Hamoo was ordered to offer his services. He agreed to accept the supremacy of Mewar and to receive the

---

7. Kaithun lies twenty kilometres south-east of Kota.

Back within the security of the walls of Chittaurgarh, the humiliated and disgraced maharana[8] assembled his army and before them took an oath. He would not taste a morsel of food so long as the castle of Bundi remained standing. No amount of pleading would make him retract his rash vow. Bundi would have to fall before the king would dine. But the castle lay sixty miles away, defended ferociously by the Hadas. To spare their sovereign from the pangs of hunger, the chiefs resorted to a childish solution. A mock castle of Bundi was erected ready to be stormed.

Koombho Bairsi and his men – Hadas in the service of the maharana – were returning from a deer hunt when the strange sight caught their attention. Koombho's blood boiled and he assembled his men.

The maharana advanced and a volley of unexpected shots surprised him. Word was brought back – Bundi would never be dishonoured, not even one of clay. What was supposed to have been a mock battle turned violent. When the last Hada had fallen, the maharana wisely decided to remain satisfied with the outcome and not drive such a daring band of men to desperation.

---

8. According to the dates available it would have to be Maharana Lakha though the impetuous behaviour matches that of his father – Maharana Kshetra Singh. The annals of Mewar, however, claim that Maharana Kshetra Singh did indeed attack and subjugate Hada lands. Kshetra Singh was killed by Lal Singh (Lallaji), the ruler of Bundi – possibly the younger son of Rao Hamoo – who had wrested the throne from his brother, Biroo. It was the generous Maharana Lakha who had restored Bundi to the Hadas.

teeka of installation from the hands of the maharana but he would not agree to unlimited attendance.

The maharana led his army to the gates of Bundi. He would make Hamoo obey or drive him from the land.

Certain that Bundi was lost, 500 men donned funereal robes of saffron and rallied around their chief. They would die with him. Hamoo attacked by night heading directly for the maharana's tent. Caught off guard, the sleeping Sisodia panicked and ran for his life.

Hamoo ruled for sixteen years and was succeeded by his eldest son.

Rao Bar Singh

Bar Singh ruled for fifteen years and is said to have begun the construction of ₍Taragarh[9], in 1411. He was succeeded by Biroo.

Rao Biroo

Biroo ruled for fifty years and left behind seven sons. The two youngest abandoned their faith and turned to Islam while his eldest, Bando, left behind a name that is immortal in the annals of Bundi.

Rao Bando

A famine struck the land in 1486. It desolated the countryside but Rao Bando's foresight saved Bundi. It was said that he had been forewarned.

Bando's younger brothers, who could not resist the temptation of power, abandoned their faith and drove him from the land. They ruled jointly under their new names, Samarkandi and Amarkandi, for eleven years.

---

9. Taragarh was named after the goddess Tara or Kali (Tara = Kali & star. Garh= Fort.). Lt Col Tod interpreted it the star fort but it is more likely that the fort was named invoking the goddess. Chauhan forts are traditionally named Taragarh and the two famous ones are in Ajmer and Bundi.

Bando, say the bards, was visited by an apparition riding a lean buffalo. Grasping his sword and shield the Hada sprang to his feet.

'Bravo Bando Hada bravo,' said the spectre, 'but your sword will be of no use against me for I am Kaal (Time).'

'Now listen, for you are the only man that has ever dared to oppose me. This land will become a desert. Fill your granaries and distribute the grain liberally. Your granaries will never be empty.'

Kaal disappeared and Bando followed every instruction faithfully. Grain was bought from every kingdom and Bundi's granaries were filled to overflowing. Two years passed and then quite suddenly the rains failed. A great famine followed. Bundi alone had food to spare.

Bando went down in history of the Rajputs as the anchor of the land.

News arrived one day that the Pathans of Mandu had besieged Chittaur. Rao Narayan Das marched at once with a band of 500 select Hadas. After several hours the army stopped for a rest. Narayan lay below a tree, having taken his usual dose of opium. The day was hot and as Narayan slept, his mouth fell open. Flies flew in and out and settled on his tongue. The young wife of a worker from the local oil press, who had come to draw water at a well nearby, was amazed by the sight. This was the great rao of Bundi, who was on his way to Chittaur.

'If this be the only help my rana should receive, then alas for my prince,' exclaimed the young woman.

Opium eaters or umuldars are known for their sharp ears and the rao sprang to his feet. 'And what did you say?' he demanded. Taking her crow bar from her hands, he beckoned for her to remain still. 'Do not fear just repeat it,' he smiled and twisting the iron bar around her neck said, 'wear my garland until I return or else in the meanwhile look for somebody strong enough to unbind it.'

The Pathans had closed in upon Chittaurgarh. The rao moved stealthily during the night entering the Pathan camp from the rear and cut his way to the general's tent. Chaos reigned among the sleeping Muslims who fled in every direction. As dawn broke, the nakarras of Bundi sounded and the Mewaris awoke to see their enemies gone. In their stead, stood their Hada allies. The chiefs of Chittaurgarh assembled to honour the Bundi rao as did the royal ladies who graced the occasion from behind the curtains. The maharana's niece made known her desire to marry the opium-eating knight. Narayan Das could never refuse a lady in love and the maharana was too wise to forbid it. The wedding of Narayan and Ketu[10] was celebrated and the victorious Hada left with his bride.

Opium overcame the rao to such an extent that he awoke one morning to discover that he had scratched his bride's face during the course of the night. Her beauty had been marred forever. Overcome with remorse the Hada handed over his opium box to the care of the lady.

---

10. The records of Marwar document the marriage of Rao Narayan Das of Bundi with Ketu, a daughter of Rao Suja of Jodhpur.

Bando retired to Matunda, in the hills, where his cenotaph still stands. Of his sons, Nirbudh inherited Matunda while Narayan Das determined to claim Bundi from his uncles. The Hadas of the plateau gathered and vowed to stand by him.

Rao Narayan Das

As soon as the period of mourning was over Narayan Das wrote to his uncles. They had no fear of a young man who had spent his life in the hills. With a small band of men, Narayan arrived at the palace and entered the room where his uncles sat unattended. At the sight of him, they ran towards a secret passage but Narayan's sword caught one and his lance the other. As he placed the heads of both traitors in the temple of Bhavani, his followers fell upon the Muslims and cleansed their land of the enemy. A slab of stone that caught a blow meant for Samarkandi forever bore the gash and became an object of devotion. It is worshipped by the Hadas every Dushera[11].

Narayan Das was famous for his strength. Fear was unknown to him and the quantity of opium that he could withstand would have killed most men. It unfortunately, left him drowsy most of the time but his gallantry remained legendary and won for him the hand of Maharana Raimal's niece.

For thirty-two years, Rao Narayan Das ruled his land peacefully. He was succeeded by his son, Surajmal.

---

11. Though recorded in the *Annals and Antiquities of Rajasthan*, the slab of stone is not to be found today.

Rao Surajmal (Soojo)

Surajmal was athletic and spirited like his father. His arms, like those of Lord Ram and Prithviraj Chauhan, reached below his knees – an unmistakable sign of a hero. Soojo, when he came to the throne, confiscated Kota from his cousin, Bhunak Singh.

The alliance with Chittaurgarh was cemented once more by intermarriages between the two houses. Surajmal's sister Sooja Bai was married to Maharana Ratan Singh (Ratna) of Chittaurgarh and Surajmal himself took as wife the maharana's sister. But Soojo remained unaware of the grudge borne against him. He had applied for the hand of the princess of Amber quite unaware of the fact that Ratna's sword had already been presented. With the death of his elder brother, Ratna had suddenly and quite unexpectedly been catapulted into the position of the heir of Mewar and with Maharana Sanga's death found himself upon its throne. The sheer stroke of good luck so dazzled the prince that he forgot all about the maiden who waited at Amber. The unhappy princess accepted Soojo, neglecting to keep him informed about the proposal from Mewar. It struck at Ratna's manhood.

Like his father, Soojo was fond of his opium. One day, while visiting his brother-in-law, he fell asleep in Maharana Ratna's presence. A nobleman of Chittaurgarh, the Poorbia chief, tickled the Hada's ear in jest. He might as well have chosen to fool around with a tiger for the drowsy Hada reached for his sword and slew the poor man in one stroke.

The son of the slain chief swore to avenge his father.

'The rao,' he said, 'had cast an eye of desire upon the women of the maharana's family while visiting his sister in the rawala.'

Ratna's passions were inflamed. The innocent Sooja Bai did not help matters much. She cooked a special meal and sat, flywhisk in hand, watching over the two men in her life, encouraging them to eat. As her brother devoured his share, her heart swelled with quiet pride. Her husband, on the other hand, toyed with his food. He seemed to have no appreciation for her culinary skills.

Bhunak Singh was partial to wine and opium. Taking advantage of the prince's inebriated state, two Pathans – Dokar and Kesar Khan attacked and occupied Kota. Bhunak was banished to Bundi while his wife, a Tomar princess of Kaithun, retired to her maternal home.

Overcome with grief, Bhunak renounced both wine and opium. He made known his intentions: he would regain Kota and be united with his family once more. The queen rejoiced and devised a way to overcome the Pathans. To go into battle would lead to a great loss of lives. She therefore decided to combine courage with strategy.

Kesar Khan and Dokar received an invitation from the Rajputni. Spring was in the air; the nip of winter a forgotten memory and 'Hindus' everywhere readied themselves for the festival of colours – Holi. As nature prepared to erupt in a burst of glory, women came out of their veiled enclosures, bearing trays of crimson powder and spray guns filled with coloured water. The Pathans felt greatly honoured. Their chests swelled in anticipation and they gave their moustaches a final twirl. The beauties of Kota awaited them.

Gathering 300 of the finest Hada youths, Bhunak's queen dressed them in swirling ghagras and flowing veils. Anklets and bangles jingled.

The Pathans came dressed in their best. They advanced to greet the ladies who awaited them. It was a joyous occasion, songs filled the air and the Pathans were smeared in colour. Yet, Kesar Khan was conscious of a strange feeling that lingered in his breast. The bells on the feet of the Rajputnis tinkled but their music was missing. The dancers moved rhythmically but there was an unusual lack of grace and the lines of their bodies had not the softness or the tenderness associated with the women of Rajasthan.

Bhunak's queen came forward. She smiled as she raised her heavy bronze plate filled with colour. Kesar's spirits lifted. The plate flew at his head and he sank to ground stunned.

This was the signal for Bhunak and his Hadas to draw swords from beneath their skirts.

The blood stained bodies of Kesar Khan and his Pathans lay strewn upon the ground among flowers and crimson powder.

Bhunak Singh was re-seated upon his throne.

'Soojo ate like a tiger while you played with yours like a boy,' she complained.

The words were salt to an open wound but Rajput hospitality would not allow Ratna to take revenge on a guest. When Soojo took leave, the maharana offered to join him during the spring hunt – the Ahairea.

The merry month of Falgun arrived and the hunters, dressed in green, ascended the slopes of the plateau. Caught up in their excitement, the men failed to pay heed to the silent words that hung in the air.

'Woe betide the Hada and Sisodia who dare forget the agony of the virgin sati of Bambaoda.'

The forest abounded with game. There were lions, tigers, hyenas and bear, every species of deer one could hope for, from the delicate gazelle to enormous antelopes; the twelve horned barasingha and the blue buck or neelgai, while jackal, fox, hare and wild dog made up the small game. Troops of beaters moved through the jungle, their drums driving out the prey. Wide eyed, their nostrils flared, the animals sniffed at the air. Neath all the excitement throbbed an undercurrent of hostility.

As both kings charged at a boar, the son of the slain Poorbia chief let fly two arrows. Soojo warded off the blow but he could not save himself from the one that Ratna struck. Unhorsed, he bound his wound and called out to his brother-in-law.

'Escape you may but Mewar is sunk.'

Ratna turned back startled and the dying Hada struck with all his strength and his sword cleaved the maharana's body from naval to neck. Both Rao Surajmal and Maharana Ratan Singh lost their lives that day and the queens of Mewar and Bundi followed them to the next world.

Cenotaphs mark the spot where each prince fell but Sooja Bai returned in death to the valley of her ancestors. Her cenotaph was raised on the highest point of the Bundi pass. It stands today looking down upon the picturesque valley below.

Ascending the gently sloping but rugged Nasairah Pass, the party halted at the summit. The eye scanned the canvas that stretched before them. Beyond the narrow strip claimed by Mewar, lay Bundi. Down in the valley upon the banks of the Chambal stood the castle of Raghunath. The black waters of the Bamni glided in the distance towards their termination near the tombs of the Saktawats. Beyond the frontier town of Dabi rose the dense jungles of Kharipur. A barren tract intervened between the forest and Nanta. Though within Bundi territory, Nanta was the personal property of the regent of Kota, Zalim Singh. It was the only piece of land that belonged to Kota west of the Chambal.

Royal hunts in India were ostentatious affairs, notorious for the opulence that went with the times. Though he never had the privilege of joining in on the Ahairea the captain did experience the Rajput style of hunting which was the same as that of the Grand Mughals. A grand hunt had been organized in his honour by the regent of Kota.

The site chosen was a large range running into and parallel to the chain of hills that separated Hadavati from Malwa. This was the site of the chief rumna. A hunting seat had been constructed half way up the gentle, thickly wooded ascent. Terraced roofs and parapets overlooked a clearing below. Here princes would await the beginning of the hunt accompanied by an army of cooks and stewards that bustled about them. Officers of the Nimach force had been deputed that day to accompany the guests and by noon they were at their positions. In anxious expectation the wait began.

The occasional deer began to appear, scudding to a halt startled at the sight of the hunters. The sounds of the approaching beaters grew louder: drums accompanied by discordant yells and all manners of noise. Soon a variety of species started to gallop past: wild deer followed by antelopes, the nilgae and the barasingha. Some wild hogs came snorting by and trotted off at a brisk pace. Soldiers of four battalions, had joined a band of ordinary huntsmen, to form a human chain that stretched across the valley from one hill to the other. As the men approached, a bevy of wild animals finding themselves trapped struggled to escape past the hunting lodge. Black nosed hyenas stopped dead in their tracks at the sight of the waiting hunters and though there were no tigers, a few wild dogs were spotted. The carnage began and by the end of the day, six camel loads of deer were carted away.

It was an exhilarating affair. The hunts cost the state an annual sum of two lakhs of rupees (£ 20,000/-). Thousands feasted, and those in the regent's favour had rewards and gratuities bestowed upon them.

Rao Surtan

Surtan succeeded to the throne of Bundi but this strange man indulged in human sacrifice. A victim of Surtan's madness was his own wife, Raj Kanwar, the daughter of Rao Maldeo of Jodhpur. Maldeo, who had married Drupda, Rao Soojo's daughter, had renamed her Rambhavati after the voluptuous apsara of the heavens, and though she bore him a son, the charm of the Hada princess stoked his insecurities. In a fit of passion he drove her from Mehrangarh and hurled a sentence upon her head. The blameless Raj Kanwar paid for her father's deeds with her life.

Surtan was deposed by his nobles and Arjun the grandson of Rao Bando was elected.

Rao Arjun

Arjun[12], the son of Nirbudh of Matunda and grandson to Bando, went to the aid of Chittaurgarh when Sultan Bahadur Shah of Gujarat declared jehaad. His sister Karmavati[13] was the late Maharana Sanga's favourite wife and the lives of his nephews – Maharana Bikramjeet and the young

---

12. Some historians maintain that Arjun had died at Chittaurgarh before Rao Surtan had been deposed. Surjan succeeded Surtan and Mewar upheld the succession.
13. According to some sources Maharani Karmavati of Bundi may have been Rao Surajmal's sister.

Uday Singh – were at stake. This was the famous Hada prince who stood guard and was blown up at his post, the Chittaurgarh burj. Though he could not save his sister's life, Bundi gave sanctuary to Uday preserving him for Mewar's future. It was the intervention of the allies that saved Chittaurgarh and reinstated Maharana Bikramjeet upon the Sisodia throne.

With Rao Arjun's sacrifice, the feud between Bundi and Chittaurgarh, over the deaths of Maharana Ratan Singh and Rao Surajmal, came to an end.

Rao Surjan

Rao Surjan, the son of Arjun, succeeded to the throne of Bundi in 1535. It was now that Sawant Singh Hada negotiated with the Afghan governor of Ranthambhor. The fortress was surrendered and handed over to Rao Surjan. For this service, Sawant Singh received a handsome grant of land and his descendents came to be known as Sawant Hada. The Chauhan chief of Baidla, who participated in the negotiations, had stipulated that Ranthambhor could be held, by Rao Surjan, but only as a fief of Mewar.

21 February 1569, the ancient walls of Ranthambhor resonated with the joyful strain of wedding pipes. Chandersen, the deposed rao of Maroo, who had raised his voice against Mughal dominance, came to marry Rao Surjan's daughter. The doli had not been lifted when Emperor Akbar came knocking at its doors.

Akbar had succeeded to the throne of Hindustan. The ambitious young man, who had overcome Chittaurgarh the previous year, longed to add the ancient Chauhan fortress to his list of conquests. With Ajmer, Chittaurgarh and Ranthambhor tucked into his belt, Akbar would be master of Rajasthan. Ranthambhor, he besieged in person. His artillery rained upon the fortress for thirty-seven days but its impregnable walls showed no signs of surrender. Eventually, Raja Bhagwan Das of Amber and his nephew, Kanwar Maan Singh, who were related to Akbar through marriage, came to negotiate on behalf of the emperor.

'Your cousin, Maharana Uday Singh, has already lost Chittaurgarh. He

Ranthambhor – the city of the pillars of war – had a long and colourful history. It was said to have been built by Jayant Chauhan in AD 1110, while others maintain that it was built by Sapal Daksha as early as AD 944. Still others claim it was built by Rati Dev, a descendent of Hasti – the builder of Hastinapur, as far back as the eighth century AD in response to the Arab occupation of Sind.

Ranthambhor had, thereafter, been a Chauhan property and a jagir of Ajmer. Its last king, Hamir Deva Chauhan, had made the fatal mistake of attracting Alla-ud-din Khalji's attention.

Since AD 1292, India had been beset by waves of Mongol invasions. These invaders had come in search of an empire and not with plunder in mind. Defeated, they settled in Delhi and came to be known as the New Mussalmans.

In the year 1299, a 200,000 strong army under Kutlugh Khwaja, a descendent of Genghis (or Chingis) Khan, crossed into Delhi. He was heading straight for Delhi leaving the countryside untouched. Alla-ud-din Khalji, the Turkish sultan of Delhi, put together all his energies into quelling this fresh onslaught but his efforts were being constantly thwarted by the enemy within. Hamir Deva granted the Mongols refuge. Secure within the Aravalli, Ranthambhor enjoyed a strategic location but Alla-ud-din's vengeance was vicious and terrible.

In AD 1300, Ranthambhor underwent a year-long siege. The first attack was successfully beaten off, a catapult claiming the life of Alla-ud-din's general. Alla-ud-din then personally took charge and a year later, the flames of jauhar served to signal the Islamic occupation that was to follow.

When Maharana Hamir Sisodia regained Chittaurgarh, Mohammad bin Tughlak, who had taken over as the new sultan, fell into his hands.

As a part of his ransom, Ranthambhor was handed over to Mewar.

For a while, Ranthambhor was lost to the sultans of Malwa and regained by Maharana Sanga. However, Sanga's defeat at the hands of Babar unearthed deep rooted scandals within the Sisodia royal family. Sanga's favourite Hada queen, Karmavati, was said to have conspired with Babar to have her son, Bikramjeet, placed upon the throne of Mewar overriding the claims of Sanga's legitimate heir.

The bribe consisted of, amongst other precious Sisodia crown jewels, the jewelled crown and belt confiscated by Maharana Kumbha from the sultan of Malwa and the fortress of Ranthambhor.

During the turbulent and overlapping reigns of Humayun and Sher Shah, Ranthambhor once again achieved a measure of independence.

is without a country. What will it be Surjan?' asked Maan Singh. 'The emperor craves Ranthambhor. Will you drive yourself to ruin in trying to preserve it?'

The rao was prevailed upon to abandon the Hada alliance with Mewar and join the Mughals. In return, Hadas would never have to give a daughter to the Mughal's royal harem, nor would their women participate in the Meena Bazaar and more importantly, never would they have to pay the humiliating jaziya. The chiefs of Bundi would never be compelled to cross the Attock nor be placed under the command of a 'Hindu' colleague. They would always be permitted to enter the Diwane-aam fully armed and never have to prostrate themselves before the emperor. Their horses would never be branded with the imperial dagh and they would hold the right to sound their nakarras up to the Lal Darwaza. The most important clause of all was that their sacred edifices and the Bundi capital would never be desecrated. Rao Surjan agreed. Sawant Singh Hada and Kotario Chauhan, who had together obtained Ranthambhor, donned the funereal robes of saffron. The ancient legacy of the Chauhans would not be forsaken without a fight. At last the Mughals took possession[14] and in the spring of 1569, Akbar entered the fortress. Since that day never has a Hada passed Ranthambhor without averting his head in shame.

Surjan was granted the title of rao raja of Bundi and he went on to serve the Mughal army with distinction. In 1564, accompanied by the Mughal general, Asaf Khan, he left for the Gondwana campaign. Queen Durgavati, the Chandel princess, who had married the Gond raja, had ruled her land wisely since her husband's death. But, the Mughals, viewed independent neighbours with distaste. Durgavati fought gallantly to the end. The capital city of Bari was stormed and the Surjanpol gate raised to commemorate the event. For this service, Surjan received seven districts, which included Benaras (Varanasi) and Chunar.

The rao raja of Bundi settled in Benaras. Beautifying Benaras became one of Surjan's passions and he worked ceaselessly for the cause of the 'Hindus'. He was succeeded by his son, Bhoj.

---

14. The fall of Ranthambhor was followed, within the year, by the taking of the Bundela Rajput fortress of Kalanjar in Bundelkhand (Madhya Pradesh).

Rao Raja Bhoj

Around the time that Bhoj inherited the throne, Akbar moved his capital from Delhi to Akbarabad (Agra). In 1572, Bhoj led the imperial army against Gujarat and, as reward for the successful campaign, was permitted to return to Hadavati every year during the annual rains.

No sooner had Akbar returned to Fatehpur Sikri, congratulating himself on a job well done, his cousins in Gujarat rose against him. A fresh expedition was arranged and with a speed that left all that witnessed it spellbound. On 2 September 1573, the emperor won himself a decisive victory.

The perpetual wars of Akbar gave the Rajputs ample opportunity to prove their valour and the Hadas were present constantly at the posts of danger and honour. It had been Bhoj Hada who, during the escalade of Ahmadnagar in the August of 1600, had clambered up the walls to confront the dowager queen of Bijapur and her force of 700. The valiant Chand Bibi had returned home to die for her father's kingdom. The Bhoj burj in Ahmadnagar was erected by Akbar to commemorate the heroic victory.

The raos of Bundi maintained meticulous diaries, in which a description of the death of Akbar and its circumstances is said to be found. Bhoj retired to Bundi upon the death of the emperor. His eldest son, Ratan, succeeded him.

Rao Raja Ratan Singh

During the reign of Rao Ratan, the house of the Emperor Jahangir fell into disarray. His sons had begun the struggle for succession. Jahangir's eldest son the blinded but much loved Khusro died under mysterious conditions while in his brother Khurram's care. Khurram then went into open rebellion. The annals of Bundi claim that while twenty-two rajas turned against the emperor, it was Rao Raja Ratan Singh alone who abided by him in the evil hour. With his younger sons, Madhu and Hari, he hurried to join Sultan Parvez and General Mahabat Khan. Khurram was defeated[16]

---

16. The forces of Mirza Raja Jai Singh of Amber and Raja Guj Singh of Marwar had also taken part in putting down the rebellion.

Jodha Bai, the empress of India passed away and national mourning was declared. Every man in court, whether 'Hindu' or Muslim, was expected to shave off his moustache and beard. The royal barbers were instructed accordingly and they made their rounds of all living accommodations in the city of Agra. But when they reached the Hada rao's place, they were chased out.

Bhoj's enemies carried the tale to Akbar[15]. It was greatly exaggerated and portrayed as insulting to the memory of the empress. In his rage, Akbar forgot the gratitude he owed his valiant vassal. He ordered that Bhoj be pinned to the ground and relieved of these tokens of manhood. He may as well have asked for a tiger to be shaved for the Hadas flew at once to their swords. It would take but the slightest incident to trigger a blood bath.

Wisdom dawned on Akbar and he went to visit the Bundi rao in person. Dismounting from his elephant he walked up to him. The rao put forward an emotional plea – this was one privilege granted to his father. Akbar bowed his head in acquiescence.

'Besides,' added the Hada, 'how can I, the unworthy eater of pork, accept the privilege of baring a lip in the honour of the empress?'

The emperor and the rao embraced each other.

---

15. The annals attribute the tale to Emperor Akbar. Historians, however, claim that Harka Bai – the princess of Amber, known incorrectly as Jodha Bai; mother to Emperor Jahangir – outlived her husband. The emperor mentioned here could then well have been Jahangir mourning his mother or a wife for Jahangir, himself, had three Rathornis in his harem, all technically daughters of the House of Jodha. Two were princesses from Bikaner: the daughters of Rai Singh and Dalpat Singh; and the third a daughter of Raja Uday Singh of Jodhpur, Jagat Gosain, who became Shah Jahan's mother. Jagat Gosain is said to have died in 1618 and though her son had been removed from her care almost immediately after his birth, to be raised by Akbar's childless first wife and cousin – Rukhiya Begum, he was said to have been so devastated by her death that both Jahangir and Mumtaz had found it difficult to console him. If it was indeed Jagat Gosain, the true Jodha Bai, who had died then the Bundi rao in question would have to be Rao Raja Ratan Singh. What is also interesting is that the shaving of the head and all facial hair, as a sign of mourning, is a 'Hindu' custom. The emperor was mourning his wife (or mother) in the manner of the 'Hindus'. But the lady would have had accepted Islam and the Hada alludes to this fact by calling himself 'an unworthy eater of pork'.

and chased to Burhanpur.

It was a full moon day in the month of Kartik, 1624, when the Battle of Hazipur was won. Both his sons had been severely wounded but the throne of Jahangir had been saved. Rao Ratan was made governor of Burhanpur and Bundi was presented with an orange flag, a symbol of honour and recognition.

Jahangir not only wished to be generous, he also wanted to peacefully curtail the growing power of the Hadas. In 1624, he granted Kota as a jagir to Madhu Singh to be held directly as a gift from the crown. Madhu would be independent of Bundi. The land of Hadavati was forever divided into two.

Gopinath, Rao Ratan's eldest son, predeceased his father but his twelve sons were marked as heirs. Among them Rao Ratan divided the principle jagirs of Bundi. Chhatra Sal had Bundi, Filodi received Karwar and Pipalda, Mohkim Singh had Anterda and Maha Singh Thanoh (Jajawar). Inder Singh founded Indergarh and Beri Sal founded Balwan.

Rao Raja Chhatra Sal

Chhatra Sal was installed on the throne of Bundi by Shah Jahan himself. The Bundi rao held a high command under Aurungzeb in the Deccan and distinguished himself in the assaults on Daulatabad, Bidar and Gulbarga. When the fort of Dhamoni fell, all of the Deccan came under the Mughals.

In the summer of 1658, Shah Jahan fell violently ill. It was surmised that he would not live. Aurungzeb declared official mourning and did not hold court for twenty days. Then he prepared to march to the capital. Learning of his hostile intentions, the emperor recalled the Hada. For Chhatra Sal, his duty lay to the throne alone. His baggage had been sent ahead and as he prepared to leave, Aurungzeb called for him.

'But why do you want to leave now when you would be going with me in a few days?'

The Mughal guards had already closed in on him. Replying that his duty lay first with the reigning emperor, the brave Hada handed the firmaan to the prince and rode off, quickly putting the Narmada between him and his pursuers.

Shah Jahan's sons launched the battle for succession. Dara, the heir, who was based in Agra had under his charge the powerful imperial troops. Shuja, the general in Bengal, moved towards Agra at the head of his army. Aurungzeb, aware that the army that he brought up from the Deccan was far smaller, teamed up with the youngest of his brothers, Murad Baksh. As they prepared to cross the Shipra near Ujjain, Dara despatched Maharaja Jaswant Singh of Marwar to meet them at Dharmat. The outcome was disastrous and the victorious Aurungzeb renamed Dharmat as Fatehabad – the city of victory. Shuja's ambitions, had in the meanwhile, been successfully curbed by Dara's son, Suleiman Shikoh.

The forces of Bundi did not serve under Jaswant Singh of Marwar on that ill-fated day, when four brothers from Kota laid down their lives at Dharmat. Maharaja Jaswant Singh returned home to find the gates barred. They had been ordered shut by his queen, Jaswant Devi – the daughter of Rao Raja Chhatra Sal of Bundi, for he had lost his chance to redeem Hindustan.

But Aurungzeb could not declare himself emperor without having first defeated his eldest brother. With Murad by side he moved to engage Dara. Their numbers were fewer; they had already gone through one battle and had marched, in the scorching heat, all the way from the Deccan. Dara positioned himself upon the banks of the Chambal ninety kilometres from Agra hoping to prevent a crossing but Aurungezeb managed to give his brother the slip. Leaving their tents behind, Aurungzeb's army crossed the river. It served as an effective decoy. Dara gave chase but by the time he caught up with them, Aurungzeb was well entrenched at Samugarh, twenty-five kilometres from Agra.

The battle of Samugarh took place on 28 May 1658. Bundi supported Dara. But it was a minor error that eventually decided the outcome of the battle. Bent upon chasing Murad, Dara abandoned his elephant and prepared to mount his horse. The sight of the empty howdah set up an alarm and the panic-stricken imperial army took to its heels. With them went the cowardly heir, even as the Hadas stood their ground.

Rao Raja Chhatra Sal died on the field that day and with him fell twelve royal princes, each the head of a Hada clan.

Of Chhatra Sal's daughters, two had had the good fortune of being married to the most powerful kings of the day. Maharani Jaswant Devi ruled Maharaja Jaswant Singh's heart and though her sister Rang (Ganga) Kanwar, had failed to win her husband's affections it was her son that succeeded to the Sisodia throne as Maharana Amar Singh II.

There is novelty in every point of view from which the fairy palace of the Hadas is seen and it burst upon us this morning, as a momentary gleam passed over its gilded pinnacles displaying its varied outline.

The capital city of the Hadas lay in a narrow valley enclosed by towering hills. The white ramparts of Taragarh encircled the top of a thickly wooded hill, at a height of 1,426 feet, guarding the palace within. A lake, still as a mirror, lay in the centre. It was perhaps the most striking in all of India. Throughout Rajputana, which boasted of many fine palaces, Bundi-ka-mahal possessed the first rank.

Every new addition had been named after its founder and each apart from being simply splendid blended harmoniously with that which existed before. The Chhatra mahal, built by Rao Raja Chhatra Sal, was the most expensive and modern of the additions. It had two noble halls with a double row of pillars, the stone – the serpentine – having been quarried from Bundi's own mines. Here, waiting to receive him were the chiefs of the vassal clans. The captain was then led to the state apartments. The view from his room was spectacular. Gigantic terraces and roof top gardens intermingled with palaces and it was in one of these that he was to be received the next day.

The maharao led the way to an open terrace where a grand court had assembled under the shade of large trees. Here, by the marble pool, neath the trellised vines waited at least a hundred courtiers. It looked down upon the Jait Sagar and the Prem Sagar set amidst their gardens. In the distance, beyond the Chambal, lay the city of Kota. On the summit of a hill, stood the Dhaibhai's (Maharao Raja Bhishen Singh's foster brother) tomb, its cupola rising above the treetops and the battlements of Taragarh. To the south-east a gorge in the valley led to the city.

Taragarh had been strengthened by Dalil Singh, the traitor of Karwar, and the walls around the city raised by Maharao Raja Budh Singh. Of these walls, Umed Singh had but one thing to say:

> They are not required against an equal foe, of no use against a superior – and will only retard re-conquest if driven out of Bundi, whose best defence is its hills.

Rao Raja Bhao Singh

All the ill will that he bore towards Chhatra Sal, Aurungzeb transferred to his descendent Bhao Singh. Atmaram Gaur, the prince of Sheopur, was sent by Aurungzeb to occupy Bundi and annex it to the government of Ranthambhor, The Hadas united, chasing him away and Atmaram was laughed out of the imperial court.

Affecting to be pleased with the Hada's bravery, Aurungzeb summoned Rao Raja Bhao to court. The hesitant rao was persuaded with promises of good will and honoured by a post in Aurungabad under Prince Muazzam. Many edifices in Aurangabad recall the days and valour of Rao Raja Bhao. He remained in Aurangabad for the rest of his life and died without an heir.

The grandson of his brother, Bheem, was declared successor.

Rao Raja Aniruddh Singh

Fifteen-year-old Aniruddh's accession was accepted by the emperor who sent his own elephant with the khelat of investiture. Aniruddh served in the Deccan and was fortunate enough to be presented with the opportunity to save the royal harem from the enemy. As a mark of honour, he was allowed to lead the vanguard in the storming of Bijapur.

There was no time to soak in the acclaim won at Bijapur for a crisis was developing back at home. Durjan Sal Hada, a senior chieftain, had occupied Bundi by force. Aniruddh rushed back to save his throne. The chieftain fled making his way to Marwar where he joined Durgadas Rathore who had sworn, in face of Emperor Aurungzeb, to uphold the rights of the heir of the late Maharaja Jaswant Singh.

Aniruddh spent his last years in the northern provinces in the service of the emperor.

Maharao Raja Budh Singh

Budh Singh succeeded his father. The ten-year-old ruled in relative peace for the next decade or so. Towards the end of his days, Aurungzeb had chosen to live permanently at Aurangabad. The dying emperor hoped to be succeeded by his elder son, Muazzam. The Mughal heir assembled all the chiefs sympathetic to his cause and among them was Budh Singh Hada.

As news of the emperor's death broke out, Muazzam advanced from Kabul and Azam, accompanied by his son Bedar Bakht, from the Deccan. The armies met on the plains of Jajav near Dholpur. Ram Singh of Kota was indebted to Azam and, casting aside the wishes of the late emperor, supported the prince of his choice. For having abandoned the cause of Muazzam, he was led to believe that he would become the next raja of Hadavati. He went ahead with declaring himself rao of Bundi. Seething with passion, the Hadas of Bundi and Kota faced each other on the field.

Muazzam succeeded to the throne of Hindustan as Emperor Shah Alam Bahadur Shah. Not one opponent lived to challenge him. But the ones who had suffered the most had been the Rajputs. All Hadas had suffered greatly but Bheem, the son of Ram Singh of Kota, was never to forget his feud with Bundi. Rao Raja Ram Singh of Kota, whose head had been filled with dreams of a united Hadavati, died that day at Jajav and Kota was attached to Bundi. Instead of Ram Singh it was Budh Singh who had honours heaped upon him. Raised to the title of maharao raja of a combined Hadavati, Budh Singh had by his side Amar Kanwar, Maharaja

Sawai Jai Singh's sister. She had been promised to the emperor but in return for Budh Singh's support at Jajav, the emperor granted the Hada the right to marry the Kachwaha princess. But physically occupying Kota was quite another thing. Their spirited Hada cousins would not yield and, after two failed attempts, Bundi left them alone.

Budh Singh enjoyed a close and warm friendship with the emperor but when Bahadur Shah died, Bundi was dropped from imperial favour. Jahandar Shah's short reign gave way to that of Farukhsiyar's. Upset with Budh Singh for having failed to attend court, the new emperor stripped him of his rank and privileges and named Bheem of Kota maharao raja of Bundi and Kota. Bundi was occupied and renamed Farukkabad.

Budh Singh worked his way back into imperial favour, helped by Maharaja Sawai Jai Singh and Kachwaha Rani Amar Kanwar. Bundi was restored. Maharao Raja Bheem Singh Hada had ruled Hadavati for two whole years but when in December 1715, he was ordered to return Bundi to Budh Singh he was most reluctant. For eight months he held on and when at last he did vacate he took with him the heirlooms that belonged with the senior Hada clan: the orange flag granted by Jahangir to their ancestor, Rao Ratan Singh, the elephant gate from Taragarh, two cannons from Ranthambhor and memorabilia precious to his Bundi cousins.

Maharao Raja Budh Singh remained loyal to Farukhsiyar but this unfortunate emperor was so beset by treachery that even Budh Singh was forced to flee. Maharao Raja Bheem of Kota made an audacious attempt on Maharao Raja Budh Singh's life even as the latter concentrated on warding off a blow meant for the emperor. Farukhsiyar was murdered and the house of the Chagatai Mongol fell into disarray. The upheaval in the centre had its repercussions on Hadavati. Maharao Raja Bheem Singh of Kota, who was held in favour by the Syyed Brothers, reoccupied Bundi and held onto it until the death of the kingmakers.

A series of puppets were offered their turn on the throne of Delhi and finally in 1719, there came a youngster named Muhammad Shah. He went by the nickname of Rangila and lived to survive for the next twenty-nine years. Bundi was restored to Budh Singh but the well-meaning Mughal youth was surrounded by treachery. He ignored the good advice of the nizam-ul-mulk, who had been in service since the days of Aurungzeb. Frustrated, the nizam raised the standard of revolt. Muhammad Shah took notice and promoted him to wazir. But finding it impossible to restore order, the old-timer chose to retire to his province in Hyderabad. Obeying orders from Maharaja Sawai Jai Singh, Maharao Raja Bheem Singh of Kota intercepted his path. But the nizam was more than a match and Bheem Singh lost his life. Following the nizam's example Avadh and Bengal seceded.

Time was ripe for treachery. Sawai Maharaja Jai Singh of Amber secretly planned to snatch Bundi from Budh Singh. Sadly, Budh Singh's Kachwaha rani was barren and intensely jealous of his second wife – the daughter of Kala Megh of Begun, one of the sixteen chiefs of Mewar. During Budh Singh's absence, she feigned a pregnancy, procured an infant and passed it off as Budh Singh's son. The maharao raja was informed of the deception and he brought it to Jai Singh's notice. When the issue was raised, Amar Kanwar, in sheer exasperation, pulled her brother's dagger from its sheath and would have had his life, had he not fled from her fury.

But it was as much an insult to Amber. Jai Singh swore to avenge his honour. Budh Singh, he determined, would have to go. On the sly, the gaddi was offered to the chief nobles of Bundi. Deo Singh of Indergarh turned it down but Dalil Singh, the chief of Karwar, who was also the fortress commander of Taragarh was unable to resist.

Jai Singh gave his guest and brother-in-law several hints.

'Remain with me in Amber,' he said. 'Accept 500 rupees a day for your needs.'

It aroused the suspicions of Budh Singh's uncle. He commanded that the Begun rani leave immediately. She was to hurry to her father's house. Then he sent a secret message to his king. Budh Singh escaped. Waiting for him by the walls of Amber was his uncle at the head of 300 Hadas.

As they headed for Bundi a band of Panchola Rajputs came riding up. A desperate encounter followed and though the enemy was vanquished, Budh Singh's uncle lost his life. The Hadas thought it best to stay away from Bundi for the moment. They turned towards Begun.

Maharao Raja Dalil Singh

Maharaja Sawai Jai Singh had Dalil Singh of Karwar installed on the gaddi of Bundi in 1729. Budh Singh's abortive attempts at recovering his throne were successfully prevented and to strengthen his own position Jai Singh arranged a marriage. Dalil Singh was made to accept the hand of a Kachwaha princess. With it went a condition. Were a son to be born of this union he was to be named heir of Bundi.

Budh Singh made many attempts to recover his kingdom. His Kachwaha rani, whom he had once accused of adultery, came once again to his aid. She recruited the help of Dalil's jealous older brother and sent him to Pune to meet with the peshwa. In April 1734, a large Maratha army, which included the generals Ranoji Scindia and Malhar Rao Holkar amongst others, reached Bundi. But Budh Singh's relief was short lived for Sawai Jai Singh soon ensured Dalil's return. Though it was a Hada that sat on the throne, the real power lay in the hands of Jai Singh.

Budh Singh died in exile in 1739, at Begun leaving behind two sons: nine-year-old Umed and the younger Deep Singh. Jai Singh's thirst for revenge had not yet been quenched. Begun was besieged and the young princes forced to flee. It was the Meenas of the plateau that took them in. Maharao Raja Durjan Sal, who had succeeded Maharao Raja Bheem to the throne of Kota, was touched by their plight. This magnanimous prince determined to help the boys recover their birthright.

During Dalil Singh's reign, the imperial capital was to witness the bloodiest sacking in its history. The Marathas who had prised Malwa and Gujarat from the hands of Jai Singh and Abhay of Marwar, appeared at the gates of Delhi. Though they were turned away, the weakness exhibited at the helm had not gone unnoticed. In 1739, a Turk appeared. Nadir Shah, an officer of the Persian army, had deposed his emperor and declared himself shah. He had come now to partake of the rich pickings of Hindustan. Not one Rajput stirred and the emperor was left to fend for himself. With cold brutality the Turk ordered the massacre of the citizens of Delhi. Emperor Muhammad Shah Rangila was reduced to begging for mercy and the ransacking of the Red Fort began. India lost its prized Peacock Throne and a beautiful diamond that Nadir Shah named Kohinoor. The Mughal emperor of Hindustan ruled now with the permission of the shah of Persia.

When news arrived that Maharaja Sawai Jai Singh had died, thirteen-year-old, Umed, put himself at the head of his clansmen and captured two cities in the Bundi territory. The son of Budh Singh had awoken and the Hadas flocked to his flag.

Ishwari Singh the new maharaja of Jaipur continued to follow his father's policies. The Hadas, he decided, would bend to his will. He attacked Kota and then turned his attention towards the heir of Bundi. A band of Nanakpuntis was sent to smoke Umed out. Five thousand tribals, armed with bows and arrows, came to the young prince's aid. While the nimble hill folk plundered the camps, the Hadas charged and slaughtered the army of Jaipur. Their kettledrums and flags fell into Umed's hands. That night as he went to seek the blessings of Ashapurna Devi, Bundi's flag flew high. Umed vowed to regain what was rightfully his.

Ishwari Singh sent an army of 18,000 men led by Narayan Das Khetri. In the formation of the gola, a circle studded with spears, the Hadas charged the Jaipur army at Dablana. Although it was cannon fire that they faced they would not give up. The losses however, grew too heavy and when Umed's steed, Hunja, was struck, the Hadas pleaded with him to save the one life they were all fighting to preserve. Umed was persuaded to ride away. If he fell, all hope for Bundi would be lost. His intestines spilling from an abdominal wound, the noble Hunja carried his master across the Sawali Pass that led to Indergarh. Here Umed dismounted and relieved Hunja of his saddle. The steed from Iraq, who had borne his father in many encounters, breathed his last. Umed Singh sat down and wept. Many years later he would build a statue to Hunja. It would adorn the city centre and keep the memory of that day at Dablana forever alive.

Deo Singh of Indergarh would not grant him sanctuary. Refusing even a drink of water within its walls, Umed headed towards Karwain. There he was received kindly. Discharging his followers and begging them to return when fortune proved kinder, Umed returned to his old home in the ruined castle of Rampura, deep in the ravines of the Chambal.

Durjan Sal of Kota, readied himself to fight for his cousin. His council and army were led by a Gujarati Brahmin bard named Bhat. Together they roped in allies. Maharana Jagat Singh of Mewar, who had a vested interest in replacing Sawai Ishwari Singh with his brother – Madho Singh, was forced to pull out as the Kachwaha brothers reached a temporary compromise. But Durjan did not back down. He applied to the governor of Gujarat and the chieftain of Shahpura. With the army of Kota backing him, Umed sent a call to his kinsmen and friends. Bundi was occupied on 28 July 1744. But continuous warfare had damaged the walls and it was difficult to hold onto the fort. A fatal shot claimed the heroic Bhat's life. To avoid panic, a sheet was thrown quickly over the body and the news of the death concealed. But Durjan would not leave Bundi in young Umed's hands. Disappointed Umed left refusing the land that was offered

Ishwari Singh leagued with the peshwa at Pune who sent in a large army marching under Jai Appa Scindia. Dalil Singh resumed his place once again and marched alongside against Kota. Kota was besieged, for several months in the course of which Jai Appa lost an arm. Both Hada kingdoms had to pay the price. By the treaty signed in May 1748, Kota paid the Marathas two lakhs of rupees and Bundi ceded Patan. Mewar and Kota lost no time in confronting Ishwari Singh. The battle of Bagru placed Umed on the throne but it wasn't long before he was evicted and the flag of Jaipur raised once more above the kangras of Deva Bango.

Umed Singh turned to the Holkar Marathas. Malhar Rao Holkar was more than forthcoming and Maharana Jagat Singh bolstered his resolve with a generous bribe. The peshwa, who had laid siege to Kota on Ishwari Singh's behalf, defected quickly to the side with the heavier purse. Maharaja Sawai Ishwari Singh, who was never quite the man of the hour, was left without support. At this crucial moment he found himself abandoned even by his subjects for he had incurred their displeasure by murdering the popular minister Kesudas. Though the sawai maharaja did succeed in stalling the Marathas several times, they returned time and again. Negotiations, bribes nothing worked for long. The king grew weary and increasingly depressed.

In the end, the sawai maharaja was forced into signing a deed surrendering Bundi. Never again would he or his descendents, lay claim to it. He applied the teeka of installation by his own hands on Umed's forehead. It was only a matter of time before he would forfeit his right to rule in favour of his younger brother, Madho Singh – the nephew of Mewar.

Deprived of his kingdom, Umed became a wanderer once again. He moved between the courts of Marwar and Mewar, never losing an opportunity to declare war on his enemy. In the course of his many wanderings, he arrived at the village of Binodia. Here lived the widowed Kachwaha rani, his father's wife and the cause of his misfortunes. He paid her a visit. Life had run its course and the old woman acknowledged that it was she who had caused ruin to visit her home. Looking at her stepson, a new emotion stirred within her. She resolved to redeem herself and set out the next day for the Deccan. On the banks of the Narmada, she came across a pillar, which bore an inscription prohibiting her race from crossing the river. The elderly Rajputni had the pillar torn down and crossed the forbidden river.

She made her way to the home of the Maratha, Malhar Rao Holkar. And Holkar pledged himself to his adopted sister. Without the accident of a noble birth, he possessed all the finesse and sentiments of royalty. He promised to restore Bundi to his nephew.

The princess of Jaipur led her supporters not to Bundi but directly onto Jaipur. Circumstances were favourable, for Ishwari, though the eldest son of Jai Singh was not the chosen one for the throne. Madho Singh, the son of the Sisodini rani and a child of Jai Singh's old age, had been marked as heir by the decree of the Rajput Federation.

Holkar's resolve was facilitated by a generous bribe of sixty-four lakh rupees paid by Maharana Jagat Singh II of Mewar.

Maharao Raja Umed Singh

Accompanied by the army of Kota, Umed arrived at Bundi and reclaimed his throne. Within three years of his accession a funeral pyre was lit for his greatest enemy – Maharaja Sawai Ishwari Singh, who, unable to swallow his disgrace, had taken his own life. After fourteen years in exile, Umed Singh sat upon the royal cushion that a traitor had pressed for close to thirty. But the means used for retrieving it had proved very expensive for Malhar Rao Holkar, the maharao's mamoo, not satisfied with mere terms of endearment, claimed for himself all lands on the left bank of the Chambal. The years in exile however, had brought with them one benefit. Dalil Singh the traitor, had fortified and strengthened Taragarh.

Umed Singh had come to the throne a year after Emperor Ahmad Shah had ascended his own. Punjab had already been lost to Ahmad Shah Abdalli (Durrani) – the Afghan minion of Nadir Shah of Persia – who upon his master's death laid claim to the Indian portion of the Persian Empire. Struggling in the grip of his dominating wazir, Safdarjung, Emperor Ahmad Shah appealed to the grandson of his father's friend – the nizam of Hyderabad. The youngster, imad-ul-mulk, successfully rid the country of the wazir, blinded and deposed the emperor who had asked his help and installed the blind elderly Alamgir II. But his own attempt at restoring the empire led to the 1757 sacking of Delhi by Abdalli – consequences of which were to strike at softer targets no longer under the Mughal's veil of protection. It was but a matter of months before the nawabs of Bengal lost their independence, on the battle-field of Plassey, to Robert Clive of the East India Company. Ignoring the merchants, Imad called for the Marathas. The peshwa's court at Pune and the Red Fort of Delhi were awash by rainbows of hallucination. Their imaginations fired, they promised to leap across to the Attock.

The fortress of Ranthambhor had until now lain in the charge of a veteran Mughal commander. Worried about a Maratha take over, he appealed to Umed Singh to accept responsibility of the ancient Chauhan fort. Under the yoke of the Marathas himself, the maharao refused. The commander had no option left but to turn to Jaipur and Maharaja Sawai Madho Singh gladly took charge.

The Maratha threat to Rajasthan was at an all time low for they concentrated upon their Indian empire. But the first step – the occupation of Lahore in 1759 – prompted the return of the Afghan. Ahmad Shah Abdalli (Durrani) came out of retirement ready for war. Imad vented his frustration upon the emperor by murdering him. The Mughal heir, Shah Alam, was not at hand for he had thought it prudent to flee to Avadh the previous year. The Third Battle of Panipat took place in January 1761. The Afghans won a resounding victory and broke the power of the Marathas. Abdalli declared Shah Alam II emperor in absentia and placed him under the protection of a Rohilla Afghan who effectively remained the ruler until 1770. Imad fled to Mecca.

Eight of the great jagirs of Bundi – Pipalda, Gainta, Karwar, Pusod, Indergarh, Khatoli, Balwan and Antardah – came technically under the Ranthambhor administration. Kota, then the more powerful of the two Hada kingdoms, convinced the chieftains to switch allegiance. It was an affront to Bundi no doubt but it directly impacted the revenue due to Jaipur. As the new master of Ranthambhor, Madho Singh saw himself as master of all Chauhan clans and entitled to the tribute that the Mughals had levied upon Hadavati. Maharao Raja Durjan Sal of Kota was equally incensed at this arbitrary assumption. The result was the battle of Bhatwara in 1761, which unfolded during the reign of Durjan's successor, Chattra Sal. It was on this occasion that a young Jhala Rajput in the service of Kota rose to make his mark. Zalim Singh won for his prince the independence of Kota but Bundi had failed to participate in the battle and redeem their tribute paying jagirs.

Umed's mind remained busy with building Bundi's economy and improving the lives of his people. The parasitic Holkar continued to claim a large share of the revenue generated. Eight years went by before Bundi could be considered prosperous enough to send the coconut to Maharaja Sawai Madho Singh. It was received with every respect due to an illustrious Rajput house. The chief of Indergarh, who not so long ago had denied the helpless prince refuge, was at the Jaipur court. Deo Singh had escaped without incurring his sovereign's displeasure. But on that day he chose to cast a slur upon the daughter of Budh Singh and the coconut was refused. It was a great insult to Bundi.

Umed went to pay his respects at the shrine of the goddess of victory,

Vijayseni Mata, at Karwar. The temple was close to Indergarh. Deo Singh was invited to join him. Despite good counsel to decline the invitation, Deo Singh obeyed and arrived with his son and grandson. In one fell swoop the three lost their heads and the line of the traitor was extinguished. The bodies were denied an honourable cremation and were cast into the lake instead. Indergarh was granted to Umed Singh's brother.

Fifteen years passed but the mind of Umed Singh remained troubled. The terrible revenge he had exacted upon Deo Singh had been completely out of character. He decided to abdicate and spend the rest of his life in penance. The impressive ceremony of yugraj was performed. The image of the maharao was cremated upon a pyre and his only son, Ajit, shaved his hair and moustache while lamentations rent the air. Ajit Singh became the new ruler of Bundi while Umed Singh, assuming the name Sriji, retired to that holy valley where Kedarnath had manifested himself to his ancestor.

Sriji determined to visit every holy spot in the land of India. Dressed in a quilted tunic, the royal ascetic bore every weapon conceivable upon his back. With a small escort, he began his travels and in time earned a reputation as an oracle. All Rajasthan revered him and every time he returned, the princes welcomed him with open arms. Homes were deemed hallowed if Sriji spent but a night. The knowledge he had gathered was admired, every word that he uttered revered and remembered.

Across the Indus, on the shores of Makran in Baluchistan lay the shrine of the terrifying Agni Devi of Hinglaz. As the warrior pilgrim made his way back through Dwarka, he was set upon by the tribe of the Kabas. The valiant Hadas overpowered the men and Sriji exacted from them a pledge. Pilgrims, on that route, would henceforth never again be molested.

Yugraj Ajit Singh

Sriji received word that his son had invited Maharana Ari Singh to hunt with him at the Ahairea. He wrote frantically:

'Remember the curse of the sati of Bambaoda.'

Ajit wrote back. It was too late for him to back out of the commitment on grounds as flimsy as an ancient curse.

Maharana Ari Singh had arrived with his army to claim the few mangoes[17] that were grown by the Meenas in the tiny village of Bileta. The crop was a small one and to save it from theft, the yugraj had had the area protected. The thieves complained to the chiefs of Mewar, who for lack of any thing better, decided to create an issue over the rights to the little village. It was Mewar's property they insisted and marched with their maharana. Ajit went to meet them and so pleased was Ari Singh with the bearing of the young man, that the issue of the mango grove was soon forgotten. In return, Ajit invited Ari Singh to hunt with him and slay a boar for Gauri. The maharana accepted happily and distributed green turbans for the occasion. The evening before the hunt, a minister of Mewar came to meet Ajit. In the most insulting language he issued an ultimatum. The mango grove would have to be surrendered by the end of the hunt; else Sindi mercenaries would be set upon Bundi. The threat rankled in Ajit's heart. The treachery under the cover of the smiles was too much for him to bear.

The hunt over the maharana, pleased with the day's events and unaware of Ajit's conversation with his chief, smilingly gave his young friend leave to retire. A half-formed idea of killing his guest flitted across Ajit's mind but unable to take a decision he left. Scarcely had he gone a few paces, when he stopped as if ashamed of himself. Turning around he rushed at the maharana throwing his lance with such force that it pierced through Ari Singh's body transfixing him to the neck of his horse.

'Oh Hada, what have you done,' exclaimed the maharana, as the sword of the Indergarh chief finished off the treacherous act.

The Hada carried off the chuthur changi, the golden sun in the sable disc – the royal insignia of the Sisodias. The panic stricken army of Mewar fled abandoning their camp and the body of their king. Not one

---

17. It appears that it wasn't a matter of mangoes but of a fort that was being raised at Bileta on the Bundi Mewar border. Maharana Ari Singh deeply resented the construction of the Hada fort and invited Ajit to hunt with him at Amirgarh. Ajit came prepared for all eventualities.

person remained behind but for a single low ranking wife, Spitting curses she climbed the pyre with her dead lord.

Sriji was devastated. Before his very eyes, his son wasted away. He was dead within two months. The chiefs of Mewar did not attempt to avenge the murder, which led to a general belief that the crime had probably been prompted by them.

One year before Ajit's death, Emperor Shah Alam II had gained the courage to return to Delhi, bringing the Marathas along as bodyguards. But he remained no more than a puppet, for a Persian adventurer had replaced the Rohilla protector.

Maharao Raja Bhishen Singh

Ajit's son, Bhishen Singh, was but a child and it fell upon Sriji to look out for his interests. Appointing a foster brother to watch over the government, Sriji took to his pilgrimages once more. He was often absent for four years at a time.

Bhishen Singh's reign bore witness to the rise of Mahadji Scindia to the post of vakil-e-mutlaq, the events of Lalsot and the blinding of Emperor Shah Alam II, by the first Rohilla regent's grandson, at Red Fort in Delhi – an event that marked the last day of the Mughal Empire. The Kingdom of Delhi and its emperor had been rescued by Mahadji Scindia who took up his new role as protector – an honour that was to be inherited by his successor, Daulat Rao Scindia.

It was a sad day when the old man, who had long renounced material life, was prohibited from entering Bundi. Selfish interests, of those that surrounded the young king, wished to keep him away from the wisdom of his grandfather. They preyed upon his mind to pronounce the sentence.

'Tell him to count his beads at Benaras.'

It was not long before the royal houses of Rajasthan vied with each other to receive Sriji in their homes. Maharaja Sawai Pratap Singh of Amber begged permission to pay homage and be granted the honour of having him live in the palace of Jaipur. Pratap offered him the thrones of both Bundi and Kota.

'They are already mine,' replied the ascetic. 'On one is my nephew and on the other my grandchild.'

Zalim Singh of Kota, who dominated this period of Rajasthani history, took control of the situation[18]. He met with Bhishen Singh. The young king was made to realise the extent of his foolishness and the court pundit sent to escort Sriji to Bundi.

The pilgrim warrior presented his sword to the young maharao saying, 'my child use this on me if you think I could harbour any ill will towards you. But do not let the unworthy defame me.'

His grandchild and sovereign wept and begged forgiveness. Sriji lived for another eight years and true to his vow, did not enter the palace again. As he lay dying, his grandson pleaded with him.

'Close your eyes in home of your father,' he said.

The dying man made no objection and allowed himself to be carried. He died that very night. Sixty years had passed since the day that a thirteen-year-old put himself at the head of the Hadas.

It was around this time that the British army under Lieutenant Colonel Monson came to put down the Holkars. The East India Company had occupied Delhi the previous December, evicted Daulat Rao from his role as protector and assumed the privilege for themselves. Shah Alam II had been reduced to a pensioner on the books of the Company. It is not known whether Sriji was aware of these matters but when the British took

---

18. Zalim Singh's intervention led to a reshuffle amongst the advisors to the maharao. The new order was sympathetic to the powerful regent of Kota. Young Bhishen Singh soon found himself son-in-law to Zalim Singh who now openly involved himself in the administration of Bundi. By 1798, matters had gone so out of hand that the chieftains of Bundi felt compelled to send word to Sriji. He returned immediately and was welcomed with a grand reception organized by Zalim Singh himself. Order was restored and Zalim's men were replaced by those who put Bundi's interests first. Maharao Raja Bhishen Singh however had to continue to watch his step for his powerful father-in-law was on easy terms with the Marathas and the Pindaris.

flight, Bhishen Singh at great risk to himself allowed the army safe passage through Bundi. The new empire that was taking shape, did not forget its debt to the maharao raja.

In 1817, the British government sent a call to the Rajput states to unite against the Marathas. Bundi was amongst the first to respond for the hateful Maratha flag had for long waved in unison with her own. Though Bundi did not have much say in the deliberations of 1817, the British remembered Maharao Raja Bhishen Singh with gratitude. The lands that Holkar had occupied for more than fifty years were returned to Bundi. The lands held by Scindia were also returned though at a depreciated value. Zalim Singh of Kota however, cleverly, managed to retain the great jagirs of Bundi under his protection.

Bhishen Singh died leaving his son under the guardianship of the British resident. His wives were instructed not to follow him on the pyre.

Maharao Raja Ram Singh was installed on the throne in August 1821.

Cholera raged through the summer of 1820. The sun had scorched the land and many had fallen victim. Those that had managed to survive the deadly combination had been left weak and drained, driven to desperation to put the Chambal behind them.

On 13 September 1820, they entered Bundi. Despite the terrible weakness that continued to assail him, the captain rejected the palki preferring to travel on elephant back. The two day march brought them to the outskirts of the capital.

Clouds of dust gradually obscuring the landscape were the first sign of the maharao's approach. Soon the sound of drums and trumpets and the tramping of horses became audible. Camel messengers were the first to arrive and announce the raja's presence. He was coming on horseback at the head of 800 horse and 1,500 foot. The captain dismounted immediately for it would have been unpardonable to have remained at an elevated height. Ignoring his weakened condition, he mounted Javadia.

The royal retinue lined up. Maharao Raja Bhishen Singh tossed his lance high into the air, bringing to mind his ancestors who had led such troops to battle. The retinue was striking, not so much from the costumes they wore as from the vigour and joyous youthfulness that pervaded it. Dashing Hada youths bewitched the onlookers with a splendid display of horsemanship. A spark was lit in Javadia's breast. Was he not the finest steed in all Rajasthan? Much to the captain's discomfort, Javadia decided that it was the moment to prove himself. Tossing his head back, striking his master's in the process, he leapt forward and in a trice, as the horrified chabukswar helplessly exhorted the name of Ali, was beside the maharao of Bundi. The two friends dismounted and embraced, going through the motions of ceremony. Finally Bhishen Singh gave the captain three hugs and said simply, 'this is your home which you have come to at last.'

Ill health continued to worry the personnel and Lieutenant Cary came to report that he had found Dr Duncan tearing up his papers and writing out his last will and testament. He had refused all food and was sinking fast. The captain left his sick bed to reason with his friend. When common argument failed, exciting his anger worked. Accusations of failing to teach by example brought a tinge of colour to the poor man's cheek and the captain's butler, Kali Khan, used the opportunity to get a tumbler of warm jelly down the doctor's throat. Kali Khan was left behind to alternately rouse and feed the patient. No sooner had the doctor recovered a little that Lieutenant Cary took a turn for the worse.

A week had passed in Bundi and litters were arranged to carry the sick. The maharaja of Thanoh at the head of a 100 horse had been appointed to escort the British to the border. They travelled through the two-mile long gorge – the famous Bunda-ka-nal. On either side were numerous gardens, temples and cenotaphs. Among them stood the memorial to Sooja Bai – silent and hauntingly beautiful. As they passed into the valley of Satur, the rocky hillside closed in on the view of the palace that reared its domes and gilded spires halfway up the mountains with the kangras of Taragarh encircling it like a crown. Bundi was completely shut in by rocks.

The night's halt was spent at Thanoh and the maharaja brought his son and heir to visit the captain. He was a fine little fellow, six years of age, who with his sword buckled by his side and miniature shield on his back, galloped his little steed over hill and dale, like a true Rajput.

The next day took them through the pass that led to Mewar. There within sight of the fortress of Jahazpur the maharaja bid farewell.

Cholera failed to distinguish between caste and creed. Nor were the sacred persons of the princes spared. The epidemic that had begun the previous summer, picked up once again in the spring of 1821. Both the captain and the maharana had their brush with death. But in the captain's case, the gravity of the situation had struck fear in every heart. The maharana ordered his nakarras be hushed. Many a rupee's worth of saffron was promised to the deities to ensure the survival of the one that had bcome so dear. Under Dr Duncan's ministrations, they had both recovered but not everyone had been as fortunate.

In July, a messenger arrived from Bundi. Maharao Raja Bhishen Singh had succumbed leaving his minor son in the captain's personal care. The queen mother, the Rathore princess of Kishangarh – Bhishen Singh's fourth wife – was anxious about the safety of her child. An immediate departure was ordered and within six days, despite the weather, the captain made it to Bundi. Speed was of utmost importance to bring home the deep interest that the British government had in the rising prosperity of Bundi. Despite having decided to travel light, the torrential rain, too heavy a load and the stress of a long and sudden march claimed the life of the best elephant. To lose the emblem of wisdom at the outset was an ominous sign. The uncomfortable day was followed by a still more uncomfortable night for a strong gale forced up the tent pins. Narrowly missing the pole as the tent collapsed about his ears, the captain used a part of it to keep the canvas propped and save himself from suffocation. All around were yells of distress, loose horses and camels. It was all half laughable and half serious but everyone was glad to pack the sodden baggage, which had consequently doubled in weight, and move on well before dawn. The country was flooded, the roads cut up and the little baggage that was left in a wretched plight. Then the crockery bearer fell smashing the contents of the box he carried.

In pouring rain, three miles outside the capital, they went through the motions of ceremony. The principal chiefs had all assembled in the face of the raging elements. The captain hastened to the palace to pay his respects and condole the prince on his loss. Anxiety was written large upon the faces of the mourners.

'My father left me in your lap; he confided my well-being to your hands,' said young Ram Singh Hada.

The crowning ceremony – the raj tilak – had been postponed by the queen mother as soon the captain's decision had been made known. She requested him to accompany her son in the teej procession. This most auspicious festival happened to coincide with the end of the mourning and he gifted the young prince a coloured dress, turban and a jewelled turban sirpech, entreating him, as was customary, to end his mourning. This honour that had been granted to the captain, was a privilege claimed by the nearest of kin alone.

6 August 1821, was chosen for the raj tilak. In the raj mahal where all sons of Deva Bango had been anointed, the young prince underwent the purification rituals. The streets were lined with citizens dressed in their best and joyous shouts of 'Jai Jai' filled the air. Among those present inside, were the prince's younger brother, faithful old chiefs and a granduncle, the venerable chief of Dugari, the only surviving son of Sriji. Here were people who remembered the desperate days the kingdom had been through and appreciated its present stability. Standing with them was Balwant Singh of Gothra, the first noble of Bundi, who twelve years ago had defied his king and captured the great castle of Naenwa. Despite tremendous bloodshed, the castle had never been recovered. Balwant cared not to obey summons nor did he dare appear uninvited. But on this day, he had come to congratulate the new maharao causing much apprehension and wonder.

The purification over, the captain was instructed to lead the prince to a temporary cushion. The prince then re-elected the royal purohit and marked his forehead with a tilak. It entitled the priest to anoint the new king as the future ruler of the Hadas. This being done, the maharao raja was led to the gaddi laid out in an elevated balcony overlooking the external court and a large part of the town. Here within full view of the citizens of Bundi, the captain anointed his forehead with sandalwood paste, using the middle finger of his right hand. He then girt him with his sword and congratulated him in the name of the British government of India. The crowds cheered and the valleys echoed as the cannons of Taragarh saluted their new sovereign. Attaching the sirpech to the maharao raja's turban, the captain placed about his neck strings of pearls and presented him with bracelets, twenty-one shields (trays) of shawls, brocades and fine clothes. An elephant and two horses, richly caparisoned with silver ornaments and embroidered velvet saddle-cloths were led into the centre of the court below the balcony. His part over the captain withdrew and the chiefs of every clan came forward to apply the tilak on the maharao's forehead, thereby accepting him as their sovereign and confirming their fealty. The maharao raja then left to visit every shrine in the city.

Though the festival of Rakhi was still a month away, the queen mother sent the captain a 'silken bracelet of adoption as brother' and requested a meeting. The conversation took place across a curtain and the queen mother was reassured about her son's safety. The captain remained in Bundi till the middle of August making certain that the government was moving in the right direction. Within this period, they celebrated the slaying of the maharao's first boar – his entry into manhood. The young king would nevertheless continue to seek mamoo sahib's appreciation by sending him samples of handwriting and choosing to take his riding lessons right in front of his tent. Less than discreet enquiries would follow in the hope of eliciting a few words of praise.

On 14 August 1821, the captain left for a brief visit to Kota. His return to Udaipur was routed once again through Bundi, to ensure all was well with his nephew and his sister – the queen mother.

Kota, lay on the far bank of the Chambal. Running parallel with the river, rose strong walls and bastions. Enclosed within, its slender minarets and cupolas rising high, was the palace. It was an imposing sight. Here ruled the forty-year-old Maharao Raja Kishore Singh and the elderly regent – Raj Rana Zalim Singh.

The Hada princes of Kota worshipped Kanhaiya (Krishna – Braj Nath) exclusively and it was zealously maintained that everything in Kota belonged to the deity. Rupees 120,000/- were granted annually to the shrine by the palace. A marvellous lake, teeming with fish, lay in the eastern part of the town under Kanhaiya's protection, the rent from the extensive lands adjoining the temple all belonging to him. It was in this lake that the captain had once cast his fly. A rider had appeared almost immediately, panting with exertion, bearing a message from the raj rana:

'Tell Captain Tod that Kota and all around it are at his disposal, but these fish belong to Kanhaiya.'

The fish were returned instantly. Two companies, of a hundred firelocks each remained constantly at their post to protect the 'dark one' from the Marathas and the Pindaris and the most valuable of shawls, broadcloths and horses made their way regularly to the temple from the office of the regent.

Having arrived on 22 February 1820, a decision was taken to spend the summer in Kota. By June, a raging epidemic of cholera (mari or death) caught the city in its grip. Four months of suffering followed. Everyone was at its mercy. Despite several changes of encampment grounds, sickness dogged the British camp. The captain himself wavered upon the brink of death. The heat and the strange transparent blue of the June sky induced a sensation of madness. Not even the breeze of a punkha was bearable. Nothing stirred for miles and Kota reposed in the stillness of death. Then the monsoon began. The rising waters of the Chambal seeped through the ground into the wells pushing mineral poisons to the surface.

The water glistened with an oily bluish gold sheen. No one escaped.

The epidemic assumed devastating proportions. Determined to be rid of this unwelcome visitor, Raj Rana Zalim Singh gathered the Brahmins of the land. A sacrificial fire was lit and in an impressive yagna a decree of banishment was pronounced upon mari (cholera)[19]. A funeral carriage was prepared and loaded with bags of blackened grain, to spare her discomfort. Driven by a pair of black oxen she was deported across the Chambal. When the maharao raja of Bundi heard of the yagna he assembled his wise men and sought a solution. Cholera would have to be stopped from entering Bundi. Accordingly, pots filled with water from the Ganga were placed upon the southern gate from which a steady stream dripped continuously. Surely, no evil could cross so holy a barrier.

The camp had been eventually shifted to the north-eastern angle of the Kishore Sagar overlooking a little fairy islet. Gardens fringed the lake and from above the treetops peeped the spires and domes of temples and mosques. The cenotaphs of the Hadas lay close at hand. They were nearly as grand as those in Mewar and Marwar. The construction of a magnificent cenotaph for Maharao Raja Umed Singh was in progress and the captain offered to put in a word to help the regent procure marble from the quarries of Kankroli in Mewar. Maharana Bhim Singh agreed to gift it to Kota.

Ceremonies marked the last days of their stay. On 10 September 1820, the departure began. It was with some amusement that the captain noted the alacrity with which his bedridden soldiers left their illnesses behind to put the Chambal between themselves and the east. Their resemblance to boatloads of ghosts crossing the Styx was remarkable. The regent's blind eyes filled with tears and his palsied hands pressed those of the captain's. A luxurious barge had been prepared to ferry the captain across, which was just as well, for fever and malaise had weakened him greatly. Fateh Bahadur the captain's elephant, on the other hand, preferred to remain behind. It was only when the howdah was removed and put into a boat

19. The germ theory of disease wasn't propounded until 1862, when Louis Pasteur published his findings and it wasn't before 1880, that Robert Koch established the principles by which germs could be identified and correlated with specific diseases. The discovery of the first antibiotic did not come about until 1928, when Alexander Fleming discovered penicillin.

that he plunged into the river in delight using his trunk as a spout. He was a third of the way across when the plight of a nervous new female elephant caught his attention. Ignoring the protests of his pigmy like mahout, the gallant, without a single thought for his master who awaited him, turned back. Too weak to ride, the captain placed his howdah on the back of a baggage elephant and the victorious warrior was made to suffer the indignity of bearing common load. A two-day march through Nanta and Talera was to take them to Bundi.

Sickness had prevented the touring of regions around Kota but an opportunity to remedy the lapse arose the next year. The maharao raja of Bundi fell victim to mari and the raj tilak of the new maharao required the political agent's presence. On 14 August 1821, the captain returned to Kota.

This time they would not be guests at the palace. Camp was set up instead at Raontha and a route chalked out that would take them from the south-eastern edge of the plateau to Malwa (Madhya Pradesh). They were to turn right from the Mukandara Pass visit the temples of Baroli, Gangabheva and Naoli then march south-east across the plains of Malwa, visit the mausoleum of Jaswant Rao Holkar that lay on the way to Bhanpura, to arrive finally at Garot. The path followed by Lieutenant Colonel Monson, during his infamous retreat of 1804, to the Mukandara Pass would then be retraced.

The early history of Kota belongs with that of Bundi. It had been Emperor Jahangir who had first formally separated Kota from Bundi. Perhaps he wished to reward Madhu Singh, the younger son of Rao Ratan, for the exemplary service rendered in the putting down of Khurram's rebellion, for the single-handed slaying of the rebel general – Khan Jahan Lodi (Peera), or perhaps because an undivided Hadavati was too much of a threat to the Mughal Empire.

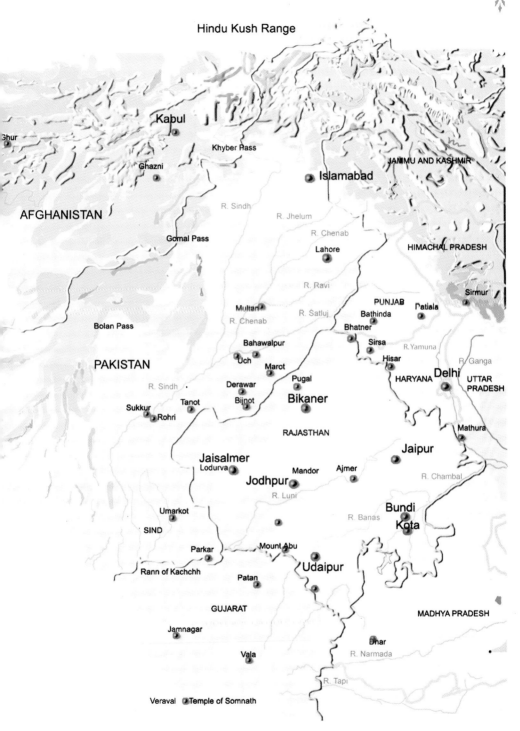

Bhati forts sprang up along the western edge of the desert

Place Spot

District Boundary

State Boundary

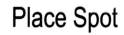 International Boundary

Rivers

Modern Road

Trails

Krishna on swing, Bikaner, Rajasthan, circa AD 1683

Krishna Imploring Radha for Love, Kishangarh,
Rajasthan, circa AD 1750

॥माधुराजिली॥हस्तालिंजिनपार्श्वस्थियाचेचनमानसः॥उष्णोरेहिविह
॥खस्यामानुरागेमुधाबजन॥५२॥

Ragini Maru, Mewar, Rajasthan, circa AD 1660

Rana Jagat Singh II of Mewar hunting wild buffaloes, Mewar,
Rajasthan, circa AD 1750

Raja Maan Singh of Jodhpur with his nobles, circa AD 1810

Lion Hunt, Ajmer Sawar, Rajasthan, circa AD 1700

Photograph: The crescent on the dome of Shah Jahan's Gul Mahal is no longer to be seen. It was however present during Captain Tod's stay in Mewar and can be seen in Captain Waugh's sketch – The Place of Jugmundur in Oodipoor Lake.

Jag Mandir: Photograph by Giles Tillotson.

Rao Madhu Singh

For his performance at Burhanpur, Madhu Singh, the son of Rao Ratan of Bundi, received Kota as a grant directly from the emperor to be held independently of Bundi. The Hada prince agreed to cross the Attock and serve as the governor of Balkh Badakshan. Madhu catapulted into imperial favour and he used it to extend the limits of his dominion. By the time he died, his lands extended right up to the Malwa border. His five sons governed the five jagirs and used the name Madhani to distinguish themselves from the senior branch at Bundi. Mokund had inherited Kota, Mohan received Palaita, Jujhar Singh given Kotra, Ramgarh and Relawan, Kuniaram had Koela while Kishore Singh was granted Sangod.

When Khurram succeeded as Emperor Shah Jahan he reconfirmed the grant of Kota to the valiant Madhani Hadas.

Rao Mokund Singh

The brothers did not forget their debt of gratitude to the Mughal throne and they all fought for the ageing Shah Jahan when his sons rose against him. Dressed in saffron, they led their armies to Dharmat. But Maharaja Jaswant Singh of Marwar, who was in command that day, took several fatal decisions. Aurungzeb and Murad were allowed to get away and Jaswant Singh himself retreated. The field was covered in gore and among the dead were the brothers of Kota. Aurungzeb renamed Dharmat as Fatehabad – the city of victory.

That night the youngest was dragged out from amongst the slain. He made a miraculous recovery and Kishore lived to become one of the most conspicuous Rajputs to have served in the Deccan distinguishing himself at the siege of Bijapur.

The young royal family had proven itself and diplomatic alliances were soon sought by Rajput houses. The first of Kota's princesses, Mokund's own daughter, was given in marriage to Mirza Raja Ram Singh of Amber.

Rao Jagat Singh

Jagat Singh, the son of Mokund, succeeded but he died without an heir and Pem Singh, the son Kuniaram of Koela, was selected. He ruled for six months but was found to be mentally feeble and was set aside by the chiefs. He returned to Koela, which remained with his line.

Rao Kishore Singh

Kishore Singh, the only brother who survived Fatehabad, was placed on the throne. When this fine specimen of a Hada died in the escalade of Arcatgarh (Arcot) there were fifty wounds to be counted upon his person. No surprise was expressed for after all why else was one born a Hada?

Ram Singh, his second son, who served in the Deccan by his father's side, succeeded to the throne of Kota.

Although, Bhishen Singh was the elder son of Rao Kishore Singh, he had been disqualified for he had failed to accompany his father to the south. The emperor granted him the jagir and royal palace of Anta instead. His son Pirthi Singh succeeded and was followed by Ajit Singh. The line of Bhishen Singh was however destined to return to the throne of Kota.

Rao Raja Ram Singh

Emperor Aurungzeb died on 3 March 1707, and his sons launched the battle for succession. Muazzam, the eldest, was far away in Kabul. Azam and Kam Baksh who were both in the Deccan lost no time in proclaiming themselves emperor and striking coins in their own names.

Ram Singh embraced the cause of Prince Azam, the viceroy in the Deccan, and was given to understand that he would receive free possession of Bundi. He celebrated by declaring himself king of Hadavati. On 23 March 1707, Ram Singh was awarded the hereditary title of raja.

The Mughal brothers raced towards Agra. Securing the treasury would decide the winner but Kam Baksh was unable to tear himself away from the Deccan in time. On 10 June 1707, Muazzam's army met Azam's at Jajav, south of Agra. Rao Raja Ram Singh was slain that day – in the battle that decided the succession to the throne of Delhi. In this memorable conflict Hada fought Hada for Budh Singh of Bundi had supported Muazzam.

Muazzam ascended the throne of Hindustan as Emperor Shah Alam Bahadur Shah and granted possession of Kota to Maharao Raja Budh Singh of Bundi. But try as hard as Bundi might their spirited cousins refused to give in. The warriors of Kota beat off two attempts by the army of Bundi.

Maharao Raja Bheem Singh

Bheem accepted service as an imperial officer and worked his way back into imperial favour. Emperor Farukhsiyar, who came to the throne, stripped Budh Singh of Bundi of his rank and honours and named in his stead, Bheem as the new maharao raja of Kota and Bundi. Bundi was occupied and renamed Farukkabad. But the honour of being master of Hadavati lasted for only two years. In December 1715, Emperor Farukhsiyar ordered the restoration of Bundi to Maharao Raja Budh Singh. Bheem resisted. He vacated eight months later bringing back with him the elephant gate from Taragarh, two cannons from Ranthambhor and every insignia of sovereign rule. Bundi's nakarras were looted, as was the 'run shunkh' – the conch shell used during battle, an heirloom inherited from the heroes of antiquity. Not even were the instruments of the army band spared. The orange flag[20] granted to Rao Ratan by Jahangir was henceforth displayed by the junior house of Kota in all its processions and battles.

---

20. Many flags are on display at the museums of Kota prominent among which is the official flag emblazoned with an image of Garuda: the bird like mythical being who serves as Lord Vishnu's personal carrier, dating from around the time that Kota became the land of the Lord (Vallabh Sampraday). Kota too had maintained an orange flag similar to the one granted to Rao Ratan, the ancestor of the Hadas of Bundi and Kota. Although Maharao Raja Bhim did bring back the original orange flag from Bundi, none of the flags in the museum of Kota can be dated to the period of Emperor Jahangir.

Many a strategy was worked out by Bundi for the recovery of the family heirlooms. Copies of keys to the gates of Kota were made, guards bribed but the plans always, at the very brink of success, failed. Ceaseless vigilance meant the gates of Kota closed at sunset and would not open. Not even for the maharao of Kota himself.

Maharao Raja Durjan Sal, the youngest son of Maharao Raja Bheem, having succeeded to the throne, returned one evening battle-weary and dejected. The sun had just gone down and the appeals fell upon deaf ears. The sentry on duty fired at him and called out in derision. Durjan was forced to spend the night at a temple nearby.

The next day, the sentry placed his sword and shield at the maharao's feet and awaited his decision. Durjan was full of praise and the sentry received, as a mark of honour, the battledress that his sovereign had worn that evening.

Maharao Raja Budh Singh had remained loyal to the imperial crown but as the unfortunate Farukhsiyar was being done to death by Maharaja Ajit of Marwar, Bheem had been unable to resist making a disgraceful attempt on the life of his cousin who was occupied, in those final moments, in defending the emperor. With Farukhsiyar dead, Bheem marched into Bundi. It was returned to Budh Singh only after the death of the last of the Syyed brothers in 1720.

With Bheem Singh, Kota prospered. He supported the cause of the Syyed brothers and received many benefits. The Syyed brothers – the kingmakers at the Delhi court – helped Kota obtain a royal grant for all the land on the plateau. This resulted in the encroachment upon the lands of the Kinchi-Chauhans and that of Bundi. The strongest castle in Hadavati, Gagraun, which had once proven invincible to Alla-ud-din Khalji, was now in Bheem's possession.

Bheem Singh aggressively expanded his territory. The Ujala or pureblooded Bhils had regained a part of their ancient lands on the southern border of Hadavati. The king of the Bhils, Raja Chakrasen, lived in Manohar Thana and commanded an army of 500 horse and 800 bowmen. Bhil tribes from Mewar to the plateau did him obeisance. This simple ancient stock of India was hunted down mercilessly and their lands annexed to Kota. From 1719, onwards, having fulfilled all his material desires, Bheem devoted himself to the exclusive worship of Braj Nath (Krishna). He assumed the name of Krishna Das – the servant of Lord Krishna – and renamed his kingdom Nandgaon after the village in which the Lord had spent his childhood in the care of his foster parents – Raja Nand and Rani Yashoda. The following year he was invested with the Mahi Maratib – the order of the fish.

Budh Singh's domestic quarrels with his Kachwaha rani had ruined his relationship with her brother turning the balance of power in Bheem's favour. Bheem threw his lot in with Sawai Maharaja Jai Singh giving him a daughter in marriage. Together they hounded the Bundi maharao. Sawai Maharaja Jai Singh of Amber and Jaipur, who saw himself as the Mughal's natural heir, eyed all Hadavati. But his energies were devoted first to the persecution of Budh Singh and his heirs.

Word arrived that the nizam-ul-mulk of Mughal India, had rebelled. Abandoning Delhi, he was making his way to the Deccan. Sawai Maharaja Jai Singh, the first lieutenant of Hindustan, commanded Bheem Singh of Kota and Guj Singh of Narwar to intercept him.

The nizam was the pugri-buddul-bhai of the Hada prince and he wrote personally to Bheem.

'Do not prevent my passage or pay heed to my enemies,' he pleaded, adding that he had stolen none of the empire's treasures and that Jai Singh was merely out to create trouble.

Replying, that he was capable of drawing the line between friendship and duty and that the emperor's orders would have to be obeyed, Bheem, like a true cavalier, gave due warning of his intentions. The courtesy of the Rajputs did not allow resentment to be mingled with hostilities. The nizam, he said, would be attacked the coming morning.

The nizam, who suffered from no such sentiment of medieval chivalry, positioned himself strategically. A large mine was laid in the only mountain pass available and covered with leaves and branches. On 19 June 1720, as the yellow clouds of dawn broke, the combined armies of Jaipur, Kota and Narwar entered the pass ready for the Battle of Pandher. Packed in a dense formation with lances protruding, they were a formidable force. Every warrior had had their opium that morning and at their head, riding their elephants were Bheem and Guj Singh. The mine exploded beneath the feet of the elephants instantly killing the entire Rajput army.

Nizam-ul-mulk went on to fulfil the glorious destiny that awaited him. Despite his rebellion, the emperor raised him to the post of wazir in 1722. But try as he might the new wazir was unable to restore order. The parasites that bred upon the empire could not be contained and finding his services unwanted he relinquished his posts of nizam-ul-mulk and wazir in 1724, and retired to rule his province independently. The emperor still thought kindly of him and in 1737, dignified him with the title Asaf Jah. He remained one of the few to have served the Mughals since the days of Aurungzeb. Under the Asaf Jahi nizams, Hyderabad – built alongside, what was once said to be the legendary Hada abode, Golconda – grew into a magnificent city. Braj Nath who had accompanied the Hadas into battle had been lost but, to their great joy, the small golden statue was returned some years later.

Bheem had ruled for fifteen years. Among his wives was a princess of Udaipur, the daughter of Maharana Amar Singh II. Bheem was the first prince of Kota to have led an imperial army of 5,000 and the first of his dynasty to have received the title of maharao. The rivalry that had begun on the battlefield of Jajav ended with the death of the cousins. They had both enjoyed their turns at holding the enviable position of maharao raja of Hadavati.

13 December 1821: Daybreak found the captain headed northwards from the city of bells – Jhalarapatan, ascending the highlands that formed Hadavati's natural boundary.

The ancient temple town had been refurbished by the regent[21]. From among its 108 temples, the Jain temple dedicated to the sixteenth teacher could alone be declared as truly belonging to antiquity. To the east lay the ancient city of Mau, the first capital of the Kinchi-Chauhans. To the north-west, enveloped in mist atop a hill, stood the fort of Gagraun.

The men followed the path trodden by Alla-ud-din Khalji when he besieged Achaldas Kinchi. Straight ahead to the north lay the antri or valley of Gagraun. Three miles wide and thickly forested, it echoed with the screams of peacocks and the calls of partridge and jungle fowl. It was here that Zalim Singh had camped for the last thirty years since his return from Mewar. He had succeeded in securing the release of his Maratha friend Bala Rao Ingle but had, in the process, lost his hold over the maharana. The palace at Kota had been proclaimed unsafe by the fortune-tellers and the regent had chosen to set up a cantonment at a site equidistant from the two southern entrances to Hadavati.

The rivers Amjhar and Ahu made their way through the plains of Malwa and surged through the chain of hills into the valley of Gagraun.

---

21. In 1838, the British government separated the state of Jhalawar from Kota. Jhalawar was granted to Jhala Madan Singh, the grandson of Raj Rana Zalim Singh. The Garh Palace was constructed in 1840 – 1845.

Flowing past the western face of the castle separating it from the town[22], they emptied their waters into the mighty Kali Sindh.

On the banks of the Amjhar, midway between Gagraun and Jhalarapatan, an upcoming town was in the process of quickly replacing the regent's camp. A short distance to the west, lay the cantonment of the Pindaris, where the sons of Karim Khan, the chief leader of the hordes, resided.

It was from Raontha, the site of his present camp at Kota, that Captain Tod, who was then in charge of the Intelligence Department, had organized the Pindari campaign of 1817 – 1818, for the predatory hordes were proving to be a menace. Thirty-two firelocks of the British guard had been sent, along with the auxiliary forces of Kota, for a surprise night attack. They had out-marched their Hada allies and had come upon the foe discovering, to their horror, a camp of 1,500 where only 500 were expected. Undaunted, the gallant little band, poured in sixty rounds before daybreak and returned in triumph, with the marauders' horses and camels laden with Pindari gold. A successful defence had been mounted against the 400 Pindaris that returned the next morning seeking to regain their lost honour. A bounty, equal to six months pay, additional pay for life for all and promotions for the non commissioned officers had been granted by Lord Hastings. The regent, who never allowed spoils of war to enter his treasury, had it sent to the British camp. With it Captain Tod proposed the building of a bridge across the Alnia, a tributary of the Chambal. The Hasteen Pul, a bridge of fifteen arches, stood in memory of Lord Hastings who had emancipated India from the scourge of the Pindaris.

It was with some amusement that the captain noted the permanent shape that the Pindari camp had taken on. An idgah had been built for while the villains believed in robbing and murdering, sparing not even a thought for helpless women or children, they continued to worship five times a day.

---

22. The colonel refers to the Ahu and Amjhar (mango forest) as confluent streams which together pass below the western face of Gagraun. The Amjhar, he says, arises from the plateau and flows past the Mukandara Pass. A waterway matching his description can be traced even today. There is another tributary called the Oojad (one who uproots), not to be confused with Amjhar, which arises from the Bhim Sagar and joins the Kali Sindh a few miles before it is joined by the Parwan.

Endless heroes have fallen defending the pass but the last hero of note was Guman Singh, a descendent of Sawant Hada who had sacrificed himself to keep Ranthambhor from the hands of the Mughal Emperor Akbar.

Maharao Raja Durjan Sal ruled Kota at the time with the help of his foujdar – a Rathore Rajput. The scheming foujdar, one day, confiscated all of Guman Singh's estates and it was with a heavy heart that the Hada made his way home.

The dark of the evening set in quickly amongst the mountains and as he entered the gloom of the pass he discovered, slinking past him though the shadows, the entourage of the villainous foujdar.

A lance fixed the Rathore to his palki and while his men held the pass, Guman Singh fled with his family to Udaipur. There he remained, until the day Kota was besieged by Maharaja Sawai Ishwari Singh of Jaipur. Maharana Jagat Singh II gave him leave to rush to Kota's defence and Guman Singh made his way across the plateau.

The army of Jaipur was present everywhere but Guman Singh was determined to reach Kota or die in the attempt. He sounded his nakarras as he made his way through the heart of the Jaipur camp. Ishwari Singh was impressed by his sheer audacity. Guman Singh Hada, the rawat of the pass, whose father had once killed a tiger with his bare hands, was brought before the sawai maharaja. Large estates were offered in exchange for abandoning the doomed Kota but all that was forthcoming was the salutation and the defiance of the Hada. The rawat was allowed to pass unmolested and on reaching his sovereign's side was deputed right away to defend a breach in the walls of Kota.

As they ascended the gentle slope of the Gagraun ridge, the view caught them by surprise. The Kali Sindh swept across the northern face of both fort and town eroding the rock to a depth of 200 feet below the level of the valley. It ploughed its serpentine way due north through three separate ranges into the plains of Hadavati. The guns on the ramparts boomed as they passed below the fort and the governor advanced to welcome the captain on the behalf of his master. Unwilling to be acquainted with the secrets of the chief stronghold of Zalim Singh, the captain suppressed a long standing desire to visit the historical castle and declined. So inaccessible was the fort that in taking it on the enemy would have had to grasp the bull by the horns. Sultan Alla-ud-din Khalji had, in the end, resorted to polluting the waters with the blood of the sacred cow in order to draw Achaldas Kinchi out of his impregnable stronghold.

There was a wild grandeur about Gagraun, which makes it well worth a visit.

Passing over the ridge of Gagraun the party descended into yet another valley. The night was passed at Narayanpur and daybreak found them making their way to the famed Mukandara Pass, one of the few passages that connected northern and southern India. Upon the summit of a ridge, midway between Narayanpur and the pass, stood the ruins of the castle of Ghati. It commanded a clear view of the plains of Malwa. At its feet, gliding through the deep woods of the valley was the Amjhar. The Kinchi and Hada, both of Chauhan descent, had once been the lords of the pass. The imprints left behind by Maharaj Kinchi's charger, as he sprang at Islamic invaders, were pointed out to the travellers as were the many cenotaphs to the slain and shrines to Shiva and his consort.

The Chaori of Bhim, where the Pandav had celebrated his wedding, lay close to the pass. Here, amongst the ruins, the most striking remains of art were still to be found though much of the material had been reused by a prince of Kota to build a palace for his tribal queen.

Every step of the way, the corridor between the Deccan and northern India, was littered with joojarhs or funeral stones.

Maharao Raja Arjun Singh

Arjun Singh, the eldest son of Bheem and his chief queen, daughter to Maharana Amar Singh II, married the sister of Madhu Singh, the ancestor of Zalim Singh Jhala. He ruled for four years and died without leaving behind an heir. His brothers began the battle for succession, which claimed the life of Shyam Singh.

Maharao Raja Durjan Sal

In 1724, Durjan Sal, the youngest son of Maharao Raja Bheem, succeeded to the throne of Kota acknowledged by Emperor Muhammad Shah Rangila. From his hands Durjan received the imperial khelat and with it a boon: the slaughter of the sacred cow was banned along the banks of the Yamuna.

It was during Durjan's reign, that the Marathas under Baji Rao Peshwa first invaded northern India. In 1732, Maharaja Sawai Jai Singh of Amber and Maharaja Abhay of Marwar had let Malwa and Gujarat fall into their hands. Kota was occupied, and allegiance forced upon the Hadas. While skirting the eastern border of Hadavati, they attacked and capturing the castle of Nahargarh from its Islamic occupants, presented it to Durjan in return for stores and ammunition. This happy relationship was not to last long. Then marching through Delhi, looting the Kalkadevi area they faced a reversal at Talkatora. Baji Rao returned to Kota. Durjan had to pay ten lakhs before they would leave.

The year 1739, saw the bloodiest sacking of the imperial capital. Nadir Shah, a Turk who had declared himself shah of Persia had observed the Marathas' north Indian expedition. Its meaning had not been lost upon him. Within two years he presented himself at Delhi. The Rajputs remained mute witnesses as the Red Fort was looted, the Kohinoor and the Peacock Throne carried away and the emperor left behind as a servant of the Turk.

The fortunes of Bundi continued to waver. Backed by the powers of Delhi, Maharaja Sawai Jai Singh of Amber had made an attempt at subduing Hadavati. Maharao Raja Budh Singh was evicted and driven into exile while a traitor – Dalil Singh, Maharaja Sawai Jai Singh's son-in-law – took his place upon the throne. The gallant Budh Singh died in exile and the puppet accepted the terms of homage and tribute. Durjan took up Bundi's cause. Maharana Jagat Singh II of Mewar joined in hoping to destabilise Maharaja Sawai Jai Singh's successor, Ishwari Singh. But Madho Singh, whose cause had taken up by the maharana, was pacified by Ishwari and Mewar was forced to pull out. Durjan persisted nevertheless. Recruiting help from Gujarat and Shahpura he drove out the traitor. But Budh Singh's heir, Umed, wanted Bundi. Not content with what Durjan had to offer he left. The army of Jaipur moved in and restored Dalil Singh.

Maharaja Sawai Ishwari Singh of Jaipur invited Raja Shahu Bhosle's help. The Maratha prime minister, Nana Sahib Peshwa, sent three of his greatest generals amongst whom was Ranoji Scindia's son – Jai Appa. Accompanying them were Dalil Singh and Surajmal's Jats. Kota was besieged in 1748, and though the outskirts of the city were vandalized, the fort did not fall. The Marathas left after three months having destroyed the trees and gardens but the Hada cannons had compelled the great Jai Appa to leave behind an arm. Kota was made to cough up two lakhs and Bundi the lands of Patan. But Durjan lost no time in teaming up with Mewar once again. This time Ishwari Singh was defeated at Bagru and Umed placed on his throne. Sadly it was not to last. Jaipur was soon back in possession of Bundi.

The days of torment, however, were drawing to a close. Ishwari Singh was ordered to the banks of the Sutlej where the Afghan minion of Nadir Shah, who saw himself as successor to his master's Indian dominion, waited with his army. But the dilemma of leaving Jaipur undefended proved too much for Ishwari. His brother's ambitions weighed on his mind to the point of driving him from his post at the battlefield. Leaving Punjab to its fate, Ishwari rushed from Sirhind and Punjab would have been lost to Ahmad Shah Abdalli (Durrani) that day had it not been for Safdarjung. All of Rajasthan sneered at the Kachwaha. Within a month, however, Emperor Muhammad Shah Rangila passed away and Abdalli returned to obtain a formal cessation.

Durjan had with him the courage and counsel of the brilliant Himmut Singh Jhala, the foujdar or commander of the garrison of Kota. The gallant maharao had helped his young cousin, Umed Singh, win back his father's throne, albeit temporarily, but it had come at a price, for it had finally been Malhar Rao Holkar who, boosted by a generous bribe from Maharana Jagat Singh of Mewar, set Umed firmly upon his throne. That year Kota was compelled to become a tributary to the Marathas. Within a year, Ishwari had committed suicide and the Kachwaha throne passed to his brother. Maharaja Sawai Madho Singh came into possession of the ancient Chauhan fort of Ranthambhor in 1753. Bundi had been too weak to accept responsibility and Emperor Ahmad Shah fully aware that it was only a matter of time before he lost it to the Marathas. Madho Singh saw himself as the Mughal's heir in Rajasthan. But included within the Mughal district of Rathambhor were eight of Bundi's great jagirs. Himmut Singh Jhala lost no time in convincing the Hada chieftains to switch allegiance to the more powerful Hada kingdom. But the actual signing of the documents took place after Himmut Singh's death.

In 1754, Durjan added to Kota several places including Phool Barod, which belonged to the Kinchis. The brilliant defence by Balbhadra Kinchi, chief of the fortress of Gugor, would have snatched from Kota the orange standard had it not been for the valour of young Umed of Bundi. It had been a meeting of rival clans, all of Chauhan blood.

The Chauhans cared little for the horrors that engulfed Delhi. Emperor Ahmad Shah was blinded and deposed the same year by imad-ul-mulk, the grandson of the first nizam of Hyderabad, and the elderly devout son of Jahandar Shah, who had been blinded by his cousin Farukhsiyar forty years ago, was raised to the throne. Alamgir II had little say in the matters of state. Imad set about recovering lost territories. The result was the return of the Afghan – Abdalli – in January 1757, which led to another sacking of Delhi. The thirty-five-year-old Afghan then announced his retirement and went home bearing with him two daughters of the imperial Mughals. The Afghan's successes were not lost upon the militant traders of Britain. In June 1757, at the Battle of Plassey, Bengal played into the hands of the East India Company.

Durjan died in August that year, remembered as an affable and valiant prince admired by all. With no children of his own, he adopted Chattra Sal, the son of Ajit of Anta. Chattra Sal was made to recount his ancestry from Durjan, Bheem, Ram and so on until Deva, Bango and Manik Rai of Aimer.

Maharao Raja Ajit Singh

When Durjan died, Himmut Singh the foujdar objected to Chattra Sal's accession for Ajit, his natural father, was still alive. It would have been unnatural for a father to be a subject to his son. The elderly Ajit was crowned instead and he ruled for two years leaving behind three sons, Chattra Sal, Guman Singh and Raj Singh. Such was the power of the foujdar.

Maharao Raja Chattra Sal

Himmut Singh died before Chattra Sal's accession. His nephew and adopted son, Zalim Singh Jhala, succeeded to the office of foujdar. And his first achievement was to conclude the negotiations with the eight Bundi chieftains whose jagirs were technically part of Mughal Ranthambhor.

It was a great slight to Bundi but there was precious little that young Maharao Raja Umed Singh could do. But Maharaja Sawai Madho Singh of Jaipur, who saw himself as the Mughal's heir in Rajasthan, would not take it lying down. He assembled his friends to subdue Hadavati.

Delhi was beset with its own worries. Having failed to rebuild the empire by himself, imad-ul-mulk had invited the Marathas' help. It filled their heads with visions of glory and a Maratha empire that would stretch to the Attock. They set about accomplishing their dreams and Lahore was occupied in 1759. Abdalli came out of retirement ready for war and Imad vented his frustrations on the unfortunate Alamgir. The emperor was murdered. But his heir was in safe hands for he had fled to Avadh the previous year. The Third Battle of Panipat loomed overhead. The Rajputs decided unanimously to have nothing to do with it. With the Marathas and the Mughals occupied they were left to their own devices.

The army of Jaipur marched towards Hadavati capturing on its way Uniara, Lakheri and Sultanpur passing through the very heart of Kota to arrive at the plains of Bhatwara near Mangrol. Here, waiting to give battle were 5,000 Hadas, united as sons of one father. But the army of Kota was tiny compared to that of Jaipur. It was now that twenty-one-year-old Zalim Singh gave the first display of his leadership qualities. Abandoning his horse, he led the soldiers on foot enthusing them with his own lack of fear. The battle had reached a feverish pitch when Zalim noticed the dejected and forlorn Holkar set up camp by the edge of the battlefield, content with watching the proceedings from afar. Fresh from his recent humiliation at the hands of Abdalli, Malhar Rao Holkar had not made up his mind as to which side to aid. Zalim mounted his horse and rushed to the Maratha.

'If you can't make up your mind at least don't lose the opportunity of plundering the Jaipur camp,' suggested Zalim.

Holkar needed no further motivation. The news that the camp had been pillaged lifted the spirits of the Hadas. The troops of Jaipur panicked and fled. The battle of Bhatwara decided forever the question of tribute. The Kachwahas gave up all pretensions of being heirs to the legacy of Delhi. But Bundi did not join the battle that day and failed to redeem its tribute paying jagirs.

Zalim Singh, who had been born the year Nadir Shah invaded India, had made his political debut immediately after the Third Battle of Panipat.

The Mughal Empire was ruled in name by the absent emperor, Shah Alam II, who preferred to live in the safety of Avadh while the empire was administered by a Rohilla Afghan appointed by Ahmad Shah Abdalli.

Maharao Raja Guman Singh

Guman Singh succeeded his brother in 1766. He was married to Ganga Bai, Himmut Singh Jhala's daughter, which made him Zalim Singh's brother-in-law. But Zalim Singh had grown too big for his boots and had been unceremoniously dismissed. Undaunted, he tried his luck at Udaipur and, when circumstances there turned against him, returned to Kota determined on making a come back.

The moment sought by Zalim appeared at the nick of time. The Holkar co-regents – Ahilya Bai and her second husband, Tukoji – laid siege to

Zalim Singh Jhala was born in 1739. A significant event marked his birth. Nadir Shah, the Turkish monarch of Persia, invaded India spelling the beginning of the end for the Mughals.

Zalim's ancestors had been petty chieftains in Gujarat. Bhao Singh had left his homeland to seek his fortune and his son, Madhu had eventually wound up at the court of Maharao Raja Bheem Singh. The services of his mercenary army were engaged and though he had but twenty-five horses with him, the young man commanded great respect. When his sister married Arjun Singh, the heir of Kota, Madhu received the estate of Nanta. The office of the foujdar was granted to him and his heirs in perpetuity. Madhu Singh became mama to the younger royals.

Zalim, who had performed so bravely at Bhatwara, soon crossed his prince's path in love. Divested of his office and his estates, the young Jhala resolved to seek his fortune elsewhere. Amber was not open to him and in Marwar, there lay no opportunity. So, to the court Mewar he headed.

The Jhala chieftain of Delwara, one of the sixteen great chiefs of Mewar, had played an instrumental role in the palace coup that had given Maharana Ari Singh the throne. As a result he wielded great power over the maharana. Several crown lands and estates that belonged to hostile chiefs had been seized and appropriated. By a most daring plan, Zalim relieved the Jhala of his life and the maharana of his bondage.

For this service, he received the title of raj rinna[23] and the estate of Chitarkhaira. He was now a noble of the second order in Mewar.

---

23. The designation was raj rinna (one to whom the kingdom is indebted) and not raj rana as Zalim used on his seal. Of this Lt Col Tod is absolutely sure, having personally inspected the royal documents of Mewar which granted Zalim Singh the title. The Jhala chiefs, who had first been granted Bari Sadri and Delwara by Maharana Raimal, had been permitted to use the hereditary titles of raj rana. But these were princes of royal blood – the descendents of Raja Raj Singh of Halvad in Gujarat. Zalim Singh on the other hand was a commoner.

Rebellion in Mewar continued and the pretender to the throne of the Sisodias sought the aid of the Marathas. In 1769, Zalim was taken prisoner during the Battle of Ujjain. But the Maratha commander – Trambak Rao, the father of Ambaji Ingle who was to later become Scindia's lieutenant – treated the Jhala kindly. A friendship formed which was to affect the later course of their lives. Udaipur was occupied by the Marathas and forced to pay tribute. Too wise to cling to the fortunes of a falling house, Zalim returned to Kota.

Maharao Raja Guman Singh had neither forgotten nor forgiven him. He refused to meet him. Without waiting for permission, Zalim burst into the royal presence begging forgiveness. He had chosen the most favourable moment. Not only was he pardoned he was almost instantly re-employed.

the castle of Bakani on the southern border of Kota. Four hundred Hadas of the Sawant Hada clan readied themselves to defend the castle. The massive doors were pulled shut and Madhu Singh, the Hada chieftain, took up his post on the ramparts. The Marathas ran a war elephant repeatedly into the castle door using its powerful head as a battering ram. The animal was on the verge of success when Madhu – a descendent of Sawant Hada, the hero of Ranthambhor – leapt onto its back. With his dagger, he stabbed the rider and with repeated blows felled the elephant. The lone Hada did not escape death but as the gates to his fort opened a flood was let loose. His clansmen came pouring out to take part in their last battle. They took with them 1,300 of Holkars' best soldiers.

The Marathas turned towards Suket and Maharao Guman Singh sent word to his garrisons. They were to preserve their lives and not sacrifice themselves for the sake of honour. Unfortunately, the forest of dry grass through which the garrison was to pass was set afire, either by accident or treachery, and many soldiers lost their lives. Enthused by this last victory, the Holkars pressed on. Guman Singh's foujdar failed in an attempt to negotiate with the Maratha and it was at this point that Zalim Singh returned. Given his history of success with Malhar Rao, Ahilya Bai's father-in-law, he was empowered with authority. A bribe of six lakhs of rupees was offered and the Marathas withdrew.

Zalim Singh regained his office. It was not long, before Guman Singh fell seriously ill. Worried about his ten-year-old son, Umed, he proclaimed his will before his chiefs and placed his son in Zalim's lap. The dying king chose, as guardian, the man who had saved Kota twice.

Maharao Raja Umed Singh I

Umed was seated upon the throne in 1771, and Zalim Singh Jhala, who was his mother's brother, held office as regent of Kota. On the day of installation, the ancient custom of teeka-dowr was revived and Kelwara grabbed from Narwar. Every thing indicated that the regent would not be a passive man. The talented prime minister, Akhairam, who had served since the days of Maharao Raja Chattra Sal, had died shortly before

Maharao Raja Guman Singh. Zalim Singh took over Akhairam's office as well. Never before in the history of Kota had both offices been invested in any one man.

The emperor returned to Delhi in January 1772, bringing the Scindia Marathas with him. The Rohilla Afghan who had been the defacto ruler of the empire had been dead for more than a year and the reins of government had passed into the hands of a Persian adventurer. Shah Alam II resigned himself to playing the role of a puppet – one that carried on until the death of the Persian ten years later.

There were many in Kota who resented the power hungry regent. Maharaj Suroop Singh, a cousin of the late maharao, conspired with the disgraced ex-foujdar and Umed Singh's foster brother. The conspiracy did not have time to hatch as the maharaj was murdered by the foster brother while cowardly ex-foujdar fled in terror. As to the reasons for the murder, it baffled everyone for the victim and the accused had had no quarrel. Zalim Singh was loud in his condemnation of the murderer and had him banished. No one felt safe in Kota any more.

Finding themselves deprived of their say in the governing of Kota, the Hada nobles withdrew and left to garner support from neighbouring kingdoms. Zalim felt nothing but contempt for this feeble display of resistance and allowed them to leave as they wished. The nobles wandered from the courts of Jaipur to Jodhpur and discovered, as Zalim had predicted, that the kingdoms, beset by problems brought on by the Marathas, were in no mood to involve themselves with Kota. When the nobles tried to return, two years later, they found their entry barred. The lands, that they had voluntarily abandoned, had been annexed. In an act of clemency, Zalim permitted them to enter but labelled as traitors.

Deo Singh of Aton granted them refuge. His estate earned him 60,000 rupees in rent and his castle was fortified. Together they determined to get rid of the regent. But Zalim calculated that Aton's resources would prove insufficient in the event of a long siege. Foreign mercenaries were hired. The siege of Aton lasted several months and when at last, the nobles surrendered, Zalim permitted them to leave unmolested. Deo Singh died in exile but many years later his son earned a reprieve and was permitted to return.

There had been several attempts at assassination but Zalim had always been on guard. Twenty years after the siege of Aton, Bahadur Singh rounded up every noble that had lost his estate. The plotting was conducted in admirable secrecy and perhaps the only other person who knew about it was the regent himself. Zalim Singh Jhala, his family and friends had been marked out for death. The regent was to be killed in open court. The very audacity of the plan was to guarantee its success. Zalim was on his way to court, when he received wind of the appointed hour. A select troop of horse, always ready at hand, was pressed into immediate action. On the verge of success, just as the prey appeared to rush into the snare, the scheme fell apart. Several conspirators were killed on the spot. Bahadur Singh managed to cross the Chambal taking refuge in a temple, but Bundi, could not shield him. He was dragged out and slain.

Umed Singh's family, which included two brothers and an uncle, were placed under strict surveillance. The brothers were soon implicated and imprisoned. Zalim too had grown weary of being relentlessly on guard for a total of eighteen plots had been hatched against him. He slept in an iron cage and worried constantly about poison.

Perhaps the most dangerous of them all was the one laid by the women of the palace. The regent had been sent for by one of the queens of Guman Singh. While he waited for the lady to address him from behind the curtains, he realised that he had been surrounded by a band of armed Rajputnis. There would have been no escape had it not been for the sudden appearance of the queen mother's attendant. A torrent of abuse had followed and Zalim Singh had been let off.

The control of Kota alone did not whet Zalim's appetite. It was Mewar that he eyed and as a result, the affairs of Kota often remained neglected. The Mughal Empire exercised no control for though the Persian at the helm had died, Emperor Shah Alam II had invested his friend Mahadji Scindia with the regency. Mahadji used it for his personal gains but a single setback, the Battle of Lalsot, had thrown the emperor at the mercy of a Rohilla youngster. This man set about searching the Red Fort for its fabled treasure and on discovering the truth, took out his frustrations upon the wretched emperor. The blinding of Shah Alam II on 10 August 1788, put an end to the Mughal Empire. What was left was called the Kingdom of Delhi, and Mahadji Scindia, who had rushed to its rescue, seized absolute control.

Zalim leagued with the Scindias and conducted his nefarious activities in the problem-riddled court of the maharana. Rivalry was to be expected and in 1791, Mahadji's lieutenant, Ambaji Ingle, manoeuvred the Jhala's expulsion from Mewar. But with Mahadji's death and the appointment of the incompetent Daulat Rao, Scindia infighting broke out giving Zalim Singh the much longed for foothold again. Allying himself with Ambaji's brother Bala Rao Ingle, Zalim vied for control over the maharana.

In a sudden swift movement in 1803, the chiefs of Mewar united and turned upon the tormentors and Bala Rao Ingle was incarcerated in the dungeons of Udaipur. For the son of Trambak Rao, Zalim would have given his life. And, though it was the maharana that he had to personally face, he succeeded. It brought him a handsome reward – the district and fortress of Jahazpur[24]. But there remained no room for him in Mewar. He was forced to return to Kota. In December, that year Lord Lake occupied Delhi and the East India Company took the blind emperor on its books. Daulat Rao Scindia, thrown out of his role as protector, set up camp in Mewar. Mewar was in anycase on the brink of ruin and held no future for Zalim. He awoke to the realization that he had been neglecting his own land in the search of a dream that was not to be. His genius was employed now in bettering Kota's prospects.

It had been Zalim's tyranny alone that had produced unploughed fields, runaway farmers and deserted villages. Food was scarce and government coffers lay empty, as the land yielded no revenue. Zalim decided to revolutionise the methods of farming. Forests were cut down and barren lands treated and prepared for planting. Twin ploughs, that had proved so successful in the Deccan, were imported and the face of Kota soon changed. Corn, lush and green, spilled over from the confines of the fields. It soon became difficult to find a path open for walking or riding. But the evil days were not over. Zalim taxed the farmers heavily, aptly naming the revenue earned lutho or loot. The success of the scheme led to the imposition of a tax on the buyer. In the midst of plenty, the people of

---

24. Ambaji Ingle – the Scindia subedar of Hindustan and the older brother of Bala Rao – died three years later, leaving his wealth, it is said, to Zalim Singh.

Kota starved. The once independent farmer with a sacred right to his land had turned into a serf. The arrival of the British and the subsequent alliances meant that Zalim had to put up a show of nurturing the downtrodden. The name lutho was changed to sawai hasil or the recovery of dues and his coffers continued to rake in money while Zalim dreamt up newer and more preposterous methods of levying taxes. Among the several absurd ones imposed, one was applied to widows who remarried and another to brooms meant for sale.

The community of the bards had had no patron since the day Zalim came to power. Their attempt at documenting the history of Kota in verse did not go down well, for it drew attention to the villainy of the period. Their lands had been confiscated and the community banished from the presence.

· Held in awe by all Rajasthan, there was not a court, nor a mercenary band that did not seek Zalim's counsel or refer to him by some term of endearment such as adoptive father, uncle or brother.

It was then in 1804, that the ill-fated army of Lieutenant Colonel Monson arrived to put down the Holkars. Zalim, with his implicit faith in the British, offered to replenish their stores and have his men escort them. But the brilliant and erratic Jaswant Rao Holkar had been underestimated. The British troops were put to flight while the Hada escort stood their ground interposing themselves in the path of the Maratha myrmidons for a cause that little concerned them. In the valley of the Amjhar, Amar Singh, the Hada chief of Koela, and his men laid down their lives while the disgraced and defeated army fled through the Mukandara Pass.

But when the panic stricken, beef eating army sought protection within Kota's walls, Zalim refused. He offered instead to escort the army till the border.

'You shall not bring anarchy and a disorganized army to mix with my peaceable citizens. I will provide you food and stores, and march alongside keeping my army between you and the enemy.'

The regent's refusal to grant them sanctuary was translated into treachery. Monson made his escape through Bundi and Jaipur and, at the enquiry conducted by Lord Lake, denounced Zalim as the cause of his misfortunes.

Because of the Hadas of Kota, the British had succeeded in escaping certain death. Jaswant Rao Holkar was livid at having lost them from within his grasp. It was at Kota that his ire was directed.

Kota's army commander, who had fallen into the Maratha hands, succeeded in securing his release by promising to furnish a bond of ten lakhs of rupees. But when he appeared at court, the regent squarely refused. The unfortunate commander committed suicide and Holkar threatened vengeance. War looked imminent. Friends of both parties intervened requesting a peaceful parley and Zalim Singh agreed provided the meeting was held on his terms.

Two boats were made ready. Rich carpets were spread and each carried twenty armed men. The negotiations were to be held in the middle of the Chambal and the guns of Kota were trained upon the site. Both Holkar and Zalim rowed to the centre of the river. The words 'uncle' and 'nephew' were bandied about in a display of affection. Amongst all the false mirth and gaiety, these two extraordinary men, who shared but one eye between them, settled for peace. At eighty-two, Zalim was nearly blind and Jaswant Rao had but one good eye left. Jaswant Rao[25] was desperate for money and agreed to settle for three lakhs though he never relinquished the threat of exacting the remaining seven from Kaka Zalim.

The treaty of 1817 was signed with the East India Company at Delhi. In March 1818, two supplemental articles were added to the treaty. These guaranteed the administration of Kota to the regent and his successors forever and were to soon place the British government in an acutely embarrassing position.

Maharao Raja Umed Sing died in November 1819, leaving behind three sons, Kishore, Bhishen and Pirthi. Kishore and Bhishen were of a placid nature, devoted to the regent and happy to leave matters to nana sahib or maternal grandfather as they affectionately called him. Pirthi the youngest was a bold Hada not happy with the bondage his father had

---

25. In November 1804, Jaswant Rao Holkar was defeated by Lord Lake and in 1818, the Holkar kingdom became a part of British India.

placed upon the family. Zalim Singh had two sons, who interested themselves in state affairs, the arrogant elder Madhu and the intelligent younger Govardhan, born of Zalim's Muslim wife – Manni Bai. Govardhan, Kishore and Pirthi enjoyed a close friendship. Madhu Singh, who had inherited the post of foujdar at a young age and was earmarked as the future regent, detested his half-brother, a feeling that was warmly reciprocated.

Maharao Raja Kishore Singh

The British agent rushed to Kota for the accession ceremony of Kishore Singh. Zalim Singh, he found, was encamped a mile away from the capital while Madhu Singh had gone on ahead to the palace. Closeted by Govardhan and Pirthi Singh, the new maharao was being tutored by the two who were desperate to break away.

It was now that the supplemental articles proved to be a stumbling block. The British government had sworn to uphold the office of the regent and Madhu Singh's right to succeed. Kishore Singh would have to remain a puppet in the hands of Madhu Singh just as his father had been under Zalim, all because the British needed to save face.

Several emotional scenes, choreographed by the British agent, were played out with Zalim Singh condemning himself bitterly and pretending to regret the difficulties he had placed his prince in. The princes in turn begged forgiveness and touched his feet. Govardhan was declared a state criminal and imprisoned. The nobles of Kota were restored to their lands. The scenes were repeated over and over again with the maharao desperate to break free and yet changing his mind every now and then. Never was there a more obsequious regent who could so completely manipulate his sovereign.

Raj Rana Zalim Singh died five years later. Though his body had worn out, his mind had not dimmed one bit.

14 August 1821: Camp was set up at Raontha and preparations were made for an extensive tour of the regions around Kota.

In their saddles before the break of dawn, they proceeded to make their way through the famous pass of Mukandara, turning abruptly to the right skirting the range that divided Hadavati from Malwa and westwards across the plains to the edge of the thickly forested plateau. As they mounted the summit the sun rose over the horizon.

Though little light penetrated through the dark foliage that stretched as far as eye could see, the sunbeams succeeded in picking out the castle of Bhainsrorgarh and a white speck, in the distance, that was the newly constructed fort of Dhangermow. Small pillars or un-inscribed tablets lay along the path marking the route used by Banjara carriers. It ran past the little monastery of Jhalaca. Here around a fire, squatted a group of ascetics. Their matted hair and beard had never known a comb. Ashes smeared their bodies, and the only evidence of human feelings lay in the loincloths they wore. Their days were spent in the adoration of Chaturbhuj – the four-armed Vishnu – and they lived off alms and the produce from a patch of land granted to them by the chief of Bhainsror. The chief ascetic, a wild looking being of about sixty, beckoned to the captain who bowed his head in quiet acquiescence as the yogi marked his forehead with sacred ash.

The captain continued on his way, following a quiet little stream that led through the woods, his new guru accompanying him. This vivacious little man turned out to be a walking mine of folklore but could only recite his tale provided he was allowed to start at the very beginning – from the moment of creation. Interruption was impossible for he would not tell the tale in any other manner save his own. His listener was obliged to mourn with Sita, bewail her abduction and go through every war waged by Lord Ram for her recovery. As to his stories, even ones as absurd as the tale of the great Sisodia ancestor who drank a measure of molten lead and lived to sire a dynasty, he believed in them as firmly as he did in his own existence.

Quite suddenly the temple complex of Baroli burst into view. The transition was amazing. From under the shadows of majestic trees that had never known an axe, steps led the way up. The temples lay enclosed in about 250 square yards of space. Writes the captain:

> To describe its stupendous and diversified architecture is impossible; it is the office of the pencil alone but the labour would be almost endless. Art seems here to have exhausted itself, and we were, perhaps now for the first time, fully impressed with the beauty of 'Hindu' sculpture.

Every individual stone within the columns and the roofing had been carved into a miniature temple. The close-grained quartz rock that had been used, though difficult to carve, was extremely durable. To protect it from the notice of vandals, it had been covered with a thick plaster of lime. Where it had peeled, the carvings appeared as smooth and sharp as the day the sculptor's fingers had imparted their last loving touch. The principal deity, Shiva, stood upon a lotus with serpents entwined about his neck, a little drum in his right hand and a skull cup in the left. To his left stood his consort, Parvati, on the back of a tortoise. The easily flowing lines of her form were peculiar to ancient 'Hindu' art. Amongst the profusion of figures, both human and animal, were flowers that filled the decorative panels and a horned lion like mythical creature that played a conspicuous role.

To the left of the temple, stood an image of the mother goddess, some thirty feet tall. Of her eight arms, all but one had fallen victim to the bigoted vandals. To the right was the shrine of Trimurti – Brahma, Vishnu and Shiva. Of the trinity, Shiva had alone been spared. The main temple itself stood fifty-eight feet high, its walls richly decorated with mythological sculpture both on the inside and outside. Within every niche stood Shiva, exhibiting his many moods from the gentle to the terrible. Here was the first representation of 'Time,' as a female personification of death, sickle in hand, bearing an uncanny resemblance to the Grim Reaper. The sanctum contained a Shivling, which was nothing but a rori or a pebble that fitted perfectly within its niche – the yoni. The slightest movement set it into motion and it would continue its revolutions until the prayers of the devotee were completed. Shiva was known locally as Rori Baroli. Yet another superb edifice, known as the nuptial hall of Raja Hun, stood twenty yards away from the temple. Outside stood smaller shrines and a fountain dedicated to the destroyer, Shiva.

Gangabheva or the circle of Ganga was other famous retreat that lay close by. The temple complex was similar to but in not so finished a style as Baroli. Though its age could not be determined an inscription bearing the date AD 955, was discovered. While Baroli marked the highest point of excellence, in Gangabheva the decline was evident. Some specimens were collected for the museum of the Royal Asiatic Society.

The village of Naoli was the next destination. Two miles to its east lay the fountain of the snake king, Takshak. It involved a climb down a precipice of nearly 200 feet and upon a little platform that perched midway upon the face of the cliff, stood two shrines, one to Takshak and the other to Dhanvantari, the physician. Takshak's fountain was 200 yards in circumference and a deep green in colour. It was watered by a stream that dropped a 100 feet in perpendicular fall while its outflow formed the Takhaili, or the serpentine, that flowed down the plateau past the eastern face of Hinglazgarh to join the Amjhar. The summit of the precipice commanded a full view of the castle of Hinglaz.

To the south by the edge of the plateau lay Bhanpura. Once a territory of Mewar, it was held at the time by the Holkar Marathas and was under the secure and peaceful rule of their diwan, Tantia Jogh. Here upon the banks of the rivulet Rewa, stood the mausoleum of the Maratha leader, Jaswant Rao Holkar, the man who had evicted Lieutenant Colonel Monson from his territory and dictated terms to Lord Lake. Prayers for his soul were chanted all day long at the altar where a life-size statue of the great leader presided. A painting depicted the Maratha astride his favourite horse, Mowah. Jaswant's steed and elephant were both pensioners here and a visit was paid to Mowah's stall. The noble animal seemed to possess all his master's aversion to the firangi for at the captain's appearance he flattened his ears and backed away. The fine chestnut coloured steed was of the famous Maharashtrian Bheemrathali breed with small pointed ears, bright intelligent eyes and a mouth so narrow that he could have drunk out of a teacup. At last, he permitted the captain to stroke him and an urzee was placed for sweeter and fresher bedding.

A thirteen-mile trek through the plains of Malwa took them to Garot.

It was delightful to walk freely without the constant reminder at every step – 'Sahib thokur'. The black loam of the plain was strewn with agate and cornelian in various shapes and tints: some veined, others plain and transparent or opaque. Since no obvious reason could be found for their presence, it was surmised that the Chambal had probably, at some time, broken its banks and inundated the land. Making their way through a dhak jungle, they arrived at the hill, which had been that morning's objective. Tents were pitched on the banks of a reservoir but curiosity would not permit a leisurely breakfast. The hill was two to three miles in circumference and about 140 feet high. The top was flat and the northern approach gentle. The southern side resembled a horseshoe and the entire crest was pierced by the caves of Dhamnar. The 170 that were counted appeared to be entrances to temples, Jain and Buddhist on one side, Shaivite and Vaishnavite on the other.

It was from Garot that the British army, led by Lieutenant Colonel Monson, had retreated. The event was as remarkable in the history of Britain as Xenophon's[26] had been in Greece. Defeated at the hands of Jaswant Rao Holkar, the humiliated army had been covered, by the forces of Kota and the irregular cavalry division led by Captain Lucan[27], until they were within the safety of the Mukandara Pass. The Hada chief of Koela, with 450 men, stood his ground fighting to the last – as did the unfortunate Lucan. It was with some sadness that the captain noted the humble tablet of clay that marked the spot where the Amar Singh Hada fell. The site would have surely been marked with a more durable monument had the regent of Kota also been a Hada.

---

26. In BC 401, Artaxerxes II and his younger brother Cyrus struggled over the throne of Persia. Cyrus recruited Greek mercenaries but while in Babylonia, at the point of victory, he was killed. The Greeks were left in the desert with no one to lead them. Xenophon was elected and he led his ten thousand countrymen through a difficult journey back home. The retreat was immortalised in *Anabasis* written by Xenophon.

27. Lucan, an English adventurer, in Scindia' service had turned traitor at the storm of Aligarh on 4 September 1803. He blew up the gate to the fort and led the British army under Lieutenant Colonel Monson in. For this he had received a captaincy in the Company's army. Lucan's fate remains unknown. Perhaps he died at the site of battle or was executed by Jaswant Rao.

Remnants of the kingdoms of Rajputana within modern Rajasthan.
Districts of Rajasthan that were once included in the kingdom of Dhundhar.

CHAPTER **5** _____

DHUNDHAR AMBER & JAIPUR

Tucked into the eastern corner of Rajasthan, a stone's throw from Delhi, lie the two capital cities of the Kachwaha Rajputs – Amber and Jaipur. The name of the Kachwaha state has long been forgotten for Dhundhar was not easy upon the European tongue. Many years before this stronghold of the aboriginal Meenas had been occupied by Rajputs, it had been made famous by the great Rajput king of Ajmer, Vishal Dev Chauhan[1].

Perhaps the land drew its name from the sacred hill made famous by Vishal Dev Chauhan's penance or from the river Dhundh that flows through it but it has always been referred to by the name of its capital city. Amber (pronounced Amer) gave way to Jaipur, which today enjoys the status of being the capital city of Rajasthan.

Its location on the leeward side of the Aravalli has spared Jaipur

_____
1.   The *Annals and Antiquities of Rajasthan* claims that Vishal Dev's name was to be found on one of the many pillars left behind by the great Emperor Ashok. Ashok ruled in the third century BC and had these great pillars placed to mark the limits of his empire. It was thought that the Rajputs, who came into being in AD 500, recognised the importance of these ancient pillars and used them to document their presence. Feroze Shah Tughlak (AD 1351 – 1388), the Turkish sultan of Delhi, had had this particular pillar brought in to beautify the city that he was building in Delhi. Ashok's message, however, was not deciphered until 1837, when James Prinsep decoded the Brahmi script. But that was five years after Lt Col James Tod had completed his book. Vishal Dev Chauhan's name did not find a mention.

Vishal Dev Chauhan had turned into a monster and had taken to preying upon his own subjects. The gods were angered and his countenance changed until he resembled a rakshas. His family shrank from him in fright but the work of evil continued. A human was killed and eaten everyday and yet his appetite remained unappeased. One day his little grandson offered himself.

Even the rakshas was horrified. An innocent child had come forward to satiate his grandfather's terrible hunger. Vishal Dev cast his wings and took to the skies. He scoured the land until he sighted a dhund – a sacrificial mound. It lay on the border of Ajmer and there he sat and meditated until the gods forgave him.

The wild land that lay beyond the dhundh came to be known as Dhundhar.

from being ravaged by the Thar. The wind, however, does manage to sneak clouds of sand, through the passes and crevices of the mountain range, depositing it in great piles along the fertile plains of the Banas as it flows through Tonk. The Jat regions of Shekhawati, dominated by the Kachwahas and the Rathores of Bikaner, lying just beyond the northern tip of the Aravalli mark the beginning of the desert.

Duleh Rai

It was either the Suryavanshi prince, Kush – the son of Lord Ram, king of Ayodhya (Uttar Pradesh) – or one of his descendents who built the famous castle of Rohtas[2]. A few generations later, Raja Nal[3] left Rohtas and founded the kingdom of Narwar or Nishida (now in Madhya Pradesh). His descendents adopted the title Pal and Narwar became the primary Kachwaha kingdom from where a branch spread to set up another at Amber.

When Sora Singh, the thirty-third king of Narwar died, his brother usurped the throne. Fear gripped the widowed queen and disguising herself as a poor peasant woman, she placed her little son, Duleh Rai, in a basket and set off towards the setting sun. She did not stop until she reached the village of Khogong[4]. Here she laid down her precious burden and rested. As she hunted about for wild berries, the exhausted woman kept an anxious watch over the basket. To her horror, a cobra slithered up and reared its hood over her child. Her screams brought a passing Brahmin running to help.

.'Rejoice,' he said. 'Your son is marked for greatness.'

---

2. Lieutenant Colonel Tod neglects to mention the whereabouts of the castle of Rohtas. Two exist today, one near Sasaram in Bihar and the other in Pakistan. The latter has been declared a world heritage site. Both forts had been occupied and modified by the Aghan emperor, Sher Shah and the dynasties that succeeded him. Rohtas in Bihar was to become the official residence of the greatest of all the Kachwaha kings, Raja Maan Singh, who was posted as the Mughal governor of Bengal.
3. Raja Nal and his queen, Damayanti, find a mention in the *Mahabharat*, which is dated traditionally to 1000 BC. Nal therefore is a mythical ancestor adopted by the Kachwahas.
4. Khogong lay five miles from the area that would in time become modern-day Jaipur.

Among the romantic ballads of Rajasthan is the song of Dhola and Maru, which is said to have been composed around AD 1000.

Dhola, the son of Raja Nal and Rani Damayanti, was still an infant in Narwar when he was married to Maru of Pugal – the northern fortress of the desert that lies within the realm of Jaisalmer. The children grew up unaware of the marriage that their parents had contracted for them. Dhola, who was by then married to Maroni (sometimes referred to as Malwani – princess of Malwa or Rewa), heard the tale from a wandering bard and determined to claim his bride. Maroni did her utmost to keep the lovers apart, as did Oomra and Soomra, two dacoits of the desert, who had lost their hearts to Maru. The tale abounds with flying camels, magicians, evil curses, tragic deaths and fairytale resurrections. Some versions end in tragedy with the deaths of the lovers and others in joyful reunion.

The song of Dhola Maru is a popular theme in gypsy lore.

The young queen made her way to the palace of the Meena raja. She begged for employment and was hired as a cook. When the raja sat down to eat, he knew at once that the new cook was no ordinary person. The queen of Narwar was adopted as sister and her son grew up as the nephew of the Meena.

Duleh Rai was fourteen, when he was sent as the Meena raja's representative to the court in Delhi. During his five years away from home, a plot was hatched with the aid of a Meena bard. When he returned, the Meenas rejoiced and gathered to celebrate Diwali with their prince. Scores of lamps were lit and as they busied themselves with the festivities the Kachwaha seized his moment. The Meenas, who had put a roof over his head, were slaughtered. The bard was put to death, by Duleh Rai's own hands, for he who had proven unfaithful to one master could never be trusted by another.

Duleh, who ruled from AD 1096 – 1136, married the only daughter of the Bargujjar chief of Dausa. With the army of Dausa he attacked and captured Manch, from its Meena ruler and re-named it Ramgarh. He then married Maroni, a princess of Ajmer, and their son was named Kankal.

Duleh died trying to subjugate the Meenas of the land.

Kankal

Kankal subjugated most of Dhundhar and his son Maidal conquered Amber from Rao Bhatto Meena, usurping the designation of rao for himself. Rao Maidal's son, Hunadev, was succeeded by Kantal whose son, Pujandeva, became a favourite with the bards. His name has been immortalised by Chand in the historical poem on the life of Prithviraj Chauhan.

Rao Pujandeva

Pujan was an important raja who had married Prithviraj Chauhan's sister and commanded a division of the Chauhan army. Posted at the frontier,

The land until this time had belonged to an ancient stock of people, the Meenas of Dhundhar. This original, pure race ruled the land, from Kali Kho, their home in the mountains. The rule of the five grand tribes or Panchwara extended all the way from Ajmer to the banks of the Yamuna. In the mountain pass, they had raised a temple to the mother goddess, Amba Mata or Ghatte ki Rani, the queen of the pass. She lent her name to the city of the Meenas – Amber.

within the Khyber Pass, Pujan had faced and repelled several attacks led by Sultan Mohammad Ghuri of Ghazni. He had overthrown the Chandels of Madhya Pradesh, becoming governor of their land and had been by his sovereign's side at the epic abduction of Sanyukta of Kannauj, losing his life covering the lovers' retreat.

The sons of Pujan ruled from their capital at Amber and amongst the famous names are those of Udaykaran, the thirteenth king since Duleh Rai and of Prithviraj the eighteenth.

Rao Udaykaran's son, Baloji, left to seek his fortune and obtained for himself a small town called Amritsar. His grandson, Shekhji, fathered a large successful clan, the Shekhawats, and Shekhawati (today the modern districts of Jhunjhunu, Sikar and Churu) became one of the great vassals of Amber.

Rao Prithviraj Singh divided his growing kingdom amongst his twelve sons, creating the bara kotri or the twelve houses of Amber. His sons formed the nobility of Amber. Amongst his queens was the sister of Maharana Sanga but his favourite was the daughter of Rao Lunkaran of Bikaner. Like Mira in Chittaurgarh, Apurva (Bala Bai) introduced the worship of Krishna to the Amber court. The year 1527 saw the Rajputs massed against the Mughals who had occupied Delhi and Agra. Prithviraj, who was amongst those that carried the wounded Sanga off the battlefield of Khanua, died later that year possibly having submitted to the Mughal for it has been suggested that Bala Bai's son, who was second-in-line, succeeded to the throne with Humayun's help. A series of murders were to follow with Prithviraj's sons clamouring for the throne. Puran Mal was said to have been assassinated by his elder brother Bheem, though the annals of Shekhawati, record that he laid down his life helping a scion of the Shekhawati family realise his claims. In 1544, Emperor Sher Shah approached Amber. Rao Maldeo's Marwar had fallen and from his belt jangled the keys of Maharana Uday Singh's Chittaurgarh. Ratan Singh, who was enjoying his turn on the throne, was quick to surrender and pay tribute. Sher Shah died the following year and all Rajputs succeeded in throwing off the imperial shackles. Ratan Singh was poisoned by his half-brother but the chiefs would not have him. And throne passed to Bharmal – a seasoned and mature politician of fifty.

Raja Bharmal

Rao Bharmal was a younger son of Rao Prithviraj and his accession meant that his nephew Suja Mal, the son of the late Rao Puran Mal, was no longer in direct line to the throne. Power hungry relatives who had to be appeased kept the new rao busy while Delhi slipped through several greasy palms: Humayun; Sher Shah; Sher Shah's son, Islam Shah; and Islam Shah's brother-in-law, Mohammad Adil Shah – who left his affairs in the hands of Hemu a shrewd 'Hindu' trader. Humayun regained the throne in 1555, but died a few months later leaving his empire to his thirteen-year-old son. Bharmal, who had submitted earlier to Humayun, presented himself to Akbar.

There was no doubting the power of the Mughal. Ajmer and Nagaur were soon wrested from Sher Shah's erstwhile slave and general – Haji Khan – and placed under Mirza Sharaf-ud-din Husain Ahrari who had married the emperor's sister – Shahzadi Bakshi Banu Begum. Supporting the cause of Suja Mal, Sharaf-ud-din attacked Amber in 1558. Bharmal sued for peace. Money changed hands; a son and two nephews were taken hostage. But Bharmal remained nervous. The way out was a matrimonial alliance. The wedding was celebrated in 1562 and fealty was sworn.

Heera (Harka, Maanmati or Jiyarani) Bai, the diamond princess of Amber, said to be Bharmal's eldest daughter born to Solankini Rani Chandravati, took her place as the first of the Rajputnis in the Mughal harem. She paved the way for Akbar's religious tolerance and was referred to as Mariam-us-Zamani (Mary of the age), by the Mughal historian Abu-l Fazl. Her son, Salim, was to succeed as Emperor Jahangir.

Bharmal accepted an office at the court of the twenty-year-old Akbar who upgraded his title to raja of Amber. Bhagwan Das – the heir of Amber, followed his father's example as did his brilliant son[5] (some say nephew) – Kanwar Maan Singh. They helped Akbar consolidate his empire. In return the loot from the conquered lands enriched their coffers. Not for them the sakas of Chittaur, the persecution by imperial forces nor the vain upholding of their women's

---

5. Maan Singh is said to be the son of Raja Bhagwan Das's Parmar queen, Bhagwati.

honour. Maan Singh's sister, Maan Bai[6], was given in marriage to young Salim and her father-in-law lent a shoulder to the doli that bore her to her new home. Like her aunt before her, Maan Bai gave to her husband his first son – Khusro.

The native people of the land, the Meenas, still held a large share of power and Raja Bharmal used Mughal backing to destroy the ancient Meena city of Naen (later called Lohan or Lowan). The Meena stronghold is remembered today only in rhyme:

Bavan Kothi Chappan Darwaza	Fifty-two fortresses and fifty-six gates
Meena Mard Naen ka Raja	The manly Meena is the king of Naen
Booro Raj Naen ko	The old king now
Jub bhoos mein bhutto mango.	Will now ask for even a share of chaff.

Raja Bhagwan Das

Bhagwan Das came to the throne and his personal ties with the emperor grew stronger. Next in line was Kanwar Maan Singh, who had already proved himself a skilled general. The princes of Amber served as successful negotiators between the Rajputs and the Mughals. Keeping the interests of their new masters in mind they had managed the surrender of Ranthambhor without bloodshed. Under their influence, Bundi quietly accepted terms of service. Amber was well on its way to glory and success.

All Rajasthan had submitted to the will of the Mughal except for Mewar. Stripped of their forts and cities, the Mewaris continued to defy the imperial army. The heir of Amber decided to have a go at the indomitable Pratap, a maharana whose court now gathered in the wilderness of woods and hills or at the only fort left with them: Kumbhalgarh. With little to claim except for his fiercely independent soul and the fidelity of his band of braves, Pratap renounced alliances with Rajput royal families that chose to associate with the Mughals. The house of Mewar that had never given a daughter in marriage to the Mughals refused to grant the hand of a Sisodia maiden to a fellow Rajput who had betrayed 'Hindu' sentiment.

---

6. Sadly, despite having given Salim his first son, Maan Bai failed to win her husband's heart. Salim who was known for his roving eye submitted ultimately to a Persian commoner – Noor Jahan, the widow of a nobleman. In her last years, Maan Bai lost her mind and the deranged Kachwaha rani committed suicide.

As a Mughal general, it was Maan Singh who had subjugated the land from distant Afghanistan to the Arakan coast of Burma. The Kachwaha bard delights in recounting his exploits from the snow capped mountains of the Caucasus to the shores of the golden Chersonese.

A delightful tale recounts the conquest of the Attock. Maan Singh was commanded to march to the troubled areas beyond the Indus and put down the rebellion in Kabul. The great commander hesitated for to the medieval 'Hindu' the river Indus was the limit. The point at which the river was traditionally crossed had been labelled by the 'Hindus' as the uttuk (Attock) or barrier.

But Akbar possessed the master key to 'Hindu' feeling. Accomplished in poetry and languages, the emperor sent Maan Singh a couplet in Rajasthani.

Sub hain bhum Gopal ka	The whole earth belongs to God
Jis me uttuk kahan?	Where is the barrier in it?
Jis ke man me uttuk hai	He whose mind has a barrier
So een uttuk hoega.	Will always find itself bound.'

Delicate sarcasm succeeded where stronger language may not have prevailed.

On his way back from a campaign in Gujarat, Maan Singh sought an interview with Pratap. The great general had been charged with securing a treaty, for the emperor's first emissary had proven himself unequal to the task. But Pratap flatly refused. Mewar, he would never permit to become a part of the empire and an office under Akbar was clearly out of the question. Pratap would come around, but it seemed that he needed time. Maan Singh chose to amuse himself in the meanwhile. Quite carelessly he took a swipe at the small state of Dungarpur that lay on Mewar's southern border. Rawal Askaran, a supporter of Pratap, lost two sons. Understandably Pratap was in no mood to negotiate. Kanwar Maan Singh made a tactical retreat and requested a third meeting. All was going well and Maan Singh arrived at Udaipur where a great feast, on the banks of the Uday Sagar, had been organised in his honour. But at the appointed hour the maharana failed to appear. In his place stood, his son and heir – seventeen-year-old Amar Singh. The heir of Mewar pleaded a headache on his father's behalf and waited upon the heir of Amber. It was clearly apparent that Pratap thought it beneath his dignity to eat with one who had given his sister in marriage to the Mughals and had broken bread with them. The Kachwaha got up seething with humiliation.

'If I do not humble your pride, my name is not Maan.'

Maharana Pratap arrived in time to witness this last moment. Mewar, he assured him, would rise to the challenge.

Spies brought back the detailed story of Kanwar Maan Singh's humiliation. The grounds on which he sat had been dug up and sprinkled with water from the Ganga. The chiefs of Mewar who had met with him had all bathed and performed ritual cleansing. Both Raja Bhagwan Das and Raja Todarmal intervened in person but Pratap's contention remained the same. The result was the battle of Haldighati in 1576. Though it ended in victory for the Mughals[7], it succeeded in immortalising the name of Pratap.

7. Some historians insist that Maan Singh prevented the victorious Mughal army from pursuing the wounded Pratap incurring Akbar's displeasure. But the farzand managed to charm his way back into the emperor's heart.

The mother goddess, in her many forms, had always enjoyed the unwavering devotion of the Rajputs. Maan Singh was personally a devotee of the ebony skinned Kali, a form worshipped almost exclusively in Bengal. He had been initiated into her rites at Varanasi by a Bengali guru. In 1612, he was ordered to the land of the goddess to put down the rebellion of the zamindars. Raja Pratapaditya had murdered his uncle and declared himself independent in Jessore. Maan Singh heard the voice of Kali call out to him. Some say she lay buried, hidden away from Muslim eyes, on the banks of the Ganga and that on that fatal day of the battle Pratapaditya had failed to complete his devotions to the Lady of Jessore. The anguished goddess commanded Maan Singh to take her away. Others claim that she appealed to Maan Singh to release her from a slab of stone thus earning herself the name Shila Devi or the goddess carved from stone. The victorious general returned with the dark skinned deity and built for her a temple in his new palace at Amber. Kali was accompanied by her priest and his descendants have continued to serve her everafter.

Maan Singh is credited with the installation of Sanga Baba in Sanganer, Hanuman in Jaipur, Shila Devi at Amber and Govind Dev in Vrindavan.

When Emperor Aurungzeb came to the throne it was feared that the temple of Govind Dev at Vrindavan was at risk and the statues of Radha and Krishna were smuggled out and kept hidden until 1714, when they were installed in a new temple within the palace complex in Maharaja Sawai Jai Singh's city of Jaipur. Many years later in 1902, the statue of Krishna would make yet another journey this time crossing the oceans in the company of Maharaja Sawai Madho Singh II as they left to attend the coronation of Emperor Edward VII.

It is an interesting observation that both Kanwar Maan Singh and Maharana Pratap shared their dates of birth – 9 May 1540[8], a fact that perhaps contributed to the vicious and almost sibling like rivalry between the two.

In 1578, father and son were posted to Punjab. Maan Singh repaired the fort of Sialkot (now in Pakistan), maintained order in the disturbed regions and kept Akbar's troublesome half-brother, Mirza Hakim – the governor of Kabul – in check. Joining forces with Rai Singh and Prithviraj of Bikaner, Maan Singh entered and occupied Kabul in 1581. The repentant Mirza was reinstated but with his death, the region was preyed upon by the Usbegs. Maan Singh crossed the Indus and obtained the surrender of Peshawar. By 1587, order had been firmly established and the emperor ordered him to Bihar.

For his services as subedar of Kabul, Maan Singh received permission to fly the pennants taken from defeated Afghans. The colours were used to design the Dhundhari Panchranga – a flag of five colours.

Mirza Raja Maan Singh

Maan Singh succeeded to the throne of Amber in 1589, a trusted and much favoured general of the great Mughal. Farzand (son) was a title that had been bestowed upon him on the eve of Haldighati. With his successes Amber prospered and the construction of a palace cum fort was begun in 1600. The close bonding with the Mughals was reflected in its architecture.

In 1594, he was appointed governor of Bengal with the express task of subjugating the Baro Bhuiyans (the landed gentry or zamindars) and the Afghan chieftains who, incited by Isa Khan, had worked up a rebellion. Akbar had personally led the first Bengal campaign annexing it to the Mughal Empire in 1576. Daud Khan Karrani the young defiant Aghan chief of Bengal had been slain but now Isa Khan, one of Daud's vassals

---

8. 21 December 1550 is another date put forward as Maan Singh's date of birth, which would make him Pratap's junior by ten years.

Maan Singh however grew too powerful and both Akbar and Salim grew wary. The dominating Mughal father and his beloved but rebellious son were estranged and Maan Singh used the opportunity to champion the cause of Khusro, his own nephew, as against that of Khusro's father, Salim. Akbar, though partial to his grandson, did not wish to disturb the line of succession and struggled to bring his wayward son to his senses. Maan Singh proved to be an obstacle in the reconciliation process.

If the diaries of the princes of Bundi are to be believed, it was at this point that the emperor decided to get rid of him. An overt attempt would have spelt disaster for the might of the Kachwaha was feared by the Mughals. A sly strategy was formulated. The emperor went to his kitchen and personally prepared a plate of confectionary – one that was laced with opium and other intoxicants, to be shared with his great general. But the final arrangement of the sweets was mixed up resulting in Akbar poisoning himself by his own hand[9].

Till this day, the cause of Akbar's death remains shrouded in mystery but in his dying moments, though denied of speech, he named his son, by means of signs, successor. The mullahs came to the deathbed to reconvert the emperor to Islam. But they failed. The head of the Din-e-Ilahi faith died without the benefit of prayers.

Salim was enthroned as Emperor Jahangir, and Khusro's rebellion ended in imprisonment. Maan Singh was too wise to identify himself with the rebellion.

---

9. The strange circumstances that surrounded Akbar's death remain a debatable point among historians. This is Lt Col Tod's version and it seems to suggest that he had studied the diaries, though their existence is denied by modern historians. That Akbar attempted to murder Maan Singh may well be a creation of the bards, but the suspicion that the great Mughal had succumbed to poison has been corroborated by historians including Vincent A Smith and Dr Percival Spear. Historian Will Durant suggests complicity on the part of Jahangir who, it is said, had discarded his robes of mourning by the evening. That Emperor Akbar died of dysentery and diarrhoea, the recorded symptoms being consistent with the administration of a 'secret irritant poison', translates into arsenic poisoning. They go on to say that the emperor, the greatest since Ashok, was buried in a hurry and without the honours of a state funeral. His was a funeral poorly attended. Akbar's grave was desecrated by Jat vandals in 1691, and his bones were set afire disallowing any modern research into the death of the great Mughal.

had risen against the empire. Maan Singh arrived in Bengal with his sons Himmat and Durjan Singh, set up a new capital city at Rajmahal – one that he named Akbarabad – and in 1596, married Kshama Devi, the Bengali princess of Koch Bihar, who bore him two sons. But the first Bengal tenure that began on a promising note ended in disaster. Both Himmat and Durjan lost their lives and the Mughal army was reduced to tatters.

Maan Singh returned to Ajmer in 1598. His heir, Yuvraj Jagat Singh, died the following year leaving behind two sons, Maha Singh and Jujhar Singh, and a daughter. With Jagat's death, his sons were no longer in direct line to the throne. They would now have to play subordinate roles. Maha Singh who had married Rani Damayanti, the granddaughter of Maharana Uday Singh of Mewar, was appointed raja of Garh. Jujhar, as the thakur of Raisar, fathered amongst others the clans of Jhalai and Isarda. It would be their sons who would fill the Kachwaha throne incase natural succession was ever in question.

In 1601, Maan Singh accepted his second tenure in Bengal effectively putting down the resistance. He returned to Agra in February 1605. Seven months later the emperor was dead and his cousin Salim ascended the throne as Emperor Jahangir. But Maan Singh had championed the cause of Khusro[10], and the new emperor, reluctant to confront the great general, ordered him back to Bengal. Maan Singh made Rohtas his home. But the future of the late Yuvraj Jagat's Singh's daughter, Koka, still played upon his mind. In 1608, Maan Singh gave his grandchild's hand in marriage to Emperor Jahangir.

Mirza Raja Maan Singh spent the rest of his life in southern India and died a peaceful death on 6 July 1614 at Ellichpur (Achalpur, Maharashtra). Accompanying him on the pyre were sixty women – both queens and wives of common origin who had sworn to live and die with him.

---

10. Among the others that supported Khusro's cause were Abu-l Fazl – counted as the foremost amongst the nine gems, wazir and hysteriographer, the author of Akbar Nama and Ain-i Akbari – and Aziz Koka (Akbar's foster brother). Akbar's drunken sons – Danial and Murad – had predeceased him, leaving Salim as the only heir. In 1602, Salim arranged to have Abu-l Fazl murdered. Bir Singh Bundela, the raja of Orchha, brought the head which Salim cast into his privy. Aziz Koka managed to survive and accepted service under Jahangir.

Meenakari – the art of enamelling upon gold and silver, which reached its pinnacle of perfection in Rajasthan, is said to have begun in Maan Singh's time. A great patron of the arts, Maan Singh is said to have had five Sikh craftsmen brought from Lahore to practice their art in Amber. The art of meenakari also flourished at the same time under Maharaja Rai Singh in Bikaner. Mughal interest in this particular art form peaked with Emperor Shah Jahan's obsession with gems and jewellery and the art of enamelling reached newer levels of sophistication.

Persian carpet weavers had been brought in to train political prisoners in the jails of Amber, Bikaner, Agra and Gwalior by Emperor Akbar. The palace at Amber boasts of a magnificent collection dating from this period.

Mirza Raja Bhao Singh

Maan Singh was succeeded by his second son, Bhao Singh. Completely overshadowed by the brilliance of his father, the son of Maan Singh failed to make a mark at the imperial court, and the princes of Marwar moved ahead taking up all the important posts.

Bhao Singh passed away overcome by the drink leaving behind no successor. The son of his nephew, the late Raja Maha Singh of Garh, was chosen as the next ruler of Amber.

Mirza Raja Jai Singh

Within a year of his accession the eleven-year-old became embroiled in Mughal politics – Khurram's (later emperor Shah Jahan) rebellion. Both Jahangir and Khurram sent word to Jai Singh. Keeping the principal of 'gaddi ki aan' in mind Jai Singh marched under the command of Sultan Parvez and General Mahabat Khan. Khurram faced a reversal and took sanctuary with Maharana Karan Singh at Udaipur. In 1623, a battle fought close to Delhi resulted in the death of Raja Bikramjit – a Brahmin upon whom Khurram chiefly relied. The rebels were dealt a crushing blow and the retreating Khurram lashed out viciously at Amber before ransacking and looting his way through Bihar, Bengal and Orissa. The imperial troops, which included Raja Guj Singh of Marwar and Rao Ratan of Bundi, caught up with him at Hazipur and on 24 October 1624, a crushing defeat was inflicted. Khurram retreated southwards and sought refuge with Malik Ambar, the one-time diwan of Ahmadnagar. Jai Singh was deputed to march, alongside Khan Jahan Lodi (Peera) – the Afghan general – against Malik Ambar. But when Peera unfurled the standard of rebellion Jai Singh stole away. Nor did he respond to Noor Jahan's call. Instead on 14 January 1628, he presented himself at Ajmer. His fidelity had not escaped Khurram. Jai Singh found himself royal favour in the new reign that was beginning. Service in the Deccan and in Kabul and Kandahar won him distinctions and Emperor Shah Jahan bestowed upon him the title mirza raja.

When the throne of Amber was ready for occupation once again, one of Jahangir's 'Hindu' wives suggested that Jai Singh, the grandson of Maan Singh, be installed upon the gaddi. Jahangir girded the young Jai and commanded him to salute Jodha Bai[11], the princess of Bikaner, who had raised him to this status. It was against Rajput tradition for a king to salute a Rajputni and the newly anointed king refused.

'I will salute any lady of your majesty's family but not Jodha Bai.'

Jodha Bai laughed. 'It does not matter. I still give you Amber.'

---

11. The daughter of Raja Rai Singh of Bikaner has carelessly been referred to as Jodha Bai (the lady of Jodhpur) – a name that popular historians appear to use wantonly. Her real name is not known, nor has the authenticity of this tale been verified. According to the *Imperial Gazetteer* and Lt Col Tod, she was Jahangir's third wife and the mother of his second son, Parvez. Other sources claim that Jahangir's fifth wife – Sahib-i-Jamal Begum Sahiba, the daughter of Khwaja Hasan – was the mother of Parvez. Jai Singh's apparent immaturity over acknowledging his benefactress is probably no more than bardic fantasy, but keeping in mind the tender age, it can perhaps be expected. The second princess of Bikaner to grace Jahangir's zenana was Rup Manjari, the granddaughter of Raja Rai Singh. Though both these women would lay claim to descent from Rao Jodha of Jodhpur, it would have to be Jagat Gosain, daughter of Raja Uday Singh of Jodhpur; wife of Jahangir and mother to Khurram (later Shah Jahan), who could truly be called Jodha Bai.
Yet another version claims that it was Empress Noor Jahan who was possibly the benefactress. Jai Singh's mother – Sisodini Rani Damayanti – lived in constant fear for the welfare of her child was threatened by the presence of Mirza Raja Bhao Singh's son. Confining both herself and her son to the fort at Dausa she sent an appeal to the empress. Bhao Singh's son died during the lifetime of his father clearing the way for Jai Singh.

Mirza Raja Jai Singh regained the powerful office held by his great-grandfather at the Mughal court. He lived to serve three emperors, see his benefactor's son raise the Taj Mahal upon lands that had once been granted to Amber and the grandson gain the throne of Hindustan. Jai Singh was one of the few 'Hindu' princes who could keep Aurungzeb's excesses in check.

The war of succession between the sons of Shah Jahan dragged the Rajputs in. Jai Singh was deputed along with Suleiman Shikoh to put down Shuja who was then governor of Bengal. It was effectively carried out and both Prince Dara and Shah Jahan sent word that the repentant Shuja be permitted to retain his province. Tied up with the Bengal affairs, Jai Singh commanded his son – Ram Singh – to join forces with Dara but was personally unable to reach Samugarh in time. The news of the disaster arrived in the emperor's own hand. With it came Aurungzeb's summons. Hastening Suleiman Shikoh's departure, Jai Singh presented himself. Shrewdly he chose to join the victor, convincing Maharaja Jaswant Singh of Marwar, at the same time, to choose preservation over a foolhardy sense of honour. Having sworn fealty he pursued Dara and Suleiman Shikoh with single-minded dedication.

In 1664, the Sikhs of Delhi approached the mirza raja. Their eighth guru, eight-year-old Harkrishan's right to succeed was being questioned by his elder brother and the emperor had him summoned to Delhi. The devotees feared for his life. Jai Singh received the child guru and his mother at his private residence, a bungalow (bangla) in Jaisinghpur[12] in Delhi, and assured them of his protection. The bungalow was then converted into a Sikh temple: the Bangla Sahib Gurudwara.

The Deccan continued to be a hot bed of trouble. The tribute paying kingdom of Bijapur was disturbed by the activities of a nineteen-year-

---

12. Jaisinghpur (the Bangla Sahib Gurudwara area), Madhoganj (Connaught Place) and Bas Hanuman (Hanuman Mandir), in Delhi, were held by the rajas of Amber and Jaipur as jagirs granted by the Mughal emperor. The lands were sold to the British Government of India in 1925. Eight acres of land in New Delhi were granted in turn for the building of Jaipur House which today houses the National Gallery of Modern Art. Jaipur gifted the Jaipur Column, which bears the Star of India, as a symbol of loyalty to the British crown. It was placed in front of the viceroy's house (Rashtrapati Bhavan), which was built upon land acquired from Jodhpur.

old Maratha adventurer. Shivaji Raje Bhonsle, who traced his descent from the Sisodias of Mewar, made his first mark by capturing the fort of Torna close to Pune. Not a rock nor an inch of ground was unknown to the rough and ready band of braves and soon forts, one after another, began to fall. Nor was treachery unknown to them. The raja of Jaoli, who refused to join the rebellion, was murdered and General Afzal Khan, whose skill in the craft of war was something the young Maratha did not wish to experience, disembowelled during a friendly meeting with a set of tiger claws. Aurungzeb sent his heir, Prince Muazzam, to the Deccan. With him went the mirza raja. Skilful diplomacy and the quick capture of the important fort of Purandhar brought Shivaji to his knees. Shivaji's services were used against the kingdom of Bijapur and Aurungzeb, paying heed to Jai Singh's advice, invited him to Agra.

Assuring the Maratha of the emperor's goodwill, Jai Singh had him sent to court. But it is said that the Maratha would not abide by the etiquettes of the imperial court and resented being treated as a commander of 5,000 instead of a sovereign prince. He refused to stand with Maharaja Jaswant Singh of Marwar, whose retreating backside he had often viewed in battle. He reportedly struck a senior court official and sat down in the imperial presence. Other accounts suggest that he was slighted. The result of the court visit was that he was placed under surveillance. But the mirza raja was not about to have his word broken. With the help of his heir, Ram Singh, he succeeded in spiriting the Maratha away in a dramatic escape on 18 August 1665. Though Ram Singh's involvement could never be proved conclusively, Aurungzeb had him demoted. Jai Singh's intentions became suspect. Adding to the list of grievances against him was his inability, despite the several attempts, to annexe the kingdom of Bijapur. The imperial treasury was forbidden to reimburse war expenses made from Jai Singh's personal account. On the verge of bankruptcy and devasted at the treatment meted out after a lifetime spent in imperial service, Jai Singh ended his days, not in the comfort of home, but on the battlefields of the Deccan.

Umdat-ul-Umara, Mirza Raja Shri Jai Singhji Bahadur, Raja of Amber fell from an elephant and died at Burhanpur (now in Madhya Pradesh) on 22 July 1667.

The mirza raja served both Jahangir and Shah Jahan and his fidelity was never in doubt. But when Aurungzeb came to the throne, Jai Singh was disillusioned. He served in the Deccan and at Aurungzeb's command, captured Shivaji. The young Maratha raja of Satara, who had envisioned a nation free from Mughal domination, was delivered into the hands of the emperor. In 'Hindu' hearts Shivaji Raje Bhosle held a special place and when realisation dawned that the honeyed words of the emperor were false and the life of the Maratha was at stake, Jai Singh personally helped him escape.

Word reached the emperor's ear: Jai Singh was to be often found playing with two cups of wine. 'This is Satara and this Delhi,' he would laugh and dash one or the other to the floor. Aurungzeb sent feelers to Kirat Singh[13] – the mirza raja's younger son, who had been named raja of Kama.

If Kirat had hoped to succeed his father, one would never know but he died in 1673, having given his daughter, Baijas Kaur, in marriage to Emperor Aurungzeb's son, Prince Muhammad Azam.

---

13. Kirat Singh has been accused by Lt Col Tod of murdering his father. Vincent Smith's *The Oxford History of India* has drawn upon the same tale and adds that Aurungzeb had rejoiced publicly and celebrated the occasion by ordering the demolition of a large temple at Mathura. That Jai Singh had been murdered, however, appears to be untrue.

Mirza Raja Ram Singh

Mirza Raja Ram Singh succeeded to the throne of Amber and held a command of 4,000 imperial troops. Soon after his accession he was commanded to Kamrup (Assam), the land of the fearsome Ahoms.

The dense steaming jungles, the heavy rainfall and above all the illnesses that bred in such regions were enough to keep invaders at bay. When the war of succession had broken out amongst the sons of Shah Jahan, Mughal Kamrup had been overrun by the Ahoms and the raja of Koch Bihar. Mir Jumla – the Persian, ex prime minister of Golconda, who had been appointed governor of Bengal, had launched a successful recovery campaign at the time but the indomitable spirit of the Ahoms had soared once again under the leadership of Raja Chakradhwaj Singha and General Lachit Barphukan. By 1667, Mughal forts began falling to the Ahom army and rumours of sorcery and the magical use of tantra abounded.

Ram Singh left for Kamrup. Accompanying him was the ninth guru of the Sikhs, Teg Bahadur, who promised to keep the magicians at bay. The imperial army sailed up the Brahmaputra to Guwahati but failed to engage the enemy. Aware of the might of the Mughals the Ahoms resorted to guerrilla tactics and Ram Singh was forced to use every method at his disposal. Bribery, corruption and even Aurungzeb's personal favourite – the planting of incriminating letters in the enemy camp – failed to work and eventually the imperialists were forced to cede the territories up to the river Manas to the Ahoms.

Mirza Raja Ram Singh was survived by his grandson, Bhishan Singh.

Mirza Raja Bhishan Singh

Bhishan Singh lived for a short time and left behind two sons, Jai Singh and Beejy Singh.

Maharaja Sawai Jai Singh

Jai Singh succeeded in 1699, in the forty-fourth year of Aurungzeb's reign and served in the Deccan with distinction. The eleven-year-old raja led his Kachwahas to take part in the emperor's wars. The important Maratha fort of Vishalgarh was captured in 1701, and Jai Singh received the title of sawai – literally, a quarter more in value than his peers. The title was inherited by his successors who took to flying two flags – one full and one a quarter sized.

When the war of succession broke out among the sons of Aurungzeb, Jai Singh allied himself with Prince Azam. Azam died in the battle of Jajav and the newly enthroned emperor, Shah Alam Bahadur Shah, punished Jai Singh by seizing control of Amber. An imperial governor and army were stationed in Amber and Jai Singh's brother – Vijay (Beejy) Singh was left in charge.

The nineteen-year-old was ordered back to his post in the Deccan. Marching alongside was the disgruntled Ajit of Marwar. The Rathore had suffered a similar fate at the hands of the emperor. Ajit, who was born raja, had been on the run for the last twenty-nine years. He was by now a seasoned warrior who had defied Aurungzeb and had even regained his kingdom for a couple of years during the tyrant's lifetime. Aurungzeb's death had given Ajit his throne back and to have it snatched yet again at such short notice left him in a dangerous mood.

The two rajas struck a deal. Deserting the Mughal army, the mutineers returned. Their newfound fervour reached all Rajput ears and Maharana Amar Singh II of Mewar advanced to meet them. The first of the Rajput federations was born. Amar at thirty-six was older than both the rajas and laid claim to an age-old authority over Rajputs. Together and without warning they entered Jaipur. The imperial garrison left quietly. Jai Singh celebrated. The gods were thanked and ritual sacrifices made. Hindustan was made aware that Jai Singh was no longer subservient to the Mughals. The new relationship was cemented through intermarriages between the three great Rajput houses. Ajit's daughter Surya Kumari married Jai Singh and revoking Maharana Pratap's ban on marriages of Sisodia princesses with Rajputs that had defected to the Mughal side, Maharana Amar gave to Jai Singh the

Worried about her son's safety, Beejy Singh's mother had him sent to her own father's house and then to the imperial court in Delhi where she had bribed in advance, Qamr-ud-din Khan, a powerful minister.

Beejy Singh sent a request to his brother and sovereign for the grant of Baswa, the most fertile district of Amber. Jai Singh was generous and Beejy's mother became even greedier. A sum of fifty million rupees and a contingent of 5,000 horses were offered to the Mughal prime minister to place Beejy Singh upon the throne of Amber. The emperor agreed to his prime minister's plan and documents for the grant of Amber were drawn up.

Jai Singh received wind of the plan from his envoy, Kriparam, who was based at the imperial court. He assembled his chiefs who had placed him on the throne of Amber and announced the news. They assured him of their support, provided he was sincere in his promise of granting Baswa to Beejy. The grant was drawn up immediately and the council of ministers sent their representative to Beejy Singh. Beejy was nervous and unsure but the ministers were confident that Jai Singh meant well. Were he to go back on his word, they would ensure Beejy's place on the throne. All Amber was anxious to see the feud, between the royal brothers, end.

The meeting was to take place at Sanganer in May 1713. As Jai Singh prepared to leave, word arrived from his mother – she wished to witness the reconciliation between the brothers. The chiefs were only too happy. Three hundred chariots were prepared for the women to accompany the queen mother. Within the queen mother's palki however, was hidden Ugrasen, the Bhati chief. Every chariot contained armed men. They arrived at Sanganer at the appointed time.

The brothers met and embraced. Jai Singh presented the grant of Baswa and magnanimously declared that should Beejy prefer to rule Amber instead, he would gladly give up his birthright and be happy to live out his days at Baswa. Beejy Singh was equally gracious. His requirements had been met and he did not wish for anything more.

When it was time to leave, word was brought that the queen mother awaited her children. The matter was referred to the chiefs who politely left the room. Jai Singh handed his dagger to the guard declaring he had no further need for it.

Beejy Singh followed his brother's lead. But as the doors closed, he found himself not within the embrace of the queen mother but in the iron grip of the Bhati chief. Bound and gagged, he was bundled into a waiting chariot and transported to the fort of Amber.

Within an hour, confirmation arrived that Beejy had been safely locked up. Jai Singh returned to where his chiefs waited. They were shocked to see him alone. Where was Beejy Singh?

'In my belly,' was the reply. 'We are both sons of one father and I am the eldest. If it is your wish that Beejy should rule then slay me. He will be as much your enemy as he is mine and all of you will perish.'

The chiefs were left dumbfounded.

It is said that Beejy spent the rest of his days in prison until 1729, when Jai Singh was made to believe that a conspiracy, supported by Maharao Raja Budh Singh of Bundi, was afoot. Beejy was then put to death.

hand of his granddaughter – the daughter of his heir Sangram.

But Sisodini Maharani Chandra Kanwar Bai Sahiba came with strings attached. She superseded all of Jai Singh's wives, becoming chief queen and mother to his heir. Unwilling to stay with the rest of his women, she lived in seclusion at the Sisodini Rani's Bagh (garden), on the outskirts of Jaipur.

The death of Bahadur Shah was followed by a period of great uncertainty. Aware that the downfall of the Mughal Empire was approaching, Jai Singh resolved to save Jaipur without having to be disloyal to the emperor. He had never really abandoned the unfortunate Farukhsiyar and when the nineteen-year-old Muhammad Shah (Rangila), having vanquished the Syyed brothers, recalled him, he served as his lieutenant in Agra and Malwa. Jai Singh used this important office to repeal the humiliating jaziya that had been reimposed upon the 'Hindus' by Farukhsiyar and to suppress the Jats who had, for long, been a thorn in the flesh of Amber. It was Jai Singh's intervention that gave to Surajmal and his Jats a kingdom of their own. Bharatpur was carved out exclusively for them and Jai Singh won Surajmal's everlasting gratitude.

For Jai Singh the death of Farukhsiyar signalled the end of the power of Delhi and as the Mughal's greatest ally he saw himself as the natural successor. Though no overt move was made to threaten the throne of Delhi, Jai Singh did begin to make his presence felt. The Hadas of Bundi were at the receiving end and Maharao Raja Budh Singh who had married the sawai maharaja's sister discovered the plot while he was a guest at Jaipur. The persecution of Budh Singh and his heirs began, one that was to be pursued by the sons of Jai Singh. With Budh Singh deposed, a traitorous chief of Bundi, who had also married into the Jaipur royal family, was raised to the throne.

In June 1724, his old friend and ally Maharaja Ajit Singh of Jodhpur was murdered. Disregarding the fact that the new king of Maroo was infact the murderer, Jai Singh was quick to snap him up for his daughter. The Rathore was of the same age as his own heir Shiv Singh. Sadly the wedding of Chatur Kanwar and Maharaja Abhay Singh was marred by an epidemic of cholera that carried off the heir of Jaipur. Where he had envisaged two dynamic young men by his side, there remained but one. Abhay was a fiery youth, known more for his brawn and a tumultuous relationship soon developed. Both father and son-in-law gave in to the vices of wine and opium and were quick to take offence as a result of which the Kachwaha and Rathore armies often found themselves face to face upon the battlefield over the most trivial of issues.

Counted as one amongst the brilliant princes of Rajasthan, a statesman and legislator far ahead of his times, it was in science that Jai Singh's interest ran deep. Emperor Muhammad Shah, who came to the throne after a long and turbulent period in Mughal history, gave him the responsibility of reforming the calendar. Jai Singh set up several observatories called Jantar Mantars with instruments of his own invention at Jaipur, Delhi, Ujjain, Varanasi and Mathura. Correspondence was set up with King Emanuel of Portugal, keeping abreast of the developments overseas. In 1728, Jai Singh completed his work on a set of astronomical tables and, as tribute to his Mughal patron, named it Zij-e-Muhammad-Shahi. That year also saw the completion of the city of Jaipur, named after its sovereign and founder. The construction and planning had been overseen by the brilliant Bengali minister Vidyadhar Bhattacharya. Vidhyadhar built for his king a city that would be rivalled by none else. It was the most modern of its time. Jaigarh[14] – the fort of victory – built to fortify the city, stood upon the hill of kites (Chil Tola) and housed the royal treasury. Legend has it that its guardians were the tribal Meenas who permitted each Kachwaha ruler but a single visit to pick out a glittering jewel for his personal use.

By 1732, Jai Singh realised that it was impossible to stem the tide of the Maratha invasions or prevent the partition of the empire. Keeping the interests of Jaipur foremost in his mind, he entered into a treaty with the Maratha minister, Baji Rao Peshwa and appointed him subedar of Malwa. His Rathore son-in-law, following his example allowed

---

14. The treasure hidden in Jaigarh was said to have been collected by Mirza Raja Maan Singh during his campaigns as Emperor Akbar's general. Under the Treasure Trove Act, Prime Minister Indira Gandhi declared the treasure to be state property. The gigantic water tanks of the fort were drained and the secret chambers that lay below searched. Nearly 600 kilograms of gold were confiscated in 1975.

Gujarat to share the same fate. Masters of Malwa, Gujarat and Bundelkhand, the Marathas gave a sudden demonstration of their power by evading the imperial army and appearing in 1737, at the gates of Delhi. They were bought off and Delhi for the moment was spared. But the loss was Hindustan's. The wavering control at the helm did not fail to attract the notice of a Turk who had just murdered his way to the Persian throne. Nadir Shah arrived in 1739. With single-minded devotion he sacked the imperial capital. Muhammad Shah Rangila was acutely embarrassed and citizens of Delhi paid with their lives. The Rajputs maintained their distance. Nadir Shah left, carrying with him the treasures of the empire: among them Shah Jahan's Peacock Throne and a great diamond that the Turk referred to as the Kohinoor. In a gesture of great condescension the bleeding empire was returned to Muhammad Shah. But Afghanistan was severed.

The Rajput federation had long been abandoned though the advantages it offered had been greedily seized. Marwar added to itself territories from Gujarat and the Kachwahas grabbed all lands around their kingdom including those of the Shekhawati federation. But for the Jats who stood their ground in Bharatpur, the kingdom of Jaipur would have extended from Sambhar to the Yamuna. The clauses that went with the alliance however, continued to rankle in the hearts of those directly affected. Shiv Singh's rights as Jai Singh's eldest son had never been threatened for the Sisodini rani bore no children for many years. When Shiv Singh died in 1724, Jai Singh's three-year-old son Ishwari Singh took his place as the undisputed heir. But then there was another brother. In December 1728, Madho Singh was born. That the sawai raja regretted this last marriage was evident from the generous grants of land that Madho Singh received. It was hoped that the law of primogeniture would be respected and Ishwari Singh's right to succeed would not be contested. A second attempt at re-establishing the Rajput Federation was made when Jai Singh's young brother-in-law, Maharana Jagat Singh II, came to the throne. But by now the dynamics between the Rajput states had altered. The maharana was the youngest among the princes and militarily Jaipur and Jodhpur were far ahead. It turned out to be no more than an exercise in futility.

Jai Singh died in 1743. Three queens and several wives followed him to the pyre. The king's women were accompanied by the greatest of Jai Singh's loves – science.

Maharaja Sawai Ishwari Singh

Ishwari Singh took his rightful place upon the throne, inheriting a kingdom with secure borders, an efficient ministry and a good army. But the presence of his younger brother was cause for anxiety. For a whole year Ishwari did not stir from Jaipur. At last the mandatory visit to Delhi could no longer be put off. The maharaja left to pay his respects to the emperor and Maharana Jagat Singh made his move. Ishwari Singh managed to return in time with the Marathas in tow. Raja Shahu Bhosle still ruled from Pune but the real power lay in the hands of his minister – the peshwa. Baji Rao Peshwa who had been Jai Singh's ally had been succeeded by Balaji Baji Rao (Nana Sahib Peshwa). The matter was stalled. Tonk was handed over to the younger prince and for the next seven years Madho Singh more or less held his peace.

Ishwari Singh nurtured his father's hopes of dominating Hadavati. Maharao Raja Dalil Singh of Bundi was a puppet in the hands of Jaipur but Kota remained aloof. The Hadas needed to be kept under control for it was common knowledge that the thirteen-year-old son of Budh Singh had the sympathy of his clansmen. Maharao Raja Durjan Sal of Kota was equally determined that his young cousin regain the throne of Bundi. The army of Jaipur attacked Kota and a band of Nanakpuntis was sent to hunt down Umed. Supported by the tribals amongst whom he spent his days, Umed won a resounding victory capturing the nakkaras and flags of Jaipur. An army detachment had to be sent in and it forced the teenager back into hiding. In 1748, Kota was attacked by the combined armies of Jaipur, the Marathas led by Jai Appa Scindia and the Jats under Surajmal. It was not a success. Jai Appa Scindia lost his arm to a cannon ball and settled for money. The war with Kota was abandoned. Umed, in the meanwhile, sought

Ishwari Singh built the Ishwar Lat or Swarg Suli: the minaret that pierced the heavens, to celebrate his victory. It stands today at the west side of the Tripolia Bazaar.

out his stepmother, the Kachwaha rani of Budh Singh, whose intriguing
had led to misfortunes of the family. The sight of her stepson stirred
emotions hitherto unknown within her breast and she swore to make
amends. The elderly Rajputni turned for help to the Deccan. She led
her recruits not to Bundi but to the kingdom of the persecutors. Sawai
Maharaja Jai Singh's sister unleashed Malhar Rao Holkar's Marathas
upon her nephew.

Ishwari Singh had proved none too popular with his own ministers
and they now proved to be his nemesis. His own Maratha allies
defected to the other side, as did Madho Singh and Maharana Jagat
Singh II. For Ishwari, the Battle of Bagru turned out to be long and
tedious. The fallout was the surrender of Bundi and a grant of more
land to his brother. But the matter was far from resolved.

Emperor Muhammad Shah passed away in 1748, in the same year
as his one time minister, Nizam-ul-Mulk Asaf Jah. Asaf Jah had
abandoned him in 1724, to retire and rule Hyderabad independently,
igniting a string of cessations. Bengal and Avadh (Uttar Pradesh) had
followed suit. Saadat Khan declared himself king in Avadh while his
Persian son-in-law – Safdarjung, who had become a minister in Delhi,
dispensed offices at will with little regard for the discomfited emperor.

A month before his father's death, the Mughal heir Ahmad Shah
had repulsed the advances of his namesake. Nadir Shah's Afghan
minion, Durrani (also known as Ahmad Shah Abdalli), had upon his
master's death, doubled back to lay claim to Punjab. Ishwari and his
men had been there that day upon the banks of the Sutlej when the
Mughal commander-in-chief, Wazir Qamr-ud-din Khan[15] fell. Some
quick thinking on Safdarjung's part had saved the day and he stepped
into the late wazir's shoes. The promise of tribute had only temporarily
quenched Durrani's greed for within days of Emperor Ahmad Shah's
accession he returned. This time he obtained a formal cessation.

Ishwari Singh's contribution had been minimal. His mind had
remained so occupied with Jaipur's defenceless state that he had lost
no time in returning home almost to the point of deserting his post.

---

15. Wazir Qamr-ud-din Khan was second cousin to the nizam of Hyderabad and had replaced
    him as wazir.

Whether it was motivated by his brother's political aspirations one will never know but his own queen received him with taunts and gibes. Ishwari was, unfortunately, not quite the man of the hour and lacked energy – without which no Rajput can command respect.

Maharaja Abhay Singh of Marwar, Ishwari Singh's powerful brother-in-law died in 1750, as did Raja Shahu in Pune. Though Maharaja Ram Singh, who succeeded to the throne of Jodhpur, was Ishwari's own son-in-law, no support appeared to be forthcoming, for Ram Singh's intemperate disposition had jeopardized the stability of his own throne. The political scenario in Pune, on the other hand, spelt great changes for the Marathas and those involved with them. The peshwa was now in absolute control.

When Malhar Rao Holkar returned in December 1750, Jaipur was eerily silent. This time Ishwari Singh offered no resistance. The kickbacks they received had kept the Marathas turning up time and again, driving Ishwari to desperation. The sons of the murdered minister Kesudas made most of the king's melancholia. An illusion was created of a vast army in full march towards Jaipur. Ishwari's spirits plummeted. The maharaja abandoned the capital to its fate and retreated to a jagir of Amber. His trusted ministers exhorted him to action. Even old Vidhyadhar dragged himself from the sick bed to rouse the tired king. Reality dawned too late – the enemy could have been tackled. Ishwari was besieged for ten days at the end of which his personal attendants emerged to announce that the sawai maharaja was no more. The twenty-nine-year-old king had shared a cup of poison with three queens. A second pyre was lit the next day for the twenty-one wives who chose to follow him.

Maharaja Sawai Madho Singh I

Twenty-two-year-old Madho Singh was seated upon the throne by Malhar Rao Holkar. That Holkar saw him as his own man was painfully evident. But Madho Singh's hands had not been soiled in this ugly affair. He had remained all the while at Mewar, while Holkar took complete responsibility for this last attempt. Consequently, he refused to see himself as a Maratha stooge and took rather a cool stance when the question of tribute was raised. But it was easier said than done and the maharaja was forced to relent somewhat. Tonk was ceded but unwilling to part with more Kachwaha lands, he gave away the jagirs of Rampura and Bhanpura instead of returning them, as he rightfully should have, to Mewar – for these had been granted to him for his upkeep during the period he was kept away from the throne.

Two years after his accession, crisis engulfed the imperial capital once again. Reduced to a puppet writhing in the hands of the sly calculating Safdarjung, Emperor Ahmad Shah sent for the grandson of his father's one-time friend and trusted governor Asaf Jah, nizam of Hyderabad. The nizam's eldest son Ghazi-ud-din, who had also served as nizam-ul-mulk, had been poisoned before he could ascend his father's throne in Hyderabad. His fourth brother had taken his place as nizam. It was the late Ghazi-ud-din's son and namesake, who responded to the emperor's distress call. But Delhi had not quite finished with its share of horrors. No one could have predicted the backlash that was to come. Safdarjung was ousted and the eighteen-year-old Ghazi-ud-din, who had been granted both the titles of nizam-ul-mulk and imad-ul-mulk, declared himself wazir in Delhi. The emperor who had called for help was blinded and deposed. Ahmad Shah gave up his throne to a new puppet: the devout and elderly son of Jahandar Shah – Alamgir II – who had been blinded forty years ago by his cousin Emperor Farukhsiyar. The year was 1754 and it saw the beginning of a strange race: that of the protector to the throne of Delhi.

The Mughal Raj spluttered like a candle in the wind. The role of protector to the throne of Delhi was a coveted one and a long line of contenders put forth their claims hoping to re-establish the empire. Though he considered himself the natural successor to the Mughals, Maharaja Sawai Madho Singh was not among the list of would-be protectors. Imad-ul-mulk's ambitions caused Abdalli's (Durrani) return and in 1757, Delhi was sacked yet again. The Rajputs let the imad and Marathas bear the brunt of the attack. The thirty-five-year-old Afghan announced his retirement and left taking the late Emperor

Muhammad Shah Rangila's fifteen-year-old daughter[16] for himself and
Emperor Alamgir's daughter – Gauhar-un-nisa – for his son and heir.
Oblivious to the ambitions of the British merchants, Imad concentrated
upon Punjab. Bengal lost its independence to the machinations of
Robert Clive in the summer of 1757 and it would be but another seven
years before Bengal was to be lost completely. But Delhi cared little.
The Marathas were called in. Fired with imperialistic dreams they
seized control of Punjab precipitating war. The Third Battle of Panipat,
in January 1761, broke the imad's hold and exhausted the Marathas.
His designs constantly meeting with frustration, the imad-ul-mulk had
had the blameless Alamgir murdered in 1759. The Mughal heir, whose
sister was married to the Afghan's son, had taken no chances and had
fled to Avadh the previous year. Abdalli confirmed the succession of
Alamgir's son but left the Rohilla Afghan chieftain, Najib-ud-daula, to
carry out the affairs of the empire. Ostensibly, Najib was to rule the
empire on Shah Alam's behalf. The emperor resolutely maintained his
distance until 1770, when Najib's death was announced.

The powers interested in Delhi paid little attention to Rajasthan and
the Rajputs were left to their own devices. In 1751, Maharaja Bakhta
in Marwar had occupied his nephew's throne but the deposed Ram
Singh was also the late Ishwari Singh's son-in-law. Jaipur found it hard
to remain indifferent. To compound matters one of Madho Singh's
wives was Maharaja Ajit's granddaughter and Bakhta's niece. She
desperately sought vengeance upon the uncle who had murdered her
grandfather. The opportunity to meddle in the affairs of Marwar soon
presented itself. A victorious Bakhta, encamped within the passes that
led to Marwar, sent word to Madho Singh to choose sides. Unwilling
to soil his own hands, Madho Singh sent his Rathorni rani. Maharani
Shri Arjun Kanwar Bai Sahiba came bearing congratulatory messages,
sweets and a robe for her uncle. By the evening Bakhta was ill and
he died within hours having named his son Vijay (Beejy) Singh
successor. In the second year of his reign, Madho Singh had succeeded
in getting rid of Bakhta. Only Beejy stood in the way of Jaipur's

---

16. Shahzadi Sahiba-us-Zamani Hazrat Begum Sahiba Padshah Bibi returned with her infant
    daughter in 1772, upon her husband's death. Mother and child lie buried, close to Emperor
    Muhammad Shah, in the Nizam-ud-din Dargah at Delhi.

candidate. A keen lookout was kept for a suitable opportunity to arise. And it did. Ram Singh aided by Jai Appa Scindia hounded his young cousin. The beleaguered Beejy abandoned by most of his chiefs and the smaller Rathore kingdoms, turned in desperation to Jaipur. He arrived in person to make his plea. Sawai Madho Singh dreamt up the most audacious of plans – Beejy was to be slain in open court. Greeting him warmly Madho Singh invited the young man to share his gaddi. But word had gotten out. Jawan Singh, the young chieftain, who led the first swords of Maroo, had stumbled upon the conspiracy at the very last moment and the sawai maharaja, at the critical moment, found a dagger at his neck. As Beejy fled the Kachwaha court, a bemused Madho Singh was left marvelling at the Rathore spirit.

It was around this time that Ranthambhor came into Madho Singh's possession. While the annals of Jaipur record it as a glorious victory, those of Bundi have a slightly different tale to relate. The Mughal commander of Ranthambhor, worried over a possible Maratha takeover, appealed to Rao Raja Umed Singh of Bundi. But Bundi itself was not out of the woods. Recovering the throne had been an expensive affair and large payments were due to the Holkars. The offer was declined and Ranthambhor's commander turned to Jaipur. As the new master of the Chauhan castle, Madho Singh expected to collect tribute from all Hada-Chauhans. Kota was incensed with this arbitrary assumption and the result was the battle of Bhatwara in 1761, which took place soon after the Third Battle of Panipat. The army of Jaipur was beaten back and the Panchranga – the Kachwaha flag with its five colours – fell into Hada hands. But Maharao Raja Umed Singh, who did not participate that day failed to redeem his tribute paying jagirs.

Madho Singh ruled for seventeen years in which time he built several cities. The beautiful city of Sawai Madhopur was built near the fortress of Ranthambhor. With his interest in science, Jaipur continued to be the city of the learned. Had Madho Singh lived long enough, this brilliant prince would have surely humbled both the Marathas and the rising Jat community, the peaceful pastoral people who, despite their lowly status as tillers of the earth, had taken to arms and were already being counted amongst the thirty-six royal races. The Jats had since grown into a formidable power and resorted to, on several occasions, vandalising the Mughal city of Agra. It was eventually through Sawai Jai Singh's intervention that they had been granted the kingdom of Bharatpur and, though they were more than a match for the finest armies that existed, they remained grateful and subservient to Jaipur. But while the brilliant Surajmal Jat regarded Madho Singh's word as law, his son and heir, Jawaharmal, was audacious and keen to break free. The reputation of the Jats was to be established without a doubt thirty-six years later when the siege of Bharatpur would turn into the first great loss in Lord Lake's career. But Madho Singh had realised that the time to rein them in was now and Jaipur chose to pick on a flimsy cause to declare war. Some peasants had taken passage through Jaipur without taking permission. It resulted in a desperate conflict, which led to the loss of many great Kachwaha chiefs. Both Madho Singh and Jawaharmal survived the encounter but within a few short months the Jat was assassinated by a rival and the Kachwaha, exhausted by the rigors of war, contracted cholera.

Maharaja Sawai Madho Singh died on 5 March 1768.

Maharaja Sawai Prithviraj Singh II (Pirthi Singh)

Pirthi Singh succeeded to the throne of Jaipur. He was still a minor and his stepmother, the mother of his younger brother, Pratap, became regent.

In 1772, four years after Pirthi Singh's accession, Emperor Shah Alam finally built up his courage to return to Delhi. The Rohilla had died over a year ago and a Persian adventurer had taken over the reins of the empire. But the East India Company that promised him protection within the realm of Avadh could not support him in Delhi. The emperor was forced to turn to the Scindia Marathas and, with them by his side, returned to sit upon his throne after thirteen long years. Mirza Najaf, the Persian, remained in control for another ten years.

The queen mother of Jaipur was from the Choondawat clan of Mewar. This ambitious woman was in love with the driver of her elephant, Feroz, whom she had made member of council much to the annoyance of the nobles. Feroz dominated her completely and through her the council. The nobles refused to attend court and remained at their estates. The queen mother decided to do without them and invited the Scindia commander, Ambaji Ingle, to forcibly collect revenue for the crown.

Three months past his fifteenth birthday Pirthi Singh died, ostensibly following a riding accident though rumours of murder were never quelled. But in the nine years that he was king, though he had never grown out of the queen mother's control, he had married several wives. His first wife had been the daughter of Raj Singh, the heir of Bikaner, who had accompanied the five-year-old sawai maharaja to Jaipur. But the cold splendour of her new home left her pining for the mother she had left behind and the little Rathorni maharani died within a few months. It was his third queen, the daughter of Maharaja Bahadur Singh of Kishangarh, who bore him a son. Maan Singh was reared at his maternal home for Jaipur was considered unsafe and his claim to the throne of Jaipur long remained an issue.

Maharaja Sawai Pratap Singh

Thirteen-year-old, Pratap Singh succeeded his brother. His mother, Feroz and Khushialiram, the new prime minister, were in charge.

The chief of Macheri (in Alwar), a vassal state of Jaipur, had along with other chiefs pointedly absented himself from the coronation ceremony. Khushialiram, who had earlier been in service with the Macheri chief, ingratiated himself with the queen mother and the elephant driver. Little did they know that it was upon his instructions that the landlords and nobles had withheld payment of taxes. Acting upon Khushialiram's advice, the Macheri chief united his army with that of a Mughal commander helping to put down a Jat uprising and earning for himself the title of rao raja with a grant that permitted him to hold Macheri directly from the imperial crown. It served to excite Feroz's imagination. The prime minister now advised that the forces

Pat rekho Pratap ka	The honour of Pratap was preserved
Nau kothi ka nath	By the lord of the nine castles (Maharaja Beejy Singh of Marwar)
Agla goona bakas dia	Offences were all forgiven
Abhi pakero haath	As now he held his hand

of Jaipur be joined with the imperial army. Keen to see Feroz in an elevated status the queen mother agreed. The elephant driver met the chief of Macheri on equal terms and a friendship was struck. A cup of poison was carefully slipped in and the embarrassment, being faced by the Jaipur court, put to an end. Pratap Singh was still too young to rule and ambitious groups soon began fighting among themselves.

All the while the Marathas stood by their promise to the emperor in Delhi and in 1785, Shah Alam II was finally able to appoint Mahadji Scindia regent.

The high point of Pratap's military career turned out to be the battle of Lalsot (Tonga) in July 1787, which in reality was no more than an exercise in diplomacy. Mahadji Scindia, who had superseded all Mughal officers, appeared in Jaipur to collect revenues that had long been overdue. With the army of Maharaja Vijay (Beejy) Singh of Marwar by his side, the twenty-two-year-old sawai maharaja personally led the operation. A generous bribe brought the chafing Mughal officers to his side and Scindia finding himself deserted upon the battlefield, retreated to Macheri. While Beejy's men rode onto redeem Ajmer, Pratap – for reasons quite unexplained – returned home. This had been his chance to completely vanquish the Maratha and he let it pass.

Mahadji's defeat at Lalsot weakened him temporarily and Delhi was seized by Rohilla Najib-ud-daula's grandson. Here was the man that would on the tenth day of August 1788, stand physically upon the emperor's chest and rip his eyes from their sockets for having failed to locate the treasure believed to be hidden within the Red Fort. That day would turn out to be the Mughal Empire's last day. The Marathas rushed to the emperor's rescue and this time Delhi was to become all theirs. It was their turn to strip what was left of the Kingdom of Delhi. Shah Alam, a blind broken man, ruled as he did before – in name alone. Mahadji Scindia for all facts and purposes had become ruler of Delhi.

Scindia returned again in 1790. His army had undergone a complete makeover under the watchful eye of De Boigne. The armies met at Patan and the Marathas won a resounding victory. Fortunately for Jaipur, Scindia was preoccupied with avenging Jai Appa's murder and

Jaipur escaped the inevitable sacking that should have followed. The taking of Jai Appa Scindia's life cost the Rathores dearly. Ajmer was lost and tribute levied upon Marwar.

Years passed. Pratap's heart longed for yet another military victory. He had outlived everyone who had participated in the two last wars. Both Mahadji and Beejy had been dead these last seven years, De Boigne had retired, his post occupied by yet another French adventurer, Perron[17], who like his predecessor had struck up a warm relationship off the field with Pratap. The opportunity presented itself in 1800. The new generation leaders, Daulat Rao Scindia and the Holkar regent Jaswant Rao, were embroiled in a personal battle. Pratap sent word to Jodhpur. Maharaja Beejy Singh had been succeeded by his grandson Bheem, who was still in the process of consolidating his own position. All rivals but one had been eliminated. This last one was the greatest threat, for cousin Maan — who was holed up in Jalor — had been named successor by their grandfather. But the prospect of shaking off the Maratha yoke was hard to resist. Despite his preoccupation with his cousin, Bheem sent his army to Malpura. But the old timers had done their work well and Rajput valour was no match for the skill and dexterity of the far smaller Maratha army now under Perron's command. The battle of Malpura turned out to be an unmitigated disaster and though the Rathore cavalry sent their Maratha counterparts packing, they, in their enthusiasm, continued chasing them well beyond the limits of the battlefield leaving their Jaipur allies exposed. The remnants of the Maratha army were quick to regroup – under commanders Major Pohlman and James Skinner – and close in on the Kachwahas. The death of his elephant signalled the end of the battle.

---

17. Pierre Cullier (1753 – 1834), better known as General Perron, became a senior general in Daulat Rao Scindia's army. What began as an honourable career turned into one of greed. Despite enjoying an income equal to that of the combined salaries of the British governor general and commander-in-chief, he took to flouting authority and is said to have begun plotting with the first consul of the French republic hoping to bring the Mughal emperor under French protection. But the with losses incurred during the Battle of Ujjain, his standing amongst his Maratha colleagues had turned shaky and the loss of Fort Aligarh on 4 September 1803, served as the final nail. He appealed to the British and was allowed free passage to the French colony of Chandernagore. A house that he had once built for himself in the Dutch Fort Gustavius at Chinsura houses the Chinsura college today.

Pratap withdrew and sued for peace.

Towards the end of his reign the sawai maharaja was to be put in an acutely embarrassing position for the deposed nawab of Avadh, appeared in Jaipur with the British hot upon his heels and a bounty of 50,000 rupees on his head. Seventeen-year-old Wazir Ali had succeeded, in 1797, to the throne of Lakhnau (Lucknow) having been proclaimed nawab by his grandmother, the bahu begum of Avadh. But his accession did not suit the East India Company. Between his rivals at court and the Company it was determined that he was to be replaced by his father's half-brother, the compliant Saadat Ali Khan. Governor General Sir John Shore took it upon himself to declare the nawab an imposter; Wazir Ali was illegitimate, that he had been smuggled into the zenana as an infant and raised by the ignorant Nawab Asaf-ud-daula who had been kept unaware of his own infertility and that the child had been disowned the moment the truth had been disclosed. Wazir Ali nawab of Avadh was stripped of his rights, evicted from his home and lands and exiled to Varanasi. Then he was asked to make another journey, this time to the confines of Fort William in Kolkata. During the discussions the British resident of Varanasi, a Mr Cherry, forgot himself. The sight of the hysterical foreigner caused the teenager to snap. Wazir Ali ran Cherry through with his sword. With the Company's army chasing him the ex-nawab arrived at Jaipur. Sanctuary was granted immediately but the British demand for surrender could not be ignored. Their military might had been proved through the recent victories over Tipu Sultan[18] of Mysore.

---

18. Tipu Sultan had inherited the kingdom of Mysore (now Karnataka) from his father – Haider Ali. Haider, a common Muslim soldier, had risen from the ranks, overthrown his master – the 'Hindu' Wodeyar raja of Mysore – and declared himself king in 1763. Tipu ruled as sultan from 1782 to 1799 and the brilliance and agility with which he defied the British was to become the stuff of legends. He was targeted and killed by the army of Arthur Wellesley, who was destined to become the first duke of Wellington (the Iron Duke) and to defeat Napoleon at Waterloo. Arthur Wellesley's brother – Richard the earl of Mornington – succeeded Sir John Shore as governor general of India.

The governor general was created marquess of Wellesley but the honour was viewed as a deliberate slight for it was an Irish title, not an English one. It was he who believed that India was ripe for unfication and that this great end made irrelevant all minor wrongs. In 1804, once Wellesley's fangs had been been irretractably embedded into Indian flesh, Napoleon chose to make his move. Britain was threatened by invasion and Wellesley was quickly and unceremoniously recalled.

In 1799, Maharaja Sawai Pratap Singh built the Hawa Mahal, or the palace of breezes. Here within the cool interiors, royal women would congregate and shielded from public view could enjoy the going-ons in the bazaar as well as witness state processions.

Reluctantly violating the Rajput code of honour and hospitality the royal fugitive was handed over in 1799. Feebly, even as they accepted the bounty, the Jaipur court exacted a promise of clemency. Little did Pratap know that the troubles that had spawned in the zenana of Avadh would visit the house of the Kachwahas sooner than could be imagined.

In 1801, in recognition of Maharaja Bheem Singh's right to the Rathore throne and in keeping with the spirit of comrades-in-arms Pratap gave to him in marriage, his daughter Anand Kanwar. Bheem gave to Pratap, as his twelfth queen, the daughter of his father's eldest brother. The Rathorni enjoyed but two years of marital bliss before she joined her husband on his pyre accompanied by her mother-in-law, the Choondawat queen mother of Jaipur. Maharaja Bheem died around the same time and Anand Kanwar returned home to Jaipur.

Maharaja Sawai Jagat Singh

Jagat Singh succeeded in 1803. Not one historian nor bard ever put down a good word for this prince. Lack of documentary evidence led to the general assumption that he was the most cowardly and dissolute of the Kachwaha princes.

The year of his accession turned out to be a significant one in the history of India, for by December Lord Lake had chased Mahadji Scindia's scuccessor, Daulat Rao, out of Delhi and usurping the Maratha's role of protector, the East India Company made itself the defacto ruler of Delhi. At a loss, Daulat Rao set up camp in Mewar and resorted to the old ways of wreaking havoc upon the Rajputs.

In 1806, twenty-two-year-old Jagat Singh vied with the twenty-three-year-old Maharaja Maan Singh of Marwar for the hand of a twelve-year-old – Princess Krishna Kumari of Mewar. Bheem of Jodhpur had sought her hand four years ago but his untimely death had spared her the flames of sati. The Rathores assumed that she now automatically belonged to Bheem's successor. But they arrived to stake their claim only after Jagat Singh's proposal was announced. Maan

Singh's succession was itself surrounded by controversy for a pretender claimed to be the posthumous son of Maharaja Bheem. Jaipur could not resist the temptation to foment trouble. The pretender was brought to Jaipur and Anand Kanwar sat him upon her knee and declared him her own true stepson. Jagat invited his nephew to eat from his plate. Together they besieged Maan Singh at Mehrangarh – the great fort of Jodhpur – and in 1808, after an uneventful five months in the desert, made their way home. Nothing had been achieved apart for some unwarranted deaths and the sacking of Jaipur by the Afghan hordes of Amir Khan.

Selfish threats continued and for the next two years the mercenary Pathan, Amir Khan, who switched sides at will, wallowed in perverse pleasure serving ultimatums to the maharana. A choice would have to be made. The kingdom of Mewar was at risk. The issue was finally resolved by the girl herself who, at the very mature age of sixteen, committed suicide at her father's command. It sent shock waves through Rajasthan as the chivalry of Mewar cowered under a shroud of humiliation and every man that responded to the name Rajput was overcome by shame. Even the ferocious khan, a seasoned mercenary in his mid forties, was stumped. He had lost his pawn upon whom lucrative bargains had been leveraged.

Little Krishna had been no more than a trophy and with her out of the way, Jaipur and Jodhpur could at last declare peace. Symbolically two princesses interchanged homes. On 3 September 1813, Jagat Singh's sister Suraj Kanwar wed the desert lord and the next day, Maan Singh's daughter became wife to Jagat Singh.

Jagat Singh next fell under the spell of his Muslim consort, Raz Kafur – the 'mystery of camphor'. Like camphor, which transforms directly from its solid state to gas, the lady's sublime charms took complete possession of the Kachwaha's reason. Despite her origin as a lowly commoner, she displaced queens of royal birth and though his nobles objected, Jagat insisted that she be granted every respect due to a legitimate queen. Half of Amber he gifted to her and placed at her disposal, Jai Singh's invaluable library. Its treasures were distributed among her relatives, coins were struck in her name and the pair rode the same elephant during ceremonial occasions. Watching the treasures of Amber being squandered, the city's ancient Meena guardians grew unhappy.

When Chand Singh of Duni was fined a sum of two lakhs for refusing to attend ceremonies over which the king's mistress presided, the nobles decided it was time to get rid of them both. Fortunately for Jagat Singh, he had a friend. This noble collected evidence against Raz Kafur, defaming her and succeeded in having her locked away in the fort of Nahargarh. There she spent the rest of her life, the queen of half of Amber, deprived of all her rights and separated from her lover.

The year 1818 brought great changes for Jaipur. For some time the court had been dallying with the Company's offer of protection. The terms of the treaty were expensive, for tribute was levied at one-fifth of the kingdom's total earnings and all subsequent rise in income was to be taxed at thirty-three percent. Furthermore Jaipur would have to accept the presence of a British resident. This last clause was the most obnoxious of them all. There were of course obvious advantages. British support had warded off an attack by Amir Khan in 1816, and with their occupation of Ajmer and their existing presence in Delhi, they had become immediate neighbours. Talks were on with Amir Khan who had agreed to disarm and settle down close to Jaipur as the nawab of Tonk. In 1818, Rawal Berisal of Samode, the wealthiest chief of Jaipur, signed the documents on behalf of the maharaja.

Maharaja Sawai Jagat Singh died on 21 December 1818, leaving no issue behind. His queens did not volunteer to keep him company in the afterlife and the Rathorni rani preferred to go home to her, by then, completely insane father.

Maharaja Sawai Jai Singh II

With no direct descendent to choose from, Jaipur turned to the senior Kachwaha house of Narwar. Mohan Singh, a son of the raja of Narwar, succeeded to the gaddi of Jaipur. The child had been chosen by Mohan Nazir, the chief eunuch at the palace. It was obvious that

Mohan intended to be regent and in the hope of a long tenure had chosen a very young child. The chiefs resented being placed under the eunuch's control, as did the queens. When it was most needed, Jagat Singh's Bhatiani rani announced her pregnancy. A committee of queens verified the facts to the visible relief of all. They took care to declare that a second baby was also on the way. The chiefs saw no reason to question the issue and the little prince of Narwar returned home with his life intact.

Maharaja Sawai Jai Singh II was born on 25 April 1819, amidst much gossip. It was said that the queens had procured the baby and passed him off as the legitimate son of Sawai Jagat Singh. The Bhatiani rani took over as regent and Rawal Berisal was appointed chief minister.

The newborn king was engaged to the princess of Bikaner but once again ugly rumours began to fly. Word reached Bikaner but it was too late to back out. It was also inconceivable that their daughter should marry beneath her. The Rathores could see no way out. In the end the little princess was administered a dose of poison and the issue was resolved.

Gratitude, honour, and fidelity, are terms which at one time were the foundation of all the virtues of a Rajpoot. Of the theory of these sentiments he is still enamoured; but, unfortunately, for his happiness, the times have left him but little scope for the practice of them. Ask a Rajpoot which is the greatest of crimes? He will reply, 'goonchor', 'forgetfulness of favours'. This is his most powerful term for ingratitude...It means, literally, 'abandoner (from chorna, 'to quit') of virtue (goon)'.

— JAMES TOD

Remnants of the kingdoms of Rajputana within modern Rajasthan.
Districts of Rajasthan that were once included in the kingdom of Jaisalmer.

CHAPTER 6

JAISALMER

Jaisalmer lies in the geographical centre of the great desert and should have rightfully been its capital city but tradition granted Mandor that privilege. Maroosthali, stretched from the flat lands in the north to the grand salt marshes in the south bordering the Rann of Kachchh (Gujarat). The Aravalli towered over the eastern boundary while the western edge of the desert blended into the valley of Sind. Its ancient Parmar kings marked the limits of their desert kingdom with a semicircle of nine fortresses: the Nau Kothi Maroo, an inheritance that was bequeathed to their Rathore successors. Pugal lay in the north, Mandor in the centre, Abu, Kheralu and Parkar (across the khar or the salt river – the modern district of Barmer) to the south, and Chotan, Umarkot and Lodurva to the west. He who possessed the nine castles was the true sovereign of the desert. While Lodurva and Arore had long been reduced to ruins Chotan (Juna Chotan in Jalor) and Kheralu (now in Mahesana, Gujarat) lived on in verse alone.

Never having personally ventured beyond, Mandor, Hisar, Abu, Neherwala and Bhuj, it became necessary for Captain James Tod to rely on the descriptions of agents. The information brought to him was corroborated by the writings of Mr Elphinstone, who had led an embassy to Kabul. *Account of the Kingdom of Kabul*[1] holds one of the very first descriptions of the Indian desert.

The first part of the route, beginning at Delhi, had lain through the British held city of Kanor along the north-eastern edge of the desert through the land of Shekhawati (districts of Jhunjhunu, Sikar and Churu) ending at Bikaner. And that had been the easy part for the miles that lay beyond Bikaner, comprised hills and valleys of loose and heavy sand. Their height ranged from a twenty to hundred feet and they shifted and changed in accordance with the winds. Clouds of moving sand made passage in summer impossible. In winter, however, the dunes appeared to gain some measure of stability for they bore grass, babul and the wild Indian jujube or ber. Occasional villages cropped up amongst these dismal conditions: a few round huts of straw with low walls and conical roofs, the whole appearance being similar to that of a little stack of corn.

The going was difficult, the terrain new and strange. A day's march could vary from anything in between fifteen to twenty-six miles but the distances covered bore no relation to the fatigue that had to be endured. Travelling in a tightly packed band, the line of men and beasts formed a two-mile long caravan. It wound its way around the dunes following tracks that had been trampled into submission, the beaten path being just wide enough to allow the passage of a single camel. One false step and the beast would sink into the sand as if it were in soft snow.

---

1. Elphinstone's efforts may have not met with the desired success but *Account of the Kingdom of Kabul* served to excite the imagination of Josiah Harlan, a Quaker in his early twenties, who had left his native Philadelphia in 1820, to flog his meagre knowledge of first aid and have himself appointed surgeon to an army division then involved in the Anglo-Burman wars. The imposter went undetected and was retained as doctor to a British garrison. It was then that he laid his hands upon Elphinstone's book. Visions filled Josiah's head. Buying himself a silver mace, he made suitable adjustments to his biodata and aquired himself a band of ruffians. Together they applied to the deposed Shah Shuja of Kabul. To this master impersonator, language proved no barrier. Soon, tucked into his belt was a governorship in Punjab and the credentials of a general of the Kabuli army. Finally he crossed the Hindu Kush, through a pass higher than the one used by Alexander, and planted the star spangled banner upon the heights. He occupied Balkh, awarded himself the title king of Ghur, and crowned himself with a band of gold that he wore around his forehead. The king of Ghur then faded away from popular notice, but Josiah lived on to inspire Rudyard Kipling who wrote *Man Who Would Be King* based on his life.

Westwards from the triple-peaked hill of Jaisal, the view included the blue waters of the Nil-ab (Indus) close to the distant edge of the sandy ocean. The entire course of the river, from Hyderabad (now in Pakistan) to Uch (also in Pakistan), could be seen snaking its way through the valleys. Little villages, dotted the few green areas that lay along its banks, where the shepherds of the desert tended their flocks. Nomads moved with their beasts in search of pastures while others indulged in more peaceful pastimes, congregating around cooking fires over which were suspended pots of bubbling 'rabri' – the maize porridge of the desert cooked in the rich milk of the camel. At length the eye could discern a long line of camels making its way through the dunes in the distance, its charun conductor keeping an anxious eye out for bands of Sehraes that waited in the shadows, astride fleet-footed horses and camels, to ambush passing caravans. A series of knots in the process of being tied, at the end of the charun's turban, served as a log of each stage of the journey that was successfully completed.

The Ghaggar that had once flowed along the northern edge had long since been absorbed, leading to a mass scale abandonment of the area. The only other river of the desert was the Luni, also known as the Khar or salt river. From its source in the Aravalli, it crossed Marwar and heading south-west entered the land of the Chauhans, dividing it into two. The eastern part, Jalor, was known as the Raj of Sooi Bai and the western, Barmer, referred to as the Parkar or beyond the Khar. The country of the Chauhans was bound to the south by giant salt marshes, which formed the Rann or Aranya (waste land). The bed of the Luni and its feeders were white with encrustations of salt. No land could have been drearier than this parched desert of salt and mud whose lone inhabitant was the solitude-loving wild ass.

Chauhans had once ruled this south-western corner of the desert – modern-day Jalor and Barmer. From their capital at Juna Chotan – the ancient Sonagir (golden mountain) – they had vanquished the Parmar kings and held sway over the kingdoms along the Luni all the way to Ajmer. In time they adopted the name of their capital, becoming the race of the Songara-Chauhans. Their kul devta (tutelary divinity of their race) remained enshrined at Sonagir. When the sons of Sihoji Rathore occupied the land, the ancient capital was renamed Jalor.

The Bhatis of Jaisalmer claim descent from Lord Krishna. Their early tales remain shrouded in myth and it wasn't until the settlement of Jaisalmer, on the western edge of the desert, that their wanderings came to an end and the formal history of Jaisalmer began.

In the days of the *Mahabharat*, the scion of the Lunar race (Chandravansh or Somvansh), Lord Krishna, ruled the Yadu (Yadav or Jadu) clan of Dwarka (in Gujarat) and distant Mathura (in Uttar Pradesh). But the mighty kingdom that stood upon the shores of the Arabian Sea was doomed for it had been said that the race of the Yadavs would not survive the death of their Lord. True to the prophecy, Lord Krishna's death was followed by a great civil war, which ended in a massacre destroying Dwarka.

Pradyumn, the heir of Dwarka – the son of Krishna and his senior queen Rukmini – lost his life. Dwarka became a city of the dead. The Yaduvansh (Yadu dynasty) would have been completely wiped out had it not been for Pradyum's son and grandsons who were away at Mathura.

Unable to bear the news, a grief-stricken Bujra lay down to die. His sons prepared to face their destiny. Vajra-Nabha, raised Krishna's Meghadhambar to shade his own brow while his younger brother, Khira, left to salvage amongst the ruins of Dwarka.

Enemies of the Yaduvansh seized the opportunity to declare war upon Mathura and Vajra-Nabha fled into the desert taking with him the only signs of his divine ancestry, the regal umbrella and insignia of Lord Krishna. He appears to have fled a great distance for he crossed the Indus and settled at the far edge within the mountainous region that is now Afghanistan.

To Khira, Dwarka was not welcoming. His son Judbhan, directed by his guardian goddess, sought his destiny among the hills of the north. Five days march to the east of the Indus, shrouded in a pall of gloom, lay the kingdom of Bhera (now in Pakistan). The king had died leaving no heir. The citizens, guided by the words uttered on the deathbed, patiently awaited the heir of Lord Krishna. Judbhan was welcomed with open arms and his new home was re-named the Hill of Jud – Jadu-ka-dang (Koh-i-Jud).

The Yaduvansh lists eighty-six kings all descended from Vajra-Nabha.

Rukmini, princess of Vidarbha (near modern Nagpur), had come of age and her father arranged for her a swayamvar. Suitors from all over the land flocked to Vidarbha. From among them Rukmini would choose her husband.

Elaborate arrangements were made and every prince was welcomed in accordance to his status. But Krishna – king of Dwarka, offended by the reception meted out to him, declined all offers and chose to camp in a garden. Rukmini's embarrassed father was prevented from making amends by the king of Magadh, Jarasandha. This was Jarasandha's opportunity to humiliate his mortal enemy.

The heavens were aghast and Indra, king of the gods, hurriedly sent his celestial umbrella – chattra – to shield the Vishnu incarnate from the heat of the afternoon sun.

An enraged, Shakti – the tutelory deity of the Yaduvansh – reached out from the heavens and snatched from Jarasandha's hand the Swang (spear) that guaranteed his immortality. The goddess earned herself the name – Swangiya-ji. The celestial weapon, now partially bent as a result of the tussle, was handed to Krishna for safekeeping.

The day of the swayamvar arrived and Rukmini garlanded Krishna.

Indra's celestial umbrella – Meghadhambar – and the partially bent Swang became a part of Krishna's royal insignia to be treasured forever by his descendents, who hereafter referred to themselves as Chattralay Yadavpati – Lord of the Yadavs who is shielded by the celestial umbrella.

Their story is one of turmoil, entwined with the creation and loss of great empires. From Mathura they migrated westwards but returned time and again in answer to a primal need that drew them to the motherland.

Subahu, the sixth king since Vajra-Nabha, set up his capital in Punjab; the site corresponds to the modern-day city of Peshawar (Purushpur).

Vajra-Nabha's grandson, Gajbahu, who inherited large parts of Kashmir, built himself a second capital in the mountains of Afghanistan – Ghazni. The construction of the Yadu fort threatened the neighbouring tribes who forced Gajbahu's successor out.

All attempts at recovering Ghazni failed until the time of Maryadpati, sixteenth in line, who not only recovered the coveted fort but also expanded his kingdom by occupying Lahore. Maryadpati's name lives on for he was the first to introduce social reforms. Intermarriage amongst related clans was banned.

The twentieth king Aprajit, however, lost half of Ghazni and anticipating further losses built himself the city of Awadhas near Mathura. It was Aprajit's great-grandson, Maghvanjit, who abandoned Ghazni for a second time and withdrew to the safety of distant Mathura.

Ghazni was too far to be effectively administered and by the time of the twenty-seventh king, Vikramsen, the Yaduvanshis had lost their hold over the great fort. Vikramsen saw wisdom in moving to Lahore, which was closer to the western border.

The Pundir Rajputs of Lahore were subjugated and six generations maintained their capital here until Uttarsen, the thirty-fourth, occupied Ghazni and re-established it as the capital of the Yaduvansh. Five generations ruled once again from the mountains.

Devasvay, the thirty-ninth, unable to face the growing power of the 'barbarians' fled all the way to Mathura. To retain a nominal hold over Ghazni, he agreed to pay tribute.

Avinijit, the forty-third king re-established Lahore as the capital and his son, Bhimsen lost his life in an attempt to move to Ghazni. Ghazni was overrun by 'barbarians'.

Chandersen, who succeeded to the throne of Lahore, stormed the fort of Ghazni avenging the death of his father. But Lahore was maintained as the capital until Chandersen's great-grandson made yet another shift to Mathura. This time the foe that threatened the Yadus was within India

In the mountainous kingdom amongst the hills of Afghanistan, Rijh's queen had a strange dream. She had been delivered of a radiant white elephant. The astrologers predicted a great future. In due course, the queen gave birth and the prince was named Guj (elephant). When he grew to manhood his cousin from the east, a descendent of Judbhan, sent the coconut offering his daughter's hand in marriage. Guj left to claim his bride but before he could return Farid, shah of Khorasan, attacked their little kingdom. The invader was defeated but Raja Rijh lost his life.

The shah of Khorasan had allied himself with the king of Room[2] to establish the Koran and the law of the prophet in the land of Hindustan. Raja Guj called his ministers and they decided to build a strong fortress in the mountains of the north. The guardian goddess of the race was consulted.

'The power of the 'Hindu' is coming to an end,' she said. 'Build a strong fort and call it Gujni.' The fort was near completion when word arrived – the foe was at hand. The astrologers were consulted and the auspicious hour was predicted. Raja Guj left with his army on the Thursday and the two armies camped within sight of each other, ready to do battle.

In the night, the shah of Khorasan was troubled by severe pains in his abdomen and by morning, he was dead. Sikander Shah Roomi was alarmed. 'While we mortals have grand schemes in hand, He holds other views,' he said.

The conch shell and trumpets sounded as the armies positioned themselves. Elephants advanced like walking mountains. The sky was dark with clouds of dust. Sunlight glinted off polished helmets and

---

2. 'Room' was a Rajput term commonly applied to both Greece and Rome. Here, it most probably refers to the Greeks for Alexander of Macedonia was traditionally referred to as Sikander Shah Roomi. The ostensible purpose of the invasion being the spread of the *Koran* seems to be a bardic foible for Alexander's invasion is dated to 326 BC, more than 800 years before the birth of Islam. The empire of the Greeks had long since been over and the Roman Empire that followed, divided into the eastern and western empires by AD 450.

soldiers rushed at each other like famished tigers. War bells rang while horses neighed in fright and the whole world trembled. Like rolling clouds, of the monsoon months of Bhadon, the armies merged into each other. Arrows hissed through the air while the clang of steel grated upon crackling bones. Mighty warriors fell and the earth was deluged in blood. Twenty-five thousand of the shah's men that lay beside the 7,000 'Hindus'. Abandoning his men, elephants and even his horses, Sikander Shah Roomi fled. To sound of the drums of victory, the Yadus returned home.

Raja Guj went on to invade Kashmir and returned with a Kashmiri princess as his bride. When their son, Salbahan, was twelve, Khorasan marched their armies once more towards India. Raja Guj locked himself within the temple of the goddess. For four days, he meditated before she graced him with her presence. 'Gujni will pass from your hands,' she said. 'Your descendents will once again possess Gujni but not as 'Hindus'. Send Salbahan to live among the 'Hindus' of the east. Command him to build a city in his own name. Fifteen sons will be born to Salbahan and his tribe will multiply. You must sacrifice yourself for Gujni but the greater reward will be yours.'

The royal family left with Salbahan for the safety of the east and Raja Guj went to meet the foe. His uncle, Rana Sehdev, remained behind to defend the fort. The shah of Khorasan had assembled a vast army. The conflict was desperate and in the end, both shah and raja lay dead on the field. For thirty days the shah's son laid siege to the fort and when at last, 9,000 Yadus had sacrificed their lives the 'barbarians' entered the famous fort of Gujni.

The tragic news reached Salbahan. Overcome with grief, he lay upon the ground and would not rise for twelve days[3]. When the period of mourning was over, he arose and began a long march. Within the land of Punjab, he chose a spot with abundant water. Here with his few surviving clansmen he built the city of Salbahanpur. Salbahan conquered all of Punjab and his fifteen sons established themselves as independent rajas.

---

3. Twelve days is the traditional period of mourning.

-- the growing power of Magadh. Too close for comfort, Mathura could not be left alone for Magadh's star was on the rise. The Yaduvanshis became feudatories to the powers of Magadh and for a while even followed the tenets of Buddhism, imitating the emperor. Charged with the responsibility of defending the north-western reaches of the empire they moved their capital back to Lahore.

Raja Rasanrap, the sixty-eighth king, who enjoyed imperial patronage, supported the reclamation of Ghazni and Kandahar. A junior branch of the family administered these far-flung areas but their hold remained tenuous.

With mounting pressure on the Yaduvanshis of Ghazni, the seventy-sixth king, Raja Hanspat was compelled to set up base at Hisar. Here a fort and a town were founded and it remained the capital of the senior Yaduvansh branch for the next eight generations.

Raja Rijhsen, the eighty-third king, who was crowned at Hisar was said to be a feudatory of the Kushans. It was he who started the work of restoring the ancient fort of Ghazni. Raja Rijhsen died defending Ghazni from marauders that coveted the great fort. His son, Gajsen completed the restoration and made it his capital. Gajsen ruled peacefully for many years and enjoyed the status of an independent sovereign. But the foreign foe returned time and again and Raja Gajsen prepared to give up his life on the battlefield. His heir, Salbahan, was sent to the safety of Punjab while Gajsen's uncle defended the fort. For thirty days, the Yadus held on and when their resources had all been depleted the first jauhar and saka in their history was held. The saka of Ghazni is said to be dated to AD 194.

Salbahan annexed for himself vast tracts of land in Punjab and built his capital, Salbahanpur[4], near Lahore. With his sons by his side he was a power to contend with. At last when he considered himself strong enough, he marched to redeem Ghazni. The Yadu flag was raised once again upon the ancient walls.

Leaving his heir, Balbandh to rule Ghazni, Salbahan returned home. Raja Balbandh became the last of Yaduvanshis. His son Bhati, who inherited Salbahanpur, changed the name of his dynasty.

---

4.   Salbahanpur is thought to be the modern-day city of Sialkot (now in Pakistan).

When Balbandh, the eldest, married the daughter of Jaipal Tomar, king of Delhi, Salbahan decided it was time. Gujni awaited redemption. At the head of 20,000 men, he crossed the Attock and regained possession of his father's fort. Leaving Balbandh behind as king of Gujni, he returned to Punjab.

Of Balbandh's seven sons, the eldest was Bhati and the second Bhoopati (lord of the earth). Kullur, the third son of Balbandh, occupied the mountains of the north-west and his clan became the notorious Kullur dacoits. Jinj, the fourth, fathered the Jinj clan.

Bhoopatis's son, Chakita, inherited Gujni from his grandfather. By this time, 'barbarians' had settled in great numbers in and around the mountain kingdom and they soon held prominent positions in Chakita's court. The 'barbarian' nobles pleaded with him to accept their faith and offered to make him the master of Baluch Bukhara. The Uzbeg king who ruled Bukhara had but one child – a daughter. Chakita married the princess to become king of all the land from Baluchistan and Bukhara to the frontier of Hindustan. He was known as the lord of 28,000 horses and from him descended the Chagatai Mughals[5].

---

5. The Chagatai Mughals are of Mongol origin. Genghis (or Chingis) Khan established the Mongol Empire and at the time of his death in AD 1227, his empire was divided amongst his four sons with the third son ruling as the supreme khan. Chagatai, the second son, received central Asia and Persia. This came to be known as the Chagatai Khanate. In AD 1369, Taimur-i-lang conquered the Chagatai Khanate in an attempt to re-establish the Mongol Empire. Amir Taimur Sahib Kiran, a self made chieftain of Turko-Mongolian descent, had established his place in Mongolian royalty by marrying women from Genghis Khan's line and assumed the name Taimur Gurkani, Gurkan being the Persian word for son-in-law. An old wound in his leg had rendered him permanently lame and hence the suffix lang. The Mughals of India claim descent from Taimur and refer to their Persian Taimurid ancestry ignoring their Mongol links for the Persians were considered the more sophisticated of the two.

Raja Bhati

Bhati, the eldest of Balbandh's sons, succeeded to his grandfather's throne, ruling Punjab from the capital city of Salbahanpur. The sons of his younger brother, Samba, came to be known as the Jareja[6] Bhatis.

Of Bhati's sons, Yuvraj Bhupat built the fort of Bhatner and Singhrao the fort of Sirsa.

Salbahan had settled his sons each with independent kingdoms of their own but the peace that he hoped for was not to be. Despite the ties of blood, each coveted the others' lands. The sons of Salbahan and Balbandh continually harassed the Salbahanpur branch. Eventually Raja Bhati resorted to enforcing discipline. His own brothers, barring the youngest, Bhoopati, who had been designated to succeed their father Raja Balbandh at Ghazni, he united under the name Bhati.

Raja Bhupat

Bhupat Bhati succeeded his father at Lahore. Soon it was time for him to contend with the ambitions of his cousin at Ghazni. Chakita, the son of Bhoopati, had set up powerful alliances with neighbouring kingdoms and had long given up the faith of his forefathers. The sons of Chakita now entertained hopes of uniting what should have been great-grandfather Balbandh's empire.

With no support from the sons of Salbahan and Balbandh, Bhupat was evicted from both Lahore and Bhatner. With his brother, Mansur Rao he sought refuge in the forest. But fortune took a turn for the better and a Suryavanshi king came forward and helped him regain Bhatner.

Mansur established himself within the jungle and his sons Abhay and Saran fathered the clans of the Abhoria Bhatis and Saran Bhati Jats Bhupat was succeeded by his sons Aterao and Bhim at Bhatner but the impoverished rulers maintained a low profile. When their nephew Saterao came to the throne, the Bhatis once again came to the forefront.

---

6. Like the Bhati, the Jareja or Jadeja is an important tribe of the Yadu (Jadu) race. Some Jarejas are of the opinion that they have descended from Shambo, who was born of Krishna's second queen, Satyabhama, while others claim descent directly from Krishna (Shyam) and refer to themselves as Shyam-putras or the sons of Shyam.

Raja Saterao

Saterao, who rose in imperial favour, sent out the call to his clansmen. The Bhatis turned upon the their one-time feudatories who had taken the opportunity to break free. The Punjab campaigns were then planned and Ghazni, so dear to the heart of the Bhatis, was retrieved. Saterao became the first Bhati ruler of Ghazni.

Raja Khemkaran

Khemkaran succeeded to his father's throne at Bhatner. Under imperial orders he shifted his capital to Lahore for the borders of his kingdom were under threat.

Raja Narpat

Narpat ruled from Lahore. The Bhatis with their experience of the border tribes and terrain were an asset to Hindustan. Family ties connected them with the rulers of these spirited and independent kingdoms that acted as buffer against the hordes that waited to gain entry.

With Narpat's death his sons began quarrelling for the throne. The elder, Gaj, abdicated in favour of his brother but as he left he carried with him the Meghadhambar and the royal insignia that marked him as the heir of Lord Krishna. He travelled west accompanied by chieftains who served the royal insignia alone.

Raja Baj

Baj had ruled for but a short while when his brother returned at the head of a foreign army. The Bhati lands were occupied but Gaj permitted his brother to retain Bhatner and Hisar.

Zhandu, son of the deposed Baj, sulked at Bhatner for a while and then the frustrated prince made his way to Bukhara bent upon vengeance. The Hun that had brought misfortune upon his father would have to pay.

Lurking in the royal gardens, Zhandu chanced upon the king's daughter. The lovely Hun princess caught the Bhati's fancy and romance blossomed.

The lovers fled, pursued by the army of Bukhara, and sought refuge at Ghazni. Unable to turn his nephew away, Raja Gaj offered safe passage.

The Hun was furious. Gaj had turned traitor. He unleashed his fury upon Ghazni.

The Bhatis put up a valiant resistance but were unable to withstand the hordes. In the end, a jauhar and saka were announced.

Raja Gaj

Gaj divided his kingdom into two. While he ruled from Ghazni, his heir Yugraj Loman Rao was made independent at Lahore.

Sadly, the enemies of Ghazni returned. The Bhatis held out for five long years. Before the saka was announced the symbols of Krishna's divine origins were smuggled out to safety.

The second saka of Ghazni, the first to be held while the Bhatis were in occupation, claimed the lives of both Loman Rao and Zhandu. The fort of Bhatner was next. Even as the flames of jauhar engulfed Bhatner, Lahore, Hisar and Mathura fell. The invader swept through every land the Bhatis called home.

The lands were parcelled amongst the old feudatories of the Bhatis. Ghazni went to the descendents of Chakita and Mathura and Bayana to the Yadavs. Salbahan's Punjab was returned to its former rulers – the Puriharas, Varaha-Parmars and the Pundirs.

Raja Ren Singh

Loman Rao's son, Rensi, fled with the family heirlooms into the Lakki jungle. Amongst his possessions was the wooden throne of Ghazni and an image of Adinarayan.

With no kingdom and no people to rule over, Raja Rensi remained but a name in the genealogy of the Bhatis.

Raja Bhoj Singh

Bhojsi inherited his father's titles but like him had no kingdom to call his own. However Toramana the Hun, who had set up his capital at Sialkot, restored Salbahanpur to him.

Raja Mangal Rao

Mangal Rao succeeded to his father's throne at Salbahanpur in AD 519. Times were precarious and though Mangal Rao had inherited less than a fraction of their once great kingdom, his cousins from Ghazni would not give up their persecution of the senior Bhati clan. An unexpected attack drove Mangal Rao into the forests.

Father and son made their way across the Sutlej. From the Parmars and the Johiyas, they wrested a piece of land close to the area known today as Bahawalpur (west Punjab). Here Mangal Rao raised a new fort. Mammanvahan was named after his son, Mandam Rao.

Mammanvahan was located strategically upon a crossroad. Here met the caravan routes that led to Delhi, Gujarat, and to the areas that were to later become Bikaner and Jaisalmer. It threatened the Parmars, who were supreme in these lands. Domination would be the obvious outcome. Wars that would necessarily follow the Bhati urge to regain Ghazni, would be fought in Multan and the Sind Sagar Doab for the Gomal Pass was the only route that led to the mountain stronghold. The Langa-Solankis of Multan swiftly crossed the river and stormed the fort.

Mangal Rao bundled his few treasures and left.

Raja Mandam Rao

Mandam Rao succeeded to his father's titles and inherited the symbols of his divine ancestry. Moving eastwards away from the banks of the Sutlej, he marched to the western bank of the Ghaggar (Hakra). Here within the realm of the Parmars of Pugal he resolved to build a fort. The Parmar clans united and the rising walls of Fort Marot were torn down as soon they came up. There was, however, no let up from the Bhati side and, despite the growing anxiety of the Parmars, a coconut arrived from the Parmar kingdom of Malwa. The Soda-Parmar king of Dhar (Malwa – now in Madhya Pradesh) was too far away to be threatened and viewed the determined efforts of the Bhatis as a sign of resurrection. He was quick to grab Yuvraj Sursen for his daughter. Grateful for such

Mangal Rao fled, abandoning Salbahanpur. He had lost everything. Taking Yuvraj Mandam Rao with him, father and son made their way into the forests.

But five younger sons had been left behind in the care of a loyal merchant, Seth Sridhar.

Satidan Tak had long borne a grudge against Seth Sridhar. Satidan was from the race of the Takshaks that had once ruled these parts. His ancestors had been evicted by the ancestors of the Bhatis and Satidan's soul ached for revenge. He sought an appointment with the king of Ghazni.

'The sons of Mandam Rao still live. They thrive in the house of Seth Sridhar.'

The seth was summoned and he stoutly refuted the charges.

'The boys are no more than sons of men like Satidan Tak who, unable to pay their dues, have left their sons as bonded labour.'

The king of Ghazni was at a loss. The opportunity to wipe out the Bhati royal family appeared to be slipping out of his grasp. But he had yet another card up his sleeve. Should these indeed be royal youths their claim to the throne would have to be erased once and for all. Seth Sridhar would have to arrange for their weddings.

Princes Khalar Singh, Mund Raj and Shivar, who declared themselves to be Jats were married to Jat women and fathered the Khullaria, Mund and Shivar Jat clans. Prince Phul Raj was married to the daughter of a nai (barber) and his sons came to be known as the Phul Nais. Kewal, the youngest, married the daughter of a kumbhar (potter) and became father to the Kewal Kumbhars.

validation, every successive generation of Bhatis considered themselves honour-bound to take as wife a Soda princess.

Rao Sursen

It took Sursen another twenty-five years, but withstanding all odds Fort Marot was completed in AD 623 and dedicated to the generations that had been rendered homeless. The inauguration was marked with great pomp and show. The neighbours could no longer deny the Bhatis. They were there to stay. Sursen was hailed as the Bhati rao.

To commemorate the event, a new calendar was established. AD 623, became the zero year of the Bhati era. The Gupta empire of Hindustan had crumbled and Harsh Vardhan, a young relative, was as yet in the process of salvaging what remained. Rao Sursen was free to declare himself an independent sovereign.

Curiously the zero year of Muslim Hizra era was AD 622 – the year Hazrat Mohammad fled from Mecca to Medina.

Rao Raghu Rao

Raghu Rao succeeded his father at Marot.
A fort of their own lent them stability and the Bhatis dug their roots in. Their obsession for the mountains of Afghanistan and the long lost lands of Punjab waned. The sands of the Thar were accepted as the new challenge.

But the desert provided no sustenance. Having lost their hold over the lush river valleys, the Bhatis took to armed robbery: raiding caravans plying the trade routes. What started as a desperate measure in difficult times soon evolved into a lucrative profession that received royal patronage.

The love story of Mumal and Mahendra.

This story has been told in Dhar, Gujarat, Sind and Jaisalmer, each version differing only slightly from the other. While Mahendra is unanimously acknowledged as the Soda-Parmar prince of Umarkot, Mumal's identity varies. She is identified variously as the daughter of Raja Brijbahan Parmar of Dhar, the daughter of Raja Dant of Kathiawar and lastly as a maidservant, in the service of the queen of Raja Salha Solanki of Gujarat, whose charms the raja was unable to resist.

In the first version Mumal and Mahendra, both being Parmars, indulged in an illicit affair as marriage within the same family group was prohibited. In the second, Mumal incurred her father's wrath and was banished for having carelessly given away the tooth of a wild animal that granted him supernatural powers. The last version holds that she was banished from Gujarat but permitted to take with her the jewels and money lavished on her by Raja Salha.

Mumal arrived at Lodurva and built herself a palace on the banks of the river Kak beside a Shiva temple. A labyrinth led to her rooms, the secret of which was known to two people alone – her sister Sumal and a faithful maidservant. One night, Mahendra Soda arrived with his sister and brother-in-law and camped by the riverside. Mumal noticed the royal entourage. Her servants were sent across with refreshments. With it was an invitation to pay Mumal a visit. But each guest would have to make his own way through the labyrinth. While Mahendra's brother-in-law returned without solving the puzzle of the labyrinth, Mahendra charmed Mumal's maid into leading him through to the interiors. Mumal's beauty and her celebrated wit matched Mahendra's own and he swore to return to her in secret every night. Raika, the camel herder, came to Mahendra's aid and Chikal, the swiftest camel in the desert, was pressed into service.

Every morning Mahendra was to be found sleeping peacefully. But his many wives failed to bear children and Mahendra's mother grew suspicious. Her daughters-in-law maintained a dignified silence. However, there was one thing that remained unexplained. Her son's hair was found drenched every morning with water dripping through the string cot upon which he lay. The resourceful mother collected some of it and took it as evidence to her husband. Mahendra's father applied the water to his blind eyes and lo his sight was restored. Their son was quite obviously returning from a tryst across the sacred Kak. Chikal was withdrawn and Raika, who received a tongue-lashing from Mahendra's wives, was left with little choice. A female camel with a pronounced limp was allotted to Mahendra.

Sumal chose that very night to insist upon a glimpse of her sister's lover and dressed as a musician she waited in Mumal's bedchamber. But Mahendra took long in coming and by the time the camel limped across to Lodurva both sisters had fallen asleep. To Mahendra it seemed that Mumal had taken another lover. Departing quietly, he scribbled upon her door a heart wrenching couplet bidding her goodbye. Mumal cursed her sister and sent many explanations to Mahendra but there was no reply. At last the sisters resolved to go to Umarkot. Sumal explained the part she had played in creating the misunderstanding and the sisters returned home. Mahendra hurried to Lodurva at the first opportunity. But he was too late. Unable to bear the separation, Mumal had taken leave of life.

Ruins still stand in Chhatral village that are referred to as Mumal ki medi or Mumal's house

Rao Mulraj

Mulraj succeeded in AD 655. Harsh Vardhan had died seven years ago and there was no one to challenge the rise of the Bhatis. Mulraj reconquered Bhatner and the lands around Mammanvahan. The borders of his kingdom approached the areas that would later be called Tanot.

Mulraj ruled for twenty-seven years and was succeeded by his son.

Rao Udai Rao

Udai Rao came to the throne in AD 682. It was during his lifetime that great changes took place in Arabia – changes that were to affect the destiny of India. Hazrat Mohammad who had begun preaching the tenets of Islam in AD 600, had been succeeded by relatives who called themselves the khalifas. Whereas Mohammad confined himself to teaching and reforming fellow Arabs, the khalifas determined to expose the world to the might of Islam. The building of the empire of Islam began. The lands that bordered Arabia were the first to witness the zeal of the would-be saviours.

Two years before Udai came to the throne, Muawiya, the fifth khalifa, had passed away. It had been Muawiya's dream to see the borders of his Islamic empire extend into the realm of Hindustan. That dream was to be realised by Khalifa Walid I, the conqueror of Spain. Within months Mohammad bin Kasim was deputed to Sind. The Islamic conquest of that first fragment of Hindustan took place in AD 712. So firmly was it established that it would never be dislodged.

However, the great general incurred his khalifa's displeasure and was put to death even as he planned to add Kannauj to his master's dominion. Walid survived his general by not more than three years but the march of Islam did not cease. Though he was unable to enjoy the credit of having added Constantinople to the crown of Islam, Walid left behind an empire that stretched from the western border of Tibet, through Afghanistan, Persia, Egypt and Carthage, to Spain.

Udai Rao ruled peacefully for forty-seven years. The Arabs did not enjoy too many successful missions within India and the 'Hindus' remained largely unperturbed by their presence.

Rao Manjham Rao

Both Manjham Rao and Bappa Rawal of Mewar were contemporaries. Junaid arrived as the governor of Sind and his immediate target was Gujarat, for there lay the important ports so valuable to the Indo-Arab sea trade. Rajput kingdoms bordering the trade route leading to Gujarat were targeted, for they lay too close for comfort. Junaid made plans for campaigns in Gujarat, Mewar, Ajmer and Ujjain.

The passage lay through Bhati lands and the Bhatis of Marot were forced into becoming willing accomplices.

Rao Kehar

Manjham Rao's son Kehar succeeded to the throne of Marot. His brother Mulraj and he were notorious. They raided with impunity the great caravans that headed west carrying spices, silk and treasure looted from the kingdoms of Hindustan. Disguised as camel merchants, the brothers shadowed Arab traders. Great mercantile towns had come up along the banks of the Indus, their citizens cousins to the Bhatis. They were all hand in glove and profits filtered through to every section of society.

Rani Kamlavati, the Jhali queen, was visited by the mother goddess in a dream. She was commanded to name her unborn son after the goddess. With Yuvraj Tanno's birth the parents gave thanks. Tanno Devi was promised a fort that would bear her name. The lands earmarked for her came to be known as Tanot. The goddess was pleased and the fortunes of the Bhatis multiplied.

The Arab influence on Multan was a new threat to contend with. A new dynasty had taken over from the descendents of Walid I and in 762, the Abbassids shifted the capital of their empire from Damascus to Baghdad. Islamic fervour was at its height. Yuvraj Tanno crossed the Sutlej

Tanno Devi made known her desires. The fattest male buffalo was to be sacrificed to her. Yuvraj Tanno set off with his Solankini wife. Sarangde was young and found the going difficult. Tanno asked his brother Bhadria to go on ahead.

Bhadria reached quickly and made the sacrifice in his brother's name. The royal couple in the meanwhile struggled over scorching sands. Finally, still twenty kos away from the devi's abode, they stopped at a hillock, the Ber Tibba, that bore a ber tree (Indian Jujube).

Yuvrani Sarangde was near exhaustion. Planting a dry twig upon the hillock she sank to her knees in prayer. She could go no further and would never have the good fortune of laying her eyes upon the devi. Sarangde pleaded for mercy.

The dry twig sprouted the next morning and the devi appeared. With her was Bhadria. The yuvrani's plea had touched her heart and blessing the royal couple, the devi chose the hillock for her temple. A wide circle of land was marked out. Here cattle would be free to graze. Out of gratitude to his brother. Tanno named the area Bhadria-ji.

The ber tree remains atop the hillock. It is said that the devi still comes to enjoy the swings that have been set up for the purpose and Ber Tibba continues to be the premier site for her worship.

Yuvraj Tanno built her a second temple within the fort of Tanot. The devi came personally to install her own image along with those of her seven divine siblings to confront the Arabs. The Langa-Solankis of Multan lost their land in the process, to the Bhatis, as did the Varaha-Parmars, Bhutta-Solankis and Channa Rajputs.

Vala – ancient Vallabhi – in Gujarat fell to the Arabs in AD 770, bringing to its end the 200-year rule of the Maitrika dynasty[7]. Kehar recognised the need for a castle powerful enough to withstand them. This was to be the devi's fort. It took him seventeen years, for the Varaha-Parmars, the deposed rulers of the region, put up a stiff opposition. It was inaugurated in AD 787, and Tanot became the new Bhati capital.

Upon the west bank of the Sutlej (now Multan, Pakistan), the construction of a second fort, that would keep watch on the activities of the Arabs, was begun.

Rao Tanno

Tanno was crowned at Tanot in AD 805. Four years later Haroun-al-Rashid, the fifth of the Abbassid khalifas, was dead. The devi appeared once again. This time in the form of Vijayseni. A son would be born and the devi put forward a demand: yet another fort.

Tanno was blessed and his heir was named Vijay Rao. Work was still going on upon the fort on the Sutlej and Tanno was pressed for the want of funds. The devi's demands were incessant and miraculously treasure was unearthed beneath a ber tree (Indian jujube).

The designated lands were occupied and the fort of Bijnot (now in Pakistan) was raised in AD 816. Around the same time a number of several successful raids were recorded in the Bhati annals. Within four years the fort on the Sutlej was complete. Rao Tanno named it Kehror after his father and within two temples were consecrated – one to Tanno Devi and the other to Vijayseni. Father and son had both devoted themselves to the mother goddess. But it was the victorious form that had chosen to be served by crown prince Vijay.

---

7. With demise of the Maitrikas, the Pratiharas (Gujjars who had assumed royal status) dominated Gujarat. In AD 960, they were overcome by the Solankis (Chalukyas), who had set up base in the Chawura-Parmar city of Anhilwara Patan.

Vijay was victorious over the Varaha-Parmars of Bathinda (Punjab) but even as he celebrated, the Langa-Solankis of Multan and the Varaha-Parmars, who had lost their lands to Tanno, united. The prince hurried towards Tanot. It was a formidable force that had arrayed against Tanot. In desperation he pleaded before his goddess:

'Accept my head before it is lost in battle.'

Setting his fears at rest, the devi slipped one of her own gold bracelets (chura) onto his arm. Churala Vijay Rao rode into battle brandishing the gold chura.

The enemy regrouped and enlisted the aid of the king of Ghazni. For four days, the defenders locked themselves up within their castle but on the fifth, their gates burst open and led by the heir of Tanot, they fell upon the attackers with such ferocity that Tanot was soon freed from all troubles.

Tanno gave himself up to religion. History is ambiguous as to whether he willingly abdicated to make way for his son or was forced into doing so.

Yugraj Vijay Rao – Churala

Vijay Rao came to the throne during the lifetime of his father and celebrated his succession by a teeka-dowr against his enemies, the Varaha-Parmars. The clans united once again against the Bhatis. Frustrated by their lack of success they took recourse to treachery.

Rao Amar, the Varaha chief of Bathinda, sent an offer of marriage to the heir of Tanot – five-year-old prince Deoraj. Rao Tanno accepted the coconut and while he remained behind at Tanot, the little bridegroom, accompanied by his father and 800 of his clansmen embarked upon their journey. The ceremony duly took place. The revelry began. But someone at an unguarded moment managed to relieve Yugraj Vijay Rao of his divine bracelet. This was the cue for the attack. The Bhatis were all slain but their little prince managed to escape.

The enemies of Tanot had been awaiting the signal. The clans rained

With his pursuers hot on his heels, Deoraj, in the arms of a cousin – a camel trainer – fled. They travelled many miles over the sands and the Varahas gave up the trail convinced that it was the wrong one. But they returned. This time with an expert tracker. The trail that led from Bathinda was picked up once again. The camel appeared to have passed beneath a tree. But as it came out of the shade it appeared to step lightly upon the sand. The tracks were no more than a few hours old. The Varahas looked about. There were no human tracks, but then they could have been meticulously covered as the fugitive made his way across the sands. They headed towards the only habitation in the vicinity.

A Brahmin worked upon his fields. By his side were five boys. The Varahas seated themselves under the shade of a tree and chewed on their beeras. As the noonday sun rose to its height, the Brahmin's wife made her way to the fields. The Brahmin, who until now had been intent upon his work, called out.

'Let the youngest as usual be fed by the eldest.'

Wordlessly, the brahmani set out the meals. The eldest of the five boys pulled the youngest towards himself. Ratan fed both himself and the little boy that had wandered upon their lands that day. No explanations had been required and the child had not resisted the sacred thread that had been placed about his neck.

The Varahas watched awhile and then having watered their camels made their way back. But in that act of graciousness, Ratan lost forever his claim to the caste of the Brahmins. His days in the home of his father had come to an end. That evening Yogi Ratan Nath left to make his own way in the world.

The child stayed amongst the Brahmins for a year and was then escorted to the village of the Bhuttas and delivered to the safety of his mother's arms. Waving a handful of salt over his head and throwing it into a pot of water, she declared, 'may your enemies melt away like this.'

Yogi Ratan had, in the meantime, stopped at Bathinda while on his way to Kashmir. He whispered in the ears of the little bride. Her husband lived. The child and her mother were overjoyed. They determined to keep it a secret. Having enjoyed their hospitality, Yogi Ratan set out once again leaving his few earthly belongings in their care.

Maintaining utmost secrecy, mother and daughter invited Deoraj to live with them. By sheer stroke of destiny, Deoraj was allotted Ratan's room. It had been a while since Deoraj had met his benefactor. The yogi had since conquered the spirit world. No longer did the material world hold any charm. For him was the simple life: robes of ochre – the garb of the ascetic. In each of his ears he wore a prickly seed earning him the epithet of the Kanferra Yogi. Among the mysteries of the universe that had been disclosed to him was the secret of alchemy. This he guarded carefully preventing it from falling into the wrong hands. The Ras Kumfa, his pot of chemicals, had been left in the care of the queen of Bathinda.

Deoraj was tidying up when a drop of elixir from Ratan's pot fell onto his dagger. The blade turned to gold. At once, the crafty Bhati knew what he had to do. Taking the pot he stole away.

At home, his maternal uncle, the Bhutta chief, was generous. 'Take as much land as can be encircled by ropes made from the hide of a single buffalo.'

Cleverly soaking the hide for several days in water, Deoraj pulled it into long narrow strips. The land it encompassed was far greater than his uncle could ever have imagined. He then proceeded to build himself a castle, which he named Deogarh or Derawar. Reports were brought back of the unusual castle that was coming up. It was fortified beyond belief and no one could have predicted that the seventeen-year-old, who had lost all his worldly possessions and had begged for a piece of land, could possibly have built such a castle. It was coming up on Bhutta land and the alarm was sounded. The chief arrived with his men determined to raze it to the ground. Deoraj's mother came out to meet the assailants. She welcomed her brother and invited him in. The 120 leaders of the Bhutta clan were requested to enter in groups of ten. Patiently they awaited their turn, oblivious to the fate that was being meted out inside. The bodies of the dead were cast over the walls.

The past, however, would not let go. Yogi Ratan came to confront a royal thief. The thief's identity had never been in doubt and Derawar had quite obviously been built with the ascetic's gold. Acknowledging his guilt, Deoraj declared himself forever the yogi's disciple. Donning the simple garb of an ascetic – a robe of ochre, a prickly seed in his ear and with a gourd in hand – he walked about his city crying, 'Alak Niranjan, god is great.' The title of rao was abandoned and he became the first Bhati rawal.

The ascetic marked his forehead with a teeka and declared him a sidhi – one who has achieved the impossible. Exacting a promise that the rites of inauguration would never be abandoned, Ratan left only to reappear every time a new rawal was crowned.

The dynasty of the Bhatis were beholden to Ratan. A temple was dedicated to Yogi Ratan Nath and his descendents were appointed as spiritual teachers to the Bhati rawals.

down upon the Bhati fort. Old Rao Tanno was shaken out of his complacence. His son was lost as were his people. Of his grandson, there was no trace. Tanot was doomed. Tanno, who had long withdrawn himself from war and politics, resumed charge once more. But the Bhatis knew they were lost.

Deoraj's mother, a Bhutta-Solankini, was spared the flames of the jauhar. With the royal insignia of the Bhatis, she made her way to the village of her father.

The saka of Tanot took place in AD 841. The enemy occupied the six Bhati forts – Tanot, Marot, Mammanvahan, Bijnot, Kehror and Bhatner.

While the Rajputs shed their own blood oblivious to the Muslim threat that loomed over their heads, the Islamic world itself was in the throes of a power struggle. Having come to distrust their own people, the khalifas had and surrounded themselves with Turks who acted as their personal bodyguards. By the middle of the ninth century the power of the khalifas came to an abrupt end with the Turks appointing themselves as the new leaders of the empire of Islam.

Rawal Sidh Deoraj

As if by miracle, the little prince escaped and grew to manhood. Helped by his maternal relatives, he built himself a new fort – Deogarh or Deorawal. The name later evolved into Derawar[8] (now in Pakistan). A new beginning was signalled with the adoption of a new title. Deoraj became the first Bhati rawal.

Anointed by his spiritual guru, Yogi Ratan Nath, Deoraj flew aloft a new flag. It was the Bawta – the royal emblem that would henceforth lead the Bhatis. It would serve as a constant reminder of their glorious ancestry. The orange shield in the centre bore a picture of the ramparts of Derawar (later said to be those of Jaisalmer) and an arm that held the bent Swang. Holding it up were a pair of stags – ones that drew

---

8. Derawar Fort lies within Pakistan. It was captured by Abbasis in 1735. The Bahawalpur Gazetteer (1904), records that in 1747, Nawab Bahawal Khan lost the fort but it was regained by the Abbasis dynasty once again in 1804.

the chariot of the moon. High above them soared a vulture – the form that Vijayseni assumed when accompanying Deoraj's father, Yugraj Vijay Rao, into battle. Inscribed below were the words Chattralay Yadavpati. At a later date, when Lanjha Beejy Rao would accept the responsibility of defending the northern approaches to Hindustan, the words Uttar Bhat Kinwar Bhati were to be added.

Reorganising the Bhati clans[9], Deoraj reclaimed Bhatner. The Varahas and Langas were beaten into submission and at last, the clans acknowledged the supremacy of the Bhatis. Deoraj built himself an extensive kingdom grabbed from the lands of the Parmars. Not even were his Bhutta-Solanki relatives spared.

The treacherous Varaha-Parmars of Bathinda could not go unpunished. When several attempts failed, Deoraj suspected the hand of his own queen. The Varaha princess, his companion since childhood, was put to death and his unborn heir seized from her womb. Bathinda was occupied and the Parmars shown no mercy. Women, children and unborn babes torn from wombs were put to the sword.

Pugal was snatched from its Parmar rulers in AD 853. This alarmed the Puriharas of Mandor, for Pugal had until now acted as a buffer state.

To the south of Derawar lived the Lodra-Parmars who ruled from Lodurva, the western fortress of the Nau Kothi of Maroo. A proposal was made for the hand of the Lodra chief's daughter. The Lodra, Raja Jasman Parmar resisted but his people, overcome by the generosity of the Bhati, pleaded on his behalf. To celebrate the wedding four reservoirs were built for Lodurva. Tradesar, named after Rao Tanno; Videsar, Yugraj Vijay Rao; Derasar, Rawal Deoraj; and Lachisar after Lachmi, Deoraj's favourite queen.

Raja Jasman suspected that it was most likely a ruse and that he was going to be victimised for belonging to the race of the Parmars. The bridegroom, he stipulated, would bring with him no more than a hundred men. He had completely overlooked one fact: there were twelve gates to his fort. On the eve of the wedding a bridegroom stood at each gate accompanied by a hundred cavaliers.

---

9. Among the armies that came to his aid were those of Jam Lakha Phulana Jareja Bhati of Kerakot, Kachchh. Lakha, an immortal name in the mythology of Kachchh and Sind was a contemporary of Deoraj.

Twenty-five kilometres to the south of Bhuj in the region of Kachchh lay Kerakot. Here ruled the jam of the Jarejas.

The traders of Kerakot had profited during the generous monsoons and hoarded great stores of grain. The wicked merchants then cast a spell and years of unending drought and famine followed. The common man despaired as prices soared.

Phula, the prince of Kerakot stumbled upon the little secret. The spell had been written on a parchment and tied to the antlers of a wild stag. As long as the parchment remained dry, Kachchh would receive no rain. The prince set off in search of the stag. The parchment was located and immersed in water. Monsoon clouds gathered and the earth was deluged. Caught in the storm, Phula was near death when he was rescued by a tribe of Ahirs. The prince married the chieftain's daughter and returned home leaving his pregnant wife with her kinsmen. A son was born and he received the name Lakha Phulana (Lakho Pulani). When the time came, Lakha succeeded to the throne of the Jarejas as the next jam.

Lakha was a renowned warrior famed for his generosity towards the needy. His name became a byword in the lands of Kachchh, Sind and Marwar. To gain a victory over the great Lakha became a quest for many a Rajput. Time and again their triumph over a mythical Lakha has been trumpeted through the annals of the subsequent eras.

Though Jam Lakha Phulana Jareja Bhati came to the throne in AD 844, three others who shared his name succeeded in the years 1250, 1320 and 1350. Sihoji Rathore, who fathered the Rathore clan of Maroo, claimed to have accomplished this glorious quest in AD 1212.

By AD 1335, another branch of the family moved from Sind into Kachchh. But the new jam soon gave up his kingdom, donating it to the charuns and dedicated himself to religion. His sons relinquished their faith and turned to Islam.

Jiskurn, a merchant of Derawar, carried on a brisk trade with his counterparts at Dhar (Madhya Pradesh). On one such visit, he found himself arrested by Raja Brij Bahan Parmar (Puar) and thrown into jail. The only way out was for him to hand over all his goods.

Jiskurn returned and displayed the marks of the iron collar around his neck. The rawal was outraged. The insult had to be avenged. Not a drop of water would pass his lips until then.

The distance to Dhar was fair bit and it was impractical to keep the rawal thirsty. A Dhar of clay was created. It would be symbolically destroyed before the army marched. But there were Parmars serving in the Bhati army who resisted. Dhar would not be dishonoured[10], not even one of clay.

Jahan Puar thyan Dhar Hai	Where there is a Puar, therein lies Dhar
Or Dhar thyan Puar	And Dhar where exists a Puar
Dhar bina Puar Nahin	A Puar cannot exist without Dhar
Or nahin Puar bina Dhar .	Nor Dhar without Puars.

Deoraj was impressed with their valour. When the last Parmar had fallen, making certain that their families were well provided for, the rawal marched to Dhar.

Brij Bahan Parmar defended his lands for five days until he fell with 800 of his men. The Bawta was unfurled in the city of Dhar and the Bhatis celebrated by shifting their capital to Lodurva.

---

10. An identical tale is related in the annals of Bundi. Maharana Lakha of Mewar, unable to dominate Bundi, declared war upon a clay model of Taragarh but to his surprise the Hada-Chauhans in his service turned against him, fiercely defending the mock structure.

Scarcely had the gates been opened when the Bhatis drew their swords. Three Lodra-Parmar princesses became unwilling brides as their relatives were put to death. Lodurva was occupied and in AD 857, it became the new capital.

The Parmar of Dhar remained the sole Parmar prince in power but he did not dare take on the might of the Bhatis. Deoraj's kingdom extended from Bathinda in Punjab to Dhat in Sind and bordered Mandor, Jalor and Abu. Twelve forts were controlled directly by him – Lodurva, Pugal, Satalmer, Kehror, Bhatner, Bijnot, Mammanvahan, Marot, Kiradu, Parkar, Rohri and Bhakkar. His kingdom came to be described as Valla Mandal.

Deoraj was assassinated during a hunt. He had ruled for fifty-five years.

Rawal Mundha.

Mundha succeeded his great-grandfather. In the robes of an ascetic, he was seated on the gaddi of Lodurva and his teeka-dowr was led against the assassins of Rawal Sidh Deoraj.

It was during his time that Turkish settlers moved into Ghazni. They retained the name that had been in use since the days of the great Yaduvanshi ancestor – Raja Gaj. Lodurva faced the brunt as Sultan Mahmud of Ghazni began his raiding expeditions to India. The fort of Mundhakot was raised upon the banks of the Indus. It was lost sometime later to the amirs of Sind and came to be known as the Aghadh-ka-kot.

Rawal Bachu

Bachu succeeded his father. He was the son-in-law of Ballabhsen Solanki, the raja of Patan. The Bhatis of the period were a part of the Chauhan empire acknowledging Govind Raj II Chauhan of Ajmer as sovereign.

The sultan of Ghazni targeted the Bhatis on several occasions in an effort to shake their hold on their ancestral land – the Hill of Jud that lay amongst the salt ranges of western Punjab. His third assault on Lodurva coincided with the sixteenth and most infamous of all his raiding expeditions. Mahmud had embarked from Ghazni in the December of AD 1023 enroute to Gujarat, his target – the fabulous wealth of the temple of Somnath. But within Bachu's lifetime, the Ghaznavid Turks came to be dominated by a new force – the Seljuk Turks.

Rawal Dusaj

Dusaj, said to be a giant of a man, succeeded to his father's throne at Lodurva. Though he had a grown son, Jaisal, it was his youngest child – the son of the princess of Dungarpur[11] – who was named successor.

The fortunate Yuvraj Beeji Rao enjoyed a rather colourful personality. Sent by his father to marry the Parmar princess of Dhar, the yuvraj came across the Solanki prince of Anhilwara Patan and Vijai Singh[12], rawal of Mewar. The three princes in a joint ceremony were to marry the three daughters of the Parmar of Dhar. With every step that the Guhilot took, water delicately scented with camphor, was sprinkled about him. He left behind a fragrant trail. The bemused Bhati ordered his people to buy up the all the camphor that was available in Dhar. A small fortune was spent and the camphor poured into the lakes and reservoirs meant for the use of the common man. Long after the wedding was over, every sip of water would bring back glorious memories of the day when the Bhati prince came to wed the daughter of Dhar. Beeji Rao earned himself the nickname Lanjha – one who is fond of the good things of life.

---

11. According to the annals of Mewar, when Rawal Kshem Singh succeeded to the throne of Ahar in 1168, two of his brothers chose to go their own way. While Rahup established the dynasty of the Sisodia ranas, Mahup annexed Dungarpur. Dungarpur was brought under the direct control of the crown by Rawal Samant Singh in AD 1172. Rawal Beeji Rao's mother, the princess of Dungarpur who had married Rawal Dusaj (1044 – 1122) therefore could not have been related to the Guhilot rawals or Sisodia ranas of Mewar.
12. Rawal Vijai Singh (1107 – 1127) ruled from Ahar.

The temple of Shahasralingas – the 1,000 lingas – and a reservoir was built at Lodurva to mark the return of the yuvraj and his bride.

Rawal Beeji Rao – Lanjha

Lanjha, who patronised a practioner of the black arts, ruled a large territory that stretched from Bhatner to the banks of the Sutlej. His wealth was attributed to his mastery over the spirit world and he made powerful alliances by marrying into prominent Rajput families of the day.

An awakening was taking place for the first time amongst the 'Hindus'. The Muslim threat could no longer be ignored. The princes that met at Anhilwara Patan, to celebrate Lanjha's wedding with the daughter of Sidh Raja Jai Singh Solanki, formed a confederation. Lanjha accepted the responsibility of defending the north-western frontier of India. His mother-in-law, while anointing his forehead with the tilak of marriage pronounced him Uttar Bhat Kinwar Bhati or the defender of the northern gate. Lanjha became the buffer that stood between the powerful Solankis of Gujarat and the armies of Islam that waited across the border.

Lanjha ruled for twenty-five years and his son by the Solanki queen was named heir.

Rawal Bhoj Dev (Bhojdeo)

Bhojdeo succeeded to the throne, much to the distress of his uncle. Jaisal, at his father's command, had given up his birthright travelled far into Punjab and had devoted his youth to extending the limits of the Bhati kingdom in the north-eastern direction. Perhaps he had hoped that the throne would be returned to him once his youngest brother died. The succession of his nephew was too much to bear.

Like his father before him, Bhojdeo was always surrounded by Solankis. That they feared the elderly Jaisal and the sympathy that he commanded amongst the Bhatis was evident in their choice of bodyguards. At last Jaisal began to conspire against his nephew. The death of Bhojdeo's grandfather,

Sidh Raja Jai Singh Solanki, served as encouragement.

Jaisal appealed to the Ghaznavid sultan's governor in Sind. Sultan Behram Shah of Ghazni had granted Mohammad Ghuri, a fugitive Turk from Ghur (in Afghanistan), asylum and the office of the governor of Sind. The man who was to one day rule all of Ghur and Ghazni; and declare himself master of all Hindustan now sent his armies to Lodurva under the command of Karim Khan and Majer Khan.

Bhojdeo, who had inherited the title of Uttar Bhat Kinwar Bhati from his father, advanced to the border. But the Bhatis were confused. What were the intentions of the invading army? Was it Lodurva that they wanted or was the real target the wealth of Anhilwara Patan? In any case Bhojdeo had sworn to defend the northern portal. The youth wrote to his uncle: Jaisal's place was by his side and that together they would uphold the honour of the Bhatis. But the mercenary army had already set out. There was no turning back.

Young Bhojdeo met his death upon the field and the sacking of Lodurva began. It continued endlessly. It is said that a warning had been issued and the people asked to evacuate before the Muslims entered. Eventually it became too much for even Jaisal to bear. The octogenarian raised his dagger. The killing of Majer Khan brought the Muslims to their senses and Karim left quietly with his men.

Bhojdeo earned himself the glory of a martyr and legends were woven around his gallantry. A temple was built in his memory upon the Asnikot road – the site of his last battle.

The vulnerability of this ancient fort had made itself all too apparent and the new rawal looked for a more secure site to build his capital.

The love song of Dhola Maru.

Said to have been composed around AD 1000, this immortal story sings of the love between Dhola, the Kachwaha prince of Narwar, and Maru (Marwani), the Parmar princess of Pugal. Several versions exist. The one prevalent in Jaisalmer was re-written during the reign of Rawal Har Raj.

Raja Nal and Queen Damayanti of Narwar lived in the era of the *Mahabharat*. The royal couple travelled to the holy lake of Pushkar to give thanks for the birth of Prince Salha, affectionately referred to as Dhola. Also visiting Pushkar with their infant daughter, Maru, was Raja Pingal and his queen. They had come to pray for their drought affected kingdom of Pugal.

The Parmar princess caught Damayanti's eye. A marriage was proposed. The infants were wed at Pushkar with the understanding that they were to be united once they came of age.

Years went by and the children grew up, ignorant of the wedding that had been contracted on their behalf.

When Dhola came of age, he took as wife the daughter of Bhim Singh of Malwa. The Malwa princess, Malwani, bent to touch her mother-in-law's feet but Queen Damayanti thought she detected a hint of arrogance on the younger woman's face. Determined to put her in her place, Damayanti revealed the secret of Dhola's first marriage. That she was a second wife, came as a shock to the new bride. Her husband remained as yet unaware and Malwani resolved to keep it that way. Guards were posted on every road that led to Narwar with orders to kill all travellers coming from the direction of Pugal.

Maru of the full moon face and swan like grace learnt of her husband in far away Narwar. She longed to be with him and grew saddened with every passing day that went without his coming to claim her. Meanwhile, it was whispered in Pugal that the union was doomed. All the young women of Pugal opted to remain single or refrained from joining their husbands for fear of adding to the burden of Maru's heart.

At last the bards of Pugal relented and one managed to slip past Malwani's guards. As the evening sky darkened, he positioned himself below the palace balcony. The poignant lyrics carried the message from the wife that waited by the desert's edge. Dhola was enchanted.

Malwani despaired. She watched her husband like a hawk. She would not sleep without securely holding his finger in her mouth. But though he offered her words of comfort, Dhola plotted a get away. As Malwani slept, he slipped a wooden finger between her lips and left. Leaping upon his camel's back Dhola spurred it on, unaware that a thread bound its tail with his queen's toe. The tug woke the sleeping woman and she rushed out brandishing her sword. But she was too late. Her sword barely glanced off the tip of its tail as the camel vanished into the night.

Dhola was united with Maru but true to the prophecy, the return to Narwar was fraught with danger.

The couple stopped for the night. To prevent his camel from straying, Dhola bent one of its hind legs at the knee and bound it with twine. As the couple rested upon the sands a venomous snake edged up to the woman. A grieving Dhola prepared to light her pyre when he was approached by a yogi and yogini – Shiva and Parvati, the celestial couple, who had assumed human forms. Parvati pleaded with her husband and the yogi agreed to revive the lifeless Maru. The benefactors departed and the couple once again prepared to resume their journey. But standing on their path, barring the way, were two dacoits.

Oomra and Soomra had long been in love with the Parmar princess. They could not bear to see her go. Dhola lost no time in mounting his camel and pulling Maru into his arms. The urgency was not lost upon the valiant beast and it responded instantly to its master's command. In a matter of moments, the dacoits found themselves left far behind. As Dhola leaned across to slash at the twine that still bound his camel's leg, a charun called out to the dacoits. 'Give up the chase for it was lost long before the camel's leg was untied.'

Back in Narwar Malwani, overcome by Maru's gentle nature, welcomed her graciously. The two queens lived peacefully ever after.

Ten miles from Lodurva, upon the summit of a rocky ridge sat a solitary ascetic, deep in meditation. Baba Isal received Jaisal's homage and pointed to a triple peaked hill. During the age of the epics, Lord Krishna accompanied by Arjun, the Pandav, had come to attend a sacrifice.

The Trikuta tugged at the Lord's heartstrings and a deep seated desire welled up: 'Here a son will come and raise a castle.'

'But where,' pointed out Arjun, 'was the water source?' Krishna struck the ground with his mace. A stream of sweet water bubbled forth. Inscribed on the margin of the fountain were the words:

'Oh prince of Yaduvansh! Come into this land, and on this mountain top erect a triangular castle.

Lodurva is destroyed, but only five kos away is Jessanoh, a site of twice its strength.

Prince, your name is Jaisal and you are of the Yadu race, abandon Lodurpura, erect your dwelling here.'

In the shimmering heart of the desert where the sunbeams set the yellow sands afire, rose the golden ramparts of Jaisal's fort[13]. It took its place as the second of the great forts of Rajasthan, Chittaurgarh being counted as the first. But unlike Chittaurgarh, Jaisalmer was never to face permanent abandonment. AD 1156, marked the beginning of their formal history and the Bhatis became the unquestioned lords of the desert.

While matters of state were continued from Lodurva, rooms in the new fort were occupied as soon as they were built. Despite an eleven-year reign, Jaisal did not live to see the completion of his fort. It took his son, Salbahan, another twenty-one years.

Located at the southern end of a low range of hills, it sat strategically up on the camel train routes leading from India to central Asia, Persia, Egypt, Arabia and Africa. Jaisalmer levied taxes upon passing caravans. Prosperity brought peace and with it flourished the arts. Elaborate mansions were built with the yellow sandstone that distinguished this corner of the desert and wealthy Jain merchants patronised the construction of temples.

A city with its network of narrow paved roads and numerous temples came up outside the walls of the fort. In time it was fenced in by another massive set of walls. At the centre the Trikuta towered bearing Jaisal's fort upon its crown proudly flaunting the standard of the Bhatis.

A desert track of fifteen kilometres led to the ancient capital of Lodurva. The old fort guarding the western edge of the desert had been left to decay. Its temples remained as the sole reminder of its days of glory.

Jaisalmer became one of the kingdoms to be included within Captain Tod's area of control.

---

13. Jaisalmer is oldest fort in Rajasthan to have remained in continuous occupation. The local yellow coloured stone that was used in its construction earned it the name the golden fort.

Rawal Jaisal

Wisely Jaisal desisted from assuming Lanjha's titles, for he had made many enemies among the powerful Solankis. The Chauhan empire was at its height and Jaisal chose to remain subservient.

He appointed as his diwan a Pahu Bhati, Biram Singh, who was a great-grandson of Rawal Bachu. Unfortunately, Jaisal's firstborn and heir, Kalan, had fallen foul of the ministers and had been banished. His younger son was named heir apparent.

Rawal Salbahan II

Salbahan's was a name famous in the annals of Jaisalmer. He was the first rawal to be crowned within the precincts of Jaisalmer.

His first expedition was led against Rao Jugbahan of Kathiawar, whose rule extended to Jalor and parts of the Aravalli. The Katthi rao was slain and Salbahan returned, the proud possessor of Katthi horses and camels.

A coconut arrived from the court of the Deora chief of Sirohi. Leaving his eldest son in charge of Jaisalmer, Salbahan left to claim his bride. He returned to find that Bijal had declared himself king. In vain did he reason with his traitorous son but finding him adamant, Salbahan left for Derawar choosing never to return.

Rawal Bijal

Bijal did not remain king for long either. His foster brother, who had encouraged him to turn against his father, grew too powerful and Bijal killed himself in remorse. Some say he was sent away to the Bhati fort of Uch while Salbahan stayed on in Derawar.

Uch became the first Bhati fort to fall (1175 – 1176), not because of any lack of ability on Bijal's part but due to the treachery of his rani, as the armies of Mohammad Ghuri, the sultan of Ghazni, embarked upon the invasion of India.

The descendents of Rawal Bachu had settled in the low-lying Kangra hills of Sirmur near the modern city of Simla. The Sirmur Bhati was without a son and appealed to Rawal Salbahan to send him an heir. Salbahan's grandson Manrup was chosen. As he made his way to Sirmur, two events took place. His wife gave birth to a son but Manrup himself did not survive the journey. With the newborn infant in her arms the grieving queen arrived at her destination. The baby had been born under a Palas tree (Flame of the Forest) and bore the name Palasia. He became the first of the Palasia Bhatis.

Jaisal's third son, Rai Hem, had long left the family hearth to seek his fortune. It was in the lush plains of Punjab, that he settled and fathered the clan of the Sidh Bhati Jats, some of whom accepted the teachings of a great preacher of the sixteenth century – Guru Nanak. They became his disciples or shishyas (Sikhs). Phula, a son of this clan, rose to prominence in the time of Akbar and his son became the ruler of the kingdoms of Nabha and Jind. Sardar Ala Singh, a descendent of Phula's youngest son, was named the first maharaja of Patiala[14] by Emperor Shah Alam II in AD 1801. Nabha, Jind and Patiala came to be known collectively as the Phulkian states.

Sadav Singh, yet another descendent, settled in the village of Ahlu near Lahore and fathered the clan of Ahluwalia Bhatis. A descendent of Sadav's brother, Sardar Jassa Singh Ahluwalia, seized Kapurthala from Ibrahim Bhati in AD 1777, and became the founder of the Kapurthala dynasty.

---

14. On 25 April 1927, an assembly of Jareja Bhatis convened at Jamnagar and allowed Lieutenant-General HH Maharaja Sir Bhupinder Singh, the maharaja of Patiala, to return to the Bhati fold without having to give up the practise of Sikhism.

Rawal Kalan

With no legitimate successor available, the chiefs of Jaisalmer sent for Kalan, the elder brother of Salbahan II. The throne of the Bhatis was returned to the rightful heir and the Pahu Bhati diwan dismissed. Though Kalan was an old man of fifty, at the time of accession, he ruled for nineteen years.

During his lifetime, Mohammad Ghuri, who had placed Kalan's father upon the Bhati throne, targeted the imperial Chauhans of Delhi. Riddled with petty jealousies, the great Rajput confederacy watched, uncoordinated and disjointed, as Prithviraj Chauhan lost the throne of Delhi and the destiny of India was sealed in blood. Rawal Samant Singh of Mewar died fighting by the Chauhan's side as the Solankis boasted of inconsequential victories. Then it was the turn of the bystanders. The Gahadwals of Kannauj were wiped out and the sultan of Ghazni returned to the mountains of Afghanistan leaving his Indian empire in the hands of a slave – Qutub-ud-din Aibak.

Indebted as they were to the sultan, it is of little wonder that the Bhatis contributed minimally to the monumental struggle that resisted the planting of the rule of Islam into the very heart of Hindustan.

Rawal Chachik Deo

Chachik defeated the Soda-Parmar prince of Umarkot and married his daughter.

It was during this time that a young man rode into the desert seeking a kingdom. Though he could lay no claim to a lineage comparable with that of the Bhatis, Sihoji wilfully suppressed his own ancestry which, though mortal and short, was none the less glorious. In an unfathomable declaration, Sihoji Rathore announced that he was the descendent of the lost Gahadwals of Kannauj. The band of Rathores that had accompanied Sihoji, settled in Parkar (Barmer) and proved to be troublesome neighbours. With the help of the Soda troops, Chachik subdued them. Chadoo Rathore pacified the rawal by offering him a daughter in marriage. The future had not been revealed for in time to come these very Rathores would vie with the Bhatis for control over the desert.

Chachik Deo was survived by two grandsons, Jait Singh (Jaitsi) the elder and the much loved Karan who was named heir. Jaitsi left and took employment with Muzaffer Balban Kishlu Khan of Gujarat.

Rawal Karan

During Karan's reign, Muzaffer Khan marched across the desert to occupy Nagaur. His men committed outrageous acts upon the citizens of Maroo and the khan himself lusted after the daughter of a landed Bhumia of the Varaha tribe. As the harried father attempted to flee by night he was intercepted. Four hundred Varahas were killed and all their women kidnapped. Word reached Karan. Rawal Karan retaliated, slaying the khan and his army of 3,000. The lands of the Bhumia were restored.

Karan ruled for twenty-eight years and was succeeded by his son.

Rawal Lakhan Sen

Lakhan Sen, who succeeded in AD 1271, was such a simpleton that his nobles were forced to replace him with his son, Punpal.

Rawal Punpal

Punpal's violent temper supposedly forced the nobles into dethroning him or perhaps it was because the clan of Sihad Bhatis, that occupied the ministerial posts, found it difficult to manipulate him. Instigating the nobles they prepared to force him to abdicate. He was to be replaced with his grandfather's elder brother who by all rights should have been rawal thirty-four years ago. Jait Singh now an old man, with grown sons had amassed great wealth having lived the life of a dacoit in Gujarat. He responded eagerly and came to claim his birthright.

Punpal was asked to voluntarily step down and he did so peacefully.

Rawal Punpal, who had ruled for two years, was exiled in AD 1276. Taking his women and children, he left for the wild lands of Pugal. The Bhils of Pugal had reasserted themselves, snatching their ancient land back from the Parmar interlopers. It was an open invitation to a Rajput in search of a kingdom.

Here Jam Kanwar, the daughter of the Deora-Chauhan of Sirohi, bore Punpal a daughter. Padmini, the lotus blossom of Pugal, was born in AD 1285. The father shuddered as he held his newborn. Words would not suffice for the exquisite beauty that was hers.

Ten years later Jaisal's fort went up in flames. The first saka and jauhar in the fort claimed all royal lives. Punpal's family had escaped.

An exile with no dowry to offer, Punpal sought for his daughter the hand of Ratan Singh, the heir of Chittaurgarh. There she would be safe, miles away from Pugal and the roving eyes of the sultan of Delhi. Mewar was more than forthcoming for the beautiful young woman was truly a treasure among her kind. Besides the two families shared long-standing ties. For was it not the son of a Pahu Bhati girl, Ranak Devi, who had once saved the Guhilot throne of Chittaurgarh?

Ranak Devi had married into the royal family of Chittaur and had become mother to Rahup, a younger son. Rahup had become the first to assume the title of rana and change his name from Guhilot to Sisodia. And it had been him who, when a Songara-Chauhan cousin from Jalor threatened to usurp the throne, had ensured its return to the rightful Guhilot occupant. The rawals of Chittaurgarh and the ranas had, ever since, maintained close family ties.

The fifteen-year-old bride left for her new home. Within a year she was queen and her kinsmen rejoiced. Little did they know that she had at her disposal but two short years. Her beauty drew to Chittaur the sultan of Delhi. Alla-ud-din Khalji was determined to have her and though Chittaur was well defended, Padmini's destiny had sealed the fate of her people. As the saka was announced the queen of Chittaurgarh led all women and children into the flames of jauhar. The line of the rawals perished and into their place stepped a descendent of Rana Rahup – the nephew of Pugal.

Pugal proudly claims to be the home of the queen of Chittaur and lovingly refers to her as Pugal-ri-Padmini – Pugal's own Padmini.

His only demand was that he be allowed to keep the heirlooms of his family. The clans readily agreed and unwarranted bloodshed was prevented. Punpal left and with him went the Uttarao and the Singhrao Bhatis – the traditional guardians of the wooden throne of Ghazni.

Punpal and his sons settled in Pugal and between them several attempts were made to regain this ancient Bhati land from the tribal interlopers that now held it. It was Punpal's great-grandson, Ranakdev, who was able to defeat the Bhil chieftain of the Thori tribe and usurp his designation of rao. In AD 1380, Rao Ranakdev installed the wooden throne in the fort of Pugal.

Rawal Jait Singh

Jaitsi came to the throne in AD 1276, an old man immensely wealthy but one who was constantly mocked by his own destiny. By his side were his two sons Mulraj and Ratan Singh. Of his eight wives, Phul Kanwar was said to be the daughter of Rao Asthan, the Rathore ruler of Kher.

Mulraj's son, Deoraj, married the Songara princess of Jalor and their son, Hamir, became a mighty warrior, whose name was to be preserved in the annals of Jaisalmer. Deoraj's second wife, the daughter of Rup Singh Purihara of Mandor, bore Kehar whose line was destined to rule.

The dynasty of the slaves of the sultan of Ghur was at its height. The riches of India ensured a flourishing trade with the empires of the world, the proceeds enriching the imperial coffers. Word arrived that a caravan was approaching – 1500 horses and 1500 mules bearing treasure were making their way through Punjab. The sons of Jaitsi, masters at their trade, made ready to ambush the caravan. Disguised as grain merchants, they set out with 7,000 horses and 1200 camels. The caravan was located by the riverside. The Bhatis camped within sight of the unsuspecting Pathans. The attack came at night, the guards were killed and the treasure carried back to Jaisalmer. This was no isolated incident. The princes of Jaisalmer kept up a constant patrol along the Indus and Jaisalmer prospered upon loot.

Sultan Balban of Delhi directed his energies towards Jaisalmer. Tidings came to Jaitsi that the army of Delhi had encamped on the banks of the

Ana Sagar at Ajmer. He prepared Jaisalmer for a long defence. Large stores of grain were accumulated. Rocks were collected and deposited on the ramparts to be hurled at the besiegers. The old, the sick and the children were moved to a location far away in the desert. The country around the capital was laid waste for many miles. Towns and cities were deserted and fields burnt. The attacking army would find no source of sustenance. Retaining two of his sons and about 5,000 soldiers by his side, Jaitsi remained behind to protect the fort while Deoraj and Hamir took up their posts outside and led the army against the invader.

The sultan stationed himself at Ajmer while his army, clad head to foot in steel, arrived at the gates of Jaisalmer. But the expected confrontation did not take place, for the walls of the fort could not be breached. For years, the invaders languished in their camps, for Deoraj and Hamir had cut off the supply routes from Ajmer. The years took their toll on the sultan's army. His generals died natural deaths and the situation looked hopeless. Reinforcements eventually made their way in under Nawab Kamal-ud-din Garg.

For ten years the fort of Jaisal withstood the siege. Jaitsi himself died of old age and his body was cremated secretly within the fort. The succession brought with it its own share of troubles. The princes had all along chafed under the prime minister's grip over their father and they now determined to be rid of him. Bikam Singh Sihad Bhati was forced to step down and Askaran Jasod Bhati took his place.

Like Jaisalmer the sultanate of Delhi was plagued by problems. Sultan Balban took leave of life and the unfortunate Kaikabad, who succeeded him, was murdered after a debauched reign of four years. The slave sultans were replaced by a minister – a Turk whose ancestor had arrived with Mohammad Ghuri – the elderly Jalal-ud-din Feroze Shah Khalji, in AD 1290. Too nervous to leave the security of Delhi, he left the management of the Jaisalmer issue to his general, Nawab Kamal-ud-din Garg and the charge of territorial expansions to his dynamic nephew and son-in-law, Alla-ud-din. The siege of Jaisalmer was not lifted. During those long years, Ratan Singh had struck up a friendship with the sultan's general. The two would meet in the shade of a date palm and enjoy a daily game of chess. They were likewise, honourable adversaries on the field of battle.

Legend speaks of Jaisalmer's two-and-a-half sakas.

During the first saka, 24,000 women and children are said to have immolated themselves at the Sation ka Pagothia.

The second, which took place because Tilaksi had stolen Sultan Alla-ud-din Khalji's favourite horse, claimed another 16,000 lives.

The last and the half saka took place in the time of Rawal Loonkaran. The wives of the Afghan, Amir Ali, had been permitted to visit the great fort. But hidden within the palanquins were the amir's men. A call was sent out to the allies but with the foe already within the walls, the Bhatis' panicked. In an act of desperation, with no time to prepare for the formalities of a jauhar, Loonkaran himself beheaded his women. The allies arrived in time to save the fort but the women and children of Jaisalmer had already been lost. This last saka has been termed the half saka[15] for the prayers of a jauhar did not precede it.

---

15. About the same time as the last saka in Jaisalmer, the Sisodia fort of Chittaurgarh experienced a fate quite similar. In 1535, Sultan Bahadur Shah of Gujarat attacked. Despite all the aid Chittaurgarh received, it appeared to be a losing battle and jauhar was announced. Women and children sacrificed themselves as the men prepared to fight their last battle. Allied help continued to pour in and the fort was liberated. Maharana Bikramjeet was reinstated upon his throne. For Chittaurgarh, however, this was not its last saka.

Rawal Mulraj

Mulraj ascended the gaddi of Jaisalmer in the midst of an ongoing war. The nawab when he came to meet Ratan Singh next, explained that the sultan had heard of the games of chess and was immensely displeased. An assault on the fort had been ordered the very next day. It duly took place and the defence was obstinate. The attackers were driven back but they returned repeatedly, backed each time with increasing reinforcements. Malik Kafur, was sent in from the Deccan and by the end of two years, the Bhatis knew that they were lost.

The chiefs assembled and made ready for a saka. The queens and the women readied themselves for jauhar. Husbands and wives would meet the next day in heaven. The night was passed getting ready for the morning. Everyone bathed and prayers were chanted. The men bid their women the last farewell and the jauhar began. Twenty-four thousand women including infants and the elderly, took release from life. Freed from their earthly bonds the men of Jaisalmer bathed and said their prayers. A sprig of the sacred basil was held between their lips and the shaligram hung about their necks. Over their armour, they donned saffron robes. The mor was placed upon the brow of the rawal and the warriors embraced each other one last time.

Ratan Singh was desperate to save his sons, Garh Singh and Kanhad Dev. He appealed to his friend and foe and the boys were sent to the nawab's camp where they were placed in the care of a Brahmin tutor.

The saka took place in 1295. The Muslims held the fort for a short while and then abandoned it when Sultan Jalal-ud-din was murdered by his nephew Alla-ud-din. Sultan Alla-ud-din Khalji devoted himself solely to the setting up the trade routes. Jaisal's great fort lay ruined and desolate for many long years. The impoverished Bhati clans that lived in the villages nearby did not have the money nor the means to restore it. Yet they had lost none of their pride.

The Rathores of Mehwa attempted a settlement amongst the ruins. Cartloads of provisions arrived under the supervision of Jagmal Rathore[16].

---

16. Jagmal Rathore was said to be the son of Mallinath of Kher, who had renounced the throne of Maroo and taken to religion. However the dates do not quite match.

Bikamsi Sihad Bhati returned to take part in the first saka. Emotions ran high and charges of corruption were levied against Askaran, the Jasod Bhati prime minister. He was asked to step down and his brothers, aghast at the developments, decided to quit the fort announcing that they would hold a saka of their own.

The eldest among them, however, refused to leave. Duda would not abandon Jaisalmer at such a moment. That night, as he slept off his opium, his brothers lifted his string cot upon their shoulders. Pretending to be on their way to cremate the dead, they left the fort.

The saka, that the Jasod brothers had promised, duly took place. Askaran returned to give his life for Jaisal's fort.

Ten queens of Duda took part in the jauhar. The eleventh waited at her maternal home for a symbol of her dead lord. An old friend, Hainfu, was despatched to obtain the needful and he approached the victorious nawab. A bag full of heads was offered to him.

It had been days since the battle and the heat of the desert made identification impossible. Hainfu sat down. Memories of the days spent with Duda came flooding back. Through his tears he uttered aloud a couplet that his friend had found irresistible. One of the heads burst into laughter. It was Duda's. Respectfully handing it over to Hainfu, the nawab bowed his head.

Cradling her husband's head, Duda's last queen mounted the pyre.

The news reached Duda and Tilak Singh (Tilaksi), the Jasod Bhati brothers. Gathering their kinsmen, they appeared at the gates of the fort and drove the surprised the Rathores out.

Rawal Duda

Duda Jasod Bhati was elected rawal. Repairs were made to the fort and the Bhatis then returned to their old ways. Tilaksi was renowned for his exploits and the impact was felt by all the neighbours. Raids were carried right into Ajmer and Tilaksi made sport of carrying away the sultan's prized breeding mares tethered at the Ana Sagar. Alla-ud-din Khalji was preoccupied and it only served to bolster the Bhati's courage. In 1309, the sultan returned to Ajmer to give thanks at Dargah Sharif – the shrine of the Sufi saint Hazrat Khwaja Moin-ud-din Chisti. A milkmaid arrived at the royal camp in tears. She had been deprived of her wares and ornaments by Tilaksi. A second attack on Jaisalmer was provoked. The six-year-long siege ended with yet another saka.

The sons of Ratan Singh, who had grown up in the care of Nawab Kamal-ud-din Garg, returned to reclaim their inheritance. Though not strictly in line to the throne, it was Garh Singh's initiative that brought Jaisalmer back to Rawal Jaitsi's descendents. Garhsi made his way to the Tughlak court in Delhi. Pleased with the service he rendered, the sultan bestowed upon him the title Ghazni ka Jaitwar – the conqueror of Ghazni and the firmaan for the grant of Jaisalmer.

Overjoyed, the Bhatis journeyed homewards when a string of strange occurrences made them stop. A study of the omens was called for. The soothsayers found it necessary to make a human sacrifice. While the men drew lots two imperial messengers rode up. They asked for directions to the fort. His suspicions aroused, Garhsi persuaded the men into parting with the letter they carried. It was addressed to the subedar of Jaisalmer. The Tughlak sultan had instructed his subedar to ignore the firmaan and kill the Bhati youths as soon as they arrived. The Bhatis consulted among themselves and it was decided that the messengers would make the perfect sacrificial offering. Two graves – the Babbar

Magra -- marked the site of the sacrifice and the Bhatis rode on.

The ignorant subedar handed over the fort unaware of the imperial displeasure awaiting him. The unfortunate man soon found himself deprived of his office and returned to seek sanctuary in Jaisalmer. He was granted the jagir of Nahawarkot and the title of wazir.

With the help of his wife Bimla Devi's Rathore relatives, Garhsi was able to overcome the claims of the other Bhati clans on Jaisalmer.

Rawal Garh Singh

Though Garhsi came into possession of the fort, he was largely ignored by the clans. The Jasod Bhatis saw themselves as heirs while there were others who supported the cause of Mulraj's descendents.

Mulraj's firstborn and heir, Deoraj, had sacrificed his life in the first saka. Of Deoraj's sons, Hamir had laid down his life by his father's side but Kehar, born of the Purihara queen, lived. He had spent the war-years in the security of his maternal home. Standing against him were the sons of Hamir -- the Hamirots -- and they were not about to relinquish their claim. As Ratan Singh's son, Garhsi had little going for him besides his enterprise and initiative.

The chaotic conditions attracted the attention of the Rathores of Kher and Rao Kanakpal advanced into Jaisalmer. His son Bhim annexed all the land right up to the banks of the river Kak. The river was declared as the new border. For a while the Bhatis were able to cast aside their differences and unite. The Rathores were slain and the Bhatis were free once again to indulge in civil warfare.

Garhsi's position remained precarious and unwarranted raids continued. He succeeded in uniting the clans for a second time in 1328, and Rao Jhalan Singh Rathore was slain. The retaliation did not take long to come. Rao Chadha imposed a tax on Jaisalmer and finding the Bhatis in a rebellious mood arrived with his army. Taken completely by surprise, the Bhatis paid up. Overcome by humiliation, Garhsi waited for an opportune moment. Mehwa was attacked and Kher occupied. In 1331, the clans unanimously elected him rawal.

Garhsi undertook the excavation of a large reservoir and sought the blessings of Dewal Charni. The site was marked out and the holy man placed within it a bowl of saffron water. An old reservoir, the Jaisalsar, built by Rawal Jaisal was enlarged and the waters of a rivulet -- the Jichai or Dhuawa -- were led into the Ranisar tank. The excess spilt over into the new reservoir, the Garhsisar (Garhsi Sarovar -- Garhsi's lake) or Gadisar.

Rawal Garhsi was a frequent visitor to the area and Tejsi Jasod Bhati, a grandson of Askaran Jasod Bhati, held a feast to honour the rawal. By then an elderly man, well past his prime, Garhsi was keen to retain the goodwill of the clans. The feasting over, the unsuspecting rawal was preparing to mount his horse when Tejsi struck. With a single blow he beheaded his guest. The rawal's horse took off in panic and made its way to the fort. As it galloped in, its saddle empty, the alarm was sounded. Swiftly assuming control, Bimla Devi ordered the gates shut. Soldiers took up positions upon the ramparts ready to attack any who dared force an entry. The Jasod Bhatis were driven away and word was sent to the Purihara village of Baru Chhayan near Mandor. For seven days Delha, an aged son of Askaran Jasod Bhati, mounted guard outside the fort until Kehar arrived and Bimla Devi rewarded him with the village of Chandan that lay on the road to Pokaran.

Then seating the nearly seventy-year-old Kehar upon her knee, Bimla Devi adopted her husband's nephew as her son. The throne was returned to its rightful occupant but with it went a clause. Kehar was forced into adopting the Hamirots -- Jaitsi and Lunkaran -- as his legal heirs. The agitation by the clans was contained with Kehar sacrificing the rights of his own sons and the sons of Garhsi's younger brother, Kanhad Dev, found no further support.

It is said that Bimla Devi completed the excavation of the lake Garhsisar[17] and when she had completed all that her husband's heart had desired she followed Garhsi to his heavenly abode.

---

17. Work on the Garhsisar reservoir was commenced once again by Rawal Devidas (1467 -- 1524) and it was eventually inaugurated by Rawal Jait Singh II (1524 -- 1528) a 160 years after the death of Rawal Garh Singh. According to the historians of Jaisalmer, the name of Bimla Devi has been needlessly attached to it.

Rawal Kehar II

A marriage was contracted between Mewar and Jaisalmer. Yuvraj Jaitsi set off to claim his bride[18]. As the bridegroom and his men made their way through Abu, ill omens made them stop. Several soothsayers came forward. Among them was the devious Mehraj Sankhla Parmar. Several allegations were made against the bride-to-be and it was suggested that the Parmar's daughter would prove a far better match. Jaitsi gave in. Kehar was furious. An important alliance had been broken without consulting him and the maharana gravely insulted. He disinherited Jaitsi immediately forbidding his entry into Jaisalmer.

For Kehar, alliances were of paramount importance. His own firstborn, Kelan, had been banished for having married beneath him. For though his ancestor, Rawal Jait Singh, had married into the newly established dynasty of the Rathores of Kher, it was not a lineage worthy of the Bhatis. By marring the daughter of Mallinath Rathore, Kelan had jeopardised his future. But Mehraj Sankhla still had a trick or two up his sleeve. He had after all picked the role of a queen for his daughter. He directed the Hamirots to Pugal.

A surprise attack was carried out by night. The elderly Rao Ranakdev defended himself valiantly and in the skirmish both Bhati brothers lost their lives. The old man was horrified when he learnt that he had killed the sons of the legendary Hamir. Discarding his clothes for robes of black, he went on a pilgrimage and on his return, fell at Kehar's feet begging to be forgiven. Kehar raised him gently. Rao Ranakdev was re-confirmed as rao of Pugal.

The way was now clear for the sons of Kehar. The exiled Kelan regained his position as crown prince and moved to a fort he had built at Asnikot. He then usurped his brother Som's lands in Bikampur. Som left to settle in Derawar. News arrived some years later that Som had passed away and Kelan left post haste to stake his claim. Having driven

---

18. It is said that the bride was Lal Bai – the ruby of Mewar – whose father was either Maharana Lakha or Maharana Mokal. Mewar made no attempt to exact revenge upon distant Jaisalmer. Lal Bai was instead given in marriage to the Kinchi chieftain of Gagraun. Sadly within a very short period Gagraun was sacked. Its women perished in the flames of jauhar leaving their men folk free to die honourably upon the battlefield.

his nephews out, Kelan went on to occupy Bhatner (Hanumangarh). It was either him or Rai Duli Chand Bhati who faced the Mongol army of Taimur-i-lang (Taimur the lame – the Mongol prince from central Asia) on 13 November 1398. Taimur did not stay for long and the possession of Bhatner remained with the Bhatis. Pugal was Kelan's next target, for the only son of the deceased Rao Ranakdev had been slain by the Rathores of Rao Chunda who had recently occupied Nagaur. Kelan wrested the fort away from Ranakdev's widow, the Soda rani, and a ceremony of adoption was forced upon her. Then on the charge that she had planned to call in the nawab of Multan for help, he had her incarcerated within a brick wall. Forbidding his clansmen from marrying into the Soda-Parmar clan, Kelan crowned himself king of Pugal.

But it was Lakhansen and not Kelan who succeeded their father at Jaisalmer. Petty warfare dominated the next few years and in a couple of generations the first Mughal invasion under Babar took place.

Rawal Jait Singh II.

Jait Singh had been on the throne for two years when the first battle of Panipat took place. The Bhati hold over Punjab, long tenuous, was lost to a new invader in 1525. Babar – a young Muslim of Mongol origin who had been thrown out of his father's kingdom – consolidated his hold over Punjab before challenging Sultan Ibrahim Lodi of Delhi. A dispassionate Rajput body watched the contest. The lessons drawn in AD 1192, had long been forgotten.

No feeling of déjà vu troubled the Rathores of Bikaner, who concentrated on clawing their way up the Rajput social ladder. While the outcome of the First Battle of Panipat was still sinking in, Bikaner could think of nothing but the Bhati fort of Bhatner. It was occupied within a year and the two neighbours busied themselves with settling petty issues and arranging matrimonial matches for their children.

The Jaitsar reservoir was excavated in AD 1528, by Rawal Jait Singh II. The Bada Bagh (large garden) came up on its banks.

A hill close by was chosen as the new crematorium and called the Satiyon ka mandap. Here stand the cenotaphs of rawals and maharawals since the day of Jait Singh II. Rawal Ramchandra's alone is missing.

Rawal Loonkaran

In the twenty years that followed since the accession of Loonkaran, the dynasty of the rawals went through a period of instability. It meant that the growing power of their immediate neighbours could no longer be ignored. Loonkaran's zenana, which included the daughter of the exalted Maharana Sanga of Mewar, was opened to the daughters of Rao Lunkaran of Bikaner and Rao Ganga of Jodhpur. The days of looking down upon Rathores were long past.

Lunkaran of Bikaner had forced the Bhatis into giving him a daughter in marriage but establishment of matrimonial relationships with Jodhpur took place under warm and friendly circumstances. With Son Baiji Lall Sahiba's arrival her brother looked forward to having a royal Bhatiani by his side and in 1537, the rawal's own daughter Ram Kanwar wed Rao Maldeo of Jodhpur. She recieved the name Uma after her wedding and was popularly known as Maldeo's roothi rani[19], the petulant queen. Loonkaran also arranged for Dheer Bai to marry Maharana Uday Singh of Mewar and though she is known simply as the Bhatiani rani, she was his favourite wife and the mother of his youngest son Jagmal. So completely did she charm her husband that he named her son his successor, overriding the claim of his firstborn. The nobles of Mewar, however were not cowed by the dying maharana's will and upon his death replaced the teenager with the thirty-two-year-old Pratap.

Imperial fugitives took passage through Jaisalmer. Chased by Sher Shah, the deposed Humayun, beset by treachery from within his own family desperately sought sanctuary for his wife, Hamida Banu Begum, who was seven months gone with child. His brothers in open rebellion, Humayun himself having barely escaped imprisonment at the hands of Rao Maldeo of Marwar, was coming to the terrible conclusion that he had but a few friends in the world. Foolishly, his men chose to slaughter a cow for their

---

19. Lusty Maldeo had been unable to keep his hands off his new bride's personal maid. Unable to forgive him, Uma shunned him. The roothi rani was in Ajmer, when news of Sher Shah's approach arrived. He had come chasing the fugitive emperor, Humayun. Maldeo recalled her instantly but the proud Bhatiani refused to return to the security of Jodhpur. Ajmer, she would not permit to surrender and jauhar was clearly out of the question. Uma promised faithfully to die on the battlefield. Fortunately Humayun left Marwar and Sher Shah did not put her to the test. Uma ended her days by her husband's side upon his pyre.

meal. Loonkaran's anger was terrible. The wells along the way were filled up with sand and for four days and nights, men and beasts were denied water. It is a wonder that Hamida survived. Delirious with thirst the pregnant woman demanded a pomegranate. The forlorn soldiers scouted the desert without hope when a miracle took place. A merchant appeared and in his hold was a single juicy pomegranate. It heartened the men; their fortunes were taking a turn and sure enough the Soda-Parmar raja of Umarkot greeted them kindly. In the small oasis kingdom deep within the desert the infant Akbar opened his eyes.

By 1545, Sher Shah the emperor of India was dead and his second son had ascended the throne as Emperor Islam Shah. Humayun, who had been forced to leave his infant son in the care of his trouble-making brothers at Kandahar and Kabul, convinced Shah Tahmasp of Persia to help him. The shah was reluctant but his sister intervened. Humayun agreed to convert to the Shia faith and gifted to the shah a great diamond – one that was to later earn the name Kohinoor. With a detachment of the Persian army he arrived in Afghanistan. Prince Kamran at Kandahar was overcome as was Prince Askari in Kabul. But every time he turned towards Hindustan, the brothers, taking advantage of his mild disposition, rose up against him. It wasn't until 1552, that Humayun was able to take firm action. Hindal, the youngest, had already died. Kamran and Askari were banished to Mecca.

Loonkaran's reign ended with the half saka of 28 May 1550. Amir Ali, ousted from his ancestral lands in Kandahar, appealed to Loonkaran for sanctuary. He was permitted to settle at Kishanghat, three kilometres north of Jaisalmer. But even as he exchanged turbans with his benefactor, he eyed the fort of Jaisal. A suitable opportunity arose the day Yuvraj Maldev left on a hunt. The amir approached his pagri-budul-bhai. His begums had requested permission to visit their Rajputni sisters. It was granted but when the palanquins had made their way in it was not the Afghan's wives but his soldiers who emerged. A desperate battle ensued and Loonkaran rushed to his palace and in a few quick words explained the situation to his family. There was no time for ceremony or for the prayers of a jauhar and as the women bent their heads, Loonkaran beheaded them. The rawal and his men all died that day but the battle drums had alerted the crown prince.

Within six hours of the attack, Maldev was inside the fort having made his way in through a secret passage. The battle took a turn and the Afghans were mercilessly put to death. The amir, it is said, was sewn into a rawhide sack and then blasted by the cannon mounted upon the southern rampart.

Rawal Maldev

Maldev succeeded his father. He was Maharana Uday Singh's son-in-law and of his two Rathorni queens, one was daughter to Rao Jait Singh of Bikaner and the other daughter to Rao Maldeo of Jodhpur.

Despite having several sons, Maldev was succeeded by his elder brother, Har Raj[20]. But it was the line of Khet Singh, Maldev's second son by the daughter of Rao Jait Singh of Bikaner that was destined to rule.

It was during Maldev's rule that the imperial crown of India encircled once more the brow of Humayun and passed on to that of his son – Akbar.

Rawal Har Raj

Jaisalmer maintained a quiet profile as the Mughals established their dominance. Har Raj paid his obeisance when the emperor held court at Nagaur. The Rathore kingdom of Bikaner had already submitted to the will of Akbar and Marwar was tottering on the brink of a takeover. Rao Maldeo had died and while his son Uday was busy ingratiating himself with the Mughals, Chandersen a defiant younger son – rose up. Usurping his brother's throne the twenty-one-year-old declared himself rao in Jodhpur.

Among Har Raj's Rathorni wives were the daughters of Rao Maldeo and Rao Kalyanmal of Bikaner. Three of his own daughters were given

---

20. Maldev's wives would have all lost their heads during the half saka and he would have most certainly remarried thereafter. It is not clear whether Rawal Har Raj was Rawal Maldev's brother or his son. Lt Col Tod believes Har Raj to be Maldev's elder brother.

away as brides to the promising young Rathore princes. The one who is remembered ironically as Saubhagyavati (she who is blessed with good fortune) was given to Chandersen of Marwar. From him the rawal recovered, through payment, the coveted jagir of Pokaran. Two daughters were given to Bikaner – one to the heir, Rai Singh, and the second – Champa Devi – to the talented younger brother Prithviraj (Peethal), who was counted amongst the nine gems of Akbar's court. A third daughter Nathi Bai was given to the great Mughal himself.

The armies of Akbar went after Chandersen and Rai Singh of Bikaner pursued him until his last day. In 1574, the deposed rao was driven into hiding. He died having lived the life of an outlaw for seven years. Saubhagyavati climbed the pyre with her husband. Her father, fortunately for him, had not lived to see the day.

Rawal Bhim

Bhim succeeded to his father's throne in 1578. Though he steered clear of Mughal politics, his chiefs and their armies were placed at the emperor's disposal. In 1610, his uncle, Kalyan Das, was appointed subedar of Orissa and soon granted a munsub of 2,000.

Jahangir succeeded in 1605, and Raja Rai Singh of Bikaner was drawn into the controversy that surrounded Khusro's rebellion. Though a supporter of Jahangir, Rai Singh earned his displeasure for failing to denounce the traitor. But with Khusro's imprisonment Rai Singh rushed to appease the emperor.

Yuvraj Dalpat, the trouble-maker of the Bikaner, had been disowned and Rai Singh named his younger son, Sur Singh, heir. In 1608, Bhim arranged a match for his elderly aunt, Rawal Maldev's daughter[21]. She became thirteenth wife to the heir of Bikaner, Sur Singh.

---

21. Several controversial statements are discovered, as the records of the kingdoms are cross-referenced. From the data available it appears that Amolakh, Rawal Maldev's daughter, would have exceeded the age of forty-six years at the time of her wedding, outlived her husband by fifty-seven years and died at the grand old age of 115.

Bhim had ruled for forty-six years but when he died the issue of succession became a disputed one. His widow, Rani Kamavati, feared for her son's life and appealed to her brother. Raja Sur Singh rushed to Jaisalmer but before he could arrive, Nathu Singh had been assassinated. In a fit of passion Sur Singh banned marriages with the house of Jaisalmer for all time to come.

The love affair with Bikaner, that had begun in the time of Rawal Loonkaran, was over.

Rawal Kalyan Das

Kalyan Das, Har Raj and Maldev's youngest brother, came to the throne. He was the father-in-law of Raja Guj Singh of Jodhpur, his daughter Lachal being the Rathore's fifth wife.

Rawal Manohar Das

Manohar Das succeeded his father. Alliances reaffirmed the bonds between Jaisalmer and Marwar. Two daughters were given in marriage to the house of Jodhpur – Udaikanwar becoming Raja Guj Singh's eleventh wife, and Jasrup Devi the first wife of Guj Singh's heir Jaswant.

A third daughter was given to Maharana Jai Singh of Mewar.

Manohar Das died without leaving behind a son to succeed him and the throne was returned to the line of Rawal Maldev.

Rawal Ramchandra

Ramchandra suffered from too many defects of personality and was soon forced to abdicate. He left for Derawar.

Rawal Sabal Singh

Sabal Singh, the grandson of Khet Singh and great-grandson of Rawal Maldev, succeeded in 1651. There had been several other contenders, but Sabal, who was a nephew of Mirza Raja Jai Singh of Amber, had distinguished himself at Peshawar. Legend has it that he rescued the contents of the imperial treasury from the hands of the Pathans and this brought him to Emperor Shah Jahan's notice. With his powerful uncle lobbying for him, Sabal became rawal but was the first to hold his kingdom as a jagir of the Mughal Empire.

The emperor commanded Jaswant Singh of Marwar to seat Sabal upon the gaddi of Jaisalmer and Nahar Khan – Mokundas Kumpawat chief of the Kumpawats – was entrusted with this duty. The powers of Delhi thought it correct to reward Nahar Khan with the grant of Pokaran[22]. Jaisalmer lost the city to Marwar forever. Yet recognizing the growing power of the Bhatis, Shah Jahan granted Sabal Singh a munsub of 1,000 and the order of the fish – the Mahi Maratib.

Jaisalmer's ties with Mewar remained strong and while Sabal's daughter married Maharana Jagat Singh I, his son, Maha Singh, settled permanently in Mewar, receiving the jagir of Moie. A match was also arranged for Sabal's grand-daughter, the daughter of his heir, Amar Singh. She became one of the eighteen wives of the heir of Mewar, Raj Singh I.

Maharawal Amar Singh

Sabal Singh's death encouraged the Baluchis and local Muslims into attacking the Bhati fort of Rohri. Amar Singh rushed with his army to Sind. Sadly the Bhatis, of the great fort upon the Indus, had been out numbered and before the heir of Jaisalmer could arrive, the saka and jauhar of Rohri had been completed. Amar Singh redeemed the Bhati fort and was crowned rawal upon the field of victory.

---

22. The annals of Jaisalmer claim that Pokaran was granted to Nahar Khan Kumpawat and that it was returned by the Mughals to Maharawal Amar Singh. Pokaran eventually became the seat of the junior Champawat clan of Marwar, which was headed by Devi Singh, a son of Maharaja Ajit. The annals of Jodhpur however count Pokaran among the crown properties since the accession of Raja Sur Singh.

From the Rajput clans that bordered Jaisalmer he extracted written promises of good conduct. Relations with Bikaner had long soured. Provoked by the ongoing nuisance created by the descendents of Rawat Kandhal of Bikaner, Amar gave leave to the chiefs of Bikampur to invade the frontier towns of Bikaner. Maharaja Anup Singh of Bikaner, who was away in the Deccan, in turn sent word that Jaisalmer was to be attacked and Bikampur razed to the ground. The sons of Kandhal who failed to do their duty would be declared traitors. Accordingly the Rathores assembled, ready to give battle, but Amar gathered his Bhatis and without waiting for an attack advanced, torching all that came his way. The Rathore army was put to the sword and Jaisalmer recovered the northern fort of Pugal and a promise of loyalty from the Rathore chiefs of the border.

But with his death in 1702, Pugal, Barmer, Phalodi and several towns were occupied by the Rathores while Daud Khan, an Afghan, grabbed a share that came to be known as the land of the Daudputras (the sons of Daud or David).

Maharawal Jaswant

Jaswant succeeded his father but ruled for a short period of six years. He died leaving behind four sons – Jagat, Surat, Isar and Tej – and a daughter who had been given in marriage to the heir apparent of Mewar, Sangram Singh II. Jaswant's heir, Jagat, gave up his claim to the throne in favour of his son Budh Singh.

Maharawal Budh Singh

No mention is made in the Bhati annals of the tumultuous conditions that prevailed in the empire. Budh Singh, who ascended the throne of Jaisalmer in 1708, witnessed a series of puppet emperors that met grisly deaths – a situation in which the princes of Marwar and Jaipur participated with obvious glee. There was no dearth of fidelity but it changed hands frequently. Eventually Muhammad Shah (Rangila) who was placed on the throne in 1719, brought a semblance of stability in the ongoing mayhem.

Budh Singh died of small pox leaving behind no issue to succeed him. The opportunity was utilised by his uncle Tej Singh, who usurped the throne. Budh Singh's brothers ran for their lives making their way to the imperial court where their granduncle, Maharawal Jaswant's brother Hari Singh was in service.

Hari Singh waited until it was time for the annual dredging of the Garhsisar. The maharawal inaugurated the ceremony by drawing out the first handful of mud and sand. He was followed by the people rich and poor alike.

Hari Singh struck during the ceremony but Tej Singh did not die immediately. He lived to name his successor – his three-year-old son Sawai Singh. Budh Singh's brother Akhai Singh gathered his allies. The castle of Jaisalmer was stormed and the child put to death.

Maharawal Akhai Singh

Akhai Singh ruled for forty years. During his reign, ancient Derawar was lost. It was snatched by Daud Khan's son, Bahawal Khan, and the kingdom of the Daudputras was renamed Bahawalpur.

The empire did not perhaps trouble Akhai Singh much. Two years after his succession Hyderabad broke away, its nizam unofficially declaring himself independent. Avadh and Bengal were the next to follow. Akhai Singh's reign bore witness to the sacking of Delhi – once by Nadir Shah of Persia and a second time by his minion – Ahmad Shah Abdalli (Durrani). The emperors of those days suffered greatly playing into the hands of rapacious ministers. Ahmad Shah was blinded and deposed and the elderly blind Alamgir II murdered by the grandson of the first nizam of Hyderabad. The Mughal throne remained unoccupied, as the heir had fled to the safety of Avadh. The Marathas, swept away by their dreams, had promised the murderer help in rebuilding the empire and had brought upon the nation the Third Battle of Panipat. As their hopes dried up, they were reduced to petty scavenging in the problem-ridden courts of Mewar, Marwar, Jaipur and Hadavati. For the moment Jaisalmer appeared to have been spared.

Akhai Singh, who had himself married a daughter of Maharaja Ajit, gave two daughters to Marwar. Sarup Kanwar married Bakhta Singh becoming his ninth queen while Vijaya Kanwar married Bakhta's grandson, Fateh Singh. In 1756, the first mint was set up in Jaisalmer and the currency referred to as the Akhai Shahi. The maharawal lived to witness the rise of the merchants of Great Britain – the Battle of Plassey of 1757, which delivered distant Bengal into the hands of the East India Company.

Maharawal Akhai Singh died a year after the Third Battle of Panipat and with his death, Jaisalmer witnessed the last of its satis.

Maharawal Mulraj Singh II

Mulraj succeeded his father in 1762, but his reign began on an inauspicious note. The wazirs of Nahawarkot, who had received their jagir from Rawal Garhsi, turned against the kingdom. In 1763, they surrendered the fort of Tanot to the Daudputras of Bahawalpur. But it was the unfortunate choice of a minister – Swaroop Singh Mehta, a Jain trader – that truly marked the beginning of Jaisalmer's misery.

Swaroop Singh's high-handed policies antagonized the chiefs. In desperation, the heir apparent, Rai Singh, conspired with others to get rid of him. The assassination was carried out in open court and as the dying prime minister clung to the maharawal, an attempt was made on Mulraj's life. Mulraj fled into the inner chambers, as Rai Singh stood transfixed with horror. This had not been a part of the plan. The events had been blown far out of proportion and appeared to be spiralling beyond his control. The panic-stricken ministers and chiefs insisted on seating him on the throne immediately. Were he to refuse, his brother would have taken his place. Mulraj had been imprisoned in his own palace but Rai Singh could not bear to physically sit upon the throne. At last a straw mat was placed on the floor before the throne and Rai Singh became maharawal of Jaisalmer.

The chief noble and conspirator soon tired of the ongoing politics and resolved to depose Rai Singh. His Rathorni wife, however, proved to be a strong-headed woman loyal to the rights of the gaddi. She called for her son, Zoravar. Instructing him to free Mulraj, she promised faithfully to climb her husband's pyre in case Zoravar was forced into taking his father's life.

Together with his uncle Arjun and Megh Singh, the chief of Baru, Zoravar freed Mulraj. The nakarras were sounded and Rai Singh dutifully gave up the throne to his father. He had been king for three months and five days. Banished from Jaisalmer, he left without a word and took sanctuary for a while at the court of Maharaja Beejy Singh of Marwar. He was eventually permitted to live out his days in the castle of Dewoh within the Jaisalmer territory.

The Mehta's son, Salim Singh, was eleven at the time and he succeeded to his father's office. But the child was obsessed with seeking revenge. Although of the Jain faith that did not permit harm to any living creature, Salim became responsible for many deaths, remaining all the while, outwardly, a soft-spoken courteous young man. All ministers, including Zoravar Singh, found themselves outlawed, their lands and estates confiscated. Soon it was the inexperienced youth's turn. He fell into the hands of the chiefs. Salim laid his turban at Zoravar's feet and begged for mercy. Zoravar spared him that day. All lands were restored but it was Zoravar alone who regained the right to attend court.

The sons of Rai Singh had been left behind with the outlawed chiefs. Mulraj pleaded in vain for the return of his grandsons. Barmer, where the children were being held, was attacked. The siege continued for six months when at last, Zoravar stepped in. He promised to escort the children personally to Dewoh. There they would live with their parents. In an unexplained fire, the Dewoh castle burnt down taking with it Rai Singh and his wife. The children managed to escape unhurt, and Zoravar, who did not trust Salim Singh Mehta, took them to the safety of the fort of Ramgarh, which lay on the border.

The Mehta now prepared to get rid of Zoravar and every Rajput of note. Treachery and poison ensured that not one of the ministers or their families survived. Nor were the sons of Rai Singh spared. The murderer proclaimed Guj Singh, the youngest grandson of Mulraj, heir.

Mulraj's troubles were no less than those being faced by the Mughals of the period. The empire continued in the grip of insatiably dominating wazirs, the emperors reduced to puppets living in constant fear for their lives. Emperor Shah Alam II returned to his throne after thirteen long years bringing with him the Scindia Marathas as his personal bodyguards. When at last he thought himself free he offered the regency of the empire to his friend Mahadji Scindia. But the defeat at Lalsot at the hands of Jaipur and Jodhpur temporarily paralysed the Maratha and Delhi was seized by the grandson of the Rohilla who had been appointed protector during the aftermath of Panipat. In a fit of madness he ripped out the emperor's eyes. 10 August 1788, the day that the dastardly deed was committed went down in history as the last day of the Mughal Empire. What was left of it would henceforth be known as the Kingdom of Delhi. Mahadji rushed to the rescue and assumed the role of protector himself – one that his successor Daulat Rao Scindia was to inherit. But in December 1803, the East India Company occupied Delhi and evicted Daulat Rao. The emperor was placed under British charge.

In 1818, Maharawal Mulraj signed the treaty of 'perpetual friendship, alliance and unity of interests' with the Honourable East India Company. Jaisalmer, one among the last Rajput states to join the British, was placed under Captain James Tod's supervision.

Mulraj died in 1820, his entire life had been spent dominated by his prime minister.

Maharawal Guj Singh

Guj Singh remained dependent upon Salim Singh Mehta. The Jain held all Jaisalmer in bondage, his honeyed words carrying no more value than a grain of sand. At his mercy were those involved in the creation of wealth. Exorbitant taxes were levied and the common man subjected to extortion by criminals employed by the state.

An exodus began. Among the many that abandoned Jaisalmer were the Paliwal Brahmins. Renowned cultivators and landlords, the Paliwals were famous for having set up an irrigation system in the desert. Their solidly constructed villages[23] lay deserted: a stark reminder of the days of prosperity.

---

23. A total of eighty-four Paliwal villages were abandoned, of which Kuldhara, Damodra and Khaba are still well preserved. Interestingly, many of the Paliwal craftsmen turned to the Jain faith perhaps to escape the persecution that went with the name.

The artful Salim strove to keep his king distracted. He contracted for him a marriage with the daughter of Maharana Bhim Singh of Mewar. The event became a coming together for all royal Rajputs. Udaipur, that had known no celebration since the unfortunate attempts to find Krishna Kumari a husband, now readied itself for a grand event. On 3 July 1820, the Hindupati gave to Maharawal Guj Singh the hand of his daughter, Roop Kanwar. The heir of Bikaner, Yuvraj Ratan Singh wed Ajab Kanwar and his brother Maharajkumar Moti Singh, Deep Kanwar. Yuvraj Mokkam Singh of Kishangarh took as wife the maharana's grand-daughter, Kika Bai.

The Sisodini rani soon became the mother to the heir of the desert kingdom. Content with life, Guj Singh devoted himself to his family and his horses. Such were the state of affairs when Captain James Tod retired[24].

Four years later Jaisalmer struggled once again to break free of the Mehta's grip. Salim Singh received a fatal wound. So terrified were those that surrounded him that even as he lay dying rumours of recovery did the rounds. It is said that it was his wife who eventually slipped him a dose of poison.

In 1829, Bikaner invaded Jaisalmer but the British government of India intervened and with the maharana of Udaipur acting as arbitrator, the dispute was settled.

---

24. Sisodini Rani Roop Kanwar of Jaisalmer remained in touch with her adopted uncle, Lt Col James Tod, through letters that carried news of her family and kingdom. Her son probably died for, after her husband's death in 1846, she adopted his nephew, Ranjit Singh, who succeeded as the next maharawal.

The lost community of Paliwal Brahmins, originally called the Nanwana Gaur Brahmins, had once been the prosperous traders of Nan-na who had been driven from their homeland by the 'barbarians' of Multan and Uch. They migrated to Marwar and received a grant of land from the Indu-Purihara ruler of Mandor. Here they built the city of Pali and settled down as raj-gurus to the Purihara dynasty. With their shrewd business acumen, Pali prospered and the Brahmins adopted the name of their new home.

Their wealth drew the notice of marauders and dacoits and the exodus from Pali began in the time of Sultan Balban. Families abandoned their homes and moved westwards. Then in AD 1256, came Sihoji Rathore. The Brahmins of Pali welcomed him. Under the guise of protector, Sihoji settled in. It was here that his son was born and visions of a glorious future gripped the new father. As the full moon heralded the joyous festival of Rakhi, the Rathores slew their hosts. Panic stricken, men and women fled into the desert. Since that terrible day no Paliwal woman has ever bound a brother's wrist with silk.

Evil days lay ahead and persecution by the sultans of Delhi continued. The final abandonment of Pali is believed to have taken place during the reign of Sultan Jalal-ud-din Feroze Khalji. Stopping at Ola, 500 yagnas were performed. Hoping that the gods had now been appeased, the Brahmins of Pali declared Jaisalmer their new home.

The land had been devastated by twelve years of war and the leading family had been lost in the first saka of Jaisalmer. The arrival of the Paliwals came as a blessing to the common man. The industrious Brahmins levelled the land employing local labour. Potters, carpenters, goldsmiths and others were employed to serve the Paliwals exclusively. Thus a caste of craftsmen known as Paliwal was born.

Through the efforts of the Paliwals, the inhospitable land and its people flourished. Reservoirs were dug to catch the little rain that came their way and a network of irrigation canals linked the fields. The bumper crops fed rich and poor alike. Once again, the passion for breeding swift camels and horses could be indulged. Money was spent in acquiring new land and and lavished upon homes, temples and cenotaphs.

The vast amounts of revenue generated from Paliwal lands brought with it royal favour and the Brahmins regained their erstwhile status of raj-guru, and moneylender. But during the reign of Rawal Jait Singh II, they were replaced by the Kshetrapaliyas.

The horrors of their past returned to haunt them in the guise of Salim Singh Mehta, the Jain minister who completely dominated the maharawals, Mulraj and Guj Singh. The Jain targeted all wealthy Brahmins and traders. The Paliwals, it is said, had refused to give him a daughter in marriage for the Mehta came from a lower caste. Armed raids were organized and unprecedented atrocities committed against men, women and children. In sheer panic Jaisalmer, that had been their home for centuries, was abandoned. Their pain and anguish remain immortalised in bardic verse.

Many communities that had added to Jaisalmer's prosperity left forever but the greatest tragedy was that of the Paliwal Brahmins. The community simply vanished. All that is left of the Paliwal name is the caste that owed its origin to these lost people.

The world is too enlightened at the present day to be in danger of being misled by any hypothetical writer, let him be ever so skilful; but the probability is, that we have been induced, by the multitude of false theories which time has exposed, to fall into the opposite error, and that we have become too sceptical...

— James Tod

GLOSSARY

Aan: Dignity.

Aghran: 'Hindu' month corresponding to 15th November – 15th December.

Ahairea or Ahota: The spring hunt where a wild boar is killed and offered to Gauri, the mother goddess.

Ahmadnagar: This Deccan sultanate, which had incorporated the sultanate of Berar (Vidarbha) within its limits, was annexed by Emperor Akbar in AD 1600 but a large portion continued to remain independent. Jahangir kept up the Deccan campaign and had good reason to suspect that Khan-e-khana Abdur Rahim was in collusion with the Abyssinian minister of Ahmadnagar – Malik Ambar. The fort submitted in 1616, and Prince Khurram was allowed to obtain a show of success. He was awarded the extravagant title of Shah Jahan. The last of the Nizam Shahi sultans, a young prince set upon the throne by Malik Ambar's son, was consigned to the dungeons of Gwalior and the dynasty came to its end in AD 1632.

Amrit: Ambrosia.

Antri: Valley.

Aonla. Phyllanthus emblica or Emblica officinalis is a medium-sized deciduous tree with fruits that are rich in Vitamin C.

Apsara: Celestial nymph.

Asar: 'Hindu' month corresponding to 15th June – 15th July.

Ashapurna Devi: A form of the mother goddess.

Asura: Demon.

Aswin: 'Hindu' month corresponding to 15th September – 15th October.

Attock: Hindi uttak meaning the barrier. The word refers to the Indus, which the 'Hindus' were discouraged from crossing. Lands that lay beyond the Indus fell into the realm of the Attock.

Avadh: Lord Ram's holy city of Ayodhya in the modern state of Uttar Pradesh became a small part of the kingdom of Oudh or Avadh or Awadh. Lakhnau or Lucknow the capital city of Oudh continues as the capital of Uttar Pradesh.

Babul: Kikar or Acasia arabica.

Bahadur: Brave warrior.

Baisakh: 'Hindu' month corresponding to 15th April – 15th May.

Banjaras: Carriers or couriers, a tribe who kept cattle especially for transportation.

Bar: Banyan tree or Ficus indica / Ficus bengalensis.

Basti: Settlement.

Battle of Plassey: The area gets its name from the brilliant red Palas flowers that bloom in the summer. In June 1757, Robert Clive of the East India Company used treachery to defeat the forces of Nawab Siraj-ud-daula and the Company earned the privilege to meddle in the affairs of Bengal. It was followed up by a decisive victory at Baksar (now in Bihar) in 1764 over the forces of Nawab Mir Kasim, who had teamed up with Nawab Wazir Shuja-ud-daula of Avadh (Oudh) and the wandering Emperor Shah Alam II. The hapless emperor, who meekly accepted the limited protection the British had to offer, granted the diwani of Bengal to the Company. Not that it was his to give away but because it awarded the British a kind of legitimacy. It would grow to become the Bengal Presidency.

Beera: Paan – a betel leaf wrapped with spices used as mouth freshener, traditionally offered at the end of a meal.

Benaras: Also called Varanasi.

Bengal Army: Between 1740 and 1757, the English East India Company raised three distinct armies in the three presidencies of Madras (Chennai), Bengal and Bombay (Mumbai). All the three maintained native troops drawn from among the local population as they were cheaper to maintain and more manageable than Europeans. By 1805, the Bengal Army had outgrown the others with the 'Hindus' of north India forming the large infantry division and the Muslims forming the smaller cavalry division.

Bengal Presidency: Also known as the Presidency of Fort William, this British province included the modern-day Myanmar, Bangladesh, West Bengal, Bihar, Jharkhand, Orissa, Uttar Pradesh, Uttarkhand (Uttaranchal), Punjab and Pakistan.

Bhadon: 'Hindu' month corresponding to 15th August – 15th September.

Bhagwad Gita: The song of the Lord – the advise proffered by Lord Krishna to Prince Arjun on the battlefield before the great battle of the Mahabharat.

Bharatvarsh: The land of King Bharat, that lies on the banks of the river Sindhu or Sindh (Arab: Hind. British: Indus) was referred to as the land of Hind or Hindustan by the Arabs. Its people – who knew themselves to be Bharatiyas – found themselves being referred to as 'Hindus'. Unable to pronounce the word Hind, the British called the land Ind or India and its people Indians.

Bhat: Genealogists by profession, Brahmins by caste, Bhats are to be found throughout India. Though the name may be spelt variously as Bhat, Bhatt or Bhattacharya, they all claim descent from a common ancestor.

Bhavani: One of the various names for the mother goddess or Shakti.

Bhiroo: A form of Kartik, the eldest son of Shiva.

Bijapur: This Deccan sultanate, that had incorporated the sultanate of Bidar within its limits, was annexed permanently by Emperor Aurungzeb in 1686.

Bhumia: Landed gentry.

Bishnoi: The sect gets its name from the twenty-nine (Bish = Twenty and Noi = Nine) principles laid down by the founder Jambaji (1451 – 1437) of Nagaur. His was supposed to have been the first attempt at conservation and his followers had been ordered to protect flora and fauna even at the cost of their own lives. This non-violent sect has made many dramatic sacrifices, embracing trees to prevent their logging and laid the foundation of the Chipko movement of the 1970s, that resisted the deforestation of the Himalayas.

Bombay: Modern name – Mumbai.

Bombay Presidency: A province of British India, which included Gujarat, the western two-thirds of Maharashtra, north-western Karnataka, Sind (now in Pakistan) and Aden (Yemen).

Brahma: The Creator.

Brahmani: The wife of a Brahmin.

Braj Nath: A form of Krishna.

Calcutta: Modern name – Kolkata.

Chabukswar: Master of the whip who was in charge of horses and training.

Chait: 'Hindu' month corresponding to 15th March – 15th April.

Chamunda: The destructive form of the mother goddess.

Chaori: The umbrella of supremacy.

Charpai: A wooden cot strung with jute ropes and stretched tight like a hammock. The jute ropes would be unstrung every morning and carried as tightly wound balls along with the dismantled frame. Cots were always freshly restrung before use.

Charun: (pronounced – cha-run) Bard. This caste of bards was known for their Rajput like valour and knowledge as extensive as that of the Brahmins. Revered throughout India, their women were worshipped as goddesses and the men referred to as deviputra (son of the goddess). To kill a bard was to invite eternal ruin, a belief exploited by the community, which would resort to self-immolation at the slightest provocation. The community is said to have four branches – Tumers from Sind, Kachhelas or Parajias from Kachchh, Marus of Marwar and the Gujjars (the name Gujjar appears to be used by both Rajputs and charuns).

Chitra-koot: Chitrang Mori's cottage. It is also a classical allusion to Chitra-koot in (modern state of Uttar Pradesh) where Lord Ram had spent some time.

Choorie: Bangle.

Churri: A narrow flexible wooden stick used as a patriarchal rod used by a shepherd to guide his flock.

Crore: A hundred lakhs or ten million.

Dada: Used to refer to both elder brother and paternal grandfather.

Dagh: Brand or identification mark.

Dhaibhai: Foster brother.

Deccan: The origin of the word lies in the Sanskrit word dakshin, which means south. The word, Deccan, traditionally refers to all lands south of the Narmada river and the Vindhya mountains. It encompasses most of central and southern India.

Dhak: Flame of the forest or Plassey / Palas.

Dhanya: Praiseworthy.

Dhai: Women of the Gujjar tribe traditionally played the role of wet nurses. They were held in great esteem, as were their sons who, as foster brothers, were referred to as Dhaibhai.

Diwali: The festival of lights celebrating the return of Lord Ram after fourteen years of exile.

Diwan: Keeper of accounts. The maharanas of Mewar who claim descent from Lord Ram – the earthly form of Vishnu, were however devotees of the five headed Shiva – Eklinga, to whom Mewar belongs. As Eklingji's diwan, the maharana is entrusted with the governing of Mewar.

Doab: Land between two rivers.

Doli: A palanquin that bears a newlywed bride to her matrimonial home.

Doonah: A cup made of leaves.

Dushera: In the epic battle that lasted for ten days, Lord Ram, assisted by the mother goddess, was able to overcome the demon king of Lanka (Sri Lanka), Raavan. But it wasn't until Dushera, the tenth and the final day, when Raavan was finally struck. Dushera is also referred to as the day of victory or Vijay Dashami.

East India Company: A group of merchants in UK obtained permission from their government in AD 1600, to monopolise trade between the UK and India. Buy cheap in India and sell dear in UK was the principle. Working capital was raised from the general public and the shareholders elected 24 directors annually who were to guide the trade in India. This became the British EIC – the Honourable East India Company – known locally as the Company Bahadur. On the Company's behalf the king's representatives met the Mughal emperor of India and obtained permission to begin trade with Indian merchants.

The directors of the Company appointed British merchants who came to India and carried out the actual process of trade. They received a nominal salary but were free to indulge in private trade so long as it did not interfere with the Company's area of monopoly. Often the directors were pressurised into appointing those with strong connections. The merchants would begin life in India as young boys of fifteen appointed to the post of writer and then make their way up. Among the large numbers of writers that arrived were: Robert Clive in 1743 and Warren Hastings in 1751.

Senior merchants formed local councils and administered the Company's possessions in Bengal, Bombay and Madras. The body of merchants in India carried out both commercial duties as well as revenue collection. They soon became scandalously wealthy, as a result of the private trade, earning the epithet of nabob or nawab, but the Company's profits did not match up to the expectations of the shareholders and the demands for increasing dividend led to a financial crisis. The British parliament stepped in and offered to take over the management of the Company. Though this crisis was tided over by a promise to pay 400000 £ annually to the government of Great Britain, it only deepened the financial crisis. In 1772, Warren Hastings was despatched as governor of the Company's possessions in Bengal with explicit orders to cut wasteful spending but the measure had come too late and directors were forced into accepting aid worth a 1,000,000 £ from the British government for the Bank of England had refused to give them a loan.

The aid, however, came with a condition. The parliament imposed the Regulating Act of 1773 by which the politics played by the manipulative shareholders came to an end. Annual elections were done away with and 6 directors were elected for a term of 4 years. A man could not be re-elected for a second term unless he had been out of office for at least one year. The Supreme Court of Calcutta (Kolkata) was set up to administer English law to Europeans and 'Hindu' or Muslim law as applicable to the Indians under its jurisdiction.

Pitt's India Act of 1784 ensured that the Company's growing possessions in India would be jointly managed by both the government of Britain and the Company's directors. The directors who were familiar with India would continue to guide the trade policies while 6 unpaid privy councillors appointed by the government would manage all other affairs. The councillors formed the Board of Control with one of them acting as president. The office of the president soon grew more powerful and the president became in effect the minister for the affairs of the EIC. Though the directors appointed and paid the governor general, he could be recalled at any time by either the Board of Control or the parliament. His primary duty was to cut the wasteful expenditures being incurred by the Company in India.

In India the governor general and his council replaced the local council that had been administering the possessions in Bengal. The council now comprised of 3 members, one of whom had to be the commander-in-chief and the other two, merchants in the Company's service. It was however made possible for the offices of both governor general and commander-in-chief to be held by one man. This ensured his ability to override the council when required. Men high in British public life were appointed to the post of governor general thereby raising his status above all his colleagues.

As the Company's possessions in India grew so did the interest of the British government. By 1813, the Company lost its monopoly over trade with India and by 1833 the directors were effectively defunct. The governor general of British possessions in Bengal became the governor general of all British possessions in India in 1834.

Governor General and Commander-in-Chief, Lord Cornwallis (1786 – 1790) who succeeded Warren Hastings separated the commercial and the revenue collecting branches. While the commercial branch continued with actual trade and lined their pockets as before, the revenue collectors accepted large salaries, strict rules that allowed no corruption and carried out administrative duties as well as the enforcement of law. This became the highly prestigious civil service, entry into which required connections and patronage. Their social status led to their contempt for the other branch. In 1853, open competition for entry into the Indian Civil Service was introduced. No longer was the Company's patronage required and the civil service was flooded with competition wallahs.

The so called dual system lasted until the uprising of 1857 and as soon as it was contained the Company was deprived of its say in the governing of the Indian possessions. The governor general, now an agent of the queen, assumed the additional title of viceroy. On 1 January 1874 the Company was formally dissolved. The president of the Board of Control became the secretary of state for India. The role of the directors in the guiding of trade policies was given to the newly created Council of India, which comprised of men who had served a lifetime in India.

In 1876, Queen Victoria was declared empress of India.

Falgun: 'Hindu' month corresponding to 15th February – 15th March.

Fateh: Victory.

Firangi: Derived from the word Frank, it refers to those of European origin.

Firmaan: Royal order.

Frengan or Firingisthan: Land of the Franks, a general term used to refer to Europe.

Gaddi: Throne or more specifically the royal cushion.

Garh: Fort.

Gauri: One of the various names for the mother goddess or Shakti.

Ghazi: Slayer of infidels (non Muslims).

Ghazni: The crown of Ghazni is said to have passed from the hands of the Yaduvansh to their descendents, the Bhatis, who eventually lost it to their cousins – the sons of Chakita. In time, it is said that the 'Hindu' kings of Ghazni converted to Islam. In AD 986, a Muslim chief of Turkish extract named Sabuktigin, Amir of Ghazni, came into notice by making his first raid into India attacking Raja Jaipal of Bathinda. In 997, the crown of Ghazni descended on the brow of his son Mahmud who styled himself as sultan. It was customary for Mahmud to quit Afghanistan in early October and spend the winter in the comfort of the plains of India, raiding and pillaging until the beginning of the hot season. It is said that he made seventeen such expeditions. In November 1001, he defeated Raja Jaipal who, unable to swallow the disgrace, commited suicide. His son Anandpal organized a league of 'Hindu' rajas and was backed by the Khokars of Punjab. The 'Hindu' army was under the supreme command of Vishal Dev Chauhan of Ajmer. But they were no match for the fierce foreign cavalry that obeyed a single master. Mahmud returned with 'jewels and unbored pearls and rubies, shining like sparks, or like wine congealed with ice, and emeralds like fresh sprigs of myrtle, and diamonds as large as pomegranates.' Orders had been left to burn the temples with naptha and fire. And thus perished the monuments and works of art that belonged to ancient India. The sixteenth and the most infamous of Mahmud's raids was the sack of the temple of Somnath. A large part of Punjab was annexed. The empire lasted for nearly 150 years eventually losing its hold over central Asia to the growing Seljuk empire.

Ghee: Clarified butter.

Ghur: The obscure principality of Ghur owed its rise to Sultan Behram Shah of Ghazni who had executed two princes of Ghur setting off a blood-feud. It resulted in the sack of Ghazni in AD 1151 and the city was devastated. All palaces and edifices of the Mahmudi kings were destroyed save for the tomb of Sultan Mahmud. By 1160, Behram Shah's son was forced to retire to Lahore by a clan of Ghuzz Turks. Some twelve years later, Sultan Ghiyas-ud-din of Ghur drove out the Turks and handed Ghazni, with its dependencies, to his brother Mohammad who became known as Mohammad Ghuri, sultan of Ghazni and conqueror of Hindustan. On Ghiyas-ud-din's death, Mohammad Ghuri added the Ghur principality to his crown but was killed shortly thereafter.

Golconda: This the fifth of the Deccan sultanates was eventually annexed by Emperor Aurungzeb in 1687.

Gondwana: Gondwana – the land of the Gonds, refers to the southern supercontinent – Antarctica, Australia, New Zealand, South America, India, Africa, Madagascar and Arabia, which broke up 160 million years ago. Continents separated and drifted apart gradually with India colliding with the Asian landmass 45 million years ago. The land of the Gonds within India includes western Orissa, Madhya Pradesh, Chattisgarh, northern Andhra Pradesh and eastern Maharashtra. Gonds are the most numerous of the Dravidian races of India.

Gopi: Female friends of Lord Krishna.

Hai: Exclamation of grief.

Hakim: Officer in charge.

Har: Shiva.

Hari: Vishnu.

Hindi: One among the many languages of north India, it was chosen as the national language after independence. The first Hindi book Shravakachar by Devasena has been dated to AD 933.

Hindupati: Defender of the ancient ways of life – those of the 'Hindus', Jains, Buddhists and the tribes.

Hindustan: India – land or sthan of the 'Hindus'. The Sanskrit word phonetically spelt as sthan is used as such in indigenous names such as Rajasthan. In Arabic or Persian derived names it becomes stan e.g. Hindustan, Pakistan, Afghanistan etc. In this text Hindustan refers to Greater India i.e. Bangladesh, India, Nepal and Pakistan. Its limits were marked by tirths or pilgrimage sites. Not only during the epic age but even until centuries later, Greater India included within its limits Myanmar, Afghanistan and the islands in the Bay of Bengal (notably Bali and Sumatra) and Sri Lanka. The way of life practised by the peoples of these lands had been the same for many eras and marriages were therefore permitted.

Holi: The festival of colours is celebrated to mark the onset of spring.

Holkar: A branch of the Marathas descended from Malhar Rao Holkar of the tribal Dhangar caste (residents of the village of Hol and shepherds by profession), who began service as a general under the peshwa.

Howdah: The wooden seat used upon an elephant's back.

Idgah: A place of worship used by Muslims.

Indian: People of India. The word is derived from Hind – the Arabic name for Bharatvarsh. At the time the name was given, the Indian people – whom the Arabs called 'Hindu' – followed the ancient ways of life known today as Hinduism, Jainism, Buddhism and the tribal faiths. The word has grown since then to include Muslims, Christians, Jews, Parsees and people of other faiths who have chosen to make this land their own.

Iran: Land of the Aryans or Persia. The ancient Persians referred to their land as Iran and this became the official name in 1935.

Jagannath: Vishnu.

Jai: Victory.

Jain: Followers of Mahavir – a tirthankar (teacher) who is dated to the sixth century BC. They are distinguished primarily by their desire to cause no harm to living beings.

Jaisht: 'Hindu' month corresponding to 15th May – 15th June.

Jaal: Web.

Jauhar: Immolation of the women and children before the warriors set out on their last battle, one from which there was no return. It was performed to save the vulnerable from atrocities at the hands of the enemy. It was also a part of a pact to be together always – in life and in death. The women would bathe, ritually cleanse themselves and dress as new brides while the priests would spend the night in prayer on their behalf, ensuring a safe passage to the heavens. The next morning, in the presence of their husbands, the women would lead the families, including the maidservants, into the designated area where blazing logs of wood doused in ghee awaited them. Chanting the verses of the *Gita* they would leap into the flames. Generous doses of opium would be used to still their fears and numb the pain.

The tradition of jauhar is said to date back to the days of Alexander.

A chronology of jauhar:
327 BC Punjab
AD 194 Yadus in Ghazni
AD 477 Bhatis in Ghazni
AD 479 Bhatis in Bhatner
AD 841 Bhatis in Tanot
AD 792, in Sind led by the queen of Raja Dahir Soda
AD 1295 Bhatis in Jaisalmer
AD 1296 Chauhans in Golconda and Asirgarh
AD 1301 Chauhans in Ranthambhor
AD 1303 Sisodias in Chittaurgarh
Chauhans in Garh Pawa, Gujarat
Parmars in Abu

Solankis in Anhilwara Patan
AD 1308 Satal Dev's family in Siwana
AD 1314 Songara Chauhans in Jalor
AD 1315 Bhatis in Jaisalmer
Kinchi-Chauhans in Gagraun
AD 1535 Sisodias in Chittaurgarh
AD 1550 Bhatis in Jaisalmer
AD 1568 Sisodias in Chittaurgarh
AD 1660 Bhatis in Rohri (Sind)

Jav: Barley (pronounced as jao).

Jaziya: A religious tax imposed upon non-Muslims. The tax could be evaded by converting to Islam. It was first implemented by Khalifa Walid I who ruled the Arabic empire of Islam.

Jehaad: Islamic holy war or struggle.

Jhul Jhulni: Festival of Teej.

Jodha Bai: The lady from Jodhpur. It is a popular misconception that Emperor Akbar's first 'Hindu' queen, the mother of his heir, was called Jodha Bai. Since the Mughal historian Abu-l Fazl referred to the emperor's wives by their given Islamic names, their original 'Hindu' names remained unknown for many years. Bards and novelists clubbed every Mughal queen of 'Hindu' origin under the generic Jodha or Jodh Bai. Ironically, never had a princess of Jodhpur or Bikaner (both royal families being derived from the house of Jodha) ever borne the name.

Jowar: Sorghum or great millet.

Joojarhs: Funeral stones.

Kaka: Uncle or more specifically the younger brother of one's father.

Kanakali: A form of the mother goddess.

Kangra Rani: The Kangra Rani or mother goddess or Shakti (power) has many forms – Bhavani, Vanmata, Sati etc. She is also worshipped as Durga, Kali, Kalika, Kanakali etc in various parts of India. All female deities in India are forms of Shakti.

Kangras: Battlements.

Kanhaiya: A form of Krishna.

Karma (karmic): A preordained duty, a result of debts accumulated during past lives.

Kartik: 'Hindu' month corresponding to 15th October – 15th November.

Kazi: Islamic Judge.

Khal: Stream.

Khalji: More correctly the Khalj dynasty, known to popular historians as Khilji.

Khan: A title with many meanings: originally commander, leader or ruler, in Mongolian and Turkish languages. (female: khatun).

Khan-e-khana: Commander of commanders.

Khelat: (pronounced khillat) A complete outfit including the head-dress and footwear. It is also called a saropa.

Khuman Rasa: (Khuman Raeso) A fictional account of the exploits of the 9th Century Rawal Khuman, which was written in 1715, during the reign of Maharana Sangram Singh II.

Khwaja: Arabic/Persian title equivalent to lord.

Koot: Cottage. Rhymes with boot. (Hindi: kootiya).

Kothi: House.

Kotri: House.

Koran: The holy book of Islam.

Kos (Coss): Though a popular measure of distance in India, it varied from place to place. Originally a kos was the distance a man's voice could travel. Every ruler gave it his own definition and thus in Akbar's time it was approximately 2 miles 4 feet, while the Bengal Presidency defined it to be about 2 miles.

Krishna: A form of Vishnu the Preserver. Of the many names of Krishna, the ones referred to in this book are Girdhar Gopal, Pitamber Rai, Braj Nath, Nath, Kanhaiya and Shyam.

Kshatriya: Warrior caste.

Kul Devta: Tutelary divinity.

Lakh: One hundred thousand.

Lalkar: To challenge.

Madras: Modern name – Chennai.

Madras Presidency: Also known as the Presidency of Fort St George, it grew to include the Indian state of Tamil Nadu, north Kerala, Lakshadweep Islands, coastal Andhra Pradesh and southern Karnataka. The grant had been made in 1639 and confirmed six years later by Ranga II, a descendent of the Vijaynagar dynasty. Despite its significance the grant went unnoticed by Emperor Shah Jahan.

Magh: 'Hindu' month corresponding to 15th January – 15th February.

Maharana: The great rana.

Maharaja: The great raja.

Maharao: The great rao.

Mahout: Elephant driver.

Mama: Uncle or more specifically the brother of one's mother. Fondly referred to as Mamoo.

Munsub: Command.

Munsubdar: Commander.

Maratha: Shivaji Raje Bhosle, a kshatriya, of Satara whose family claimed descent from Sujan Singh, son of Rana Ajay Singh Sisodia of Mewar, created a platform, which permitted the rise of brilliant generals from diverse castes and backgrounds. Having established a strong Maratha kingdom, Shivaji led his Marathas against the Mughals. The Chitpavan Brahmin, Balaji Vishvanath Bhat or Baji Rao Peshwa, who functioned as prime minister or peshwa in the reign of Shivaji's grandson, Raja Shahu, invaded northern India establishing the Maratha empire. The Maratha clans that have not found a mention in this book are the Gaekwads of Baroda (Vadodara in Gujarat) and the Bhosles of Nagpur. The Bhosles of Nagpur, who are said to share a common ancestry with the Bhosles of Satara, claim descent from Banbir Sisodia. Shivaji's descendents ruled independently for a while from Kohlapur in southern Maharashtra and Thanjavur in Tamil Nadu. The peshwa then had the capital moved from Raigarh back to Pune once relative peace had been established. The Scindia, Holkar and Gaekwad generals rose to powerful positions under the peshwas and were granted independent jagirs. They continued in the service of the peshwas until the fall of the peshwai dynasty when they declared independence and vied with each other for control of the Maratha empire.

Maratha History – a summary: The two arch enemies, Shivaji and Aurungzeb, both succeeded in extinguishing the other's empire. The rise of the peshwas that followed Aurungzeb's death ended with the Third Battle of Panipat. Madhu Rao Peshwa, who took over soon after Panipat and succeeded in maintaining central authority with the help of Nana Fadnavis, died a premature death in 1772. The quarrels over succession brought in the East India Company.

The next thirty years saw a murderer – Raghunath Rao (Raghoba) – and Nana Fadnavis as leading figures while the Scindias and Holkars, who had shaken off central authority, vied for control over Sawai Madhu Rao II. Mahadji Scindia, who had been in occupation of the Kingdom of Delhi since 1788, defeated the Holkar co – regents Tukoji and Ahilya Bai – in 1792. Fadnavis, who had no personal army, posed no competition. In 1794, upon the very brink of success, Mahadji died leaving his kingdom to the inept Daulat Rao and his troops to the correspondingly inferior Perron. If Scindia was incompetent then Jaswant Rao Holkar, who gained control of Holkar fortunes in 1799, was brilliant but unbalanced. Fadnavis died in 1800, and with him went the last voice of reason. Holkar's victory over Peshwa Baji Rao II in 1802, precipitated British intervention. The peshwa signed the treaty of Bassein and was granted 6,000 troops in exchange for 2,600,000 rupees annual revenue. Daulat Rao refused to accept the treaty and organised a Maratha coalition – one which Holkar cared not to join.

Arthur Wellesley, the brother of the governor general, who already had the defeat of Tipu Sultan to his credit crushed the coalition in 1803, and later that year General Lake defeated Scindia at Laswari and occupied Delhi taking Shah Alam II under the protection of the East India Company. But Holkar proved to be a basket of surprises. Lt Col Monson, who was sent to rein him in, lost miserably and was sent packing. But by the end of 1805, both Scindia and Holkar had signed subsidiary treaties.

From 1814, the Marathas were once again restless. Daulat Rao Scindia was hostile, fearful and slow moving, the peshwa scheming but irresolute while the Holkars were torn by internal feuds. Gaekwad's envoy to Pune had been murdered in July 1815, by the peshwa's favourite – Trambak Dengle. Elphinstone, then resident at Pune insisted upon a trial and incarcerated the culprit at Thane. In a romantic turn about, in October the next year, Dengle escaped helped by a syce who wove directions into Marathi songs sung outside the prisoner's window. By the following spring he was raising an army. Pressed by Elphinstone, the peshwa, who had denied all knowledge, soon ran out of courage. Dengle was renounced and the Treaty of Pune signed in July 1817. Meanwhile earlier that year in February, Appa Sahib had murdered the imbecile Bhosle of Nagpur, seized control and considered himself free of the British.

In October 1817, Lord Hastings began to move on his grand plan – net the Pindaris and intimidate the Marathas at one go. There after it became a matter of dates.

On 5 November 1817, Daulat Rao Scindia signed a treaty agreeing to cooperate against the Pindaris and non-interference in the Rajput states and during war. Scindia saved his state by a hair's breadth by giving up his supremacy in Rajputana. On the day Scindia signed up, the peshwa struck Pune. Elphinstone beat off the attack at Kirkee and launched a counter attack. The peshwa retreated. Then within a few days Appa Sahib was attacked and he fled to the court of Maharaja Ranjit Singh in Punjab. Raghuji III, the grandson of Raghuji II took Appa Sahib's place in Nagpur.

Tulsi Bai, the Holkar regent, was inclined to accept terms similar to those of Scindia's but she was murdered by her rivals. The Holkars were then defeated on 21 December. The Holkar state was shorn of Tonk, which was granted to Amir Khan the Pathan, and the remainder under the able administration of Tantia Jog began to revive.

By early 1818, nineteen Rajput kingdoms had signed treaties with Metcalfe in Delhi – these included Jaipur, Mewar and Marwar.

The peshwa surrendered to John Malcolm on 2 June 1818. His dominions were annexed by the Presidency of Bombay. Through the generosity of Malcolm, much regretted by Hastings, he was allowed to settle at Bithur on the Ganga with a pension of eight lacs per annum. He died in 1851, leaving his claims and grievances to his adopted son, Nana Sahib.

Shivaji's descendent was restored to Satara.

Gaekwad alone gained territory as a reward for his fidelity to the British.

Medpat: The ancient Sanskrit name for Mewar.

Meena Bazaar: A fete that was held by high-ranking women both 'Hindu' and Muslim. Mughal princes were the only men that could attend it and frequently claimed the ladies who caught their fancy, regardless of their marital status.

Meru: Mountain.

Mirza: The word is derived from amir-zada or son of the amir. Taimur, from whom the Mughals claim descent, used the title of amir. The hereditary title of mirza was bestowed by Emperor Akbar upon Raja Maan Singh of Amber but it was his grandson, Raja Jai Singh, who became popularly known as the mirza raja.

Mor: The crown or the mor was worn during a wedding – with an earthly maiden or when courting death in the arms of a heavenly nymph.

Mughal: It is derived from the root word Mongol.

Munsub: Office of an army commander.

Mussalman: Muslim. These are the followers of Islam and include people from many races and countries.

Nahar: Tiger.

Nakarras: Kettle-drums. Every raja had his own signature tune, which announced his presence. Subordinate rajas would silence their drums in the presence of higher-ranking rajas.

Nine gems: Emperors liked to surround themselves with the brightest and the most talented people and the nine that qualified were referred to as the nav ratna or the nine gems. Among those of Akbar's court were Mia Tansen – the Dhrupad singer, Raja Birbal of the ready wit, Peethal the poet and Abu-l Fazl the hysteriographer.

Nizam-ul-Mulk: Controller of the realm.

The dynasty of the nizams of Hyderabad traces their descent through the direct male line from Shaikh Shihab-ud-din Suhrawardy, of Suhrawada, in Kurdistan, a celebrated Sufi mystic who lived in Persia, and from Khalifa Abu Bakr who was married to Prophet Hazrat Mohammad's daughter. Shaikh Mir Ismail was the first to come to India.

Shaikh Mir Ismail's son Khwaja Abid who accompanied him entered Mughal service in 1641, under Emperor Shah Jahan. He was soon appointed subedar of Ajmer and Multan, faujdar of Bidar and granted the titles of Azam Khan and Qilich Khan Bahadur in 1680. Both father and son died during the attempt to annex Golconda. Abid's son and grandson both entered Mughal service and it was the grandson, who was named Mir Qamr-ud-din Khan Bahadur by Emperor Aurungzeb, that became HH Asaf Jah I. 'The star of destiny shines on his forehead.' These had been Aurungzeb's words as the child was presented to him. In 1697, Aurungzeb invested him with the title Chin Qilich Khan.

But after Aurungzeb, the power of the Mughals waned. Mir Qamr-ud-din Khan Bahadur Chin Qilich Khan was raised to subedar (viceroy) of the Deccan, Moradabad, Patna, Malwa and Gujarat, faujdar of Carnatic (Karnataka and parts of Andhra Pradesh , Maharashtra) and granted the titles of khan-e-khana, nizam-ul-mulk fateh jang on 12 January 1713 by Farukhsiyar. The series of emperors that succeeded Farukhsiyar were murdered and finally Muhammad Shah (Rangila) found himself on the throne in 1719. But the nizam-ul-mulk found his good advice and services rejected and he raised his standard of revolt for the first time in 1720. But he was too important a man to labelled as traitor and in 1722, was appointed wazir. He still found it impossible to bring the government to order and in 1724, chose to retire to his province in the Deccan where, though he never actually declared independence from the central government, he governed without interference. Having given up his appointments as wazir and nizam-ul-mulk he was henceforth referred to as the nizam. Quite naturally Delhi nominated fresh appointees to the imperial offices of nizam-ul-mulk and wazir. In 1737, the nizam visited Delhi and was well received – for he had been in imperial service since the days of Aurungzeb – and granted the title of Asaf Jah I (equal in dignity to Solomon's minister – Aesop). This honour came about despite the fact that he had been forced to concede Malwa to the Marathas. Nizam Asaf Jah I died peacefully in 1748, and was succeeded upon the throne of Hyderabad by his fourth son, his eldest, Ghazi-ud-din – who had taken over his father's imperial office of nizam-ul-mulk – having been killed before he could reach Hyderabad. Nizam-ul-Mulk Ghazi-ud-din had been present during Nadir Shah's sack of Delhi. The Persian emperor had left Emperor Muhammad Shah with a warning – the nizam-ul-mulk appeared too ambitious by far.

Mir Muhammad Fazil, the grandson of Shaikh Mir Ismail's younger son, had replaced his second cousin Nizam-ul-Mulk Mir Qamr-ud-din Khan Bahadur Chin Qilich Khan (Nizam Asaf Jah) as wazir in Delhi. He was known as HH Wazir ul-Mamalik-i-Hindustan, Itimad-ud-daula, Nawab Qamr-ud-din Khan Bahadur, Nusrat Jang. He had repulsed the advances of Ahmad Shah Abdalli (Durrani) at Sirhind but had in the process lost his life. He was succeeded by Safdarjung, nawab of Avadh, who was eventually ousted by Nizam Asaf Jah's grandson – the son of the unfortunate Ghazi-ud-din. This lad, who inherited all his father's titles and his name was popularly known as imad-ul-mulk, occupied the post of both nizam-ul-mulk and wazir.

Having made use of the services of the Marathas to evict Safdarjung, Imad then turned against the emperor -- the beleaguered man who had appealed for his help. Emperor Ahmad Shah was blinded and deposed in 1754. The elderly devout Alamgir II – son of Jahandar Shah – who had been blinded forty years ago by his cousin Farukhsiyar, was set upon the throne. Imad set about recovering the empire and it prompted Abdalli's fourth coming in 1757. Delhi was sacked and the Rohilla Afghan chief, Najib-ud-daula, appointed guardian. Imad called in the Marathas once again this time against the Afghan. In 1759, the Marathas occupied Lahore and Abdalli (Durrani) returned ready for war. Imad's frustrations were vented on the hapless Alamgir who was murdered in 1759. The Mughal heir, Gauhar Ali (later Shah Alam II), who had fled to Avadh the previous year, remained out of Imad's reach. Abdalli, who was victorious in the Third Battle of Panipat, succeeded in breaking the Maratha power. But the Mughal throne slipped from within his grasp. His own army was up in arms clamouring for pay and leave to go home. Faced with the mutiny, Abdalli confirmed the succession of the absent Shah Alam as vassal emperor and left Delhi in the care of Najib-ud-daula who ruled until his death in 1770. Imad fled to Mecca to escape punishment.

Seven generations of nizams, who continued to write nizam-ul-mulk as one of their titles, ruled independently until Hyderabad merged with independent India. The first nizam, it is said, had visited the saint, Hazrat Nizam-ud-din, at Aurangabad. The saint had offered him some bread – kulchas – of which seven were accepted. Wrapping the bread in a yellow cloth the saint had explained its significance. The seven kulchas represented the seven generations that would rule. For his flag Asaf Jah chose a yellow fabric adorned by a white kulcha.

Nuzzer: To be brought to notice.

Nuzrana: Offerings made to acknowledge a superior presence.

Umara: Noble.

Pandav: The sons of Prince Pandu, the heroes of the epic *Mahabharat*.

Panipat: Panipat, located in the modern state of Haryana, is a historical site said to have been founded by the Pandavs during the period of the *Mahabharat*. Three historic battles took place here – ones that sealed India's destiny. The first was fought between Babar and Sultan Ibrahim Lodi on 21 April 1526 AD, the second between the 'Hindu' trader Hemu, who represented Mohammad Adil Shah (of Sher Shah's line), and the newly crowned, thirteen-year-old Akbar on 5 November 1556. Hemu was beheaded personally by Akbar, which allowed him to assume the title ghazi. The third battle was fought between the Marathas and Ahmad Shah Durrani (Abdalli) – the Afghan emperor, on 13 January 1761.

Paras Patthar: Philosopher's stone.

Pathan: Pathan or Pashtun are part of an ethno-linguistic group of Afghans living primarily in eastern and southern Afghanistan, North West Frontier Province, Federally Administered Tribal Areas and the Balochistan province of Pakistan.

Paus: 'Hindu' month corresponding to 15th December – 15th January.

Peela Khal: Yellow River.

Peepul: Ficus religiosa.

Persia: Iran.

Peshwa: Prime minister to the Maratha kings of Satara. It was a hereditary post held by a Chitpavan Brahmin family of Bhats long involved in the service of the state.

Phoopha: Uncle or more specifically the husband of one's father's sister.

Pindari: These were dacoits known since the days of Aurungzeb. They started out as adventurers who attached themselves to Maratha chiefs but proved more elusive and ruthless than the Marathas. Drawn from varied backgrounds and religions, their only tie lay in their leader and in their common objective of plunder. Unlike the Marathas and the Pathans they had no organized army and were devoid of any form of national pride. The fleet footed Pindaris evaded escape but Lord Hasting's widely and loosely cast net managed to close in on them. The leaders – Karim Khan and Vasil Muhammad – were killed in action while Chithu, the most daring of the lot, fled into the jungle and fell to the jaws of a tiger.

Pir: A Sufi saint – the master who has accepted responsibility of his disciple's spiritual growth.

Piya: Beloved.

Pitamber Rai: Lord Krishna dressed in garments of yellow.

Prithviraj Raso: Composed by Chand Bardai, the court poet of Prithviraj Chauhan, *Prithviraj Raso* documents the historical events of the time. It is unanimously agreed that only a portion of what is available today can be a part of the original. Much of it appears to be additions made after the 15th Century. A 1300 verse manuscript preserved in Bikaner seems to be the closest to the original text.

Pugri-badal-bhai: Men who have exchanged turbans sealing their relationship as brothers.

Pundit: Priest and scholar.

Purohit: Priest.

Raj mahal: Palace.

Rajputni: A Rajput woman.

Rajwara: Land of the Rajputs which would encompass all lands occupied by Rajputs. Technically it would cover most of Hindustan.

Rakshas: Demon.

Rawala: Women's quarters within a Rajput palace.

Rori: Pebble.

Rumna: Hunting grounds.

Rupee: Currency of India. During the 1800s, one rupee was equivalent to one tenth of an English Pound i.e. £1/- = Rs 10/-.

Safawi: The Safawi dynasty of Persia dates from the twelfth century AD and takes its name from Sheikh Safi-ud-din 'Abdu'l Fath Ishaq founder and grand-master of a Sufi religious order established at Ardabil in 1301. His descendant Sheikh Junaid, on receiving charge of the order, converted it into a Shia movement with the intention of creating an empire. His influence spread over large areas of North Western Persia, Anatolia, Syria, Mesopotamia and Armenia. In 1501, the grand-master established himself as Shah Ismail I. Through their waxing and waning fortunes the Safawis continued to be recognised as shahan-shahs or emperors until the last shah of the dynasty was finally deposed and exiled to India in 1786.

Sahib: An Arabic word meaning sir or master. It was probably introduced into the India by the Arabs in the eighth century AD and has been in use since by Indian royalty. (Sahib = Lord; Sahiba = Lady). The word was later used to address Europeans. Today, it is a popular misconception that word is used to refer to Englishmen.

Saka: Hindi equivalent of the English word sack. When the sacking of a castle looked imminent the saka was announced. The women and children would first immolate themselves in the flames of jauhar and then the men, having undergone ritual cleansing, would embark upon their last battle dressed in funereal robes of saffron holding leaves of the sacred basil (tulsi) within their mouths.

Sangam: A confluence of streams.

Sati: This form of the mother goddess had committed suicide. The practise of wives immolating themselves on the funeral pyres of their husbands came to be popularised and the women earned the right to be equated with the sacred feminine or Sati.

Sawai: Equal to one fourths more than the standard measure.

Scindia: Also referred to as Shinde – of lower caste origin – descended from Ranoji Scindia, who served as a general under the peshwa.

Shahzadaa: Son of the shah.

Shahzadi: Daughter of the shah.

Shaivite; The followers of Shiva

Shaligram: A fossilised mollusc, which is worshipped as a form of Lord Vishnu or Narayan.

Shenvi Brahmins: These are the Saraswat Brahmins of Maharashtra who claim origin from Sage Saraswat who lived upon the banks of the now extinct Saraswati river in Punjab. With the rise of the Maratha empire many Shenvi Brahmins attempted to get into government service but faced stiff competition from the Chitpavan Brahmins who had long held powerful government positions and the office of prime minister (peshwa).

Shiva: Mahadev, Eklinga, Trambak.

Shyam: The dark man – refers to Lord Krishna.

Sind: Refers to the state of Sind now in Pakistan. The land that the river Sindhu or Indus belongs to, i.e. India, was known to the Arabs as the land of Hind – a mispronounced version of Sind.

Sindh: Sindhu river or Indus.

Sindi: People of the state of Sind.

Sirpech: Aigrette, turban ornament.

Solankini: A woman of the Solanki clan.

Sravan: 'Hindu' month corresponding to 15th July – 15th August.

Sufi: The mystic branch of Islam, which believes that the ego centred self has to be destroyed before the devotee can experience Allah.

Sur: The dynasty of Sher Shah, known to popular historians as Suri.

Suraj: Sun.

Surya: Sun.

Talab: Lake.

Teej: A festival to welcome the monsoons and thank the mother goddess. Women in north India celebrate by setting up swings and decorating their hands with a paste made from the leaves of the mehendi (henna – Lawsonia inermis) plant.

Teeka: Ceremonial mark placed on the forehead.

Thali: A metal platter.

Thokur: An obstacle against which an un-mindful traveller could trip.

Tilak: same as a teeka.

Torna: Also called a toran. It is a wooden triangle with an effigy of a peacock at its apex, which is hung from the gate of the bride's city. As the groom enters on horseback, he tears it down with his lance as the bride's companions, sing wedding hymns and shower him with a crimson powder made from the dried petals of the Palaas or the Flame of the Forest.

Trambak: Shiva.

Trimuti: The combined form of Brahma, Vishnu and Shiva.

Triveni: A confluence of three streams.

Turk: Natives of Turkey. The Rajputs however referred to all Muslims as Turks.

Unnadaata: Provider of food.

Urzee: Request.

Vaid: Physician.

Vaishnavite: The followers of Vishnu.

Vakil: Lawyer.

Varaha: Vishnu in his form of the divine boar that saved mankind from destruction.

Vikramaditya: This title was assumed by many kings in India, notably Chandra Gupta II (375 – 413 AD), of the Gupta dynasty. The legendary Vikramaditya was said to have been a king of Ujjain (a Parmar according to Rajput sources) who ruled from 56 BC, which marked the beginning of the Vikram Samvat era. He is associated with a number of legends notably the *Vetal Pachisi* – Twenty-five vampire tales and the *Singhasan Battisi* – Thirty-two tales of the throne. Kalidas, the famous poet, whose dates are wildly uncertain, could have been a luminary at the court of either Vikaramaditya.

Vishnu: The Preserver.

Wazir-e-azam: Chief minister or prime minister, one who also held the revenue portfolio i.e. the office of the diwan.

Yagna: Sacrificial rite where offerings are made to Agni, the God of fire.

Yogi: Ascetic.

Yoni: The female reproductive organ.

Yugraj: A prince who becomes king during the lifetime of his father.

Yuvraj: Crown Prince.

Zenana: Women's quarters.

TOD FAMILY TREE

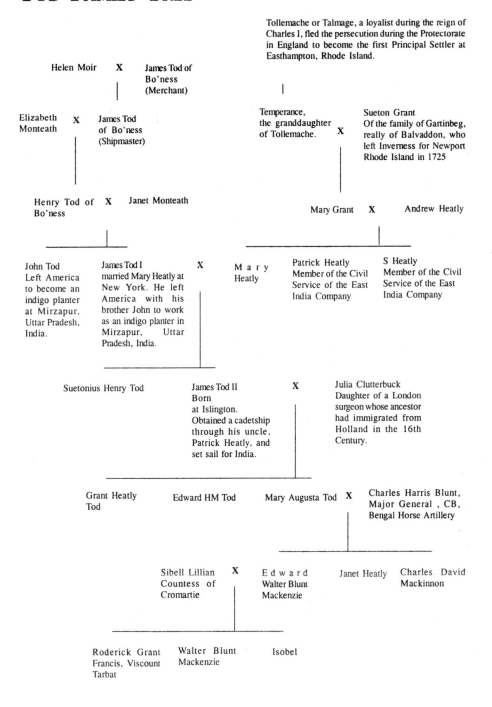

Tollemache or Talmage, a loyalist during the reign of Charles I, fled the persecution during the Protectorate in England to become the first Principal Settler at Easthampton, Rhode Island.

Helen Moir   **X**   James Tod of Bo'ness (Merchant)

Elizabeth Monteath   **X**   James Tod of Bo'ness (Shipmaster)

Temperance, the granddaughter of Tollemache.   **X**   Sueton Grant Of the family of Gartinbeg, really of Balvaddon, who left Inverness for Newport Rhode Island in 1725

Henry Tod of Bo'ness   **X**   Janet Monteath

Mary Grant   **X**   Andrew Heatly

John Tod Left America to become an indigo planter at Mirzapur, Uttar Pradesh, India.

James Tod I married Mary Heatly at New York. He left America with his brother John to work as an indigo planter in Mirzapur, Uttar Pradesh, India.   **X**   Mary Heatly

Patrick Heatly Member of the Civil Service of the East India Company

S Heatly Member of the Civil Service of the East India Company

Suetonius Henry Tod

James Tod II Born at Islington. Obtained a cadetship through his uncle, Patrick Heatly, and set sail for India.   **X**   Julia Clutterbuck Daughter of a London surgeon whose ancestor had immigrated from Holland in the 16th Century.

Grant Heatly Tod

Edward HM Tod

Mary Augusta Tod   **X**   Charles Harris Blunt, Major General , CB, Bengal Horse Artillery

Sibell Lillian Countess of Cromartie   **X**   Edward Walter Blunt Mackenzie

Janet Heatly

Charles David Mackinnon

Roderick Grant Francis, Viscount Tarbat

Walter Blunt Mackenzie

Isobel

The trails followed by Captain Tod:

Passage to Jodhpur – travels through the Aravalli

Udaipur, Pallana, Nathdwara, keeping the Banas to the left, Usarwas, Samecha, elephant's pool, Murcha, the Bargula nal Pass led to Nathdwara and another to Rincher, the celebrated temple of Vishnu, Uladar, Kelwara, Kumbhalgarh Fort – Jain temple, temple of Mama Devi and memorial to Prithviraj Sisodia and Tara Bai, pass descending into Marwar, Hathidwara, Godwar, Nadol, Indara, Pali, Khankani, Jhalamand, Jodhpur.

Visit to Mandor

Jodhpur, Sojat Gate, road to Nagaur, Maha Mandir, along the mountain range, through gorge leading to Mandor, cenotaphs of the Rathores, follow the course of the Nagda to the Pushkunda (Panchkunda), past a well dedicated to the memory of Nahar Rao Purihara, the palace of the Puriharas, Thana Pir, return to Pushkunda, gardens and palaces of the Rathores, the caves dedicated to the heroes of the desert.

Return

Jodhpur, Nandla, Vishalpur, Pachkalia, Pipar, Lakka Phoolana, Madreo, Bharunda, Indawar, Merta, Jharau, Rian, crossing of the stream Luni, Alniawas, Govindgarh, crossing the Saraswati at Nandla, crossing the Saraswati at the entrance of the Pushkar, valley of Pushkar, through the northern hills of the valley turning right to enter the Dhar-l-Khair, Ajmer, Vishal Talab, Ajmer Fort, Ana Sagar, castle of Bhimgarh in Merwara, Bhilwara, Bhunai, Deolia, Dabla, Banera, Mandalgarh, Pur, Rashmi, Mairta, Debari, Ahar, Udaipur.

Passage to Bundi and Kota – travels through the plateau of central India.

1. Udaipur, Kheroda, Hinta, Morwan, Nikumbh, Marla, Nimbahera, Kanera, Dhareshwar, Ratangarh Kheri, Little Attoa, Singoli, Bhainsrorgarh, Dabi, Kharipur, Sontra, Nanta, Kota city.

Return

Kota city, Nanta, Talera, Navagaon, Bundi, Thanoh, Jahazpur, Kajuri, Kachhola, Damnia, Manpura, Mandalgarh, Baghit, Birslabas, Amba, Hamirgarh, Siyana, Rashmi, Jasma, Sunwar, Mavli, Toos and Mairta, Udaipur.

2. Udaipur, Mairta, Mavli, Pahuna, Bhilwara, Jahazpur, Bundi, Raontha, Mukandara Pass, Baroli, whirlpools of the Chambal close to Bhainsrorgarh, Gangabheva, Naoli and the fountain of Takshak, Bhanpura, Mausoleum of Jaswant Rao Holkar, Garot, caves of Dhamnar, Pachpahar, Kanwara, Jhalarapatan, Narayanpur, Gagraun, Mukandara Pass, Kota city, Bundi.

Return

Bundi, Bijolia, ruins of Morakara, Menal, Bambaoda, Begun, Basi, Chittaur, Mairta, Udaipur.

BIBLIOGRAPHY

James Tod, *Annals and Antiquities of Rajas'than*, volumes I&II (New Delhi, Rupa & Co, 1997)

Hari Singh Bhati, *Annals of Jaisalmer*: A Pre-Mediaeval History (Bikaner, Kavi Prakashan, 2002)

Vincent A. Smith, *The Oxford History of India*: edited by Percival Spear (New Delhi, Oxford University Press, 1994)

Christopher Buyer, *Royal Ark*, India Salute States, Persia (Internet, January 2001 – September 2006)

Henry Soszynski, *Indian Princely States* (Brisbane, Internet, 2001)

Ian Austin and Thakur Nahar Singh Jasol, *The Mewar Encylopaedia* (Udaipur, Maharana Mewar Institution Trust, 2001)

William Wilson Hunter, *Imperial Gazetteer of India*, Volume 14, edited by James Cotton Sutherland, Richard Burn, William Stevenson Meyer (New edition, published under the authority of His Majesty's secretary of state for India in council. Oxford, Clarendon Press, 1908-1931)

R S Tripathi, *History of Kanauj to the Moslem Conquest* (Delhi, Motilal Banarsidass, 1964)

Abu-l Fazl, *Akbar Nama* volumes I & II: Translated from Persian by H. Beveridge (New Delhi, Low Price Publications, 1993)

Will Durant, *Our Oriental Heritage*, The Story of Civilization I, (New York, Simon and Schuster, 1954)

Vyas Dev, *Mahabharat*, Retold by Kashi Das (Calcutta, Dey's Publishing, 1987)

Valmiki, *Ramayan*, Translated by Arshia Sattar (New Delhi, Penguin Books India, 1996)

Aman Nath, *Dome over India*: Rashtrapati Bhavan (New Delhi, India Book House Pvt Ltd. 2002)

Isaac Asimov, *Asimov's Chronology Of The World*: The history of the world from the big bang to Modern Times (New York, HarperCollins Publishers, 1991)

Gopa Sabarwal, *The Indian Millenium*, AD 1000 – 2001 (New Delhi, Penguin Books India, 2002)

Kishore Singh, *A History of Bikaner* (New Delhi, Cross Section Publications Pvt. Ltd. 1988)

Karni Singh, *The Relations of the House of Bikaner with Central Powers* (New Delhi, Munshiram Manoharlal Publishers. 1974)

Giles Tillotson, *Jaipur Nama*: Tales From The Pink City (New Delhi, Penguin Books India, 2006)

Sir Jadunath Sarkar, *A History of Jaipur*, edited by Raghubir Singh (Hyderabad, Orient Longman, 1984)

Romila Thapar, *The Penguin History of Early India*: From The Origins To AD 1300 (New Delhi, Penguin Books India, 2002)

Narayan Bareth, *Indian ex-royals lose battle for gold* (United Kingdom, BBC News, 27 June 2002)

T F Mills, *Regiments.org; Land Forces of Britain, the Empire and Commonwealth* (Internet, 2005)

Rumer Godden, *Gulbadan*, Portrait of a Rose Princess at the Mughal Court (New York, The Viking Press, 1981)

Rima Hooja, *History of Rajasthan* (New Delhi, Rupa & Co, 2006)

INDEX

M